LOVE & WAR

By

Dr. Joseph Micah Ragland, J.D., LL.M., LL.D., Esquire

**Personal Injury Trial Lawyer, Legal Counselor, Joyful Good News
End of the Age Speaker, and World Evangelist-Ordained Minister.
Former Law Professor, Mississippi College School of Law, and
Member of the American, Mississippi, and Tennessee Bar Associations.
Email: *joeragland@raglandministries.org***

Joe M. Ragland

PRESENTED IN TWO VOLUMES
VOLUME 1
'Let Justice Roll!'
(Amos 5:24)

Library of Congress Number: 2015908700
ISBN: 978-1-878957-77-1

**Eternity! No other book will prepare you for Eternity better than *Love & War* you are holding in your
hand. *Love & War* is not a fictional work, as it reveals actual legal secrets, is full of reliable evidence, and has
the most joyful ending of any recorded book, to which the Adventurer is invited to participate.**

***Love & War* is a celestial and earthly adventure across time, space, and the invisible, *having no previous
examples,* and will help make you God's masterpiece now and in the coming ages if you will diligently let it!**

The Great Commission
By
Jesus, the Son of God
"All power (authority) is given unto Me (Jesus) in Heaven and on Earth.
Therefore, go (Kingly command) and make followers (disciples) of all people
(who will repent, receive Jesus as Savior, and confess Jesus as Lord) in the world (nations),
baptizing them in the name of the Father and of the Son and of the
Holy Spirit, and teaching them to obey everything I (Divine King Jesus) have taught (commanded) you.
And surely I am (Divine Presence) with you always, even until the end of this (Earth) age."
(Jesus, Matthew 28:18-20)
"I (Jesus, Son of God) am the way and the truth and the life.
No one (no exceptions) comes to the Father (God for salvation) except through Me."
(Jesus, John 14:6)
"The time (final hour) has arrived to gather the harvest, for the Earth's crop (people of their own '
free will,' choosing to accept or reject the Great Gospel of Salvation) is fully ripened!
Do not keep secret the words of the prophecy of this book, because the time is near.for all this to happen.
Let whoever is doing evil continue to do evil. Let whoever is unclean (vile, impure, filthy) continue to be
unclean (vile, impure, filthy) Let whoever is doing right (justice, seeking truth) continue to do right (justice, seeking
truth). Let whoever is holy (ever cleansing a born again one of sin by the Blood of the Lamb)
continue (to overcome) to be holy."
(Part of the Apostle John's vision regarding the end of this age, Revelation 14:15), 22:10-11).
"D*aniel, keep the Message (*preserved it*) a secret, seal the Book, until (*this '**Secret Message**' to the people of
the world should be further revealed at*) the end of the age. Many shall run to and fro (*global travel;
Internet communication*) and knowledge (*understanding God's hidden revealed end of the age Message to
Daniel and to others, with great advancement in* technology in both war and business*) shall increase."*
(This Heavenly Message to Daniel to be further amplified at the end of the age, Daniel 12:4)

Great Commission End of the Age Technology

Technology has so increased that **Love & War** you are holding in your hand is presently available to millions of people on the Earth from amazon.com in English throughout the USA, Canada, United Kingdom, France, Germany, Spain, and Italy. As others translate **Love & War** from our international copyrighted file, using a translation tools such as Babel, into French, German, Spanish, and Italian, in these countries having Amazon, besides the English, the people can obtain **Love & War** in their native language, to be printed and mailed to them within their own country. **Great Commission End of the Age Technology** is here! Also, Portuguese, Russian, Chinese, and other languages can be made available by alternative means. You are invited to choose to be a part, with Jesus faithfully promising to be with those faithful to Him, "even until the end of this Earth Age!"
Technology is available now to allow an implant of a tiny chip under the skin of a person to show a person's identity, where they are, and what they are doing. The Bible warns that many will be deceived to worship the Beast/Antichrist and to receive his mark. **Love & Wa**r will timely reveal hidden overcoming and salvation secrets including,

(1) Enabling one courageously not to worship the Beast/Antichrist or to receive his mark "on their right hand or on their forehead," without which no one can "*buy or sell*" (Revelation 13:16-17), as if taken, this will seal the taker's doom (Revelation 14:9-12) first in Hell and later in the Lake of Fire. We must warn all throughout the world not to worship the Beast/Antichrist nor to take his mark urging them to receive Jesus as Savior, repent and confess Jesus as Lord, trusting the Lord Jesus to give them a way of escape, '*But when you (a born again Christian) are tempted, God will also provide a way out (escape) so you can stand up under it.'* (1 Corinthians 1013).

(2) Receiving a blessed invitation to the "Marriage Supper of the Lamb" (Revelation 18:9) described in joyful detail in Volume 2 of **Love & War.**

(3) Qualifying to dwell with God on the New Earth (the present Earth will pass away as further shown in Volume 2 of **Love & War** and in Volume 3 of the musical play **Hallelujah** obtainable from amazon.com, Books, by Joe Ragland*)*. The Apostle John had this vision of the truth regarding God's dwelling with His people on the New Earth,"*Behold, God's dwelling (on the New Earth) is with His (born again ones adopted into the family of God) people, and He will be their God."* (Revelation 21:3)

ii

LOVE & WAR

Affectionately and earnestly
dedicated to the

The Father,
The Son, and
The Holy Spirit,

Ministers, Evangelists, and Witnesses
throughout the world proclaiming
the Gospel of Jesus Christ,

Lost Souls of the world for whom
Jesus died on a cross to save,
who will receive the truth, repent,
overcome, and obtain the promised
wonderful, abundant, eternal life,
as shown in *Love & War,*

You Adventurer holding in your hand
this message to the people of the world!

The best part of **Love & War** is that the teachable Adventurer is shown how to discover and be a part of this secret eternal joy. If an Adventurer has only time to read one book besides the Bible, in this day of going to and fro by various means throughout the Earth, let it be the joyful unabridged **Love & War** and the musical version **Hallelujah** end of this Earth's Age critical and timely messages to the people of the world, revealing secret truths and how to walk in them, including,

(1) **Love** – Ever since time began, nothing has ever been found stronger than walking in *"unfailing love!"* (1 Corinthians 13:8).

(2) **Joy** – "For the **joy** of the Lord (Jesus is your Lord and Father God is Jesus' Lord) is your *strength"* (Nehemiah 8:10). *"**Delight** yourself in the Lord; trust in Him and He will make your righteousness shine like the dawn, the justice of your cause (*including your presenting Jesus as Savior and Lord to others*) like the noonday sun."* (Psalm 37:4-6). "Consider it **pure joy** *when you face trials of many kinds, because* you know that the testing of your faith develops perseverance." (James 1:2). "This is the day (as a precious gift) the Lord (Jesus is Lord) has made. Let us (born again ones) rejoice and be glad (in the now moments) in it!" (Psalm 118:24). "Instead of shame My (God's) people will receive a double portion . . . and everlasting joy will be theirs." (Isaiah 61:7).

(3) **Rewards** – When the *"Lord (Jesus is my Lord) has tried me, I shall come forth as* (without impurities as pure) *gold!"* (Job 23:10). *"Eye has not seen, nor ear heard, neither have entered into the heart of humans (on Earth), all (the wonderful eternal rewards) God has prepared for them that love Him (those who repent, receive Jesus as Savior, confess Jesus as Lord, obey, and overcome to the end)."* (1 Corinthians 2:9). *"Bless (eternally joyful) are those who wash their robes (clean as the fresh fallen white snow in the blood of the Lamb, Jesus), that they may have the right to eat the fruit from the tree of life and may go through (enter as part of the adopted family of God) the gates into the (New Jerusalem) city."* (Revelation 22:14). *"For where your treasure is, there will your heart be also.."* (Matthew 6:21)

†TABLE OF CONTENTS†

VOLUME 1

✞FOREWORD✞

SECRET! THE WORD STIRS curiosity! We all want to be in on a secret, especially if it relates to the truth that affects people greatly and answers the ultimate question of life itself.

One of the greatest secrets was initially and partially stirred in a place called "Nothing." In this place, having no place to stand or sit, the eternal, invisible, Father God laughs as He meditated on a glorious and joyful secret known only to Him.

Shortly, Word, God's Son, and the Holy Spirit, also invisible, join in the laughing not having a clue about why they are laughing. Adventurer (reader), yes, there is one person of the Father, another of the Son, and another of the Holy Spirit, but the Godhead of the Father, Son, and the Holy Spirit is one God.

The adventure continues with the creation of Lucifer, a cherub[1] angel having a "free will," to lead the music and worship in Heaven. All created beings, as an act of their own "free will," could love, worship, and obey God or rebel. God made no robots and will not override a person's "free will" to choose right from wrong, good or evil, and ultimately love or war.

The Adventurer (reader) eavesdrops, similar to being a spectator in a balcony in a court of law, in on the Divine Godhead. Lucifer desired more and more of the worship and praise for himself. Lucifer schemes, plans, and ultimately commits an act of war after his scientists invent at his direction, what he mistakenly believes is the ultimate weapon for the destruction of the Godhead.

The Adventurer (reader) will see Lucifer, as attractive as a Spanish prince and as supremely gifted in music, politics, flattery, communication, allurement, charm, persistence, deceit, and craftiness. Lucifer offers ultimate freedom, independence, and pleasures to those who will choose of their "free will" to worship and follow him. He initially convinces a third of the angels in Heaven to join him, and many on Earth join his war efforts as he convinces them he would eventually win.

Starting in the heavens before time begins, *Love & War* moves through the First, Second, Third Earth Ages to the time of the New Earth, when time, as known today, will be no more. It is a sweeping epic containing love and conflict, revealing (exposing) what might have been, some of which more than likely were. Secrets of the origins and mysteries of life are revealed giving prior evidence and purpose of the dinosaurs and the great fall of the historic city of Atlantis.

Dr. Ragland paints a legal and spiritual struggle between love, good, and peace and hate, evil, and war in two dominions – the celestial and the terrestrial. He shows how pride, disobedience, and selfishness degraded the highest angels. In contrast, love, obedience, and self-control raised flesh and blood to overcome, endure, and win the ultimate prize of being adopted as children into the eternal family of God.

Dr. Ragland has prepared and trained himself over thirty years to look at both sides of a position (here God and Lucifer). Dr. Ragland invites the Adventurer (reader) to be eternally blessed by his respective legal presentation, backed by footnotes, setting forth various truths and probabilities much as he would in presenting a case before a carefully-selected jury.

---

[1] See Ezekiel 28:14.

In this compilation, God's secrets are slowly revealed line upon line and precept upon precept. One can benefit from this jurisprudential presentation without knowing supporting Scriptures, definitions, precedents, and legal rules outlined in the footnotes. However, the Adventurer (reader) of *Love & War* will find that the supporting footnotes, add immeasurably to understanding the intricate interplay of what likely have occurred in the first, second, third Earth ages, going into the mystery of the New Earth period when time as known today will be no more.

For the romantic at heart, *Love & War* contain love stories, which could have been, and many probably were, involving attractive chemistry between men and women down through the ages. Dr. Ragland often laughs when he ponders, "All's fair in love and war! I don't know about war!"

Throughout, Dr. Ragland advances that the only thing necessary for evil to triumph is for good people to do nothing, giving guidance to many perplexing and fundamental questions, including:

† How can love and good (right) overcome hate and wickedness (evil)?

† How does one refuse to receive a mark on the right hand or forehead, without which no one can buy or sell, as foretold in Revelation chapter thirteen, verses 16-17?

† How does one escape the upcoming great tribulation (just ahead) to be, "*such as has not been since the beginning of the world to this time, no, nor ever will be again.* " (Matthew 24:21)?"

† How does one obtain the "*blessing of being invited to the wedding supper of the Lamb (Son) of God* (Revelation 19:9)?"

† How does one become part (a personal obsession) of the Great Commission (command) assignment to "*go and teach (the truth to) all (every person on the Earth) nations* (Matthew 28:19)?"

Thesis: Ever since time began, nothing has ever been found that is stronger than love! Check your love walk. Read *1 Corinthians 13:4-8* and strive to emulate the characteristics of God's love. On each page of Love & War enjoy the power and participate in God's love, and enjoy God's supernatural grace and protection. Adventurer, please share a testimony of this truth to *joeragland@raglandministries.org* (please start your subject line **Love & War** giving your first and last name, and location on planet Earth) in your own life or in the life of another with whom you have shared *Love &* War or the companion amazon.com, Book *Hallelujah* by Joe Ragland. God planned this moment in your life for you to discover how to live and participate in God's love enjoying days of Heaven on Earth now and forever throughout **Eternity!**

God gave Dr. Ragland unabridged (full-length) episodes of the hidden treasures of dreams and visions in a Message from Heaven to the people of the Earth. They are "*holy to the Lord*" and contain a blessing of Heaven for the people of the world having ears to hear. Our assignment is to put these before the people. Some religious will not approve, and others will bless God and have the blessings of Almighty God upon them. The blessings of Heaven and the eternal God be upon all those meditating on, translating, publishing, printing, and distributing to others *Love & War*.

This recorder lawyer would appreciate receiving your helpful reviews *via* emails of what ministered to you, any typesetting or reference errors you might spot, and your personal wisdom about how to further distribute this Message to more and more of the over seven billion people on the Earth. About 10 percent of Americans say they do not believe in God. (Pew and Gallup, polling firms in America) About 20 percent of the people in the European Union, and about 61 percent of the people in China report they do not believe in God. (See Atheism, *Wikipedia, The Free Encyclopedia.*)

The Bible declares all the millions of atheist throughout the world, '*The fool says in his heart, 'There is no God.*' (Psalm 14:1). Atheism often undermines morality and is contrary to common sense. Dr. Ragland presents admissible evidence of the intelligibility of Creation, why God sent His Son, Jesus, to the Earth, the death of God's Son on a cross, the empty tomb, the five hundred eyewitnesses observing God's Son risen from the dead and ascending back up into Heaven. *Love & War* present evidence proving that God exists and loves those made in His image.

The Adventurer is enabled of their own '*free will*' to have faith to receive Jesus, the Son of God, as Savior, knowing their name is written in the ***Lamb's Book of Life***.

'*Without faith (obtain from reading the Bible and even **Love & War**) it is impossible to please God, because anyone who comes to God must believe that God exists and that He rewards those who earnestly seek Him.*' (Hebrews 11:6).

No other book, besides the Bible, will build up faith for salvation and prepare one for eternity better than the evidence, testimonies, and messages from Heaven presented in ***Love & War,*** having the most joyful ending of any book ever written to which the Adventurer is invited to be a part.

"*I* (**Apostle John in a vision**) *saw a New Heaven and a New Earth, for the First Heaven and the First Earth had passed away, and there was no longer any (roaring) sea (only still waters representing peace and security). . . . Now the dwelling of God is with people (saints), and He will live (in the same location on the New Earth) with them. They will be His people, and God Himself will be with them, and be their God. He will wipe away every tear from their eyes. There will be no more death or mourning (sadness) or crying (no stress or worry) or pain, for the old order of things has fled (passed) away.* He (Jesus) who was seated on the throne said, 'Look! *I am making everything new*! (John) **write** this (to prepare all people, who will repent, receive Jesus as Savior, and confess Jesus as their Lord), because **these words are true and to be trusted** (for in God you are to trust to the utmost)!" (Revelation 21:1-5) [Emphasis added.]

Please consider praying, even if you are born again, as you proceed 'line upon line, line upon line, a little here, a little there' (Isaiah 28:10) with truth building upon truth in your adventure of adventures in Love & War. If you get bogged down like regarding Job's first wife please do not stop, but skim over to the next truth and proceed running your race to the grand conclusion on the New Earth to which you Reader is invited to be a part.

"***Dear Father God in Heaven, Thank You for loving those in the world so much that you gave Your one and only Son, Jesus, that whosoever*** (that's me) ***believes in Him shall not perish*** (in Hell) ***but have eternal life. (John 3:16) I know I am a sinner. I am sorry for and repent of my sins. I do believe Jesus is Your Son and that You sent Him into the world to die on a cross to pay the penalty I owe for my sins. Father, I believe You raised Jesus from the dead. Now of my own free will, I receive Jesus as my Savior and confess Jesus as my Lord! I ask the Holy Spirit to come into my heart and join with my human spirit and make me born again. I will not be ashamed to confess the name of Jesus to others! Father, please give me wisdom and understanding now as I proceed through the Message in Love & War, supported with Scripture, to the people of the world recorded by Dr. Joe M. Ragland. I offer Hallelujahs, Thanksgivings, Praise, and Worship for Your saving love for me. In Your Son Jesus' name, Amen*** (So be it!)!"†

Again, you are invited to receive End-Time emails (we will not share your email with others) updates from the Author of ***Love & War*** and **Hallelujah,** Dr. Joe M. Ragland, a friend of Jesus, rejoicing that his name is written in the **Lamb's Book of Life**. (Luke 20:10) As you communicate with joeragland@raglandministries.org, please start with **Love & War** or *Hallelujah,* introduce yourself, what has ministered to you, include your first and last name, your talents and gift(s), and your location on the Earth. God has lost people He loves throughout the world to reach. Every life that's touched is a life we reach together. Let us join in Hallelujahs now and throughout eternity for such a joyful salvation as we bring glory to the Lord Jesus Christ! Rest assured your communication shall be appreciated very much! Bless you!

†A Lawyer's Sidebar: Please review only the portion of this lawyer's Personal Privileged[2] Prologue[3] below you desire as the adventurous evidence, testimonies, and message to God's people begins below in Book One, Episode 1.†

†PROLOGUE†

THE COUNTRY ROAD STRETCHED AHEAD with a field of white bolls (called balls after picked) of cotton peeking through the trees on the right side as songbirds filled the forest trees with singing, with the mockingbirds echoing with expertise. In thankful joy to be alive, I sang,

> When through the woods and forest glades I wander
> and hear the birds sing sweetly in the trees.
> When I look down, from lofty mountain grandeur
> and see the brook and feel the gentle breeze.
> Then sings my soul, My Savior God, to Thee;
> How great Thou art! How great Thou art!

I heard distant thunder rolling in like waves of the sea. I continued joyously singing,

> O Lord my God, when I in awesome wonder
> Consider all the works Thy Hands have made,
> I see the stars, I hear the rolling thunder,
> Thy power throughout the universe displayed.
> Then sings my soul, My Savior God, to Thee;
> How great Thou art! How great Thou art!

I further lift my voice in Thanksgiving and Praise choosing to sing some of the greatest lyrics[4] ever written,

> And when I think, that God, His Son not sparing;
> Sent Him to die, I scarce can take it in;
> That on the Cross, my burden gladly bearing,
> He bled and died to take away my sin.
> Then sings my soul, My Savior God, to Thee;
> How great Thou art! How great Thou art!

I was joyfully looking up at the swaying lush green tree limbs with glimpses of a lavish blue sky with one glowing fluffy white cloud in the eastern sky as I further sang,

> 'You may ask me how I know
> My Lord (Jesus) is real?
> You may doubt the things I say
> And doubt the way I feel.
> But I know He's real today,
> He'll always be.
> I can feel His hand in mine
> And that's enough for me.
> He holds my hand
> He will guide each step I take
> And if I fall, I know he'll understand
> Till the day, He tells me why
> He loves me so.

---

[2] "The matter may be '*personal privilege*,' where it relates to some action to be taken or some order of proceeding expressly enjoined (such as free speech) by the constitution." Quoting from *Privilege* from *Black's Law Dictionary*.

[3] A prologue from the word pro (before) and logos (word) is the opening that establishes the setting and gives background detail. See Prologue at *Wikipedia, The Free Encyclopedia*.

[4] Billy Graham once said, "The reason I like *How Great Thou Art* is that it glorifies God! It turns Christian eyes toward God, rather than upon themselves. I use it as often as possible because it is such a God honoring song."

I can feel His hand in mine
That's all I need to know.
I can feel His hand in mine
That's all I need to know.'[5]

I was on the Lord's Day fasting and praying, "Father God, '*the great and awesome God, who keeps His covenant of love with all who love You and obey Your commands,*'[6] I repent of my sins. I seek You 'by turning from my sins and giving attention to Your truth.'[7] 'Give me insight and understanding.'[8] 'I offer my body as a living sacrifice, holy and pleasing to God.'[9] 'I throw off everything that hinders . . . and run with perseverance the race marked out for me.'[10] In the name of Your Son, Jesus. Amen!

Suddenly, there was a sense of anticipation in the very atmosphere. The birds hushed their singing; the wind stilled, and a strange joyful silence and calmness came into the forest. I sense I was standing on holy ground in the presence of God as I had been before in such rare sacred moments. I gently and quietly removed my shoes and tied them on the top my backpack. I kept on walking barefoot feeling the pleasant cool dust and soft grass under my feet. I had a sense that something grand and wonderful was about to happen! I softly sang from memory,

You are not a God
Created by human hands
You are not a God
Dependent on any mortal man
You are not a God
In need of anything we can give
By Your plan, that's just the way it is.
You are God alone
From before time began (Eternity)
And right now, in the good time and bad, You are on Your throne
You are God alone.
You're the only God (no other God)
Whose power none can contend
You're the only God
Whose name and praise (to Him) will never end (Eternity)
You're the only God
Who's worthy of everything we (I) can give
You are God; that's just the way it is.
Unchangeable,
Unshakeable,
Unstoppable.
That's Who You are![11]
[A time of silence and meditation.]
Oh, I wish I was in the land of cotton,
Old times there are not forgotten.
Look away, look away, look away, Dixie Land![12]

I 'looked away' through the trees into a snow-white cotton field seeing two majestic creatures, wearing clothing dazzlingly white as light, looking over at me, and I heard a message like a trumpet,

'You are highly esteemed'[13] and 'a friend of God!'[14]

---

[5] Lyrics to *His Hand in Mine* previously sung by Elvis Presley.

[6] Daniel 9:4. NIV.

[7] Daniel 9:13. NIV.

[8] Daniel 9:22. NIV.

[9] Romans 12:1.

[10] Hebrews 12:1.

[11] Music lyrics from *You are God Alone* by William McDowell.

[12] "*Dixie*, also known as *I Wish I was in Dixie, Dixie's land*, and other titles, is a popular American song. The song was a favorite of President Abraham Lincoln: he had it played at some of his political rallies and at the announcement of General Robert E. Lee's surrender." *Wikipedia, The Free Encyclopedia.*

War, perilous times, and great tribulation (destruction), such as has not been from the beginning of the world,are coming on the Earth![15] Write a message to God's people!

Blinking my eyes and looking again the majestic creatures had vanished. From that spot, two white doves were streaming away flying over a distant abandoned white stone church with a well-preserved cross on its steeple. I thought, 'Jesus, thank You for paying the punishment due for my sins with Your life's blood on a cross!' Soon the fast flying doves disappeared from view into the one white fluffy cloud.

I glanced over at a nearby historic Raymond Ridge, dotted with white morning glories. I could faintly imagine the Union cannons slaughtering the gallant, but greatly outnumbered Southern gentlemen of the Confederacy, on that same yonder bloodstained ridge. 'Hush little baby don't you cry, you know your daddy is bound to die.'[16] They died for a cause that was wrong in seeking to take away the free will of men, women, and children to choose! This lawyer apologizes to all descendants of slaves, and I ask on behalf of myself and the white race for your total forgiveness as slavery was wrong! I love and care for all descendants of slavery and thank you for forgiving me and all members of the white race and let us live together in love and harmony as Jesus taught this critical truth, '*For if you forgive others for their sins (transgressions; failings; trespasses) against you (and against your ancestors), your Heavenly Father will also forgive you. But if you do not forgive others their sins, against you (and your ancestors) your Father will not forgive your sins.*' (Jesus, Matthew 6:14-15).

The simple answer is the love of Jesus in our hearts, as we love our neighbors as ourselves, and keep His commandments! O for a thousand tongues to sing the love of God and the gift of eternal life to all who will from the heart, repent, receive Jesus as Savior, and confess before others, "Jesus is my Lord." I reasoned back to my early writing, 'Death is a trip to eternity. No one can tell how soon he or she may be at the gates of death. Everyone has a free will to choose Jesus as Savior or to reject such a great offer of salvation. Without Jesus, the richest man is poor, and with Jesus, the poorest man is rich. Jesus is the only way to Heaven!'[17]

I noticed the beautiful morning glories also climbing the remains of a red brick chimney of a burnt-out, once eloquent, antebellum mansion. I then remembered the words of the beautiful Southern Belle, Scarlet O'Hara,

'I'll think of some way to get him (Rhett, the man she thought she loved) back. After all, tomorrow is another day.'[18] Being a Southern gentleman, earning the right to wear the courtesy title Esquire,[19] like Scarlet I had both won and lost in romance. I smiled as I thought of the beautiful Scarlet as she flirted with competing suitors 'in the cool shade of the porch of Tara, her father's plantation.'[20] She broke hearts only at the end to have her own heart broken – all '*gone with the wind!*'[21]

I sought to take my romantic thoughts captive. I reasoned, "Today, I am not going to think of the Civil War 'days of wine and roses and (romantic) you,'[22] and of the beautiful Southern women who wore elaborate dresses having some twelve yards of billowing material over hoops. 'Why did she have to go? I don't know; she wouldn't say.'[23] [A time of silence and meditation.]

I continued walking barefoot feeling the grass and the dust under the refreshing 'shadow of the Almighty,'[24] under overhanging majestic tree limbs reaching across my pathway as if to kiss each other. I was walking on a delightful abandoned portion of *the original* Natchez Trace, an old Indian trail beginning in Franklin, Tennessee and

---

[13] Gabriel spoke this to Daniel in James 2:23.

[14] Spoken of Abraham in such verses as James 2:23, 2 Chronicles 20:7, and Isaiah 41:8.

[15] See Luke 21:5-36.

[16] See words song by Elvis Presley – An American Trilogy – I wish I was in Dixieland."

[17] Quoting from *Jesus is Coming Sooner Than You Think* track written by Joe Ragland.

[18] Ending lines from Margaret Mitchell's *Gone With the Wind*. "Did Scarlet get Rhett back?" Miss Mitchell consistently said she did not know. To her the book ended where it ended. Or will anyone ever know, for on August 16, 1949, in Atlanta, Georgia U.S.A., Margaret Mitchell died after having been struck down by a taxicab."

[19] "Esquire is a courtesy title used in the United States largely for lawyers and in the United Kingdom for certain members of the gentry." *Wikipedia, The Free Encyclopedia.*

[20] Among the opening lines from Margaret Mitchell's *Gone With the Wind*.

[21] *Id.*

[22] *Days of Wine and Roses* from Andy Williams' Lyrics.

[23] *Yesterday* a song written by John Lennon and Paul McCartney.

[24] Psalm 91:1.

ending at the then crystal blue Mississippi River in Natchez, Mississippi. This walking path was trodden out by many moccasin steps before Christopher Columbus discovered 'the New World.'[25]

Delighting in the beauty of this 'day the Lord has made,'[26] I sang,

"How can I say thanks for the things, You have done for me?
Things so undeserved,yet You gave to *prove* Your love for me;
the voices of a million angels could not express my gratitude.
All that I am and ever hope to be, I owe it all to Thee.
To God be the glory. To God be the glory, To God be the glory
for the things, He has done.
With His (Jesus') blood, He has saved me, with His power (Holy Spirit joining with
my born again spirit) He has raised me; to God be the glory for the things, He has done.
Just let me live my life, let it be pleasing, Lord to Thee,
and if I gain any praise, let it go to Calvary.'[27]

Then suddenly out of the corner of my eye, I noticed a single white dove coming from the direction of the same white fluffy cloud. I was pleasantly surprised by waves of joy, feeling like the honey barrel spilled over me from Heaven, inquiring within, "*What is this?*"

I heard in my born again spirit, "*Heaven again has smiled upon you! You have been chosen and anointed for a critical end-time work! Write down in full for the people spiritual truths you are to witness and experience, some of which have been hidden before the foundation of the world! 'Woe to those (not born again) who laugh now, for your laughing will turn to mourning and sorrow.'[28] War and perilous times will come on the earth!*"

Responding in thought, "*War? Lord, You know I am for peace and not for war! I have no desire to study war! Heaven might choose someone else as the subject of war does not interest me. Still, I often 'pray for the peace of Jerusalem!'[29] In Bible School, I once memorized this Scripture, which I am waiting to come to pass,*

*'O God, do not keep silent; be not quiet, O God, be not still.
See how Your enemies are in tumult, how Your foes rear their heads.
With cunning, they conspire against Your people They plot against those You cherish.*

'Come,' they say, 'Let us destroy them (in war) as a nation, that the name of Israel be remembered no more.'[30]

I further thought, "*I know this war is coming. Also, the Antichrist will promise peace, safety, and prosperity to all who will take his mark and those who refuse to take his mark 'can neither buy nor sell.'[31]*"

At that moment one whose face glowed clear and bright, wearing clothing dazzlingly white as light, being bare-foot like myself, was seated on a huge abandoned millstone. When he stood and was rushing straight toward me, I immediately also stood looking at him coming fast and hearing him say,

'Greetings, you who are highly favored! The Lord is with you!'[32]

Feeling the anointing and the power of the Lord flowing through me, I stretched out my opened right hand toward the unidentified creature closing in fast on me. Suddenly a white light shot out like a laser beam from my right hand striking the creature on the chest, with the creature falling back sitting down in a dazed condition on the abandoned millstone.

I inquired, "Are you or are you not, a ministering messenger angel from Heaven? An anointed beam of power coming out of my right hand has happened before. I as a born again Christian am 'an ambassador for Jesus Christ.'[33] Jesus promised, 'the works I do, you will also do.'[34] According to the Bible, it is recorded regarding a

---

[25] Christopher Columbus recorded, "It was the Lord who put it into my mind. . . . I could feel His hand upon me. . . .There is no question the inspiration was from the Holy Spirit because He comforted me with rays of marvelous illumination from the Holy Scriptures." *Christopher Columbus* – from his diary, in reference to the discovery of 'the New World.'

[26] Psalm 118:24.

[27] *My Tribute* by Andre Crouch. [Emphasis added,]

[28] Luke 6:25.

[29] Psalm 122:6.

[30] Psalm 83:1-4 NIV.

[31] Revelation 13:17.

[32] Luke 1:28.

[33] 2 Corinthians 5:20.

[34] John 14:12.

band of men rushing to arrest Jesus, '*As soon as He (Jesus) said unto them, I am He they went backward and fell to the ground.*'[35]

You likewise were coming at me too fast without an introduction and 'Satan himself masquerades (disguises himself) as an angel of light (trying to fool people into thinking he is from God).'[36] As a Christian lawyer, I remind you that the term Christian (means little Christ) and we Christians are to examine and prove (much like a lawyer) the spirits. Therefore, it is commanded,

'*Do not believe every spirit, but try (test like an attorney) the spirits to see whether they are from God.*'[37]

'*Do you not know that we (Christians) will judge (try) angels? How much more the things of this life.*'[38]

"Creature, do you confess that 'Jesus Christ came to the Earth in the flesh! That He was sacrificed by being nailed to a cross, was resurrected from the dead the third day, and will come again to 'judge the living and the dead,'[39] 'yes' or 'no.'

The angel visibly stunned responds, "Yes!"

"Right answer! Angel from Heaven let us start all over by properly introducing ourselves. My name is Joseph, and I am a lawyer, an ordained minister, public speaker, and a born again citizen of Heaven. My name is in the 'Lamb's Book of Life.'[40] Jesus is my Savior, Lord, and 'elder brother.'[41] What is the purpose of your visit on this 'Lord's Day?'[42]

"Counselor, forgive me for being presumptions and coming at you so fast. That is a bad habit of mine, which I believe you have finally broken!

I nodded a '*yes*,' assuring, "You are forgiven! Please introduce yourself."

"My name is Raphael.[43] I am an angel of the Lord in Gabriel's division. I am in John Milton's Paradise lost regarding my assignment from God to expound to Adam about the war in Heaven, in which Lucifer and his angels '*fell like lightning from Heaven*'[44] to the Earth.

Today, I have an assignment from Heaven to join myself to you. I respectfully ask you to write messages you will receive in dreams and visions from Heaven to God's people of the Earth with ears to hear. You have read the end-time warning by Jesus,

'*For then shall be great tribulation (destruction), such as has not been from the beginning of the world . . . and never to be equaled again.*'[45] [Emphasis added.]

I replied, "Raphael, I have no clue regarding the tribulation in the Earth at the beginning to which Jesus was referring! In reading the Bible, the Word of God, I knew something happened as the Bible declares,

'*In the beginning, God created (formed and fashioned) the Heaven and the Earth.*

The Earth became (some great tribulation took place) without form and empty (a wasteland void of life on its surface).'[46j]

I know Jesus while on Earth taught, '*I have much more to say to you, but they are too much for you (to bear) now.*'[47] Also, the Apostle Paul '*was caught up (to Heaven) and heard inexpressible things – things that man may not tell.*'[48] Am I too going to be caught up to Heaven?"

The angel nods a '*no.*'

---

[35] John 18:6.

[36] 2 Corinthians 11:14.

[37] 1 John 4:1.

[38] 1 Corinthians 6:3.

[39] 2 Timothy 4:1.

[40] See Revelation 3:5; 13:8; 17:8; 20:15; 21:27.

[41] Hebrews 2:11.

[42] Revelation 1:10.

[43] See Raphael in *Archangels* at *Wikipedia, The Free Encyclopedia*.

[44] Luke 10:18.

[45] Matthew 24:21.

[46] Genesis 1:1-2.

[47] John 16:12.

[48] 2 Corinthians 12:2-4.

"Raphael, I know that tribulation is coming, but who on the Earth today knows what the 'tribulation was in the beginning' to which Jesus was referring? What are the names of the other two magnificent angels that spoke on this Lord's Day from the cotton field?

Raphael answers, "Please lawyer, one question at a time!

The angel that delivered the message to you from the cotton field was Gabriel,[49] and the other angel beside him with the sword was Michael.[50] They are now delivering messages, restraining war and protecting the nations of Israel and the United States as plans are being made to detonate simultaneously atomic bombs near the coasts of Tel Aviv and New York.

Paul, the evangelist, wasn't permitted to reveal such things, and he was 'determined not to know anything save Jesus Christ, and He crucified.'[51] Counselor, one can search the whole world over, and not one soul will know about this great tribulation (destruction) the Son of God, Jesus, expounded that occurred at the beginning of the Earth. No, not one!"

"Counselor, wouldn't you like to have some insights regarding the 'tribulation at the beginning of the Earth' to which Jesus was referring?" I nod a 'yes.'

Raphael continues, "*Your 'prayers and alms have come up for a memorial before God.'*[52] You praise, worship, and are thankful to God. You hear from Heaven and act on what you hear until the task is closed. You '*seek first God's kingdom and His righteousness.'*[53]

When you miss it, you are quick to repent and turn away from that sin. 'The blood of Jesus (is ever) cleansing you from every sin.'[54]

'*As you confess your sins, God is faithful and just to forgive you of your sins and purify you from all unrighteousness.'*[55] You '*overcome him (the devil and his crew) by the blood of the Lamb and by the word of your testimony.'*[56]

Heaven is now in need of your faithful services using your Bible knowledge, computer skills, and legal gifting in the jurisprudence of presenting evidence. Heaven has found you '*diligent in your business.'*[57] As you work on an assignment, you do it '*with all your might.'*[58]

"Raphael, in deep humility, I respectfully seek to complete each assignment from Heaven giving my utmost and all the glory for His Highest, the Father, the Son, and the Holy Spirit. Of my service, it is written,

'*When you have done (fully performed) all these things (work assignments) which are commanded you, you should say, 'We are undeserving servants (no personal praise due), we have only done the work (in the Kingdom of God) which was our duty (obligation and responsibility) to do.'*[59]

Raphael replies, "For such a reply this is why you are anointed and chosen for this unique and extraordinary assignment! Heaven considers you more than a servant, but an anointed 'friend of the Bridegroom (Jesus).'[60] You are the anointed man for the task – '*for such a time as this!'*[61]

Counselor, you will see as if through a '*glass darkly'* as in dreams some '*reflection of* truths'[62] as you write '*line on line, line on line. A little here, a little there.'*[63] Some of what you will see and hear had or will happen or be close to that way and other parts will be like parables often used by Jesus to illustrate a moral or spiritual truth.

---

[49] See Gabriel delivering a message to Daniel. Daniel 9:21-27.

[50] '*There was war in Heaven: Michael and his angels fought against the dragon (Lucifer; Satan), and the dragon fought and his angels, and prevailed not; neither was their place (Lucifer and his angels) place found any more in Heaven.'* Revelation 12:7-8.

[51] 1 Corinthians 2:2.

[52] Acts 10:4.

[53] Matthew 6:33.

[54] 1 John 1:7. Present active tense meaning that the blood of Jesus is ever purifying from all sin as believers confess and repent of their sins.

[55] 1 John 1:9.

[56] Revelation 12:11.

[57] Proverbs 22:29.

[58] Ecclesiastes 9:10.

[59] Luke 17:10.

[60] John 3:29.

[61] Esther 4:14.

According to the Bible, '*In the last days, God says, 'Your young men will see visions, and your old men will dream dreams.*'[64] '*And Joseph dreamed a dream, and he told it.*'[65] '*The Lord appeared to Solomon during the night in a dream, and God said, 'Ask for whatever you want Me to give you.' Solomon answered, '. . .Give your servant a discerning heart to govern your people and to distinguish between right and wrong.' So God said to him, 'I will give you a wise and discerning heart.' Then Solomon awoke – and he realized it had been a dream.*'[66]

'*God was pleased to use the message that sounds (or reads) foolish (like folly) of what was (is) preached (written and oral) to save those who believe.*'[67]

Counselor, you are to record as a scribe the messages to God's people of the Earth in a manner it had never been written before, with no prior examples. Remember that Jesus guarded His teaching in parables so as not to cast '*pearls before swine.*'[68]

For those judgmental ones, who would like to challenge what you will record, use your law skills to cite supportive jurisprudence in the footnotes. Some will attempt to debate and argue, 'Bible or no Bible, I believe another doctrine. '*Where is this coming (back to the Earth) He (Jesus) promised? Ever since our ancestors died, everything goes on as it has since the beginning of creation.*'[69] '*Do not be anxious (worry) about how to respond or what to say. For at that time, you will be given the things to say (or be led to remain silent).*

It will not really be you speaking, but the (Holy) Spirit of your Father (God) speaking through you. God will give you the right words at the right time.'[70] The Apostle Paul wrote to those with a teachable spirit,

'*For the invisible things of Him from the creation of the world are seen, being understood by the things made, even His eternal power and Godhead; so they (who do not believe in such a great offer of salvation) are without excuse. . . . And even as they did not like to retain God in their knowledge, God gave them over to a reprobate mind, to do those things that are not convenient; being filled with all unrighteousness, fornication, wickedness, covetousness, maliciousness; full of envy, murder, debate, deceit, malignity; whisperers, backbiters, haters of God, despiteful, proud, boasters, inventors of evil things, disobedient to parents.*

Without understanding, covenant breakers (divorce included), without natural affection, implacable, unmerciful: Who knowing the judgment of God, that they which commit such things are worthy of death, not only do the same, but have pleasure in them that do them.'[71] [Emphasis added.]

To some, your recorded messages will sound like folly. To those '*hungering and thirsting after righteousness*'[72] the recorded messages will contain nuggets of wisdom, counsel, joy, and revelation from Heaven worth more than fine gold. Some of these truths have been '*hidden before and 'from the foundation of the world.*'[73]

One will seek to debate that the Apostles Creed, 'I believe in God, the Father, Almighty, Creator of Heaven and Earth,' written by the Apostles themselves, to prove that God the Father was the Creator and not His Son, Jesus. Reply in love that the Apostles could not have written this as the Bible teaches that it was Jesus, the Son of God, who created the Heaven and Earth,

'*He (Jesus, Son of God) is the image of the invisible God (the Father), the firstborn over all creation. For by Him (Jesus), all things were created: things in Heaven and on Earth . . . . All things were created by Him (Jesus) and for Him. He is before all things, and in Him, all things hold together.*'[74]

---

[62] 1 Corinthians 13:12

[63] Isaiah 28:10.

[64] Act 2:17.

[65] Genesis 37:5.

[66] 1 Kings 3:5, 9, 12, 15.

[67] 1 Corinthians 1:21.

[68] Matthew 7:6.

[69] 2 Peter 3:4.

[70] Matthew 10:19-20.

[71] Romans 1:20, 28-32 KJV.

[72] Matthew 5:6.

[73] Matthew 13:35.

[74] Colossians 1:15-17. Legend has it that the Apostles wrote The Apostles' Creed on the tenth day after Jesus ascension into Heaven. In error it declares: "We believe ... the Father . . . maker of heaven and earth, of all that is, seen, and unseen," contrary to the Bible truth that through Jesus all thing were created, e.g., see Colossians 1:16, John 1:3, Hebrews 1:2), and some versions in error declare, We

'In the beginning was the Word (Jesus, the Son of God), and the Word was with God, and the Word was God. He was with God in the beginning. Through Him (Jesus), all things were made; without Him, nothing was made that has been made. . The Word (Jesus) became flesh and lived for a while among us.'[75]

Counselor, some doctrines of men are beneficial, and others contain harmful untruths. Many in the world are taught and believe that Jesus is not the Son of God, nor was He crucified and died on a cross (shedding His life's blood to pay the penalty owed for sins). Those believing this will believe a lie and be damned (to Hell).

The main thing is that the person enters the Kingdom of God by being born again after repenting, receiving Jesus as Savior, and confessing Jesus as Lord. The messages you will record are so needed by the people of the Earth. Jesus declared these foundational truths,

'In vain do they worship Me (Jesus), teaching as doctrines the commandments of men.'[76]

'I tell you the truth, unless a man is born again, he cannot see the kingdom of God.'[77]

'I (Jesus) am the way and the truth and the life. No one can come to the Father except through Me.'[78]

'Blessed are those who wash their robes (in the blood of Jesus), that they may have the right to the tree of life (and live forever) and may go through the gates into the city. Outside are the dogs, those who practice magic arts (drugs), the sexually immoral, the murderers (includes those killing in the name of a false religion), the idolaters and everyone that loves and practices falsehood.

I, Jesus, have sent My angel to give you this testimony for the churches. I am the Root and Offspring of David, and the bright Morning Star.

The Spirit and the bride say, 'Come!' And let him who hears say, 'Come!' Whoever is thirsty (for the truth), let him come, and whoever wishes, let him take the free gift (not of works) of the water of life. . . .The grace of the Lord Jesus be with God's people. Amen.'[79]

Jesus known as the 'Wonderful Counselor'[80] counseled such self-righteous to see themselves as they were and not as they perceived themselves to be. Jesus spoke of such,

Woe to you, teachers of the law and Pharisees, you hypocrites! You are like whitewashed tombs, which look beautiful on the outside, but on the inside are full of the bones of the dead and everything unclean.'[81]

Many will say to Me (Jesus) on that (Judgment) day, 'Lord, Lord, did we not prophesy in Your name, and in Your name drive out demons and in Your name perform many miracles?

Then I (Jesus) will tell them plainly. 'I never knew you. Away from Me, you evildoers!'[82]

'Unless you repent (critical) you also will all perish (in Hell).'[83]

Counselor, a friend of Jesus, I know you are for peace, but war and perilous times are coming on the Earth! The messages you write will be considered acts of war by the 'whitewashed tombs' and by Hell itself. Legal counselor remain with your refreshing sense of humor and keep holding *'up the shield of faith, with which you can extinguish all the flaming arrows of the evil one. Take the helmet of salvation and the sword of the Spirit, which is the word of God.'*[84]

Counselor, you are now a Heaven's seventh choice to compile the *'Unabridged Messages'* to the people of the world in a book entitled **Love and War**. Six before you have turned this offer down to write these revealing messages to God's people! In rejecting the offer they gave various excuses: 'I have obligations to my spouse; my parents are old; my business is taking off; I don't have time; too expensive to finalize such an unabridged book containing all the original content; my peers and those at the church I attend would not understand; persecution will come if I told it as it truly is; I do not like to be scorned or mocked; some of the truths I will receive may go against many traditions of men, some to which I dearly embrace, et cetera.

"believe in the Holy Spirit, the Lord," (No, Jesus is Lord, e.g. see Romans 14:1, Philippians 2:10).

[75] John 1:1-3, 14.

[76] Matthew 15:9.

[77] John 3:3.

[78] John 14:6.

[79] Revelation 22:14-17- 21.

[80] Isaiah 9:6.

[81] Matthew 23:27.

[82] Matthew 7:22-23.

[83] Luke 13:3.

[84] Ephesians 6:16.

Counselor, this will not be an easy assignment to finish. Record with joy the messages *'fixing your eyes on Jesus, the pioneer, and perfecter of your faith. For the joy set before Him, He endured the cross, scorning its shame, and sat down at the right hand of the throne of God.'*[85]

'For nothing is impossible with God!'[86] *'Behold, I am the Lord, the God of all flesh. Is there anything too hard (difficult for Me?'*[87] God promises to confer a *favored saint's blessing* upon the one who will accept Heaven's offer and compile these messages to God's holy people,

'Now to Him (God) who is able to do immeasurably more than all we (born again believers) ask or imagine, according to His power (Holy Spirit's anointing) that is at work within us, to Him be glory in the church and in Christ Jesus throughout all generations, forever and ever (throughout eternity)! Amen.'[88] *'Those who honor God, He (God) will honor.'*[89]

"Raphael, 'Heaven can look no further for an anointed chosen vessel to record Heaven's messages to God's holy people if I can be assured of these precious promises, *'God's Presence will go with me!'*[90] *'The Lord was with Joseph, so he succeeded in everything he did.'*[91]

Raphael, you know I detest and hate war! A man of God has the right to defend themselves *'for the battle is not yours, but God's.'*[92] I daily hold up the shield of faith and put on the spiritual armor.[93] Paul explained of his salvation, "I keep my body (flesh) under so that after I have preached to others, I will not be disqualified (become a castaway).[94] I stand on this precious promise, *'Now to God, who is able to keep me from falling and to make me stand (keep me from stumbling) and to present me (saved) before His glorious presence without fault (washed in the blood of His Son) and with great joy.'*[95]

I respectfully with fear and trembling accept your challenge to compile these messages for God's people as I devote my utmost for His Highest! Such as *'I do have I give in the name of Jesus Christ,'*[96] whom I love! Lord, use me for Your glory, as I seek no glory for myself. How does one begin?"

Raphael responds, "Remember that God-given dreams and visions are not always given in the night. Some include what God paints on the canvas of your born again spirit. These dreams and visions are powerful and are real, being a part of God's plan and design, and you are to record these messages for God's people. 'Do not despise the days of small beginning, for the Lord rejoices to see the work begin.'[97] Your goal at the end of your exciting and abundant time on Earth is to hear,

'Well done, good and faithful servant! You have been faithful with a few things (in your lifetime on Earth), and I will put you in charge of many things (in your future eternal life with Jesus). Come and partake in your Master's happiness!'[98]

Persecution, war, and tribulation, the likes of which have not been since the tribulation at the beginning of the Earth are coming again on the Earth! In part, these terrible times are described,

'There was a great earthquake. The sun grew black like sackcloth made of goat hair. The whole moon turned (red) like blood.

---

[85] Hebrews 12:2.

[86] Luke 1:37.

[87] Jeremiah 32:26.

[88] Ephesians 3:20-21 NIV.

[89] 1 Samuel 2:30.

[90] Exodus 13:14.

[91] Genesis 39:3.

[92] 2 Chronicles 20:15.

[93] Ephesians 6:10-18.

[94] 1 Corinthians 9:27. Can an original believer be lost? "23,000 fell in one day." (1 Corinthians 10:8); "Ye are fallen from grace." (Galatians 5:4); "Later end worse than first." (2 Peter 2:20); "A servant cast out." (Matthew 25:30); "Fall away." (Hebrews 6:6, Luke 8:13); "Faith shipwrecked." 1 Timothy 1:19. 20); "Cast out and burned." (John 15:6); "Christ will spew out." (Revelation 3:16), and "Take heed lest ye fall." (1 Corinthians 10:12).

[95] Jude 1:24.

[96] Acts 3:6.

[97] Zechariah 4:10.

[98] Matthew 25:23.

. . .They (not born again ones in the Kingdom of Heaven) called to the mountains and the rocks. 'Fall on us and hide us from the face of Him who sits on the throne and from the wrath of the Lamb (Jesus, Son of God)!'[99]

'During those days (of the great tribulation) people will look for a way to die (to escape the great persecution, but they will not find it. They will long (desire) to die, but death will flee (making it impossible to die) from them.'[100]

You will dream about the 144,000 evangelists, who will have *'His (Jesus) name and His Father's name written on their foreheads.'*[101] They will help reap a great harvest during the great tribulation.

According to the Bible, those accepting Jesus as the Messiah will include,

'These are they (born again ones), who have come out of the great tribulation; they have washed their robes (finally accepted Jesus as Savior, repented, and confessed Him as Lord), and made them white (pure) in the blood of the Lamb.'[102]

'How can they believe in the One (Jesus, Lamb of God) whom they have not heard? How will they hear without someone preaching to them? And how can they preach unless they are sent? As it is written, 'How beautiful are the feet of those who bring good news (of salvation)!'[103]

'The Kingdom of Heaven has been forcibly advancing, and forceful men take it by force (as a precious prize).'[104]

Counselor, you like the 144,000 evangelists are one of the forceful men! Now take it by force! Write down what has happened, what is now, and what will take place and put the messages in an unabridged (complete) book form en*titled* **Love & War** for the people![105] Don't fear, the Lord will be your 'refuge and fortress.'[106]

'The day of the Lord Jesus will come just like a thief in the night. While people are saying (bragging), 'We have peace, and we are safe,' then destruction will come upon them suddenly like labor pains on a woman with child, and they will not escape!'[107]

'The preaching of the cross (seems like) sheer absurdity and foolishness to those who are lost (headed for destruction in Hell and the Lake of Fire), but to us who are being saved it is the (manifestation) of the power of God.'[108]

'The present heavens and the Earth are reserved for fire, being kept for the Day of Judgment, and destruction of ungodly men. But do not forget this one thing, dear friends: With the Lord, a day is like a thousand years, and a thousand years are like a day. The Lord is not slow in keeping His promise, as some understand slowness. He is patient with you, not wanting anyone to perish, but everyone to come to repentance. But the day of the Lord will come like a thief. The heavens will disappear with a roar; the elements will be destroyed by fire, and the Earth and everything in it will be laid bare. Since everything will be destroyed in this way, what kind of people ought you to be? You ought to live holy and godly lives as you look forward to the day of God and speed its coming.'[109]

Raphael concludes, "Counselor, you are anointed and equipped to complete this assignment. Ask a blessing of the Lord! A nearby wealthy landowner has a born again daughter believing for a husband, and she is a virgin and looks remarkably as beautiful as Scarlet O'Hara."

I respond, "Charming, but no thanks! I will ask initially in prayer what Solomon and Jabez asked,

'Give your servant an understanding heart . . . that I might discern between good and evil.'[110]

'And enlarge my territory, that Your hand would be with me, and that You would keep me from evil, that I may not cause pain (to myself or to others).'[111]

---

[99]   Revelation 6:12, 16.

[100]   Revelation 9:6.

[101]   Revelation 14:1.

[102]   Revelation 7:14.

[103]   Romans 10:14-15.

[104]   Matthew 11:12.

[105]   See Revelation 1:19 being similar words given to John on the island of Patmos.

[106]   Psalm 91:2.

[107]   1 Thessalonians 5:2-3.

[108]   1 Corinthians 1:18.

[109]   2 Peter 3:7-11.

[110]   1 Kings 3:9.

[111]   1 Chronicles 4:10.

Raphael concludes, "Amen! Blessings and anointing from Heaven are in and on you!

'The Lord takes pleasure in the prosperity of His servant.'[112]

'And all these blessings shall come upon you and overtake you, because you obey the voice of the Lord your God.'[113] *'The eternal God is your refuge, and underneath (to hold you) are His everlasting (strong) arms.'*[114]

'How we (born again ones) praise God, the Father of our Lord Jesus Christ, who has blessed us with every spiritual blessing in the heavenly realms because we belong to Christ.'[115]

Counselor, now you lay me down to sleep and receive the dream of dreams, the vision of visions, and record the messages to God's people fully. I am being called back to headquarters!"

As I rubbed my eyes, Raphael vanished from in front of me.

Feeling drowsy, I looked down at my blanket. I then looked again toward the abandoned millstone as a white dove was flying rapidly away low over the cross on the steeple of the distant abandoned white stone church then disappearing into the same fluffy white cloud.

Laying my Bible behind my head as a pillow, and pulling half the quilt over me, I prayed, "Father God, now I lay me down to sleep. I pray my spirit, soul, and body. You will keep. May Your angels and the Holy Spirit guide me in these promised dreams and visions to be compiled for Your people. In Jesus' name. Amen!"

As I closed my eyes, it was like the word ETERNITY was stamped on my eyeballs. Perceiving – "I am about to go where no man has ever gone before – back in Eternity," I fell into a supernatural deep *'sweet sleep.'*[116]

I dreamed[117] a dream witnessing a rapid rewind like a video tape traveling back in time through the world wars, when the Earth was covered by water, the lush Garden of Eden, the ice age, the Earth looking like a huge mud ball, and finally back to a vast nothingness.

In my dream I reasoned, 'Lord, here I exist before the creation of Heaven, Earth, stars, or any other physical matter! Not possible for a mere mortal man, but I know according to the Bible, *'For nothing is impossible with God!'*[118]

Soli Deo Gloria†[119]

---

[112] Psalm 35:27.

[113] Deuteronomy 28:2.

[114] Deuteronomy 33:27.

[115] Ephesians 1:3.

[116] "When you (one trusting in God) lie down, you will you won't be afraid. When you lie down, you will sleep in peace." (Proverbs 3:24).

[117] "The day shall come . . . (when) your old men will dream dreams, your young men will see visions." (Joel 2:28).

[118] Luke 1:38.

[119] *"Soli Deo Gloria* is a Latin term for *Glory to God alone.* It has been used by artist like Johann Sebastian Bach, George Handel, and Christopher Graupner to signify that the work was produced for The sake of praising God. ." *Wikipedia, The Free Encyclopedia, Soli Deo Gloria.*

†BOOK ONE†

†BOOK ONE – Episode 1†

[†**Sidebar Scriptures**: "Joseph had a dream and promptly reported all the details (Genesis 37:5)."
"The Lord revealed to me what the evil ones were doing and planning and showed me their wicked plots (Jeremiah 11:18)."
"The word of the Lord came to Abram in a **vision**. . . . A **deep sleep** came upon Abram . . . . (Genesis 15:1, 12)."
I witnessed and experienced "dreams and visions, and I described all I had seen to instruct many (Daniel 7:1, 11:33)."†][1]

Back in Eternity

"**ETERNITY** – Without beginning or end.
'*The high and lofty One (God) who inhabits eternity.*'
Isaiah 57:15
God has existed from eternity."
(Noah Webster)[2]

AS I HIKED DOWN the old Natchez Trace, I sat down to rest in a pleasant place.
My ***Bible*** fell   open to this passage,
'*So we fix our eyes not on what is seen, but on what is unseen.*
For what is seen is temporary, but what is unseen is ETERNAL.'[3]
Laying my Bible behind my head as a pillow, I closed my eyes, and it was like the word **ETERNITY** was stamped on my eyeballs. Perceiving

Laying my Bible behind my head as a pillow, I closed my eyes, and it was like the word **ETERNITY** was stamped on my eyeballs. Perceiving – "*I am about to go 'where no man has ever gone before'*[4] *– back in Eternity.*"
I soon fell into a supernatural deep '*sweet sleep.*'[5]

In this pleasant sleep, I dreamed[6] a dream and witnessed a rapid rewind like a video tape traveling back in eternity – through the world wars, then when water covered the Earth, the ice age, then with the Earth looking like a huge mud ball, and finally back to a vast emptiness, where I eavesdropped in on the Godhead of the Father, the Son, and the Holy Spirit, being one God.

Opening my born again spiritual eyes and ears in my dream, I witnessed, God the Father, an invisible Spirit, being asked by His invisible Son, the Word,

"Eternal Father, the 'I am who I am,'[7] what is the name of this place in which we are located?"

The Father answers, "I call this place, ***Nothing***."

---

[1] The Apostle Paul wrote, "For now I see through a glass darkly, but then (in eternity) I shall see clearly face to face." (1 Corinthians 13:12). God-given dreams are not always given in the night. Many are like what God paints on the canvas of one's heart. The Apostle Peter explained that such visions and dreams are to be expected from God, **Error! Main Document Only.**"*In the last days, God says . . . your young men will see visions, your old men will dream dreams (Acts 2:17).***Error! Main Document Only.**" I often laugh when I receive a vision and dream from the Lord whether I am a young man or an old man!

[2] *Eternity* from *American Dictionary of the English Language* by Noah Webster 1828.

[3] 2 Corinthians 4:18. [Emphasis added].

[4] Where no man has gone before is a phrase originally made popular through its use in the episodes of Star Trek television series.

[5] "*When you (one trusting in God) lie down, you will you won't be afraid. When you lie down, you will sleep in peace.*" (Proverbs 3:24).

[6] "*The day shall come . . .(when) your old men will dream dreams, your young men will see visions.*" (Joel 2:28).

[7] Exodus 3:14.

Pondering the Father's reply, the Son inquires, "What is on the other side of **Nothing**? Is there anything else out there?"

"No," the Father replied, "On the other side is nothing. A good future definition of the term "Nothing" will be, '*Not anything; denies the existence of anything; (a) non-entity; opposed to something. The world (to be) was created from nothing.*'[8]

Then the Father inquires, "Son if there was a wall, what would be on the other side of the wall? Many will advocate a big bang, but they cannot answer the simple question, 'Who made the matter that blew up?' There is neither another god nor anything anywhere, but Us. We are the center of all this nothing. Nothing else to hear. Nothing else to feel. Nothing to see. Only empty darkness. Nothing, but nothing. Just Us! We three in One – no more. Son, it is not good to have just nothing. Initially, there has to be nothing because nothing has been created. I have a wonderful plan and out of the nothing, You will create the Heaven, the Earth, the sun, the moon, the planets, stars, angels, man having a free will in Our image (likeness), animals, birds, fish, and all things in Heaven and on Earth, visible and invisible."

"Father, I can hear You, but I can hardly see You or Myself as I too am an invisible Spirit. Do I look like You? I see Your form – Your face, hands, and feet. I move in and out of You. I can look down and see a shadowy outline of My almost invisible hand. Are we separate, or are we One? I hear you laugh, and even so I laugh separate from You. How can We be One, yet separate? You are '*greater than I*'[9] and '*My food (nourishment) is to do Your will (pleasure).*'[10] Father, I '*delight in You and You give Me the desires of My heart*'[11] so others will know '*I love My Father, and I do exactly what My Father has commanded Me!*'[12] Father take Me to a place called at least 'There' with something there. I realize it is now nothing from the beginning as nothing has been created."

Son, "Hold My hand, and I'll take You to a 'There'[13] place."

The Son reaches out His spiritual hand, and His hand goes into the spiritual hand of His Father. The place called 'Nothing' comes alive with the auditory sensations of music with a glorious light pulsating to the rhythm of the music. The Father smiling decrees, "Son, it will be written about this special time back in eternity,

'*In the beginning, there was the Word (eternally existing Son of God). The Word was with God (the Father), and the Word was (wholly) God. He was with God in the beginning. All things (created) came to be by (through) Him (the Son of God), and nothing came to be (created) without Him (the Son of God).*'[14]

'*He (the Son of God) is the image[15] of the invisible (Father) God.*'[16]

---

[8] Nothing (made up of) no and thing.
  See *American Dictionary of the English Language* by Noah Webster 1828.
[9] John 14:28.
[10] John 4:34.
[11] See Psalm 37:4.
[12] John 14:31.
[13] From the song, "*Somewhere*" (There's a Place for Us) Lyrics.
[14] John 1:1-3.
[15] The Hebrew word of image in (Genesis 1:27) is teselem. Tselem translates as 'an outline or representation of an original as a shadow is the outline of the original.' Also, see *A Concise Dictionary of the Words in the Hebrew Bible* by James Strong, S.T.D., LL.D., 6754, teselem. God making man in His own image (likeness; resemblance).
[16] Colossians 1:15.

Son, we are Spirit – one person of Me, the Father, another of You, My Son, and another of the Holy Spirit, but the Godhead of the Father, Son, and the Holy Spirit is one God. There is no other, but Us."

"Father, who made Us?"

"My Son, the Godhead had no beginning. We are the One and only God. There has never been another god. '*We are from everlasting to everlasting*,'[17] an uncreated, eternal Spirit[18] Being.

Us three in One – no more. It is the desire of Your heart to testify of Your love for Me to others. Also, it is My will that You will soon be creating others, giving them a 'free will' to choose to love or war against Us. I am soon letting You come out of the pure Spirit realm and to give You '*flesh and bones*'[19] so others can see, hear, touch, and believe We love them. You shall be God manifested in the flesh (physical body)!

I will love those You create so much I will give You, My one and only Son, that '*whoever exceptions) believes in You (making You sincerely their personal Savior, repenting of sin, and confessing You as their Lord) shall not perish, but have eternal life.*'[20] They can choose of their own 'free will' to receive You as Savior. They can choose to worship Us and love Us back with all their heart, mind, soul, strength, and body, and love their neighbor as themselves.[21] They can choose to be born again into Our family, or they can reject selfishly, our free offer of salvation, and even war against Us with it being written of Us, '*The Lord is a man of a war. . . .*'[22] Presently, My Son, you are a Spirit, with a will, emotions, and mind, but soon you will be '*spirit, soul,* (with a flesh and bone) *body.*'[23]

Son, regarding Your body, this is a future dialog between You and one of Your disciples,

'Though the doors were locked, Jesus came and said, 'Peace be with you.' Then He said to Thomas, 'Put your fingers here (on My flesh and bone body); see My hands. Reach out your hand and put it into My side (a hole from a spear wound by a Roman soldier received after being nailed to a cross by Our enemies). Stop doubting and believe.'

Thomas said to Him (after touching the nail holes and wound in His body), 'My Lord and my God!'

Then Jesus told him, 'Because you have seen Me (touching the wounds in My body), you have believed; blessed are those who have not seen (direct evidence) and yet have believed (faith and obedience working in love pleases Me the most).'[24]

Son, in Your flesh body You will look like a shadow image of Me, an invisible, eternal Spirit. Your face in the flesh will look like My invisible face, with a slight hump on Your nose. You dimly see in Me what Your congregation will see in You. Here, look intently at My eternal face, as I was not created by another's hands since I have always been. 'I am who I am.'[25] During this part of eternity, the Holy Spirit and I will stay mostly invisible, for reasons of My own. "No one (human) can see My face and live.'[26] Again, Son, it will be written of You,

'*He (Jesus, the Son of God made flesh) is the image of the invisible God.*'[27]

---

[17] Psalm 90:2.
[18] See John 4:24.
[19] See Luke 24:39.
[20] John 3:16.
[21] Luke 10:27.
[22] Exodus 15:3.
[23] 1 Thessalonians 5:23.
[24] John 20:26-29.
[25] Exodus 3:14.
[26] Exodus 33:20.
[27] Colossians 1:15.

Suddenly, without warning, God the Father commences again a joyous contagious laughter, which sounds to the natural ear as claps and peals of thunder.[28] God the Son and God the Holy Spirit, as part of the One Godhead,[29] join in the joyous laughter.

The Eternal Son giggling bursts forth with the jubilant expression, "Shalom![30] Almighty Father, You are love![31] Lord, the Mighty One, no enemy can ever stand against You. How great Thou art! You are perfect in love, power, and purity of holiness. You always have been and always will be. You had no beginning, and You will have no end. Love (that is You) never fails![32] I too am love and have always been Your begotten Son, delighting to do Your will. I have been and will always be, faithful to do Your will and not My own,[33] for You are greater than I.[34] At Your right hand there are pleasures and joy (eternally) forever.[35] The glory[36] of being with You now before the creation of material substance is so majestic! I am so thankful to be Your Son, and I delight in hearing and doing Your will and plans. I bless and honor You, My Father! There is such joy in doing Your good pleasure."

With that introduction [intense laughing], God the Son is silent a few moments, then cheerfully inquiries of the Father, "Why are We laughing? You have not let Me in on Your secret. My cup is overflowing with joy! Laughing and giggles are evidence of joy overflowing. The honey barrel has fallen over Me.

I feel like I am under the waterspout where the glory is rushing out going through Me filling all this nothing. From where is the wonderful music and light coming? I know it is Your glory to conceal a matter, but it is My glory to search it out.[37] So, why are We laughing? I am thoroughly soaked, and I can't stop giggling!"

The Father smiling looks into the gentle and compassionate spiritual eyes of His only begotten Son, whom He loves, speaking, "This is the *ab initio*[38] '*wisdom of God (the Father) in a mystery, even the hidden wisdom, devised and decreed before the ages.*'[39] Shalom back to You, because at the end of all things I am planning, You and I are going to have a good laugh that will last forever!

---

[28] "*Then a voice (Father God) came from Heaven . . . . The crowd that was there and heard it said it had thundered . . . .*" (John 12:28-29).

[29] The one God is revealed as the Father, the Word (the Son of God), and the Holy Spirit. The Word (Son) of God is the express image of the Father and has always been Divine. The one Godhead consists of the Father, the Word (Son), and Holy Spirit.

[30] Shalom meaning peace, completeness, prosperity, and welfare and can be used to mean both hello and goodbye.
See *Wikipedia, The Free Encyclopedia.*

[31] 1 John 4:8 NIV.

[32] 1 Corinthians 13:8.

[33] *Jesus declared, "Father, if You are willing, take this cup from Me; yet not My will, but Yours be done."* (Luke 22:42 NIV).

[34] Jesus declared, "*If you loved Me, you would be glad that I am going to the Father, for the Father is greater than I.*" (John 14:28 NIV).

[35] "*In Your presence is fullness of joy, at Your right hand there are pleasures for evermore.*" (Psalm 16:11 NKJV).

[36] "*I have gloried You down here on the Earth by completing the work that You gave me to do. And now, Father, glorify Me along with Yourself and restore Me to such majesty and honor in Your presence as I had with You before the world existed.*" (John 17:4-5).

[37] "*It is the glory of God to conceal a matter; but to search out a matter is the glory of kings.*" (Proverbs 25:1 NIV).

[38] *Ab Initio* – "From the beginning . . . in the inception." *Black's Law Dictionary.*

[39] 1 Corinthians 2:7.

Trust Me, You and I will have the greatest laugh ever between a Father and Son, and this time You will lead it. Here is a clue to this marvelous mystery from a greatly loved future servant, John the Baptist, who in his day will deliver to those with ears to hear a portion of the greatest secret ever delivered among men,[40] and will reveal in part this mystery and secret in this testimony,

'I am not the Messiah (Christ), but I am one sent to prepare the way for Him. He who has the bride is the bridegroom (Messiah). But the friend (a wedding guest – invited to the wedding party) who stands by and listens to Him is full of joy when he hears the bridegroom's voice.'[41]

My Son, You will further reveal from Me, *'Can the wedding guests (not talking about the bride, but the friends of the bridegroom) fast (abstain as in mourning from food and drink in this time of great joyful celebration) while the bridegroom (preparing to receive the bride) is with them?'*[42]

In these Scriptures are clues to this mystery, which will point you in the right direction."

The Father again commences peals of laughter as He throws out this riddle of riddles and marvelous mystery of mysteries.

The Son, giggling and looking at God the Holy Spirit, speaks, *"My Father has more might and foreknowledge than I."*[43]

The Holy Spirit replies, "Here we have a joyful bridegroom (with friends) who is about to receive a bride. Could He be talking about You, Word? How could the Son of God, being an invisible Spirit with no substance, have a bride? Seems impossible, but *'nothing is impossible with God (the Father).'*[44]"

After a few moments of silence, God the Holy Spirit further speaks as the music and light magnify, "This is the greatest Shekinah Glory ever! Love and joy are also flowing out of Me like a mighty rushing golden river.[45]

There has never been such glory in the eternities of eternities! Something is about to happen of magnificent proportions in whatever God the Father is planning. I also thank Him for His goodness and for His being love..[46]

He is laughing about something good in the middle of all this nothing!"

The Father's face is glowing, and He smiles decreeing, "Yes, Spirit, for My new plan is to be revealed in stages, like the unrolling of a precious scroll. Otherwise, My family relationship would forever be just confined to the two of You making up the Godhead – three in One! "

The Spirit replied, "We have been with You from infinity past; and, yes, 'We are One Triune God.' The Godhead consists of You, Your Son, and Me; and We are the One and only eternal God. Are We not family enough?"

"O, Spirit, how I love My Son and You," replies the Father. "I will reveal My plan in stages to My Son. He will speak My Words, and You Spirit will move, hover and brood[47] like a dove over the face of the situation to assure that My will and good pleasure are perfectly accomplished.

---

[40] Matthew 11;11-14.

[41] John 3:28-29.

[42] .Mark 2:19 See also Matthew 9:15 and Luke 5:34.

[43] John 14:28.

[44] Luke 1:37.

[45] *"For the kingdom of God is not meat and drink; but righteousness and peace and joy in the Holy Spirit."* (Romans 14:17).

[46] "God is love." (1 John 4:8).

[47] The Spirit of God was moving, (hovering like a dove, brooding) over the face of the waters. And God said, *'Let there be . . . ."* (Genesis 1:2-3 AMP).

5

Nothing can stop My will from being accomplished! Spirit, may no part of My plan grieve You, but rejoice in My Son doing My will always,[48] as I desire to have a comprehensive family circle to love and worship Us in return[49] – a family that will delight in doing all Our commandments,[50] rejoice in Our glory in their inner being, and present their bodies to Us unselfishly as a living sacrifice, and as a *'reasonable act of worship.'*[51]

Some will choose to give to Us true and faithful love! I am a God of love and war; many will choose war, but the friends of the Bridegroom and the bride will choose love.

The Spirit interjects, "Please tell Me more!"

"There is something even more wonderful, which brings Me great joy. I will choose a **bride** for My beloved Son because even He, the Son of God, needs an intimate helper to share this joy. Sweet Spirit, it will be written,

'And I heard, as it were, the voice of a great multitude, as the sound of many waters and like loud peals of thunder, saying, 'Alleluia! For the Lord God Omnipotent reigns! Let us be glad and rejoice and give Him glory, for the marriage of the Lamb has come, and His wife had made herself ready' And to her it was granted to be arrayed in fine linen, clean and bright, for the fine linen is the righteous acts of the saints (friends of the bride). . . . Write: 'Blessed are those who are called (invited and accept the invitation) to the wedding banquet of the Lamb!'[52]

With great expectations, the Spirit projects, "I am looking forward to an invitation to the greatest marriage banquet ever to be!"

The Son still invisible to the natural eye remains silent. Spiritual tears flow from His spiritual eyes running down His cheeks and dripping off the bottom of His spiritual chin as He looks into the face of His loving Father and in a soft voice speaks, "O Father, I am crying for joy! Me a bridegroom? A bride for Me?"

"My Father, how could I be more joyful than I am right now by Your side?"

"My Son, You don't know what You are missing You think You have all of the joy, pleasures, and adventure now, but this is before You win the love of a godly bride who is passionately determined to stand by her Man. However, it will be written about the Son,

*'For the **joy** set before Him, He endured the cross (shedding His life's blood for sinners*[53] *who will receive Him as Savior and confess Him as Lord), scorning its shame, and sat down at the right hand (place of power) of the throne of (Father) God.*[54] *None of the princes of this world hath known (this mystery); for had they known it, they would not have crucified the Lord of glory.'*[55] [Emphasis added.]

Blood and water will flow from Your pierced side as it will when You take a rib near the heart of a man known as Adam, and from that flesh, bone, and blood You make him a bride. He will never desire Us to give his rib back, nor will You regret the wound in Your side legally opening up a way for You to be presented later with an eternal bride."

"Father, I am a Spirit, and I do not have a body of substance. How can my side be pierced?"

"Son, presently the Holy Spirit and I will mostly remain invisible for reasons of My own, but it will be written about You,

---

[48] *"Rejoice in the Lord always. Again, I say rejoice."* (Philippians 4:4).

[49] *"Then Jesus said to him, "be gone Satan! For it has been written, 'You shall worship the Lord your God, and Him alone shall you serve"* (Matthew 4:10 AMP).

[50] *"Keeping God's commands is what counts."* (1 Corinthians 7:19 NIV).

[51] *"In view of God's mercy . . . offer your bodies as living sacrifices, holy and pleasing to God – which is your spiritual worship."* (Romans 12:1 NIV).

[52] Revelation 19:6-9.

[53] See Romans 5:8 and Ephesians 2:4-6.

[54] Hebrews 12:2.

[55] 1 Corinthians 2:8.

'In these last days God (the Father) has spoken to us (those created in God's image) through His Son. God has appointed His Son to be Heir and lawful Owner of all things, and through Him, He made the worlds and the reaches of space and the ages of time – (that is) He made, produced, built, operated and arranged them in order.

He (the Son) is the sole expression of the glory of God (the Father) . . . and He (the Son) is the perfect imprint and the image of God (the Father) . . . .

But to the Son, He (God the Father) says to Him, 'Your throne, O God, is forever and ever (no ending through the eternal ages); and the scepter of Your kingdom is a scepter of absolute righteousness – of justice and straightforwardness.

You (the Son) have loved righteousness – You have delighted in right, integrity, virtue, and uprightness in purpose, thought and action – and You have hated wrong (lawlessness, injustice, and sin).

*Therefore, God (the Father), Your God, has anointed You with the oil of exultant **joy and gladness** [emphasis added] above and more abundantly than Your companions.*

And You, Lord (the Son), in the beginning did lay the foundation of the Earth, and the Heavens are made by Your hands.'[56]

Son, it will be written about this moment in eternity when You come out from Me into a body I prepared for You,

'You are My Son, today I have begotten You (that is, established You in an officially prepared body as King and Lord). I will be to Him a Father, and He will be to Me a Son.'[57]

'You (Father God) have made ready a body for Me.'[58]

Out of the light and music floats in the nothing a body dressed in a white robe with the Father inquiring, "Son, will you receive this gift and permit Me to place Your eternal Spirit in this flesh and bone body? Your name in this new body I have prepared for You will be Jesus, which means 'Savior,' as You will save many from sin and death. Their human spirit will be born again by believing in and receiving You as Savior and confessing You as Lord. True saving faith is trusting in You alone for eternal life. My Son, it will be written regarding Your body on Earth, having precious and holy blood,

'Now it came to pass as He (Jesus) took bread, blessed and broke it, and gave it to them. Then their eyes were opened, and they knew Him (to be Jesus), and He vanished from their sight.[59]

*. . . Now, as they said these things, Jesus Himself stood in the midst of them and said to them, 'Peace to you.' But they were terrified and frightened and supposed they had seen a spirit. And He (Jesus) said to them, 'Why are you troubled? And why do doubts arise in your hearts? Behold My (pierced) hands and my feet, that it is I (Jesus) Myself. Handle Me and see, for a spirit does not have **flesh and bones** [emphasis added] as you see Me (Jesus) have.'*

*When He (Jesus) had said this, He showed them His hands (containing marks where Romans had nailed Him to a wooden cross) and His feet (also containing marks from being nailed to a cross). But while they still did not believe, for **joy** [emphasis added] and marveled, He said to them, 'Have you any food here?' So they gave Him a piece of a broiled fish and some honeycomb. And He took it and ate in their presence.'*[60]

Son and Holy Spirit, questions?

Hearing none, are you ready, My Son, for Your Spirit to enter this body I prepared for You?"

"Yes, My Father, I am ready!"

Jesus' invisible Spirit leaps into the prepared body, and He examines in a full length mirror His body testifying, "I am a skinny preacher. My face in this flesh and bone body resembles Your face. Those who see Me will see You. My voice sounds a lot like Your authoritative voice. You have no blood in this body, as this is not needed yet.

---

[56] Hebrews 1:2-5, 8-9 (see *The Amplified Bible*, abbreviated AMP).

[57] Hebrews 1:5.

[58] Hebrew 10:5.

[59] Luke 24:30.

[60] Luke 24:36-40.

However, with this flesh and bone body, those in the congregation can see and hear Me preach. I could even ride a swift horse I could create. I receive with thanksgiving this body prepared by You to do Your will."

The Father spoke, "This body is My creation, a chip off the old block so to speak, but You will create the rest through my counseling. It will be written about the body I created for You,

'He (Jesus) has no (royal, kingly form) to make us notice Him;
there was nothing in His appearance to make us desire Him.
He was despised (hated) and rejected and forsaken by men,
a Man of sorrows and suffering and acquainted with grief.
People would not even look (hid their faces from; turned their backs on) at Him.
But He took (bore in His own body) our suffering on Him
and carried our sorrows and pain.
We saw His suffering and thought God (the Father) was punishing Him.
But He was wounded for the wrong we did (our transgression);
He was beaten for our iniquities (the evil we did).
The punishment, which brought us wholeness and peace, was given Him,
and we (those who received Him as Lord and Savior and overcome the flesh,
the world, and the devil) are healed because of wounds (bleeding lacerations
from the stripes (lashes) on His back, with His hands, feet, and side being pierced).[61]
. . . But He bore (carried away) the sins of many (those who receive Him as Savior and Lord and overcome the
flesh, the world, and the devil) . . . .'[62]

The Father lovingly says, "Jesus,[63] I am omnipresent, and all things are open and naked before My eyes. I see and comprehend all things both present and future. My foreknowledge is absolute! My will is to make the creatures as free moral beings. No robots! I desire no bride for You who does not love You of her own *'free will.'* No bride will ever love a husband more than Your bride will love You. One woman's junk is another woman's treasure. You will be treated like junk by many, but by the friends of the Bridegroom and by the bride herself You will be believed upon, loved, respected, cherished, and honored." The Son blushing for the first time in His new body of substance replies, "I offer no debate as I am ready to receive a pure bride, who so loves and respects Me. How long do I have to wait for My marriage to the one I already love in faith without seeing her? Father, I can wait forever if it does not take too long! [Laughter] Sincerely, how long must I wait?"

"Son, I am now planning the marriage and the marriage banquet of the Lamb (that is You) in the fullness of time. Only I, not You, nor the Holy Spirit, but only I know the times for such as it is to be written, *'No one knows about that day or hour, not even the angels in Heaven, nor the Son, but only the Father.'*[64]

'At that time, the Kingdom of Heaven will be like ten virgins who took their lamps and went out to meet the bridegroom. Five were foolish, and five were wise. The foolish ones took their lamps but took no oil with them. The wise, however, took oil in jars along with their lamps. The bridegroom was a long time in coming, and they all became drowsy and fell asleep.

At midnight, the cry rang out: 'Here's the bridegroom! Come out to meet him!'

---

[61] Isaiah 53:2-5.

[62] Isaiah 53:12.

[63] Those who argue and insist on calling Jesus by his Hebrew name, Yeshua, are concerning themselves with trivial, as English speakers simply call Him Jesus with a "J" that sounds like 'gee." Spanish speakers call Him Jesus, with a "J" that sound like "hey." Portuguese speakers call Him Jesus, with a "J" that sounds like "sjeh;" and this list goes on.

[64] Matthew 24:36.

Then all the virgins woke up and trimmed their lamps. The foolish ones said to the wise, 'Give us some of your oil; our lamps are going out.'

'No,' they replied, 'there may not be enough for both us and you. Instead, go to those who sell oil and buy some for yourselves.'

But while they were on their way to buy the oil, the bridegroom arrived. The virgins (friends of the bridegroom) who were ready went in with him to the wedding banquet. And the door was shut.

Later the others came. 'Sir! Sir! They said, 'Open the door for us!'

But he replied, 'I tell you the truth, I don't know you.'

Therefore, keep watch, because you do not know the day or the hour.' [65]

'Let us (friends of the bridegroom) rejoice and be glad and give Him (Bridegroom) glory! For the wedding (marriage) of the Lamb has come, and His bride has made herself ready. [66]

'As many as receive Jesus (as Savior and Lord), He (Jesus) gave the right to become (born again) children of God.' [67]

'Blessed (born again, saved ones) are the peacemakers, for they shall be called the children of God.' [68] *'Blessed are those who are invited to the wedding banquet of the Lamb.'* [69]

Your bride will be ready, and the wedding guest coming in will be excited. The bride I am choosing for You will be like a daughter to Me. I also desire many other born again sons and daughters to love Me and for Me to love. Man is to be made in *'Our image, according to Our likeness.'* [70] It will be written, *'Then God said, 'Let Us (Godhead of the Father, Son, and Holy Spirit) make man in Our image, in Our likeness.'* [71]

'But for Adam, no suitable helper was found. So the Lord God (that's You, My Son) caused the man to fall into a deep sleep, and while he was sleeping, He took one of the man's ribs and closed the place with flesh. Then the Lord God made a woman (meaning a human being with a womb [72]*) from the rib He had taken out of the man, and He brought her to the man.'* [73]

Son, notice that the bride is not taken from Your foot as if You could walk on her, nor from Your head, as if she could rule over You. She is to be taken from Your wounded side to walk hand-in-hand, to stand toe-to-toe, looking at You eye to eye, giving You lip to lip kisses, and front on embraces (hugs). *'. . . Her breast (small, firm, and pointed) will satisfy you always (throughout the eternity of eternities).. . . . You will ever be exhilarated (delighted) in her (romantic marital) love.'* [74]

The Son looking down at His flat skinny flesh and bone chest exclaims, "Wow!"

"However, Son, for a short season You will have to leave My right side and be born of an obedient and courageous young virgin woman named Mary, who will speak of carrying the Son of God in her female body's womb,

'My (Mary, mother of Jesus, having formed in her womb, a flesh, bone, and blood body) soul praises (exalts; glorifies; magnifies) the Lord; my heart (spirit) rejoices in God my Savior . . .' [75]

---

[65] Matthew 25:1-13.
[66] Revelation 19:7.
[67] John 1:12.
[68] Matthew 5:9.
[69] Revelation 19:9.
[70] Genesis 1:26 NKJV.
[71] Genesis 1:26.
[72] "Woman . . . a compound of womb and man."
     American Dictionary of the English Language Noel Webster 1828.
[73] Genesis 2:20-22.
[74] Proverbs 5:19.
[75] Luke 1:47.

At your birth, Your virgin mother, Mary will clean and wrap Your body now containing Holy and pure blood. She will lay you in a manger from which cattle had been fed, in the village of Bethlehem, Israel, of which it will be written,

'In those days (at just the right time) Caesar Augustus issued a decree that a census should be taken of the entire Roman world. (This was the first census that took place while Quirinius was governor of Syria.) And everyone went to his own town to register.

So Joseph also went up from the town of Nazareth in Galilee to Judea, to Bethlehem the town of David, because he belonged to the house and line of David. He went there to register with Mary, who was pledged to be married to him and was expecting a child. While they were there, the time came for the baby to be born; and she gave birth to her firstborn, a Son. She wrapped Him in cloths and placed him in a manger, because there was no room for them in the inn.

And there were shepherds living out in the fields nearby, keeping watch over their flocks at night. An angel of the Lord appeared to them, the glory of the Lord shone around them, and they were terrified. But the angel said to them, 'Do not be afraid. I bring you good news of great JOY (emphasis added) that will be for all the people. Today in the town of David a Savior (emphasis added) has been born to you; He is Christ the Lord. This will be a sign to you: You will find a baby wrapped in strips of cloths and lying in a manger.'

Suddenly a great company of the heavenly host appeared with the angel, praising God and saying, 'Glory to God in the highest, and on earth peace to men on whom His favor rests.'

When the angels had left them and gone into Heaven, the shepherds said to one another, 'Let's go to Bethlehem and see this thing that has happened, which the Lord has told us about.'

So they hurried off and found Mary and Joseph, and the Baby (Jesus), who was lying in the manger. When they had seen Him, they spread the word concerning what had been told to them about this child, and all who heard it were amazed at what the shepherds said to them. But Mary treasured up all these things and pondered them in her heart. The shepherds returned, glorifying and praising God for all the things they had heard and seen, which were just as they had been told.'[76]

You will be both at the same time – all man and all God."

The Son inquires, "Father, in the fullness of time I am leaving Your right side to be born a baby having blood in a flesh and bone body?"

"Yes, My Son, from My right side for a short period of time. Our enemy will inspire his cohorts to nail Your fleshly hands and feet to a rugged wooden cross at a place called Calvary and to pierce Your side with a spear between Your ribs into Your heart.

Your bride will come forth because of the cleansing blood (shed to pay the penalty due for her sins) and water (her repentance and leaving her sins (past, present, and future buried in the watery grave of baptism) from Your pierced side and of the testimony of her love and faith in You as her Savior, her Lord. In a covenant of marriage, You will be her precious beloved Husband throughout the eternity of eternities!

Again, Jesus, My flesh and bone Creator, You will open Adam's side near his heart to create from his rib, blood, and flesh his wife, Eve. She will be to him, *'A lovely doe, a graceful deer with her breast satisfying him at all times . . . .'*[77] Likewise, You being the '*Second Adam*'[78] will suffer Your own side to be pierced opening the way for Your own bride to be legally brought to You, representing all who will repent, receive You as Savior, be baptized, and testify You are their Lord becoming born again with their names added to the **Lamb's Book of Life**.

Jesus, You will die as My perfect sacrificial Lamb for the sins of those who choose their own 'free will' to receive You as Savior, confess you as their Lord, and choose to joyfully worship You. It will be written,

---

[76] Luke 2:1-20 .

[77] Proverbs 5:19.

[78] 1 Corinthians 15:45.

'*And the twenty-four Elders fell down and worshiped the Lam (Jesus), Who lives forever and ever.*'[79]

When You take the sins of the whole world on that cross as My sacrificial Lamb, I will have to turn My back on You, as I cannot look upon sin. I will legally accept Your life's Blood shed on the cross to pay the price owed for the sins of all those that will receive You as their personal Savior and add their names as adopted sons and daughters to the ***Lamb's Book of Life***. You will trust with the faith of a child, that My right arm and the works of the Holy Spirit will raise You from the dead."

"Father, You mentioned other sons and daughters. Are they going to be co-heirs with Me?"

"Yes, Jesus, but You are My One and only begotten Son, and We have been One God together in all the eternities past, and We will always be One God in all future eternities. Today You have received a flesh and bone body needed to preach truths such as these, '*I (Jesus) am the way, the truth, and the life: **no one comes to the Father, except through Me.***'[80] [Emphasis added.]

'*I (Jesus) told you that you would die in your sins; if you do not believe that **I am** [emphasis added as this is a self-identification that He is God from Exodus 3:14] the One, I claim to be . . . .*'[81] '*Salvation is found in no-one else, for there is no other name (than Jesus alone) given to men by whom to be saved from sin.*'[82]

'*For there is one God and one mediator between God and men, the man (the second Adam in the flesh) Christ*[83] *Jesus, who gave Himself as a ransom for all men (who will receive Him as Savior, repent of sin, and confess Him as Lord)!*'[84]

Here is a key Scripture for You, My Son, '*The joy of the Lord is your strength.*'[85]

My Son, You will challenge Your enemies who did not believe You are My Son,

'*When the Pharisees had come together, Jesus asked them. 'What is your opinion about The Anointed One (Messiah)? Whose son is He? 'David's son,' they said. He said to them, 'How, then, does David in the (Holy) Spirit, call Him Lord,' when He says, 'The Lord said to my Lord, 'Sit on my right hand, till I put your enemies beneath your feet.' If David calls Him Lord, how is He (the Messiah) his son?' And no one could give Him any answer.*'[86]

Son, here you are quoting from King David, speaking by the Holy Spirit, in His Psalm 110:1, '*The Lord says to my Lord: Sit at My right hand.*' The First Lord is Me, Your Father God; the second Lord is You, the Messiah."

The Son decrees, "The joy of My Lord, Father God, is My strength. I can do all things through My Father, My Lord, who strengthens and anoints Me. I enter fully into the joy of My Lord today in my new fresh and bone body."

---

[79] Revelation 5:14.
[80] John 14:6.
[81] John 8:24.
[82] Acts 4:12.
[83] Christ meaning anointed is a translation of the Hebrew, the Messiah.
   See *Wikipedia, The Free Encyclopedia.*
[84] 1 Timothy 2:5.
[85] Nehemiah 8:10.
[86] Matthew 22:41-46.

The Father smiling explains, "My being Your Lord means My joy is Your strength at all times. It will be written, '*Be full of joy in the Lord (Father for the Son and the Son for those who believe on Him) always, I will say again, be full of joy (rejoice).*'[87]

"The Good News is I am Your Lord and the sheep following You will have protection and strength in You, being all God and all man as You are their Lord and Good Shepherd. As a Man (a reference to His earthly life in the flesh), You will be born a descendant (through His mother Mary) of the seed of David. You through the Spirit of holiness, You will be declared (evidence presented) to be God's Son with great power when God (the Father, through God, the Holy Spirit) raises You (Jesus) from the dead. It is to be written,

'*If you (repentant believer) confess with your mouth, 'Jesus is (my) Lord,' and if you believe in your heart that God (God the Father and God the Holy Spirit) raised Jesus (God the Son) from the dead, you will be saved.*'[88]

The Father teaches through King David regarding the Son of God, "Although You have been eternally My Son, it will be written,

'*Now I recount to You what the Lord (Father God) has declared: He said 'You are My Son.*

Today I have become Your Father.'[89] "*God (the Son), Your throne will last forever. You will rule Your kingdom with virtue, so God (the Father) has anointed You . . .He has set You apart with the oil of joy.*'[90]

The Son looking over His fleshly separate body decrees,

"Father, You are My Lord, and I will be Lord to those who love, obey, and receive Me as Savior, repent, and confess Me as their Lord."[91]

The Father explains, "To confess You as Lord sincerely means that You, My Son, will be that one's Supreme Ruler being given first place in their lives. It is to be written,

'*He (Jesus, God's Son) is the image of the invisible God, the firstborn over all creation. For by Him (Jesus) all things were created, both in the Heavens and on the Earth, visible or invisible, whether thrones of dominions or rulers or authorities – all things have been created by Him and for Him and He is before anything was made and in Him (Jesus, God's Son) all things hold together.*'[92]

While the Messiah (The Anointed One) is in the generation line of David, from Mary, Jesus' mother, You are My Son, and I am Your Father, always listening and being present with You. Rejoice and trust in Me always as **Your Lord**, knowing that My love for You never fails. **Having My joy in You is now Your eternal secret weapon!** I decree that as You look to Me as Your Lord that **My joy will be Your strength** and as others abandon themselves to Your Lordship over them, Your joy will be their strength. Their part is to believe the words.

You will teach, repent, trust, and obey as it will be written,

'*The things I (Jesus) taught (preached) were not from Me. The Father, who sent Me, commanded Me what to say and what to teach (preach). And eternal life comes from what the Father commanded. So whatever I say is what the Father told me to say.*'[93]

---

[87] Philippians 4:4.
[88] Romans 10:9.
[89] Psalm 2:7.
[90] Psalm 45:6-7. [Emphasis added.]
[91] Romans 1:4.
[92] Colossians 1:15-16.
[93] John 12:49-50.

12

'I (Jesus) was sent by the One (Father God), who is true, Whom You don't know. But I know Him (Father God) because I am from Him, and He sent Me.'[94]

The Father adds that it will be written of them who believe on You and make You Lord,

'The Lord is the God (the Son) who lives forever,
*   Who created the ends of the Earth.*
He (God's Son) does not become tired or weary.
No one can fathom how great His wisdom is.
He gives strength to those (who sincerely make Him Lord) who are tired
*   and more power to those who are weak.*
Even youths become tired and weary,
*   and young people trip and fall (in exhaustion).*
But the people who trust the Lord (Jesus, Son of God) will become strong again.
They will rise up with (strong) wings like an eagle in the sky;
*   they will run and not grow weary;*
*   they will walk and not faint (fall and be put to shame).'*[95]

"Son, many will love You, Jesus Christ; but in contrast, many known as antichrists will war against You, despise and hate You, and even deny that You 'came to Earth in the flesh.'[96]

My Son, Your integrity is a further key, *'Thou lovest righteousness and hatest wickedness: therefore (Father) God. Thy (Lord) hath anointed Thee with the oil of gladness (exceeding joy) above Thy fellows.'*[97]

"Son, You are going to have such gladness in creation, preaching, in destroying the works of Our enemies, in saving the lost, giving those who confess You as Lord strength, wisdom, and joy, healing the sick and raising the dead, loving righteousness and hating wickedness, making others kings and priests, and being about Your Father's business. It will be written of You, My Son,

*'For the (even more) **JOY** set before Him, He endured the cross, scorning its shame, and sat down at the right hand (place of power) of the throne of (Father) God.'*[98]

King David will write by the Holy Spirit,

*'In Your presence (Father being Lord of His devoted Son and the Son being Lord of devoted born again believers) is **fullness of joy**; at Your right hand there are pleasures for evermore.'*[99] [Emphasis added.]

'And God raised us (born again devoted believers) up, (being a legal position) with Christ (God's Son) and seated us with Him in the Heavenly realms in Christ Jesus, so that in the ages to come He might show the exceeding riches of His grace by being kind to us (born again ones) in Christ Jesus (Son).'[100]

"Jesus, You are My Preacher, My Ambassador, My only-begotten Son, and *'the Apple of My Eye,'*[101] now having a body I have prepared for You so others You will create can see, touch, and hear You preach. Son, give everyone a free will to believe, trust, love, and obey Us or disbe-

---

[94] John 7:16-18, 28.
[95] Isaiah 40:28-31.
[96] 2 John 1:7.
[97] Psalm 45:7.
[98] Hebrews 12:2. [Emphasis added.]
[99] Psalm 16:11.
[100] Ephesians 2:6-7.
[101] Zechariah 2:8.

lieve, or to reject Your messages. No robots! They can even choose to hate and war against Us. When they confess You as Lord, the joy of Your salvation will become their strength! We will have a young man in a future Earth age named Saul, who later after he confesses You as Lord and has Your joy as His strength, will change his name to Paul as it will be written,

'But Stephen full of the Holy Spirit, looked up to Heaven and saw the glory of God and Jesus standing at the right hand of God. 'Look,' he said, 'I see Heaven open and the Son of Man (Jesus) standing (to honor him) at the right hand of God.

At this, they covered their ears . . . and stoned him.

. . . And Saul was there, giving approval (guilty as an accessory to the murder) to his death.'[102]

It will be further written by Saul (later called Paul), who saw Your body and heard Your voice, *'Saul was still breathing out murderous threats against the Lord's disciples. He went to the high priest and asked him for letters to the synagogues in Damascus, so that if he found any there who belonged to the Way, whether men or women, he might take them as prisoners to Jerusalem. As he neared Damascus on his journey, suddenly a light [Shekinah Glory] from Heaven flashed around him. He fell to the ground and heard a voice say to him, 'Saul, Saul, why do you persecute Me?'*

'Who are you, Lord?' (Confessing in faith the Heavenly Being as Lord.) Saul asked.

'I am Jesus, whom you are persecuting,' He replied. 'Now get up and go into the city, and you will be told what you must do.' . . . In Damascus, there was a disciple named Ananias. The Lord (Jesus) called to Him in a vision, 'Ananias!' 'Yes, Lord,' he answered.

The Lord told him, 'Go to the house of Judas on Straight Street and ask for a man from Tarsus named Saul, for he is praying. In a vision, he has seen a man named Ananias come and place his hands on him to restore his sight.'

'Lord,' Ananias answered, 'I have heard many reports about this man and all the harm he has done to your saints in Jerusalem. And he has come here with authority from the chief priests to arrest all who call on Your name.'

But the Lord said to Ananias, 'Go! This man is my chosen instrument to carry My name before the Gentiles and their kings and before the people of Israel. I will show him how much he must suffer (in My strength to endure) for My name.' . . .

Then Ananias went to the house and entered it. Placing his hands on Saul, he said, 'Brother Saul, the Lord Jesus, who appeared to you on the road . . . sent me so you may see again and be filled with the Holy Spirit.' Immediately, something like scales fell from Saul's eyes, and he could see again. He got up and was baptized; and after taking food, he regained his strength.'[103]

"My Son, Paul will later write about the importance of confessing You as Lord and always having joy, *'That if you (sincerely in faith) confess with your mouth, 'Jesus is (my) Lord,' and believe in your heart that God (the Father) raised Him (His Son, Jesus), from the dead, you will be saved.*

For with your heart you believe and are justified (just as if one had never sinned), and with the mouth you confess (the Lordship of Jesus) and are saved. As the Scripture says, 'Everyone who trusts in Him (Jesus) will never be put to shame. . . . Everyone who (sincerely in faith) calls on the name of the Lord (Jesus) will be saved.'[104] *'Rejoice in the Lord (Jesus) always. I will say it again: Rejoice!'*[105]

---

[102] Acts 7:52-59, 8:1.
[103] Acts 9:1-5, 10-17.
[104] Romans 10:9-12.
[105] Philippians 4:4.

14

"Son, those who hear Your preaching with faith with sincere repentance, receiving You as Savior and confessing You as Lord gladly and willing will be saved. However, it will be written of those who hardened their hearts and reject Your Good News, '*Everyone will have to answer (give account) of themselves to God.*'[106]

'The day of the Lord Jesus will come just like a thief in the night. While people are saying (bragging), 'We have peace, and we are safe,' then destruction will come upon them suddenly like labor pains on a woman with child, and they will not escape.'[107]

My Son let no evil creature or circumstance rob You ever of your fullness of joy for he or she does not reject You but rejects Me, who ordained and sent You out from the throne to preach. My joy is Your strength! There is no enemy that can stand against You! Are You ready to preach?"

Here is a poem and a Scripture You will preach regarding those receiving You as Lord,

'The King of Angels Army will follow His Lord, Father God.
And born again believers will follow the King of Heaven
in Whom, the high Father God hath breathed a secret thing.[108]
"His Lord said to him, 'Well done, thou good and faithful servant:
thou hast been faithful over a few things,
I will make thee ruler over many things:
enter thou into the (abundant, eternal) joy of thy Lord.'[109]
'He (that's You, Son, having Me as Lord, and those truly obeying and abandoning themselves to You as Lord) that dwell in the secret (not many will know it – the greatest secret ever for those who have ears to hear and act on the truths from Your preaching) shall remain stable, safe, protected (like in a mighty fortress) under the shade of the Almighty (a protective place).'[110] *'Behold, My Son, 'Make all things (to be created) new!*'[111]

'*How can they hear the Good News that You are the way, the truth, and the life and that no one*[112] *can come to Me, the Father, except through You, the Son) without someone preaching to them? And how can they preach unless they are sent? It is written, 'How beautiful are the feet of those who bring good news.*'[113]

The Son responds, "Ready, My Lord, to give You My utmost, having in Your eyes, beautiful feet as I preach the good news! Your everlasting joy gives Me constant strength. I will walk in love and peace knowing You guard Me. Let creation and preaching, giving You all the glory, begin! For such a time as this! Amen! [So be it]!"†

---

[106] Roman s 14:12.

[107] 1 Thessalonians 5:2-3.

[108] King Arthur's *Knights of the Round Table* were singing about the royal wedding in Tennyson's *Idylls of the King:* "The King will follow Christ, and we the King in whom high God hath breathed a secret thing."

[109] Matthew 25:21.

[110] Psalm 91:1.

[111] Revelation 21:5.

[112] See John 14:6.

[113] Romans 10:14-15.

†BOOK ONE – Episode 2†

[†**Sidebar Scriptures**: "*Joseph had a dream and promptly reported all the details (Genesis 37:5).*"
"*The Lord revealed to me what the evil ones were doing and planning and showed me their wicked plots (Jeremiah 11:18).*"
"*The word of the Lord came to Abram in a* **vision**. . . . *A* **deep sleep** *came upon Abram . . . . (Genesis 15:1, 12).*"
I witnessed and experienced "*dreams and visions, and I described **all** I had seen to instruct many (Daniel 7:1, 11:33).*"†]

The Creation of the Throne,
Heaven, and the Original Earth

GOD THE SON, now in His new flesh and bone body, bows before His Father with His hands passing right through the almost invisible feet of His Father. The Father laughingly acknowledges the Son's efforts to reach out and touch Him, sharing, "It is a truth that a single flesh-and-bone man of good upbringing must be in want of an affectionate, pure, tender, warm, loving, flesh and bone bride to kiss, hug, touch, to be His beloved companion in marriage. and to give him a home!   One cannot kiss oneself on the lips. [Laughter]"

The Son, swallowing hard nods *yes* and speaks, "Father, no debate! I love and miss her already by My side. It will be worth it all to win such a prize. I am Thine, My Lord! I submit my flesh and bone body as a living sacrifice, holy, consecrated, and well pleasing to You Father, which is My reasonable service and worship.[1]

The Holy Spirit suddenly transformed Jesus' body in a bright glory cloud, known as the Shekinah[2] Glory, to be later described in the Scripture,

His (Jesus') appearance underwent a change in their presence, and His face shone clear and bright as the sun, and His clothing became white as light. . . . A shining cloud (composed of light) over-shadowed them (Disciples Peter, James, and John), and a voice from the cloud (Father God) said, 'This is My Son, My Beloved, with Whom I am (and have always been) well pleased (delighted in His Son always). Listen to Him!'[3]

The Apostle John wrote,

'*The Word (Jesus) became human (flesh, bone, and blood) and lived among us. We saw His glory – the glory that belongs to the only begotten Son, who came from the Father – and He was full of God's gracious love and truth. John (the Baptist) testifies concerning Him and cries out, saying, 'This is the One I told you about: The One, who comes after me (in time) is greater than I am because He existed (Jesus' preexistence) before me.'*[4]

Peter bore witness,

'*When we made known to you about the powerful coming of our Lord Jesus Christ, we were not telling just clever stories that someone invented (or cleverly-concocted myths). But we were eyewitnesses of His Majesty when He received honor and glory from God, the Father. The Voice (Father God) said (testified),*

---

[1] Romans 12:1.
[2] "Shekinah . . . denotes the dwelling or settling of the Divine Presence of God . . . . Where references are made to the Shekinah as manifestations of the glory of the Lord associated with His presence, Christians find numerous occurrences in the New testament . . . ." Quoting from *Shekinah* in *Wikipedia, The Free Encyclopedia.*
[3] Matthew 17:1-2, 5.
[4] John 1:14-15.

'This is My Son, whom I love and am very pleased with Him.' We heard that Voice (of Father God) from Heaven while we were with Jesus on the sacred mountain.'[5]

The Father speaks, "Son, it is My will that You will not be so transfigured and gloried when You are preaching or hanging on the cross, paying the penalty owed for the sins of many who will receive You as Savior.

This is My will, *'God (the Father) chose the foolishness of preaching to save those who believe.'*[6]

'I (Paul preaching the Good News that Jesus Saves) did not come preaching God's secret (message) with fancy (superior; eloquent) words. . . . My teaching and preaching were not with words of human wisdom that entice people, but with a demonstration of the (Holy) Spirit and of power. . . . We speak God's secret wisdom, which He has kept hidden before the world began. None of the rulers of this age understood it. If they had, they would not have crucified the glorious Lord (Jesus).'[7]

"Son, go out there dressed in a white robe, barefoot or with simple sandals, and humbly preach as My Ambassador to all who are unselfish enough to have teachable spirits and ears to hear the messages I give You. It will be written of those who believe, trust, love, and obey Your words,

'What eye has not seen, and ear has not heard, and has not entered into the heart of man,(all that) God has prepared – made and keeps ready – for those that love Him (that is, for those who hold Him in affectionate reverence, promptly obeying Him, and gratefully recognizing the benefits He has bestowed).'[8]

'He that does not love (God and fellow man) has not become acquainted with God – does not and never did know Him; for God is love.'[9]

During one of Your preaching sessions, You will be asked, and You will reply,

'Teacher, which is the greatest commandment (to obey) in the law?'

Jesus replied, 'Love the Lord your God with all your heart and with all your soul and with all your mind. This is the first and greatest commandment. And the second is like it: 'Love your neighbor as yourself.'[10]

When those who love Us in unselfish unity are worshiping Us in Spirit and in truth, the Shekinah presence of the Holy Spirit may roll in as shown in these upcoming Scriptures:

'It came to pass, as the trumpeters and singers were as one, to make one sound to be heard in praising and thanking the Lord, and when they lifted up their voice with the trumpets and cymbals and instruments of music, and praising the Lord, saying,

'For He (God) is good, and His love (mercy) endures forever (eternal): then the house was filled with a cloud (Shekinah) even the house of the Lord;

So the priests could not stand to minister by reason of the cloud: for the glory of the Lord had filled the house of God.'[11]

"My Son now fashion Us a throne as You in that body I prepared for You will at times need to sit down." [Laughter]

---

[5] 2 Peter 1:16-18.

[6] 1 Corinthians 1:21.

[7] 1 Corinthians 2:1, 4, 7-8

[8] 1 Corinthians 2:9 AMP.

[9] 1 John 4:8 AMP.

[10] Matthew 22:37.

[11] 2 Chronicles 5:13-14.

"Father, what am I going to create from as I have no building material?"

"Create it from nothing using Your faith. You will preach to those having at first little faith, *'If you have faith as small as a mustard seed, you can say to this mountain, "Move from here to there,' and it will move. Nothing will be impossible for you.'*[12]

The Son boldly in faith speaks, "In My Father's name, Throne **Be**!"

An eloquent golden throne appears sitting on nothing.

The Father observes the new throne saying, "This throne is inadequate!"

Jesus responds, "In what way is it inadequate? We three in One are right here."

The Father replies, "My Son, look at your seat at My right hand. Your flesh and bones body will fill it. Your left arm has an armrest. It has to be expanded to prepare a place for Your bride, representing all those beside her making up the guests of the Bridegroom, You.

It will be written of them that believe in You and are born again friends of the Bridegroom, *'And He (Father God) raised us (born again believers) with Jesus Christ and seated us (born again believers) with Him in Heaven.'*[13]

Your eternal bride and believers will also have glorified bodies, just like Yours, as it will be written about them, *'But our citizenship is in Heaven. . . . By His power to rule all things, He will change (transform; transfigure) our humble bodies and make them like His own glorious body.'*[14]

Your bride will sit at Your right hand when she is not sitting in Your lap. [Laughter] I tell you the truth; this will be the greatest love story of all time and the most contested. Holy Spirit, she must be prepared spirit, soul, and body by You to be a perfect fit for My Son to share a seat beside Him on Our throne. I will experience the "slopped-over" [Laughter] joyful blessing of just watching the romance between My Son and His loving bride having a passionate love affair, which will never come to an end. Never! Everlasting! (Smiling) She is to be the purest inside and out – but not prideful. She is to be made in Our image and having a 'free will' to love You. She will not be a robot, and she will not be just brought to You as We will bring Eve to Adam."

The Son inquires, "Father, how am I going to find the one I already love?

Son, "Here is a song I inspired just for such a time as this,
'Climb every mountain,
Search high and low,
Follow every highway,
Every path you know.
Climb every mountain,
Forge every stream
Follow every rainbow,
'Till you find your dream.
A dream that will need
All the love you can give . . . .'[15]

Son, You will know when Your earthly heart beats faster. You will recognize her. You and Your bride will look as if you go together because you do. Your love will be better than wine, than the finest wine.[16] Both your heads will spin with love. A severe joyful and frisky romance!

---

[12] Matthew 17:20.

[13] Ephesians 2:6.

[14] Philippians 3:20-21.

[15] *Sound of Music*, Lyrics from "*Climb Every Mountain*."

[16] *'Let him kiss me with the kisses of his mouth – for your love is more delightful (sweeter) than wine.'* (Song of Solomon 1:1.)

18

However, when you turn sideways, you will both have a little hump on your noses. Clue: If she has no hump, she is not the one! [Laughter]

The Holy Spirit is not to give a nose job, as I have a purpose for that hump, known only to Me. She will even joke with her people, 'Don't mess with our noses or our Moses.' [Laughter] When You are dancing, You will often give each other Eskimo Kisses[17] pleasantly rubbing noses together as you two have the right noses to do it. [Laughter] What love she will have for You for eternity and You for her! Your kisses on the lips will be very passionate and pleasant to both of You. You will kiss after a prayer of thanksgiving before each meal.

We will not make a Steve for Adam, but an Eve with breasts and curves – romance in marriage. Dazzling fireworks! Many that see you two together will just say, 'Awe, what a beautiful couple!' You will be so happy to be loved by her and her by You. She will be so thankful and glad to belong to You and to have Your eternal love. Let the dance soon begin as I can hardly wait to see those noses rubbing together." [Laughter]

The Son replies, "Wow! Thank You, Father, for giving Me a bride. I will be so pleased to have this beloved companion by My right side. I see Your wisdom in giving Me a wife. No one could ever love a wife more, being a 'female partner in a continuing marital relationship.'[18] I need someone to love and to love Me back – to be a friend and to be My bosom pal. [Laughter] Well, as My bride, her breasts will satisfy Me always.[19] [Laugher] If she is sitting in My lap, she is not a frigid (cold) woman! Right?" [Laugher]

"Right, My dear Son! I would not give You a cold wife, for there is almost nothing as useless as a cold wife. [Laughter] Can you think of something? [Silence – then laughter]

She will save her first kiss for You, but because of the strong chemistry, you will kiss a few times before your wedding date. [Laughter] You did not sin as the aggressor, and neither did she as the responder. You cannot kiss your own self on the lips. [Laughter.]

However, You will have an enemy, a prince of darkness, who will declare war on Us and whose representatives will try to rape and murder her, but You will rescue, protect her, and be her hero. Even one good-looking representative will slyly seek to steal the first kiss from her, but the Holy Spirit helped defend her in those days. She will even bend in approaching kissing Your good looking enemy's representative, but she will exercise self-control and pull back just in the nick of time. All Heaven will rejoice with her not being deceived and seduced into giving her first kiss away to Your enemy's representative. Our enemy in pride thinks he is something else, being his own Lord, but it will be written, "It is Mine to avenge; I will repay.[20]"

The Son replies, "Father, I assume. Our enemy who will declare war on Us and his representative are good looking – no hump in their nose like Me [Laughter] – and both charmers."

"Yes, My Son, but all will bump their nose hard when they try to touch Your eternal bride. After that, We can call them flat nose! [Laughter] Looks are not everything to a pure woman. Are they?" [Laughter and silence.]

The Son inquires, "Father, could not You reconsider making Me a little better looking?" [Laughter and then further silence]

---

[17] "When early explorers of the Arctic first witnessed this behavior (noses of lovers rubbing together) they dubbed it Eskimo Kissing." Quoting from *Eskimo Kissing* from *Wikipedia, The Free Encyclopedia*.

[18] "A wife is a female partner in a continuing marital relationship . . . applied to a woman in a legally, loyally and sanctioned marriage . . . ." Quoting from *Wife* from *Wikipedia, The Free Encyclopedia*.

[19] *'Let her be as the loving hind and pleasant doe (tender, gentle, attractive); let her bosom satisfy me at all times: and always be transported with delight in her love.'* (Proverbs 5:19 AMP)

[20] Romans 12:19 NIV.

The Son concluding from the silence, "Father, if My looks please You that is the most important thing to Me. I will rescue My bride and be her Champion, and she will see My heart of compassion and love for her. This good-looking dark prince representative, whom You have not hinted who he is, has to be the most stupid of all to declare War on You." [Laughter]

"My Son, 'yes,' I would say 'ignoramus dodo bird' as this handsome prince of darkness, who charms with high sounding words of *'tongues of men and angels'*[21] will convince a large following that he will be able to destroy Us, and he should be worshiped in Our place.

You will have to guard even Yourself against this bragging, prideful, good-looking, effeminate[22] ['yes,' I said effeminate like a homosexual] charmer as to give Our enemy no place as in every way You will be tempted,[23] but You will stand against and overcome him and be without sin. Give him no place. None!

Your bride, who when you first meet her will have no outstanding outward beauty to make her desirable, but even now I am seeing her in the future sitting by Your side looking over smiling at Me with such joy, without having a spot or blemish and looking so radiate in glorious feminine beauty and splendor."[24] You, Jesus, will be highly exalted throughout the eternities of eternities and 'given the name above every name.'[25] You are the center of it all. Your wife will "exult and thrill with inexpressible and glorious (triumphant) joy"[26] at Your Side."

"Father, I pray right now, before the foundation of Heaven and Earth, that You will give My bride 'ways of escape'[27] from Our enemy's snares as he tries to rape her and steal her first kiss, which belongs only to Me alone. You know, Father, this will be My first romantic kiss from the lips of a woman.

I will save My first romantic kiss for her. I am determined with Your help, to do this, but you indicated that I will not be able to refrain from kissing the one I love until the wedding day." [Laughter]

"Son, you have the power to refrain, but things will be just right, and it is not a sin to kiss, before marriage, the one You love and plan to marry. All the stupid plans of Our enemy will not prevail and stop this divine wedding. My Son, I will let you in on a little secret; even before the foundation of the Heavens and the Earth, that all these plans of Our enemy will be laughable to Me for it will be written,

'The rulers take counsel together, against the Lord (Father God) and His Anointed One – the Messiah, the Christ. They say,

'Let us break Their bands (of restraint) asunder, and cast Their cords (of control) from us.

He Who sits in the heavens laughs; the Lord has them in derision (in supreme contempt He mocks them).

He speaks to them in His deep anger and troubles (terrifies and confounds) them in His displeasure and fury, saying,

Yet have I anointed (installed and placed) My King (firmly) on My holy hill of Zion.

'You are My Son (Jesus); this day (I declare) I have begotten You.'[28]

---

[21] 1 Corinthians 13:1.

[22] See Daniel 12:37. Related Scriptures are 1 Corinthians 6:9 and Revelation 9:8.

[23] Hebrews 4:15 NIV.

[24] Ephesians 5:27.

[25] Philippians 2:9.

[26] 1 Peter 1:8.

[27] 1 Corinthians 10:13.

[28] Psalm 2:3-4, 6 AMP.

Hold on to Your seat as it will shake while I laugh now as Our future enemy thinks he will win." [Thunderous Laughter from the Father]

"Father, *'in Your presence is fullness of joy, at our right hand there are pleasures for evermore (eternal.,'*[29] Back to My discourse on the delights of My promised bride. [Laughter] Her smile, as she looks into My face will be such a delight. It sounds as if our noses give us a tremendous romantic advantage. Could we beside a few kisses, at least, rub noses before we say, I do? [Silence] I guess we better not rub noses unless we might be *'tempted above what we are able to bear.'*[30] [Laughter]

Father, let the dance of romance begin. We will bloom together for Your glory and delight to do all Your will. We in the joy of the Lord (You, My Lord, and I, her Lord[31]) will have the strength to overcome and stand against all premarital temptations. May the term 'bridegroom and bride' be soon turned into 'husband and wife,' making all things new and lawful."

"My Son, are you ready for the time to begin in this dispensation of many dispensations throughout the eternities of eternities. The eternal Zoe romantic life I will bestow upon Your marriage will be the best reward I can ever give You. For now, cast[32] the identity of your bride and the timing of your wedding upon Me and hold your questions about her. You will know when romantic love blows Your way. My foreknowledge is absolute, and in Your body, You are going only to know in part and joy in Me as Your Lord.

When born a baby, Your mother named Mary will teach You about the Messiah, the Son of God, in the Scriptures. It will be written about You as a twelve-year-old child as You go to Jerusalem for the Passover Feast,[33] celebrating the shed blood of innocent lambs allowing My people to depart from Egypt, as You ask the teachers of the law questions and answer their questions,

'And all who heard Him (Jesus) were astonished and overwhelmed with bewildered wonder at His intelligence and understanding and His replies.

... And He (Jesus) said to them (mother Mary and her husband Joseph), How is it you had to look for Me? Did you not see and know that it is necessary for Me to be in My Father's house, and about My Father's business.

But they did not comprehend what He was saying to them . . . and His mother kept and guarded these things in her heart.

And Jesus increased in wisdom, and stature and years, and in favor with God (His Father); and men (who received Your preaching).'[34]

Those choosing to receive and obey You or to reject Your message from Me delivered by You, My Preacher, have nothing to do with My foreknowledge of who will receive or reject Your preaching as I desire You to create all free moral beings, and no robots! My secret to You is always to remember that the joy of Your Lord, Me, Your Father, is Your strength. Likewise, the strength of a free moral being making You Lord is his or her strength,

'The joy of the Lord is your strength.'[35]

---

[29] Psalm 16:11 AMP.

[30] Quote from 1 Corinthians 10:13.

[31] "Sarah obeyed Abraham (following his guidance and acknowledging his headship over her by) calling him Lord (master, leader, authority)." 1 Peter 1:6 AMP.

[32] See 1 Peter 5:7.

[33] See Deuteronomy 16:1-8.

[34] Luke 2:47, 49-52.

[35] Nehemiah 8:10.

Son, You will stand at the door and knock through preaching,

'I stand at the door (of one's free will) and knock. If anyone hears My voice and opens the door, I will come in and eat with them, and they will eat with Me (including at the marriage supper of the Lamb).'[36]

'Come, let us (those who believe and obey), bow down in worship, let us kneel before the Lord our Maker; for He is God, and we are the people of His pasture the flock under His care.

Today, if you hear His (My Son's) voice, do not harden your hearts . . . .

So I declared on oath in my anger, they (who do not believe and obey My Son) shall never enter My rest.'[37]

Son, You will preach the Good News (Gospel) to all that have ears to hear. But Your preaching (message; teaching) will not help many because they heard it (half-heartedly) and did not with their own free will accept (to obey) it with faith. However, those who believed (obeyed) can enter and have My rest, as it will be written,

'It still remains that some will enter that rest, but those who formerly heard the way to be saved (the Good News that Jesus saves and is Lord of all) did not enter because they did not obey (believe; remain faithful).

. . . Today (when My Word is preached), listen to what He (Jesus and His preachers) says (intently listen and obey) if you hear His (Jesus and His preachers') voice do not (the hearers responsibility) harden not your hearts.'[38]

Son, are You ready?"

"Yes, Father, let both time in this dispensation and the dance begin for Me winning the joyful love of My bride."

"My Son, Amen, So be it! I decree this to be the dispensation to be the 'Beginning,' and it will be written of this first day of this beginning,

'Before the mountains were formed, or the Earth and the universe were created, You were God from all eternity and forever.

. . . For a thousand years in Your sight are but as yesterday when it is past, and as a watch in the night.'[39]

My Son, I am looking so forward to the Wedding Banquet and Marriage of the Lamb, You, and hearing those words, 'You may now kiss the bride.' You will have lip-to-lip romantic passion and not just rubbing noses. [Laughter] However, as Our private inside joke, you two will often rub your humped noses together, just to make Me laugh. While rubbing your humped noses together will not compare with the pleasure of kissing on the lips, I decree it will be a very delightful and joyful experience.

One group of people, Eskimos, will discover and delight in this joyful experience. Also, how beautiful will be the lovely smile of your pure, eternal bride toward Me as she delights in My bringing you two together. I see You holding hands and embracing with such joy. It takes two – one cannot kiss themselves on the lips. [Laughter]

You will after you two are married and settle in as husband and wife, having absolute trust in Me, declare, *'It was worth it all! Father knows best! My Father has given abundant life now and eternally. It is not good for man to be alone. Thank You for inventing marriage.'*

---

[36] Revelation 3:20.
[37] Psalm 95:6-8. 11.
[38] Hebrews 4:6-7.
[39] .Psalm 90:2, 4.

With Your wife, I will have an eternal daughter, who loves Me and delights to do My will. She will have the pleasure of ruling with Us on Our throne as a 'joint heir'[40] with You throughout the 'ages to come.'[41] Yes, she will give wise counsel as Your 'helpmeet.'[42]

My Son, it will be written about this unique moment in eternity,

'The Lord has established His throne in the heavens, and His kingdom rules over all.'[43]

Now through You, My Son, Our new throne is to be placed on a new celestial sphere called Heaven. I will also make through You a new terrestrial sphere called Earth. Please start with a beautiful rainbow over Our new throne, and all the way to its foundation make it out of the finest material for opulent magnificence.

Then create the glorious globe Heaven for it to be set. Heaven will be a great place of joy and delight and a place to rejoice with Your bride at Your side. She will enjoy rubbing noses with You [Pause with laughter] and being close to You in her romantic seat on her throne beside You. The desires of her pure heart, as she delights in Us, will be bestowed[44] upon her.

Your bride will have grand taste, especially in the Man she will love and marry. [Laughter] Are You ready?"

"Father, how? I do not have any building material. Am I to make Heaven and Earth out of nothing?"

"Yes, A+ answer, My Son, My only-begotten Son, whom I love, You will make something visible out of something invisible by Your faith-filled words. The thesis, 'Nothing comes from nothing,' does not apply to the Godhead.' [Laughter] You can make visible matter or substance with just Your faith-filled words. Why? Because I decree it to be so! Now use faith for creation is My plan! God, My Son, it will be written about My words spoken through You,

'For with God nothing (even creating substance out of nothing) is ever impossible, and no word from God shall be without power or impossible of fulfillment.'[45]

'He it is Who spreads out the northern skies over emptiness and hangs the Earth upon or over nothing.'[46]

The Father turns to the Son directing, "My Son, in whom I delight, now speak with bold faith[47] words as You create two worlds. Our 'Heaven' in a spiritual dimension and the Earth, in a terrestrial dimension. The Earth, at first, will be a little watery mud ball, which I will call '*My footstool.*'[48]

In the heart of the Earth create a place call Hades, having on the North side a beautiful place called Paradise, and over a great gulf on the South side a place named Hell by Our enemy. My servant, Attorney Job, will see this truth in a dream,

'The Underworld (Hades) lies open (uncovered; nothing was hidden) in God's eyes.'[49]

---

[40] See Romans 8:16-17.

[41] See Ephesians 2:7.

[42] Term used in Genesis 2:18.

[43] Psalm 103:29 AMP.

[44] *'Delight yourself in the Lord, and he will give you to desires of your heart.'* (Psalm 37:3b)

[45] Luke 1:37 AMP.

[46] Job 26:7.

[47] *'By faith we understand that the worlds were framed – fashioned, put in order and equipped for their intended purpose -- by the Word of God, so that what we see was not made out of things which are visible.'* (Hebrews 11:3 Amp.)

[48] Isaiah 66:1; Acts:7:49.

[49] Job 26:6.

Now, My Son decree by using words to '*make all things new*'[50] and through You and by You all things will exist and hold together in Heaven and on Earth.[51] Spirit, are You ready for My Son to create Our new throne room and the planet Heaven for it to be placed?"

"Ready, amen!"

The Son, looking so youthful and vibrant, arose dressed so Kingly majestically holds up His right hand speaking, "It all begins! I make everything new. Throne of the one living and true God – **Be**!"

Word further spoke, "Spiritual world Heaven and physical world Earth – **Be**!"

The Holy Spirit excitedly proclaims, "Wow, Word, what Your faith words are creating right in front of Our eyes. First, I see a glorious celestial Heavenly globe in one dimension, being a world of beautiful landscaping, with blue lakes, purple mountains, and valleys so majestic. Now I see in the dim light the beautiful city like a feather gently falling with the throne being placed in its center coming down so gently and quietly coming to rest like an eagle gently entering her nest."

The Father proclaims, "Spirit, now watch the horizon of Heaven above the mountains."

"The Spirit describes,, "Wow, I see a sun forming to shine upon the mud ball with light on one side of the mud ball toward the light and darkness on its side away from the light. Not total darkness on the side away from the sun since I see a little moon reflecting like a mirror light down from the greater light on the dark side of the mud ball. Now I see a blue and golden atmosphere forming a warm misty covering, which will water with dew the Earth in the mornings making it like a giant greenhouse. Now I see the water beneath the atmosphere being collected into one giant ocean. The dry land now appears also containing, as in our Heaven, beautiful purple mountains, valleys, rivers, lakes, and landscaping.

What a beautiful Earth in this other terrestrial dimension reflecting the beauty of our celestial Heaven. I see it hung on '*nothing*'[55] going around the sun, and I see the moon as a giant mirror having one side always facing the Earth as it rotates around the Earth. Wait, now, I see beautiful and majestic stars appearing throughout the vast expanse. Look one set of stars is in the form of a cross, which can only be seen from the Southern portion of the Earth, which I will call the 'Southern Cross' by which sailors on the sea can navigate. I like this footstool with the ocean all in one place and a great mass of land connected in one accord. No one had better touch the Father's footstool!"

The Father replied, "Holy Spirit, Our enemy will declare war on Us. It will look like Our enemy, and his forces will have totally wrecked My beloved footstool making it look worse than the little watery mud ball My Son first formed before He separated the land and the sea. It will be reported about Our enemy, that he comes '*to steal, kill, and destroy*,'[56] and his destructive ability will result in,

'*The Earth was (became) without form and an empty waste . . . .*'[57]

---

[50] Quoting Revelation 21:5.

[51] See Colossians 1:16.

[55] For Millennia Generations various false theories were advance of what supports the Earth – elephants, giants and other fantastic means – were accepted by mankind as truth; but the **Bible** makes no absurd error. How could Job possibly have known that God "hangs the Earth on nothing" (Job 26:7) except by divine inspiration?

[56] John 10:10 NIV.

[57] Genesis 1:2 AMP.

24

My footstool's axis will be knocked off thirty-seven degrees, and the 'Green House Canopy' over it making it so lush and vibrant will be destroyed. All it will be an empty waste and void of life on its frozen solid surface. It will come so quickly that one of the dinosaurs will be frozen in a glacier with a buttercup it is eating frozen in its mouth.[58] The Earth will become formless and empty with darkness over the quickly frozen surface, as the sun itself became for a season frozen and could not give its light. However, there was a foreboding light shining in Hell in its heart with Our enemy setting up his black onyx throne from which to rule his forces as he made further plans to murder both Myself, the Holy Spirit, and My Son."

The Holy Spirit inquired, "Will the surface of the Earth ever be recreated back to its original beautiful one blue ocean and large one land mass?"

"Yes, but the Earth will become so wicked that My servant Noah will warn and warn the people of the Earth to repent. At this time I will destroy the surface of the Earth with a great flood because they choose not to worship and love Us as Our enemy had so corrupted the Earth again. I do everything legally and according to My plan. Noah, who loves and serves Us, will find grace in Our eyes, but he will only be able to save eight souls, including himself and his wife, by preaching Our repentance message. It will be written about one of Noah's righteous descendants,

'*To Eber were born two sons: the name of one being Peleg (meaning division), because (the inhabitants of) the Earth was divided up (North and South American splits from Europe and Africa) in his days. . . .*'[59]

When the large land mass You see will be divided in Eber's day, the second land mass separated from Europe and Africa will later be known as North and South America.

Holy Spirit, it will be written about this beginning day,

'*In the beginning (of creating physical substance out of nothing), God created the Heavens and the Earth.*'[60]

Now, Son and Spirit, let Us sit on Our new throne. Son, You are to sit at My right hand and You, Holy Spirit, to sit at My left hand."†

---

[58] "Dinosaurs came before the Ice Age because scientist discovered dinosaurs frozen in ice and that is how they found out what they eat by finding the frozen food (quick freeze) in between the teeth of the dinosaurs." Quoting from Hunter Dietrich's books at Google.

[59] Genesis 10:25 AMP.

[60] Genesis 1:1.

†BOOK ONE – Episode 3†

[†**Sidebar Scriptures**: "*Joseph had a dream and promptly reported all the details (Genesis 37:5).*"
"*The Lord revealed to me what the evil ones were doing and planning and showed me their wicked plots (Jeremiah 11:18).*"
"*The word of the Lord came to Abram in a* **vision**. . . . A **deep sleep** *came upon Abram . . . . (Genesis 15:1, 12).*"
I witnessed and experienced "*dreams and visions, and I described* **all** *I had seen to instruct many (Daniel 7:1, 11:33).*"†]

The Splendors of the Throne of Heaven, and Word (Son of God) Being Ordained as King and Preacher of Heaven

THE HOLY SPIRIT dictates into Heaven's Archives, "Spectacular! I see a golden throne room of majestic elegance sitting on the highest place in the Celestial City of God. Let Me record a few splendors of the new throne room and the surrounding Celestial City.

Today, the City of God is peaceful and as eloquent as a bride chamber awaiting its occupants.

Jesus, are You going to create flowers?"

"Oh, yes, Spirit, but the Celestial flowers in Heaven will always be looking either toward the throne or will turn to look at the person passing by them. If one steps on Heaven's flowers, the flowers will not be crushed, as the flowers in Heaven will spring right back up. However, the terrestrial flowers on Earth can be crushed and even eaten by animals. In fact, My Father, in His foreknowledge looking at a future age reported observing a dinosaur preserved in ice eating a buttercup flower, when the dinosaur was quickly frozen. The lushness of the Earth's initial greenhouse will produce 'black gold' held in pools beneath the Earth needed for fuel in a future Earth age. Each age in Heaven and on Earth will have its beauty and splendor as it will be written,

'*The beauty (splendor; glory) of the Heavenly bodies is one kind, and the beauty (splendor, glory) of the Earthly bodies is another.*'[1]

The Spirit resumed recording, "Glory! Immediately behind the throne room is the Father's house with 'many mansions'[2] to be filled with treasures, as it will be written as Jesus will advise and preach to those on Earth,

'*But gather and heap up and store for yourselves treasures in Heaven, where neither moth nor rust nor worm consume and destroy, and where thieves do not break through and steal; for where your treasure is, there will your heart be also.*'[3]

These mansions will be further eloquently furnished and prepared by the Son for those who love Him, repent, overcome, and who will choose to occupy these many mansions. Yes, they with a free will must choose.[4] It will be written about those having a free will made in Our imag,

'*This day I call Heaven and Earth as witnesses against you that I (God) have set before you life and death, blessings, and curses. Now choose life, so you and your children may live and that you may love the Lord your God, listen to His voice, and hold fast to Him. For the Lord is your life, and He will give you many years in the land . . . .*'[5]

Archives, We now await the Father and the Son to be seated. We have one large throne of the Son to sit at the right hand of His Father when He is not preaching, and a place prepared be-

---

[1] 1 Corinthians 15:40.
[2] John 14:2.
[3] Matthew 6:20-23 AMP.
[4] See Joshua 24:14-15.
[5] Deuteronomy 30:19-20 NIV.

side the Son for His beautiful bride. I wonder why there is no arm rest between the Son and His future wife. [Laughter]

Jesus' bride, when you watch this Celestial Archive Preservation (CAP) I would like to *nunc pro tunc* (now for then) tell you, 'Welcome aboard. It will be a joyful eternal ride.' After the joyous honeymoon, you being truly an inquisitive woman may desire one day to view these recordings. From the beginning of creation, We just wanted you to know that you were on Our mind. Bride of Jesus, it will never be a dull moment with you sitting with Us on the throne. [Laughter] Also, a place is on the left of Father God for Me to sit when I am not out on assignment as I usually am. [Laughter]

The Father spoke, "Holy Spirit, there will be, after the marriage of My Son, You will have for a season a time to relax with fewer assignments. In the fullness of time, My Son will leave His place here on this throne, according to My will, to be born as a baby in the Earth beneath. When He returns to sit at My right hand again, then Holy Spirit I will send You back to Earth to give power and comfort to all those on the Earth, who fully received My Son.

It will be written,

'*When the day of Pentecost came, they were all together in one place. Suddenly a sound like the blowing of a violent wind came from Heaven and filled the whole house where they were sitting. They saw what seemed to be tongues of fire that separated and came to rest on each. All of them were filled with the Holy Spirit.*'[6]

Woe to those that grieve You, Holy Spirit as all Your works, are so precious, but know that My enemy will also try to destroy You and My Son. He will disguise himself as an angel of light and will deceive both himself and his followers into believing a lie that he and his forces are strong enough to destroy the Godhead so he can sit as a (false) god."

The Spirit frowns and grieving spoke, "Why are You going to permit this?"

"Spirit, Our enemy, is going to have a free will, and it is he that chooses war over love. I will permit this futile effort for reasons of My own so I will have a family that most truly loves Me of their own 'free will.' No robots – each being given many opportunities to love and to obey My Son.

Spirit, now put a smile on Your face for We will have a good laugh that will last forever at the end of these things. [Laughter] I laugh so much when Joy finally takes her seat beside My Son. When the bride turns looking My Son in the eyes, it will be recorded in the Archives of that moment of ecstasy, 'Righteous bride and the Prince of Peace, King of kings, and Lord of lords, My Son, have kissed each other.'[7] [Laughter] Spirit, You will be given many critical and difficult assignments to accomplish My perfect will before the bride arrives. Are you ready? Are you truly ready?"

The Spirit replied, "I am most truly ready! I will give My utmost. Let love roll! Please know that I delight in all My assignments from eternity to eternities. I love what I do. I want no one else to have My job. [Laughter] Let the Archive video continue to roll!"

Father smiles, "Spirit, no one can accomplish some of Your seemingly impossible assignments. It will be written,

'*The things impossible with men are possible with God.*'[8]

The Spirit responds, "The more responsibility and the more impossible, seemingly Your assignments are, the more I like them since I know there is nothing impossible with You!

---

[6] Acts 2:2-4 NIV.

[7] "*Righteousness and peace have kissed each other (go together)*." (Psalm 85:10).

[8] Luke 18:27 KJV.

You are love, and love never fails! I will not have any dull moments. I am sure I will not with the bride around." [Laughter]

"Spirit, You, like My Son, do all things well! Also, with You I am well pleased. Thank you for Your faithfulness to help accomplish My will. You will be My recorder in Heaven and will move on My servants on Earth to record the Word of God, later to be collected in a precious holy book known as the Bible. It will be written of My Son's spoken words and those recorded in the **Bible**,

'*Heaven and Earth (that You see today) will perish, and pass away, but My Words will never perish or pass away.*

But of that day or that hour, not a (single) person knows, not even the angels in Heaven, nor the Son, but only the Father.'[9]

The Holy Spirit's dictation continues to be recorded in the archives, "I see twenty-four smaller thrones near the right side of Our throne."

The Father explains, "Yes, Spirit, it will be written, '*The twenty-four elders fall down before Him, who sits on the throne, and worship Him who lives forever and ever. They lay their crowns before the throne and say,*

You are worthy, our Lord and God,
to receive glory and honor and power,
for You created all things,
and by Your will they were created
and have their being.'[10]

The Spirit continues to record, "Also, on the side of the golden throne I see another 'Great White Throne'[11] overlooking a vast plain as far as the eye can see."

The Father further explains, "Spirit, everyone on Earth that dies and rejects my Son's great offer of eternal life will appear before that white throne; and it will be written about them,

'*Then I saw a great white throne. . . . . The dead were judged according to what they had done . . . . If anyone's name was not found in the book of life, that person was thrown into the lake of fire.*'[12]

The Spirit continues recording in the archives, "I further see in front of Our throne twenty-four thrones, outside the sliding glass doors I see an outdoor arena, a beautiful choir loft, stationary seats and spacious land behind for several thousand to stand to hear Word, the Son of God, preach."

The Spirit interjects, "Father, I have a special gift for Word, the Preacher, of a diamond preaching pulpit to use as He preaches with purity the truth to the assembled congregations of Heaven."

At the moment, a glorious, magnificent diamond preaching pulpit appears.

The Son interjected, "Thank You, Holy Spirit! It is very elegant. I will not give my bride any diamond on a ring that big for her finger. [Laughter] I am so pleased that My Father and also You Spirit have such a view of the podium through the one-way glass from this throne room and can see and hear the praise and worship and the preached Word of God. I am beyond excited. I am ready to be My Father's preacher and to take my place on Our new throne at the Father's right hand. "

The Spirit inquiries for the archives, "What is the name of our new throne?"

---

[9] Mark 13:31-32 AMP.
[10] Revelation 4:10-11.
[11] Revelation 20:11.
[12] Revelation 20:11-12, 15.

The Father responds, "Spirit, this newly-designed golden throne is presently known as "The Throne of God." However, its name will be changed after my Son is raised from the dead; and You will help open the eyes of My first Martyr Stephen, to whom in front of this throne My Son will give a standing ovation as Our enemies also murdered him,

'But Stephen, full of the Holy Spirit, looked up to Heaven and saw the glory of God, and Jesus standing at the right hand of God. 'Look, he said, 'I see Heaven open and the Son of Man standing at the right hand of God.' At this they covered their ears and yelling at the top of their voices, they all rushed at him, dragged him out of the city and stoned him. Meanwhile, the witnesses laid their clothes at the feet of a young man [approving of his death] named Saul. While they were stoning him, Stephen prayed, 'Lord Jesus, receive my spirit.' Then he fell on his knees and cried out, 'Lord, do not hold this sin against them.' When he said this, he fell asleep (in death).' [13]

In this wonderful age of grace, there has been nothing like it before or ever will be afterward. Our throne's name will be changed to "*The Throne of Grace*,' for it will be written,

*'Let us, therefore, come boldly unto the **throne of grace**, that we may obtain mercy and find grace to help in time of need.'* [14]

Holy Spirit, regarding our 'throne of grace,' You will later give one of the worst of sinners, John Newton, the truth in the inspirational song 'Amazing Grace,'

'Amazing Grace! How sweet the sound, That saved a wretch like me!
I once was lost, but now am found, Was blind, but now I see.
Twas grace that taught my heart to fear, And grace my fears relieved;
How precious did that grace appear The hour I first believed!
Thro' (through many dangers, toils, and snares, I have already come;
Tis grace hath bro't (brought) me safe thus far, And grace will lead me home.
When we've been there ten thousand years, Bright shining as the sun,
We've no less (fewer) days to sing God's praise Than when we first begun.' [15]

The Holy Spirit reflects on the upcoming 'age of grace' and continues to enter the events of this day in the archives of Heaven saying, "I am ready to record Our truly being seated.

The Son humbly and respectfully standing at the right hand of the Father smiles up at His Father. The Father so tenderly speaks, "Eternal Son, in whom I am well pleased, You have played as a child from eternity. You will always have the joy and hope of a child. I have enjoyed Our tag games across the cosmos, but today You are ordained (consecrated) to be My preacher. Those who see You see Me and those that hear You hear Me.

You will preach, 'If you have seen Me (Jesus), you have seen the (invisible) Father for I speak My Father's words.' You are my beloved Son and My preacher. Your preaching will not include speaking childish things. Believe Me, You will have such joy, love, and hope in Your preaching. You will not miss out on any adventure or happiness. For at My right hand are pleasures for evermore (eternally). This day I have begotten Thee as a man's man, a champion of champions, and a preacher of preachers.

No weapon formed against You will prosper. For the Joy set before You, You will endure the cross. [16] No man, but You would be man enough to bear it. No one else but You would pay the price to overcome. No one else could accomplish My perfect will. Only You, dear Son, Whom I love. The greatest work ever is Your dying on the cross to pay for the sins of those who will receive You as their Savior. They had better hear You as You Son is the **only** way to Me, the Father! You will tell them without any exception,

---

[13] Acts 7:55-60.
[14] Hebrews 4:16.
[15] *Amazing Grace* by John Newton, 1725-1807.
[16] Hebrews 12:2.

'I am the way and the truth, and the life. No one comes to the Father (God) except through Me.'[17]

Before we take Our seats today, Son, I have three unique gifts for You to save to wear in due time. You being humble will wear a simple white robe and often preach barefoot when You sense You are standing on holy ground. I concur, but these three gifts I desire You to wear in the fullness of time. My first gift is a regal kingly robe, which will be dipped in Your own blood and made as white as the driven snow with Your titles on it,

KING OF KINGS
LORD OF LORDS"

The Son receives the robe with His shoulders held back and with a happy and joyful spirit putting on the kingly garment, saying, "Thank You, Father, it's a perfect fit. It is so eloquent! Thank You!"

"My next gift, My Son, is these sandals of peace as You will also be known as the Prince of Peace,

'For to us a Child is born, to us a Son is given (sacrificed), and the government will be on His shoulders. And He will be called Wonderful Counselor, Mighty God, Everlasting Father, Prince of Peace. Of the increase of His government and peace, there will be no end. He will rule on David's throne and over his kingdom, establishing and upholding it with justice and righteousness from that time on and forever. The zeal of the Lord Almighty will accomplish this.'[18]

My Son, You will be for peace, and Your enemies will be for war. You will preach and teach peace and silence them with truth such as,

'Hearing that Jesus had silenced the Sadducees, the Pharisees got together. One, an expert in the law, tested him with this question: 'Teacher, which is the greatest commandment in the Law?' Jesus replied, 'Love the Lord your God with all your heart and with all your soul and with all your mind.'[19] *The first and greatest commandment And the second is like it, 'Love your neighbor as yourself.'*[20]

. . .While the Pharisees were gathered together, Jesus asked them, 'What do you think about the Christ? Whose son is he?' 'The son of David,'' they replied. He said to them, 'How is it then that David, speaking by the Spirit, calls Him Lord? For he says, 'The Lord said to my Lord: 'Sit at my right hand until I put Your enemies under Your feet.'[21] *If then David calls him 'Lord,' how can He be his son?' No one could say a word in reply, and from that day on no one dared to ask Him more questions.'*[22]

My Son, the Prince of Peace, it will be written about those that trust in You, *'You will keep him in perfect peace, Whose mind is stayed (focused) on You because he trusts in You.'*[23]

'The Lord gives strength to His people; the Lord blesses His people with peace.'[24]

The Son stands barefoot, wearing a simple white robe in His new body of substance and steps into His Gospel of Peace Sandals, responding, "Father, thank you! A perfect fit."

"Son, talking about a perfect fit, I am going to give for Your bride's beautiful feet, who is a representative of all those that love You, a matching pair." [Laughter] It is to be written,

---

[17] John 14:6.
[18] Isaiah 9:6-7 NIV.
[19] Quote from Deuteronomy 6:5 NIV
[20] Quote from Leviticus 19:18 NIV.
[21] Quote from Psalm 110:1 NIV.
[22] Matthew 22:34-36 NIV.
[23] Isaiah 26:3 NKJV.
[24] Psalm 29:11 NIV.

30

'How beautiful on the mountains are the feet of those who bring good news, who proclaim peace.'[25]

I will give both of you matching robes. You two will have matching gold crowns later designed by the twenty-four Elders. Nothing will be so lovely as this romantic and joyful marriage."

The Son laughing within has a flash of His beautiful bride by His side. Such marital romance is above all I could *'ask or imagine!'*[26] I love My secret love and trust My Lord Father to reveal her to Me in His timing. I can wait forever if it doesn't take too long!" [Laughter]

"My Son, we will both have to be patient. She has to first of her own free will receive You as her Savior, be washed as pure as snow in Your blood, and confess You as her Lord.

'The joy of the Lord (You are her Lord, and I am Your Lord) is your strength.'[27]

She will be worth waiting for I assure You. Your covenant wedding rings and the marriage covenant to each other will be a sign throughout eternity of the joy of union in marriage. Yes, she will often speak of her feelings on various topics. The final decisions will be Yours to make, but at times, she will have strong emotional pleas for Your consideration. Often I will say to You and You will say to her,

'Come now, and let us reason together.'[28]

My third present to You today for our right ring finger will be at first invisible to others, which is My special-designed royal signet ring, having a white stone with a red cross in the middle, signifying Your death on the cross to pay the penalty due for the sins of those who receive You as Savior and Lord. With My invisible signet ring, You are given under my Lordship all authority in Heaven and on the Earth![29]

The Son inquires, "In my flesh and bone body on Earth may I give my Power of Attorney to others to exercise My kingly authority?"

"Yes, My Son, it will be like Your giving them also an invisible signet ring. In my absolute foreknowledge, I see you doing this with seventy-two You were sending out,

'The Lord appointed (Jesus delegated His Power of Attorney to act for Him) *seventy-two and sent them two by two ahead of Him to every town and place where He was about to go. He told them, 'The harvest is plentiful, but the workers are few.*

. . . When you enter a town and are welcomed, eat what is set before you. Heal the sick that are there and tell them, 'The kingdom of God is near you. But when you enter a town and are not welcomed, go into its streets and say, 'Even the dust of your town that sticks to our feet, we wipe off against you, Yet be sure of this: The kingdom of God is near.' I tell you, it will be more bearable on that day [of judgment] for Sodom than for that town.

Woe to you, Korasin, woe to you, Bethsaida (Towns in Galilee, where Jesus preached and ministered) for if the miracles performed in you had been performed in Tyre and Sidon, they would have repented long ago, sitting in sackcloth and ashes. And you, Capernaum (another town in Galilee, where Jesus lived, preached, and ministered), will you be honored (exalted/lifted up) in Heaven? No! You will be cast down to the depths (Hell).

He who listens to you listens to Me; he who rejects you rejects Me, but he who rejects Me rejects Him (Father God) who sent Me.'

The seventy-two returned with joy and said, 'Lord, even the demons submit to us in Your name.'

He replied, 'I saw Satan fall like lightning from Heaven (to the Earth). I have given you authority (Power of Attorney as they wore Your Kingly signet ring representing the power of the Holy Spirit in these dedicated believers) to trample on snakes and scorpions, and to overcome all the power of the enemy; nothing will harm you. However, do not rejoice that the (evil) spirits submit to you, but rejoice that your names are written in Heaven.'

---

[25] Isaiah 52:7.

[26] Quote from Ephesians 3:20.

[27] Nehemiah 8:10.

[28] Isaiah 1:18.

[29] Matthew 28:18.

. . . Jesus, full of joy through the Holy Spirit, said, 'I praise You Father, Lord of Heaven and Earth, because you have hidden these things from the wise and learned (being proud; advancing they know it all), and revealed them to little children. Yes, Father, for this was your good pleasure.

All things have been committed (all authority in Heaven and on Earth) to Me by My Father.'[30]

Son, I do all things legally, not willing that any should perish in Hell, and You counseled Your disciples when you sent them out to the cities of Israel. *'And whoever will not receive you, nor hear your words, when you depart from that house or city, shake off the dust from your feet.*

Behold, I send you out as sheep in the midst of wolves. Therefore, be wise as serpents and innocent as doves. . . . All people (who reject your message) will hate you because you follow Me (as Savior for all who will believe and repent), but those (few) people who endure (standing firm; enduring; overcoming) until the end (not how one that starts the race, but how they end it) will be saved.'[31]

My Son, to Your eleven disciples, after one had betrayed You, You delegated Your royal power I am giving You today, as it will be written,

'All authority in heaven and on Earth has been given to Me. Therefore, go and make disciples (of those who receive the Son of God as Savior) of all nations, baptizing them in the name of the Father and of the Son and the Holy Spirit, and teaching them to obey everything I have commanded you. And surely I will be with you (on every occasion) always, to the close and consummation of this (Earth) age.'[32]

It will further be written of the eleven disciples that believed (their part) and received Your power of attorney,

'Go into all the world and preach the good news to all creation. Whoever believes (their part) will be saved (as they continue to walk in the light and overcome the flesh, the world, and the devil), but whoever does not believe will be condemned [to hell]. And these signs will accompany those that believe: In My name (Jesus) they will drive out demons, they will speak in new tongues (the Heavenly language the devil and his crew cannot understand), they will pick up snakes (evil trying to hinder them) with their hands, and even if they drink deadly poison (enemy seeking to murder them), it will not hurt them; they will place their hands on sick people, and they will get well.'

After the Lord Jesus had spoken to them (delegated them authority), He was taken up into Heaven, and He sat at the right hand of God. Then the disciples preached everywhere, and the Lord kept working with them and confirming the message by the attesting signs and miracles that closely accompanied it.'[33]

"Son, this signet ring is never to be worn on your left-hand ring finger as We are saving that finger for your wedding ring, a symbol of Your eternal love for Your bride. Yours will be a glorious wedding full of surprises.

'The marriage of the Lamb (Jesus) has come, and His bride has made herself ready. . . . Blessed are those who are invited to the wedding supper of the Lamb.'[34]

'But about that day or hour, no one knows, not even the angels in Heaven, nor the Son, but only the Father.'[35]

---

[30] Luke 10:1-21.
[31] Matthew 10:16-22.
[32] Matthew 28:16-28.
[33] Mark 16:15-19.
[34] Revelation 19:7, 9.
[35] Matthew 24:36.

The Son inquires, "Father, if it can be Your will, would You please reveal just one of these surprises."

"Son, those invited to the wedding supper, will be introduced on Your wedding day for the first time to the twenty-fourth Elder. Also, an anointed singer born in Mississippi, USA, is chosen to sing My favorite song *How Great Thou Art* at Your wedding was assigned in his lifetime by many religious to the lowest part of Hell. A man looks on the outward appearance, but I look on the heart! A thief crucified on a cross beside You will be the head usher seating one couple, who left their spouses to marry each other. On Earth, he performed dressed in black, but with his sins forgiven, he and his wife June will be dressed in white at Your wedding. Whose sin You forgive, are eternally forgiven! No matter how horrible their sin, where there is life there is hope of repentance, salvation, and the blessing of being invited to the wedding supper of the Lamb.

Your wedding will be glorious. None of the wedding guests will know who the twenty-fourth Elder will be. Many will concur in the selection affirming, 'Oh, yes, he is the one!'

For the relatively few that will receive You as Savior, repent, and confess You as Lord, they will look around and notice those missing at the Marriage Supper of the Lamb. I will wipe away every tear, and I will take away all remembrance of those that have rejected such a great offer of eternal salvation. No more surprise secrets from Your Father should be revealed now. Wait in patience and see what a joyful blessing I have for You!

I shall have a family that loves Us of their own free will. I will help them in their days of salvation as I am '*not wanting anyone to perish, but everyone to come to repentance.*'[36] The free will of all will be tested and tried as gold in the fire. However, I will not permit those that receive and obey My Son's teaching to be tempted beyond what they can bear, but when tempted, I will also provide a way out that they may stand up under it.[37]

Those made in our image will not be robots. They will of their own free will have to overcome[38] the flesh, the world, and the devil by the name and the blood of Jesus and the words of their testimony. Yes, I said 'relatively few' as it will be written,

'*For wide is the gate and broad (appearing easy, rich, and pleasurable) is the road that leads to destruction (a ruin in Hell), and **many** enter through it. But small is the gate and narrow (requires true repentance and overcoming the flesh, the world, and the devil) the road that leads to (eternal) life, and only a **few** find it.*'[39] [Emphasis added.]

Yes, my Son, I said relatively '**few**' of those who are invited (by hearing the Gospel)." [Silence in Heaven]

The Son, standing dressed in His royal robe, His sandals of peace, and wearing the Father's invisible to others signet ring, respectfully submits, "Father, I will do Your perfect will and present the Good News of Eternal Life and true repentance to all that will receive it.

I will delegate the authority in this signet ring, backed by the power of the Holy Spirit, to those few that will pay the cost of overcoming and 'enduring to the end.'[40] I will give them 'the right to eat from the tree of life'[41] for the ones that eat from it will never die."

---

36 2 Peter 3:9 NIV.
37 1 Corinthians 10:13 NIV.
38 Revelations 12:11.
39 Matthew 7:13-14.
40 See Matthew 10:22.
41 Revelation 2:7; Genesis 3:23.

The Son bows His head and looks down at His Father's signet ring knowing He has received all authority in Heaven and on Earth and realized what He must suffer by dying by being nailed to a cross to save those who will believe on Him.

Spirit inquires, "How much influence am I to exert on the heart and soul of those that have sinned to help them see and feel the sinfulness of sin?"

"Spirit, I must have a family that loves Me of its own 'free will' (volition)! They will stumble in their love toward Me, and My Son's blood will cleanse them if they truly repent and boldly approach Our Throne of Grace. I am permitting evil and sin to be for My own reasons, not now fully revealed. *'He that has been forgiven much will love Us much, but to him whom little is forgiven, the same loves little.'*[42] In true repentance, Spirit, You will help sinners see and feel the sinfulness of sin, to urge them to forsake them utterly, and with full purpose of heart to yield in obedience to My Son's commandments in the future. There is only one thing powerful enough to wipe away the stain of sin, of those that sincerely desire to be part of My family."

The Holy Spirit exclaimed, "Your Son's pure and precious blood?"

"Yes, Spirit, for there is no forgiveness of sins without the shedding of My Son's blood.[43] My Son's precious blood will be poured out when He is murdered as an innocent man, shedding His life's blood for those that believe, trust, and obey Him. I accept that one who sincerely repents and receives My Son as Savior and Lord as righteous in My sight for the sake of My Son."

The Spirit responds, "The shedding of Your Son's precious life's blood is truly a mystery of mysteries to demonstrate Your wisdom, compassion, mercy, and the merciful grace to many becoming a part of Your family."

Spirit, today I see everything My Son has made in both the Celestial and in the Terrestrial. I do everything legally, and I will have a family that will love Me and believes, trust, and obeys what My Son preaches. These few will be eternally blessed and honored as My Son will preach,

'He that loves his life will lose it, and he that hates his life in this world will keep it for eternal life. If anyone serves Me, let him follow Me, and where I am, there My servant will also be. If anyone serves Me (that person loving and honoring the Son), My Father will honor.'[44]

For it will be further written,

'Now has come the salvation and the power and the kingdom of our God and the authority of His Christ. . . . They (that hear and obey My Son, and repent) overcame him (My enemy) by the blood of the Lamb and the word of their testimony; they did not love their lives so much on shrink from death. Therefore, rejoice, you Heavens, and you that dwell in them! But woe to the Earth and the sea, because the devil has gone down to you! He is filled with fury because he knows that his time is short.'[45] My Son, are you willing to drink this bitter cup and have Your blood poured out for the forgiveness of the sins of many, We will adopt into our family to enjoy Us, and for Us to enjoy them forever? They will be joint heirs with You with a right and title to eternal life." [Silence]

"Father, it is a cup I rather not drink, but not My will but Thy will be done." [Silence]

Yes, Father, I am willing. I know it is the most painful of deaths, but for the **Joy** set before Me, I will do it. " [The Son smiles]

---

[42] Luke 7:47 NIJV.

[43] *"Without the shedding of blood there is no forgiveness."* (Hebrews 9:22 NIV.)

[44] John 12: 25-26 NIV.

[45] Revelation 12:10-12 (NIV.)

"My eternal Son, You do all things well, even the beautiful creation of Our Throne of Grace adorned with various shapes and figures. You will later create The Great White Throne[46] to judge those that do not keep My words spoken through You. So many will be crying on that day as they witness the rebels that were their friends and relatives on Earth. In fact, I will personally throw these rebels into the lake of fire. For those remaining as part of Our family, I will wipe away all tears[47] as they mourn over those that were repeatedly warned and prayed to receive You, My Son, as their Savior from their sins and choose to overcome. When I wipe away their tears, I will take away all their remembrance of the damned.

My Son, I stand in awe sitting down for the first time on Our new golden throne. Look out over this dimly-lit holy city and off into the Southern horizon as I see majestic mountains and in the Southern distance My new beautiful footstool hanging on nothing in our cosmos having a vast blue sea and a barren land mass. It is all so pleasing to My eyes. Thank You for being such an obedient, faithful and artfully skilled Son, Whom I love."

"You are most kindly welcome, My dear Father. I am so blessed to have You as My loving and caring Father, whom I most truly love with all My heart, mind, soul, and strength. I shall delight to do Thy will throughout the eternities of the eternities."

"Yes, My preacher, You will do all My will, and Your overcoming virgin bride will delight in You. Your bride is going to enjoy this beautiful golden throne to be later named 'Throne of Grace' during the age of grace. There will never be a daughter that will have more joy and graciousness than your bride She has been made as pure as the driven snow by Your words and Your blood shed for her. JYour brode will fill both of your hearts, beating eternally as one, as you hold each other tightly and give each other passionate and romantic kisses of true love!

I see Myself having good laughs with your bride. I even see Myself on my back rolling on the throne room floor laughing with her as she had just told Me a joke. [Laughter] She will have such a sense of humor and be such a joy. She will so delight in Me, and she will especially delight in You as her husband. She is so thankful and happy to be Your bride. Are you ready for such joy? [Laughter]

"Yes, I can hardly wait to have My bride at My right side in this place prepared for her before the foundation of the world. Father, what is going to happen when I finally sit down and take My place at Your right hand on Our new throne? [Laughter] Anticipation of all Your surprises is so pleasant!"

"My Son, it will be a surprise. Now, My Son, whom I love, sit down on your portion of the throne at My right side and receive Your best present ever of a romantic bride. The place beside You at Your right side, as you know, is reserved for Your lovely virgin bride, Joy, and when she takes her seat, I will have a surprise for her also.

In My presence is the fullness of joy, and at My right hand, there are pleasures for evermore.[48] This throne you designed is totally regal and masculine, and I do like it.

---

[46] *"Then I saw a great white throne . . . . The dead were judged according to what they had done . . . . If anyone's name was not found written in the book of life, he was thrown into the lake of fire."* (Revelations 20:11-12, 15 NIV.)

[47] *"And I heard a loud voice from the throne saying, 'Now the dwelling of God is with men, and he will live with them. They will be his people, and God himself will wipe every tear from their eyes. There will be no more death or mourning or crying or pain, for the old order of things has passed away.'"* (Revelation 21:3-4 NIV.)

[48] *"You will show me the path of life; in Your presence is fullness of joy, at Your right hand there are pleasures for evermore."* (Psalm 16:11 AMP.)

I comprehend both male and females. The male generally leads and initiates. The female is the responder and is to be a helper.

That is why I God the Father and You My Son are masculine. We initiate! The woman is refined – not made of clay, but from the rib out of the side of man.

I am telling You in advance, turning and smiling at the standing Son preparing to be seated, do not be surprised if Joy adds here and there a few of her feminine touches. We both will have to at times brace Ourselves as a woman thinks pleasantly different than a man. [Laughter]

Nothing makes a man feel more like a man than to have a real feminine woman beside him. [Laughter] For Us to have long hair would be a shame,[49] but her beautiful flowing hair down below her breast, like Eve before her, will remind us of Arabian goats flocking together in the wind going down Mount Gilead.[50] So beautiful and so pleasing to a man. Patience, My Son. Patience! [Laughter]

"Wow," says the standing Son. "I almost can't wait to run My fingers through her beautiful hair, but for now, I am ready for My surprise!"

"Son, all You have to do, is take Your place beside Your Father's right hand and see what happens as You are seated. Holy Spirit, You first sit at My left hand and record, in addition to what You have just recorded in the Archives of Heaven this day one, what happens."

The Spirit inquires, "What number is day one?

"Spirit, the sand of My cosmic hourglass will start running when My Son takes His seat. The sand will end to be turned over to start again after You, Holy Spirit, place My Son's Spirit into the egg of a virgin girl named Mary, who lives in the town of Nazareth, a small city in Galilee.[51] Some nine months later My Son, who left this throne, will be born of Virgin Mary one starlit night in Bethlehem, the town of David.[52] Time in the Third-Earth age will start over at 1 A.D. because it will be written about those then living on My footstool,

'For God so loved the world that He gave His one and only begotten Son, that whosoever believes in Him, should not perish (in Hell), but have everlasting life.'[53]

Now in My gigantic cosmic hourglass filled with grains of sand, they will stream down quickly, but in reality, each grain represents a day. To Us, a day is like a thousand years and a thousand years is as a day or like a watch in the night.[54] *So this creation, beginning first day, starts counting down to the last grain of sand falling through on the day of My Son's birth at which time the hour class will be turned over. Son, the sooner the sand starts falling, the nearer You will be to Your marriage day, so let the celebration begin. Now take Your place at My right hand and be My preacher."*

The Son, full of heroic manly adventure with a sparkle in His eye, smiles with such joy enjoying every mini-second slowly sits down, taking His place beside His Father with the Holy Spirit recording, "Archives, 'it is day one of the beginning. When the Son was seated, the whole Celestial City lit up wonderfully bright, and a mighty river, known as the 'River of Life,' flowed out from under the throne into the celestial city. Also, appearing was a ' Rainbow, resembling an emerald that encircled the throne. '[55]

---

[49] *"Does not the very nature of things teach you that if a man has long hair, it is a disgrace to him, but that if a woman has long hair, it is her glory?"* (1 Corinthians 11:14 NIV.)

[50] *"How fair you are, my love, he said, how very fair. Your . . . hair (makes me think of the black, wavy fleece) of a flock of (the Arabian) goats which one sees trailing down Mount Gilead (beyond Jordan on the frontiers of the desert)."* (Song of Solomon 4:1 AMP.)

[51] Luke 1:26.

[52] See Luke 2:4.

[53] John 3:16 KJV.

[54] *"For a thousand years in your sight are like a day that has just gone by, or like a watch in the night."* (Psalm 90:4 NIV.)

[55] Revelation 4:3 NIV.

'From the throne came flashes of lightning, rumblings, and peals of thunder. Before the throne, seven lamps were blazing. . . . Also, before the throne, there was what looked like 'a sea of glass, clear as crystal.'[56]

The Father speaks, *"Holy* Spirit, it will be written about the Son, Jesus, to be born of a virgin, who chose to do My will and as an innocent Lamb be crucified on a cross and shed His life's blood to pay in full the sins of those that will receive Him as Savior, repent, overcome, and confess Him as Lord,

'The city had no need of the sun, neither of the moon, to shine in it: for the glory of God illuminated it. The Lamb is the light thereof.

. . . And he showed me a pure river of water of life, clear as crystal, proceeding from the throne of God and of the Lamb.

. . . And the Spirit and the bride say, 'Come!' And let him that hears say, 'Come!' And let him who thirsts come. Whoever desires, let him take the water of life freely."[57]

"Father, I am ready to speak words to plant some Trees of Life on each side of the River of Life and landscape, both Heaven and Earth with beautiful flowers and plants of all shapes and varieties."

The Holy Spirit inquires, "Will Your Son's words always be used to create such beauty?"

"Spirit, My Son's Words are so powerful that it will be written about His coming on His stately white horse named Abundant Life that just the words of His mouth will utterly defeat Our enemies,

*'I saw Heaven standing open and there before me was a white horse, whose rider is called Faithful and True. With justice, He judges and makes war. His eyes are like blazing fire, and on His head are many crowns. . . . He is dressed in a robe dipped in blood, and His name is the **Word of God**. The armies of Heaven were following Him, riding on white horses and dressed in fine linen, white and clean. **Out of His mouth comes a sharp sword** with which to strike down the nations. . . . On His robe and on His thigh he has this name written:*

KING OF KINGS AND LORD OF LORDS.

*. . . Then I saw the beast and the kings of the Earth and their armies, gathered together to make war against the Rider on the horse and His army. But the beast was captured, and with him the false prophet who had performed the miraculous signs on his behalf. With these signs, he had deluded those who had received the mark of the beast and worshiped his image. The two were thrown alive into the fiery lake of burning sulfur. The rest of them were killed with the **word that came out of the mouth** of the Rider(Jesus) on the horse, and all the birds gorged themselves on their flesh.'"*[58] [Emphasis added.]

The Father smiles and instructs the Son, "Wait on creating the 'Trees of Life' to bear twelve fruits to line the River of Life. Also, wait upon creating the flowers, vegetation, plants of all varieties throughout our glorious spiritual Heaven. Your first Creation of life itself will be Your song leader. I see the first grain of sand has fallen through the hour glass. Let us rest this evening and in the morning, 'The 'Creation Celebration' will begin."

"Son, let us enjoy the moment and let us start laughing now because We are all going to have a good one at Your wedding that shall last forever. " [Laughter]†

---

[56] Revelation 4: 5-6 NIV.
[57] Revelation 21:23; 22:1, 17 NKJV.
[58] Revelations 19:11-16, 19-21 NIV. [Emphasis added as the Father spoke.]

†BOOK ONE – Episode Four†

[†**Sidebar Scriptures**: "*Joseph had a dream and promptly reported all the details (Genesis 37:5)."*
"The Lord revealed to me what the evil ones were doing and planning and showed me their wicked plots (Jeremiah 11:18)."
"*The word of the Lord came to Abram in a* **vision**. . . . A **deep sleep** *came upon Abram . . . . (Genesis 15:1, 12)."*
I witnessed and experienced "*dreams and visions, and I described* **all** *I had seen to instruct many (Daniel 7:1, 11:33)."*†]

Creation of Heaven's Song Leader and Word (Son of God) Begins Preaching

THE SON OF GOD, Word, wearing a simple white linen ephod[1] being the bodily image of His invisible Father God stands barefoot behind a simple preaching pulpit containing these Scriptures;

'*In the beginning was the Word, and the Word was with God. He was in the beginning with God (the Father). All things came into being through Him, and without Him, not one thing came into being.*[2]

No one has seen God the Father, but God the only Son, who is at the Father's side, has made Him known.[3]

The Lord is One. Love the Lord your God with all your heart, soul, mind and strength.

. . .Love your neighbor as yourself.[4]

Whoever does not love does not know God, because God is love.[5]

Heaven and Earth will pass away, but My words will never pass away.[6]

For I (Word) did not speak of My own accord, but the Father, who sent Me, commanded Me what to say and how to say it. I know that His command leads to eternal life. So whatever I say is just what the Father told Me to say.[7]

If anyone loves Me (Son), he will obey My teaching. My Father (God) will love him . . . .He who does not love Me will not obey My teaching. These words you hear are not My own; they belong to the Father, who send Me.'[8]

Word (Jesus) turns His eyes up to His Father awaiting His directions. The Father smiles, speaking with His thunderous voice:

"My Son, it will be written about You,

'*The Son is the radiance of God's glory and the exact representation of His being, sustaining all things by His powerful word. After He had provided purification for sins (for those who receive Him as Savior, repented, overcome, and confessed Him as Lord), He sat down at the right hand of the Majesty in Heaven.*

. . .Your Throne (Word), O God, will last forever and ever, and righteousness will be the scepter of Your kingdom. You (Word) have loved righteousness and hated wickedness; therefore, God, Your (Father) God, has set You above Your companions by anointing You with the oil of gladness.'[9]

Word, this day I ordain You, Jesus (your name meaning the Lord is Salvation) as My Preacher, the Savior (only by Your blood, the Lamb of God, is anyone saved)! I am not the Savior, as I do not have blood.

No one is saved except by Your shed Blood as it is to be written, '*They (believers in Jesus) overcome him (the devil and his crew) by the blood of the Lamb (shed by Jesus being crucified on a cross) and by the word of their (own]) testimony.* '[10]

---

[1] King David is described as wearing 'a linen ephod (a priest's upper garment) joyfully dancing before the Lord with all his might.' (2 Samuel 6:14).

[2] John 1:1-3.

[3] John 1:18.

[4] Mark 12:30-31.

[5] 1 John 4:8.

[6] Matthew 24:35.

[7] John 12:49.

[8] John 14:23-24.

[9] Hebrews 1:3, 8-9 NIV.

[10] Revelation 12:11.

'Without the shedding of Blood (of Jesus), there is no forgiveness (for the believer).'[11]

Son, You will preach My Word boldly in Heaven and in the fullness of time on the Earth in various Earth ages. Your authoritative preaching will be a sign and wonder to many. I decree every Word You preach will come about just as You preach them. You will preach fearlessly for all authority[12] is delegated to you, and I will back your every word. I see this beautiful meeting place packed with a great convocation. Many will listen with profound attention to every word You preach, and two-thirds initially will choose to love and obey Your words with such joy and thanksgiving of their own free will. It will be written of those choosing to love and obey Your words in future Earth ages,

'Then the King (Jesus) will say to those on His right, "Come, you who are blessed by My Father, inherit the kingdom prepared for you from the foundation of the world. (This is now.) For I was hungry, and you gave Me drink. I was a stranger, and you welcomed Me. I was naked, and you clothed Me. I was sick, and you visited Me. I was in prison, and you came to Me. Then the righteous will answer Him, saying, 'Lord, when did we see You hungry and feed You, or thirsty and give You drink? And when did we see You a stranger and welcome You, or naked and clothed You? And when did we see you sick or in prison and visit You? And the King (Jesus) will answer them, 'Truly, I say to you, as you did it to one of the least of these My brothers, you did it to Me.'[13]

"Father, not My will but Thine be done, but could You consider giving me a deep preaching voice like You?" [Laughter]

"No, my Son, I like Your voice, face, and nose just the way they are. Your features, including Your humped nose, bring Me joy. [Laughter] You are a chip off the old block, to be known, along with Me, as the Ancient of Days,[14] rightly meaning We existed before days were created. It will be written,

'In my vision at night, I looked and there before me was one like a son of man (Jesus in bodily), coming with the clouds of Heaven. He approached the Ancient of Days (God the Father) and was led into. His presence. He (Son of God) was given authority, glory, and sovereign power; all peoples (who receive the Son as Savior), nations and men of every language worshiped Him. His dominion is an everlasting dominion that will not pass away, and His kingdom is one that will never end (be destroyed).'[15]*'As I watched, the (evil) horn was waging war against the saints and defeating them until the Ancient of Days (Jesus, Son of God) came and pronounced judgment in favor of the saints of the Most High. The time came when they possessed the kingdom.'*[16]

Son, You and I will be criticized by experts. They will not like Our noses, Mine they cannot even see, or Our Moses. The funniest joke in both Heaven and Earth will be, "I wonder if God is stressed over this?" [Laughter] It will be written,

'The rulers gather together against the Lord (Farther God) and against His Anointed One (Son of God). 'Let us break their chains,' they say, 'and throw off their fetters.'

The One enthroned in Heaven laughs; the Lord scoffs at them. Then He rebukes them in His anger and terrifies them in His wrath, saying 'I have installed My King [Jesus] on Zion, My holy hill.'

. . . Be warned, you rulers . . . Serve the Lord with fear and rejoice with trembling. Kiss the Son, lest He be angry, and you be destroyed in your way, for His wrath can flare up in a moment. Blessed are all who take refuge in Him.'[17]

---

[11] Hebrews 9:22.

[12] Matthew 28:16.

[13] Matthew 25:34-41.

[14] Daniel 7:9.

[15] Daniel 7:13.

[16] Daniel 7:21.

[17] Psalm 2:2-6, 10-12 NIV.

. . .A little while and the wicked will be no more; though you look for them, they will not be found. But the meek will inherit the land and enjoy great peace. The wicked plot against the righteous and gnash their teeth at them, but the Lord laughs at the wicked, for He knows their day is coming.'[18]

My Son, the saints are not being drawn to You because you have a regal appearance or an eloquent voice. Your form is de-emphasized, and Mine remains invisible. [Laughter] They will be drawn by Your love, mercy, forgiveness, precious promise of salvation, character, compassion, hatred of evil, and good works. When lifted up on a cross, You will draw all men to You, both those who accept or reject Your preaching, the latter who will of their own free harden their own heart. You will later preach,

'Now is the time for judgment on this world; now the prince of this world will be driven out. But I, when I am lifted up from the earth, will draw all [by the preached Word] to Myself.'[19]

Son, carry Your shoulders high with a joyful bounce in Your step and a song in Your heart as You look forward to the JOY set before You. [Laughter] I *'anoint you with the oil of gladness (joy) more than on anyone else.'*[20] Your cup and Our throne will at the conclusion of all this overflow with the joy of marriage for You. [Laughter] Let Us laugh now as we will have a good one that will last forever!" [Laughter]

"What is your input, Holy Spirit, of My Son creating a song leader gifted in music and having a free will for His preaching?"

Holy Spirit replies "To be, or not to be, that is the question."[21] For such a powerful creation, a song leader, with a *'free will'* with a musical gifting is risky. You could put a governor on that 'free will' as he might desire the praise and worship for himself! Then what? Just a little puppet string for Us to jerk him back into line. Also, just a little line on Our congregation to keep them from worshipping the created music leaders more than the Creator.

Word remember how We would dance and sing before the beginning at the feet of Father God until we all started that precious, joyful laughter? Word, You might lead Your own singing and then do the preaching? Word, let's try singing again. I will provide you some background music."

Word behind the pulpit sings out with a not-so-attractive singing voice,

'I sing praise to My Lord, My Father!
I worship the Lord with joy and come before Him with a happy song!
I will never forget that My Father knows best for Me throughout eternity.
I enter His sanctuary with thanksgiving and His courts with praise.
I give thanks to Him and praise Him.   ,
My Lord's love is eternal, and his faithfulness and goodness last forever.'[22]
Shalom! Amen!"

The Father smiles, "You are My beloved Son and with You I am well pleased. I gifted You in preaching, not singing! To Me, your singing will be a joyful sound! [Laughter]

I will permit You to have this separate song leader gifted in music for reasons of My own. We will do all things legally!

Holy Spirit, You will use your influence only to draw everyone who gives particular and special attention to hearing and obeying the preached Word of My Son, choosing Him as Savior,

---

[18] .Psalm 37:10-13 NIV.
[19] John 12:31, 32 NIV.
[20] Psalm 45:7.
[21] Shakespeare's play Hamlet, Act 3, Scene 1.
[22] Adapted from Psalm 100.

repenting of sins, and worshipping Him as Lord of their own 'free will.' No puppet strings! You are not to override a created being's 'free will!'

"Now, Son, You will need both a congregation and a song leader each with a 'free will.' You will need to create them out of nothing using just Your words. First, it is My will that You create, according to the pattern I will show, Your song leader. Let Your song leader be an Anointed Cherub (not an archangel), gifted with plenteous musical abilities.

He will be Your first creation of life, having a *'free will'* in both the celestial world and in the terrestrial world below, Earth being My footstool.[23] Jesus, I now instruct You to create Your music leader to be filled with every gift of musical ability and give him totally a *'free will'* to choose to hear and 'obey or not to obey Your preaching, that is the real question' for Me now to only know the answer. His *'free will'* gives him the right to choose to obey or rebel, to err and sin, or to keep himself pure and free from sin, to love Us or to hate Us, to fellowship and be a part of Our family, or seek to set up his own kingdom, or even seek to kill, steal, and destroy, and ultimately to be a blessing or to be a curse."

"Father, what name would You like Me, to give My song leader?"

"Son, I will name him Apollyon Lucifer, but You are only to first call him Apollo or friend. Apollyon is not to be made in Our image, not a likeness to Your face or Our matching noses. [Laughter] For example Apollyon's internal settings and mountings are to be made of gold.[24] Are You Ready for Your first creation of life itself?"

"Yes, Father, this Cherub, a bearer of music and who covers with his beauty, is going to be a powerful first creation as My song leader. I agree with the Holy Spirit that giving him totally a 'free will' is risky! Nevertheless, not My will, but Thine be done. I am content just to leave things alone. I heard You say once, 'If it is not broke, don't fix it!' I heard You say once, 'Speak now or forever hold Your peace.' I desire You to know of My concerns about giving him totally a 'free will' with such gifting in music and a beautiful appearance."

"I know Your concerns, My Son."

"Well, Father, as long as You '*know*,' then I am satisfied."

[Word cups His hands and cast this concern back onto the Father, His Lord.[25]]

"My Son, as much as I love You and Enjoy Our fellowship, I now desire a large family that chooses to love Us of their own 'free will.' We could have a robot, and You could pull a string on its back, and it would say, 'I love you. I love You. I love You. Let us fellowship. Pull my string again.' [Laughter] No way, Hosea!

While you feel You are content and somewhat resist change, it is not good for You to be alone. I know You have the Holy Spirit and Me. A wife as a companion and helpmate to adore You and cherish You would be a delight and be good for You. My Son, whom I love, as she would be the best reward I could ever give You. I rest My case!" [Serious look on the Father's face.]

"Father, You never have, nor will You, ever lose a case. What a closing argument! You have won Your case hands down. You are right as always, but I have a feeling that I am going to have some tears."

---

[23] "This is what the Lord says: 'Heaven is My throne and the Earth is My footstool." (Isaiah 66:1 NIV).

[24] "Your settings and mountings were made of gold; on the day you were created they were prepared." (Ezekiel 28:23 NIV).

[25] See 1 Peter 5:7.

The Father nods 'yes' and indicates that it will be written, '*Weeping may endure for a night, but JOY comes in the morning!*'[26] [Laughter]

'*God will wipe every tear from their eyes. There will be no more death or mourning or crying or pain, for the old order of things has passed away.*

He who was seated on the throne said, 'I am making everything new!'

. . .I am Alpha and Omega, the Beginning and the End. To him who is thirsty, I will give to drink, without cost from the spring of the water of life. He who overcomes will inherit all this, and I will be His God, and he will be My (adopted born again) son. But the cowardly, the unbelieving, the vile, the murderers, the sexually immoral, those who practice magic arts, the idolaters, and all liars – their place will be in the fiery lake of burning sulfur.'[27]

The Father smiles as the Son nods, indicating that He is ready. The lighting in the great convocation arena lowers for the Son's creation of the first life.

The Father in a still small voice says, "Let Your preaching commence!"

The Son looking up at His Father's face in absolute trust and oneness speaks: "Apollo, Cherub, My music leader I create you – be!"

Appearing in front of the pulpit was the loveliest creature, dressed in dazzling white apparel, the first of life itself. As Apollo was awakening and wiping his closed and slowly opening eyes, he arose looking himself over and admiring his reflections, deep from within the pulpit partially block by inscribed Scripture. He then turned with widespread arms to the empty arena and sang out in the most beautiful voice ever,

"My music be glorified!

Beautiful so all can hear and see!"

Apollo's voice exploded in musical sound vibrating throughout the empty arena in song,

"Come in. Come in.

Let the service begin!

Let the service begin!

Come in. Come in with a grin."

The Son of God, dressed casually in a white linen ephod garment and being barefoot, standing on the sideline, is to be described later in the Scriptures,

'*He had no beauty or majesty to attract us to Him, nothing in His appearance that we should desire Him.*'[28]

Apollo then turns and asks, '*Are you, the gardener?*'[29]

Without waiting for an answer, Apollo, turns his attention away from the One he supposes to be the gardener and focusing on looking at his hands and then continues speaking like a cross-examining lawyer asking,

"Who am I?

What am I?

Where am I?

How am I?"

Focusing down on his body, Apollo exclaims, "I am beautiful and wonderful. Is there a pool or a mirror around here other than this pulpit covered in writing in which I can see my face?'

I feel like singing more!"

---

[26] Psalm 30:5 NIV.

[27] Revelations 21:4-8 NIV.

[28] Isaiah 53:2.

[29] Mary Magdalene later made this same assumption, "Jesus said to her, Woman, why are you crying [so]? For whom are you looking? Supposing that it was the gardener, she replied, Sir, if you carried Him from here, tell me where you put Him and I will take Him away." (John 20:15 AMP.)

The Word, waiting to get a word in edgewise, answers, "No, I am not the gardener!" [Word laughs about being thought He was the gardener with the Father joining in with thunderous laughing from the throne room.]

Apollo looking up at the throne room asks,

"Who, what, where is the thunder coming from as I see no one."

Word responds, "It will later be written about my Father God,

'No one has ever seen God, but God the only Son, who is at the Father's side, has made Him known.'[30]

Let Me introduce Myself. My name is Word, God's Son. My Father God, My Lord, has chosen and ordained Me to be the preacher of Heaven. You are My song leader. I created you out of nothing. You can call Me Lord, Word, and even later you may call Me 'friend.' Your name is Apollo, and later with your permission, I may call you 'friend.' In the services, we will call each other 'Apollo' or 'Word.' At times, you may refer to Me as the 'Son of God' or Jesus. You know little now, but you will learn quickly.

I am God the Son, who just created you to be the song leader of Heaven. You are to prepare with songs the congregation to worship My Father God as He preaches His words through Me. It will be written,

'The true worshipers will worship the Father (God) in spirit and in truth, for they are the kind of worshipers the Father seeks to be His worshipers. God is Spirit, and His worshipers must worship in spirit and in truth.'[31]

Apollo replies, "Do we also worship You, Son of God?"

Word responds. "Yes, for it will be written of the Son,

'Come, let us bow down and worship Him; let us kneel before the Lord (Son of God) our Maker, for He is our God, and we are the people of His pasture and the sheep of His hand. To-day, if you hear His voice, harden not your heart.'[32]

Apollo averred, "As your first creation and song leader I assume that it will be appropriate for the lesser creatures also at times to fall down and worship me?"

Word answers, "No! Neither you nor any other created being is ever permitted to receive worship exclusively reserved for the Godhead. It will be written about created creatures wor-shipping other than the Godhead,

'They exchanged the truth of God for a lie and worshiped and served created things rather than the Creator . . .

Because of this, God gave them over to shameful lusts. Even their women exchanged natural relations (with husbands) for unnatural ones. In the same way, the men also abandoned natural relations with women (as wives) and were inflamed with lust for one another. Men committed indecent acts with other men and received in them-selves the due penalty for their perversion.

Furthermore, since they did not think it worthwhile to retain the (true) knowledge of God, He gave them over to a depraved mind to do what ought not to be done. They have become filled with every kind of wickedness, evil, greed and depravity. They are full of envy, murder, strife, deceit, and malice. They are gossips, slanders, God-haters, insolent, arrogant and boastful. They invent ways of disobeying evil; they, disobey their parents; they are senseless, faithless, heartless, ruthless. Although they know God's righteous decree that those who do such things deserve death, they not only continue to do these very things but also approve of those who practice them.'[33]

---

[30] John 1:18 NIV.
[31] John 4:24.
[32] Psalm 95:6-8
[33] Romans 1:25-32

43

Apollo, questions, "How many sermons have You preached? Who else is living other than You and me?

Word, replies, "Please, one question at a time. You sound like a Philadelphia lawyer. You were not supposed to be that gifted in jurisprudence as your gifting is to the utmost in music as My song leader. Today is My first day of on-the-job experience behind this new pulpit. The Holy Spirit has just given Me this pulpit, and so it is special to Me. I have preached no sermons as yet, but I plan to preach one after your singing today.

On-the-job experience for both of us starting with no congregation, yet to which to sing or to preach. [Word gives an encouraging smile.] There are no other living beside the Godhead and you. You have been specifically honored as being My first living creation. You have been given a free will to choose whether you truly desire to be My friend. A faithful friend requires being loyal in heart, thought, and spirit. That decision will be yours to make alone. You might like to have time to think about it as friendship involves covenant and loyalty."

Apollo interjects, "No, I don't need time. I am your best friend! Who else? [Self-laughter] You can always count on me. I will never leave you nor forsake you. In me, you can trust! I am faithful. I will identify with your plans, purposes, and pursuits with my whole mind, body, and spirit. I have your backside covered!"

"Apollo, My new friend, up in the throne room also is the Holy Spirit, who is presently sitting at the left hand of My Father God. He, like my Father, is also invisible, but you will at times feel His presence in the services. When the Holy Spirit chooses to manifest Himself in a spectacular manner once things are just right in one of the services this manifestation will be what is called the *Shekinah Glory*. It is one of the most rewarding experiences one will ever know."

Apollo interjected, "This is a poorly designed pulpit. All the writing on it takes away from it. What about a large black onyx top? Is it just for Your preaching, or may I lead singing behind it? We could have separate but equal pulpits. A black one for me and this glass one with all the writing for you."

Word responds, "Of those Scripture words on the pulpit to which you are referring it will be written,

'*Heaven and Earth will pass away, but My words (Scriptures) will never pass away.*'[34]

"Friend, you have a free choice to lead singing from anywhere in this great convocations. However, you are not to preach (speak words), but you are chosen only to lead the singing. You are not to do any preaching, but just singing! Also, with My voice, I will not seek to lead any of the singing." [Word, smiling at His own limitations]

"Word, you will, unquestionably, with your voice, not be singing in my choir! [Laughter] Also, the one above, who sounds like thunder, will also not be singing in my choir! What does he look like?"

"Friend, if you have seen Me you have seen the invisible God, My Father, as it is to be written,

'*The Son is the image of (visible representation of) the invisible (Father) God.*'[35]

'*The Son reflects (shines forth) the glory of God (the Father) and is an exact representation of His (God, the Father) very being. He holds everything together with His powerful Word*'[36]

---

[34] Matthew 24:35
[35] Colossians 1:14.
[36] Hebrews 1:3.

No one will see God (the Father), who is a pure spirit. But God the only Son, who is Himself God, is beside the Father, and He shows the likeness of God the Father. Let me explain, there is one person of God, My Father, another of God, the Holy Spirit, and the one that speaks to you is God, the Son. The Godhead of the Father, the Son, and the Holy Spirit is One God. I am the Son of God and have always been divine. I am the express image of the Father. I am the Word of God from eternity before time began.

I always was and always will be. A creative being is to choose of their own *'free will'* to both love and obey God or to rebel and disobey. Do you understand?

"No," responds, Apollo, "I have so much to learn. How can three (3) be one (1)? Impossible!"

Sounding again like thunder, but to the ears of the Son the words His Father spoke were,

"Let the first service begin!"

With a nod from His Father, the Son turns to Apollo and invites him to lead the empty congregation in a song, and Word steps back with Apollo taking front and center.

Apollo in perfect pitch sounding like an entire orchestra, booms in song,

"Let me celebrate the One true God, who through Word created me and gave me life and gifting. I celebrate and lift my song up into the throne room to the invisible God and to the invisible Holy Spirit and to the Son, the Word of God, being Immanuel, God visible to me. I have ears to hear the words of the Son of God and I will trust and obey.I cherish in my heart the words of the Son of God. Hallelujah!"

Apollo makes a prideful bow, knowing he spoke what he believed Word wanted to hear. He then steps back from the pulpit. With a gesture of his hand, he turns the service over to Word. Apollo quickly selects the most chief seat in the front row center, feeling so esteemed after delivering such an important part of the first service in Heaven.

The First Sermon

The Son of God, looking up and receives the Father's smile, under the anointing, preaches His first sermon,

"Everyone that acknowledges Me before men and confesses Me (out of a state of oneness with Me), I will also acknowledge before My Father, Who is in Heaven. . . . But whoever denies and disowns Me . . . I also will deny and disown before My Father, Who is in Heaven.'[37]

'I do nothing on My own but speak just what the Father has taught Me.'[38]

'The Father loves the Son and has placed everything in His hands. Whoever believes in the Son has eternal life, but whoever rejects the Son will not see life, for God's wrath remains on him.'[39]

'I tell You the truth, the Son can do nothing by Himself; He can do only what he sees the Father doing . . . . The Father judges no one, but has entrusted all judgment to the Son, that all may honor the Son. . . . He that does not honor the Son does not honor the Father, who sent him.'[40]

' I (the Son) am the Way and the Truth and the Life; no one comes to the Father except by (through) Me. . . .

He that hath seen Me hath seen the Father . . . .

Believe Me, that I am in the Father and the Father in Me . . . .

If a man loves Me, he will keep My words, and My Father will love him . . . .

The word which ye hear is not Mine, but the Father, who sent Me.'

If a person (truly)) loves Me, he will do My word – obey My teaching, and My Father will love him, and We will come to him and make Our home (abode, special dwelling place) with him.

---

[37] Matthew 10:32, 33 AMP.
[38] John 8:28 NIV.
[39] John 3:35-36 NIV.
[40] John 5:19, 22, 23 NIV.

Anyone that does not (really) love Me does not observe and obey My teaching. And the teaching you hear and heed is not Mine, but (comes) from the Father, Who sent Me.[41]

'The Word of the Lord endures forever.'[42]

'Heaven and Earth will pass away, but My words will never pass away.'[43] Amen! [So be it.]"

Word, steps from behind the pulpit after delivering with boldness the first sermon in Heaven. Word responds further to Apollo's statement that it seemed impossible to him that the one person of the Father, another of the Word, and another of the Holy Spirit, making up the Godhead of the Father God, the Word, and the Holy Spirit is one God,

'For with God nothing is ever impossible, and no word from God shall be without power or impossible of fulfillment.'[44] *'Hear . . . The Lord our God, the Lord, is One. Love the Lord your God with all your heart and with all your soul and with all your strength. These commandments I give you today are to be upon your heart.'*[45]

'Love your neighbor as yourself.'[46]

Apollo interrupts, "Where do I live? Will I have any neighbors?"

Word gently points saying, "Yes, you will have fellow angels living near you. Do you see that lovely lighted pink mansion on yonder mount off to the left?"

"I've never seen anything so beautiful! Whose is it?"

Word answers, "You never saw anything until you opened your eyes a few moments ago. [Laughter] All in Heaven and on Earth belong to My Father, but He has given Me authority to grant temporary lease legal rights in property such as this mansion and grounds. You as my song leader and a friend may use it."

Apollo inquires, "What do I have to do to earn this right?"

Word responds, "God's graciousness cannot be earned or deserved, less anyone should boast. It will later be written about God's free, gracious gift of eternal life,

'For the wages that sin pays is death, but the (bountiful) free gift of God is eternal life through (in union with) Jesus Christ our Lord.'[47] *'For it is by free grace (God's unmerited favor) that you are saved (delivered from judgment and made partakers of Christ's salvation) through faith. And this (salvation) is not of yourselves – of your own doing, it came not through your own striving – but it is the gift of God: Not because of works (not the fulfillment of the Law's demands), lest any man should boast. – It is not the result of what anyone might do, so no one can pride himself in it or take glory to himself.'*[48]

Your free gift is the right to use this mansion containing a choir loft and orchestra pit stocked with various musical instruments. You will discover a special room designed to compose praise and worship music for our services.

Apollo urges, "Oh, please let me go see what is mine at once. I almost can't wait to see this beautiful pink mansion. Pink is one of my favorite colors. Also, I want to see my image in the water as I would like to look at my face. Do I have a plain face, sort of like yours? Do I have a hump on my nose? It feels straight when I run my hand over it. Is my voice soft like yours? Also, I am hungry is there anything to eat?"

"Friend, remember one question at a time. No, you are not made in My image. You look like a Spanish Prince, wavy black hair, dark skin, with no hump on your nose. [Laughing as Word points to a hump on the top of His nose.]

---

[41] John 14:6, 11, 23-24.

[42] Isaiah 40: 8; 1 Peter 1:25 NKJV.

[43] Luke 21:33 NIV.

[44] Luke 1:37.

[45] Deuteronomy 6:4-6 NIV.

[46] Matthew 22:39 NIV.

[47] Romans 6:23 AMP.

[48] Ephesians 2:8, 9 AMP.

Your voice is not like My soft voice, but is deep and sounds like music, which is your gifting. Your voice is very gifted, especially when you are singing. You can eat or not eat, '*For the kingdom of God is not a matter of eating or drinking, but righteousness, peace, and joy, in the Holy Spirit.*'[49]

Since you are hungry, my friend, as My second creation of life, I will create a garden of delight on the song leader's grounds. You have a right to use this garden, and you can easily enter it from a sliding glass door in the kitchen. This Garden of Delight will contain dates, figs, grapes, nuts, various fruit trees, and delicious vegetables like carrots. beets. broccoli, brussels' sprouts, cauliflower, celery, eggplant, sweet potatoes, tomatoes, and much more, for you, your staff, and choir members to eat when they come to the song leader's mansion to rehearse and plan for the services.

'Garden of Delight' – **Be**!"

"Word, how am I going to pick the fruit and gather the vegetables?"

"With your right hand. One at a time." [Laughter]

"Do I put them in my pockets or under my arm?"

"You can, but I would suggest neither. I see your gifting is not gardening! [Laughter] You might consider simply going to the kitchen and selecting a large light crystal container and gather all the delicacies you like. It will be an honor for any subject to be invited by you to eat with you out on the veranda. I hope you will invite Me some day yourself after you have selected your choir. This evening you can eat until you have eaten sufficiently. Enjoy it!"

"Thank you, Word for offering me all my needs." Apollo turns stepping toward the pink palace.

Word responds, "Apollo, you are most kindly welcome! '*Eye hath not seen, nor ear heard, neither has entered into the heart of man, the things which God hath prepared for them that love Him.*'[50] Those who love and obey My teachings will not want any good thing! Friend, let me point out the two roads between this mansion and the throne room behind Me. The first broad road has a wide gate, which will automatically open to your voice or even to you approaching it. The second narrow road has a small gate,[51] which you will, with minimum effort, have to push open and securely close behind you. Since you are taller than Me, get down on your knees to enter that small gate, but this narrow road, less traveled, has many advantages, and I advise you to choose that one."

"Okay, let me go as I want to see all this!"

"Friend, let us meet back here tomorrow at 3:00 P.M. Here is an 18 karat gold watch for you to enjoy. It keeps perfect time down to the very atomic second. Others will ask you for the perfect time so they can set their clocks. [Laughter]

It is best that we always start our services on time. Not even an atomic second late as, '*Everything should be done in a fitting and orderly way.*'[52]

Again, tomorrow for you and some plants I have just created are the only life created. We will be just practicing together again."

Apollo appears keen to leave to see his gifts says with a higher pitched voice, "Well, until tomorrow then! "

---

[49] Romans 14:17 NIV.

[50] 1 Corinthians 2:9.

[51] "For wide is the gate and broad is the road that leads to destruction, and many enter through it. But small is the gate

and narrow the road that leads to life, and only a few find it." (Matthew 7:13-14).

[52] 1 Corinthians 14:40 NIV.

"Apollo, I would like to give you the assignment to compose a song of "Thanksgiving" to My Father God for you to sing tomorrow. As the previews of coming attractions, the song leader's pink palace has the word "HALLELUJAH," in pure gold above the entrance door.

The door is surrounded by every precious stone – a ruby, topaz, emerald, chrysolite, onyx, jasper, sapphire, turquoise and beryl. The door will automatically open as it hears your voice or notices you approaching. The kitchen will have a beautiful outside dining a veranda, with a view of the mountains, adjacent to your individual garden stocked with delicious food and delicacies for you to pick and freely eat. It has a 'bread tree' you will especially enjoy. Also, you will have a walk-in closet full of beautiful clothes, and you will have access to a large full-length dressing mirror from which you can see every side of your attire. Since it will be just the two of us tomorrow, let us both dress casually. I plan to wear another white linen ephod, and I will preach barefoot as we are standing on holy ground. Friend, I will look forward to seeing you back here tomorrow at 3:00 P.M."

Apollo, looking over his shoulder at the pink palace licks his lips and quickly turns his back on Word as he walks, almost with a run, swiftly toward the pink palace, not giving a thought to Word standing beside the throne behind him before the Holy Throne Room. Word watches Apollo gliding along at a good clip until he comes to the two roads. Apollo looks for a split moment at the small gate and narrow road and chooses the easy way by stepping in front of the wide gate saying, "Open for me, I am Apollo, the gifted song leader of Heaven." It quickly opens not causing any delay for him to enter this easier broad and wide way.

Shortly Apollo comes to a crystal clear pool of water. He hurries over to it to see his image on the surface of the water upon which, when he sees himself, he proclaims, "*Whoa, handsome! No hump nose. No plain face. I'll be the center of attraction.*" He leaped about six inches in the air as he admired his own good looks saying further to himself,

"*Wow, what beautiful black wavy hair, what beautiful dark eyes, what sparkling white teeth, what a physic – muscles everywhere!*

I am thankful that I am not plain like Word. I was concerned when I saw him thinking He was the gardener. The people will be so drawn to my good looks and deep singing voice. I've got to remember to write the song of thanksgiving to the Thunderer, Word's Father. I wonder how Thunderer looks. I picture a bearded old man with an unattractive face, and an ugly humped nose. [Self-laughter] Word said if I have seen him I have seen the Father. That doesn't make sense – the three are one. Impossible in logic for three to be one. What kind of game is being played on me here? I have a good thing going. If it is not broke, don't fix it – so three equal one. [Laughter to himself] However, all this walking is broke, and needs to be fixed. There has to be a faster way to travel. I've got it! Tomorrow I will ask Word for a swift horse to ride back and forth on this broad road as it is just right for racing. Faster than a speeding bullet, whatever that means! [Laughter] I will further look even more like a Spanish Prince on my beautiful black horse. What name should I give my attractive horse?"

The Son, observing all these things, turns looking up into the throne room shaking His head and hearing the Father say, "Come up hither, My beloved Son."

The Son quietly sits down at the right hand of the Father with the Father speaking, "Son you rightly created Your song leader as a free moral agent having the privilege to choose his own way and to know right from wrong. We do not want robots! Apollo has a choice to serve others or to serve himself.

I am a God of love, legality, and patience '*not wanting anyone to perish, but everyone to come to repentance.*'[53] I will give everyone, including Apollo, ample opportunity to obey your preaching and to repent of disobedience. However, on the 'Day of Judgment' when You sentence those who choose the broad selfish way to Hell, it will be written,

'*Many will say to Me on that day, 'Lord, Lord, have we not prophesied in Thy name? And in Thy name have cast out devils and in Thy name done many wonderful works?' And then will I profess unto them, 'I never knew you: depart from Me, ye that work iniquity.*'[54]

"Father, what is to become of My new song leader? I can see that he is already selfish and vain because of his beauty and gifting."

"Son, fret not! Enjoy the trip, as will I, with You being described in Scripture, "*Who for the JOY set before Him endured the cross, scorning its shame, and sat down at the right hand of the throne of God.*'[55]

"Father, Your **JOY** argument wins Me over immediately every time." [Laughter]

"Son, for now, it is My will that Apollo be invited to be Your friend. The time will come when he will truly just be interested in three people – 'Me, Myself, and I.' My Son, there will be two types of people coming to your services. One will say, "Here I am." The other will say, "There you are, my Lord." [Father smiles] Many will pray "Bless my plan, Lord!" Others will humbly inquire, "What's the plan, Lord?" [Father again smiles]

"Father, what's the plan?" [Laughing]

"My Son, I am going to permit selfishness for reasons of My own, not fully revealed even to You. Now relax and enjoy the literal ride as Apollo is going to ask you for a horse tomorrow, and I want you to enjoy riding together with Apollo as a friend."

"Father, what if Apollo asks Me for the moon? Am I to give it to him to continue his own selfish desires?"

"Yes, My Son, only a temporary right to use, as soon Apollo will ask you what he feels is the wealthiest real estate. I want you to give him only the right to use it – not a title deed. For now, if he wants to use the moon, let him. [Smiling] No title deed to anything, only the right to use it! I am instructing you not to tell Apollyon directly what to wear or who to choose for his staff or choir members or seek to control his selfishness. Of course, for the benefit of the congregation you certainly can request that Apollo consider a subject or a previously sung song for an upcoming service. However, you will boldly preach in your portion of the services. You will '*teach (preach) as One who has authority!*'[56]

Apollo will ask you for many selfish favors, which you may, or may not, fully grant him. You will preach the truth from the pulpit! All who hear You will have a free will to obey or disobey or even to ignore or neglect to lift a finger toward doing what You preach, but they had better each earnestly continue to work out their own "*salvation with fear and trembling . . . .*"[57] They will not be robots, and it is My will that they all obey Your preaching."

"Father, I know You know all things. I know You prefer Me not to ask such questions before you choose to reveal Your will to Me, but will My new friend Apollo choose to obey Our message?"

---

[53] 2 Peter 3:9 NIV.
[54] Matthew 22:23.
[55] Hebrews 12:2 NIV.
[56] Mark 1:22.
[57] Philippians 2:12 NIV.

"My Son, it will be like a wife, which most of the time is faithful to her husband. Partial faithfulness is disobedience She may spuriously defend herself before the judge that she just very seldom committed adultery and that most of the time she was a faithful wife. The judge will rule that out of her own mouth, she admitted that she broke her marriage covenant – divorce granted – and then she is to be separated from her husband forever and ever and ever. My Son, I will always answer your questions, sometimes with a yes, other times with a no. Often You will have to wait for the appointed time to learn My perfect eternal will fully as I like to conceal a matter.

However, regarding Apollyon, or Apollo, the name You will for a season call him, in My foreknowledge, since you have specifically asked Me, it will be written regarding him in part:

'In the pride of your heart,
 you say, 'I am a god;
I sit on the throne of God
 in the heart of the seas.'
But you are a man and not a god,
 though you think you are as wise as God.
. . . By your wisdom and understanding
 you have gained wealth for yourself
. . . You were the model of perfection,
 full of wisdom and perfect in beauty.
. . .You were anointed as a guardian cherub,
 for so I ordained you.
You were on the holy mount of God . . . .
. . .Through your widespread trade
 you were filled with violence, and you sinned.
So I drove you in disgrace from the mount of God,
 and expelled you, O guardian cherub . . . .
Your heart became proud
 on account of your beauty
and you corrupted your wisdom
 because of your splendor.
So I threw you to the earth . . . .'[58]
'. . .How you have fallen from Heaven,
 O morning star, son of the dawn!
You have been cast down to the Earth,
 you who once laid low the nations!
You said in your heart,
 'I will ascend to heaven,
I will raise my throne
 above the stars of God.
I will sit enthroned on the mount of assembly
 On the utmost heights of the sacred mountain.
I will ascend above the tops of the clouds;
 I will make myself like the Most High.'
But you are brought down . . .
Those who see you stare at you,
 they ponder your fate:
 'Is this the man who shook the Earth
 and made the world a desert,
 who overthrew its cities
 and would not let his captives go home?'[59]

---

[58] Ezekiel 28:1, 4, 5, 11, 13-17 NIV.

"Father, I never question Your wisdom or your will, but I see that Apollo is going to make Your footstool a desert (wasteland)."

"My Son, it is a desert (wasteland) now as You have not created any vegetation on it. [Father smiles] Therefore, since Apollo is going to make it a desert again, let him go down with You, and see what kind of plants and living creatures he would like on it before he destroys all of them. Some will even mess up a free meal, and this is not an exercise in futility. Yes, My footstool is going to groan and moan.

In fact, I am going to destroy its surface twice Myself, once with water and then with fire. I want you to show Apollo the land having much gold. Specifically, point the temporary riches out to him."

"Yes, I will. Father, not My will, but Thine be done. I once heard You warn, "*Pride goes before destruction, and a haughty spirit before a fall.*"[60] Therefore, I will preach the importance of unselfishness and choosing to obey our commandments. I will give the prideful and selfish many opportunities to repent and to humble themselves under Your mighty hand. They will not have to perish if they repent and turn after I have warned them."

"Father, how am Apollo and I going to travel to the Earth?"

"You are going to ride your horses – zoom! [Laughter]

"Father, although We have played all over the cosmos together, I have never even seen or ridden a horse. What is to be My horse's name?"

"Your horse will be known as 'Abundance Life,' and it will be written about You and your famous horse,

'*I saw Heaven standing open, and there before me was a white horse, whose Rider is called Faithful and True. With justice, He judges and makes war. His eyes are like blazing fire, and on His head are many crowns. He has a name written on Him that no one but Himself knows. He is dressed in a robe dipped in blood, and His name is the Word of God. The armies of Heaven were following Him, riding on white horses and dressed in fine linen, white and clean. Out of His mouth comes a sharp sword with which to strike down the nations. He will rule them with an iron scepter. He treads the winepress of the fury of the wrath of God Almighty. On His robe and on His thigh he has this name written:*

KING OF KINGS AND LORD OF LORDS.'[61]

'*The thief (Apollo will become, the ultimate evil one) comes only to steal and kill and destroy. I (Jesus) have come that they may have life, and that they may have it more abundantly.*'[62]

Son, for your information, no other horse can beat Your 'Abundant Life.'† [Laughter]

[59.] Isaiah 14:12-17 NIV.

[60] .Proverbs 16:18 AMP.

[61] .Revelations 19:11-16 NIV.

[62.] John 10:10.

†BOOK ONE – Episode 5†

[†**Sidebar Scriptures**: "*Joseph had a dream and promptly reported all the details* (Genesis 37:5)."
"*The Lord revealed to me what the evil ones were doing and planning and showed me their wicked plots* (Jeremiah 11:18)."
"*The word of the Lord came to Abram in a* **vision**. . . . *A* **deep sleep** *came upon Abram . . . .* (Genesis 15:1, 12)."
I witnessed and experienced "*dreams and visions, and I described* ***all*** *I had seen to instruct many* (Daniel 7:1, 11:33)."†]

Word (Son of God) and the Song Leader Apollo's
Association in Heaven Continues

FATHER GOD SPEAKS, "God, the Holy Spirit, I love You. For there is one person of Me, the Father, another of the Son, now having a flesh and bone body from which to preach, and another person of You, mighty Holy Spirit. We are one Triune God. As a person, You have feelings, Holy Spirit, and when Your feelings are hurt My feelings are hurt. I inquire as if I didn't know, 'Why are you grieving?'[1]

The Holy Spirit responds, "Because Apollo did not esteem the Word of God, nor offer any worship to the Father nor the Son. He has sinned from the beginning[2] with the first words out of his mouth, 'My music be glorified.' Me, myself, and I. He even desired to remove the Holy Scriptures from the pulpit, I gave Word, for others to see and meditate on."

Word responds, "He is My first creation, now a friend, and we laugh together. I will go down to the preaching pulpit to meet again today with My new song leader, Apollo. Again, since I have never been stressed or grieved, I will this day endure all this for the JOY set before me! My Father is always right! Once I thought He may have been wrong, but He was right! Father knows best!"

Word walks down from the throne room at 2:50 P.M. and is waiting at the preaching pulpit for the 3:00 P.M. scheduled meeting. It is now 3:06 P.M. and Apollo, arrive briskly walking up from the broad road averring, "Here I am. Hi. It is such a beautiful day in Heaven.

About the gift you gave me to use, as I approached my gorgeous mansion, I saw a beautiful lighted water fountain spraying water high into the air with every color of light, except black, radiating from inside the water. As you explained, as I approached the gold-lite word HALLELUJAH above the elegant front door, surrounded by many precious jewels – a ruby, topaz, emerald, chrysolite, onyx, jasper, sapphire, turquoise and beryl – I demanded, 'Here I am, Apollo,' and the door swung wide open inviting me in with beautiful music.

I stepped into the foyer, and it contained a nice harp with engraved musical notes. The foyer had tall ceilings with a glass crystal front viewing the lighted water fountain. I could see all the way to my singing pulpit and up to the magnificent throne room, sitting on the top of the mount. It had gold crown moldings containing various musical notes with precious stones between them. Everything is perfect and so stunning! Sparkling furniture, drapes, and mirrors. Everything fits my personality and tastes down to the last detail. A lot of gold and marble, and there was on my table in the foyer a director of music's yawn that would bear glorious different color lights at its tip keeping beat with the music as I practiced waving it as if I was conducting the orchestra and choir. I meant to bring it today, but You have not yet created anyone for me to direct. [Laughter] Everything throughout my mansion is elegant."

Word inquires, "Apollo, do you desire anything changed or rearranged?"

---

[1] "Do not grieve the Holy Spirit of God." (Ephesians 4:30).
[2]. "The devil has been sinning from the beginning." (1 John 3:8).

"No, but I did rearrange my staff room, making it into three sections containing six thrones. I mean chairs, each. I pictured my instructing the first group of six, the second group of six, and the third group of six. It was great as we conspired and planned. What power in unity! I like the numbers 666.

A spotlight shone down on me as I sat on my throne, I mean eloquent director's seat, as I practiced instructing my staff. I demonstrated my musical ability by playing and explaining in practice last evening every musical instrument. It took me almost all night to learn to play all of them – it was a piece of devil food cake and so easy. [Self-laughter] I then remembered that I was hungry, and I walked to a crystal door, and it opened for me. I found myself in a magnificent garden with a small fountain shooting water into the air filled with all different colors of light. I enjoyed eating delicious dates, figs, grapes, fruit, and nuts until I was stuffed. It was the best meal I ever had."

The Son laughing said, "It is the only meal you ever had! [Both laughing] Apollo, once I said to My Father that I was 'stuffed.' He instructed me, 'Don't say, My Son, 'I am stuffed,' but say, 'I have eaten sufficiently.' [Laughter]

Apollo, replies, "Last evening I truly had eaten sufficiently, and I mean exceedingly sufficiently. [Laughter] After I had eaten my fill, sufficiently, I went into the master bedroom and opened all the drawers. Look at these gold rings and the gold necklace adorned with a ruby, topaz, emerald, chrysolite, onyx, jasper, sapphire, turquoise, and beryl. It was so late that I decided to take a nap. I awaken a little late, and I walked as fast as I could to get here. I had no opportunity to compose the song on 'Thanksgiving,' but I am looking forward to hearing your sermon today on that subject. Please forgive me for not doing your first assignment."

"Apollo, My friend, 'You are indeed forgiven!' Confession[3] and repenting (being sorrow for sin and making a U-turn away from doing it again) restores fellowship."

"I mean it! I ask you to forgive me."

"Apollo, I do not know what you are talking about as it has been cast into the 'depths of the sea'[4] of My forgetfulness. This is removed as far as the east is from the west.[5] Picture yourself going east. Will you ever reach the west? [Laughter] Picture Me casting your confessed sin in the deepest part of the sea on Earth. Then see the confessed and repented of sin sinking beneath the water to the floor of the ocean never to be seen or heard of again."

"Word, I have a request to make to help me get here faster from my pink palace. I need a horse to match my hair. Your hair is light brown, and you might consider a brown horse for yourself so we can tell them apart. [Self-laughter]

"Apollo, you are not a robot; so you can choose the color of your horse and the clothes you wear." "Word, every color of clothes was in my huge walk-in closet, but I chose this black sparkling outfit as it matched my wavy black hair, my dark eyes, and dark skin. Also, black shows off my jewelry better." [Self-laughter]

---

[3] "If we confess our sins, he is faithful and just and will forgive us our sins and purify us from all unrighteousness." (1 John 1:9)

[4] Micah 7:19.

[5] "As far as the east is from the west, so far has He removed our transgressions from us." (Psalm 103:13).

"Apollo, let us both have horses to ride together and we can ride tomorrow up into the mountains for a view of views. If you like, we can even take a ride to Earth and explore that beautiful desert ball, which my Father calls His footstool, and I can show you a land of unusual raw materials, including gold."

"Wow, resources, including gold! Yes, Word, that would be fun. Make mine black and fast! There is nothing as useless as a slow horse." [Self-laughter]

Jesus responds, "Several other things may be more useless. [Laughter] Two horses, **Be!**"

Apollo felt a push on his back, and as he turned around, he saw his lovely black horse. He proclaimed, "Your name will be, "Black Shadow," and you will be fast. You will always hold your head high in a prideful manner as you are the best as you carry me as the first created prince."

Behind Black Shadow was Word's horse standing respectfully with Apollo smirking, "And Your name will be called "Slower" as you will never win a race over Black Shadow."

Word spoke, "Never say never!" [Laughter]

"Look at my beautiful horse. I like black better than plain Vanilla. You could call your horse Vanilla. May I now ride Black Shadow to my pink palace?"

"Certainly, and your horse will have a beautiful stable home to live in on the mansion grounds. Black Shadow will like living there. However, the Name of My white, not brown, horse will be 'Abundant Life.' Remember Apollo, 'You take the black one, and I'll take the white one.' [Laughter]

"What a strange name for a horse – 'Abundant Life!' I like the name 'Black Shadow' much better as it is descriptive. Well, Word, would you like to practice your preaching? You indicated the theme today, 'Thanksgiving.' I will sit in the middle seat on the front roll and try not to watch Black Shadow. I am excited about riding him. I needed him to get here on time today. If I had him today, I would not have been late, but would have been even a few minutes early."

Word hands Apollo a song and respectfully requests its singing before the preaching. Apollo holding the sheet music in his right-hand raises his left hand, increasing the brightness of the lights throughout the arena. He then with an eloquent voice projected his voice using his unique gifts of music throughout the arena,

'*Praise the Lord, Sing to the Lord a new song, His praise in the assembly of the saints.*
Let Israel rejoice in their Maker; let the people of Zion be glad in their King.
Let them praise His name with dancing and make music to Him with tambourine and harp.
For the Lord takes delight in His people; He crowns the humble with salvation.
Let the saints rejoice in this honor and sing for joy on their beds.
May the (high) praise of God be in their mouths and a double-edged sword in their hands,
to inflict vengeance on the nations and punishment on the peoples, to bind their kings with fetters, their nobles with shackles of iron to carry out the sentence written against them. This is the glory of all His saints.
Praise the Lord.'[6]

Apollo walks out from behind the pulpit and down the steps and chooses the chief center seat on the front row.

Word in quietness and holiness stands behind the pulpit and looks up into the throne room and nods back and opens His mouth,

'Worship the Lord (only) with gladness
    Come before Him with joyful songs.
    Know that the Lord (Jesus) is God.

[6.] Psalm 149:1-9 NIV.

It is He (Son of God) who made us
and we belong to Him (not belonging to ourselves) . . . .
*Enter into His gates with songs of **Thanksgiving**,*
*and into His Courts with songs of **Praise**;*
*be thankful unto Him, and **Bless** His name.*
For the Lord is good and His love endures forever . . . .[7]

'*Praise God in His sanctuary (holy place);*
Praise Him in His mighty Heaven.
Praise Him for His acts of power;
Praise Him for His surpassing greatness.
Praise Him with the sounding of the trumpet,
Praise Him with the harp and lyre,
Praise Him with tambourine and dancing,
Praise Him with the strings and flute,
Praise Him with the clash of cymbals,
Praise Him with resounding cymbals.
Let everything that has breath (life) praise the Lord.
Praise the Lord.'[8]

Thanksgiving is distinct from *Praise*, which is distinct from *Worship*!

The first step is to be **thankful** for the deeds God has done in the past as we from the heart believe that God can do now what He has done in the past. *Thanksgiving* of one's own '*free will*' gets us into the gates.

'*Let them sacrifice (of their own 'free will') thank offerings.*'[9]

We are to turn our eyes away deliberately from self and our concerns and humbly thank God for His goodness and mercy to us!

'*In everything (all you do) give thanks, for this is (Father) God's will for you in Christ Jesus.*'[10]

Amen (So be it.)"

Apollo clapping avows, "Word that was marvelous! I will obey of my own '*free will*.' I am looking out over the mountains to the right and the fields of the city, and they appear like a desert. What about some greenery in Heaven like in my garden for us to ride on our horses, and maybe some flowers with a sweet smell."

"Apollo, be back here in the morning at 10:10 A.M., and we can go riding together on the green grass. I have prepared a horse stable, divided into separate stalls, which cannot be seen from the pulpit for Abundant Life and your horse off to the left, to keep you from being distracted. [Laughter] They both will be just fine until the end of the services, and we can often take refreshing rides together after the services if you desire."

---

[7] Psalm 100:2-5. [Emphasis added.]
[8] Psalm 150 NIV.
[9] Psalm 107:22.
[10] 1 Thessalonians 5:18.

55

"Apollo avers, "'Black Shadow' is a little distracting. He is so beautiful, and I am sure he is faster than a speeding bullet, whatever that means? A perfect match for me. We will go as one unit."

"Yes, my friend, you will find that he will zoom!" [Laughter]

With that Apollo mounts Black Shadow and orders, "Zoom!" [laughing to himself] with Apollo steering him directly to the 'wide gate.'[11] Apollo never gave a thought to seeing whether Black Shadow might get on his knees and go through the small gate for this first ride together down the delightful narrow road[12] less traveled.

The Son looks up into the throne room and hears His Father say, "Well done, 'Come up hither.'[13] Your preaching blessed Me!"

The Son humbly speaks, "Father, I do like Apollo as a friend. We have horses and will ride together, but you see his selfishness. Please have 'goodness and mercy'[14] follow Me and Abundant Life tomorrow as I am not used to such selfishness. It is not stressful, but it concerns me. I'm too blessed to be stressed!" [Laughter]

"Yes, My Son, 'goodness and mercy' will follow You and I want you to enjoy this season of fun, friendship, and working together as Apollyon Lucifer leads the singing. You do the preaching! Those tuning in their ears will be blessed by hearing and obeying Your preaching. From time-to-time, as You already know, include in your sermons the importance of walking in humility and unselfishness. I am 'not wanting anyone to perish [in the fires of Hell] but everyone to come to repentance.'[15] Emphasize at times in your preaching that eternal fire is a place to avoid at all cost. If Hell must be filled, at least, let it be filled in spite of Your repeated warnings, and let no one go to destruction unwarned and uncalled on to repent of sin and receive You as Savior and confess You as Lord.."

"Father, is there any other Kingdom business We need to discuss?"

Father adds, "Apollyon, desires You to create all the beautiful flowers, trees, and vegetation throughout the Celestial City and in our planet Heaven. For a season do not create the *Tree of Life*, to bear twelve different fruits or create golden streets, walls, and gates here in Heaven. Just wait on landscaping the Earth until you two ride down on your horses and be careful with my heated footstool. [Laughter] There is no way that 'Black Shadow' can outrun 'Abundant Life.' [Laughter] Nothing beats my Son's *Abundant Life* as You will preach,

'*The thief cometh not, but for to steal, and to kill, and to destroy: I (Jesus) have come that they might have life and that they might have it more abundantly.*'[16]

The Son rising to His feet and standing beside the Father looks into the Father's smiling face and then looks out over the Celestial City and out over the horizon of Heaven and speaks,

"Flowers, **be**!"

Throughout Heaven, the scent of flowers goes forth.

"Now the green grass, trees, grape vines, shrubs, hedges, and all types of plants, vegetables, and vegetation be!"

The planet Heaven was filled with plant life.

---

[11] Matthew 7:13-14.
[12] See Matthew 7:13, 14.
[13] Quoting from Revelation 11:12.
[14] "Surely goodness and mercy will follow me . . . ." (Psalm 23:6 KJV).
[15] 2 Peter 3:9.
[16] John 10:10 KJV.

Word patting 'Abundant Life' on the head the next morning observes Apollo racing up the Broad Road on his black horse toward the hidden stable near the preaching pulpit and when Apollo dismounts he lands on both feet and exclaiming,

"Here I am. I like my gold watch – 10:9 and 54 seconds, 55, 56, 57, 58, 59 – 10:10." [Laughter] Six seconds early. That is a record for me.

I told you I could be on time if I had my black racing horse. Today I set a new record for racing the some 666 furlongs up the Broad Road on the beautiful Kentucky Blue Grass. That would be a good place for you and me to race. Talk about racing, we will set a record time today when we race to your Father's footstool."

Word is laughing, replies, "I guess so. No one has ever traveled there before."

Apollo turns around with his thumbs on each side of his riding britches, also wearing a black riding jacket with a silk pink open lace blouse, showing some wavy black chest hairs bordered with a Lavender scarf with a jeweled necklace saying, "Am I not a sight for fashion?"

"Yes, you are a sight, but who is going to admire you other than the flowers and horses and right now the Earth is a little dusty for pink silk." [Laughter]

Apollo, patting his black horse on the head and smiling at Word says, "The flowers are beautiful. They turned and looked at me when I rode by them. It could have been the wind of my speed going by them that turned them. [Laughter] I was a little disappointed because they cannot sing."

"Apollo, they can sing, but you have to get on your knees and put your ear right up to the blossom to hear. I am going to create angels with voices of all types, and you are going to select and train them to make the lovely sounds of Heaven, their singing in Heaven will be glorious."

Apollo inquires, "Am I an angel?"

"Yes, you are the highest type of angel – a 'guardian cherub.'[17] I will be creating cherubs, archangels, and other types of angels and heavenly beings all having various different functions and gifts. Friend, today as we ride horses would you like to hear some beautiful singing of birds flying in the sky above us? At times, these created flying creatures will be serenading you outside your music studio while you write songs for the worship and praise services."

"Oh, yes. That would be good for me to hear."

Word decrees, "Birds fly and to sing, **Be!**"

Beautiful songbirds appear freely flying and singing in the sky of Heaven, and they were especially drawn to and attracted to Apollo, who would sing with them.

As Apollo mounts Black Shadow, a songbird lands on Black Shadow's head and sings Apollo a lovely song.

Apollo joking at the bird declares, "You are the first chosen for my choir." [Laughter]

Word turns to Apollo and says, "You ride on the left. We will take the scenic path to the right up to the pinnacle of Lookout Glory Mountain. No racing yet." [Laughing]

Apollo laughs, "You did say, 'yet.'"†

---

[17] Ezekiel 28:14

†BOOK TWO†

†BOOK TWO – Episode 1†

[†**Sidebar Scriptures**: "*Joseph had a dream and promptly reported all the details (Genesis 37:5).*"
"*The Lord revealed to me what the evil ones were doing and planning and showed me their wicked plots (Jeremiah 11:18).*"
"*The word of the Lord came to Abram in a* **vision**. . . . *A* **deep sleep** *came upon Abram* . . . . *(Genesis 15:1, 12).*"
I witnessed and experienced "*dreams and visions, and I described* ***all*** *I had seen to instruct many (Daniel 7:1, 11:33).*"†]

First Earth Age Begins

Word and Apollo Having a Friendly Horse Ride to Planet Earth

WORD, THE SON OF GOD, and Apollo, the song leader of Heaven enjoy each other's fellowship as they horseback ride together in friendship on a scenic trail, lined with beautiful flowers, plants, and trees, up the final steep slope to the pinnacle of Lookout Glory Mountain. They laugh with each other as the two horses touched noses as if to celebrate, "*We made it!*" At that happy moment, the Earth below rises above the horizon as if to say, with a lovely twinkle waving and saluting, "*There you are, my Creator! Thank You for creating and loving me!*"

Word spoke, "What a fantastic friendship ride. I so much enjoyed the trip up here with you. Such views of both the Celestial City and the rising planet Earth are even more spectacular when shared with a friend, My song leader. Your music can be a foundation for worship if offered with unselfish love and humility for My Father! '*God is spirit, and His worshipers must worship in spirit and in truth.*'[1] Father God is omnipresent, meaning He is present everywhere at all times and is ominisent (knows everyting).

'*Has it not been told you from the beginning?*
Have you not understood since the Earth was founded?
He sits enthroned above the circle of the Earth,
and its people are like grasshoppers.
He stretches out the heavens like a canopy,
and spreads them out like a tent to live in.'[2]
"*He (God) has total knowledge,*
and He knows everything."[3]
'*O Lord, You have searched me,*
and You know me.
You know when I sit and when I rise;
You perceive my thoughts from afar.
You discern my going and my lying down;
You are familiar with all my ways.'[4]
'*The word of God is living and active.*
Sharper than any double-edged sword,
it penetrates even to dividing soul and spirit, joints and marrow;
it judges the thoughts and attitudes of the heart.

---

[1] John 4:24.
[2] Isaiah 40:21-23.
[3] 1 John 3:20.
[4] Psalm 139:1-3.

Nothing in all creation is hidden from God's sight.
Everything is uncovered and laid bare before the eyes of Him
to whom we must give account.'[5]

Remembering that Father God is omnipresent and omniscient, let us again practice."

With a preaching pulpit appearing, Word hands Apollo a song sheet.

Apollo, as he pats Black Shadow on the head choosing not to get behind the pulpit, releases an orchestra of sound, as he lets his gift of music flow,

'The Earth is the Lord's and everything in it . . .
for He hath founded it upon the seas and established it upon the waters.'[6]
'Praise the Lord from the heavens, praise Him on the heights above . . .
Praise the Lord from the Earth . . .
Let them praise the name of the Lord, for His name alone is exalted;
His splendor is above the Earth and the heavens.
He has raised up for His people a horn, the praise of all His saints . . . . Praise the Lord.'[7]

Apollo hands this service over to Word. He sits down in front of the pulpit on a stone with his eyes on Black Shadow eating leaves from a Mulberry tree. Word preaches, "It is to be written,

'The reverent and worshipful fear of the Lord
is the beginning . . . of knowledge –
that is, its starting point and its essence . . . .'[8]
'Lean on, trust, and be confident in the Lord with all your heart and mind
and do not rely on your own insight or understanding.
In all your ways know, recognize, and acknowledge Him,
and He will direct, and make straight and plain your paths.
Be not wise in your own eyes: reverently fear and worship the Lord
and turn (entirely) away from evil.'[9]
'Receive My instruction in preference to (striving for) silver,
and knowledge rather than choice gold.
For skillful and godly Wisdom is better than rubies or pearls,
and all the things that may be desired are not to be compared to it.
I, wisdom (from God), have made prudence My dwelling,
and I find out knowledge and discretion.
The reverent fear and worshipful awe of the Lord includes the hatred of evil.
Pride, arrogance, the evil way, and perverted and twisted speech I hate.[10]
By the fear of the Lord, one departs from evil.'[11]

Apollo ignoring Word's preached Scriptures seeks to change the subject, "Wow, did you see all the flowers turning and worshiping us as we rode by; and what beautiful fragrances they gave off as offerings. When am I going to have my staff and choir members as I am ready to launch?"

World replies, "Apollo, within a few days you can go exploring the Celestial City and meet some of the newly created inhabitant angels and start inviting them to come to the studio for auditions. You will choose some to play instruments in the orchestra and others to sing in the choir, and some from these two groups can be your music staff members. I am leaving the choices of whom you select to you. I respectfully ask you not to put undue (excessive) pressure on anyone to join the choir or orchestra as they, like you, have a free will."

---

[5] Hebrews 4:12-13.
[6] Psalm 24:1 NIV.
[7] Psalm 148:1, 7, 13, 14 NIV.
[8] Proverbs 1:7 AMP.
[9] Proverbs 3:5-7 AMP.
[10] Proverbs 8:10-13 AMP.
[11] Proverbs 16:6 NKJV.

"I like that. I can hardly wait. Am I going to be in charge of virtually everything?"

Word responds, "You are in charge only of the music for praise and worship of God. Next, I will create two chief archangels having different gifts and responsibilities.

"Word, I'll give them a prominent place in my choir."

"No, My friend, for neither Michael nor Gabriel will be given singing voices so they will not be candidates for your choir. [Laughter] All three of you will be directly under My authority, which means you are not to seek to give each other orders or assignments. Remember that your mission solely is to be in charge of the music. However, Michael and Gabriel will also have horses, and the four of us can ride together or the three of you, at times, may enjoy riding, fellowship, and even exploring together. You, Apollo, as the elder creation, should seek to form a friendship bond between you three. Each of you is My delegated heads of three separate areas, similar in rank, but each having entirely different areas of responsibilities. Remember, your area is limited to music, a foundation for praise and worship!"

Word and Apollo Explore Planet Earth

"Word, I see a rounded rock like a dome down on the Earth, having light reflecting off it."

"Yes. That is Mount Moriah,[12] a special place on My Father's footstool."

Apollo 'throwing down the gauntlet'[13] advancing, "Let's race! I bet I can beat you there!"

Apollo, not waiting for a response to his challenge, looking like lightning falling from Heaven, zooms on Black Shadow in a straight line to land right beside Mount Moriah. Apollo looks back with a proud look and with a smirk on his face because he got the jump at the gate on Word, or, at least, he thought he had. However, when Apollo turns his head back toward the Earth, he shockingly sees Abundant Life standing beside Mount Moriah with Word kneeling barefoot in prayer on the summit. Apollo landing beside Mount Moriah inquiring, "Word, in what way did you do that? How? Impossible!"

Word responded, "Nothing beats My Abundant Life! For your further information, I do not gamble, race, or bet as this is not part of the abundant life I preach. I will in my future preach the command, 'Thou shalt not covet . . . .'[14] I am instructing all My angels not to race each other, gamble or bet with each other, as the greatest among you will be the servant of all. Again, I consider gambling or betting, a form of greed. Many will hear of the gamblers at Golgotha, who gambled for My garment when abundant blessings were right there above their heads. They never even looked up as they threw the dice with greed in their eyes."

Apollo exclaimed, "I did not see you pass me! How did you do that?"

Word explains, "I can travel at a speed faster than the speed of light. At that speed, I become invisible, and time stops and even goes backward. I have been here a while praying to My Father waiting for you."

Apollo replies, "That's impossible! Will you give me a clue?

---

[12] "Then Solomon began to build the temple of the Lord in Jerusalem on Mount Moriah, where the Lord had appeared to his father David. It was on the threshing floor of Araunah the Jebusite, the place provided by David."
(2 Chronicles 3:1 NIV).
[13] Throwing down the gauntlet was one knight's method for challenging another knight. "To 'throw down the gauntlet' is to issue a challenge." See Gauntlet in Wikipedia, The Free Encyclopedia.
[14] Exodus 20:17 KJV.

Word responds, "With the Godhead, as I have already explained, nothing is impossible. I'll give you a short formula, $E=MC^2$."

Apollo complains, "This place is a desert! It looks like a worthless and empty dust bowl with a moon going around it appearing just as dry and bare."

Word responds, "Apollo, you might be surprised what can be made out of dust and a rib! [Word smiles] Near here we have the 'land of Havilah, where there is gold.'[15] with untapped assets. The gold here differs from the gold in Heaven as it represents great riches."

Apollo replies, "We could build a gold dome on this rock, and everyone from Heaven could see it at times when the sun reflects off of it."

Apollo smirked to himself thinking, "*He who has the gold, makes the rules. Control! Control!*"

Word speaks, "Yes, there will be a gold dome built over this very rock, but it will be none of My or My Father's doing, but just false doctrines and a shrine of men. Now, we will travel to the '*Land of Havilah, where there is gold . . . and onyx.*'[16]"

"Word, I like the combination of gold and onyx. As you can see, I chose a gold ring with a black onyx stone from my jewelry collection to wear on my left ring finger. Why don't you wear a ring on that finger like me?"

Apollo, I am saving that finger as I anticipate being given a special ring, which will represent unending love, absolute purity, devotion, and a covenant commitment for eternity. I am saving Myself and that finger for that special person. I am patient, but I can hardly wait. However, I possibly could wait forever if it did not take too long?" [Laughter]

Apollo reasons, '*He must desire me to give him an eternal friendship ring in our relationship as he calls me friend*, further inquiring, "Word, is the ring to be made out of earthly gold or heavenly gold?" Word answers, "It is going to be made out of 18-karat Earth gold, but the eternal covenant will be sealed in Heaven."

"Word, I saw you gaze over at that nearby hill, which is the most desolate spot possible. It looks like a dried-out skull. Is that where the Earth gold is?"

"Apollo, there is no natural gold in that hill known, as Golgotha, which means 'The place of the Skull.'[17] The path you can see leading to it is known as the 'Via Dolorosa.' A way of great suffering producing great joy. I will choose to walk that narrow road out of the love (agape) God has for all men made in Our image. All the way to die like a pure Lamb on Calvary to take away the sins of all who will receive Me as Savior. Please stay here and let Me practice walking that path, and when I reach the top of Golgotha, I will motion for you sing this song I am handing you. I will further practice preaching."

"Word, we are doing a lot of practicing. Is all this preparation necessary? I think I am ready for the crowd and the actual performance. After this practice, then can we go to the land where there is gold?"

Word walks down and locates the starting spot and walks barefoot down the "Via Dolorosa" in Jerusalem with Thunder from Heaven sounding with Word nodding back.

Word pauses some twelve[18] times on his westerly route down the "Via Dolorosa."

---

[15] Genesis 2:11 NIV.

[16] Genesis 2: 11, 12 NIV.

[17] John 19:16 NIV.

[18] These twelve pauses are (1) Jesus is condemned to death; (2) Jesus receives the cross; (3) Jesus falls the first time; (4) Jesus meets His grieving mother; (5) Simon of Cyrene helps Jesus to carry His cross; (6) Veronica wipes the face of Jesus; (7) Jesus falls the second time; (8) Jesus speaks to the daughters of

Apollo thinks, "*He sure isn't traveling at a speed faster than light as this is getting excessively long and wasting my time. I am bored! I am ready to get me some of that gold.*"

Ultimately, Word reaches the summit of the hill known as Golgotha (Calvary) and He lets His outer garment fall into the dust hitting His knees (having a vision of a crown of thrones on His head, His back profusely bleeding, saying not a word, knowing He would be nailed to a wooden cross to pay the penalty due for the sins of all who will receive Him as Savior, and Jesus motions to Apollo to sing.

Apollo bellows out still standing at the side of Mount Moriah glancing over at Black Shadow,

> '*He was oppressed and afflicted;*
> *yet He did not open His mouth;*
> *He was led like a Lamb to the slaughter,*
> *and as a sheep before her shearers is silent,*
> *so He did not open his mouth.*'[19]

Apollo thinks to himself, "*Why? The person I was singing about must not be able to speak, or does not speak well, so as not even to open his mouth, but this is only a practice and not the real deal. I am ready to be in the spotlight – front and center.*"

Word looking up to Heaven nods and preaches His first sermon on Earth . . .

"Shalom!

'*Let those with ears use (of their own free will) them and listen!*'[20]

'*I must preach the good news, the Gospel, of the kingdom of God . . . .*'[21]

'*Blessed – happy, to be envied, and spiritually prosperous (that is, with life-joy and satisfaction in God's favor and salvation, regardless of their outward condition) – are the poor in spirit (the humble rating themselves insignificant), for theirs is the kingdom of heaven!*'[22]

'*The silver is Mine, and the gold is Mine, declares the Lord Almighty.*'[23]

'*Who have believed Our message, and to whom has the arm of the Lord been revealed?*

He grew up before Him like a tender shoot, and like a root out of dry ground.

He had no beauty or majesty to attract us to Him, nothing in His appearance that we should desire Him, He was despised and rejected of men, a man of sorrows, and familiar with suffering.

Like one from whom men hide their faces, He was despised, and we esteemed Him not.'[24]

'*My God, My God, why have You forsaken Me?*

Why are You so far from saving Me,
> *so far from the words of My groaning?*

O, my God, I cry out by day, but You do not answer,
> *by night, and am not silent.*

In You our fathers put their trust;
> *they trusted, and You delivered them.*

Yet You are enthroned as the Holy One;
> *You are the praise of Israel.*

In You our fathers put their trust;
> *they trusted, and You delivered them.*
> *They cried to You and were saved;*

Jerusalem; (9) Jesus falls the third time; (10) Jesus is stripped (naked) of His garments; (11) Jesus is nailed to the cross; (12) Jesus is lifted up on the cross between Heaven and Earth where He dies for the sins of all who receive Him as Savior.

[19] Isaiah 53:7 NIV.

[20] Matthew 11:15.

[21] Luke 4:43 AMP.

[22] Matthew 5:3 AMP.

[23] Haggai 2:8 NIV.

[24] Isaiah 53:1-4.

in You they trusted and were not disappointed.
But I am a worm and not a man,
    Scorned by men, and despised by the people.
All who see Me mock Me;
    they hurl insults, shaking their heads:
'He trusts in the Lord;
    let the Lord rescue Him.
Let Him deliver Him,
    since He delights in Him.'
Yet you brought Me out of the womb;
    you made Me trust in You
Even at My mother's breast.
From birth I was cast upon You;
    from my mother's womb, You have been my God.
Do not be far from Me,
    for trouble is near,
    and there is no one to help.
Many bulls surround Me;
    strong bulls of Bashan encircle Me.
Roaring lions tearing their prey
    open their mouths wide against Me.
I am poured out like water,
    and all My bones are out of joint.
My heart has turned to wax;
    it has melted away within Me.
My strength is dried up like a potsherd,
    and My tongue sticks to the roof of My mouth;
You lay Me in the dust of death.
Dogs have surrounded Me;
    a band of evil men has encircled Me;
    they have pierced my hands and My feet.
I can count all My bones; people stare and gloat over Me.
They divide My garments among them
    and cast lots for my clothing.
But You, O Lord (Father God is Jesus' Lord and He is Lord of His sheep), be not far off;
O, My Strength, come quickly to help Me.
Deliver My life from the sword,
My precious life from the power of the dogs.
Rescue Me from the mouth of the lions;
    save Me from the horns of the wild oxen.'
'If anyone would come after Me, he must deny himself
and take up his cross and follow Me.
For whoever wants to save his life
    will lose it, but whoever loses his life for Me and for the gospel will save it.
What good is it for a man to gain the whole world, yet forfeits his soul?
Or what can a man give in exchange for his soul?
If anyone is ashamed of Me and My words in this adulterous and sinful generation,
    the Son of Man will be ashamed of him when He comes in his Father's glory with the holy angels.'[25]
'This is My beloved Son, in whom I love; with Him, I am well pleased. Listen to Him.'[26]
'You cannot serve God or money (deceitful worldly riches); you cannot serve both.'[27] [Brief silence.]

---

[25] Psalm 22:1-21 and Mark 8:34-37 NIV.
[26] Matthew 17:5 NIV.
[27] Matthew 6:24 NIV.

Father God, I have delivered Your truth in My first sermon on Earth for Your glory. He that has a willing spirit to hear, let him hear and act accordingly to his own '*free will*.' He that believeth not is condemned already."

Apollo acts as he did not hear or care about the sermon and changes the subject advancing, "Zoom! Which way to the pay dirt!"

After riding a brief distance, Word comes to a halt. Apollo inquires, "Is this desolate desert the Land of Havilah? It looks again like a worthless and empty dust bowl. I see no gold."

"Apollo, you can't tell the contents of a book by its cover. We have to dust the cover off and look inside. [Laughter] Let us leave our horses here as I reveal to you, my friend, the richest and poorest place in all creation."

Word and Apollo proceeded on an almost hidden, and nearly impassable trail. When they come to the top of a large innocent looking dark charcoal boulder shaped like a giant spider with six legs, Apollo speaks,

"This climb was not easy as it is steeper than the steepest slope of Lookout Glory Mountain. I don't think I ever want to come back up here. The book cover looks terrible. It must be the poorest, most desolate place on this planet. What is the name of this place?"

Word answers, "This entrance tunnel is known as the 'Abyss' going down into a deep place in the heart of the Earth. On the right side is a lovely vibrant place called 'Paradise' and on the left side is a different no named place.' I would counsel you of your own '*free will*' to enjoy the abundant refreshing life of 'Paradise' and stay far away from the region not presently named, which is full of the pleasures of sin for a season, and not even touch or explore it. You will see a way of escape. Take it! You have been given a unique gift of knowing 'good from evil' and a '*free will*' to choose right from wrong. I would further counsel you as My friend to choose good, right, and life and to stay by My side in giving your worship, praise, and glory to My Father God, who is LOVE and not evil! You have been given such an opportunity to choose the right and the better part and to enjoy eternal life for evermore (eternally) as My song leader in Heaven."

Apollo grabs the keys from Word's hands and sticks the largest key into the entrance gate to the Abyss, which opens revealing steps going down to a locked iron gate Behind that gate were more winding steps further going down, down, down, into a cavern deep beneath the Earth.

"Word, hands Apollo a powerful atomic light, saying, "This is it, the richest on one side being Paradise and the poorest on the other side, presently having no name, of any place in all the Earth."

Apollo turns on the bright light thinking to himself, "*Seeing is believing. How can this be the richest and poorest place at the same time? Contradiction. Impossible!*"

"Apollo, I have just been summoned back for a meeting with My Father. I never have personally went down into this dark pit. I will leave the exploring and discovery to you. Remember, to be obedient to obey the preaching you have just heard! I counsel you to choose Paradise and stay far away from the unnamed place. You have a '*free will*,' and you can do this as you think about worshiping and praising My Father in song at My side throughout eternity, being a position of honor giving an opportunity to serve many.

The set of keys you have taken from my hand will open all the gates you will find inside. One narrow straight path leads to Paradise. That is the narrow path you need to take! As you put the key in the lock, speak a password. It can be a set of three letters, numbers, or a combination as this password further lets the key open the gates.

Let us meet tomorrow at 3:00 P.M. sharp at the podium! I will introduce to you, My first creation, to My second and third creations, Michael and Gabriel, the head of two other divisions in Heaven. You might compose a song for this occasion. I will preach after the new song.

Apollo as you enter, shut the entrance to the Abyss behind you, and if you lose the key in the pit you will be trapped inside, and I will have to come and get you out tomorrow. Remember, you cannot open the entrance gate to leave without both the key and your chosen password. Any treasures you might see inside just leave for they all belong to My Father."

Fastening the set of keys to a black sash he had worn around his waist, Apollo, speaks to himself, *"You will not have to rescue me. I am the great Apollo. See these muscles. I may have to rescue the second and third creation, and even You and, yes, even your father, whom I have not seen, but only heard making that disturbing laugh. He must be very old (ancient) and feeble with Word is the sole heir. How rich is He? He probably summoned Word to get Him a cup of tea. A selfish old man. How dare he separate us on our holiday of riding our horses together as I wanted to race Word back to Heaven. What kind of love is that to spoil our holiday? He dishonored me today by separating me from my faithful friend, leaving me all alone in this desolate place. How dare Him! How great I am! Number 2 is not my favorite spot."*

With a look of pride and greed on his face, Apollo hastily enters the opening and descends the staircase. Looking up, he notices a stone handle on the underneath side of the slab and tries to move it shut. It would not budge. He thinks to himself, *"No need to shut it."* Then he placed the key in the slot and spoke the code, "The password is 666 so designates the great Apollo," and the main entrance door shuts by itself. Apollo, experimenting further, places the key back in the spot and speaks "666 open;" but the entrance remains shut. Then, using the key again, he demands, "I am Apollo, 666 open," and it quickly opens wide again.

"I must not lose this key, nor will I give Michael and Gabriel a duplicate of my key nor my password. No one but me will know even the code. It will only be shared with my most loyal subjects, and I will put this number on their foreheads or the back of their hands invisibly so they can do commerce and freely enter into my works. What they don't know won't hurt them as they have to agree of their own free will to keep to themselves all of our dark secrets and to pay me 666% of the wealth I allow them to keep. Such great riches I will have and none richer than I." [Apollo with a greedy look laughs to himself.]

With great anticipation, Apollo inserts a key into the second iron gate saying, "I am Apollo, 666." It opens, revealing two paths – one narrow and difficult to pass through and the other broad and rich looking. Apollo chooses, without even a second thought, the broad and rich looking path.

Apollo then comes to an eloquent stairwell containing 666 steps down to a large chamber having a solid black pearl looking gate entrance. Apollo lifts up his hands as if to lead music and smirks, *"I am the light bearer in this kingdom of darkness!"*

Apollo shines around the light Word had given him, revealing a beautiful huge black onyx chamber having veins of what appear to be gold, silver, and all precious stones running throughout the rock. Apollo exclaims, "Wow! I'm filthy rich. I especially want all this gold."

Apollo, exploring the onyx room, coveting (with a strong greedy desire) thinking, *"It is all mine! What a place for a black onyx throne for me to rule as the prince of this terrestrial Earth."*

Then he notices off to the left an onyx tunnel containing further what appeared to be veins of gold, silver, and precious stones. Apollo, laughing to himself, further thinks,

"I am the richest creation of all! Well, until Michael and Gabriel are created, I am the only creation (inward laughter). I wish Word were not creating them. Two is company – a preacher and a song leader, but three or four is a crowd. All Word needs is me, his best friend, as his song leader. I don't see why they are necessary as I could run it all. Well, I legally deserve all these riches as I am the first creation. The elder is the legal heir of all things after the death of the owner.

Word says this is His Father's footstool. He must be old and rich to put His feet up so. I call Him the Thunderer. I have never seen Thunderer. Legally, if Thunderer and Word die, then I, as the elder creation, would be the sole heir and be number one. If I can control the wealth, I can control at least the world for sure and someday who knows even Heaven itself. How can I get control? No one is as clever as I. Let me devise a plan. I like the way those flowers, worship me. For now, let me see where this onyx shaft leads."

Descending the onyx tunnel, Apollo comes to another chamber and walking in he discovers a mirror type walls on all sides. He states to the mirrors,

"Mirror, mirror on the Apollo's wall, is not Apollo the most beautiful of them all? Look at my wavy black hair and my fine features, belonging only to me! How do you like my black velour riding outfit? I need a gold signet ring with a black onyx stone. I could even add a crest of my very image in the center of this ring."

Apollo turns from every angle admiring his reflection in the mirror thinking.

"*I look exactly like a Spanish Prince. I declare and appoint myself Prince of this World. All who see me in this world will bow to the great Apollo and do my will – or else severe punishment awaits them. Mirrors, you don't lie. I am so beautiful I will make this room my private dressing chamber to house my kingly black robes and riding outfits. Let my ruling of this kingdom of darkness begin!*"

Gleefully skipping along Apollo descends a long corridor. He further discovers another beautiful chamber filled with what appeared to be gold nuggets and every precious stone. Apollo slips six of the most brilliant gold nuggets, six of the precious stones, and six pieces of black onyx into his pockets as souvenirs saying to himself, "*These will never be missed. I could make me a signet ring with a gold crest bearing my image, some earrings, neck chains, and bracelets out of these.*"

Apollo goes along on this broad and wide way and by chance notices a hard to see a straight and narrow crack, which would require someone to get on their hands and knees and crawl into to enter with difficulty. Apollo thinks, "This is that secret passageway to Paradise, and I will find it again some night. *Now I'd rather have all this wealth and title deed to this side first. Let me explore one side at a time. I might spot this again someday when I have nothing better to do and can wear some work clothes to crawl through to explore for further riches. I will send a servant first. Let me gather the wealth today here. I have enough gold on this side.*"

Apollo premeditates and chooses not to obey the Son of God's counsel to go down that straight and narrow way over to Paradise, located under the land of Havilah, where there is much gold.

Apollo staying on the broad and wide way comes to another locked iron gate, and placing in the lock, his key he orders, "This is Apollo, '666,' obey me."

This gate swings open, revealing an Abyss shaft going high to the surface of the Earth and looking over into what appeared to be a bottomless pit, having beautiful nooks and crannies. One niche is giving off a fiery glow housing what appeared to be pure melted gold. He mused to himself,

"*Wow! All I would have to do is have my workers dip out the melted gold and pour it into molds for gold coins, gold bars, and for reward signet rings for my fanatical subjects to wear on their left ring finger to show their covenant and allegiance to me.*

I will add to it a beautiful onyx stone and gold crest with my image. I might even give a left finger friendship ring in the distant future to Word as he keeps saying over and over again that I am his friend. I have an opportunity to control and manipulate the economy and wealth of this entire world. 'He who has the gold, that's me, makes the rules.' [Self-laughter]

Rule one, 'I am in control and the god of this world.' Possession is nine-tenths of the law.

Rule two, 'I have the key and the 666 password and will give them legally to whomever I choose.'

Rule three, 'No one comes to this wealthy place, but by obeying and being loyal to me.'

Rule four, 'My subjects have to take an oath not to reveal my dark secrets.'

Rule five, 'My subjects who take my mark in Heaven, on the Earth, and under this Earth, will eternally belong to me and no one else.'

66

Rule six, 'I am lord, prince, and ruler of all the powers that be here.'
I claim this domain. I discovered it. I own the title deed. I stake it out and legally claim it is mine and mine alone. I own it and am not sharing this wealth with Michael or Gabriel, or to even tell them about it."

Apollo proudly walks to the main entrance. Looking down, he panics in confusion as he sees he has lost the key to Hell. Holding his bag of stolen treasures, he runs in terror of being trapped in as he retraces his steps screaming "Apollo, 666 open." All the gates open without using a key. He finally spots his key on the floor near where he picked up and stole the six black onyx stones. Smiling, he returns to this main gate. He places the key in the slot and speaks to the iron gate, he had left wide open, "This is Apollo, close – 666" and the gate closes with a clang by itself. Apollo then gives the gate a slight tug to make sure it is securely locked. He then turns back and winks with his eye to the gate saying, "I will return! I will return! I command you in the name of Apollo, 'Let nobody else in but me and my guest, and I mean no one!'"

Apollo further runs back up the 666 stairs and springs like a Jack-in-the-box out of the hole as he had carelessly not slid shut the slab cover. Apollo places the atomic light on the top step down in the hole for future use. He touches the concealed outside handle commanding, "Shut tightly in the name of the great Apollo, 666, and let no one enter you, but Apollo and my guests and I mean no one! It would not move. Apollo then remembers to place the key in the slot. He demands of it again, "Shut tightly in the name of the great Apollo, 666, and let no one enter you, but me and my guests, and I mean no one!"

The gate with a groaning sound, this time, slid tightly shut, making a clicking, crashing noise.

"Apollo thought to himself, "*I must be careful not to lose these keys, or I cannot get out of this pit. A nice seal. I almost can't see it myself, and I am standing right on top. Let me further cover it by sprinkling on the crack dust from the ground. What's next?"*

"Black Shadow, get here now, wherever you are!"

Black Shadow almost immediately appears bowing his left knee in worship as Apollo had previously trained him to perform. Apollo declares as night is falling in the Land of Havilah, where truly there is gold, "Black Shadow. Black Shadow! We are rich! Well, I am rich, as you cannot spend silver or gold! You take care of me, and I will take care of you. I'll name this dark charcoal-colored stone mountain "Dark Kingdom Mountain," but for short, we will call it "Dark Mountain." I can tell everyone that I named it Dark Mountain since 'darkness' was approaching in the Land of Havilah, and it is also a dark gray color. I like darkness. The dimness and darkness here in Hell are so entreating as light at times is so distracting and blinding." Apollo mounts Black Shadow with a fun jump on his back and orders,

"Black Shadow, remember this place that we call "Dark Mountain" and take me to Apollo's 'Pink Palace' as I have some scheming and planning before I sleep."†

†BOOK TWO – Episode Two†

[†**Sidebar Scriptures**: "Joseph had a dream and promptly reported all the details (Genesis 37:5)."
"The Lord revealed to me what the evil ones were doing and planning and showed me their wicked plots (Jeremiah 11:18)."
"The word of the Lord came to Abram in a **vision**. . . . A **deep sleep** came upon Abram . . . . (Genesis 15:1, 12)."
I witnessed and experienced "dreams and visions, and I described **all** I had seen to instruct many (Daniel 7:1, 11:33)."†]

Creation of Michael and Gabriel

WORD OF GOD, having been requested to return to His Father God, humbly and respectfully speaks, "Father, will Apollo, My friend, ever repent of his sins of pride, arrogance, greed, vanity, conceit, and trusting in his own power and resources, and being so selfish? Will he choose to obey and love Us and serve Us in Heaven and enjoy eternal life, or will he of his own 'free will,' choose that place of 'darkness' in the heart of the Earth he has named 'Hell' over our 'Kingdom of Light?

The Father responds, "Yes, he will choose Hell. No robots! He rather reign alone in Hell than serve Us in Heaven! Apollo of his own *'free will'* will prefer *'darkness rather than light'*[1] because his deeds are evil?" As for You, dear Son,

'Preach the word; be prepared in season, and out of season.'[2]

I am working My plan for the 'Joy set before You.'[3] It was My will that You created Apollyon Lucifer to know good from evil and to have a free will to choose to love and obey Us or to war against Us. Yes, he has truly been *'sinning from the beginning.'*[4] Son, it is not Your fault as You preach repent and confess your sins and your sins will be forgiven. Notwithstanding My foreknowledge, Apollyon Lucifer and men made in Our image are free moral beings. Holy Spirit, I direct that all the archives of Heaven be sealed and not opened in the distant future. I desire You to record such events in Heaven, on the Earth, and under the Earth in Our 'Annals of Heaven.' Our archives will demonstrate when unsealed by My Son that I am a loving, good, and just Father God and that I did everything legally according to law. My Son, since You asked, it will later be written about Apollyon Lucifer,

'He who does what is sinful is of the devil because the devil has been sinning from the beginning. The reason the Son of God appeared was to destroy the devil's work. . . .This is how we know who the children of God are and who the children of the devil are: Anyone who does not do what is right is not a child of God; neither is anyone who does not love his brother.'[5]

Father, "Not my will, but Thine be done. Nothing is impossible with You. Is it truly worth it to have a family who truly loves Us? I heard you once say, 'If it's not broke, don't fix it.'"

"Yes, the reason I am permitting all of this is that I desire to have a family who will choose to love, trust, and obey Us. A relative few faithful ones will obey, follow, and love Us. The winning of the love of these family members is worth it. I have counted the cost, and it is worth it. I cherish Your love, but I need a larger family to love and to love Me. Remember the *'Joy* (Father God has) *set before You.'*[6]

Your bride doesn't want a fragile floating lily pad [Laughter] as her husband. You will become both My and her faithful 'Champion' – a man's man.

---

[1] John 3:19.
[2] 2 Timothy 4:2.
[3] Hebrews 12:2.
[4] 1 John 3:8.
[5] 1 John 3:7, 8, 10 NIV.
[6] Hebrews 12:2.

Your work of overcoming and dying on the cross will be the bravest and manliest work of all. Your bride will sing this song applicable to You, My Son,

'Let Him kiss me with the kisses of His mouth
for Your love is more delightful than wine (makes one light-headed).
. . . Take me away with You – let us hurry!
The King has brought me into His chambers.
. . . How handsome You are, my Lover!
. . . He has taken me to the banquet hall,
and His banner over me is love.
. . . His left arm is under my head,
and His right arm embraces me.
. . . Thus, I have become in His eyes
like one bringing contentment.
. . . Come away, My Lover . . . .'[7]

"Father, You always win Your case with Me with the 'Bride Argument!' [Laughter]

Now My Son, fashion the beloved Archangel, Michael, our warrior, the keeper of the peace, and the commander, under you, of the army of Heaven. Do not make him in Our image. Make him valiant, loyal, and strong to the uttermost!"

Father, "Do you desire I also give Michael a free will to choose to love, trust, and obey Us and to know good from evil?"

"Certainly, and for Gabriel also. I do not desire any robots in Heaven. I am not going to force anyone to love, trust, or obey Us!"

"Father, would you want me to make him more beautiful that Apollo?"

"Beauty is for the feminine side of creation – Your bride. Real men are tall and ruggedly handsome, but not beautiful! Don't get Me on this soapbox. 'Ugh, Sodom and Gomorrah!'[8] Give Michael a stern chiseled masculine face. Make both Michael and Gabriel men of steel with utmost courage. Later it will be recorded, and often repeated as a warning to those on Earth, about a visit Michael and Gabriel make to the Earth,

'The two angels (Michael and Gabriel) arrived at Sodom in the evening, and Lot was sitting in the gateway of the city. When he saw them, he got up to meet them and bowed down with his face to the ground. "Sirs," he said, "please turn aside to your servant's house. You can wash your feet and spend the night and then go on your way early in the morning."

'No,' they answered, 'we will spend the night in the square.'

But he insisted so strongly that they went with him and entered his house. He prepared a meal for them, baking bread without yeast, and they ate. Before they had gone to bed, all the men from every part of the city of Sodom — both young and old — surrounded the house. They called to Lot, 'Where are the men who came to you tonight? Bring them out to us so we can have sex with them.'

Lot went outside to meet them and shut the door behind him and said, 'No, my friends. Do not do this wicked thing. Look, I have two daughters who have never slept with a man. Let me bring them out to you, and you can do what you like with them. But do nothing to these men, for they have come under the protection of my roof.'

'Get out of our way,' they replied. And they said, 'This fellow came here as an alien, and now he wants to play the judge! We'll treat you worse than them.' They kept bringing pressure on Lot and moved forward to break down the door.

But the men (Gabriel and Michael) inside reached out and pulled Lot back into the house and shut the door. Then they struck the men at the door of the house, young and old, with blindness so they could not find the door.

The two men said to Lot, 'Do you have anyone else here – sons-in-law, sons or daughters, or anyone else in the city who belongs to you? Get them out of here, because we will destroy this place. The outcry to the Lord against its people is so great He has sent us to destroy it.'

---

[7] Song of Songs 1:2, 4, 16; 2:4,6; 8:10, 14 NIV.
[8] See Genesis 19:1-28 NIV.

So Lot went out and spoke to his sons-in-law, who were pledged to marry his daughters. He said, 'Hurry and get out of this place because the Lord is about to destroy the city!' But his sons-in-law thought he was joking.

With the coming of dawn, the angels urged Lot, saying, 'Hurry! Take your wife and your two daughters, who are here, or you will be swept away when the city is punished.'

When he hesitated, the men grasped his hand and the hands of his wife and of his two daughters and led them safely out of the city, for the Lord was merciful to them. As soon as they had brought them out, one of them said, 'Flee for your lives! Don't look back, and stop nowhere in the (flat) plain! Flee to the mountains, or you will be swept away!'

But Lot said to one of them, 'Sir, please don't force me to go so far! Your servant has found favor in your eyes, and you have shown great kindness in sparing my life. But I can't flee to the mountains; this disaster will overtake me, and I'll die. Look, here is a town near enough to run to, and it is small. Let me flee to it – it is small, isn't it? Then my life will be spared.'

He said to him, "Very well, I will grant this request too; I will not overthrow the town you speak of. But flee there quickly, because I can do nothing until you reach it."

. . . By the time Lot reached Zoar, the sun had risen over the land. Then the Lord rained down burning sulfur on Sodom and Gomorrah – from the Lord out of the heavens. He overthrew those cities and the entire plain, including all those living in the cities–and also the vegetation in the land. But Lot's wife looked back, and she became a pillar of salt.'[9]

Word speaks, "Father, I am committed to doing Your will. We could go much faster than the speed of light and go back in time and change all of this and start over with no Apollo. Father, I heard You once say, 'A bulldog can whip a skunk anytime, but sometimes it's simply not worth it?' No one ever will be sprayed with such bitter hate when the devil and his crew nail Me to a cross, but I hear sweet victory coming through My dying lips, 'It is finished!.'[10] Is it truly worth it?"

"Yes, My Son! Remember, you will have to win the love of Your bride! She will respect and admire You so much for rescuing her. You will fall in love with her and she with you. Her romantic and affectionate love will be Your best reward throughout eternity. It is entirely worth it. I rest My case." [The Son smiles, nodding acceptance of the Father's plan.]

"My Son, regarding Apollo, You will soon notice that he is wearing gold earrings and at times diamond earrings. Apollo brags that his hair is 'beautiful,' and he will let it grow long like a woman's hair. Say nothing to him directly about this, but only indirectly in your sermons. You will start noticing that others filled with pride will begin worshipping him, wearing their hair like his, and will greatly desire a set of Apollo earrings. On Earth, later a great Ishmaelite army under his influence will come against Israel all wearing feminine gold earrings.[11]

My servant Gideon, with Michael's invisible assistance, will destroy them with the earrings being collected from their dead bodies as part of the spoils of war. However, I will greatly enjoy the feminine earrings of what You will say regarding the bride's beauty,

'How beautiful you are, my darling!

Oh, how beautiful!

Your eyes are doves.

. . . Your cheeks are beautiful with earrings,

  your neck with strings of jewels.

---

[9] Genesis 19:1-26 NIV.

[10] John 19:30.

[11] "But Gideon told them, '*I will not rule over you, nor will my son rule over you. The Lord will rule over you.*' And he said, '*I do have one request, that every man of you give me the earrings (removed from earlobes of the dead enemies) from your share of the plunder.*' (It was the custom of the Ishmaelites (evil prideful men) to wear gold earrings.)" (Judges 8:24).

We will make you earrings of gold,
* studded with silver.*
. . . How beautiful your sandaled feet . . . .
Your neck is like an ivory tower,
Your eyes are the pools of Heshbon . . . .
Your head crowns you like Mount Carmel;
Your hair is like royal tapestry;
* the king is held captive by its tresses.*
How beautiful you are and how pleasing,
* O love, with your delights!'* [12]

"Father, I thank You for giving Me love through the precious gift of a beautiful bride. I receive her future love with thanksgiving and anticipation."

Are you ready for Me to create Michael?"

The Father nods and the Son decrees,

"Michael, the commander of the angelic host, and my loyal, faithful, and courageous warrior, **Be!**"

On his knees before the King of Kings and Lord of Lords, Michael lifts his left hand with a sword in his right. He opens his eyes, looking into the smiling face of His beloved Creator, the Word of God, and declares,

"My Creator, I am a 'soldier of the cross' reporting for duty. To get to you, they will have to step over my dead body.

Word, laughing declares, "Amen! Let us laugh now because we will have a good one, which will last forever." The Father joins in the laughing, sounding like thunder, with Word explaining,

"You are My second angel creation in this celestial realm. Your name is Michael, which means that you are like Me although not made in My image. You will help assure that the will of My Father God is fully carried out and accomplished with a 'Yes and Amen!' [13]

Michael, I introduce you to My Father God, who is sitting at My left, and on the other side of Him is the Holy Spirit. They are both invisible. As you see Me, you have seen the Father. My Father desires a family who will love Him, which includes a bride for me, who will in the fullness of time be seated here at My right hand. Her place beside Me has been reserved for her before the foundation of the world. My Father is a God of love, but when war is declared on Him, He legally has a right to defend Himself and all that belongs to Him. You will defend and protect My to-be bride and those in the Kingdom of Light to the uttermost! We will have a war, both in Heaven and on Earth.

I am the 'Commander-and-Chief' and you as My 'Seven Star General,' are to orchestrate and direct the Army of Heaven. Holy Spirit, please show Michael a portion of what is to come."

The Holy Spirit permits a scroll to be unrolled before Michael's eyes . . .

'He (Son of God, Word) is the image of the invisible God . . . .For by Him all things were created: that are in Heaven and on Earth, visible and invisible. . . . All things were created by Him and for Him. And He is before all things, and in Him all things consist. . . .That in all things He may have the supremacy.

---

[12] Song of Songs 1:10-11, 15; 7:1, 4-6 NIV.
[13] 2 Corinthians 1:20.

It pleased the Father that to have all His fullness dwell in Him (Jesus), and by Him to reconcile all things to Himself, whether things on Earth or things in Heaven, having made peace through the blood of His cross.'[14]

'And war broke out in Heaven: Michael and his angels fought with the dragon, and the dragon and his angels fought back. They (Satan and his angels) did not prevail, nor was a place found for them in Heaven any longer.

So the great dragon was cast out, the serpent of old, called the Devil and Satan, who deceives the whole world; he was cast to the earth, and the angels (who worshiped him) were cast out with him.'[15]

'And when the servant of the man of God (Elisha) was risen early, and gone forth, behold, a host (under the influence of the devil) compassed the city both with horses and chariots. And his servant said unto him, 'Alas, my master how shall we do?'

And he answered, 'Fear not: for they that be with us are more than they that be with them.'

And Elisha prayed, and said, 'Lord, I pray Thee, open his eyes, that he may see.' And the Lord opened the eyes of the young man; and he saw: and, behold, the mountain was full of horses and chariots of fire (led by Michael) round about Elisha.

And when they came down to him, Elisha prayed unto the Lord, and said, 'Smite this people, I pray Thee, with blindness.' And he (Michael) smote them with blindness according to the word of Elisha.'[16]

'On the appointed day Herod, wearing his royal robes, sat on his throne and delivered a public address to the people. They shouted, "This is the voice of a god, not of a man" Immediately, because Herod did not give praise to God, an angel (Michael) of the Lord struck him down, and he was eaten by worms and died.

But the word of God continued to increase and spread.'[17]

'The Angel (Michael) swung his sickle, harvested earth's vintage, and heaved it into the winepress, the giant winepress of God's wrath. The winepress was outside the city, and blood flowed out of the press, rising as high as the horses' bridles for a distance of one hundred and eighty miles.'[18]

Then the Apostle John heard the sound of massed choirs singing,
'Hallelujah!
The Master reigns,
our God, the Sovereign-Strong!
Let us celebrate, let us rejoice.
Let us give Him the glory!
The Marriage of the Lamb has come,
His wife has made herself ready.
She was given a bridal gown
of bright and shining linen.
The linen is the righteousness of the saints.

---

[14] Colossians 1:15-19.
[15] Revelation 12:7-9 NKJV.
[16] 2 Kings 6:15-18 NIV.
[17] Acts 12:21-25 NIV.
[18] Revelation 14:19-20.

The Angel said, 'Write this:
'Blessed are those invited to the Wedding Supper
(part of the marriage ceremony) of the Lamb.'[19]

The Apostle John would further record these truths,

'Then I saw Heaven open wide and there before me was a white horse and its Rider.
The Rider named Faithful and True, judges and makes war in pure righteousness.
His eyes are a blaze of fire, on His head many crowns.
He has a Name inscribed that's known only to himself.
He is dressed in a robe soaked with blood, and He is addressed as 'Word of God.'
The armies of Heaven mounted on white horses and dressed in dazzling white linen, follow Him.
A sharp sword comes out of His mouth so He can subdue the nations,
then rule them with a rod of iron. He treads the winepress of the raging (furious) wrath of God,
the Sovereign-Strong. On His robe and thigh is written,
'KING OF KINGS, LORD OF LORDS.'
... I saw the Beast assembled with him, earth's kings and their armies,
ready to make war against the One on the horse and His army.
The Beast was taken, and with him, his puppet, the False Prophet, who used signs
to dazzle and deceive those who had taken the mark of the Beast and worshiped his image.
They were thrown alive, those two, in the Lake of Fire and Brimstone.
The rest were killed by the sword of the One on the horse, the sword that comes from His mouth.
All the birds held a feast on their flesh.
I saw an Angel (Michael) descending out of Heaven.
He carried the key to the Abyss and a chain – a huge chain.
He grabbed the Dragon, the old Snake – the Devil, Satan himself! –
chained him up for a thousand years, dumped him into the Abyss,
slammed it shut, and sealed it tight. No more trouble out of him, deceiving the nations –
until the thousand years are up. After that, he has to be (legally) let loose briefly.'[20]
Michael on his knees worships with hands lifted,
'Holy, holy, holy, is the Lord God Almighty, who was and is, and is to come.
... You are worthy, our Lord and God, to receive glory and honor and power,
for You created all things, and by Your will they were created and have their being.'[21]

Word places His hand on Michael's head decreeing, "None more gifted in war than you. *'Be strong and courageous . . . for the Lord your God will be with you wherever you go.'*[22]

Michael's response, "I will give You, my Creator, 'My Utmost for Your Highest' in times of war and in times of peace and love. You will always remain on Your throne. You are,

Eternal!
Unbeatable
Unshakable!
Unstoppable!
That's who You are!

I love You, and I pledge all I have and ever hope to be, my utmost allegiance and loyalty, throughout the eternities of eternities."

---

[19] Revelation 19:5-9 The Message Bible (MSG).
[20] Revelation 19:11-16, 19-21, 20:1-3 (MSG)
[21] Revelation 4:8, 10.
[22] Joshua 1:9.

Word replied, "Michael, mighty warrior, I commission and ordain you to direct under Me the mighty Army of Heaven against all the powers and schemes of darkness. My Father is a God of love and peacemaking, but at times, his enemies are for war. When war is declared upon Us, We shall defend Ourselves, and with you being My seven-star general of the Army of Heaven, We will never be defeated.

'*No weapon forged against you (Us) will prevail.*'[23]

"You are not to communicate with others what you have seen and heard this day nor let anyone know about this upcoming battle of battles in Heaven and again, later on, Earth. My Father insists that everything has to be done legally. He has a legal right to defend Himself when war is declared on Him or on His faithful subjects. Defender, you are to watch over everything. Your motto is, BE PREPARED,[24] which means you are perpetually in a state of readiness in spirit, soul, and body to do your DUTY with all your force. You will know the right thing to do at the right moment and be willing to finalize it. Few or no words!"

However, it is My Father's will that you are friendly and speak some with My first creation, Apollo, my song leader. Work hand-in-hand with My soon to be third created being, My beloved communicating and sounding the alarm archangel, Gabriel. For your further confidential information, My song leader, Apollo, has been prideful and sinning from the beginning, but We will give him every chance to turn and REPENT, but for your information he will choose not to repent, and his music gifting and beauty, (yes, I said 'beauty) will enable him to deceive one third[25] of Our beloved to be created angels in Heaven to worship him and to join his kingdom of darkness. Later on Earth, some 'two hundred million'[26] will join him to attack Us. It will be written about My Father God.

'The One enthroned in Heaven laughs:
The Lord scoffs at them;
Then He rebukes them in His anger
and terrifies them in His wrath, saying,
I have installed My King
on Zion, My holy hill.'[27]

The Father laughs, sounding like thunder, at the thought of someone attacking His Son, who is King of kings and Lord of Lord. Word says to Michael, "My Father wants you to have previews of things to come and to know about a created creature deceiving himself and his followers into thinking that he can destroy My Father, the Holy Spirit, and Myself. Questions?"

Hearing none, I now leave this confidential briefing to you and declare this would now be the time to create Gabriel. 'To everything, there is a season, a time for every purpose!'[28]

Word looks over to His right into the face of His invisible Father, and Word nods a yes saying,

"Gabriel, my faithful and devoted announcer, messenger, and communicator, **Be!**"

Kneeling beside Michael was Gabriel. He opened his mouth and raised his right hand holding a blank scroll and writing kit declaring,

---

[23] Isaiah 54:17 NIV.
[24] See *Scout Motto* at *Wikipedia, The Free Encyclopedia.*
[25] Revelation 12:4 NIV.
[26] Revelation 9:16 NIV.
[27] Psalm 1:4 NIV.
[28] Ecclesiastes 3:1 NKJV.

"Glory to God in the highest! My Creator, I pledge faithfully and truthfully to serve You with my utmost throughout the eternities of eternities. I know that for nothing is impossible with You! There is 'nothing too hard'[29] for You. I commit to faithfully and accurately deliver Your messages."

Word speaks, "Holy Spirit, please show Gabriel a portion of what is to come."

The Holy Spirit permits a scroll to be unrolled before Michael and Gabriel's eyes showing previews of future events,

'I, Daniel, was the only one who saw the vision; the men with me did not see it, but such terror overwhelmed them, that they fled and hid. So I was left alone, gazing at the great vision. I had no strength left, my face turned deathly pale, and I was helpless. Then I heard him speaking, and as I listened to him, I fell into a deep sleep . . . .

A hand (Gabriel) touched me and set me trembling on my hands and knees. He said, 'Daniel, you who are highly esteemed, consider carefully the words I am about to speak to you and stand up, for I have now been sent to you.' And when he said this I stood up trembling.

Then he (Gabriel) continued, 'Do not be afraid, Daniel. Since the first day you set your mind to gain understanding and to humble yourself before your God, your words were heard, and I have come in response to them. But the prince (evil spirit of darkness being assigned over by Satan) of the Persian kingdom resisted me twenty-one days. Then Michael, one of the chief princes, came to help me because I was detained there with the king of Persia. Now I explain to you what will happen to your people, for the vision concerns a time yet to come.'[30]

'In the sixth month, God sent the angel Gabriel to Nazareth, a town in Galilee, to a virgin pledged to be married to a man named Joseph, a descendant of David. The virgin's name was Mary. The angel said, 'Greetings, you who are highly favored! The Lord is with you.'

Mary was greatly troubled at his words and wondered what kind of greeting this might be. But the angel (Gabriel) said to her, 'Do not be afraid, Mary, for you have found favor with God. You will be with child and give birth to a Son, and you are to give Him the name Jesus. He will be great and will be called the Son of the Most High. The Lord God will give Him the throne of King David, His ancestor (Mary is also a descendant of King David). He will reign over the house of Jacob forever; His kingdom will never end.'

'How will this be,' Mary asked the angel, 'since I am a virgin?'

The angel answered, 'The Holy Spirit will come upon you, and the power of the Most High will overshadow you. So the Holy One to be born will be called the Son of God. Even Elizabeth your relative will have a child in her old age, and she who was said to be barren is in her sixth month. For nothing is impossible with God.

'I am the Lord's servant,' Mary answered. 'May it be as you have said.' Then the angel (Gabriel) left her.'[31]

'This is how the birth of Jesus Christ came about: His mother Mary was pledged to be married to Joseph, but before they came together, she was found to be with child through the Holy Spirit. Because Joseph her husband was a righteous man and did not want to expose her to public disgrace, he had in mind to divorce her quietly.

---

[29] Jeremiah 32:27.
[30] Daniel 10:7-14 NIV.
[31] Luke 1:26-38 NIV.

But after he had considered this (divorcing her), an angel (Gabriel) of the Lord appeared to him in a dream and said, 'Joseph, son) of David (Mary also a descendant of David), do not be afraid to take Mary home as your wife, because what is conceived in her is from the Holy Spirit.

She will give birth to a Son, and you are to give Him the name Jesus, because He will save his people (who receive Him as Savior) from their sins.'

All this took place to fulfill what the Lord had said through the prophet:

'The virgin will be with child and will give birth to a Son, and they will call him Immanuel' [32] *– which means 'God with us.'*

When Joseph woke up, he did what the angel (Gabriel) of the Lord had commanded him and took Mary home as his wife.' [33]

'I declare to you, brothers, that flesh and blood cannot inherit the kingdom of God; nor does the perishable inherit the imperishable. Listen, I tell you a mystery: We will not all sleep, but we will all be changed – in a flash, in the twinkling of an eye, at the last trumpet. For the trumpet will sound (by Gabriel), the dead will be raised imperishable, and we will be changed. For the perishable must clothe itself with the imperishable, and the mortal with immortality. When the perishable has been clothed with the imperishable, and the mortal with immortality, then the saying written will come true: 'Death has been swallowed up in victory.' [34]

'Where, O death, is your victory?
Where, O death, is your sting?' [35]

The sting of death is sin, and the power of sin is the law. But thanks be to God! He gives us the victory through our Lord Jesus Christ.

Therefore, my dear brothers, stand firm. Let nothing move you. Always give yourselves fully to the work of the Lord, because you know that your labor in the Lord is not in vain." [36]

Word looking over at His left received direction from the Father and nodded back to the Father and spoke,

"Seraphim angels to stand beside and hover above the throne and serve as attendants, **be**!"

Word spoke to one of the Seraphim,

"Seraphim, please escort Michael and Gabriel into the Grand Mansion. Michael is to have the specially prepared top floor suite from which he can view the entire Celestial City, the convocation grounds, and planet Earth. Gabriel is to have the lush garden suite specially prepared for him.

Michael and Gabriel, please meet Me here at the throne room tomorrow at 2:30 P.M. The three of us will go down to the podium a few minutes before 3:00 P.M. for Me to introduce both of you to My friend Apollo, My song leader. Apollo will lead us in song, and I will preach. Afterward, I have delightful gifts of two white horses (both brothers of My white horse 'Abundant Life.'). 'Star' for Gabriel as he is the fastest besides My horse 'Abundant Life.' 'Trumpet' for Michael as one day while sitting on him the Trumpet of the Lord will sound blown by Michael announcing My return to the Earth. Until tomorrow! Shalom!"†

[32.] See Isaiah 7:14.
[33] Matthew 1:18-25 NIV.
[34] See Isaiah 25:8 .
[35] See Hosea 13:14.
[36] 1 Corinthians 15:50-58 NIV.

76

†BOOK TWO – Episode 3†

[†**Sidebar Scriptures**: "*Joseph had a dream and promptly reported all the details (Genesis 37:5).*"
"*The Lord revealed to me what the evil ones were doing and planning and showed me their wicked plots (Jeremiah 11:18).*"
"*The word of the Lord came to Abram in a* **vision**. . . . *A* **deep sleep** *came upon Abram . . . . (Genesis 15:1, 12).*"
I witnessed and experienced "*dreams and visions, and I described **all** I had seen to instruct many (Daniel 7:1, 11:33).*"†]

Initial Meeting of Michael, Gabriel, and Heaven's Song Leader (Apollo)

APOLLO AT THE PINK PALACE instead of preparing for the song service revised and amended his plan to ask Word for the title deed to "Dark Mountain," and for some surrounding 666 acres of desert land. He also made sketches of monster animals and other life he would ask Word to create. Apollo reasoning,

"I will explain to Word that I would also like a convocation center on Earth for the worship of Thunderer. I better refer to Thunderer as Word's father. I sometimes wonder if Thunderer actually exists? I certainly have not seen any evidence of him, nor have I seen the Holy Spirit. Word says they are one, and that if I have seen him, I have seen his father. Maybe Word is all that is left that can speak down through the eternities of eternities. They are googols of years old. Perhaps Word's father died, and He remains the only heir. How could something always exist? Impossible! Everything has to have a beginning. Who created them, and who created the one who created them? Infinity back to some beginning (origin). The universe is strongly expanding, and I witnessed part of its beginning as Word created it out of nothing. How could He create something out of nothing? It must have been a trick. Whatever exists has a cause. Don't I have a cause? I'm not a rebel without a cause. I 'will be the ruler of this world.'[1] *Am I not the first creation of life?*

I have heard something that sounds like thunder and wondered what, or who does that sound. Word is nodding back at something or somebody. Well, someday if I arrive early at our pulpit or Word is elsewhere, I might venture a peek into the throne room.

Now, first things first to promote my cause and make my plans. Not a hint of any of this great wealth as I meet Michael and Gabriel today! I will say nothing and Word might not bring it up before them. I hope they don't look like me. I have always desired to be one of a kind. I would like to ask Word to create for me on earth furry little creatures about four feet tall that walk upright like me and whom I could teach to sing in a convocation. I need to be silent about my plan. These furry little creatures can keep my grounds and mine the ore from the nearby mountains with which I could do great commerce. I have the gold, so I make the rule – the true golden rule. [Smirking within] We could create a nearby city for them to live. I can call them Gremlins covered with thick hair, male and female so they can populate the Earth, build cities, and produce wealth for me. I will tell Word we need them for Him to practice.

Word said He had never been down into that pit. I can privately explain to him that nothing was down there except a meeting room for my most trusted music staff to plan music for the services here in Heaven and a special service even on Earth. Again, we could have a great black convocation center just outside the nearby city for those from Heaven to hear my earthly choir made up of my Gremlins. Again, I can tell Word it is to worship Thunderer. I suppose I should say Word's father. This plan should work. Word will not deny His first creation, the Great Apollo, the most beautiful of all, a convocation center on Earth to worship his father and give him a place to preach. On the surface, it is just a worthless desert, but I can make the kingdom beneath it a habitation of ecstasy, pleasures, delights, lushness, power, and lavishness. No one but me will know. I will name this superb place, which I will prepare for myself and my angels and gremlin servants, Hell, from these words,

        H   **H**abitation for
        E   **E**cstasy in
        L   **L**ushness and
        L   **L**avishness

---

[1] John 16:11.

Wow, what a brilliant and catchy name! HELL! Since I named it, Hell is mine! I will sing of the delights and pleasures of Hell. Also, I would like the Earth to be my hothouse under my lordship, covered with exotic vegetation, lush flowers, and with colossal sea, land, and air creatures. Let me now draw some of the tropical trees, huge flowers and plants, and enormous creatures of all types, and my little furry Gremlin friends, to show Word. I will ask him if He will create these for my amusement."

Apollo spends the entire evening drawing and drawing and drawing sketches, e.g., vegetation, including tropical trees and flowers, with his prize drawings being what he called dinosaurs of all types, dragons, beautiful reptiles, including hooded cobras, and what he describes as sea monsters, large wooly mammals, and his most prideful drawing of a large insect type creature with a blue tail and enormous wings by which to fly. He further drew small furry creatures about four feet tall. They stood upright like Apollo so they could see better and could work with their hands, which he showed harvesting the vegetation and riding creatures having a front body and a head like his Black Shadow. They had a single horn in the middle of their foreheads, powerful hind legs like a stag deer, and the tail of a lion.[2] Apollo laughs thinking almost out loud, *"I hope 'Black Shadow' is not jealous as I am going to have to race one of these creatures, which I will call Unicorns."*

Looking at his artwork, Apollo prided himself on such artistic ability with his further thinking,

"We need male and female parts of all the plants and animals so they can multiply and replenish this barren desert. They are to have a short life span and die both fertilizing the ground and eventually being collected beneath the surface of the ground, like my Hell, in what I call 'black gold,' which my subjects can later purchase if they have my mark on their hands or foreheads. When the Gremlins (Ape Men) die, like the animals, plants, and worker bees, they will be like a dog called 'Rover' – dead all over – or might their spirits serve me in Hell?

Perhaps today I can challenge Word and 'Abundant Life' to a horse race up to the top of Lookout Mountain to watch the earth rise. It would be a good setting for me to present my plan to Word if I can isolate Him away from Michael and Gabriel. I will discourage them in desiring to stay right with us. I trust Black Shadow has had a restful evening as we now have a full day of racing ahead."

Black Shadow, hearing his name, paws outside the door, with Apollo looking down at his beautiful gold watch Word gave him, further thinking, *"Where has the time gone? I've got to go, or I'll be late. I again forgot to compose a song. With my gifting, I can wing it and compose it on the spur of the moment. Word might hand me a song on a sheet, as this is easier for me. 'One cannot attend (serve) two masters (lords), my agenda and his.'[3] I've been so freaking busy getting richer and richer."*

Apollo opens a side door of the Pink Palace and sees Black Shadow and says, "Kneel the knee as I taught you, and worship me! I am your master and lord!"

---

[2] Webster defines in part, "Unicorn," "a fabulous animal generally depicted with the body and head of a horse, the hind legs of a stag, the tail of a lion, and a single horn in the middle of the forehead."

[3] Matthew 6:24 reads, "No man can serve two masters: for either he will hate the one, and love the other; or else he will hold to the one, and despise the other. Ye cannot serve God and money."

Black Shadow immediately bows his left knee. Apollo thinking, "*I am glad no speed limits are posted on 'Broadway' as the flowers worshipping and singing to me may barely see me when I fly by.*"

Putting the drawings in the saddlebags, Apollo jumps on Black Shadow commanding, "Push the pedal to the metal, whatever that means. Zoom! Soar! 'Full speed ahead, damn the torpedoes,'[4] whatever that means, to Apollo's and Word's pulpit. Go! Faster! Speedo! Wow, we are almost flying! Next time, you will beat Abundant Life and win the black and gold ribbon. Thar's gold in them thar hills!'[5] It's mine! Mine all mine! I discovered it yesterday! Rich! I stake my claim, and nobody had better touched it. I see a cow made of this prized gold. I like that image."

The Father Counsels His Son, Jesus

Back at the "Throne Room," the Father counsels His Son, "Apollyon is going to ask You for the title deed to what he calls Dark Mountain, based upon his greed to **control** the large quantity of gold and other wealth he believes he discovered under the surface of the earth. He speaks of this place as his **H**abitation for **E**cstasy in **L**ushness and **L**avishness, which he will refer to as HELL He will lie about, and seek to cover up, what he believes is discovered wealth from the beginning.

I do not desire You to give him a title deed to anything, but I want You to give him a temporary day-to-day lease to the Hell portion only. Apollyon will set up tight security at the entrance of Hell. He will even trespass on some of Canaan Land by putting up an iron fence to guard further the entry to the Abyss leading down into the heart of Hell. His scientist and evil counselors think I cannot see what is going on in Hell as the walls and ceiling are lined with lead. My Servant David, made in Our image, will later write a song explaining about My knowledge of what's going on,

'Where can I go from Your Spirit?
Or where can I flee from Your presence?
If I make my bed in Hell, behold, You are there.'[6]

Apollyon will even later steal the temporary lease to the surface of the Earth. We will give to Our first creation in the Second Earth Age, Adam, made in Our image,[7] as Our earthly son[8] in the flesh. Apollyon will legally have both a temporary lease to Hell beneath the Earth and a temporary lease to the surface and atmosphere as the "*prince of this world . . . .*"[9] However, all Apollyon's legal rights and temporary leases will end when Michael throws him, and those who worship him and his idols, into a lake of fire.[10]

---

[4] Phrase used by Union Admiral David Farragut in winning on August 5, 1864, a great victory in the Battle of Mobile Bay. See David Farragut at *Wikipedia, The Free Encyclopedia*.

[5] Quoting from the Digital Library of Georgia *Thar's Gold in Them Thar Hills. Gold and Gold Mining in Georgia 1830s-1940s*.

[6] Psalm 139:4 NKJV.

[7] "*May your whole spirit, soul, and body be kept blameless at the coming of our Lord Jesus Christ.*" (1 Thessalonians 5:23 NIV).

[8] "*Let Us make man in Our own image, in Our likeness . . . .* (Genesis 1:26 NIV) See also Luke 3:37.

[9] "John 14:30 NIV

[10] "*And the devil, who had deceived them was thrown into the lake of fire and sulfur . . . .*" (Revelation 20:10 NKJV).

It will then be written about Apollyon,

'Through your widespread trade
you were filled with violence,
and you sinned.
. . .Your heart became proud
on account of your beauty,
and you corrupted your wisdom
because of your splendor.
So I threw you to the Earth . . .
. . . By your many sins and dishonest trade
you have desecrated your sanctuaries.
So I made a fire come out from you,
*and it **consumed you,***
*and I **reduced you to ashes** . . . .*
All the nations who knew you
are appalled at you;
you have come to a horrible end
*And will **be no more**.'*[11] [Emphasis added.]

"Father, 'a horrible end, reduced to ashes, and then to **be no more**!' Both our first creation and those who choose of their own free to join his kingdom of darkness to '**be no more**?' Apollo is My best friend, besides You, and tears for him are even now falling from My eyes and for those who will join in his war efforts against Us. You are love; how can You permit this? You will have to be the ultimate judge as I cannot pronounce such a judgment of '**be no more**' on My best friend."

"My Son, I commit all judgment to You. We do all things legally. Your wedding supper cannot take place until all Our enemies will '**be no more**.' I have given everyone a measure of faith, a free will. Whoever repents of sin and receives You as Savior, confesses You as Lord and King, and overcomes and endures to the end will be saved. I will add their name to the Book of Life for it will be written,

'Then I saw a great white throne and Him (that's You, My Son) who was seated on it. . . . Then death and Hell gave up the dead in it, and each person was judged according to what he had done. Then death and Hell were thrown into the lake of fire. The lake of fire is the second death. If anyone's name was not found written in the book of life, he (or she) was thrown into the lake of fire.'[12]

"Father, show me the Book of Life."

Appearing before the throne was the "Book of Life" with the Son of God opening the dedication page, which read:

Dedicated to All Who Repent, Receive My Son, Jesus,
As Savior, are baptized for Remission of Sins,
Confess Jesus as Lord, Overcomes the World,
The Flesh, and the Devil,
And are Born Again into My Family!
By: Father God

---

[11] Ezekiel 28:16-19 NIV.
[12] Revelation 20:11-12, 15.

The Son opens the second page, and it was blank. Then the Father rolls time forward to that final Day of Judgment with the names of countless appearing in alphabetical order by their first name and something about them.

The Son scrolls down and finds with a smile the name,

Joy Christ, the Pure Wife of the Son of God

"My Son, I am giving everyone a 'free will' and a measure of faith! I refuse to override a person's 'free will' and if they choose to do wrong, vile, filthy, and sinful things, unless they repent and receive You as Savior and confess You are Lord, before Your marriage, they must legally '**be no more**' I will make them legally void with no remembrance of such before Your pure and holy wedding day!.

I desire an adopted daughter and a bride for You and a large family to love and who loves Me! It is enough for Me to tell You right now that I am going to legally permit Lucifer to exercise his own idiotic 'free will' for further reasons of My own. I will share with You more of My reasoning from time-to-time in the eternities of eternity. All has to be prepared and judged legally. Apollyon will be doing various illegal things such as lying, deceiving, stealing, and murdering. Even now he is planning to surround "Dark Mountain" with a high iron fence for some 666 acres, without asking Our permission, which fence is a continuing legal trespass on My footstool and the Land of Canaan.

Also, he desires selfishly to make the Earth, for this First Earth Age into his lush greenhouse for his own pleasure and sport. Since he cannot create life, he will ask You to create giant plants, trees, and vegetarians of all sorts, according to his drawings. The land vegetation will primarily be watered by a mist coming up each morning from the Earth, and all the plant life will significantly increase the oxygen level balance in the Earth.

Next, he will ask You to create for his giant creatures to fill the sea, the land, and the sky, according to his proud drawings. At first, they will eat the vegetation and live at peace with each other. Afterward, he will cause such agitation they will hate and devour each other.

He will also ask You for some creatures he calls Gremlins.

Please create Elders and helper wives in Our image (including the hump on Our noses) from the dust of Canaan Land, for these and many of their descendants of the First Earth Age will be part of Our family as You will preach,

*'I am the Good Shepherd; I know My sheep, and My sheep know me – just as the Father knows Me and I know the Father – and I lay down my life for the sheep. I have **other sheep, not of this sheep pen (age)**. I must bring them also. They too will listen to My voice, and there shall be one flock and one Shepherd.'*[13] [Emphasis added.]

It will be written about many who reject and despise You both in this First Earth Age, in the Second Earth Age before the flood, and in the Third Earth Age,

'He is despised and rejected by men,
A Man of sorrows and acquainted with grief.
And we hid (as in shame) our faces from Him;
He was despised, and we did not esteem Him.
. . . And He bore the sin of many (only those who receive Jesus as Savior),
And made intercession (prayer) for the transgressors.'[14]

---

[13] John 10:14-16 NIV.
[14] Isaiah 53: 2-3, 12 NKJV.

Apollyon will indicate to You he needs the Ape Men in his choir on Earth to praise and worship Us, but do not give them a singing voice as he only wants them as his slaves.

Apollyon has designed one insect-like creature having oversized wings and a sting in its blue tail, which he calls Beelzebub, which he would like to keep as a pet in Hell. He desires to talk with this insect, which he proposes will rule over similar insects as Apollyon's seeks to control those all over the Earth. These flies are pure harassment, but their maggots are needed to consume the animals that eventually die. However, give it weak wings so it cannot fly over sixty-six (66) miles from the coast of the island Atlantis so this hideous insect will not spread to the mainland. I will feel like sounding out to You Spirit,

"Hand Me a giant fly swatter as they are so foul and evil!" [Laughter]

Beelzebub, with Apollyon's encouragement, will introduce cock-fighting, gambling, dirty morals, and every cruel and evil work all being an abomination to Me.

The Holy Spirit inquired, "What is cock-fighting?"

"Spirit, cock-fighting occurs when two male roosters with little razor-sharp spears fashioned to their claws cruelly and furiously fight each other until one dies from injuries received by the other. Often the one that wins will eventually die also of the wounds received. The spectators cheer and bet on which one will win.

The Holy Spirit further inquired, "Will Word create these furry little creatures to worship Us?

"No, Spirit! Word will create on the Earth first the elders out of the dust of Canaan Land, made in Our image, who have a free will and who will choose to worship, love, and obey Us.

Spirit, let me give you some previews of what is to take place. Apollyon will present all his plans and drawings to Word on top of the Lookout Glory Mountain as they await the rising earth on the horizon. Apollyon will emphasize the need to have a congregation to worship the Father. Because Apollyon cannot see Me, he doubts My existence, or at the most he thinks that I am very old and decrypted. [Laughter] Word will be silent as He hears Apollyon's presentation; and as the Earth rises, Word will invite Apollyon, Gabriel, and Michael to ride down to a dome-shaped rock reflecting the sun. Apollyon leaves to go to Dark Mountain, and then Word will create the first earthly congregation made up of elders.

Apollyon will many years later specifically ask Word to inform Me and You, Holy Spirit, of a special concert in a large coliseum with his building Us a room from which to view the service. We will agree to attend. Michael and Gabriel will be with Us. However, during the concert, Apollyon will give the order to set off an I-Bomb his scientist created, in his effort to murder Us.

Afterward thinking We are all frozen to death, as with everything else on the earth, he will enter Heaven with one-third of the angels in Heaven bowing down and worshiping him, calling him king and lord. Michael will enter the throne room leading the Army of Heaven, and Apollyon and his angels will then fight against Michael and his angels. Michael will throw Apollyon Lucifer and his angels back to the frozen earth.

They will fall so fast to the Earth they will look like a streak of '*lightning from Heaven*'[15] hitting the frozen Earth. Like roaches because of the extreme cold, they will all scramble to enter the hot chambers of Hell and to shut the outside gate behind them.

They will soon discover that not only did he not kill Us, but all the saints living on the surface of the earth were transferred in an atomic second into the chamber of Hades known as Paradise. Paradise has a '*great gulf*'[16] fixed between it and Hell.

---

[15] Luke 10:18.

All on the surface of the Earth will remain frozen solid for a span of time. Later explorers in a subsequent Earth age will discover in ice a dinosaur with a buttercup in his mouth frozen to prove just how fast the Earth froze and other fossils making the oil in this first Earth age. This lengthy period will be 'The Ice Age'[17] with thick ice covering the entire Earth with water beneath the ice.

From deep in Hell I could hear Apollyon Lucifer (then known as Satan or the Devil) in thought lamenting,

"It is me, Satan. Satan the banished. The humiliated. The accursed one! Expelled from my heavenly mansion, Empyrean,[18] crashing me to the Earth. With time still ticking on my lease of Hell, I will not be idle. If I could do it over, I believe I could have won. How did they escape a split second before the I-Bomb exploded? I assume Thunderer if he exists, escaped also. One more second and I would have won. I hate Thunderer, Word, and those goody saints who also escaped. One day I will win! My Scientists say they are on the verge of a greater scientific breakthrough. All I need is another chance, and I will win this time. We will invest all my deep scientific secrets to developing the ultimate weapon for the final battle."

Word inquires, "Father, how long will the Earth remain frozen?"

"My Son, the Earth will remain frozen without form and void for some time. Then we will create new creatures, being another fold[19] of people in addition to those saints who died or were rescued out of the First Earth Age to live in Paradise. You will be Man enough to take being nailed to a cross for the JOY set before You! Your dying on the cross will be the greatest work of all! Enough questions joyful Bridegroom, as My desire is for You to walk in love, friendship, and to enjoy the drama as the scroll unrolls. Patience! [Laughter]

Michael and Gabriel Arrive In the Throne Room

At this point, the Son nods and a Seraphim respectfully announces, "Michael and Gabriel are presenting themselves."

Michael and Gabriel humbly bow their knees with hands raised in joyful thanksgiving, praise, and worship. Word honors them by standing and extending His right hand first to Gabriel and then to Michael saying, "This is your first full day of a joyful and adventurous eternity together. Today We have no messages to be delivered and no war, yet declared against Us.

Now laugh with Me at two of My Father's private jokes, "He says about the future Earth, the three fastest means of communication are – Telephone, Telegraph, and Tele-a-woman, – and 'All's fair in love and war! Well (a deep subject), I do not know about war!' We will do all things lawful, in love and legal even in times of war.

You will notice I am in a flesh and bone body. I will be murdered in an act of war and raised from the dead in this flesh and bone body. For reasons of His own, My Father gave Me a skinny body with a humped nose. [Laughter].

With this challenge, I will win a flesh and bone bride, also with a humped nose. [Laughter] To My right is My bride's reserved seat. First war and then romance!

---

[16] Luke 16:26.

[17] The Greenland, Arctic, and Antarctic ice sheets starting in the ice age still exists. See *Wikipedia, The Free Encyclopedia* "Ice Age."

[18] Webster defines in part, "*Empyrean*" as, "The highest heaven or heavenly sphere . . . the true and ultimate heavenly paradise."

[19] John 10:16.

To My left is My invisible Father God and to His left is the invisible God, the Holy Spirit. I am the express visible image of the Father. My Father God Himself would like to welcome you,"

Father God in His deep voice speaks, "Michael and Gabriel welcome as part of Our unbeatable team. Be prepared, for war will be declared on Us. Our prideful enemy, who has been given a free will has been given great beauty and charm.

He will convince a third of the angels in Heaven to worship him and join his war efforts. Also, a sea of flesh and blood people on the Earth in the First, Second, and Third Earth Age will join his war efforts. If they are not for Us, then they are against Us.[20] No one can be neutral. We do all things in love, but we defend Ourselves if attacked to the uttermost. Michael, I delegate you full power to defend Us. I will back you and the Army of Heaven to which you will lead. It will be written about you, Great Defender,

'I looked and seated on the cloud was one 'like the Son of Man' (My Son in a flesh and bone body) with a crown of gold on His head and a sharp sickle in His hand. . . . The angel (Michael) swung his sickle on the Earth, gathered the grapes, and threw them into the great winepress of God's wrath. They were trampled in the winepress outside the city; and blood flowed out of the press, rising as high as the horse's bridle for a distance of 1,600 stadia (that is about 180 miles; being also about 300 kilometers).'[21]

'And I saw an angel (Michael) standing in the sun, who cried in a loud voice to all the birds flying in midair. 'Come, gather together for the great supper of God, so you may eat the flesh of all people, free and slave, small and great.'

Then I saw the beast and the kings of the Earth and their armies, gathered together to make war against the Rider (God's Son) on the horse and His army. But the beast was captured, and with him the false prophet who had performed the miraculous signs on his behalf. With these signs, he had deluded those who had received the mark of the beast and worshiped his image. The two were thrown alive into the fiery lake of burning sulfur. The rest of them were killed with the sword that came out of the mount of the Rider (God's Son) on the horse, and all the birds gorged themselves on their flesh.'[22]

'When the thousand years are over, Satan will be released from his prison and will go out to deceive the nations in the four corners of the earth – Gog and Magog – to gather them for battle. In number, they are like the sand on the seashore. They marched across the breadth of the earth and surrounded the camp of God's people, the city He loves. But fire came down from Heaven and devoured them. And the devil, who deceived them, was thrown (by Michael) in the lake of burning sulfur, where the beast and the prophet had been thrown.'[23]

Michael, you will be like Me, the Son of God, and My power will back you. I give you this signet ring from my right pointer finger containing a star of David and the word Jerusalem, as you will protect Jerusalem, the city I love, to the uttermost.

Now look over to that beautiful **Lamb's Book of Life** as this will contain the names of all who receive My Son as Savior, repent of their sins, confess Him as Lord, and endure and overcome to the end. Now open it as I have written the first name in faith."

Michael, turns to page, reading the dedication page,

---

[20] Matthew 12:30.
[21] Revelation 14:14, 19-20 NIV.
[22] Revelation 19:17-21 NIV.
[23] Revelation 20:7-10 NIV.

Dedicated to All Who Repent, Receive My Son, Jesus,
As Savior, are baptized for Remission of Sins,
Confess Jesus as Lord, Overcomes the World,
The Flesh, and the Devil,
And are Born Again into My Family!
By: Father God

Michael, turning the page, and reads the only name written in the *Lamb's Book of Life*,

Joy Christ, the Pure Wife of the Son of God

With a tear of joy in His invisible eye the Father laughing next speaks to Gabriel asking, "How was your first evening and morning in Heaven?"

Gabriel respectfully answers, "It was heavenly!" [Laughter]

Michael, nodding his head yes affirming that it was likewise heavenly for him.

Gabriel, having a way with words, further speaks, "Lord, I am Yours. I love You with all my heart, soul, strength, and mind. Thank You for creating me, loving me, using me, and for the lovely home and garden, you prepared for me."

Michael, nodding, making this his statement.

Word, replies, "There is no place like home! You two are home. Gabriel, you will be My messenger, and My power will back you. I take this signet ring from my middle right finger containing 'The Trumpet of the Lord' in gold on a white background and place it on your right middle finger. Here in this Trumpet Case is 'The Trumpet of the Lord,' and My beloved Apostle Paul will write about a time when you will blow it,

'*Listen, I tell you a mystery (secret). . . . In a flash, in the twinkling of an eye, at the last trumpet. For the trumpet will sound, the dead will be raised imperishable, and those who have not died will be changed. For the perishable must clothe itself with the imperishable, and the mortal with immortality.*'[24]

I will always back both of you – never be afraid. Speak My words, use My name, and the authority granted to Me by My Father. It will be written,

'*But even the archangel Michael, when he was disputing with the devil about the body of Moses, did not dare to bring a slanderous accusation against him, but said, 'The Lord rebuke you!'*[25]

"Gabriel and Michael, My Father ordained Me as His preacher. I have been practicing with My song leader for some time. Let us go down for another practice session, and this will be our last practice session for it is now My Father's will shortly to create through Me the first flesh and blood inhabitants on Earth known as the Elders. Soon after this, I will create numerous angels here in Heaven, which will make up the original convocations from which Apollo will be choosing the choir and orchestra here in Heaven."

Michael inquisitively, "We both brought our note-taking journals entitled *Sermon Notes* we found in the center of our library table for we esteem Your words to the uttermost. Should we take notes while You are delivering Your sermons?"

---

[24] 1 Corinthians 15:52-53.
[25] Jude 9 NIV.

Word replying, "Everyone else should, but I desire both of you to be constantly watching and on guard, and I am gifting each of you with an instant recall for you to write down the sermons later.

Take your journal in your hand with you today and write only Word's Practice Sermon on the top of a blank page to be filled in later. I am so pleased that you have honored Me with this question. Everyone, including Apollo, will have these journals, and they can take, or not to take, notes from My sermons. All seats have a unique pull-up table for taking sermon notes.

I would suggest you read the sermon notes over and over again and say to each other, 'It is written in my journal' this truth. The day will come when My words will be written in a book, known as the Bible, for all to read and to confess. There will be those who will seek to burn and destroy My Bible and to keep it from others. It will be written about My words:

'*Heaven and Earth will pass away, but My words will never pass away.*'[26]

Further questions?

Gabriel asks, "We have worn our dazzling white linen robes laid out for us and sandals, but we see that you are barefoot for the upcoming sermon. Would you desire, we also are barefoot during the sermon, and where would you want us to stand?

Word, replies, "I wish you to stand behind Me on each side – like the Champions you are – with Michael on My right and Gabriel on My left. The podium and pulpit area where the word is preached is especially holy ground. As examples, I would respectfully ask you also to remove your sandals, but you will need them later for your first and many trips to Earth. It is dusty in the land of Canaan, so I placed for you some riding garments and riding sandals in your lockers in the dressing room, and you can change back upon return to Heaven. Have you more questions?" [Both nod a no.]

Word blesses them by laying His right hand on each of their heads directing, "My Champions now stand to your feet, and let us go down to the diamond pulpit the Holy Spirit gave Me."

The word stands near the diamond pulpit, and Michael and Gabriel stand behind Him on each side, all three barefoot. Word says to Michael and Gabriel, "See that black streak coming up the broad road, that is My song leader, Apollo. He was late the first day, but I gave him what he calls a '*Time Master*' watch, and using it he has not been late, never early either. He will do it today again by a whisker." [Laughter]

Apollo, jumping off of Black Shadow, with his sandals making a slapping sound with each step, runs up to the podium. He looks at his gold watch saying, "Two fifty-nine and fifty-four seconds. Six seconds early! Hi, I'm Apollo. These must be Michael and Gabriel. I'm Word's song leader, the first creation. Can you sing? You must be Gabriel."

Michael responded, "You had a fifty-fifty chance, but I am Michael." [Laugher]

"Oh, well," says Apollo.

Word laughs, "That is a deep subject. Let me formally introduce you three: Apollo, this is Michael [Michael responds with his right hand raised opened], and this is Gabriel [who likewise extends his opened right hand). Apollo, My song leader, has a song for our practice session today."

Word, Michael, and Gabriel step away from the pulpit with Apollo taking no thought of removing his sandals. Apollo pridefully winging it takes his place behind the pulpit and opens his mouth with his booming voice,

"I am Apollo. Let us sing together,

---

[26] Luke 21:33 NIV.

'God is blessing me. He honors me today. I am on the fast road to success. I have confidence in myself now. I live excited! I hope in prosperity. All things are at my disposal. I am rich.'"

Apollo takes his usual place in the center of the front row thinking to himself, "*That Michael is one hunk of a man. Such bulging muscles. Look at Gabriel's fantastic hair and thick lips. I am still the most beautiful of all, but they both are very attractive young men. Why are they barefoot? They both have very attractive and appealing feet. Why are they both wearing dazzling bright white linen?*

What is that book they are carrying and why are they standing behind Word on each side instead of sitting by my side on this choice front row?"

Word walks barefoot to the pulpit and looks out over the vast Celestial Auditorium and up to the Throne Room nodding back and preaches,

'Lord, who may dwell in Your sanctuary?
Who may live on Your holy hill?
He whose walk is blameless
and who does what is righteous,
who speaks the truth from his heart
and has no slander on his tongue,
who does his neighbor no wrong
and casts no slur on his fellowman,
who despises a vile man
but honors those who fear the Lord,
who keeps his oath
even when it hurts,
who lends his money without usury
and accepts no bribe against the innocent.
He who does these things
will never be shaken.'[27]
A good name is more desirable than great riches;
to be esteemed (respected) is better than silver or gold.'[28]
*The Earth is the Lord's, and **EVERYTHING** [emphasis in speech added] in it!*
. . .Who may ascend into the hill of the Lord?
Who may stand in His holy place?
He who has clean hands and a pure heart;
who does not lift up his soul to an idol
or swear by what is false.
He shall receive the blessing from the Lord,
and vindication from God his Savior.'[29]
*'The silver is Mine, and the **GOLD** [emphasis in speech added] is Mine, declares*
the Lord Almighty.'[30]
'Speaks the Lord God of Israel, saying: Write in a
book for yourself all the words that I have spoken to you.
'Show me Thy ways, O Lord,
teach me Thy paths;
guide me in Your truth and teach me . . . .
. . . He guides the humble in what is right
and teaches them His way.'[32]

---

[27] Psalm 15:1-5 NIV.
[28] Proverbs 22:1 NIV.
[29] Psalm 24:1, 3-5 NIV.
[30] Haggai 2:8 NIV

'Let not the wise man boast of his wisdom
or the strong man boast of his strength
or the rich man boast of his riches,
but let him who boasts boast about this:
that he understands and knows Me (the eternal God).'[33]
'Trust in the Lord with all your heart
and lean not on your own understanding;
in all your ways acknowledge Him,
and He will make your paths straight.
Do not be wise in your own eyes;
fear the Lord and shun evil.'[34]
Amen, so be it!"

Apollo comes up to politic with Word and holds up his watch for Michael and Gabriel to see asking, "I seldom make it early and now never late." [Laughter] How do you like my gold, Time Master?

Word replied, "*'It is more blessed to give than to receive.'*[35] Today I have more gifts for each of you. Gabriel, here is a present for you!" Word turns to Michael saying, "And here is a present for you!" I've already given Apollo this gift, but I have something else for all three of you."

Apollo watches as Gabriel gently removes the purple bow and opens the neatly wrapped present and smiles as he sees a solid gold watch exactly like the one Word had given Apollo. A frown comes on Apollo's face.

Michael, who had been watching, as his first thought is always the protection of Word, not thinking of how he can please himself, opens his present, being an identical gold watch. Apollo frowns to Gabriel averring, "They are both exactly like mine. These watches are accurate to the atomic second. See all three are exactly together on the second. Others will ask you for the exact time. It's a beautiful timepiece, which I have named 'Time Master.' Word likes to start the services exactly on time. I've never been late to the service since Word gave me this T.M. (Apollo alone laughs) However; I like to receive presents. What's next?"

Word says, "Patience, *'There is a time for everything, and a season for every activity under Heaven.'*[36] Apollo, we will go together down to the hidden stable." Upon arrival 'Black Shadow' bows his left knee to Apollo. Coming out of a cloud was a white horse having a blue six-pointed Star of David on his forehead with Word presenting this horse as a present to Michael.

Michael responds, "Thank You so very much. What a magnificent present. His name shall be Star!"

Coming out of a cloud was another white horse having a golden trumpet on his forehead with Word giving this horse as a present to Gabriel.

Gabriel responded by saying, "Thank You so very much. What a delightful present. His name shall be Trumpet!"

"I have for each of you matching gifts, which will go with your watches, and Word hands the first eloquently wrapped box to Apollo."

Apollo first rips into his present laughing as he sees the content being a gold and silver horse's bridle saying, "This is what I've always wanted."

---

[32] Psalm 25:4-5, 9 NIV.
[33] Jeremiah 9:23-24 NIV.
[34] Proverbs 3:9-7 NIV.
[35] Acts 20:35 NIV.
[36] .Ecclesiastes 3:1 NIV.

88

Word laughs responding, "Apollo, you have not been here long enough to declare you 'always wanted one of these.' [Laughter] A plain one came as standard equipment with the original present, but I thought I would dress it up a little. I must admit that I also gave Myself one of these for My white horse, 'Abundant Life.'"

Apollo fitting his gold and silver horse's bridle, challenges 'Gabriel and Michael, "We are all going to go riding up to the top of the Lookout Glory Mountain? Maybe we can race!"

Word replied, "No racing or competition among you. You each have been given different gifts. '*One has this gift and another that gift.*'[37] You three are not to compete among yourselves as we are about serious kingdom business."

With all four brightly shining horse bridles in place, they proceed side by side. Word was front right and Apollo at his left with Gabriel behind Word and Michael at his left they traveled up a little broader trail than before up to the top of Look Out Mountain. Apollo says to Gabriel and Michael, "Now you two stand right here and watch the horizon. As our matching watch hands reach 3:24 P.M., you will see the blue-green jeweled Earth rising so stunningly."

As Gabriel and Michael are set to watch the view, Apollo turns and says to Word, "Walk over with me to this boulder as I would like to share some propositions with you and show you some of my magnificent sketches."

As they arrived, Apollo lays his sketches on a boulder and presents his case, "You could consider preaching at times on the Earth, and if you like my ideas, you will need a congregation. I drew these hairy little creatures I call Gremlins (Ape Men) as my helpers. Also, I drew this tropical vegetation. Look at what I call dinosaurs of all types, beautiful reptiles, sea monsters, and huge wooly mammoths. One of my favorite drawings is to be a friend – a large insect type creature with a blue tail and enormous wings. Also, look here at some unicorns having a single horn in the middle of their foreheads, and many snakes and spiders.

Beneath what I call 'Dark Mountain;' I found an ideal meeting hall in which I could go for a retreat to write and plan the music for our heavenly meetings and at times when you preach on the Earth. Please be so kind as to give all this to me. My winged insect could stay there and keep it all dusted and clean with his wings. Well, will you give all this to me?"

Word, replies, "My Father has the title deed, but you may have a temporary lease. Those unicorns you drew are going to be hard to saddle break. Even if one of those hairy little creatures could ride a unicorn as a race jockey, it still could not beat 'Abundant Life.'"

Apollo, laughing, responds, "That remains to be seen!"†

---

[37] 1 Corinthians 7:7.

†BOOK TWO – Episode 4†

[†**Sidebar Scriptures**: "Joseph had a dream and promptly reported all the details (Genesis 37:5)."
"The Lord revealed to me what the evil ones were doing and planning and showed me their wicked plots (Jeremiah 11:18)."
"The word of the Lord came to Abram in a **vision**. . . . A **deep sleep** came upon Abram . . . . (Genesis 15:1, 12)."
I witnessed and experienced "dreams and visions, and I described **all** I had seen to instruct many (Daniel 7:1, 11:33)."†]

The Creation of Dinosaurs and Dragons

WORD AND APOLLO WALK back over to rejoin Michael and Gabriel standing on the pinnacle of Lookout Glory Mountain with the wind of Heaven blowing through their hair, resulting in their hair dancing like the waves of the sea. At that moment, the blue and brown Earth rises above the horizon with Michael and Gabriel saying simultaneously, "Wow!"

"Apollo, seeing the light reflecting off the dome of a rock, with a smirk, turns Black Shadow's head as a gesture to challenge both Michael and Gabriel thinking, *"No one beats the great and beautiful Apollo!"*

Apollo speaks, "See these sketches. That brown you see will soon be green giving us a blue-green planet. See that rounded rock like a dome down on the Earth having light reflecting off it; that is the place where we are going. Word, what was the name of that rock?"

Word interjects, "That is Mount Moriah,[1] an exceptional place on My Father's footstool.

'The Earth is the Lord's, and everything in it.'[2]

Throwing down the gauntlet as in invitation to compete, Apollo declares, "Word, are You sure we cannot race? Black Shadow and I have been practicing. I bet I can beat all of you by miles."

Word responded, "Nothing beats My Abundant Life!" [Laughter]

Apollo seeks to wage, "I bet my Time Master gold watch that Black Shadow can beat Abundant Life!"

Word speaks sternly, "Be wise never to lose your atomic 18-karat gold watch as I only made three for each of you to enjoy. I am instructing all creation not to bet or to gamble on who can be first in a race or physical contest. In the Kingdom of God, the last shall be first, and the first shall be last, and the greatest will be the servant of all for it will be written,

'Whosoever would be first among you, shall be your servant. For whoever exalts himself will be humbled, and whoever humbles himself will be exalted.'[3]

'But many who are first will be last, and many who are last will be first.'[4]

Why go through life in a hurry and race to accomplish something that in eternity will amount to nothing or be less than nothing. Now let us take a casual ride side by side down to Mount Moriah, and you can look back with your angel eyes and see the planet Heaven, which is even more spectacular. You three have eyes to see both some things in the celestial and some things in the terrestrial, but there are many other realms you cannot see.

---

[1] 'Then Solomon began to build the temple of the Lord in Jerusalem on Mount Moriah, where the LORD had appeared
   to his father David. It was on the threshing floor of Araunah the Jebusite, the place provided by David.'
   (2 Chronicles 3:1 NIV) .
[2] Psalm 24:1.
[3] Matthew 23:11-12 NIV.
[4] Matthew 19:30 NIV.

The terrestrial creatures on Earth cannot unless their eyes are further opened, see planet Heaven or angels. My Father's footstool is always near enough for Him to prop up His invisible feet.

My Father's will is that I preach in a flesh and bone body. I choose to have a controlled lack of knowledge[5] as I am made more like those[6] I am ministering so I can identify better with their nature. So My feet will not reach from Heaven to Earth, but His will. My Father God is present everywhere at all times,[7] and He knows everything.[8] I never have throughout all eternity ever seen My Father hurrying or stressed. In My Father's Kingdom, the one who wins is the one who can wash the most feet."

Apollo's responds, "I am going to lose that one on purpose." [Laughing inside]

Upon arriving side by side on Mount Moriah, Apollo pulled out his sketches from his saddle bag and asked, "Which one first?"

Word standing barefoot, with Michael and Gabriel, who had also removed their sandals, respond, "Let Me first put a wall with gates, which can be shut at night around Zion. Otherwise, the dinosaurs and dragons *et cetera* Apollo has drawn will at times try to explore and check-in for the night at the Jerusalem Hotel. Some weigh tons and snore loudly." [Laughter]

Immediately a magnificent wall appeared with beautiful gates around Zion. Word turned and looked at a beautiful gate behind them, which swung open wide as if to say, '*Welcome at last. Thank you for creating me as a gate to lovely Zion. All her foes shall be confounded, and no weapon formed against her will prosper. Your great power will keep Zion. Happy Zion! How blessed are the people abiding within her walls!* '*Pray for the peace of Jerusalem.*'[9]

Word smiles at the happy gate speaking in a low tone with Apollo's not focused as he had gone to his saddle bags for his sketches,

'Blessed are those who wash their robes (in My blood), that they may have the right to the tree of life and may go through the gates into the city. Outside are the dogs, those who practice magic arts, the sexually immoral, the murderers, the idolaters, and everyone who loves and practices falsehood. . . . The Spirit and the bride say, 'Come!' And let him who hears say, 'Come!' Whoever is thirsty, let him come, and whoever wishes let him take the free gift of the water of life. . . . The grace of the Lord Jesus is with God's people. Amen.'[10]

Apollo, returning holds up for Word again, his sketches of various gigantic trees, tropical plants, dinosaurs, dragons, cobras, scorpions, reptiles, and sea monsters, saying, "I am ready!"

Word decrees, "Let the City of Zion and of the surrounding Canaan Land "bring forth living plants, tasty fishes of some twenty-four variations, in the Sea of Galilee, delicious fowl, cattle, sheep, camels, and other creeping things such as camels, horses, oxen, and other social animals.

Beloved Zion will be a pleasant, blessed[11] land flowing with milk and honey.

---

[5] See Philippians 2:6-11.

[6] See Hebrews 2:17.

[7] Omnipresent. The prefix omni comes from the Latin meaning "all." So, to say that God is omnipresent is to say that God is present everywhere at all times.

[8] God is omniscient meaning that all things are open and naked before His sight.

[9] Psalm 122:6.

[10] Revelation 22:14-15, 17, 21 NIV.

[11] A Jewish historian, Josephus, will write regarding the blessed Canaan Land's fertility, "One may call this place the ambition of Nature, where it forces those plants that are naturally enemies to each other to agree together: it is a happy contention of the seasons, as if each of them nourishes different sorts of autumnal fruits beyond man's expectation, but preserves them a great while. It supplies men with the principal fruits -- grapes and figs continually during the ten months of the year, and the rest of the fruits, as they ripen together through the whole year."
(Josephus War III, x 8).

It will be covered with flowers, vegetables such as lettuce, radishes, celery, cucumbers, broccoli, cauliflower, wheat, and barley, with seed-bearing plants and trees bearing delicious fruit such as figs and dates and olives for oil, grape vines, according to their various kinds."

Immediately it was accomplished. Appearing were lush grasses, beautiful and sweet smelling flowers, fruit trees, cedar and other trees for lumber, with songbirds, cattle, sheep, camels, horses and other animals, and fish abundantly appearing throughout Canaan Land.[12]

Apollo, looking disgusted because not one of his sketches appeared among the vegetation and livestock, held up his sketches with him, this time, complaining, "What about these?"

Word spoke, "May there now be a greater 'greenhouse effect'[13] throughout the remainder of this one continent, which one day will be divided[14] into two continents, containing all the living beings in Apollo's drawings. **Be** the various species of dinosaurs, dragons, reptiles, cobras, and scorpions, unicorns, et cetera, and his drawing of a winged insect, which is now waiting for him at the entrance to the Abyss and is desperately wanting in.

Apollo declares, "Great! Can I let my pet inside and observe and meet some of my creatures I drew, especially the dinosaurs and the unicorns?"

"Yes, Apollo, you are excused to let your winged insect into Hell and to go see the dinosaurs. Today is Sunday, the first day of the week, and tomorrow the Celestial City will be populated with angels, many having discoverable gifts of music. You will need to start interviewing the inhabitants of the Celestial City and the surrounding areas tomorrow for the choir and orchestra. Soon you will need to start musical instrument and voice lessons, as well as draft some music for our first service with a congregation in Heaven. How long do you feel you will need to get truly ready for this first service?"

Apollo, answering, "Let me shoot for sixty-six days, six hours, and six minutes. I would suggest the first service starts at 6:00 P.M. on that day. I will begin knocking on doors tomorrow throughout the Celestial City and the surrounding area recruiting those for the choir and the orchestra. I can fit the perfect angel with the right instrument and the exact angel voice together in a tuneful blended sound.

I am a can-do person! I can do anything better than . . . ." [Apollo checks his sentence thinking the word '*you refers to Word.*']

Word responds, "Giving you an extra month, day and hour for the first service will be July 7th at 7:00 P.M., being the three sevens, 777. I will preach a message after the praise and worship music portion. Remember, it is of one's own free will to be in your choir, to play an instrument, and even to attend the services. Put no undue pressure on anyone to participate."

Apollo replied, "See you on July 7th at 7:00 P.M. I am a can-do person! Bye"

Apollo mounts Black Shadow and whispers, "Go as speedily as a unicorn to 'Dark Mountain'– show them your racing speed."

Shortly Apollo spots Dark Mountain, smiling about all the riches inside, thinking, "*I am glad I was not questioned about all the gold and wealth inside. I got over that hurdle. It's*

---

[12] '*The whole land of Canaan, where you are now an alien, I will give as an everlasting possession to you (Abraham) and your descendants after you; and I will be their God.*' Genesis 17:8 (NIV).

[13] "The *greenhouse effect* is a process by which thermal radiation from a planetary surface is absorbed by atmospheric greenhouse gases, and is re-radiated in all directions. Since part of this re-radiation is directed back towards the surface and the lower atmosphere, it results in an elevation of the average surface temperature above what it would be in the absence of the gases."
Wikipedia, The Free Encyclopedia.

[14] '*One was named Peleg (means division), because in his time the Earth was divided.*' Genesis 10:29 (NIV).

stimulating to be so rich! I can eat, drink, and be merry with my pet. It's all mine, and I will not share!"

As Apollo lands on Dark Mountain near the entrance to the Abyss into Hell, his winged-insect pet wagging its blue tail waiting to get in immediately greets him. Apollo exalts himself, "Beelzebub, I am the great rich Apollo. I designed and created you. You are a sight to behold. I am your master and lord. When I approach, you are to bow and worship me. Black Shadow, show Beelzebub, how it is done!"

Black Shadow bows his left knee to Apollo and Beelzebub follows suit, also bowing and worshiping Apollo.

Apollo declares, "That is more like it! Put as much emotion and feeling into it as possible, as I am worth it. Let me show you to your new quarters. Apollo takes a key from his pocket and places it into a hidden slot on top of Dark Mountain and commands, "This is the great Apollo, and the password is 666. Open! I command!" The abyss quickly springs open like a hungry jaw to receive its first tenant, Beelzebub.

Apollo enters the open slot and leaves it open instead of shutting it. He picks up the atomic light with Beelzebub following him closely wagging his blue tail as they go down the 666 steps until they reach the iron gate. Apollo inserts the key into the main iron gate and commands, "I am Apollo, 666, open!" The gate opens with a little cry as though it needed oiling. Apollo and Beelzebub, hurrying down another 666 steps, enter a large chamber with a black onyx gate.

Apollo declares, "Beelzebub, this is my throne room. You are to keep this place spotless. If anything gets in here, sting it with your tail as this is private property. 'No Solicitation!' I have set up a series of reflection mirrors from where the molten gold and flames are given off a darkened light to give the throne room some atmosphere.

Now, I will leave you here to go look for the dinosaurs, dragons, and sea monsters I designed, as I did you, of my own creativity. Make yourself at home until I return whenever that may be. I brought you this package of food and water from my saddle bag, which should hold you over. The food from Heaven is a little blah. If all goes as planned, we will be enjoying a dinosaur steak together. This large place seems to be in the shape of a body, and we are in the head portion. You have a lot of exploring you can do. I saw a few mushrooms growing under a rock over the left big toe if you run out of food before I return.

It looks as if I will be gone for at least 66 days. Do not singe your wings in those delicious flames. Make yourself at home, because you cannot get out as I have the only key, and no one ever will take this key away from me. I guard it, as it is a key to my palace containing great riches. You are now officially a citizen of Hell. You are my first loyal recruit! Hell is a grand place to be? Congratulations.

Later you can brag to tell all the inhabitants you were the first occupant. That is something of which to be proud (lofty)! How do you like Hell so far?" [No response.]

Apollo grabs Beelzebub, by his blue tail being careful to avoid the stinger, sets him upright, and pats him on the head saying, "Bye. See you in several months as I have important work in Heaven to do. I am the song leader of Heaven. I am the king of music! Take good care of my place and be careful not to fall over on your back; otherwise, I will use your dead body to grill me a dinosaur steak."

Apollo, proceeding to shut the black iron gate, exited the abyss, and shouts, "Black Shadow, let's go!" Black Shadow arrives bowing his left knee.

Apollo mounts and orders, "Let's get out of this barren land of Canaan and go to the lush equator, where the mist forest will be the thickets, and let's explore for dinosaurs!"

Shortly they arrive at the equator with the ground temperature being 106.66 degrees with Apollo shrieking, "Look, Black Shadow, there is one of my Behemoths[15] eating out of the top of the tree. He weighs tons and tons. Wow! Look, there are my Diplodocus[16] and Apatosaurus![17] I see some unicorns[18] grazing in that clearing. Let's land and see if you are skilled enough to politic one of them."

Apollo mounted on the back of Black Shadow as he gallops over to the herd of unicorns. Black Shadow is accepted and rubs noses with one of the unicorns avoiding the horn to keep it from jabbing him. Apollo says, "They like you, Black Shadow. I might take one for a test drive. I know one of these can beat Abundant Life. I don't like to lose."

Apollo stands up on his saddle on Black Shadow and jumps on the back of the unicorn with which Black Shadow has been rubbing noses and demands, "I designed you. You are faster than a speeding bullet!" The unicorn immediately bucks and gallops into the forest sideswiping trees and thorny bushes, leaving strips of Apollo's trousers hanging from thorn to thorn and from limb to limb. The unicorn designs and makes a sudden hateful stop at the bank of a swamp with Apollo sliding over the unicorn's head and off the end of its horn and landing head first into the swamp filled with sticky mud and underbrush.

Apollo's concern grows as he cannot free himself, and in his thoughts, he dials for help, "*666.*" Immediately a serpent with four legs comes to his help pulling his head out of the mud and marsh with its tail. Apollo, feeling humiliated, hangs onto the snake's tail as it with great effort pulls Apollo free of the swamp and underbrush. Apollo, visibly shaken, gets to his feet having lost the rest of his trousers holdings up his fist saying, "I curse you unicorns. I regret ever designing you. I will see that every last unicorn is destroyed and become extinct. I designed you, and I can take you out.

My key to Hell! Where is it located? It is the only key! It is in my trouser pocket, which I lost in the swamp. Serpent, if you will retrieve my trousers, I will have a wonder name and position for you in my kingdom." The Serpent wags its tail as if to say, "*I accept your offer,*" diving off the bank back into the dark swamp and shortly appears with Apollo's trousers. Apollo in desperation looks into each pocket for the key to Hell. Finally, in the last pocket, he pulls the key out saying, "No one is ever going to take the keys of Hell from me!"

Serpent, "Your name shall be Herpein, meaning a creeping serpent, and you will be honored by being invited to join me as my second guest in the enchanting Dark Mountain. I designed you as one of the most stunning of creatures having every color going through your scales.

Now travel north starting where the Jordan River empties into the Dead Sea, and follow it up 666 meters. Then take a left at the salt rock for another 666 meters and then travel up to the top of Dark Mountain and guard it for me with those poisonous fangs.

Also, enjoy sunbathing on top of 'Dark Mountain.' I will be over two months in returning as I have some important matters to attend to as the great music leader of Heaven.

---

[15] Behemoth is a beast mentioned in Job 40:15-24.

[16] "Diplodocus . . . whose fossils were first discovered in 1877 . . . . Its great size may have been a deterrent to the predators Allosaurus and Ceratosauris . . . ." *Wikipedia, The Free Encyclopedia.*

[17] "Apatosaurus . . . is one of the largest land animals known to have ever existed, with an average length of 23 meters (75 feet) and a mass of at least 16 metric tons . . . ." *Wikipedia, The Free Encyclopedia.*

[18] '*Will the unicorn be willing to serve thee, or abide by thy crib. Canst thou bind the unicorn with his band in the furrow?*' Job 39:9-10 KJV.

I am looking forward to introducing you to the first resident of Hell, Beelzebub. Here, let me show you a sketch of my pet. In your journeying, if you see a female version, please bring her along promising her great riches. Beelzebub needs a mate to help me populate the kingdom of Hell and to do my work in the Earth. Do not provoke her as she can sting you with her tail. I will let you in when I return. Now watch and imitate how Black Shadow worships me!"

Apollo commands, "Black Shadow here, now!" Black Shadow arrives bowing the knee in worship. Likewise, the Serpent bows down on one knee and worships Apollo.

Apollo, mounting Black Shadow, looks down at Herpein saying, "That is it. Go and wait for your prize. I will be back at "Dark Mountain" after two months. "

Holding on to his key tightly and in relief Apollo, throws his wet, torn, and shredded trousers back into the muddy swamp. He hears both a splash and a clunk, sounding like a small stone also hit the water, saying,

"A little littering will improve the looks of things around here. It is an embarrassment and humiliation to be thrown off and to have lost my pants. I better not go see my dragons looking like this."

As Apollo rises in the air on Black Shadow, he looks down and sees that unicorn in question looking at him from behind a Palm Tree. It seemed in Apollo's mind that the unicorn was laughing at him. Apollo points his finger in a cursing manner avers, "You think you won, and now you laugh at the one that designed you. I curse you and wish you dead for trying to hurt and embarrass me and for being so selfish and prideful as not to give the great Apollo a little ride. No one turns down or laughs at the great Apollo.

I will put out the word to my furry little friends, which I also have not met yet that unicorn steak is a luxury of luxuries, and soon you all will be extinct. I will ask some of my furry friends to draw your picture on some cave walls to preserve your image since you were my design. Your horns will soon decorate my throne room as a reminder to all those that could try to hurt the great Apollo. I will never slide down one of your sharp horns again, but your flesh will slide down the throats of many. Your horn will not do you any good against our fiery darts and arrows. I might have a few bites of you myself and feed the rest of you to my pet Beelzebub.

Well, since I have on only my underwear, these pink mud stained bikini speedos, not by choice, Black Shadow fly me over the sea in search of my Leviathan. I do not want the dragons to see me without my full dignity obtained through politicking, as they will have to obey me as I have job assignments for them.

Skimming the surface of the sea, they soon spot the largest creature in the sea – a huge and fast swimming Leviathan,[19] which Apollo had named on his drawing as 'Kronosaurus.'[20]

Apollo thinks, "*I am not going to take him for a test run as I might soon be 666 leagues under the sea. A unique design if I say so myself.*"

"What a day, Black Shadow, take me fast to Apollo's pink mansion for some well-deserved, earned rest so I can take a shower. I will cover my exposed beautiful legs in those black silk leotards, which I have never worn. Tomorrow I start politicking and making friends by visiting every habitation in the Celestial City. I mean every residence!

---

[19] Leviathan is described extensively in Job 41:1-34 and mentioned in Isaiah 27:1.

[20] "Kronosaurus was a marine reptile . . . carnivorous, and had many long, sharp teeth. Curremt estimates put Kronosaurus at around 9-10 meters (30-33 feet) in length." *Wikipedia, The Free Encyclopedia.*

My name will be a household name even more than Thunderer. I will leave everyone with a musical note paperweight with my name on it and have each angel to complete a detailed information sheet. Who knows, they may together want to elect me mayor. Control!"

As Apollo was preparing for his shower, he whined, thinking, "*Oh, no! I lost my watch. It probably was knocked off on one of those sideswiped trees, or that was the clunk in the water I heard when I littered the swamp by throwing away my torn trousers. At least, I retrieved my key to Hell. One out of two is not too bad. Easy come, easy go. I rarely ever looked at it. I might send Herpein back to search for it, but it would be like looking for a needle in a haystack or a pink grain of sand at the bottom of the ocean in that large swamp. I have to remember to look at the house clock, be on time, and wear extra-long sleeves so they will not notice I am not wearing my watch. A day of great loss for me on Earth.*

That unicorn will smoke soon at the end of my fork. I decree that unicorn and all other unicorns, will not desire proper sexual union of the male to the female unicorn. Because they will not be bearing young, they will soon die out and be no more for a male with a male rubbing against each other cannot produce offspring.

I had better get some shut eye. Politically, I will make many friends as I systemically commence tomorrow my campaign of knocking on all the doors starting with the inhabitants at the Southern end of the city, furthest away from the throne. It will be three secrets to my winning the hearts of the inhabitants to follow me – Flatter, Flatter, Flatter![21] *I will control and influence the angels-to-be of my choir and orchestra, and I will control them as I control my earthly vault containing great riches in the heart of the earth. Great wealth! Great riches! Good night, good looking. Beautiful one. Good night, rich Apollo!*"

Apollo's sleep escaped him most of that evening because of the desire to murder in his heart toward the unicorn robbing him of his gold 'Time Master.' Also, he was planning and purposed to publish a weekly newsletter to all the potential angel choir members in Heaven with his thinking, "*I will name my newsletter 'Apollo's Glorious Music Weekly.'*

The application to be part of my choir or my orchestra will ask the sixty-six dollar question, 'List all your talents!' Any who list watchmaking, I could have them make 666 'Apollo Glorious Music' watches with black faces. Those who list a gifting in science I could assign them to find out what is meant by the formula $E=MC^2$?'†

---

[21] '*A flattering mouth worketh ruin.'* Proverbs 26:28 Flattery is praise designed to deceive someone into doing what the flatterer wants them to do. It is a form of lying because it is not sincere. It is poison in a spoonful of honey -- crafty, friendly, and subtle – holding out false promises.

96

†BOOK TWO – Episode 5†

[†**Sidebar Scriptures**: "Joseph had a dream and promptly reported all the details (Genesis 37:5)."
"The Lord revealed to me what the evil ones were doing and planning and showed me their wicked plots (Jeremiah 11:18)."
"The word of the Lord came to Abram in a **vision**. . . . A **deep sleep** came upon Abram . . . . (Genesis 15:1, 12)."
I witnessed and experienced "dreams and visions, and I described **all** I had seen to instruct many (Daniel 7:1, 11:33)."†]

The Creation of the Heavenly Host of Angels

WORD, MICHAEL, AND GABRIEL had taken off their sandals off on Mount Moriah for the place they were standing was holy ground, where love abounds. Word, Jesus, bows on both knees looks up toward the Celestial Planet Heaven hovering in open space, resting on nothing, shining in all its fullness, and appearing seven times larger than the moon. After offering thanksgiving to His Father, He nods a yes with a smile toward the throne room. Word decrees with overflowing joy,

"A stairway from Mount Moriah to Heaven **be**!

The angels of Heaven, **be**!"

Numerous created occupants of the Celestial Planet Heaven appeared on a golden '*stairway resting on the Earth, with its top reaching to Heaven, and the angels of God were ascending and descending on it.*'[1]

The Son of God greets the host of Heaven,

"Welcome, ministering spirits, the inhabitants of Heaven, who were created to worship God alone and serve those made in God's image on Earth. You all have free wills to choose to worship God, to serve or be served, and I instruct you, '*Whoever wants to be first must be a servant of all. For even the Son of Man[2] did not come to be served, but to serve, and to give His life as a ransom (to pay the penalty due for sin) for many.*'[3] I will leave Heaven to become the Son of Man (having like flesh and blood) in the Earth below by being born as Savior of the world. My mother will be an obedient young virgin girl, who consents to be mocked, despised, and scorned as an unwed mother, and of her obedience it will be written,

'*God sent the angel Gabriel (standing as I speak to you at My left) to Nazareth, a town in Galilee, to a virgin pledged to be married to a man named Joseph, a descendant of David. The virgin's name was Mary (also a descendant of King David). The angel said, 'Greetings, you who are highly favored! The Lord is with you.' '. . . You will be with child and give birth to a Son, and you are to give Him the name Jesus. He will be great and will be called the Son of the Most High. The Lord God will give Him the throne of His father David, and He will reign over the house of Jacob forever; his kingdom will never end.' 'How will this be,' Mary asked the angel, 'since I am a virgin?' The angel answered 'The Holy Spirit will come upon you, and the power of the Most High will overshadow you. So the Holy One to be born will be called the Son of God.' . . . 'I am the Lord's servant,' Mary answered. 'May it be to me as you have said.' Then the angel left her.*'[4]

Many of you will be part of the celebration of My birth for it will be written,

'*She gave birth to her firstborn, a Son. She wrapped Him in strips of cloth and laid Him in a manger, because there was no room for them in the inn. And there were shepherds living out in the fields nearby, keeping watch over their flocks at night. An angel of the Lord appeared to them, and the glory of the Lord shone around them and they were terrified. But the angel said to them, 'Do not be afraid. I bring you good news of great **joy** that will be for all the people.*

---

[1] Genesis 28:12 NIV.

[2] "Son of Man" implies the Son of God being in a flesh and bone body. He would be born of a virgin. All man and all God.

[3] Mark 10:44-45 NIV.

[4] Luke 1:26-28, 30-35, 38 NIV

*Today in the town of David a **Savior** has been born to you; He is Christ.*[5] *This will be a sign to you: 'You will find a baby wrapped in strips of cloths and lying in a manger.' Suddenly a great company of the heavenly host appeared with the angel, praising God and saying, 'Glory to God in the highest, and on Earth peace to men on whom His favor rests.' When the angels had left them and gone into Heaven, the shepherds said to one another, 'Let's go to Bethlehem and see this thing that has happened, which the Lord has told us about.' So they hurried off and found Mary and Joseph, and the baby, who was lying in the manger. When they had seen Him, they spread the word concerning what had been told them about this child, and all who heard it were amazed at what the shepherds said to them. But Mary treasured up all these things and pondered them in her heart. The shepherds returned, glorifying and praising God for all the things they had heard and seen, which were just as they had been told.'*[6]

"I, the Son of God, Your Creator this day, am to be that baby Jesus to be born having a flesh, bone, and blood body. It will be written,

'God (the Father) never said to any of the angels,
>   *'You are My Son.*
>   *Today I have begotten You (in a flesh and bone body).*
Nor did God say of any angel,
>   *'I will be His Father,*
>   *and He will be My Son.'*
And when God brings His firstborn Son into the world, He says,
>   *'Let all God's angels worship Him (the Son of God).*
. . . God said this about His Son:
>   *'God, Your throne will last forever and ever.*
>   *You will rule your kingdom with a just and righteous scepter;*[7]
You love righteousness and hate evil (rebellion, wickedness; lawlessness) so
>   *God (Your Father and Lord) has anointed You above anyone else;*
>   *He has set You apart with much JOY.*
God (the Father) also says (to His Son),
'   Lord, in the beginning, You made the Earth,
>   *Your hands made the heavens.*
They will be destroyed, but You (Son of God) will remain forever;
. . . And God (the Father) never said this to an angel:
>   *Sit by Me at my right side until I put Your enemies under Your feet.*
. . . All the angels are spirits and are sent to serve those who will receive
(the Son of God as Savior) salvation.'[8]

"Citizens of Heaven, this day, I, the Son of God, being the Word of God from eternity, according to My Father God's commandment have created each of you angels having a *'free will.'*

Each of you is given unique individual gifts, *'For each man (as well as each angel) has his own gift from God; one has this gift, and another has that gift.'*[9]

---

[5] Or Messiah. "The Christ" (Greek) and "the Messiah" (Hebrew) both mean "the Anointed One."

[6] Luke 2:7-20 [Emphasis added.]

[7] A scepter symbolizes royal kingly authority.

[8] Hebrews 1:5-11, 14.

[9] 1 Corinthians 7:7. Seventh book of New Testament, Seventh Chapter, Seventh verse. Affectionately known as the three 7s, with 777 representing the threefold perfection of the Trinity, in contrast to 666 in Revelation 13:18 representing, , the number of perfected evil, *"for it is* (evil) *man's number. His number is 666."*

I am God the Son, My Father is sitting above on the Throne, and the Holy Spirit is sitting on His left hand. I sit at the Father's right hand. The Father and the Holy Spirit are both invisible in this dispensation. This golden stairwell upon which you are worshiping and praising God symbolizes the uninterrupted communion the Godhead desires between those in prayer, living on this terrestrial planet Earth and the throne room of the celestial planet Heaven. Those on the Earth like you will also have *free wills*, and they have a large part to play in keeping this communion open as they speak forth the truths in My Words as it will be written,

'The Lord has established His throne in Heaven, and His kingdom rules over all. Praise the Lord, you His angels, you mighty ones who do His bidding, who obey His word. Praise the Lord, all His heavenly hosts, you His servants that do His will.'[10]

When you hear words spoken on Earth, contrary to My Word you will have to fold your wings and sit back and do nothing. Those on Earth will be warned regarding speaking stout words, contrary to the Word of God and provoking you as it will be written,

'See, I am sending an angel ahead of you to guard you along the way and to bring you to the place I have prepared. Pay attention to him and listen to what he says. Do not rebel against him; he will not forgive your rebellion since my Name is in him. If you listen carefully to what he says and do all that I say, I will be an enemy to your enemies and will oppose those who oppose you. My angel will go ahead of you and bring you into the land of the Amorites, Hittites, Perizzites, Canaanites, Hivites, and Jebusites; and I will wipe them out. Do not bow down before their gods or worship them or follow their practices. You must demolish them and break their sacred stones to pieces. Worship the Lord your God and His blessing will be on your food and water. I will take away sickness from among you, and none will miscarry or be barren in your land. I will give you a full life span. I will send my terror ahead of you and throw into confusion every nation you encounter. I will make all your enemies turn their backs and run . . . .'[11]

We, the Godhead, are one God and consist of the eternal Father, the eternal Son, and the eternal Holy Spirit, to whom you only shall worship and praise. There is no other god to worship! I reiterate, "No other!"

Upon hearing this, each of the created angels on the stairway bow in humble worship, praising, admiring, and giving thanksgiving to the one true God.

Word holds out His right hand, teaching, "Your love and worship to God ministers to Us greatly. It will never go unnoticed and will be rewarded. It will be written regarding some of you angels on this ladder ministering to Me,

'When Jesus saw Nathaniel approaching, he said of him, 'Here is a true Israelite, in whom there is nothing false.' 'How do you know me?' Nathaniel asked. Jesus answered, 'I saw you while you were still under the fig tree before Philip called you.' Then Nathaniel declared, 'Rabbi, You are the Son of God; You are the King of Israel.'

Jesus said, 'You believe because I told you I saw you under the fig tree. You shall see greater things than that.' He then added, 'I tell you the truth, you shall see Heaven open, and the angels of God ascending and descending on the Son of Man (Jesus born on the Earth of a woman).'[12]

The host of Heaven, please be seated in the Great Convocation Center in front of the top of the ladder, and you will be given a map of the location of your respective abodes. I am sending up Gabriel and Michael on their white horses to welcome you formally to Heaven.

---

[10] Psalm 103:19-20 NIV.
[11] Exodus 23:20-27 NIV.
[12] John 1:47-50 NIV.

Some of you of your free will may desire to apply to be a part of 'The Army of Heaven' under the leadership of Gabriel. He will select a limited number, and a few of you will be chosen to serve in this capacity. Right now, we have to study war, but the time will come when,

'Nations will no longer raise swords (weapons of war) against other nations; nor will they train (study) war no more (ever again).

Everyone will sit (restfully in peace) under his own grapevine and fig tree,[13] *and no one will make him afraid, because the Lord Almighty, of Heaven's Army (hosts), has said (decreed) it.'*[14]

Until then, it will be a special honor to be part of Heaven's Army, headed by Michael, who defends the Kingdom of Heaven. It is a position of great humble service and those who serve faithfully will be greatly rewarded in the eternities of eternities.

Likewise, others might desire to apply to be part of Heaven's Communication Network, headed by Gabriel, and even deliver top-secret messages. You may share none of the contents of your messages with others, but again for those who serve faithfully in this area, there will be great eternal rewards.

Also, both groups will be unique *'ministering spirits sent to serve those who (on Earth) will inherit salvation.'*[15] These are service-oriented positions and may be time-consuming. Now each has a free will, and you have the right not to be part of either of these strictly confidential teams or even to sing in the choir or to be part of the orchestra, which will also take a lot of preparation and practice to learn either your instruments or your singing parts.

For your information, after the praise and worship songs, I will be further preaching the Word to you. You will each have a notebook in which you may, or may not, choose to take notes from My sermons. Also, you have a free will to obey or not to obey My words. None of you are a robot. I strongly advise you to wait at least twenty-four hours before making such an important service decision. You may be just a part of the Celestial City. While you are not even required to come and hear My teaching and preaching, it will be written about one who focus upon My words,

'As Jesus and His disciples were on their way, He came to a village where a woman named Martha opened her home to Him. She had a sister called Mary, who sat at the Lord's feet listening to what He said. But Martha was distracted by all the preparations that had to be made. She came to Him and asked, 'Lord, don't You care that my sister has left me to do the work by myself? Tell her to help me!' 'Martha, Martha,' the Lord answered, 'you are worried and upset about many things, but only one thing is needed. Mary has chosen what is better, and it will not be taken away from her.'[16]

I have requested Gabriel to communicate with you, as you take a seat in the Great Convocation Center, as to your respective places of residence. Michael and Gabriel will meet with you in twenty-four minutes before the Throne of Heaven. Questions?

Hearing none, the Son of God smiles and returns to a kneeling position of worshipping His Lord, Father God, on Mount Moriah. The golden stairway from Heaven to Earth disappears from view, and Gabriel and Michael mount their nearby white horses and proceed to the Great Convocation Center.

Upon putting their white horses in the stable, Michael and Gabriel notice two large containers full of eloquently printed gold maps of the Celestial City with each angel's name and address, and application forms to serve in the Army of Heaven, or in the Communication team, or in the choir or orchestra.

---

[13] Symbols of prosperity.
[14] Micah 4:3-4.
[15.] Hebrews 1:14.
[16] Luke 10:38-41 NIV.

Gabriel and Michael each carry a container of maps to the front and right side of the podium and directs each angel to take one copy. Shortly each angel had received a copy and had located his proper abode. Each angel has his distinct name on his robe.

Gabriel respectfully communicates with the angels,

"In the name of the Living One God, whom I serve, I welcome you to your first day in the beautiful Celestial City located on planet Heaven. Each day will be like a blank scroll for you, of your own 'free will,' to write about your service to God, others, and truths you learn. My name is Gabriel, an archangel of Heaven and a fellow servant of the Most High God! This is the day of the week called Sunday, the first day of our seven-day week – Sunday, Monday, Tuesday, Wednesday, Thursday, Friday, and Saturday. Saturday is a day of quiet worship to God alone, rest, and meditation on how you have grown in the grace and knowledge of God and how you have served God and others during the past week. Let me introduce Michael, also an archangel, and fellow servant of the Most High God, who has an announcement."

Michael addresses the angels with authority under the headship of the Word of God,

"The Word of God is the Commander and Chief and leader of the Army of Heaven. I am a servant of God just as you. You can choose of your own 'free will' to be a part of the choir, orchestra, communication team, or army.

I respectfully invite you to consider being a part of serving in the Army of Heaven. I will be meeting back here Thursday at 3:00 P.M. to receive any of your applications containing essays of a hundred words or less of why you sincerely would like to be considered to serve in the Army of Heaven. These have been placed in the center drawer of your desk in your abode marked 'We Need a Few Good Angels.' I turn you back over to you Gabriel."

Gabriel further announces, "I will meet back here Friday at 3:00 P.M. to receive from some of you your applications entitled, 'Messengers from God.' Likewise, please include your essays of a hundred words or less of why you would indeed aspire to serve as a 'Messengers from God.' Likewise, copies of these forms have been placed in the top center drawer of your desk in your abode.

Also, I will suggest that the music leader, Apollo, consider meeting with some of you who may desire to sing in the choir or play an instrument in the orchestra. You possibly could meet back here with him this upcoming Wednesday at 3:00 P.M. Any of you have a question or comment?"

One angel raised his hand and spoke, "My name is Mercury – none faster than I – and I see that I live near Apollo. I would be happy to take Apollo some maps and to advise him of the suggested meeting date and time of those that desire to be in the choir or play an instrument in the orchestra, being this Wednesday at 3:00 P.M. However, Michael, I aspire to be a part of your great communication team as I am very speedy."

Gabriel delivers to Mercury several maps for Apollo and advises, "There are two ways to travel to Apollo's pink abode to transport these. One is the broad and wide way, and the other is the straight and narrow way. You chose the path you take. I suggest you take the straight and narrow route less traveled, having more beautiful and delightful scenery."

Michael and Gabriel watch as Mercury starts running at a chosen speed of six (6) miles per hours calculated to make him arrive at Apollo's in only six (6) minutes and six (6) seconds. Mercury holds the maps rolled in his hand like a relay runner as he turns the corner and first looks at the straight and narrow less traveled road. Upon seeing he would have to get down first on his knees to enter through that narrow gate, he chooses to run on the broad way to the Pink Palace.

Shortly, Mercury was knocking on the door with Apollo coming to the door dressed in tight black leotards and a black opened shirt proudly displaying his black chest hairs.

Apollo, with a forced grin, says, "You must be one of the newly-created angels. Can you sing or play a musical instrument?"

Mercury responds, "I have no idea, but I can carry messages faster than anyone else. None as swift as I. Taking the way that is broad, running at six (6) miles an hour, I covered the six miles (6) from the throne room in six minutes (6) and six (6) seconds. No brag, just plain fact. I also know about scientific things. Gabriel himself selected me out of all the rest to bring you these maps showing the names and the abodes of all the created angels. Also, Gabriel suggested those present, who desire to sing in your choir or orchestra could meet you at the Great Convocation Center this Wednesday at 3:00 P.M."

Apollo thinks, *"That time frame is too short as I need time for politicking. I may have to make it clear to Gabriel he is not to make any schedules for me, the Song Leader of Heaven. He is over his area, and I am over my area. I will do my own scheduling. I want to befriend each angel by making a personal visit. I may have multiple choirs and orchestras and social events. I may need to draw the line in the sand and cancel this meeting Michael scheduled for me Wednesday. Maybe I should cancel, but again maybe I shouldn't or again maybe I should. Why am I double minded? I don't need Gabriel's help!"*

Apollo, coming out of his distracted reasoning asked Mercury, "What does E=MC² mean to you?"

Mercury gloats, "That is a formula for energy, which could be used for producing a powerful weapon of mass destruction such as possibly an I-Bomb (Ice Bomb) if you did it in reverse. I am a scientific genius, and I have an idea or two on how to construct such a bomb. But remember first, 'I am fast!'"

Apollo propositions, "Instead of being a lowly runner, you could be head of my entire communication department. I will outfit you with wings on your helmet and your shoes so everyone will know an important message is arriving from me. Mercury[17] you would be the messenger of the gods in the know as you deliver our top-secret messages. You alone would be in on the important top secrets of Heaven. Tomorrow, Monday, is my planning and scheming day. You could even start Tuesday morning delivering my first important, urgent message to the citizens of Heaven. Also, I have a headquarter on Earth, and you would be head of communications on Earth as well. How does that sound to you?"

Mercury further gloats, "Great, I accept! By by Gabriel! I now work exclusively for Apollo. I am CEO of 'Lightning Communication' even if I may not be able to sing, tap dance, or play the accordion. [Laughter] In this position, I will have the inside scoop on just about everything as I am fast and cunning. I deliver! What time would you desire me to report for duty tomorrow?"

"Be here at 6:06 A.M. on Tuesday morning as I am going to print out a communication for you to start delivering. We will start off walking and circling to our left with you on one side of the street and me on the other. Later I will obtain you a fast horse like my Black Shadow. Maybe we could race down the Broadway. It will be as if your horse has wings on his hoofs, but I doubt if any horse could beat Black Shadow. You had better lose on purpose, as I do not like to be beaten. You are the first on my team.

---

[17] *Webster's New Collegiate Dictionary* defines, *Mercury*, in part as, ". . .the messenger of the gods . . . a bearer of messages or news . . . .."

I will design for you black attire for you to wear Tuesday containing your name with gold wings on each side along with a flat musical note on one side and a sharp musical note on the other side in gold so everyone will know you are truly part of my team. On the map, I see you live near. Until Tuesday morning at 6:06 A.M. then you are dismissed. Bye."

With that, Apollo closes the door and lays out his strategy to visit personally, with utmost political pressure, each angel in the Celestial City and to draft the communique to put Gabriel in his place.

Gabriel and Michael Teaching Angels on Personal Service

Back at the Great Convocation Center, Gabriel and Michael cordially in the utmost love and respect have been fellowshipping with many angels who wanted to meet and talk with them and learn more about the rewarding life of unselfish personal service. Having met briefly with all those who desired to speak, Gabriel communicates, "Lord willing, we will see some of you again this week. Michael, Lord willing, will meet back here Thursday at 3:00 P.M. with those desiring to be part of 'The Army of Heaven' with the Son of God being Commander and Chief. I will be here, Lord willing, Friday at 3:00 P.M. to meet with you who would like to be part of the communication team to deliver messages from Heaven to Earth and throughout Heaven. I stress that both of these positions require utmost trust and confidentiality and with almost little personal recognition, but it will be an opportunity for you to serve faithfully and to know that you unselfishly gave, 'Your Utmost for His Highest.'

Beloved, welcome again to Heaven of which you are a part. Shalom!"

Gabriel and Michael Returning to Watch Over the Son of God

Gabriel and Michael mount their horses and soon arrive back at Mount Moriah. They quietly remove their shoes and return to their respective spots bowing on one knee each watching over the Son of God. The Son of God continues bowing before His Father on both knees, with His face to the ground, praying fervently to His Father. His prayers continued all night until the first break of dawn.

The Son of God smiling looks up with joy overflowing to the Throne Room of Heaven confessing, "I worship and love You Father, My Lord, with all My heart (My Spirit), soul (mind, emotions, will), and strength in My flesh and bone body as the joy of My Lord is My strength (physically and emotionally). Likewise, bless those who love Me as their Savior and confess Me as their Lord, to have My joyful strength (physically and emotionally) and a precious anointing to love their neighbor as they love their own self. A focus on worshipping Me as their Lord, and the joyful strength this provides, is a key secret few will discover. Again, I worship My Father as My Lord, and His joy gives Me strength. All accepting Me, in faith as their Savior, are to worship Me as their Lord! All who worship Me, as their Lord, mercy, deliverance, honor, forgiveness, salvation, favor, goodness, love, and mercy shall follow them. I shall surround them and satisfy them on Earth with long life, and will eternally set them on high! For there is one person of the Father, another of the Son, and another of the Holy Spirit, but the Godhead of the Father, Son, and the Holy Spirit is one God! You are also to worship God, the Holy Spirit, and God, the Father!"†

†BOOK THREE†

†BOOK THREE – Episode 1†

[†**Sidebar Scriptures**: "Joseph had a dream and promptly reported all the details (Genesis 37:5)."
"The Lord revealed to me what the evil ones were doing and planning and showed me their wicked plots (Jeremiah 11:18)."
"The word of the Lord came to Abram in a **vision**. . . . A **deep sleep** came upon Abram . . . . (Genesis 15:1, 12)."
I witnessed and experienced "dreams and visions, and I described **all** I had seen to instruct many (Daniel 7:1, 11:33)."†]

The Creation of Elders and Apollo Making His Plans to Choose Members of His Choir, Orchestra, and Staff

THE SON OF GOD, on Mount Moriah, at the dawning of the day, further looks up to the Throne Room in Heaven after having prayed all night to His Father, further confesses, "Father, I thank You that You always hear Me. I am ready to create the twenty-four Elders, save three to be chosen later."

The Father speaks from Heaven, "You are My beloved Son, in whom I am well pleased. Create the twenty-four elders, less three for another time and place. They will hear and humbly and faithfully serve Us through each subsequent Earth age and throughout eternity."

Word nods a yes back to His Father in Heaven, and cups the dust from the ground of Mount Moriah, as a Potter would make a vessel from the finest dust of the ground mixed with the purest water. Word formed twenty-four Elders, less three, from the dust of Zion's holy ground and breathed into them the breath of life. They became living beings made in the image of God. They manifest in dazzling white apparel, and each had an olive leaf crown on his head. Word introduces Himself,

"Twenty-four elders, less three more to be added later, you have been given a free will to worship God or not to worship God. The eternal God is revealing Himself to you as Father, Son, and Holy Spirit. I am the Son of God and have always been divine. You are to worship Me as God manifest in the flesh. I am before you in a visible flesh and bone body and am the express image of My invisible Father God. There is one person of the invisible Father, another of the Son, and another of the invisible Holy Spirit, whose presence you feel, but the Godhead of the Father, Son, and the Holy Spirit is one God.

Upon hearing the Son of God's teaching, the Elders all bow in worship and love at the feet of the Son of God.

"Elders, I am in a flesh and bone preaching body, but in the fullness of time, I will be God manifested in a flesh, bone, and blood body (Immanuel) like unto you. This is legally required as it will be written,

'I (Word) had to be made like His brothers in every way, so that He might become a merciful and faithful high priest in service to God and that He might make atonement for the sins of the people. Because He suffered in the flesh (as the Son of Man) when He was tempted, He is able to help those who are being tempted (to pass the test of obedience to God).'[1]

My brethren, I will call Myself the 'Son of Man,' as My mother, Mary will give me birth in the flesh and call me Jesus (Savior). I will have skin, bone, and blood. I will humble Myself to die a cruel death on the cross for the sins of all those who receive Me as Savior.

---

[1] Hebrews 2:17-18.

You are My first sheep, and you will hear and obey My voice and serve Me faithfully even to the point of death.

It will later be written,

'Do nothing out of selfish ambition or vain conceit, but in humility consider others better than yourselves. Each of you should look not only to your own interests, but also to the interests of others.

Your attitude should be the same as that of Christ Jesus, Who, being in very nature (being the eternal God, the Son) in the form of God (God, the Father), did not consider equality with God (the Father) something to be grasped, but made Himself nothing, taking the very nature (or the form) of a servant, being made in human likeness. And being found in appearance as a man, He humbled Himself and became obedient to death – even death on a cross! Therefore, God exalted Him to the highest place and gave Him the name above every name, that at the name of Jesus every knee should bow, in Heaven and on Earth and under (in Paradise and ultimately in Hell itself) the Earth, and every tongue confess that Jesus Christ is Lord, to the glory of God the Father.'[2]

Later, My enemy, that old serpent, the devil, will deceive My created woman, Eve, having like you a free will, by presenting her the prospect of being as God, knowing good and evil, if she would just disobey a simple commandment of God not to eat the forbidden fruit. Those who willingly disobey will not be blameless. When God prohibits something, it is for His creatures' own good. You twenty-four, three later to be added, need to set an example of obedience and service.

Many others will choose to disobey and *'enjoy the pleasures of sin for a season.'*[3] They will believe the lies of the devil and follow his pride with all its selfishness, ambitions, and sin. However, those who sincerely believe in Me and receive Me as Savior and confess Me as Lord will become what the Father would have all you, *'called to be saints (God's born again people).'*[4] For whom *'the Son sets free is free indeed'*[5] and will inherit eternal life and all things pure and good. For it will be written, *'When the Son of Man comes in His glory, and all the angels with Him, He will sit on His throne in heavenly glory. All the nations will be gathered before Him, and He will separate the people one from another as a shepherd separates the sheep from the goats. He will put the sheep on His right and the goats on His left.*

Then the King will say to those on His right, 'Come, you who are blessed by My Father; take your inheritance, the kingdom prepared for you since the creation of the world. For I was hungry, and you gave Me something to eat; I was thirsty, and you gave me something to drink; I was a stranger, and you invited Me in; I needed clothes, and you clothed Me; I was sick, and you looked after Me; I was in prison, and you came to visit Me.'

Then the righteous will answer Him, 'Lord, when did we see You hungry and feed You, or thirsty and give You something to drink? When did we see You a stranger and invite You in, or needing clothes and clothe You? When did we see You sick or in prison and go to visit You?'

The King will reply, 'I tell you the truth, whatever you did for one of the least of these brothers of Mine, you did for Me.'

Then He will say to those on His left, 'Depart from Me, you
who are cursed, into the eternal fire prepared for the devil and his angels.
For I was hungry, and you gave Me nothing to eat; I was thirsty, and you
gave Me nothing to drink. I was a stranger, and you did not invite Me in,
I needed clothes, and you did not clothe Me; I was sick and in prison,
and you did not look after Me.'
They also will answer, 'Lord, when did we see You hungry
or thirsty or a stranger or needing clothes or sick or in prison
and did not help You?'
He will reply, 'I tell you the truth, whatever you did not do
for one of the least of these, you did not do for Me.'

---

[2] Philippians 2:3-11 NIV.

[3] Hebrews 11:25.

[4] 1 Corinthians 1:2.

[5] John 8:36.

Then they will go away to eternal punishment, but the
righteous to eternal life.'[6]

Your message at times will be – 'Repent (turn around and flee away from your life of sin) and of your free will choose,

ETERNAL LIFE? OR ETERNAL PUNISHMENT? IT'S YOUR CHOICE! ETERNITY IS AT STAKE!'

It will be written as you go after individual lost sheep,

'What do you think? If a man owns a hundred sheep, and one of them wanders away, will he not leave the ninety-nine on the hills and go looking for the one that wandered off? And if he finds it, I tell you the truth, he is happier about that one sheep than about the ninety-nine that did not wander off. In the same way, your Father in Heaven is not willing that any of these little ones should be lost.'[7]

You will be strategically placed on the Earth in the First Earth Age for good works and to present the "Good News" of salvation to the lost as you instruct them in part,

'Enter through the narrow gate. For wide is the gate and broad is the road that leads to destruction, and many enter through it. But small is the gate and narrow the road that leads to life, and only a few find it. 'Watch out for false prophets. They come to you in sheep's clothing, but inwardly they are ferocious wolves. By their fruit, you will recognize them.'[8]

Twenty-one of you will be here in the land of Zion, and two more of you will be on the Island of Atlantis, and another will be announced after My resurrection. *'Whatever you bind on Earth will be bound in Heaven, and whatever you loose on Earth will be loosed in Heaven.'*[9] None of the elders will die in the First Earth Age. Each of you and your families will be raptured up and then down into Paradise in the First Earth Age before war results in the Earth's surface destruction, to rescue you allowing you to live and die in a later Earth Age. Legally, *'It is appointed unto men once to die, but after this (death on Earth) the judgment.'*[10]

It will be written,

'Then I saw a great white throne. The dead were judged according to what they had done. . . . If anyone's name was not written in the book of life, he (or she) was thrown into the lake of fire.'[11]

'Eye hath not seen, nor ear heard, neither has entered into the heart of man, the things which God has prepared for them that love Him.'[12]

'Here you have no enduring city, but you are looking for the city to come.'[13]

Some of you will face hardships and persecutions, but your labor in the Lord will be eternally joyful and rewarding."

'These trials come so the proven genuineness of your faith – of greater worth than gold, which perishes even though refined by fire – may cause praise, glory, and honor when Jesus Christ is revealed (as Savior and Lord to those who receive Him by faith).'[14]

---

[6] Matthew 25:31-46 NIV.
[7] Matthew 18:12-14 NIV.
[8] Matthew 7:13-16 NIV.
[9] Matthew 16:16.
[10] Hebrews 9:27.
[11] Revelation 20:11-12, 15.
[12] 1 Corinthians 2:9.
[13] Hebrews 13:14.
[14] 1 Peter 1:7.

Your love, humility, faith, obedience, and valor will assist My Father in acquiring a willing, loving, devoted, and obedient family, even a beloved bride for Me, and ultimately destroying the works of Our enemy. You will testify in the eternities of eternities, 'Through it all I have stood upon His Word. It pays to serve the living God and stay in the center of His holy will as you do it God's way. It will be written of some of you and some of your disciples in the Third Earth Age,

'Now faith is being sure of what we hope for and certain of what we do not see. The (faith) is what the ancients (that's you) were commended. By faith . . . the universe was formed at God's (the Son's) command, so what is seen was not made out of what was visible.'[15]

You all have a free will, and I, your Savior, Lord, and the Son of God will never force you to serve. In My foreknowledge, I see that each of you will humbly serve of your free will, and evangelize many into eternal life, as you live the adventure of adventures. It will be recorded from a future vision by my disciple John after My enemy failed at murdering him by placing him into a pot of boiling oil, and then exiling him to the 'island of Patmos because of the word of God and the testimony of Jesus,'[16]

'There before me was a throne in Heaven with someone sitting on it. And the One who sat there had the appearance of jasper and carnelian. A rainbow, resembling an emerald, encircled the throne. Surrounding the throne were twenty-four other thrones, and seated on them were twenty-four elders. They were dressed in white and had crowns of gold on their heads.

. . . Whenever the living creatures give glory, honor and thanks to Him who sits on the throne and who lives forever and ever, the twenty-four elders fall before Him, who sits on the throne, and worship Him who lives forever and ever. They lay their crowns before the throne and say: 'You are worthy, our Lord and God, to receive glory and honor and power, for You created all things, and by Your will they were created and have their being.'[17]

'. . . And the twenty-four Elders, who were seated on their thrones before God, fell on their faces and worshiped God, saying: 'We give thanks to You, Lord God Almighty, the One, who is and who was because You have taken your great power and have begun to reign. The nations were angry, and your wrath has come. The time has come for judging the dead and for rewarding your servants, the prophets, and your saints and those who reverence your name, both small and great – and to destroy those who have corrupted the Earth.'[18] Amen!"

Just as I created you today, having a free will, the first creation of life was Apollyon Lucifer, known and called now for a season, Apollo, who is My song leader in Heaven. When you are old and gray-headed in this First Earth Age, My song leader Apollo will hold a music concert on the Island of Atlantis. You Elders will view same on a large screen, and the Triune God will sit in a special throne box looking down on the preaching platform.

However, that afternoon Apollyon Lucifer will try to destroy and murder the Father, the Son, the Holy Spirit, and those living on the Earth. Apollo has a temporary lease to a place beneath the surface of the Earth he named Hell in Hades. However, there is another chamber in Hades across from Hell, with a great chasm fixed between, engulfed with burning sulfur. That chamber in Paradise is in the form of a cross, which is to initially house those who believe and act on My message that I will die on a cross to pay the penalty for sin for those who believe in Me as Savior, repent, and confess Me as Lord. It will be written about Elder Abraham,

'A (specific) rich man was dressed in purple and fine linen and lived in luxury every day. At his gate was laid a beggar named Lazarus, covered with sores and longing to eat what fell from the rich man's table. Even the dogs came and licked his sores.

---

[15] Hebrews 11:1-2 NIV.
[16] Revelation 1:9 NIV.
[17] Revelation 4:2-4, 8-10 NIV.
[18] Revelation 11:16-18 NIV.

The time came when the beggar died, and the angels carried him to Abraham's side (in Paradise). The rich man also died and was buried. In Hell, where he was in torment, he looked up and saw Abraham far away, with Lazarus by his side. So he called to him, 'Father Abraham, have pity on me and send Lazarus to dip the tip of his finger in water and cool my tongue because I am in agony in this fire.' But Abraham replied, 'Son, remember that in your lifetime you received your good things while Lazarus received bad things, but now he is comforted here, and you are in agony.

And besides all this, between us and you a great chasm has been fixed, so those who want to go from here to you cannot, nor can anyone cross over from there to us.' He answered, 'Then I beg you, father, send Lazarus to My Father's house, for I have five brothers. Let him warn them, so they will not also come to this place of torment.' Abraham replied, 'They have Moses and the Prophets; let them listen to them.' 'No, father Abraham, he said, 'but if someone from the dead goes to them, they will repent.' He said to him, 'If they do not listen to Moses and the Prophets, they will not be convinced even if someone rises from the dead.'[19]

Elders, an atomic second before Apollo's freeze bomb goes off seeking to kill the Godhead and all of you, including those who believe and trust in God in Atlantis, all will be transported into the safe haven of Paradise beneath the Earth. Elder Abraham, for a season you will be the one in charge before We send your spirit back to the surface of the Earth to continue your ministry. Most of you will die in future Earth ages. However, several of you again will be taken from the surface of the Earth before death. It will be written,

'Just as man is destined to die once, and after that to face judgment, so Christ was sacrificed once to take away the sins of many people, and He will appear a second time, not to bear sin, but to bring salvation to those waiting for Him.'[20]

It will be written about Enoch, who did not die as he was raptured up and then back down into Paradise in the Second Earth Age,

'When Enoch had lived sixty-five years, he became the father of Methuselah. And after he became the father of Methuselah, Enoch walked with God three hundred years and had other sons and daughters. So all the days of Enoch were three hundred and sixty-five years. And Enoch walked with God, and he was no more (on the surface of the Earth) because God took him away.'[21]

Elder Elijah, it will be written about you, *'Elijah said to Elisha, 'Tell me, what can I do for you before I am taken from you?' 'Let me inherit a double portion of your spirit,' Elisha replied. 'You have asked a difficult thing,' Elijah said; 'yet if you see me when I am taken from you, it will be yours – otherwise not.'*

As they were walking along and talking together, suddenly a chariot of fire and horses of fire appeared and separated the two, and Elijah went up to Heaven in a whirlwind.'[22]

It will be written about the two of you in a later Earth Age, *'And I will give power to my two witnesses, and they will prophesy for 1,260 days, clothed in sackcloth. These are the two olive trees and the two lampstands that stand before the Lord of the Earth. If anyone tries to harm them, fire comes from their mouths and devours their enemies. This is how anyone who wants to harm them must die. These men have the power to shut up the sky so it will not rain during the time they are prophesying, and they have power to turn the waters into blood and to strike the Earth with every kind of plague as often as they want. Now when they have finished their testimony, the beast that comes up from the Abyss will attack them and overpower and kill them.*

---

[19] Luke 16:19-31 NIV.
[20] Hebrews 9:27-28 NIV.
[21] Genesis 5:21-24 NIV.
[22] 2 Kings 2:9-11 NIV.

Their bodies will lie in the street of the great city, which is figuratively called Sodom and Egypt, where also their Lord was crucified.

For three and a half days men from every people, tribe, language and nation will gaze on their bodies and refuse them burial. The inhabitants of the earth will gloat over them and will celebrate by sending each other gifts because these two prophets had tormented those who live on Earth.

But after the three and a half days, a breath of life from God entered them, and they stood on their feet, and terror struck those who saw them. Then they heard a loud voice from Heaven saying to them, 'Come up here.' And they went up to Heaven in a cloud, while their enemies looked on.'[23]

Elders, greatly beloved, each of you will now be handed a key by My angel, Michael, and that key is to your numbered homes on Elder Circle, Jerusalem. Your home is within walking distance, and you can see the circle of homes just North of here. Your homes look very humble of white stone from the outside, but many treats are inside for you. Your homes will be Elder Circle 1 - 21. They are in a circle to show that no Elder is to be above or beneath another Elder. You have a high stone wall connecting each abode for privacy and protection. Your kitchens are stocked with vegetables and fruit. You each have fruit trees and vegetables growing for each of you behind your portion of the stone wall.

Each of you will soon receive a warm, loving wife to help you populate Zion. Three other Elders will be added later. Paul returning to Earth in the Third Earth Age will not marry, but will be given the gift of singleness[24] because of the intense persecution he is ordained to receive in the Third Earth Age.

The identity of the twenty-fourth Elder will be kept secret and revealed after I have resurrected from the dead. It is so necessary for us to do everything legally as My invisible Father is a God of legality and love. He will do nothing illegal. He laughs when I say, "All is fair in love and war! Well, I don't know about war!" [Laughter] My prayer for us ALL is for true romantic love that will eternally grow for the glory of the Father, who invented holy and faithful marriage, between one man and one woman. It is not good for a flesh and bone man to be alone. Love forever true is rare, but it is not impossible to laugh, hug, kiss and have your virgin bride by your side every day throughout eternity. The joy of My Lord, Father God, is My strength and the joy of your Lord, the Son of God, will be your strength.

'This is the work of God (the Father): to believe in the One (Son of God made flesh) He has sent – that you cleave to, trust, rely on, and have faith in His Messenger (the Son, your Savior and Lord).'[25]

I am appointing and gifting in jurisprudence, Elder Paul, to be the attorney for Zion, and, Elder Job, to be the attorney in Loveland on the Island of Atlantis.

I will preach in the role of an invited evangelist, known only by one of My favorite names Melchizedek[26] (meaning King of Jerusalem) for the inhabitants of Atlantis, with many repenting and receiving salvation, and being relocated to Paradise to be with you.

---

[23] Revelation 11:3-12 NIV.

[24] Paul will write in the Third Earth Age under severe persecution of the saints, "*I wish that everyone were like me [having a gift of singleness so as not to marry] . . . . Now for those who are not married and for the widows I say this: It is good for them to stay unmarried as I am. But if they cannot exercise self-control (to remain sexually pure), they should marry. It is better to marry than to burn with sexual desire.*' (1 Corinthians 7:7-8.)

[25] John 6:29.

Now, it will be a delightful walk, but a little dusty, to your abodes and back again here in the morning. Take the straight-and-narrow way home. Remember that all of you have a free will to love God and rejoice in Him. I pronounce this truth for all of you to meditate, '*If anyone (really) loves Me (Jesus, Son of God), they will obey My teaching.*

My Father will love them, and We will come to them and make our home with them. Those who do not love Me will not obey My teaching. These words you hear are not My own; they are front the Father, who sent Me.'[27]

Please meet Me back tomorrow at 10:00 A.M. on Mount Zion as I have a secret surprise for each of you. Shalom and Good evening!

The Conspiracy of Apollo and Mercury to Pressure Angels to Join Apollo's Choir and Orchestra

At 6:06 A.M. Mercury knocks on the door of the pink palace with Apollo opening and handing him an expandable, black folder with announcements in pink lettering and musical notes on Black Paper reading,

*Needed: Gifted Singers and Musicians
for the Heavenly Choir and Orchestra!
Auditions for Choir this Thursday at 3:00 P.M.!
Auditions for Orchestra this Friday at 3:00 P.M.!
WHERE: Apollo's Pink Palace Choir and Music Room.
(See map below.)
Refreshments will be served, and designer shirts will be given out!
NOTE: The Wednesday Meeting for 3:00 P.M. at
the Great Convocation Center has been cancelled.*

Mercury praises Apollo, "Perfect. You did not miss a trick. Now we will have the first bite at the apple. How can we deliver this communication to thousands of angel homes in three days?"

Apollo schemes, "Simple! Remember the word KISS (Keep it simple, stupid) and let us kiss them on the cheek if necessary, gross. We will have them eating out of our hands, and then we will have them 'hook, line, and sinker' and 'lock, stock, and barrel,' whatever that means. Let me do the talking and win them over to my side. I will make the singing and the playing of musical instruments so glamorous and attractive. I will flatter them. The big 'I' and personal honor should win them over. We will solicit as we are exiting from those we manage to make a personal recruiting visit, 'How would you like to be our mouth and hands and give out some of these announcements?' We have a special gift for those who can recruit even six (6) for our team.'

The delegation of work is a means to use as we are only two among so many angels. Understand?" Mercury nods, '*yes*.'

Apollo further orders, "Also, as you exit your politicking inquire, 'What do you feel is your gift?'

Make a note of each angel's name, address, and gifting, especially a scientific gift, like the one you have, as I can later use some of these endowments.

---

[26] "See Genesis 14:18 "*Melchizedek king of Salem,*" identified with Jerusalem or Zion on the basis of Psalm 76:2, "*His tent is in Salem, his dwelling place in Zion.*"

[27] John 14:23.

Here is a black journal address-recording notebook, as you will deliver messages back to those joining our camp such as, 'Apollo needs to see you!'

Flash, I mean Mercury, time is a wasting. Now let us go immediately into the Celestial City to do massive solicitation. Let us lasso them in a ring of political fire. They may later see a personal benefit of electing me Mayor of the Celestial City. Then I will be politically in charge of this entire city. Let us go with a flash!"

The Next Day Meeting of Elders on Mount Moriah

After having walked up the beautiful dusty road back to Mount Moriah, the twenty-one Elders take off their sandals at the door. They enter quietly the Prayer Meeting Room on Mount Moriah, which now contains twenty-one chairs in a circle.

As they experience the presence of God, Word appears in their midst, and they bow at His feet. The Son of God, holding a towel and a basin for water, welcomes,

"Beloved Elders, I receive your worship and be seated and put your bare feet out in front of you. The lesson today is that the greatest among you will be the servant of all.

Please be seated in the numbered chair that corresponds to your house number and open your note-taking journal to page one."

The Son of God removes His outer garment and with a white towel around His waist maneuvering over a basin of warm water placing the first Elder's feet in the basin. He then washes each Elder's feet carefully with a washcloth and white soap and carefully dries them with a fresh white towel for each, leaving the towel under the clean drying feet and announces,

"'*You are clean.*'[28] As you have seen Me serve, you will also be used to serve others. My friends, the secret of secrets of those living in flesh and blood bodies, is '*the joy of your Lord is your strength.*'[29] It is commanded,

'*Love the Lord your God with all your heart and with all your soul and with all your strength and mind,*' and '*Love your neighbor as yourself.*'[30]

Love your God first, your neighbor as yourself, shun hideous pride, die daily to self and sin, and often bow down and worship God, and sincerely repent from the heart saying, '*God, have mercy on me, a sinner.*'[31] Elder John, you will write, "If *we confess our sins, God is faithful and just and will forgive our sins and purify us from all unrighteousness. If anyone claims they have not sinned, they make God out to be a liar and God's word has no place in their lives.*'[32]

Let Me now open your eyes to the Celestial world and introduce My companions, whom you usually cannot see in this terrestrial realm unless they reveal themselves to you. To My right is Angel Gabriel, who will bring you important messages from time to time On My left, is Angel Michael, who is in charge of the defense of Heaven and the saints on Earth. Both will have under them other mighty angels who will communicate, deliver, protect, and guard you.

Elder Peter, it will one day be written about you when King Herod was planning to sentence you to death after a mock trial,

---

[28] John 13:10.
[29] Nehemiah 8:10.
[30] Luke 10:27.
[31] Luke 18:13.
[32] 1 John 1:9-10.

'So Peter was kept in prison, but the church was earnestly praying to God for him. The night before Herod was to bring him to trial, Peter was sleeping between two soldiers, bound with two chains, and sentries stood guard at the entrance. Suddenly an angel of the Lord appeared, and a light shone in the cell. He struck Peter on the side and woke him up. 'Quick, get up,' he said, and the chains fell off Peter's wrists. Then the angel said to him, 'Put on your clothes and sandals.' And Peter did so. 'Wrap your cloak around you and follow me,' the angel told him. Peter followed him out of the prison, but he did not understand that what the angel was doing was really happening; he thought he was seeing a vision. They passed the first and second guards and came to the iron gate leading to the city. It opened for them by itself, and they went through it. When they had walked the length of one street, suddenly the angel left him. Then Peter said, 'Now I know without a doubt that the Lord sent his angel and rescued me from Herod's clutches and from everything the Jewish people were anticipating.'[33]

Likewise, Elder Paul, it will one day be written about you when you were in a violent (fierce) storm at sea,

'When neither sun nor stars appeared for many days, and the storm continued raging, we finally gave up all hope of being saved. After the men had gone a long time without food, Paul stood up before them and said: 'Men, you should have taken my advice not to sail from Crete; then you would have spared yourselves this damage and loss. But now I urge you to keep up your courage because not one of you will be lost; only the ship will be destroyed. Last night an angel of the God whose I am (was assigned to watch over Paul) and whom I serve stood beside me and said, 'Do not be afraid, Paul. You must stand trial before Caesar, and God has graciously given you the lives of all who sail with you.' So keep up your courage, men, for I have faith in God it will happen just as He told me. We must run aground on some island.'[34]

It will be written about each of you, and all who love and serve Me faithfully, "You who dwell in the secret (not many know it) place of the most High shall abide under the shadow (protection) of the Almighty.

You will say of the Lord, He is my refuge, and my fortress: my God; in Him will I trust.

Surely He shall deliver me from the snare of the fowler and from the noisome pestilence.

He shall cover me with His feathers, and under His wings shall I trust; His truth shall be my shield and buckler.

You will not fear the terror of night, nor the arrow that flies by day nor the pestilence that stalks in the darkness nor the plague that destroys at midday.

Nor for the pestilence that walks in darkness, nor for the destruction that wasteth at noonday.

A thousand may fall at your side, ten thousand at your right hand, but it will not come near you.

You will only observe with your eyes and see the punishment of the wicked.

Because you make the Most High your dwelling – even the Lord, who is your refuge – then no harm will befall you, no disaster will come near your dwelling (home).

For He will command His angels concerning you to guard you in all your ways.

They will lift you up in their hands so you will not strike your foot against a stone.

You will tread upon the lion and the cobra; the young lion and the dragon shalt thou trample under feet;

Because you have set your love upon Me, therefore, will I deliver you: I will set you on high because you hath known My name.

You shall call upon Me, and I will answer you: I will be with you in trouble; I will deliver you And honor you.

With long life will I satisfy you, and show you My salvation.'[35]

'The eternal God is your refuge, and underneath are the everlasting arms'[36]

Questions? [Silence]†

---

[33] Acts 12:6-11 NIV.
[34] Acts 27:20-26 NIV.
[35] Psalm 91:1-16.
[36] Deuteronomy 33:27.

112

†BOOK THREE – Episode 2†

[†**Sidebar Scriptures**: "Joseph had a dream and promptly reported all the details (Genesis 37:5)."
"The Lord revealed to me what the evil ones were doing and planning and showed me their wicked plots (Jeremiah 11:18)."
"The word of the Lord came to Abram in a **vision**. . . . A **deep sleep** came upon Abram . . . . (Genesis 15:1, 12)."
I witnessed and experienced "dreams and visions, and I described **all** I had seen to instruct many (Daniel 7:1, 11:33)."†]

The Creation of the Brides for the Elders

ON A BEAUTIFUL BANK of the Jordan River, birds, bees, flowers, and gentle small animals all celebrating the mating time surround the Elders. Each Elder feels somewhat trapped in a body having healthy sexual desires with no holy or natural means of relief, being strengthened by the Lord Jesus to remain pure until marriage as none was given the gift of singleness.

The Creator, Word, Jesus, appears dressed in a white robe barefoot in the midst of the Elders with each falling prostrate worshiping and loving Him with all their being and strength. Word instructs the Elders, "Besides worshipping Me, as God the Son, the Savior and Creator, you are also to worship God, the Holy Spirit, and God, the Father, Who gave His Son as the Lamb of God before the foundation of the world to shed His life's blood to pay the penalty due for the sins of all who receive the Son as Savior, repent, and confess the Son as their Lord. As you worship the Son as your Lord, then the joy of your Lord will be your strength.

For there is one person of the Father, another of the Son, and another of the Holy Spirit, but the Godhead of the Father, Son, and the Holy Spirit is one God! Now, "Rise to your knees and lift your hands toward Heaven and also worship God the Holy Spirit, and Father God as it is to be written,

'*Yet a time is coming and has now come when the true worshipers will worship the Father in spirit and truth, for they are the kind of worshipers the Father seeks. God is spirit (invisible), and His worshipers must worship in spirit and truth.*'[1]

Brethren, God's enemies also desire worship. It will be written,

'*Men worshiped the dragon (devil) because he had given authority to the beast, and they also worshiped the beast and asked, 'Who is like the beast? Who can make war against him?'*

The beast opened his mouth to blaspheme God and to slander His name and His dwelling place and those who live in Heaven. He was given power to make war against the saints (on the Earth) . . . . All inhabitants of the Earth (not raptured up to Heaven) will worship the beast – all whose names have not been written in the book of life belonging to the Lamb (Jesus, Son of God,) slain from the creation of the world.'[2]

Word proceeds to lay His hands of blessings firmly on each side of each elder's head, proving to each that He also is flesh and bone. Word in pronouncing individual blessings also cites the Scriptures as He moves from one elder to another,

'*The Son of Man (God in the flesh like His brethren) must be delivered into the hands of sinful men, be crucified and the third day (after His death) be raised again.*

Look at my hands and My feet (nail holes and scars from the crucifixion nails). It is I Myself. Touch Me and see a spirit does not have flesh and bones, as you see I have.'[3]

'*The Lord God said, 'It is not good for the man (flesh and bone) to be alone. I will make a helper (wife also of flesh and bone) suitable for him.*'[4]

Stand up Elders as I desire to give each one of you a manly hug with my flesh and bone body. We are brethren, and will be friends throughout eternity.

---

[1] John 4:23-24.
[2] Revelation 13:4-8.
[3] Luke 24:7, 39.
[4] Genesis 2:18.

Let me explain, in part,

Back in eternity, I was once an invisible Spirit. There was one Spirit person of the Father, another Spirit person of the Holy Spirit, and another Spirit person of Me, the Son, but the Godhead of the Father, Son, and the Holy Spirit was, and always will be, one God. We each have different thoughts and personalities, or one of Us would not be needed. I never once thought of the words *romance, marriage,* and the *union* of husband and wife. My Father in a place called 'Nothing' out of the blue declared, 'It will be written one day,

'*Romance – A fabulous relation or story of adventures and incidents, designed for the enter-tainment of readers; a tale of extraordinary adventures. . . And often extravagant, interesting the sensibilities of the heart or the passions of wonders and curiosity. . . . It treats of great actions and extraordinary adventures. It vaults or soars beyond the limits of fact and real life and often of probability. The first romances (written by men and women on the Earth) were a monstrous (impressive) assemblage of histories, in which truth and fiction were blended without probability; a composition of amorous adventures and the extravagant ideas of chivalry.*'[5]

My Father, laughing, expressed, "While Romance will start on Earth with the Elders and their romantic, faithful wives, Your day, My Son, will also come with Your romance being the most chivalry of all romances."

Therefore, Elders, yours are to be the first romances – to be beautiful and exciting. It will be written,

'*Live happily with the woman you love through the fleeting days of life (on the Earth), for the wife God gives you is your best reward down here for all your earthly toil. Whatsoever thy hand findeth to do (includes romancing your wife), do your best (with joyful strength).*'[6]

Elders, you are blessed, and all dearly loved. I have the best reward for each of you – a warm, loving wife created especially for you. I made you from the dust of the Earth, but she will be removed out of you. I desire each of you now to give Me a rib from your side close to your heart with the blood and flesh around it. If you consent, please raise your right hand."

Twenty-one right hands were raised.

Now take hold of the lever on the left of your seat, pull it up, and push back and you will lay back as you are falling into a deep sleep. While you are sleeping, I will take one of your ribs and the blood and flesh around it and have a blessing for you when you awake."

While they were sleeping, Word took one of the ribs from each of the twenty-one elders' side and closed the bleeding incision with flesh. From each rib, flesh, and blood, Word fashioned a woman as a helper suitable for the prior owner of the rib. Each fashioned woman was dressed in a modest white linen wedding gown with baby's breath in her hair and a veil over her face. Each wife was holding a bouquet of no thorn, red roses with baby's breath in her right hand.

As the men were awakened and recovering from the surgery, Word instructs, "Now push down the lever and sit up. You have lost blood, for this is a blood covenant, and you may be a little weak as you were originally made from the dust of Canaan Land.

Now arise and gently lift up her modest veil placing it behind her long hair and look her in the eyes and give her a smile of acceptance, and say,

'*This is now bone of my bones
    and flesh of my flesh;
she shall be called woman,
    for she was taken out of man.*'[7]

---

[5] "Romance" as defined in part in *American Dictionary of the English Language* by Noah Webster 1828.
[6] Ecclesiastes 9:9-10.

114

Now look what I sculptured for you from your rib. She is lovely, adorable, and beautiful! A perfect fit in every way. The chemistry between you two will be just right for there is nothing as useless as a cold woman. [Laughter] She was made for you. You were not made for her, as it will be written,

'A man ought not to cover his head, since he is the image and glory of God, but the woman is the glory of man. For man came not from woman, but the woman for man; neither was man created for women, but woman for man.'[8]

Now grasp her left hand and hold it as you would never let go. Good, now turn and face Me, for she will stand by her man and walk by your side – not walking before you are behind. Each man was caressing the feminine, soft, and affectionate left hand he held tightly in his right hand.

I have one question for you, "Does anybody want his rib back? Speak now or forever hold your peace!"

Romance, laughter, and joy filled the room as each man further tightened his grip as he held onto the lovely soft hand of his soon to be bride.

Word spoke, "Abraham, is not Sarah beautiful? Her eyes are large and healthfully bright like *'the blue. Pools of Heshbon, by the gate of Bath Rabbim'* and her slightly humped *'nose, is like the tower of Lebanon looking toward Damascus '*[9]

All Abraham could do was to gaze at Sarah, swallow hard, and nod as tears of joy filled his eyes, thinking, "*I love her so much already it hurts. How could I be so loved by my Creator as to be given such a priceless and beautiful gift?*"

The Son of God, smiling, speaks, "Daughters of Zion, let me introduce Myself to you. I am Word, the Son of God, and I have always been Divine. I am the express image of the invisible Father God. The eternal God consists of the Father, Son, and the Holy Spirit. You are to love the one Triune God with all your heart, mind, soul, and strength. There is one person of the Father, another of the Son, and another of the Holy Spirit, but the Godhead of the Father, Son, and the Holy Spirit is one God. This is the beginning of this First Earth Age for you, but I want you to know that I have always been the Word of God from eternity, and it will be written,

'In the beginning was the Word, and the Word was with God, and the Word was God. He was with God in the beginning. Through Him, all things were made; without Him, nothing was made that has been made. In Him was life, and that life was the light of men. The light shines in the darkness, but the darkness has not understood it.'[10]

As a further foundation, it will be written, *'There came a man sent from God; his name was John. He came as a witness to testify concerning that light, so through Him, all men might believe. He was not the light; he came only as a witness to the light. The true light that gives light to every man was coming into the world. He was in the world, and though the world was made through Him, the world did not recognize Him. He came to that which was His own, but His own did not receive Him. Yet to all who received Him, to those who believed in His name, He gave the right to become children of God – children born not of natural descent, nor of human decision or a husband's will, but born of God.*

The Word became flesh and made His dwelling among us. We have seen His glory, the glory of the one and only Son, who came from the Father, full of grace and truth.'[11]

John the Baptist further testified regarding the Word being in the flesh,

'This was He of whom I said, 'He who comes after me has surpassed me because He was before me.' From the fullness of His grace, we have all received one blessing after another. For the law was given through Moses; grace and truth came through Jesus Christ. No one has ever seen God, but God the Son, who is at the Father's side, has made Him known.'[12]

---

[7] Genesis 2:2 NIV.
[8] 1 Corinthians 11:7-8
[9] Song of Solomon 7:4.
[10] John 1:1-3.
[11] John 1:6-14.
[12] John 1:15-18.

'Let Me further teach. Abraham – your name means 'father of many nations;' and, Sarah your name means 'princess.' You two will have twenty-three children in this first earth age, and neither of you will die in this First Earth Age. Also, you will remember nothing except an occasional shadow about this First Earth Age. However, Sarah will again be your beloved bride in Third Earth Age where she will give you a son named Isaac, which means 'laughter.' Oh, the joy of serving the living and giving God!

Daughters of the Most High God, I will be born in this world in the Third Earth Age of a pure virgin, just as you are all pure virgins today. I will be crucified on a cross for the sins of all who will receive Me as their Savior, repent of their sins, and confess Me as Lord. On the third day after I have died on the cross, it will be written,

'*After the Sabbath, at dawn on the first day of the week, Mary Magdalene and the other Mary went to look at the tomb. There was a violent earthquake, for an angel of the Lord came down from heaven and, going to the tomb, rolled back the stone and sat on it. His appearance was like lightning, and his clothes were as white as snow. The guards were so afraid of him, they shook and became like dead men. The angel said to the women, 'Do not be afraid, for you are looking for Jesus, who was crucified. He is not here; He has risen, just as He said. Come and see the place where He lay. Then go quickly and tell His disciples: `He has risen from the dead and is going ahead of you into Galilee. There you will see Him.' Now I have told you.' So the women hurried away from the tomb, afraid yet filled with joy, and ran to tell his disciples. Suddenly Jesus met them. 'Greetings,' he said. They came to Him, clasped His feet, and worshiped him. Then Jesus said to them, 'Do not be afraid. Go and tell my brothers to go to Galilee; there they will see Me.'*

While the women were on their way, some of the guards went into the city and reported to the chief priests everything that had happened. When the chief priests had met with the elders and devised a plan, they gave the soldiers a large sum of money, telling them, 'You are to say, 'His disciples came during the night and stole him away while we were asleep.' If this report gets to the governor, we will satisfy him and keep you out of trouble.' So the soldiers took the money and did as they were instructed. And this story has been widely circulated among the Jews to this very day.

Then the eleven disciples went to Galilee, to the mountain where Jesus had told them to go. When they saw Him, they worshiped Him, but some doubted. Then Jesus said, 'All authority in Heaven and on Earth has been given to Me. Therefore, go and make disciples of all nations, baptizing them in the name of the Father and of the Son and of the Holy Spirit, and teaching them to obey everything I have commanded you. And surely I am with you always, to the very end of the age.'[13]

Elder Peter, it will be written of you regarding your testimony and sermon about Me as you will preach,

'*God has raised this Jesus to life, and we are all witnesses of the fact. Exalted to the right hand of God, He has received from the Father the promised Holy Spirit and has poured out what you now see and hear. For David did not ascend to Heaven, and yet he said, 'The Lord said to my Lord: 'Sit at my right hand until I make your enemies a footstool for your feet.'*[14] *Therefore, let all Israel be assured of this: God has made this Jesus, whom you crucified, both Lord and Christ.*'[15]

'*When the people heard this, they were cut to the heart and said to Peter and the other apostles, 'Brothers, what shall we do?' Peter replied, "Repent and be baptized, every one of you, in the name of Jesus Christ for the forgiveness of your sins. And you will receive the gift of the Holy Spirit. The promise is for you and your children and for all who are far off — for all whom the Lord our God will call.' With many other words, he warned them, and he pleaded with them, 'Save yourselves from this corrupt generation.' Those who accepted his message were baptized, and about three thousand were added to their number that day. They devoted themselves to the apostles' teaching and to the fellowship, to the breaking of bread and to prayer. Everyone was filled with awe, and many wonders and miraculous signs were done by the apostles.*

---

[13] Matthew 28:1-20 NIV.
[14] Psalm 110:1 NIV.
[15] Acts 2:37.

. . . They broke bread in their homes and ate together with glad and sincere hearts. And the Lord added to their number daily those being saved.'[16]

Word spoke to Peter, "Step forth and preach this Good News first to yourself and to all flesh and blood present this day."

Peter stepping forth addresses the congregation,

All confess this after me,

Father God in Heaven,

I come to You in the name of Your Son, Jesus.

I believe with all my heart that Jesus will die to pay the penalty for my sins on a cross.

After He has died for my sins, Father God will raise Him from the dead

I receive Jesus into my heart as my Savior, and I confess, 'Jesus is my Savior and Lord!'

He will never leave me nor forsake me.

From this moment forward, I belong to Jesus and will follow Him forever and forever.

I will not be ashamed of Jesus, and I will confess Him before men.

Thank You, Jesus, for being my Savior and for saving me.

Jesus, You are Lord and Master over all aspects of my life.

I will obey You.

Jesus, take all of me!

Thank You, Heavenly Father, for giving Your Son for me that I might have life and have it more abundantly. I am saved! I am continually washed clean in Your Son's blood.

'Whom the Son sets free, that man is free indeed.'[17]

I am part of the family of God!

In the name of my Savior and Lord, Jesus. Amen!'

Everyone is smiling, filled with love, delight, and joy, with Jesus saying, "O Happy Day!" And with that, the Son of God breathed on them saying,

'Receive the Holy Spirit (to join with your human spirit). If you forgive anyone his sins, they are forgiven; if you do not forgive them, they are not forgiven.'[18]

You are my brothers and my sisters. Welcome as the first fruit into the family God."

A voice from Heaven, sounding like thunder, spoke,

AMEN! *'THIS IS MY BELOVED SON (JESUS) IN WHOM I AM WELL PLEASED!'*[19] ALWAYS HEAR AND OBEY HIM! I WELCOME YOU INTO OUR FAMILY! THE JOURNEY IS GOING TO BE A JOYOUS AND EXCITING ONE! NO WEAPON EVER FORMED AGAINST YOU WILL PROSPER! SHALOM! "

Peter returns to his place to hold the hand of the woman he loves.

Jesus instructs, "Each of you men drop down on your left knee only. You are never to worship a woman, but sincerely ask her in your own words, Will you marry me?"

Each woman with a smile of joy on her face responds "Yes, I will marry you!"

The men arose and with the women turn toward the Son.

The Son of God, then took bread, and when He had given His Father God thanks, He broke it and gave a piece of the broken bread to each of the men and women standing before Him saying,

'This is My body, which is (to be broken) for you; do this in remembrance of Me.'[20]

---

[16] Acts 2:36-43, 46 NIV.

[17] John 8:36.

[18] John 20:22 NIV.

[19] See Matthew 3:17.

[20] 1 Corinthians 11:24 NIV.

As the Lamb of God, I will suffer, receiving stripes on my back for your healing, and will die by being nailed to a wooden cross in a future third earth age. My death on a cross legally pays the penalty for the sins for all those who receive Me as Savior.'

Each took a piece of the broken bread. The Son of God spoke,

'*Take and eat, this represents My body to be broken for you.*' After each had eaten the broken bread, the Son of God took a cup of non-alcoholic wine saying,

'*This cup is the new covenant in My blood, do this, whenever you drink it, in remembrance of Me.*'[21] My life's blood will be shed for the forgiveness of your sins in a third earth age. Now drink from it, all of you."

As often as you partake, do this in remembrance of Me. I desire you each morning upon awakening as your first act of worship to partake of this communion bread and cup and to repeat the same each evening before enjoying sweet sleep. For you will overcome all temptation and any pressing besetting sins by applying My blood over the situation, for it will be written,

'*I overcome by the blood of the Lamb and by the word of my testimony.*'[22]

'*Because of sexual (impure) temptations, each man should have sexual relations with his own wife, and each woman should have sexual relations with her own husband. . . . Do not refuse sex to each other (in marriage), unless you both agree to stay away from sexual relations for a time so you can devote yourselves to prayer. Then resume your sexual relationship so Satan cannot tempt you because of a lack of self-control.*'[23]

"Ladies and future brides of these twenty-one elders, these protecting angels will escort you to the white bridal chamber to be fitted with your wedding dresses as you 'make yourselves ready'[24] for the marriage where you all will abide until your wedding day. You will have fun getting to know each other.

Sons and daughters of the Most High God, look each other in the eyes, and say, 'I'm saving my first kiss for our wedding day! [Laughter]

Elders watch and wave at your wives as they are walking right over that rise out of sight to the Bridal Chambers!✝

---

[21] 1 Corinthians 11:25 NIV.

[22] Revelation 12:11 NIV.

[23] 1 Corinthians 7:2-5.

[24] "*Let us rejoice and be glad and give Him (God) glory! For the wedding of the Lamb [Son of God, Jesus] has come (to Earth in the flesh), and His bride has made herself ready.*" (Revelation 19:7).

[†**Sidebar Scriptures**: "Joseph had a dream and promptly reported all the details (Genesis 37:5)."
"The Lord revealed to me what the evil ones were doing and planning and showed me their wicked plots (Jeremiah 11:18)."
"The word of the Lord came to Abram in a **vision**. . . . A **deep sleep** came upon Abram . . . . (Genesis 15:1, 12)."
I witnessed and experienced "dreams and visions, and I described **all** I had seen to instruct many (Daniel 7:1, 11:33)."†]

Apollo Politicking in Heaven and the Elders on Earth Being Taught About Walking in God's Love

TUESDAY MORNING THE ELDERS, leaving their sandals at the door assemble outside the meeting hall on Mount Moriah preparing to be seated in the numbered chairs with names arranged in a circle. Elder John announces, "This morning it is my high privilege to wash everyone's dusty feet."

John had already washed his feet and had each Elder sit on a long bench. Moving down the line, John places their feet in heated water from the River Jordan in a white with a star of David wash pan. He washes them with the finest white soap floating on top of the water, dries them with white towels, and invites them to take their respective place in the circle of chairs so no Elder would appear to be above any other elder.

Apollo Meeting With Inhabitants of the Celestial City

Back in the Celestial City Apollo and Mercury Speedo, which Apollo called M. S., knocks six times on the first angel's front door. The door opens, and an angel appears and steps outside with the conversation commencing,

"I am Apollo, the first creation of life in the Celestial City, and I am the song leader of Heaven. Beside me is my assistant, M. S. We see your name and address on the map, and I wanted to introduce myself and hand you an announcement about recruiting you for either my choir or my orchestra. What kind of angel are you?"

"I am a Guardian Angel."

"Guardian Angel, who do you guard?"

"I assume my future duties would be by my assignments from the Throne Room. Praise Him forever, who sits upon the Throne!"

"You certainly can praise by either singing in our choir or playing a musical instrument. I would give you a lot of personal freedom, keeping you in the know. I would be proud to have you be a part of my team, and you would, in turn, be proud to be such an important part of such an illustrious group. Also, with your lungs, you might consider playing a horn. Another alternative, with those mighty hands of yours, I could appoint you as a lead cymbal player, a prominent position as the cymbals have to clash at just the right moment. Of course, you would receive some neat outfits like those M. S. is wearing today, letting everyone know you are part of our elite music, team – 'all for one, one for all.'[1] At times, all eyes are on the cymbal player, and this would be a highly honored position.

The angel responds, "Chief Cymbal Player. Wow! "I will certainly acknowledge the Lord first in all my ways, and He will direct my paths."[2]

---

[1] See "*The Three Musketeers*" at *Wikipedia The Free Encyclopedia*.
[2] See Proverbs 3:5-6.

M. S. in passing inquiries, "Besides music do you feel you have any special gifts?

"I feel I have a gift of guarding and protecting. Also, maybe some scientific gifting for witty inventions."

M. S. responds, "I may desire to get back with you on your scientific gifting. We have many houses to visit. Bye!"

The mighty angel turns and goes back into his abode. M. S. turns to Apollo and inquires, "How did I do?"

"You got out of him his scientific gifts. Valuable future information and those indicating 'scientific gifting' probe a little deeper. I see a group of six angels walking toward us on the other side of the red brick street. Give them a stack of the communication announcements and ask them to read them and pass them out and to consider singing in our choir or playing an instrument in our orchestra. By the way, you forgot to hand that last angel the communication announcement or to ask him to pass some out, but he is bound to see one as we will be scattering them everywhere."

M. S. runs to the six angels walking on the other side of the brick street (presently no golden streets in Heaven). He hands them the announcement brochures saying, "I am M. S. and across the street dressed in black is Apollo, the song leader of Heaven. We would like to honor you by inviting you to be part of our team."

M. S. runs up the street and catches up with Apollo's backside as he walks toward the next prospect's house. Apollo turns and says, "You're the best. Remember to give this angel some announcement brochures and ask him to give them out. You are learning my ways."

Word and Elders Meeting

As Peter was finishing washing and drying the last foot of John, the Word of God enters the room with all the twenty-one Elders falling prostrate in praise and worship.

The Word of God declares, "'*You are (all) clean,*'³ both spiritually and physically! '*You have received the Holy Spirit, and He lives within you. So just as He has taught you, abide in Him.*'⁴

Tomorrow will be David's turn to come early and to wash your feet. Be patient, beloved, for all your turn will come to wash each other's feet. [Laughter] I will at times wash your feet Myself as an example of one who serves.⁵

Beloved Elders, for your information our future mutual prideful enemy is interviewing, even as I speak, angels in Heaven seeking to attract them over into his camp. His underlying message being that they can gain personal independence and benefits from him apart from obeying God's commandments to live a humble and unselfish life putting others first.

One-third of the angels will eventually join him as he and his scientists seek to murder the Father, the Son, the Holy Spirit, and each of you. The ice explosion, he will set off will turn this Earth into an empty waste frozen land 'without form and void'⁶ of life. You will be transferred beneath the surface of the Earth where you will live in Paradise separated by a great gulf where the devil and his fallen angels and demons will live in a place called Hell.

---

³ See John 13:10.
⁴ See 1 John 2:27.
⁵ See John 13:1-17.
⁶ See Genesis 1:2.

Elder John Appointed Minister of Love

Today, I am appointing the Beloved Elder John, who has just washed your feet as our 'Minister of Love.' My Father is love, but He knows how to defend Himself when an act of war is declared against Love. At the end, all the enemies of God will be defeated and thrown into the Lake of Fire to be no more. It will then be '*Love and Peace*.' Until then it will be '*Love & War*.' War often comes before peace.

Agape Love Partially Defined

Remember that love – the *summum bonum*[7] – is the strongest power in the universe and never fails!' Elder John now read a portion of Scripture about the supreme good of walking in love."

Elder John picks up a scroll, and when he found the place, he reads with emphasis,

'*If I speak in the tongues of men and angels, but have not love, I am only a resounding gong or a clanging cymbal.*

If I have the gift of prophecy and can fathom all mysteries and all knowledge, and if I have faith that can move mountains, but have not love, I am nothing.

If I give all I possess to the poor and surrender my body to the flames, but have not love, I gain nothing

Love is patient; love is kind. It does not envy; it does not boast; it is not proud.

It is not rude; it is not self-seeking, it is not easily angered; it keeps no record of wrongs.

Love does not delight in evil but rejoices with the truth.

It always protects, always trusts, always hopes, and always perseveres.

Love never fails! *But where there are prophecies, they will cease; where there are tongues, they will be stilled; where there is knowledge, it will pass away.*

For we know in part, and we prophesy in part, but when perfection comes, the imperfect disappears.

When I was a child, I talked like a child, I thought like a child, I reasoned like a child. When I became a man, I put childish ways behind me.

Now we see, but a poor reflection as in a mirror; then we shall see face to face. Now I know in part; then I shall know fully, even as I am fully known.

And now these three remain – faith, hope and love. But the greatest of these is love.'[8]

"Thank you, Beloved John, and I ordain you this day as the Elder of Love. You will have the honors of writing about the ending of the third earth age in part reading,

'*Let him who does wrong continue to do wrong; let him who does right continue to do right, and let him who is holy continue to be holy.*

Behold, I [Jesus] am coming soon! My reward is with Me, and I will give to everyone according to what he has done. I am the Alpha and the Omega, the First and the Last, the Beginning and the End.

Blessed are those who wash their robes (keep themselves clean and holy) that they may have the right to eat the fruit from the tree of life and may go through the gate into the city. Outside are the evil people (those who refuse to receive Jesus as Savior and confess Him as Lord), who practice magic arts (drugs; sorcery), the sexual immoral (sex outside of marriage of all types), the murderers, those who worship idols (anything instead of God), and everyone who loves and practice falsehood (liars).

I Jesus am the Root and Offspring of David (through Mary, the mother of Jesus).

The Spirit and the bride say, 'Come!' And let him who hears say, 'Come!' Whoever is thirsty, let him come, and whoever wishes, let him take (receive Jesus as Savior and confess Him as Lord) the free gift (cannot be earned or deserved, but must be received by faith) of the water of (eternal, abundant) life.

---

[7] "*Summum bonum* . . . meaning 'the highest good' . . . while in Christianity, the highest good is usually defined as the life of the righteous and/or the life led in Communion with God and according to God's precepts." *Wikipedia, The Free Encyclopedia.*

[8] 1 Corinthians 13:1-13 NIV [Emphasis added].

. . . He (Jesus) who testifies to these things says, "Surely I come quickly (to receive believers in Jesus) unto Himself.

. . . The grace of the Lord Jesus is with God's people (saints). Amen [so be it].' [9]

'Satan will go out to deceive the nations of all the Earth – Gog and Magog – to gather them for battle. In number, they are like the sand on the seashore. They march across the breadth of the Earth and surround the camp of God's people (to destroy the nation of Israel [10]*). But fire came down from Heaven and devoured them. And the devil, who deceived them, was thrown into the lake of fire, where the beast and the false prophet had been thrown.*

. . . Then I saw a great white throne and Him (Jesus, Son of God) who was seated on it. . . . And I saw the dead, great and small, standing before the throne, and books were opened. Another book was opened, which is the book of life. Each person was judged according to what he had done. The sea gave up the dead in it, and death and Hell gave up the dead. Then Death and Hell were thrown into the lake of fire. The lake of fire is the second death. If anyone's name was not found written in the book of life, he (or she) was thrown into the lake of fire.' [11]

Today I hope that all of you wear an undergarment of love in this time of war, and that your love grows throughout the eternities of eternities. It will be written about Me,

'The Lord is a man (having flesh and bone) of war.' [12]

Please do not be discouraged Peter, and others, if you cannot out love John. [Laughter] None of you is perfect as you are made of the dust of the ground, and all of you will miss the mark of walking in love. There are three secrets – Practice, practice, practice! [Laughter] One day Elder James and Elder John will get angry when certain people did not welcome Me, and this is what they will propose,

'And He sent messengers on ahead, who went into a Samaritan village to get things ready for Jesus; but the people there did not welcome Him because He was heading for Jerusalem (Samaritans believed proper to worship at Mount Gerizim and not in Jerusalem). When the disciples James and John saw this, they asked, 'Lord, do you want us to call fire down from Heaven to destroy them?' But Jesus turned and rebuked them, and He said, 'You do not know what kind of (unloving) spirit you are of, for the Son of Man (Jesus in the flesh) did not come to destroy men's lives, but to save them. And they went to another village.' [13]

Elders James and John, you are to have a loving spirit about you and exercise tough love even to the unlovely. It will be written, *'If anyone will not welcome you or listen to your words, leave that home or town and shake the dust off your feet'* [14] and move on still in tough love to another home or city. Most of you will die for the glory of God in the Third Earth Age. However, death is nothing to you, and this is how My Father describes death,

'Precious in the sight of the Lord is the death of His saints.' [15]

Questions?"

Peter inquires, "Will we learn from our encounters requiring us to exercise love in this First Earth Age and be able to apply what we learned in a later Earth Age?"

"Not directly, as you will not be able to remember except for shadows your life in this First Earth Age, as you enter the Third Earth Age, since you will not die in this First Earth Age, but will be taken to Paradise as a holding place for future assignments. Experiences of this First Earth Age will be like faint impressions that follow you. You will sense that you existed before and that you have further good works to do in an Earth Age to come.

---

[9] Revelation 22:11-17, 20-21.

[10] *"Come,"* they say, *"let us destroy them as a nation, that the name of Israel be remembered no more."* (Psalm 83:3).

[11] Revelation 20:7-10, 11-15.

[12] Exodus 15:3.

[13] Luke 9:52-56.

[14] Matthew 10:14 NIV.

[15] Psalm 116:15 NIV.

For all men made of flesh must die once, including Me, as I will be born of a woman in the Third Earth Age, as will also most of you. We will have to grow '*in wisdom and stature and favor with God and man.*'[16] I will die to pay the penalty (sanction due for the sins of those who will receive Me as Savior, for it will be written,

'*Just as man is destined to die once, and after that to face judgment, so Christ was sacrificed (died once to take away the sins of **many** people, and He will appear a second time, not to bear sin, but to bring salvation to those who are waiting for Him.*'[17]

You, like Me, will be severely tempted, but remember to walk in love, quote and use the Scriptures as a sword, and invoke the power of My Name,[18] confess Scripture, and as a lawyer 'plead My Blood,' for it is written,

'*And they (who believe on Me) have overcome (conquered as in war) him (the devil and his cohorts) by means of the blood of the Lamb (Jesus sacrificed on a cross to pay the penalty for the sins of those who will receive Him as Savior) and by the utterance (confessing out loud with words) of their testimony (like giving the truth in a court of law), for they did not love and cling to their lives even when they were faced with death (for their witnessing).*'[19]

My Father and I take delight in the death of His saints, as it will be written,

'*Precious in the sight of the Lord is the death of His servants.*'[20]

John, you will be an example of love throughout eternity. John, you will write about yourself and Me in part in your Gospel of John,

'*Peter turned and saw that the disciple (John), whom Jesus loved, was following them. . . . When Peter saw him, he asked, "Lord, what about him?"*

Jesus answered, 'If I want him to remain alive until I return, what is that to you? You must follow me.'

Because of this, the rumor spread among the brothers this disciple would not die. But Jesus did not say he would not die; He only said, 'If I want him to remain alive until I return, what is that to you?'

This is the disciple (John) who testifies to these things and who wrote them down. His testimony is true.'[21]

Love is the greatest thing on earth and in Heaven. John, you are to wear a thick undergarment of love, and you will die of old age only after you have completed your life's work. The Roman Emperor Domitian will order your execution by throwing you into a cauldron of boiling oil.

When you didn't die you continue preaching from the cauldron[22] and Domitian was so angry that he exiled you to the isolated island of Patmos, where he thought you could not preach to anyone, but your love enabled you to send the critical preaching of your **Book of Revelation** to the churches.

---

[16] Luke 2:52 NIV.
[17] Hebrews 9:27-28 [Emphasis added.]
[18] See John 16:23.
[19] Revelation 12:11.
[20] Psalm 116:15 NIV.
[21] John 21:20-24 NIV.
[22] Tertullian (160-225) may have been first to describe it as a historical event.

Walking in God's love, known as agape, takes practice, and you all are first to practice on each other. When you fail, just confess your failure in prayer and receive your forgiveness as the prior recording of that sin will be erased and removed from you *'as far as the east is from the west.'*[23] It will be written,

'And if any man sin, we have an advocate (a defense attorney) with the Father, Jesus Christ the righteous.'[24]

'If we confess our sins, He is faithful and just to forgive us our sins, and to cleanse us from all unrighteousness (iniquity; everything wrong).'[25]

You humans in the flesh will not operate perfectly in love in your beginning, but as you keep at it, you will get better and better. In the end, you will be perfect, even as My Heavenly Father is perfect, for I will preach, *'You have heard that it was said, 'Love your neighbor*[26] *and hate your enemy.' But I tell you: Love your enemies and pray for those who persecute you, that you may be sons of your Father in Heaven. He causes his sun to rise on the evil and the good, and sends rain on the righteous and the unrighteous. If you love those who love you, what reward will you get? Are not even the tax collectors doing that? And if you greet only your brothers, what are you doing more than others? Do not even pagans do that? Be perfect, therefore, as your heavenly Father is perfect.'*[27]

'As God, who called you, is holy, be holy yourselves in all your conduct; for it is written, 'You shall be holy for I am holy.'[28]

Beloved Elders, you will develop and walk in agape love, the love of God. When those in the world seek to harm you because you appear weak, they will run into My unseen power of divine protection. Agape love never fails, and you will walk in My protection. By walking in agape love, you release a force of faith to work on your behalf – a force that has all the appearance of weakness but is much stronger than any force of darkness.

Today the gifted angels have you and your wives, who are longing to see you, a tasty buffet with the catch of the day from the nearby Sea of Galilee. Please take the beautiful walk back here tomorrow for a 10:10 A.M. meeting. Gentleman as you walk in the God kind of love (Agape), I will give you a discernment key. Our enemy can counterfeit a lot of things such as pretending to work miracles, claiming to heal the sick, false prophecy, and deceiving many as the antichrist, but our enemy cannot counterfeit 'Agape love!' 'By their fruit you will know them,'[29] and you will not be deceived. Remember this key point,

'Trust in the Lord with all your heart and lean not on your own understanding; in all your ways acknowledge Him, and He will make your paths straight.'[30]

Now enjoy the excellent buffet prepared for you. I have asked John to bless the bread and water and the tasty St. Peter fish you are about to receive as you immediately arrive back with your wives. Shalom!†

---

[23] Psalm 103:12.
[24] 1 John 2:1.
[25] 1 John 1:8-9.
[26] See Leviticus 19:18.
[27] Matthew 5:43-46 NIV.
[28] 1 Peter 1:3:15-16.
[29] Matthew 7:20.
[30] Proverbs 3:5-6.

†BOOK THREE – Episode 4†

[†**Sidebar Scriptures**: "Joseph had a dream and promptly reported all the details (Genesis 37:5)."
"The Lord revealed to me what the evil ones were doing and planning and showed me their wicked plots (Jeremiah 11:18)."
"The word of the Lord came to Abram in a **vision**. . . . A **deep sleep** came upon Abram . . . . (Genesis 15:1, 12)."
I witnessed and experienced "dreams and visions, and I described **all** I had seen to instruct many (Daniel 7:1, 11:33)."†]

David Leads the Music in Jerusalem and Apollo Continues Building His Choir and Orchestra in Heaven

David Washes Elders Feet

[Wednesday morning the elders, leaving their sandals at the door of the assembly room, take their respective places on a long bench outside the circle of seats. David, wearing only a linen ephod[1] washes everyone's dusty feet[2] as the elders take their respective seats in a circle of desk chairs with a note-taking journal on top containing each elder's imprinted name.]

Apollo sends Mercury Speedo to Convocation Center and Continues Recruitment of His Choir and Orchestra

Back in the Celestial City Apollo and Mercury Speedo [M. S.] continues knocking on doors and winning recruits and scattering the announcement brochures *via* delegation throughout the Celestial City. Some distance from the Convocation Center, Apollo assigns to M. S.,

"In a few minutes, I want you to start briskly walking, (you need your horse with wings on its hoofs) so you will be at the Convocation Center at 3:00 p.m. today, just in case anyone missed the announcements that the meeting set today, without my permission by Michael, had been cancelled by me. Michael was way out of line in scheduling this meeting without first consulting me! I will get him back someday! Take this backside route, which we have not covered, and try not to miss giving anyone you see some of the announcement brochures. You can give the announcement brochures out to those on the way that is broad as you return to the Pink Palace. The end justifies the means!

It would be amusing to have a unicorn steak this evening! I will never forgive that skunk for making me lose my atomic watch. See you later, and you can brief me if anyone did not get our communication and showed up. Go as a flash, Speedo. I will win a large number to my group today before the conflicting meetings on Thursday and Friday. I will not even rest Saturday as advanced by Word, but will continue recruiting those to my choirs and orchestras. Politicking is just telling them what I want them to believe. "

David Leads the Music and Brings in the Shekinah Glory

David instructs, "Please be seated. It will be written,
'*It is the glory of God to conceal a matter;
but the glory of kings to search out a matter.*'[3]

---

[1] See 2 Samuel 2:14.

[2] "*Now that I (Jesus, Son of God) , your Lord and teacher, have washed your feet, you also should wash one another's feet. I have set you an example that you should do as I have done for you.*" (John 13:14-15 NIV).

[3] Proverbs 25:1. NKJV.

David starts skillfully stroking his harp stating, "Today the Lord Jesus has requested me to play the harp and lead you in praise and worship and respectfully to teach you regarding 'The Shekinah[4] Glory' or the manifest presence of God! Word had shared many of these truths before with the present song leader of Heaven, Apollo, but indicates that Apollo's mind was focused upon other things choosing not to take even a single note in the journal Word had given him. Please take out your journal for notes and worship God in song in one accord as the words will be on the large screen."

David continues skillfully stroking the harp sounding like the flow of many rivers of water and leads in song,

'The Lord (Jesus) is my shepherd; I shall not want.
He maketh me to lie down in green pastures:
He leadeth me beside the still waters.
He restoreth my soul.
He leadeth me in the paths of righteousness
for His name's sake.
Yea, though I walk
through the valley of the shadow of death,
I will fear no evil,
for Thou art with me;
Thy rod and Thy staff
they comfort me.
Thou preparest a table before me
in the presence of mine enemies:
Thou anointest my head with oil;
my cup runneth over.
Surely goodness and mercy will follow me
all the days of my life:
and I will dwell in the house of the Lord forever.'[5]

David plays flowing runs with his hands on the harp and lifts up his hands in worship leading further in a song,

"Let everything that has breath praise the Lord;
Praise the Lord."[6]

Praise God from whom all blessings flow;
Praise Him all creatures here below,
Praise Him above, ye heavenly host,
Praise Father, Son, and Holy Ghost.'[7]

---

[4] Shekinah – the visible symbol of God's presence with His people. God spoke to Moses through the "shekinah" out of a burning bush. (Exodus 3:1-2). *'Moses could not enter the Tent of Meeting for the (shekinah – Hebrew word meaning to settle, inhabit, dwell) glory rested on and in it.'* (Exodus 40:35). Shekinah is often manifested as a form of great joy, love, peace, reference, and holiness. It can quickly leave in a praise and worship service by someone shouting, clapping, and otherwise calling attention to oneself or by playing or singing the wrong song. *"And now, bring me for a musician (to play the harp), and it happened that when the (harp) music played, God's hand rested on him (Elisha).'* (2 Kings 3:15).

[5] Psalm 23:1-6 KJV.

[6] Psalm 150:6 NIV.

[7] A doxology by Thomas Ken (1637-1710 A.D.).

THANKSGIVING

David further entreated, "Let us in one accord lift high our hands and worship God in song,

'Make a joyful noise unto the Lord (Jesus, who will die for my sins), all ye lands.
Serve the Lord with gladness;
come before His presence with joyful singing.
Know ye that the Lord, He is God.
It is He (God) that hath made us, and not we ourselves (no bragging on self, but on God).
We are His people and the sheep of His (the Good Shepherd) pasture.
Enter into His gates with Thanksgiving
and into His courts with Praise;
give thanks unto Him and bless (praise) His name.
For the Lord is good, and His (Agape) love is everlasting,
And His truth and faithfulness continues through all generations (to those who love Him).'[8]

Selah! Let us in one accord pause and meditate on this stanza and let us focus and perform the fourth stanza again,

*'Enter into His gates with **Thanksgiving,** and into His Courts with **Praise;***
*give thanks unto Him, and **bless** His name.'*[9]

Thanksgiving is Distinct from Praise, which is Distinct from Worship

Let us search out and review these stages or steps.

The first step is to be **thankful** for all the good things you receive from God. These include your daily food, health, family, work to do, all the blessings of life, for your salvation, and for all that includes having faith that God can do today what He has done in the past.

Thanksgiving gets us into the gates. **Praise takes us into the Court**. What is this gate and Court? Let me briefly explain,

In Heaven above, a model Tabernacle is right off from the throne room of God from which an earthly Tabernacle is to be patterned[10] in the early part of the Third Earth Age, with an outer gate on the east. Next, one goes through the gate into the outer court containing the altar of burnt offerings and the bronze laver.

Inside the Tabernacle itself, still going west, next is the Holy Place containing three pieces of furniture: (1) the table of Showbread, (2) the golden lampstand, and (3) the golden altar of incense. Continuing going west in the Tabernacle is the Holy of Holies or the Most Holy Place, hidden by a veil or curtain. [Later on, it will contain the Ark of the Covenant.]

God's presence dwells in the Holy of Holies evidenced by the Shekinah Glory Cloud. My sacred goal in praise and worship is to bring us right through the veil into the Holy of Holies entreating the Shekinah glory or presence of God. In one accord, let us now together go for this ultimate blessing of blessings as we lift our hands, on our knees, high in worship, and raise our hands and praise,

'Oh, that men would praise the Lord for His goodness,
and for His wonderful works to the children of men!
And let us offer (of our free will) the sacrifices of thanksgiving,

---

[8] Psalm 100:1-5.
[9] Psalm 100:4. [Emphasis added.]
[10] See Exodus 25:9; 36:30.

127

and declare His works with rejoicing.'[11]

We are to turn our eyes deliberately away from self and our concerns and humbly thank God for His goodness and mercy to us!

It will later be written in the Third Earth Age,

'Make sure nobody pays back wrong for wrong,

but always be kind to each other and to everyone else.

Do not put out (quench) the Spirit's fire.'[12]

We are never placed in circumstances in which there is not something for which we should thank God. Let us remember the good things we have received.

It will be written and commanded in the Third Earth Age,

'Giving thanks always for all things unto God and the Father,

in the name of our Lord Jesus Christ.'[13]

Thanksgiving and praise are to be key points of the psalms and hymns. We humbly and heartily give thanks for God's goodness and loving-kindness to us and for blessing the works of our hands. We have an abundant cause for thanksgiving as we are saved from our sins and have the promise of eternal life. The Son of God, the Savior of the world, had agreed before the foundation of the world to shed His life's blood to pay in full the penalty for the sins of all who receive Him as Savior.

Praise Invites the Divine Presence of God

Elders of Zion, the yielding and focus of one's *'free will'* dictate the level of praise in the outer court as one enters the holy place. We should be filled with a profound sense of the majesty and goodness of God with souls bursting forth in expressions of both Thanksgiving and praise.

'Praise waiteth for Thee, O God, in Zion.'[14]

Praise is humbly setting aside selfishness and one's own agenda and includes with all our being, affectionately exclaiming such as,

I boldly proclaim God is good, He is always right, and He is in charge of my life. I love God and rejoice in Him. I please God as I praise Him!

O God, I am going just to look at You and think about You and offer You the praise of my heart. I will praise God for His love, joy, peace, patience, kindness, mercy, goodness, majesty, power, grace, strength, faithfulness, gentleness, wisdom, and understanding He freely gives to His covenant-adopted children. And then I will think of other attributes for which to praise Him. I will lift up my hands in the sanctuary and praise the Lord. Let all that is in me adore the Lord. Hallelujah!

'Praise ye the Lord from the heavens. Praise ye Him, all His angels; praise ye Him, all His hosts. Praise the Lord from the earth, ye dragons, and all deeps (large sea animals, like Leviathans).'[15]

---

[11] Psalm 107:21-22 KJV.

[12] 1 Thessalonians 5:15-19 KJV.

[13] Ephesians 5:20.

[14] Psalm 65:1 NIV.

[15] Psalm 148:1-2, 7 KJV.

128

The praises and sincere love of the lips and heart are the emotional thrusts that can bring one up to and into the highest praise and hopefully through the veil into the act of worship. A sacrificial fragrance rises up into the nostrils of God and makes Him well pleased.

'Thou art holy, O Thou that inhabits the praises of Israel.'[16]

This is the final stage of the highest praise we are invited to enjoy before hopefully going through the veil and moving into the presence of God's Shekinah Glory.

God's Shekinah Glory

A future account of God's manifest Shekinah Glory will be recorded,

'All the priests had consecrated themselves. . . . All the Levites who were musicians . . . playing cymbals, harps, and lyres. They were accompanied by 120 priests sounding trumpets. The trumpeters and singers joined in unison, as with one voice, to give praise and thanks to the Lord. Accompanied by trumpets, cymbals, and other instruments, they raised their voices in praise to the Lord and sang: "He is good; His love (mercy) endures forever." Then the temple of the Lord was filled with a cloud, and the priests could not minister by reason of the cloud, for the glory (heavy anointing) of the Lord filled the temple of God.'[17] Then Solomon stood in front of the whole assembly of Israel.... He said (preached in prayer):

'O Lord, God of Israel . . . Who keeps Your covenant of love (mercy) with Your servants who continue wholeheartedly in Your way. Hear from Heaven, Your dwelling place, and when You hear, forgive. . . . Teach them the right way to live. Forgive, and deal with each man according to all he does, since You know his heart (for You alone know the hearts of men), so they will fear You and walk in Your ways all the time they live in the land You gave our fathers.'[18]

'When Solomon finished praying, fire came down from the sky and consumed the burnt offering . . . and the (Shekinah) glory of the Lord filled the temple. . . .When all the Israelites (standing outside) saw the fire coming down and the glory of the Lord above the temple, they knelt on their faces to the ground, and they worshiped and gave thanks to the Lord, saying, He is good; His love (mercy) endures forever.'[19]

WORSHIP

A Congregation will not always enter the Holy of Holies. Even as a Congregation moves from Thanksgiving, into Praise, and then hopefully into the high praises, they are to wait for the divine invitation of God to come into His actual presence. When the invitation to come into the presence of God is given, the song leader must be sensitive to it. He can repeatedly ruin that special moment by drawing attention to himself, saying the wrong words, singing the wrong song, or misdirecting the service. Also, others can grieve the Holy Spirit by shouting, clapping, or drawing attention to themselves. Solomon warned,

'Guard your steps when you go to the house of God. . . . Do not be quick with your mouth. God is in Heaven, and you are on Earth; so let your words be few.'[20]

However, when that moment happens when the (Shekinah) glory comes as a manifestation of the Divine presence of the God it is glorious. It is the 'now moment' of God, the Holy Spirit! A Congregation must be taught to respond to that 'now moment' and to move collectively at the invitation of the Holy Spirit. Some may fall bowing the knee and others may lie prostrate on the floor with an overwhelming sense of the presence and power of Almighty God. At other times, the members will go into a hushed silence.

Being in the presence of God is a great miracle. It is one of the most joyous blessings a creative being can experience! My responsibility as song leader and teacher today was to bring us as a congregation to this place of worship of God in Spirit and in truth.[21]

---

[16] Psalm 22:3 KJV.
[17] See 2 Chronicles 5:11-14.
[18] 2 Chronicles 6:14, 21, 27, 30-31 NIV.
[19] 2 Chronicles 7:1-3 NIV.
[20] Ecclesiastes 5:1,2 KJV.
[21] John 4:24.

This is a place of special blessings for created beings, which at times include on Earth divine healing for man made in the image of God. At the right moment, the song leader may bring the congregation slowly out of worship to prepare them for the ministry of the preached Word. The preacher in Heaven is Word, the Father's chosen vessel, who would teach the Word of God and minister and preach a blessed and timely message to the congregation. The Song Leader of Heaven is to turn the service at this point over to the Word of God. Either the Word of God or His chosen ministers would preach a message to the congregation. We have a God infinitely good and knows what He is doing."

Rolling in is the Shekinah Glory

Rolling in unnoticed on the surface of the floor from the North was the Glory Cloud when David announced, "I invite us in one accord to apply what we learned while I gently play the harp and in one accord sing,

> *O Lord, my God, when I in awesome wonder, Consider all the works[22] Thy hands have made,*
> *I see the stars, I hear the rolling thunder, Thy power throughout the universe displayed.*
> *Then sings my soul, my Savior God, to Thee; How great Thou art! How great Thu art!*
> *Then sings my soul, my Savior God to Thee; How great Thou art! How great Thou art!*
> *How great Thou art! How great Thou art![23]*

The manifest presence of God in the form of a "Shekinah Glory Cloud" then filled the meeting room as each Elder like a slain man hits the floor with a gentle thud as they are engulfed by the Shekinah Glory Cloud.

Mercury Speedo arrives at the Convocation Center

Mercury Speedo arrives at the Convocation Center at 3:06 P.M. licking his lips as he sees 666 potential applicants for the choir and orchestra, with M. S. Smirking,

"Sorry, I'm late. [Inside laughing] You must not have gotten the word spread throughout the Celestial City that this meeting today had been canceled by Apollo, the song leader of Heaven, the first creation of life, as he is going to have the meetings at his Pink Castle. I only have sixty-six announcements left as I have been giving these out all day. Here, pass these around the best you can and all look over one. See most of you Thursday or Friday at the times outlined in Apollo's announcement. Bye."†

---

[22] The late George Beverly Shea, soloist for the Billy Graham Evangelistic Association, changed the original word "works" to "worlds" indicating only that it sounded better when it is sung. Jurisprudentially, there is no evidence that God created other "worlds" inhabited by those made in His image. This world through the various Earth Ages will produce a joyful one bride for the Son of God. There is one person of the Father, another of the Son, and another of the Holy Spirit, but the Godhead of the Father, Son and Holy Spirit, is one God. The Son is not a bigamist having brides from different worlds because it sounds better. Logic mandate that the writers chosen word "works" was correct. I rest my case.

[23] Song, *"How Great Thou Art"* by Stuart K. Hine.

[†**Sidebar Scriptures**: "Joseph had a dream and promptly reported all the details (Genesis 37:5)."
"The Lord revealed to me what the evil ones were doing and planning and showed me their wicked plots (Jeremiah 11:18)."
"The word of the Lord came to Abram in a **vision**. . . . A **deep sleep** came upon Abram . . . . (Genesis 15:1, 12)."
I witnessed and experienced "dreams and visions, and I described **all** I had seen to instruct many (Daniel 7:1, 11:33)."†]

Apollo Has His First Meeting with Potential Choir Members, and Mercury Speedo Travels to the Convocation Center to Spy on Those Desiring to Join the Army of Heaven

John Washes Elders Feet

THURSDAY MORNING THE ELDERS, leaving their sandals at the door of the assembly, enter the vestibule. John, having cleaned his feet and standing barefoot in deep humility, carefully and lovingly washes everyone's dusty feet.

Apollo Has His First Meeting with Potential Choir Members

Back in the Celestial City Apollo and Mercury Speedo prepare the Pink Palace with enticements as they anticipate a big crowd at 3:00 p.m. of those wanting to join their team as part of the choir. Tomorrow they will meet at the same time with those desiring to be part of the orchestra.

Apollo boasts, "We are going to have a spectacular turnout today. I will flatter them and win their hearts. I can control them for a Cherubim such as I am superior to these lower classes of angels. About 3:06 p.m. I may have you sneak away and take Black Shadow for a spin up the Broadway to the Convocation Center to give me an estimate of how many show up for Michael's army. Why does he even need an army?"

David Leads the Congregation in Praise and Worship

Stroking his harp, David leads the congregation in a hymn entreating the presence of the Holy Spirit, who comes in this morning as a gentle refreshing breeze. The Son of God appears in the midst of the Elders, with the Elders falling prostrate in worship at the Son of God's feet.

The Son of God Speaks on Loving One Another

The Son of God quotes, from what would be written as foundational instruction to the Elders, and commences His sermon to them.

'*Do not love the world or anything in the world. If anyone loves the world, the love of the Father is not in him. For everything in the world – the cravings of sinful man, the lust of his eyes and the boasting of what he has and does – comes not from the Father but from the world. The world and its desires pass away, but the man who does the will of God lives forever.*'[1]

---

[1] 1 John 2:15-17 NIV.

This is the message you heard from the beginning: We should love one another. Do not be like Cain, who belonged to the evil one and murdered his brother. And why did he murder him? Because his own actions were evil and his brother's (actions) were righteous. Do not be surprised, my brothers, if the world hates you.

. . . This is how we know what love is: Jesus Christ laid down His life for us. And we ought to lay down our lives for our brothers.

. . . Dear friends, if our hearts do not condemn us, we have confidence before God and receive from Him anything we ask, because we obey His commands and do what pleases Him. And this is His command: to believe in the name of His Son, Jesus Christ, and to love one another as He commanded us. Those who obey His commands live in Him, and He in them. And this is how we know He lives in us: We know it by the (Holy) Spirit (joined with our born again human spirit) He gave us.[2]

'Dear friends, let us love one another, for love comes from God. Everyone who loves has been born of God and knows God. Whoever does not love does not know God, because God is love. This is how God showed His love among us; He sent His one and only (begotten) Son into the world that we might live through Him. This is love: not that we loved God, but that He first loved us and sent His Son as an atoning sacrifice for (or as the One, Who would turn aside God's wrath, taking away) our sins. Dear friends, since God so loved us, we also ought to love one another. No one has ever seen God (the Father), but if we love one another, God lives in us and His love is made complete in us.

We live in Him and He in us, because He has given us His (Holy) Spirit. And we have seen and testify that the Father has sent His Son to be the Savior of the world. If anyone acknowledges that Jesus is the Son of God, God lives in him and he in God. And so we know and rely on the love God has for us.

God is love. Whoever lives in love lives in God, and God in him. In this way, love is made complete among us so that we will have confidence on the day of judgment because in this world we are like Him. There is no fear in love. But perfect love drives out fear, because fear has to do with (anticipating) punishment. The one who fears is not made perfect in love.

We love because He first loved us. If anyone says, 'I love God,' yet hates his brother, he is a liar. For anyone who does not love his brother, whom he has seen, cannot love God, whom he has not seen.

And He has given us this command: Whoever loves God must also love his brother.[3]

'Everyone who believes that Jesus is the Christ is born of God, and everyone who loves the Father loves His child (Jesus and those born again). This is how we love the children of God: by loving God and carrying out His commands. This is love for God: to obey His commands. And His commands are not burdensome, for everyone born of God overcomes the world. This is the victory that has overcome the world, even our faith. Who is it that overcomes the world? Only he who believes that Jesus is the Son of God.

. . . Anyone who believes in the Son of God has this testimony in his heart. Anyone who does not believe God has made him out to be a liar because he has not believed the testimony God has given about His Son. And this is the testimony: God has given us eternal life, and this life is in His Son. He who has the Son has life; he who does not have the Son of God does not have life.

. . .This is the confidence we have in approaching God: that if we ask anything according to His will, He hears us. And if we know that He hears us – whatever we ask – we know that we have what we asked of Him.
. . . We also know that the Son of God has come and has given us understanding so we may know Him who is true. And we are in Him who is true – even in His Son Jesus Christ. He is the true God and eternal life.

---

[2] 1 John 3:11-13, 16, 21-24 NIV.
[3] 1 John 4:7-21 NIV.

Dear children, keep yourselves from idols.'[4]

The Son of God decrees, "You Elders are My preachers to proclaim that My Blood will be shed to pay the penalty owed for sin for all those who will repent and receive Me as Savior. At first, you will preach that I am the only Savior to your own children, then to your grandchildren, and then to your great grandchildren, then to those populating the Earth in various Earth ages.

The beloved, Elder Paul, in the Third Earth Age, will clearly explain that only Jesus saves,

'For Christ (the Son of God) sent me to preach the Gospel (Good News that Jesus, the Son of God, paid with His own blood being named to a wooden cross the penalty due for the sins of all those who would receive Jesus as Savior) – not with words of human wisdom, lest the cross of Christ be emptied of its power.

For the message of the cross is foolishness to those who are perishing, but to us being saved, it is the power of God. For it is written:
'I will destroy the wisdom of the wise; the intelligence of the intelligent I will frustrate.'[5]
'Where is the wise man? Where is the scholar? Where is the philosopher of this age? Has not God made foolish the wisdom of the world? For since in the wisdom of God the world through its wisdom did not know Him (Jesus), God (the Father) was pleased through the foolishness of what was preached to save those who (be faith) believe. Jews demand miraculous signs (evidence of eyewitness proof) and the Greeks look for wisdom (with a mathematical certainty), but we preach Jesus Christ crucified (paying the penalty for sins by being nailed to a cross of all those who receive Him by faith as their personal Savior). For the foolishness of God is wiser than man's wisdom, and the weakness of God is stronger than man's strength.

Brothers, think of what you were when you were called. Not many of you were wise by human standards; few were influential; few were of noble birth. But God chose the foolish things of the world to shame the wise; God chose the weak things of the world to shame the strong. He chose the lowly things of this world and the despised things – and the things that are not – to nullify the things that are, so that no one may boast before Him. Because of God (the Father), you are in a relationship with Christ Jesus, who has become for us wisdom from God – that is, our righteousness, holiness, and redemption. Therefore, as it is written: 'Let him who boasts boast (only) in the Lord Jesus).'[6]

When I (Paul, highly educated) came to you, brothers, I did not come with eloquence or superior wisdom as I proclaimed to you the testimony about God. For I resolved to know nothing while I was with you except Jesus Christ and Him crucified (Jesus alone paid the penalty owed for sin). I came to you in weakness and fear, and with much trembling. My message and my preaching were not with wise and persuasive words, but with a demonstration of the Spirit's power, so your faith might not rest on men's wisdom but on God's power.

We do speak a message of wisdom among the mature, but not the wisdom of this age or of the rulers of this age, who are coming to nothing. No, we speak of God's secret wisdom, a wisdom that has been hidden and that God destined for our glory before time began. None of the rulers of this age understood it, for if they had, they would not have crucified the Lord of glory. However, as it is written: 'No eye has seen, no ear has heard, no mind has conceived what God has prepared for those who love him, 'but God has revealed it to us by His Spirit. The Spirit searches all things, even the deep things of God.'[7]

---

[4] 1 John 5:1-5, 10-12, 14-15, 18-21 NIV.
[5] See Isaiah 29:14.
[6] 1 Corinthians 1:20-31.
[7] 1 Corinthians 2:1-10.

Son of God Further Teaching the Elders

The Son of God, Jesus, further teaches the Elders, "You are all to ' doing *the work of an evangelist*.'[8] They are not rejecting you, but Me, and My Father, who legally sent you. Do not grow weary in preaching My gospel, nor be discouraged, but 'be content (in your victory in Me as your Savior and Lord) and in whatever circumstances you find yourself.'[9]

Elder Noah, My preacher of righteousness, will warn in his preaching for 120 years that a flood is coming as a judgment on the ungodly people, who refuse to repent and receive Me as Savior. Elder Noah with all that preaching you would have only eight souls saved – your three sons, their wives, yourself, and your precious wife. You were counted as righteous by obeying Me in building a large vessel right here up high for all to see on My holy hill with no water anywhere. Not even a drop falling from the sky.

Elder Noah, you will be laughed at, cursed, and spit on as you preach My repentance and overcoming by My Blood for those who will receive Me as Savior and confess Me as Lord, as you warn of the coming destruction. Your wife will stand by your side and 'laugh at the days to come.'[10] It will be written,

'*Noah was a righteous man, blameless among the people of his time, and he walked with God.*
Noah had three sons: Shem, Ham, and Japheth.
Now the Earth was corrupt in God's sight and was full of violence. God saw how corrupt the Earth had become, for all the people on Earth had corrupted their ways. So God said to Noah, 'I will put an end (in this Second Earth Age) to all people, for the Earth is filled with violence because of them. I am surely going to destroy both them and the Earth. So make yourself an ark of cypress wood; make rooms in it and coat it with pitch inside and out. . . .You are to bring into the ark two of all living creatures, male and female, to keep them alive with you.
Two of every kind of bird, of every kind of animal and of every kind of creature that moves along the ground will come to you to be kept alive.
Noah did everything just as God commanded him.
. . . And Noah and his sons and his wife and his sons' wives entered the ark to escape the waters of the flood. . . . The animals going in were male and female of every living thing, as God had commanded Noah. Then the Lord shut him in.

For forty days the flood kept coming on the Earth, and as the waters increased they lifted the ark high above the Earth. . . . Every living thing on the face of the Earth was wiped out; men and animals and the creatures that move along the ground and the birds of the air were wiped from the Earth. Only Noah was left and those with him in the ark. By the twenty-seventh day of the second month, the Earth was dry.
. . . So Noah came out with his sons and his wife and his sons' wives. . . . All the animals and all the creatures that move along the ground and all the birds – everything that moves on the Earth came out of the ark, one kind after another.
Then Noah built an altar to the Lord; and, taking some of all the clean animals and clean birds, he sacrificed burnt offerings on it. The Lord smelled the pleasing aroma and said in His heart, 'Never again will I curse the ground because of man, even though every inclination of his heart is evil from childhood. And never again will I destroy all living creatures, as I have done.

'*As long as the Earth endures,*
seed-time and harvest,
cold and heat,
summer and winter,

---

[8] 2 Timothy 4:5.
[9] Philippians 4:11.
[10] Proverbs 31:25.

day and night
will never cease.'
. . . Then God blessed Noah and his sons, saying to them,
'Be fruitful and increase in number and fill the Earth.'[11]

Elder Noah, you were a great success, and from you will come, King David,[12] from which I, the Son of God, will be born of David's heir, Mary, a virgin. Also, My precious bride will be from King David!

Elders, remember Noah when people reject your preaching of righteousness. Also, many in Heaven and on Earth will reject My preaching and teaching, and many likewise will reject of their own free will your preaching. It is written when I was preaching in My flesh, bone, and blood body, as you will do,

'Just as the living Father sent Me, and I live because of the Father, so the one who feeds on Me will live because of Me. This is the bread that came down from Heaven. Your forefathers ate manna and died, but he who feeds on this Bread (Son of God in the flesh) will live forever.'

. . . On hearing it, many of his disciples said, "This is a hard teaching. Who can accept it?"

Aware that His disciples were grumbling about this, Jesus said to them, 'Does this offend you? What if you see the Son of Man (in the flesh) ascend to where He was before! The Spirit gives life; the flesh counts for nothing. The words I have spoken to you are spirit, and they are life. . . . From this time, many of His disciples turned back and no longer followed Him.

'You do not want to leave too, do you?' Jesus asked the Twelve.

Simon Peter answered him, Lord, to whom shall we go? You have the words of eternal life. We believe and know that you are the Holy One of God.'[13]

Noah, you will have your same precious wife in this age and at the end of the Second Earth Age, and at the beginning of the Third Earth Age, and she will greatly encourage and help you. Questions?

Elder Peter inquired, "What happened to all those who rejected Noah's preaching?"

The Son with a tear in His eye replied it will be written,

'In a flaming fire (as they fall down from the surface of the Earth into Hell in the heart of the Earth will they be) . . . To them, that know not God, and that obey not the gospel (good news) of the Lord Jesus Christ.'[14]

Further questions?" [Silence]

---

[11] Genesis 6:9-14, 19-20, 22; 7:7,16, 23; 8:13, 18-20; 9:1 NIV.
[12] Luke 3:31.
[13] John 6:57-63, 66-69 NIV.
[14] 2 Thessalonians 1:8.

Buffet Lunch for Elders and Wives

Hearing none, My loyal angels have prepared a delicious buffet lunch with your precious wives again invited, as they are your best reward. Ask Mrs. Noah, Naamah[15], meaning 'pleasant, beautiful,' after Elder Abraham's prayer of thanksgiving to share the joke she made up about the pair of hippopotamuses. As a shadow of this age, Naamah will remember this joke in the Second Earth Age after the severe storm outside becomes calm as they float along under a full moon and bright stars. She will have the entire boat laughing. She will be one of the most pleasant and joyful women ever, and we will all enjoy her so much throughout eternity. Noah, enjoy your wife Naamah's humor and beauty to the uttermost, as she is your best reward down here. I hear her saying to you Noah, 'If it were not for the storm outside we could not stand the stink in here! Grab your shovel and wheelbarrow.' [Laughter]

Apollo Has His First Meeting with Potential Choir Members

Crowds of potential angelic choir members congregate on the beautiful large lawn at the Apollo's Pink Palace. The number was 666 x 6 or 3,996. M. S. was passing out the detailed applications with a unique black gift pen containing the in gold the words "Apollo's Choir" with musical notes. The application included detailed and personal questions and asked the applicants to list all their different gifts. As the applications were collected, Apollo whispers, "M. S., Black Shadow is pawing and ready to race. Bring me back a report of how many angels show up for Michael's recruitment scheduled at the same time today and report back whatever else you can hear being said. .I can take it from here. Bye, my spy."

Mercury Speedo Travels to the Convocation
Center to Spy on Those Desiring to Join the Army of Heaven

M. S. Mounts Black Shadow and enters Broadway pridefully orders, "I am the great Mercury Speedo, the first selected angel of the Great Apollo, now go the speed of sound x 6."

M. S. arriving at the stable of the Convocation Center spying on Michael addressing 700 angels. He hears Michael tells about a future story to be about the Army of Heaven, riding on either horses or in Chariots of Fire. Because a brisk wind was blowing in the trees, M. S. could not hear every word Michael was sharing from a future Scripture,

'This enraged the king of Aram. He summoned his officers and demanded of them, 'Will you not tell me which of us is on the side of the king of Israel?'

'None of us, my lord the king,' said one of his officers, 'but Elisha, the prophet, who is in Israel, tells the king of Israel words you speak in your bedroom.'

'Go, find out where he is,' the king ordered, 'so I can send men and capture him.' The report came back: 'He is in Dothan.' Then he sent horses and chariots and a strong force there. They went by night and surrounded the city.

---

[15] "Although the *Book of Genesis* in the *Bible* does not give any further information about the four women that were aboard Noah's Ark during the flood, there are substantial extra-Biblical traditions regarding these women and their names." See "Wives aboard Noah's Ark" at *Wikipedia, The Free Encyclopedia*. Jewish Rabbinic literature speculates "the name of Noah's wife to be Naamah daughter of Enoch."

When the servant of the man of God got up and went out early the next morning, an army with horses and chariots had surrounded the city. 'Oh, my lord, what shall we do?' the servant asked.

'Don't be afraid,' the prophet answered. 'Those who are with us are more than those who are with them.'

And Elisha prayed, 'O Lord, open his eyes so he may see.' Then the Lord opened the servant's eyes, and he looked and saw the hills full of horses and chariots of fire all around Elisha.

As the enemy came down towards him, Elisha prayed to the Lord, 'Strike these people with blindness." So He struck them with blindness, as Elisha had asked.

Elisha told (his now blind enemies) them, 'This is not the road, and this is not the city. Follow me, and I will lead you to the man you are looking for.' And he led them to Samaria.

After they entered the city, Elisha said, 'Lord, open the eyes of these men so they can see.' Then the Lord opened their eyes, and they looked, and there they were inside Samaria.

When the king of Israel saw them, he asked Elisha, 'Shall I kill them, my father? Shall I kill them?'

'Do not kill them,' he answered. 'Would you kill men you have captured with your own sword or bow? Set food and water before them so they may eat and drink and then go back to their master. 'So he prepared a great feast for them, and after they had finished eating and drinking, he sent them away, and they returned to their master. So the bands from Aram stopped raiding Israel's territory. '[16]

Finally, the noise of the wind quieted down with M. S. hearing about feeding those who attacked Aram, with M. S. reasoning, *"They gave them a little slap on the wrist. What kind of army feeds its enemies. I only count 700 angels. Apollo today had six times that number just for his choir. Let me get back and report all this to the Great Apollo as I desire to watch my master perform."*

Michael, watching M. S. choose the broad gate and road, remarks,
*'For wide is the gate and broad is the road that leads to destruction, and **many** enter through it. But small is the gate and narrow the road that leads to (abundant, eternal) life, and only a **few** find it!* '[17]

I am not promising that Heaven's Army will never be at war as we have to defend ourselves if attacked. However, the Son of God, our Lord, will give us His strength and joy forever if we remain on His side and give Him all the honor and glory.

Apollo Gloats Over Low Turn Out for Heaven's Army

Apollo sees M. S. returning smirks and inquires, "How many?" M. S., replies, "Only 700, with a bizarre story about feeding their enemies, if the angels join Heaven's Army."

Apollo replied, "My offer to be a part of my grand choir is superior to what Michael is offering."

Apollo Steals the Hearts of His Choir Members

Apollo appears before the angels dressed in a tight black outfit with his name on his opened shirt pocket having musical notes on each side. He further dramatizes his appearance by having sixty-six black streamers blowing with fans on the stage, having various flashing lights, with the sound booming with his playing on a guitar and singing a spellbinding song,

---

[16] 2 Kings 6:18-23 NIV.
[17] Matthew 7:13-14. [Emphasis added.]

"This is the great day of conspiring together.
Nothing is as powerful as the music of the cosmos.
Singing it, you will be free and as light as a feather.
To be part of this team is something about which to boast."

The crowd sees Apollo glowing from hidden black lights and hearing Apollo's enchanting performance and entreating voice almost in unity with their drooling mouths open saying in unison, "Awe!"

Apollo responds with a guitar presentation with these additional words,
"Dazzling you will be a part of the Awe!
Independence, fun, and adventure will be yours.
All that is free and beautiful you will draw.
To those hearing your voice, you will allure."

The audience, spellbound drools further in unity replying, "Awe! The king of music!"

Apollo continues politicking, "I am Apollo, the first creation of life. I feel like I am the mayor of this Celestial City, and I know each one of you by name. I have in fact visited many of you in your homes and plan to call upon numerous more of you. Members of the choir, you will be able to harmonize with me and produce a sound of sounds as you heard today. No problem. I can teach you. You are shrewd to have chosen this most exciting, with never a dull moment, stunning and enticing area of music. If you have ever been done wrong or have a need, I will see that you receive swift justice and welfare. I am on your side. Welcome to my world of music and excitement. Let me teach you a little song,"

'*I sing because I'm delighted to have a part*
Also, I am excited because I sing.
For music, I give my whole heart.
Hitting every note, I do ring!'"

The crowd responds again in drooling unity,
"Wow! We choose you to teach us to sing and perform!"

Apollo with a self-satisfied smirk exclaims, "I commission and appoint each of you this day as my official charter member of my choir. We have enough members for six choirs making up 666 members each enabling us to give six simultaneous services throughout Heaven instead of putting all our eggs in one basket at the Convocation Arena.

Choir 6 will rehearse this Saturday evening starting at 6:06 a.m. into the dark night. I prefer the more dismal and dark nights for my work. A different choir will practice starting at 6:06 each evening for six days, and on that sixth day we will double up and really labor for perfection We have six boxes of song sheets with words and music notes with the number of your choir and orchestra at the top. One rotten apple (missed note) can spoil the whole barrel (performance)!

Look to your left for the black path to the goodie tent. We will serve you a dark brown, almost black devil food cake with some tasty green punch with pink ice cream. I am planning on later to serve unicorn steak from the planet Earth below. [Smirking in himself at the sworn revenge, he was planning.]

We will have refreshments every evening, and a black offering box for everyone to give something substantial to pay for expenses and the redistribution of the wealth so all of you will be equal. I believe in "Liberation Theology"[18] letting poorer angels share in the wealth of the richest angels. Politically, we can accomplish this as the socialist end justifies the means. Starting tonight, and throughout eternity, I would like everyone to give a generous donation in the offering box at every rehearsal. All are to give their best offering. I will know (lie) what each of you each time give. You give me your best offerings, and I will treat you with much pleasure. You are dismissed for the refreshments. Get to know each other as being a part of an exclusive music club. Our team will win all. The means justify the end. See all of you at the first of many rehearsals. Bye."

Applications of Heaven's Army Reviewed

Michael, having reviewed the applications, announces,
"Each of you 700 is highly qualified. If you desire to enlist, lock the door of your dwellings, tell no one that you have enlisted, and be here in the morning at 5:00 a.m. sharp. I inform you that those in the Army of God will be away from their pleasant dwellings at times for extended periods. So please do not feel obligated to enlist in the morning, but for those who are sure, please sign under the great seal of Heaven and bring back with you the following:

ARMY OF HEAVEN LOYALTY PLEDGE OF ALLEGIANCE

I, _____, an angel of Heaven, do solemnly affirm before my Creator that I have not yielded, nor will I yield, support to any pretended god or created being or an alleged power being hostile, unfriendly, having the temper of an enemy, being adverse, hostile, hurtful, or repugnant to the Godhead of the Father, Son, and the Holy Spirit, making up the one Triune God. And I do further pledge with the best of my ability and strength to support and defend the Kingdom of God against all enemies, foreign and domestic; that I will bear true loyalty and allegiance to same; that I take this obligation freely, with no mental reservation; that I do this with a full determination, pledge, and purpose; and that I will confidentially and faithfully discharge the duties of the high office of a soldier of the Kingdom of God on which I am about to enter: So help me God the Father, God the Son, and God the Holy Spirit – the One Triune God.! Amen [So be it!]"

_____
Signed Under the Seal of Heaven†

---

[18] An article entitled "*Liberation Theology*" by S. Michael Houdmann at Google answers *inter alia* as follows: "Simply put, *Liberation Theology* is an attempt to interpret Scripture through the plight of the poor. . . . It started when Marxism was making great gains among the poor because of its emphasis on the redistribution of wealth, permitting poor peasants to share in the wealth of the colonial elite and thus upgrade their economic status in life. As a theology, it has very strong Roman Catholic roots."

†BOOK FOUR†
†BOOK FOUR – Episode1†

[†**Sidebar Scriptures**: "Joseph had a dream and promptly reported all the details (Genesis 37:5)."
"The Lord revealed to me what the evil ones were doing and planning and showed me their wicked plots (Jeremiah 11:18)."
"The word of the Lord came to Abram in a **vision**. . . . A **deep sleep** came upon Abram . . . . (Genesis 15:1, 12)."
I witnessed and experienced "dreams and visions, and I described **all** I had seen to instruct many (Daniel 7:1, 11:33)."†]

Gabriel's Communication Team, Michael's Army of Heaven, Apollo's Choir and Orchestra, and the Marriage Ceremony of the Elders

Angels Joining the Army of Heaven

FRIDAY MORNING BEFORE 5:00 A.M., all 700 loyal recruits, who had respectfully submitted the signed loyalty pledge of allegiance to serve faithfully in the Army of Heaven, quietly arrive in a secret place known as *Camp King Jesus*.

Michael welcomes, "You are all given linen garments, dazzling and clean, and a splendid white horse, white armor, and a sharp two-edged sword, as we ride our horses down to the City of Zion on planet Earth. We are honored by being invited to attend and assist at the marriage of the Elders, who will *'judge angels.'*[1] It will later be written, when you will ride your white horses and wear fine linens, white and clean, back to the Earth,

> *'I saw Heaven standing open and there before me was a white*
> *horse, whose Rider is called Faithful and True (King Jesus, the Son of God).*
> *With justice, He judges and makes war.*
> *His eyes are like blazing fire, and on His head are many*
> *crowns. He has a name written on Him that no one knows but He.*
> *He is dressed in a robe dipped in blood, and His name is the Word of God.*
> *The armies of Heaven were following Him, riding on white*
> *horses and dressed in fine linen, white and clean.*
> *Out of His mouth comes a sharp sword with which to strike*
> *down the (enemy) nations. 'He will rule them with an iron scepter.'*[2]
> *. . . He treads the winepress of the fury of the wrath of God Almighty.'*[3]

The enlisted angels arrive at Camp David, Zion, Israel. They travel in perfect formation to the dazzling white Zion Wedding Chapel shaped like the blue Star of David, overlooking the sparkling Sea of Galilee. Their assignment is to guard, assist, and join in the joyful celebration of the 7:00 P.M. wedding.

Peter Washes the Feet of the Elders

Friday morning, the Elders, leaving their dusty sandals at the door of the sanctuary and wearing plain white linen robes, enter and take their seats. Peter, having washed his own feet previously, considering this lowly task as a privilege of privileges washes the dusty feet of every Elder.

---

[1] 1 Corinthians 6:3.
[2] See Psalm 2:9.
[3] Revelation 19:11-15.

Apollo Prepares for Potential Orchestra Members

Back in the Celestial City, Apollo and Mercury Speedo conspire as they lay out tables in the Pink Palace with spices, treats, and musical souvenirs as they anticipate another large crowd at 3:00 P.M. on this Friday afternoon of those wanting to join their team as part of the orchestra. Apollo boasts of himself,

"Six choirs need six orchestras. We have done our politicking. They will be here. Just watch – we are going to have another spectacular turnout today. I will again flatter them and demonstrate some of the musical instruments, and their hearts will be **captured** *forever. About 3:06 p.m. I may have you again sneak away and take Black Shadow for a spin up the Broadway to the Convocation Center to give me an estimate of how many show up for Gabriel's communication team. I have the best and fastest communicator!"*

Special Worship and Preaching Service in Zion

While Peter was drying the last Elder's feet, David was playing on his harp and led the congregation in praise and worship,

'The Lord has dealt with me according to
my righteousness; according to the cleanness of my hands, He has rewarded me.
For I have kept the ways of the Lord; I have not done evil
by turning from my God.
All His laws are before me; I have not turned away from His decrees.
I have been blameless before Him and have kept myself from sin (wickedness).
The Lord has rewarded me according to my righteousness,
according to my cleanness in His sight.
'To the faithful, You show Yourself faithful, to the blameless
you show Yourself blameless, to the pure you show Yourself pure,
but to the crooked you show Yourself shrewd.
You save the humble, but your eyes are on the haughty (proud) to bring them low.'[4]

The gentle breeze of the Holy Spirit blows in as the Shekinah Glory, with the sound of a gentle dove's wings, filling the very atmosphere. At that special moment, the Son of God appears in the midst with each Elder falling to the floor in deep worship. The Son of God helps each Elder stand to their feet and gives each a hug, a smile, and decrees,

"Beloved Elders, you will, this day and evening, be entering into a scared Blood Covenant of Marriage.

My blood, your blood, and your bride's blood.

(1) My blood to be shed on the cross in the fullness of time as a sacrifice for the sins of many who will receive Me as Savior. Until then, each family must sacrifice a lamb[5] without spot or blemish yearly to roll your sins forward. *'Without the shedding of blood, there is no forgiveness.'*[6]

(2) Your blood I will request this day, of your 'own free will' if you desire a wife. You agree to donate one of your ribs with its flesh and blood nearest your heart from which your bride will be formed.

(3) Your bride's blood will be given in romantic love, this wedding night from her ripped thick hymen, which before, partly closed the entrance of her vagina when you consummate the marriage with her.

---

[4] 2 Samuel 22:21-28 NIV.
[5] Leviticus 5:10.
[6] Hebrews 9:22.

You must guard your daughters for it will be written as part if the Law of Moses to ensure the bloodline would be pure for the promised Seed (the Messiah) of the woman is to crush the serpent's head,

'*But if the thing (loss of virginity) is true, that evidence of virginity was not found in the young woman (by shedding blood upon consummation of marriage by her husband), then they shall bring out the young woman to the door of her father's house, and the men of her city shall stone her to death with stones (severe in those days to keep the bloodline pure for the promised Messiah), because she has done an outrageous thing (not saved her virginity to marriage) in Israel by having sexual relations before she was married. So you shall purge the evil from your midst.'* [7]

Now celebrate the pure consummation of your marriage and your wife's shed blood as proof of her purity as she gives you her most precious gift of her virginity. The day will come on Earth when many females will lose their virginity for a piece of bread and deprive (rob) their husband of the joy of marrying a pure virgin. Woe to those who cause My little ones who are pure to stumble and lose their virginity. Likewise, many males will do indecent and filthy (lewd) acts robbing their wives and themselves of the joy of entering into a pure marriage.

Your marriage bed is to be kept pure and holy. You all have free will! If you desire no wife with all those hugs, kisses, and encouragement she will give you, speak now or forever hold your peace. [Laughter]

"Again, speak now or forever hold your peace! I don't want any of you coming to Me later asking for your rib back.[Laughter] Also, you can't give back any of your children born of this union no matter how they behave. [Laughter] You men don't spare the rod of correction when they do wrong. It is the greatest act of love you can show them, but afterward, give them words of encouragement and speak words of faith about their future. It is written,

'*He who spares the rod hates his son, but he who loves him is careful to discipline him.*' [8]

'*Do not withhold discipline from a child, if you punish him with a rod, he will not die.*' [9]

Last chance, Elders! Does anyone desire to keep his rib?

Hearing not a peek, I decree you have this day waived all objections." [Laughter]

The Word of God further instructs, "Gabriel, you have an appointment at the Convocation Center, but be back in time for the seven o'clock wedding at the Zion Wedding Chapel, located where the Jordan River enters into the beautiful Sea of Galilee.

We invite your entire communication team to attend. Michael's Army of Heaven will already be in place. The more, the merrier as it will be such a joyful and delightful evening. The angels will be seen by the bridegroom and brides and are invited to join in the celebration of these marriages this evening and in My future glorious wedding Elder John will later describe as follows,

'*Then I (Elder John) heard what sounded like a great multitude, like the roar of rushing waters and like peals of thunder, shouting:*

'*Hallelujah!*
For the Lord God Almighty reigns.
Let us rejoice and be glad
and give Him (God) the glory!
For the wedding of the Lamb (Son of God, in the flesh) has come,
and His bride has made herself ready.
. . . Then the angel (Gabriel) said to me (Elder John),

---

[7] Deuteronomy 22:20-21.
[8] Proverbs 13:24.
[9] Proverbs 23:24.

'Write: 'Blessed are those who are invited to the wedding supper of the Lamb!' And he (angel) added, 'These are the true words of God.'[10] Shalom! "

Mercury Speedo Travels to the Convocation Center to Spy on Those Desiring to Join Michael's Communication Team

A crowd of potential Angelic orchestra accumulates on the beautiful large lawn at the Apollo's Pink Palace. The number is 666. Politically, Mercury dispenses detailed applications with a unique black pen with the words in gold "Apollo's Orchestra" with musical notes on each side of the lettering. The application contained detailed and personal questions and asked the applicants to list all their peculiar gifts.

The completed application forms are collected by Mercury and are brought in and laid on the left corner of Apollo's desk as he composes sheet music.

Apollo, not looking up, grunts, "Mercury, my Spy, Black Shadow is pawing and is ready to practice racing. Bring me back a report of how many angels come to Gabriel's recruitment scheduled to be held at the same time today, and report back on whatever else you witness. Let me review what we have caught in our music web. Now flash and return with some evidence."

Mounting Black Shadow this command is given, "I am the great Mercury Speedo, the first selected angel of the Great Apollo, now zoom the speed of sound times six (6) to the rear of the stable in front of the Throne Room."

Mercury arrives going into the rear of the stable at the Convocation Center, and sliding a spy board, he observes and hears Gabriel's addressing seven hundred 700) angels. Mercury hears only bits and pieces because of the heavy wind popping a Star of David flag on top, about someone, who because they did not believe Gabriel's words, could not be able to speak,

'Zechariah asked the angel, 'How can I be sure of this? I am an old man and my wife is well on in years.'

The angel answered, 'I am Gabriel. I stand in the presence of God, and I have been sent to speak to you and to tell you this good news. And now you will be silent and not able to speak until the day this happens, because you did not believe my words, which will come true at their proper time.'[11]

Mercury thinks, *"Stupid flag, shut up!. Apollo's black widow spider flag should be flying over all Gabriel only sanctioned the man who didn't believe him with the temporary loss of his voice. Why didn't he just kill him? What kind of a communication system has such light sanctions? I only count 700 angels. They beat Apollo's orchestra number today by only 34 angels. Apollo will not like that! Let me sneak back and report all this to the Great Apollo. I desire to watch my master perform on the various musical instruments."*

Mercury returns and enters his 666 door code, and steps inside. Apollo looks up with a smirk inquiring, "How many?"

Mercury reports, "Only 700 with a far-fetched story about a man's losing his ability to speak because he didn't believe Gabriel's message."

Apollo complains, "I have to watch Gabriel. He beat me by thirty-four, but I outnumbered them all with my combined choir and orchestra. If Gabriel has the power to take away someone's voice, he could hurt us. We had thirty-three more marking scientific gifting making a total of sixty-six (66).

Pull back the black curtain revealing all our magical musical instruments, and invite the angels to gather before the stage as I twist their minds."

---

[10] Revelation 19:6-9.
[11] Luke 1:18-20 NIV.

Apollo dressed in a tight black velour outfit, showing black chest hairs, having his name on his opened shirt pocket, with musical notes on each side, dramatizes his appearance, *coming through* a revolving door opening onto the plush outdoor stage. As he enters, 66 black decorated streamers roll out blowing by fans, with various spectacular and stunning images of Apollo being produced by ultraviolet black lights and neon paint. Apollo's hair and lips appear fire red, with his face, hands, and arms glowing with shades of green, blue, and red alluring neon paint. Apollo commences playing on a golden fiddle a spellbinding sound and when all are spellbound and enchanted he sings,

"This is the big day of linking together.

Nothing is as powerful as the music of the cosmos.

Play your selected instrument and you will be free and as light as a feather.

To be part of this unique orchestra is something of which to boast."

The crowd, hearing Apollo's incredible playing and his entreating voice, almost in unity with their mouths open, whispers, "Ah!"

Apollo responds on a black guitar, decorated to the utmost with neon paint, presentation, pulling his hearers in like in a black web with these additional words,

"Dazzling you will be a part of the 'Ah!'

Independence, fun, and adventure will be yours.

All that's free and stunning you will draw.

To those hearing your voice, you will allure and charm."

Many in the audience whisper, "Awe! The king of music!"

Apollo in a seductive voice bids, "Welcome to my cosmos of music! I am Apollo, the first creation of life. I feel as if I am the mayor of this Celestial City, and that I know each one of you by name. In fact, I have visited many of you in your homes and have plans to visit numerous more of you. Members of the orchestra, you will be able to harmonize with me and produce a sound of sounds like those sounds you heard from me today. No problem here! I can teach you how. You are shrewd, cunning, and crafty to have chosen this most exciting, with never a dull moment, charming, entreating, and the loyal world of music.

If you have ever been done wrong or have a need, I will see you receive swift justice and welfare. I am always on your side. Count on me to meet all your needs. Let me demonstrate as I play some of my Apollo songs, which I have written, on various instruments as you select this night the particular musical instrument you would desire to learn to play.

I enthrone you under me this day as an official member of my orchestra. We have enough members for six choirs making up 111 each. Choir six (6) rehearses this Saturday evening starting at 6:06 A.M. as I prefer working in the dark evenings. A different choir will practice starting at 6:06 each evening. We have six boxes of songs and music for you to take one set each and memorize. You can see by the way I am dressed I am a perfectionist. [Smirking]

Look to your left toward the black tent. We will serve you a dark devil food cake, pink ice cream, tasty green punch, with enjoyments always.

We will have refreshments every practice evening and an offering box to help pay for expenses. I would like everyone to do your utmost and give something in the offering box every rehearsal so everyone will look and sound the best. You give me your best, and I will give you my best.

You are dismissed to enjoy the refreshments and to rub shoulders with each other, being a marked, prominent, and a notorious charter member of the 666 Fraternity. Ours is a fraternity that will win! It's the end that counts."

Gabriel's Communication Team Invited to the Wedding of the Elders

Gabriel confidently declares to his chosen communication team, "Each of you has been provided with a confidential aphone (angel phone), and when it beeps you are to read the message and respond appropriately. At present, each one of you is receiving the same secure beep. You are to read it immediately and memorize each confidential (ultra private) message (you are not to speak out any secret messages or information you might learn to anyone). The present one to be erased in seven minutes reads as follows,

> *Please attend the wedding of the Elders*
> *this evening on Earth at 7:00 P.M. overlooking the*
> *Sea of Galilee in Zion, Israel! Proceed to the Agape*
> *Communications Center to be beamed down.*

We all will be shortly gathering in the Agape Communication Center to change into fresh white wedding garments. Only step into the circle of light and you will be beamed down to the earth, to attend the wedding of the Elders, who will later judge angels. We are all ministering spirits, and we will communicate confidential messages between the Throne of God and the Elders, their wives, and those whose names are in the Lamb's Book of Life. Spies will seek information from you. The penalty for any breach of confidentiality will be severe. Do not be tricked! Look straight ahead when confronted and say **NOTHING**!"

Wedding of the Elders in First Earth Age

Word, Jesus, the Son of God, officiating the wedding speaks, "Dearly beloved, we are gathered together before our Father in Heaven, who is love and has given us the gift of love, to join each of these precious couples in Holy Matrimony. How long will your love last? When the present Heaven, Earth, and stars all have passed away, your great love story placed in your heart today will be there. Now reach out and hold each other's hand and look each other in the eyes with a smile:
Grooms, all repeat,
I love God, and I love you!
Brides, all repeat,
I love God, and I love you!
Grooms, all repeat,
I make a blood covenant with you to be faithful to you and not to '*look lustfully (leer) at another woman or virgin girl.*'[12]
Brides, all repeat,
It is my prayer and desire that in me you, my husband, will find the help meet the Son of God designed especially for you. I confess,
Where you go, I will go, and where you stay, I will stay. Your people will be my people and your God my God.[13]

---

[12] Job 31:1.
[13] Ruth 1:16 NIV.

Grooms, all repeat,

I promise to love you with an unselfish devotion. I will care for you with tenderness, will always seek to strengthen you, comfort you, encourage you and hold you up daily in prayer before our Heavenly Father, in the name of His Son.

Brides, all repeat,

I promise to love you with an unselfish devotion. I will always seek to honor and respect you, comfort you, encourage you and hold you up daily in prayer before our Heavenly Father, in the name of His Son.

Grooms, all repeat,

With the deepest joy, I receive you as my wife and life's partner that together we may be one.

Brides, all repeat,

With the deepest joy, I receive you as my husband and life's partner that together we may be one flesh.

The Son of God, laying hands on each couple, speaks a blessing over each and instructs,

It is important that others know you are married. In a subsequent Earth Age, you will not remember this marriage or your life together in this First Earth Age (except for a faint shadow now and then). Later you will remember in eternity this wedding today. All you do will be recorded in the 'Archives of Heaven.' For example, Abraham and Sarah, you two will improperly pretend, by removing your wedding rings in another Earth age, that you are not married, and it will be written,

'Now there was a famine in the land, and Abram went down to Egypt to live there for a while because the famine was severe. As he was about to enter Egypt, he said to his wife Sarai (named later changed to Sarah, meaning princess), 'I know what a beautiful woman you are. When the Egyptians see you, they will say, 'This is his wife.' Then they will kill me but will let you live. Say you are my sister so I will be treated well for your sake, and my life will be spared because of you.' When Abram came to Egypt, the Egyptians saw she was a very beautiful woman. And when Pharaoh's officials saw her, they praised her to Pharaoh, and she was taken into his palace. He treated Abram well for her sake, and Abram acquired sheep and cattle, male and female donkeys, menservants and maidservants, and camels. But the Lord inflicted serious diseases on Pharaoh and his household because of Abram's wife, Sarai. So Pharaoh summoned Abram. 'What have you done to me?' he said. 'Why didn't you tell me she was your wife? Why did you (lie to me and) say, 'She is my sister,' so I took her to be my wife? Now then, here is your wife. Take her and go!' Then Pharaoh gave orders about Abram to his men, and they sent him on his way with his wife and everything he had.'[14]

I desire the man and woman to always wear matching wedding bands giving evidence to all they have acquired exclusive rights in marriage to each other to which it will be written,

'But since there is so much immorality, each man should have his own wife and each woman her own husband. The husband should fulfill his marital duty to his wife, and likewise the wife to her husband. The wife's body does not belong to her alone but also to her husband. In the same way, the husband's body does not belong to him alone but also to his wife. Do not deprive each other except by mutual consent and for a time, so you may devote yourselves to prayer. Then come together again (sexually) so Satan will not tempt you because of your lack of self-control.'[15]

[The Son of God next goes down the line, placing an 18-karat matching gold wedding band in each of the man's right hand and matching 18 karat wedding band in each of the woman's right hand and instructs,]

Grooms, now slightly place the wedding ring on just the tip portion of your partner's left ring finger and repeat, *'Just as this purest gold ring is in a circle without end, my love for you is eternal! With this ring, I seal today my vow of marital love for you, my darling. Wear my wedding ring with love and joy being happy and contented that God has brought us together here on Mount Moriah in Jerusalem, Israel. By this ring, all the world will know that I am yours, and you are mine. I now push this ring on your finger as an eternal seal so all who see it will know my love for you. With this ring I thee wed, in the Name of the Father, the Son, and the Holy Spirit. Amen!'*

Brides, now all slightly place the matching wedding ring on just the tip portion of your partner's left ring finger and repeat after Me,

'Just as this purest gold ring is in a circle without end, my love for you is eternal! With this ring, I seal today my vow of marital love for you, my darling.

---

[14] Genesis 12:10-20.
[15] 1 Corinthians 7:2-5.

Wear my wedding ring with love and joy being happy and contended that God chose me as your wife. By this ring, all the world will know that I am yours, and you are mine. I now push this ring on your finger as an eternal seal so all who see it will know my love for you. With this ring I thee wed, in the Name of the Father, the Son, and the Holy Spirit. Amen! The Son of God, smiling, decrees,

By the authority vested in Me, by My Father God, as His ordained preacher, I pronounce you husband and wife. Husbands, you may now kiss your brides for the beginning of many kisses. I desire each of you to spend a few moments together, holding hands and kissing and looking each other in the eyes. Then gather outside in front of the chariot of fire drawn by twenty-four white horses as I prepare to transport you in style to your honeymoon villa on the Sea of Galilee for it is a truth,

'Those who honor Me I will honor.'[16]

Tomorrow is the Sabbath, being the seventh day of the week, and this day of rest is made for man and not man for the Sabbath.[17] Enjoy this special day of your honeymoon together to the uttermost!

We will have delicious meals on your veranda overlooking the Sea of Galilee throughout the honeymoon, which incidentally will be for twenty-four days and evenings, to honor each one of your marriages. This evening meal will be private for just you two with candles, flowers, and moonlight, and will feature the tasty Peter's fish, being the catch of the day from the Sea of Galilee. Please be cautious in eating the Peter fish as it has plenty of bones, but it is so tasty. Nothing even in Heaven itself can match its taste. The bones and bumps in the road are part of the adventure. Enjoy the ride and don't worry about tomorrow. Elder Luke is our resident medical doctor in Suite 12 if a bone gets stuck in your throat. His medical emergency number is e777. However, he needs no medical business this evening. [Laughter] Also, you women have been given a little extra blood for your first romantic evening, and you won't need a doctor.

Always remember that you are flesh and blood, and it is appointed unto you all once to die on this Earth, but in the eternities of eternities you will have celestial bodies like the angels who do not give and receive in marriage or multiply themselves. Hint! [Laughter] Remember to come up for air! [Laughter] Now take your respective seats on the open chariot drawn by twenty-four white horses and look up at the heavenly host of stars as they twinkle down rejoicing in your marriages. Shalom! It will be written,

The Lord came to Abram in a vision. . . . He took him outside and said, 'Look up at the heavens and count the stars – if you can count them.' Then He said to him, 'So shall your offspring be.'
Abram believed the Lord, and He credited it to him as righteousness.'[18]
'Those who are wise will shine like the brightness of the heavens, and those who lead many to righteousness, like the stars forever and ever.'[19]

The couples with each Elder's right arm around his bride, so much enjoy their moonlit carriage ride to the Honeymoon Villa overlooking the Sea of Galilee. As they rode, the full moon turned off its light briefly. Then the skies out of the North became full of bright meteorites entering the atmosphere, giving off a fireworks celebration of both the marriage and the upcoming honeymoon. Each couple in loving anticipation enters the lobby and is directed by an angel to a private suite filled with wedding gifts and pleasures.†

---

[16] 1 Samuel 2:30.
[17] Mark 2:28.
[18] Genesis 15:1,5-6.
[19] Daniel 12:3 NIV

†BOOK FOUR – Episode 2†

[†**Sidebar Scriptures**: "Joseph had a dream and promptly reported all the details (Genesis 37:5)."
"The Lord revealed to me what the evil ones were doing and planning and showed me their wicked plots (Jeremiah 11:18)."
"The word of the Lord came to Abram in a **vision**. . . . A **deep sleep** came upon Abram . . . . (Genesis 15:1, 12)."
I witnessed and experienced "dreams and visions, and I described **all** I had seen to instruct many (Daniel 7:1, 11:33)."†]

The Elders' Honeymoon and Apollo Meeting with His Scientists

EACH COUPLE EXCITEDLY LOCATES their suite entrance. Abraham at Suite 7 says to his bride, Sarah, "You are altogether lovely, thank you for accepting my proposal of marriage."

Sarah laughs, "Who else? [Laughter] I am glad you did not give your rib back. Abe, I have never had so much fun in all my short life, as it is as if the honey barrel of joy has fallen over me. I do so love you, my husband! You are my handsome and gifted man – all man! God took out of you, anything feminine and put it in me. I am so blessed to be your bride and lover. You are my master[1] under God!

Abraham puts his fingers over her beautiful lips whispering, "Darling, you don't have to call me Master. You are the glorious one. Men will want to worship such beautiful women as goddesses and be their servants and slaves."

Sarah compellingly replied. "No! You must never worship me! I was made for you from one of your ribs. The Lord gave me some kissable lips and some curves for you to enjoy. Jesus explained to us brides to be this Scripture,

'*The head of every man is Jesus Christ (He is Lord and Master), and the head of the woman (wife) is man (her husband). The woman (wife) is the glory of man. For man came not from the woman, but the woman from the man; neither was man created for woman, but woman for the man.*
. . . Because of the angels (not to grieve them by a reversal of the roles of husband and wife) does not the nature of things teach that if a man has long hair, it is a disgrace to him, but that if a woman has long hair, it is her glory? For long hair is given to her as a covering.'[2]

"Darling, Abraham, my precious husband, you are the man of my dreams. Whatever I have is yours anytime you want it. The Son of God shared with me it will be written of my example to other women,

'*Wives should yield (submit; be subject) to your (own) husbands and adapt yourselves to them. Then, if some husbands do not obey God's teaching, they will be won over (to obey) with no one (wife) saying a word to them. They will be won over by the way their wives live. . . . Your beauty should not come from outward adornment, such as braided hair and the wearing of gold jewelry and fine clothes. Instead, it should be that of your inner self, the unfading beauty of a gentle and quiet spirit, which is of great worth in God's sight. For this is the way the Holy women of the past who put their hope (trust) in God used to make themselves beautiful. They were submissive to their own husbands, like Sarah, who obeyed Abraham and called him her master (her lord on Earth).*
Husbands, in the same way, be considerate as you live with your wives, and treat them with respect as the weaker partner and as heirs with you of the gracious gift of (eternal) life so nothing will hinder your prayers.'[3]

---

[1] Genesis 18:12.
[2] 1 Corinthians 11:3, 7-10, 14-15.

Each Bride Being Carried Over the Threshold

Abraham, replying, "I already love you so much it hurts. Only God could have thought up something as beautiful and grand as marital romance. Let me gently pick you up and carry you, my darling, over our first threshold. To God be the glory – let our dance of romance commence!"

Sarah blushingly smiles as she places her arms around Abraham's neck as he lifts her like a feather, and she takes the opportunity, as their lips come close, to give him her second of many kisses right on his lips with tears of joy flowing down her face declaring,

"I know where you are going, and I want to go with you. It is an eternal city, isn't it?"

As Abraham steps in and closes the door, he replies,

"Yes, my rib! [Laughter] Together forever! But first, *'The Lord will bless us out of Zion. We will see the goodness of Jerusalem all the days of our lives.'*[4] Later we will enjoy, *'a New Heaven and a New Earth, for the first Heaven and the first Earth had passed away . . . . '*[5] The Lord revealed that it will be written about us in the second earth age,

'By faith Abraham, when called to go to a place he would later receive as his inheritance, obeyed and went, even though he did not know where he was going. By faith he made his home in the promised land like a stranger in a foreign country; he lived in tents, as did Isaac and Jacob, who were heirs with him of the same promise. For he was looking forward to the city with foundations, whose architect and builder is God.

'By faith Abraham, even though he was past age (being a hundred years old) – and Sarah herself was barren (being ninety years old in the Third Earth Age) – was enabled to become a father because he considered Him faithful who had made the promise. And so from this one man, and he was as good as dead, came descendants as numerous as the stars in the sky and as countless as the sand on the seashore.'[6]

A Wedding Note Left in Each Room from the Son of God

Sarah observing a golden note addressed ***Abraham*** ♥ ***Sarah*** lying on a satin pillow on top of beautifully wrapped in white wedding gift inquiring,

"My master, do you want to open it?"

Setting Sarah down with her bare feet hitting the floor he directs,

"My darling, you open the note first, and I will read it."

Sarah's fingers break the red wax seal on the back of the envelope containing in its center a ✝ (cross), and she hands the opened envelope to her husband who reads,

'Astra Petamus!'[7]

You two will shine forever (bright) as the (present) stars! 'You are (even now) the lights in the world. Let your light shine before men, that they may see your good deeds and glorify your Father in Heaven.'[8]

'Do not (ever) let your hearts be troubled and do not be afraid.'[9] *I (Son of God) am your Third Strain in your beautiful marriage. I will never leave nor forsake you. I am your Good Shepherd, and you shall not want!*[10]

Delight in Me, and I will give you the desires of your heart.[11] *Rejoice in the Lord (Son of God) always.*[12] *The joy of My Lord, Father God, is My strength, and likewise, the joy is your Lord (Son of God), is your strength.*

---

[3] 1 Peter 3:1-7.

[4] Psalm 128.5.

[5] Revelation 21:1.

[6] Hebrew 11:8-12 NIV.

[7] *Ad Astra*: Latin "To the Stars"; *Altiora Petamus*: Latin "Let us seek higher things."

[8] Matthew 5:14, 16 NIV.

[9] John 14:27.

[10] Psalm 23:1.

[11] See Psalm 37:4.

I will in the Third Earth Age seek to explain, 'What do you think about the Christ? Whose Son is He?' 'The Son of David.' they replied.

I said to them, 'How is it then that David, speaking by the (Holy) Spirit, calls Him 'Lord'? For he (David) said, 'The Lord (Father God) said to my Lord (Son of God): 'Sit at My right hand until I put your enemies under your feet.'[13]

Abraham your strength is the joy of your Lord, Me, the Son of God. Sarah's strength is the joy of her lord, Abraham, her husband. A key Scripture is, 'The joy of the Lord is your strength![14]

Abraham, you and Sarah will receive this secret revelation truth, giving you great eternal joy and strength. However, this secret of joyful strength is so rare to be obtained that Scripture will record of King Solomon's observation in his day, 'While I (Solomon) was searching and not finding, I found one man (having the joy of the Lord, being free and upright) among a thousand. But I (Solomon) found no woman (who understood this truth) among all these.'[15]

Sarah, the Son of God, has set you free to be all a wife should be. Let the dance and adventure begin. You two will tell the story of how great a romantic marriage can be. Hold his hand and touch and hug him. Romance! Happiness! Just have joyful, fun! You two are the sweethearts of sweethearts! You will love each other in the eternal when the present Earth, Heaven, and stars have passed away. Your love is here to stay, and you will love even more than you love each other on this your wedding day. Such true romantic love of a wife is the golden crown that makes her husband feel like a joyous king. Sarah give Abraham all your kisses every spring, summer, winter, and fall, and throughout eternity. Sarah, you will have a surprise eternal bosom friend. I see you two women of God 10,000 years from today dressed in glorious white laughing as you spot your joyful husbands taking about the affairs of the cosmos walking toward you. You both run barefoot into the arms of your respective husbands giving them kisses and hugs. You two married women, will be the darlings and delight of all Heaven. Amen.

Agape and Eternal Friendship,
Jesus (Son of God)

P.S. My wedding gift contains matching his and her keys to your wedding present, a glorious mansion with a romantic master bedroom, various other eloquent rooms, kitchen and patio, furnishings, wardrobes, and all the trimmings. We may take an air tour soon to all the Elders mansions and businesses. Your estate is near here known initially, 'Hallelujah A & S Plantation.' Behind its protective stone walls and gates are delicious fruit trees and vegetable gardens. Abundant livestock, camels, and donkeys are grazing on the lush green hills. Its lakes are full of tasty fish. Further, Number 7 Elders Row in the City of Zion will be used for your townhouse to which you will have a title deed. You two will live in Number 7 Elders Row at first. Abraham, did you remember to make the bed and wash the dishes? [Laughter] My ministering spirits will help you maintain these two estates as you two are obeying, *'be fruitful and multiply'.*[16] [Silence]

Sarah in a gentle and submissive voice speaks, "Darling, master Abraham, Abe Darling, look the Son of God also included our wedding album and two A&S Cameras.

Abe, the first photograph is you looking down the aisle, smiling at me, your bride soon to be. The wedding photographs climaxed with our first kiss after the Son of God offered, "You may now kiss your bride!" I was shaking with excitement thinking, *'Let him kiss me with the kisses of his mouth.'*[17]

Abraham replied, "I am looking forward to our third kiss. Darling, please know that I will be gentle with you. Only God could have thought up something as beautiful as marital romance. It will be well written,

'Now to Him (Jesus), Who can do immeasurably more than all we ask or imagine, according to His power (Holy Spirit joined with our born again human spirit) that is at work within us.'[18]

---

[12] Philippians 4:4.
[13] Matthew 22:43-44.
[14] Nehemiah 8:10.
[15] Ecclesiastes 7:28.
[16] Genesis 1:22.
[17] Song of Solomon 1:1.
[18] Ephesians 3:20.

Abraham and Sarah Celebrating their Marriage
[Warning Note: The judgmental religious may
should not read this nor the Song of Solomon.]

Sarah whispers, "Abe, '*perfect love casts out fear.*'[19] I was made for you, and I am not afraid. What is a little pain and loss of blood for the eternal joy set before us? Our God so lovingly gave us to each other in sacred marriage, and to make us a perfect fit as we become one flesh."

Abraham with a look in his eye moves toward Sarah and Sarah smiles,

" Abe I smell that St. Peter's fish out on the veranda are you ready for our first dining experience together?"

Abraham's stomach growling with hunger reluctantly delays the joy by giving Sarah the yes nod.

Walking out to the veranda and holding hands, they find an eloquent crystal round table with another round turning table in the middle containing crystal covered delicacies. Sitting on the heart-shaped table are a dozen red roses with no thorns, red heart-shaped placemats, with several spice candles lighting each dish. Abraham pulls out a choice heart shaped seat for Sarah positioning it to overlook the beautiful Sea of Galilee. Then out of the Northern skies, rain a flurry of meteorites (shooting stars) as if to say, "Let the Celebration Begin!"

Abraham bows to his knees and gives thanks to His Creator for what they are about to receive – both food and romance. Sarah joins him at his side also on her knees, holding his hand as they have the first of many prayers together,

Our Father in Heaven,
    Hallowed be Your name.
Your kingdom come,
 Your will be done,
    on Earth as it is in Heaven.
Give us today our daily bread.
Forgive us our debts,
    as we also have forgiven our debtors.
And lead us not into temptation,
    but deliver (rescue) us from the evil one.[20]

We bless Thee, Father, for giving us Your Son to die for our sins.

This evening you have prepared for us a feast of both romance and bread.

We come to you in love and Thanksgiving.

We look forward to the Marriage Supper of the Lamb, Your Son.

Bless our marriage in every way. Here we are, Lord, use us to give You glory.

We thank you for the meal we are about to receive and for our romantic marital love.

In Your Son's Name, Jesus, we agree on Earth in prayer. Amen!"

Sarah squeezes the Abraham's hand and whispers so gently, "Amen – so be it!" Abraham seats Sarah back into a soft, comfortable heart-shaped red seat and moves it up closer to a heart-shaped table. A burst of meteorites fills the northern sky as if to confirm, "Amen – Be it unto Abraham and Sarah as they prayed. Let it happen. So be it!"

Abraham turns to Sarah and gives her a kiss of joy on the lips and makes an eternal decree for them,

---

[19] 1 John 4:18.
[20] Matthew 6:9-13 NIV.

151

"Let us kiss each other on the lips before every meal. Let us often partake of the Lord's Supper in remembrance of the upcoming sacrifice for our sins by the Son of God to satisfy God's justice that our sin must be punished. The Son of God directed, 'As often as you partake of the Lord's Supper do this in remembrance of Me.' Often means, 'Frequently; many times; not seldom.' [21] *I desire us to partake often. Many times we will partake daily the Lord's Supper right before we retire in the evening and also at times upon waking in the morning. Also, I desire us to give each other a special good-bye kiss even when we are to be separated* even *briefly."*

Sarah responded, "Amen – so be it! Wow. I am so completely in love with you. I will kiss you back with my lips made of your rib, flesh, and blood."

Abraham focuses on Sarah's inviting, beautiful lips at the same time opens the crystal container containing the St. Peter's fish. He places the largest whole piece on Sarah's plate and one on his plate as they both obtain helpings of all the delicacies from the dishes as they spin the center turntable.

Abraham holding a piece of bread breaks half for each and looking up to Heaven says, "Father, I thank you for this meal and romance we are about to receive. In Your Son's Name. Amen!

Abraham kisses Sarah on the lips as they dine both in anticipation of the real desert of their first lovemaking as husband and wife.

Once they had eaten Abraham laughs, "Peter is probably stuffed by now on this fish named after him."

"Sarah gently corrects, "No, he has eaten sufficiently."

Abraham laughs, "That's a better way of saying it. I knew you would be a blessing. It was not good for man to be alone. Let's take a tour of the facility."

Sarah stands as she folds the cloth napkins and arranges the table. She places her hand in Abraham's hand walking as on-air by his side saying,

"Look, Abraham, separate bathrooms with fluffy white towels, toothbrushes, and all the accessories. I assume the blue bathroom and closet are for you, and the pink bathroom and closet are for me. [*Laughing at the thought of Abraham having anything to do with pink.*] Look, Abraham, I have shelves and hangers full of undergarments, robes, and nightgowns. What would you think about my wearing this nightgown tonight? Is it too thin?"

Abraham gulped hard having a loss of words. Sarah laughingly says,

"Well, you are man enough to take it! So this one will be the one. Here is a robe I can wear over it until right before I crawl under the sheets with you."

Abraham remaining silent with Sarah exploring,

"Let's see your wardrobe. Look at these blue pajamas. Let me count the buttons, as I cannot see in the dark. [Laughing] You did not think God would give you a cold woman, did you?

We will always keep the marriage bed pure, but we will also always keep our marriage bed warm, which may at times be an understatement. Strike the word *warm* and contrast the word *cold* with the word *hot*. Hotter *than* a "pepper sprout" for us!

Abe, please do not bring your council meetings or war strategies to discuss with me in our marriage bed, as that must wait for the morning after breakfast. Likewise, I will not be talking to you about a problem in our sewing circle right before bed. I will focus on my love for you darling. Pure, passionate, warm, warmer, and hot, my precious husband!"

---

[21] See *American Dictionary of the English Language,* Noah Webster 1828, *"Often."*

152

Abraham replied, "Amen. Let's both take a shower or you a bath and meet for prayer and the Lord's Supper kneeling at the side of our pure marriage bed."

Abraham came out first sporting his blue pajamas and looked at himself in the full wall mirror thinking, *"Lord, thank you for making me a man and for giving me a warm and romantic woman. Patience, Abraham, patience!"* [Self Laughter]

Abraham prepares the Lord's Supper on the night tray as he patiently awaits his beloved finally coming out of the pink bathroom. Abraham had prepared the bread and the non-alcoholic red grape wine, on the nightstand. Abraham pacing for a few minutes kneels in prayer. In a few minutes, Sarah finally comes out wearing her thick robe over her nightgown, and she kneels barefoot beside Abraham kissing him on his left cheek. Abraham ministers,

"The Son of God taught us He would give His body as He receives stripes from a brutal whipping with cords containing cutting metal on His back for our healing. He subsequently would be nailed to a wooden cross to pay the penalty due for our sins and for of all who would receive Him as Savior saying

'This is My body, which is (to be broken) for you; do this in remembrance of Me.'[22]

Abraham gently picks up the small piece of bread, blesses it and gives thanks and brakes it and hands one piece to Sarah and retaining one piece saying,

"Take and eat as this represents our Lord's body to be broken for us. We do this in remembrance of Him!"

After each had eaten the broken bread, Abraham takes the cup having about an ounce of non-alcoholic red wine saying, "Our Lord taught,

'This cup is the new covenant in My blood, do this, whenever you drink it, in remembrance of Me.'[23] Sarah, our Lord's life's blood will be shed for the forgiveness of our sins in the third earth age. As often as we partake of the bread and wine, we do this in remembrance of our Lord and Savior. Again, I hope we partake of the bread and wine each morning upon awakening as our first act of worship, and again receive this communion bread and cup each evening before enjoying sweet sleep together. I will try not to separate from you at night unless it may be necessary to do His will."

Abraham hands the small cup to Sarah, and she drinks a sip. He drinks the remaining amount, and he arranges the elements on the nightstand for them together in the morning upon awakening to partake again.

Abraham on his knees with Sarah at his side prays,

"Father in Heaven, in the Name of Your Son, we praise and magnify Your holy name and for showing us your great love, salvation, and for giving us each other in marriage this day. Thank You for being ever watchful over us, even in the stillness of the night. We thank You for our marriage and Your love, goodness, and kindness toward us. In the Name of Your Son, our Savior and Lord, Jesus. Amen!

Sarah in a soft voice responds in a whisper, "Amen! Darling, please turn out the light as I am about to bounce this hot robe off the wall and climb on your side first. No use my going to the other side in this king size bed as in a few moments nothing will separate us. I have already noticed the birds and the bees, and like them, I rejoice in anticipating our marriage act."

Upon the light's going out, there was a thud against the wall. The rest is history!

---

[22] 1 Corinthians 11:24 NIV.
[23] 1 Corinthians 11:25 NIV.

In the morning, Abraham with a smile on his face and dressed back in his blue pajamas was already on the side of the bed praying. Sarah opens her eyes with her lovely hair looking like a flock of goats, which had recently gone through a windstorm. Sarah spoke, "I can't find my gown. Would you be so kind as to go over to that wall and hand me my robe so I can join you in prayer and partake of the wonderful Lord's Supper for the second of many times together?

Abraham retrieves the robe and with Sarah, having the sheets pulled up to her chin hands it to her.

Sarah suggested, "Now turn your back while I put on my robe?

"Why, I'm your husband?

Sarah responds, "Husbands are moved by sight, and I want us to focus upon the Lord's Supper."

"Abraham turned his back and replied, "Thank you, Lord, for giving me such a wise and warm woman who knows what turns me on."

Sarah joined Abraham kneeling at his side holding his hand in prayer with Abraham praying,

"Father in Heaven, Thank you for awakening us to this new dawning. We begin this day, rejoicing in You. We commit this Sabbath day of rest to You and commit ourselves to do Your will on earth. May we magnify and glorify Your great name in all we do and say. We bless You and thank You for Your love and goodness toward us! We pray this in the mighty name of Your Son. Amen!"

After they had received together the blessed Lord's Supper, Sarah spoke, "Abe, my man, please turn your back again as our marriage bed is a bloody mess. I will fold up our linens and put them out in the hall. Please, don't even glance at this mess."

Abraham, taking a quick peek, gasps at all the blood. Then, upon hearing the door open and shut, spoke, "Thank you for giving me your love. We have a blood covenant, and you will always be my pure virgin. Now, what?"

"Abe, as for me, I am going to wash my tangled hair. It feels like I have been rolled through a hay field. Would you like me to wear it straight today or in pigtails?"

What's a pigtail?

"Oh, never mind. I will keep it kosher! [Self-laughter] I will wear it straight for you today. You might desire a shower too. I know you like to dress, but please wear some casual restful clothes today." Sarah immediately got into her shower and Abraham into his in the blue bathroom. Upon Abraham's exiting his shower, he hears Sarah yell, "Abraham, do you have some more shampoo. This little bottle was not enough for my flock of goats."

"Abraham responds, "I just used a little from my bottle of shampoo. I nearly have an entire bottle."

Sarah said, "Well, I am in the shower, bring it to me. If you like, you can help me shampoo this flock of goats and rinse it out."

Abraham gulped again as he enters Sarah's feminine pink bathroom wearing around him a small towel. He pushes the shower door back with her turning, facing him with the water running on the back of her hair as she gives him a kiss and pushing her pointed breast against his chest insisting, "Well, pour some of the shampoo on my hair and lather it up. What are you waiting for?"

So Abraham gulped at the sight of such beauty and did as he was instructed and soon had her flock of goats fully lathered. "Abe, now help me rinse it out. Come on and use your fingertips. On my hair, not on my body."

"Oh, Sarah, 'How could God create such beauty for a husband as your pointed breast."

Sarah loosens the knot on Abraham's towel, letting it fall to the floor, reminding him, "Did not our Lord say, 'Have fun. What are you waiting for?" '

Abraham swallowing hard, "How can two people be this close?"

"Sarah corrects, "Now we are one flesh, not two! Enter me for you are ready, and I am ready – we are a perfect fit. My body belongs to you. Enjoy it to the uttermost. My body is holy and pure, and I give it to you without reservation. How else are we going to have 24 babies and help populate the Earth in this First Earth Age?"

Drying each other after the act of marriage, Abraham going shirtless slips on white paints ending beneath his knees. Sarah puts on another beautiful gown and covers herself with a thinner cooler robe. They walk arm in arm out on the veranda and find the crystal containers filled with delicious breakfast treats.

After a delightful breakfast and conversations, Sarah exclaims,

"Look, Abe, our bed has been remade and this time with soft cotton sheets with the smell of spices. How about an after-breakfast nap?"

Abraham nods, "Let's first brush our teeth. A nap? I'm not sleepy." [Laughter]

Sarah exits her bathroom first removes her robe and climbs in his side of the king-size bed. After Abraham finishes brushing his teeth, he puts on some pajama bottoms and slips in beside Sarah with her snuggling up close to him.

Abraham asks, "Nap?"

Sarah passionately kisses him on the lips suggesting, "Afterward, my darling! Our morning exercise first."

Apollo Meeting with 66 of His Scientists
Prior to the First Choir Rehearsal

Apollo had directed Mercury Speedo to invite 66 promising scientists on this Sabbath to a special called meeting at the Pink Palace to be held before the planned first of many lessons on *Music Theory and Appreciation*

Apollo rolls out the black carpet and meets with the 66 chosen in a luxurious dark basement room being lined on the walls, floor, and ceiling with lead as suggested by Speedo as a way to enhance security.

Apollo with a flattering smirk presents himself,

"Trusted members of the Choir and Orchestra of Heaven, I wanted to in strict confidence inform you that I have uncovered a plot to harm us. Naturally, I must come to you for your expert help. Mercury Speedo, you can call him Speed or Flash for short, has an idea for the perfect ultimate weapon, which we may need to defend ourselves. How many of you can I, Apollo, personally count on to be part of our defense? Raise your left hand."

All 66 left hands were raised.

"Speedo take your time and brief this group of the cleverest scientists ever to assemble to conspire with you on your shrewd hypothesis. I will be leaving you, for now, to go work on a great and unforgettable lecture on *Music Theory and Appreciation*. You are in crafty hands with Speedo."

Speedo bows to his waist to his anxiously awaiting team proclaiming,

"Outstanding musicians and scientist, what a magnificent combination you are! I can neither sing nor play a musical instrument, and I envy you for having such additional talents. Wise Apollo advisers we need to be prepared as we have an enemy out there seeking to take away our independence and control us as slaves. I have a theory for the creation of an I-Bomb. It is the exact opposite of a regular hot bomb. Like cool, dark is the opposite of hot, light. Instead of creating extreme heat, it produces extreme cold.

So cold that nothing, not even a spirit, can survive it. We could create it in portions as we will need to assemble it in our main experimental facility located in the heart of the Earth below. Apollo owns the richest and the best place on Earth, and we will shortly visit his resort.

Many of you are in the choir and orchestra, and Apollo has a brilliant lecture planned today as the first of many on *Music Theory and Appreciation*. Let us meet back here tomorrow, the first day of the week at 6:06 p.m., and work into the night. It has been my experience that a lot more can be accomplished in the dimness of the evening than in the bright light of the day. Each one will have his workstation. If we are in unity, there is nothing we can't accomplish. How many see the I-Bomb as a reality? Raise your left hand."All 66 left hands raise.

Abraham and Sarah Continue Celebrating their Marriage
[Warning Note: The judgmental religious should not read
this next section nor the Song of Solomon]

Back in Suite 7 Abraham awakens out of a deep refreshing nap and looks intensively at Sarah's face with her eyes gently shut beside him on a pillow. Abraham begins softly romancing her with these words, '

How beautiful you are, my darling!
   Oh, how beautiful!
   Your eyes . . . are doves.
Your hair is like a flock of goats . . . .
Your teeth are like a flock of sheep . . . .
Your lips are like a scarlet ribbon;
   your mouth is lovely.
. . . Your neck is . . . built with elegance.
. . . Your two breasts are like two fawns,
   like twin fawns of a gazelle
   that browse among the lilies.
. . . I will go to the mountain of myrrh
   and to the hill of incense.
All beautiful you are, my darling;
   there is no flaw in you.
. . . You have stolen my heart, my sister, my bride;
   you have stolen my heart
   with one glance of your eyes. . . .
How delightful is your love, my sister, my bride!
Your lips (in kisses and words) drop sweetness as the honeycomb, my bride!
You are a garden locked up (my pure virgin), my sister, my bride;
   you are a spring enclosed, a sealed fountain.
. . . You are a garden fountain,
   a well of flowing water (so refreshing to your husband.'[24]

Sarah without opening her eyes responds,

---

[24] Song of Solomon 4:1-7, 9-12 NIV.

156

'Awake, north wind,
and come south wind!
Blow on my garden,
that its fragrance may spread abroad.
Let my love come into his garden
and taste its choice fruits.'[25]

Abraham gently kisses Sarah on the lips with her putting her arms around his neck, drawing him close to her as he gently removes her gown throwing it against the wall romancing,

'I have come into my garden, my sister, my bride;
I have gathered my myrrh with my spice.
I have eaten my honeycomb and my honey;
I have drunk my wine and my milk.'[26]

After the third act of marriage this morning, Abraham speaks, "All your love is so beautiful and satisfying. It is wonderful to drink refreshing water out of one's own well (wife).[27] Thank you for every refreshing and satisfying kiss!"

Sarah responds, "You are most kindly welcome, my Master! Thank you so very much! It is a two-way street. Let us put on some play clothes as I saw a picnic basket and light blankets and pillows. I smell our dinner out on the veranda. I will pack us a picnic and let us have a picnic and breathe some fresh air. This air has gotten a little steamy." [Laughter]

Abraham replied, "Wonderful idea, my love. I noticed on our carriage ride back from the baptism service a beautiful solitary place under a grape arbor high on a hill overlooking a bend in the Jordan River. The perfect place for a picnic. Let's go!"

Sarah carried two large light blankets, one long pillow, and two fluffy towels. Abraham, carrying the picnic basket, joyfully spotting a walking trail leading up to the solitary place that Abraham had noticed the night before. The path was delightful as little rabbits hopped before them, and the birds sing romantic songs. Even the birds and the bees were celebrating the mating time. Upon reaching the beautiful grape arbor with a soft wind blowing in, Sarah selects a choice spot and spreads the blanket and neatly places the covered dishes down in a semi-circle."

Abraham takes both of Sarah's hands as they bow in prayer,
"Our Heavenly Father,
We worship You and Your Son, and we thank You for blessing our food and water. Thank you for giving us Your Son, Jesus, Who will shed His life's blood on a wooden cross the pay the penalty owed for our sins. We receive Jesus as our Savior. Your will be done on Earth! We praise you for all the blessings we already have received from You on this our first Sabbath together as husband and wife. You have promised never to leave us, nor forsake us.[28] Thank for blessing our lives and marriage for Your Glory.
In the Name of Your Son, we humbly pray.
Amen!"
Sarah softly agrees, "Amen! So be it!"

Abraham was pleasantly surprised as Sarah orderly opened the trays revealing all the delicious entrees and preparing colorful matching plates of the delicious food.

They had a delightful meal together.

Sarah spoke gently,

"I am not sleepy. With your permission, my Lord, from whom I also find my joy and strength, I would like to take a refreshing swim in the crystal clear Jordan River."

---

[25] Song of Solomon 5:1 NIV.
[26] Song of Solomon 5:1 NIV
[27] See Proverbs 5:15.
[28] Deuteronomy 31:6.

Abraham responded, "You didn't bring anything to swim in."

"So, no one is around."

Sarah picks up two towels as Abraham follows her down the path to the beautiful River Jordan with Sarah assuring, "See no one is around."

Abraham questions, "I don't know about this?"

"Master, if you forbid me, I will not go swimming."

Abraham remains silent.

"Abe, why don't you turn around?"

"Sarah hung her play clothes on some tree limbs and wades into the warm crystal clear Jordan. When the water was up to her neck, she announced, "Abe, you can turn around. The water temperature is perfect. I'll turn around while you enter, and I will race you to that beautiful white rock yonder on the other side."

After Sarah had turned around, shortly she heard Abe dive in heading for the finish line. Sarah took off holding a good head start. Upon seeing, she would slightly beat her husband Sarah slows down and lets him pass her to win. On the other hand, did she win by letting him win? Abe touches the rock and turns around with her swimming right into his arms. He hugs her tightly against his body, and she hugs him back. He kisses her passionately, and she passionately kisses him back saying, "Underwater?"

Abraham replied, "This is holy ground, my love."

Sarah responded, "So? We are a holy couple hotter than a pepper sprout of Damascus! Why not add the pleasures of the Jordan to our romance experiences? We might as well be the first couple underwater. With twenty-four children and the world full of people around, this may be our last opportunity. Let's take advantage of this beautiful romantic place."

Abraham replies, "Why not? You won your case! What is the boiling point of this holy river? [Laughter] Thank you for giving me your love."

After the act of marriage, they swam back together side-by-side toward the tree in which both their play clothes were hanging. Abe took a towel and dried off Sarah, and Sarah took a towel and dried off Abe. Sarah spoke first,

"Abe, you are so handsome! I am not ashamed to be seen naked by you! What about you, my darling?

"No, my rib. [Laughter] You are beautiful. Curves everywhere. Let us put on our play clothes, and even though I had my dessert – you, I saw a container of delicious smelling desserts.

Sarah prepared Abe a big plate of various desserts and sweet fruits giving herself about half the serving she had given him. She reasoned, '*I don't want Abe to lose weight – he is just right for me.*'

Abe blessed the deserts, putting the largest piece of cake back, and gave thanks and broke the silence,

"We have an enemy out there, my darling. Stay near me as we keep each other's backside covered. It was not good for me to be alone, as I needed you. You know even right now our enemy might be planning our destruction.

While he might think he is going to win, I can assure you that no weapon formed against our Savior and Good Sheperd will prevail.[29] The battle is the Lord's,[30] and we are his humble instruments of service."

---

[29] See Isaiah 54:17.

158

Sarah, enjoying the wisdom of her husband as she smiles in perfect contentment, thinking, *"Lord, what a man you have given me. Thank you so much! He is truly the desire of my heart."*

Sarah cleared the containers off the bottom sheet and made a bed for a delightful nap together.

Apollo's Lectures on Music Theory and Appreciation

Back in the Celestial City Apollo begins his first of many lectures on *Music Theory and Appreciation* emphasizing the delightful obsession (addiction) to his music. He encouraged them to show sorrow and condemnation to those not similarly addicted, seeking to pull them into the magic. The time came for his Choir 6 and Orchestra 6 to rehearse. While all sounded so grand and perfect, Apollo had an underlying hidden message beneath the surface of personal independence and complete freedom of not subjecting oneself to being controlled by another person's will. He would say such things as, "It is wrong for another to seek to control you." Many were nibbling at his poisonous bait as he planned an act of war with the goal to make himself a lord to be worshiped and obeyed."

Abraham and Sarah Set a World Record – Seven in One Day

Sarah awakened first on the picnic blanket from the sound of the humming of mating bumblebees and joyous singing of some songbirds, all celebrating the mating time. She rubbed her hand through the hairs on Abe's chest and kissing him softly on his face while he slept laying her body dressed in the play clothes directly on top of him. Abe awakens pulling down the straps on each arm to Sarah's play clothes saying,

"I am certainly happy that the Lord gave me a warm and loving woman to be my wife. We are in Suite 7 and we can have a roll now under the grape arbor this afternoon. I will plan to have you again for dessert after our evening dining out on that soft lounge chair on the Veranda. Number seven (7) will be in our beautiful marriage bed right before our evening prayer. We cannot let anyone ever know about our seven (7) in one day as they would never forget it and would not understand. Our Lord hinted that we were going to hold the record and that no other Elder and his wife would ever be able to catch us. You make me feel so much like a man. Thank you!"

Sarah responds, "You are most kindly welcome my lord and master. I like the number seven (7). I believe we set a world record of seven (7) in a day, which may not be broken in this First Earth Age. I overheard the Son of God explaining to you that since we will not die in this First Earth Age, we would be allowed to come back and marry again in the Third Earth Age. At least, let us have a chance at the world's record in that age as well. Eight (8) in one day would be a new beginning number. [Laughter]

You make me feel like a fulfilled married woman. I have never had so much fun in all my life! Thank you again! Let us go back and see what we are having for dinner, as you are also my dessert.

Tomorrow is the first day of the week, and I saw the most modest of robes for me to wear at your side as we attend a special 3:00 p.m. worship service. I know where you are going, and I want to go with you! Through thick and thin, I am sticking with you like glue. I wonder where we will have a worship service tomorrow?"†

---

[30] See 2 Chronicles 20:15.

†BOOK FOUR – Episode 3†

[†**Sidebar Scriptures**: "Joseph had a dream and promptly reported all the details (Genesis 37:5)."
"The Lord revealed to me what the evil ones were doing and planning and showed me their wicked plots (Jeremiah 11:18)."
"The word of the Lord came to Abram in a **vision**. . . . A **deep sleep** came upon Abram . . . . (Genesis 15:1, 12)."
I witnessed and experienced "dreams and visions, and I described **all** I had seen to instruct many (Daniel 7:1, 11:33)."†]

Apollo's Scientists Convene, and the Son Announces
Abraham and Sarah to Have a Son

Apollo's Scientists Meet in the Lead-Lined
"Operation Black Room" in the Basement of the Pink Palace,

APPOLO, DRESSED IN LUXURIOUS black tight fitting apparel with his shirt opened, revealing black hairs on his chest beneath a gold chain, wearing a matching gold bracelet, and diamond earrings greet every scientist individually and flattering[1] each one to the uttermost. Apollo mentions an outstanding and unique individual attribute, assuring all he was their best friend. Each of the sixty-six (66) scientists being seated in a "U" shape and Apollo as the center attraction in the lead lined conference room exalts them,

"Inventors, I have come to admire the cleverness in each of you. You are my elite, the select, the cream that rises to the top, and the very best of the best. You are all my close friends, and I will always have your backside covered. United, there is nothing impossible for us to accomplish. He who is not with us is against us. Great rewards, lavish wealth, and territories to rule over will be provided in the future for individual scientific accomplishments. You will be a part of the team that has invented the ultimate weapon, which is our best defense. Our team will be known only to us as the "M.A.N. Project – Magnificent – Atomic –Neutralization.

We start with a leaked clue – $E=MC^2$. Each of you sixty-six (66) scientists has been provided a workstation, and all of you are to work independently. After 66 days, we will meet again, with each presenting his progress. Now go to work. You are the best, the elite, the select, the cream of the crop! We will have unity as we speak the same language and have the same goal 'then nothing we plan to do will be impossible for us.'[2] War! [Uttered in a low tone so others could not hear.]"

Father God Laughing and Fellowshipping with His One and only Begotten Son

On the throne, the Father laughs with the Son, and the Holy Spirit joins in.
Finally, the Holy Spirit asked, "Why are We laughing?"
The Father responds, "Apollyon Lucifer has convinced himself that he can create the ultimate weapon to destroy Us. He has been a liar and murderer from the beginning[3] and now he actually hates Us. I will permit him to proceed for reasons of My own. One reason, but not the only reason, is that I desire a family who will choose Me as Father of their free will. The special gift I give to the angels and man is the freedom to choose.

Also, out of all of this will come forth a determined bride that chooses You, My Son, over all others. She will be determined to accept Your marriage proposal.

---

[1] "Flattery" is defined in the *American Dictionary of the English Language, Noah Webster 1828*, as "False praise; commendation bestowed for the purpose of gaining favor and influence or to accomplish some purpose. Direct *flattery* consists in praising a person himself; indirect *flattery* consists in praising a person through his works or his connections."

[2] Genesis 11:6.

[3] See John 8:44.

There is nothing more determined than a woman in love! [Laughter] Her words are 'mot juste'[4] (just right and appropriate) and what a joy she will add to the throne.

Talking about love, brief Us, My Son, on the twenty-one (21) brides you designed, created, and gave in marriage to the beloved twenty-one (21) Elders."

The Son replies, "Right now they are all enjoying their honeymoon, and I am happy to report that all are 'occupied with gladness of heart.'[5] Your invention of sexual romance in marriage is being enjoyed by all. However, Abraham has been the only one to ring the dinner bell of Heaven. We send a human spirit to join with his sperm, which yesterday joined with Sarah's egg under the Grape Arbor, right where we will have the anointed service this afternoon. [Laughter] Yes, We will soon hear the 'pitter-patter'[6] of little feet from Isaac. Isaac will accept Me as his Savior at the early age of accountability, adding his name to the **Lambs Book of Life**[7] and who will likewise rejoice with his wife, Rebecca."

The Father laughs, "Abraham is My friend, a man's man in the flesh as You will be in the Third Earth Age. I am not surprised that he of his own 'free will would select such a holy spot for a romantic picnic. His son Isaac will also be Our friend, and We will also delight in and bless him.

Are you going to let the others know the details of Isaac's conception?"

"Well?"

"That is a deep subject, My Son." [Laughter]

"Father, yes, I am going to let the other Elders know about the home run. I will give no other details as the others will not forget the details and will think about them at times when they see them. This way Abraham and Sarah will know that I am a trusted Friend, Savior, and Lord to them. The location is a funny secret, which I will not tell others, but someday in eternity, they will disclose it, relating to Isaac's birth in the First Earth Age, on themselves. We will all have a big laugh then. Until they tell it, silence is My lip.

The Couples Fellowship as they Assemble in the Lobby, Joyfully Board the Carriage and Shortly Arrive Under the Grape Arbor Overlooking the Crystal Clear Jordan River

Back on Earth, each of the twenty-one couples has joyful fellowship in the lobby showing their wedding rings and photo albums and being silent about their intimacy.

"*All Aboard*" respectfully announce the angel carriage driver.

Arm-and-arm each couple boards with joy taking their respective seats. Abraham acknowledges the Lord's goodness and offers a prayer of Thanksgiving, with each couple in unison saying, "Amen!" The white gold-trimmed convertible carriage, drawn by twenty-four white horses, proceeds in perfect harmony and rhythm toward the Jordan River turning into a side grass road leading up to the Grape Arbor, being the same location that Abraham had previously noticed and under which they had spread a picnic yesterday.

---

[4] Mot justice from French meaning, "The perfectly appropriate word or phrase for the situation. " *Wiktionary, Open Content Dictionary.*

[5] Ecclesiastes 5:20 (NIV).

[6] Pitter-patter, "the sound of rapid succession of light beats or taps, as rain or footsteps." *The Free Dictionary by Fairlex.*

[7] See Revelation 21:27.

Abraham announces, "This is holy ground. Let us leave our sandals in the carriage and walk up the narrow yellow dirt road."

Abraham and Sarah look at each other, and Abraham whispers, "I thought you said this spot was private!" Sarah giggles and laughing, getting Abraham giggling and laughing with her saying, "Something or someone[8] in me is making me laugh."

Abraham and Sarah Being Seated over the Same Spot they had Spread a Blanket the Day Before and Sarah Not Able to Stop Laughing and Giggling

As they were seated over the exact grassy spot where Sarah had spread the blanket the day before, Sarah continues giggling and whispers to Abraham, "Did I do anything wrong? Did you have any idea this was our holy meeting spot? What is making me laugh?"

Abraham giggling replies, "The answer to your first question is 'no,' the second is, 'I had no prior knowledge,' and the third answer I suspect, my darling, is related to His commandment for us to have fun. God is not a spoiled sport! He did not frown on our picnic and lovemaking here yesterday. He told us to have fun. I can imagine no one ever having more fun together than we had yesterday, especially on this spot of spots. You made me feel the way a married man should feel. Thank you very much! Remember that seven in one day is our secret." [Laughing in a low tone together.]

"Abraham, something or someone in me is causing me to laugh and giggle."

At that moment, Michael and Gabriel appear on each side of the crystal pulpit with Gabriel blowing a Shofar. A future to-be-written Scripture appears on a screen reminding the Lord's servants, they should imitate their Lord's previous example of washing their feet,

'You call me 'Teacher' and 'Lord', and rightly so, for that is what I am. Now that I, your Lord and Teacher, have washed your feet, you also should wash one another's feet. I have set you an example that you should do as I have done for you. I tell you the truth, no servant is greater than his master, nor is a messenger greater than the one who sent him. Now that you know these things, you will be blessed if you do them.'[9]

Each elder rose and went to a nearby table and poured water from a pitcher into a basin and picking up a bar of white soap, two wash clothes, four towels, and the pitcher of water. They returned and sat down on the ground, instead of kneeling, and placed their beloved wife's feet in the basin and soaped her feet using a washcloth. Holding the wives' feet, they rinsed them by pouring on the crystal clear water from the pitcher and then dry them with a towel. Each wife being seated with her sparkling clean feet resting on a white towel.

Abraham is thinking, "*Sarah, how beautiful are your feet.*"

Sarah smiles, looking Abraham in the eyes announces, "Now husbands, it's your turn for us, blessed daughters of Zion, to wash your handsome feet."

---

[8] Isaac from the Hebrew means "he will laugh."
 See *The New Name Dictionary - Modern English and Hebrew Names* compiled by Alfred J. Kolatch.
[9] John 13:13-17 (NIV).

Each wife seats on the ground, being careful not to kneel, except Sarah kneels on one knee as she refers to Abraham as her 'lord (master).'[10] While the men are seated, each wife picks up her husband's feet and places them in the basin and lovingly soaps them into a rich lather with the washcloth removing all the dust. The wives then pick up the husbands' feet pouring clean water on them and dry them with the towel, with Sarah using her hair to dry Abraham's feet. Sarah smiling takes her place beside her husband with Abraham so pleased taking her left hand in his right hand.

The invisible hands of ministering angels remove the washing elements, drying and shaping Sarah's hair, giving it a glorious glow and beauty, above the other women, with the couples feeling every bit clean.

David under the anointing arises and going over to his harp with these words appearing on the screen as he softly plays,

'How beautiful on the mountains
    are the feet of those who bring good news,
who proclaim peace,
    who bring good tidings,
    who proclaim salvation,
who say to Zion, 'Your God reigns!'
Listen! Your watchmen lift up their voices; t
    together they shout for joy.
When the Lord returns to Zion,
they will see it with their own eyes.
Burst into songs of joy together,
    you ruins of Jerusalem,
for the Lord has comforted His people;
    He has redeemed Jerusalem.
The Lord will lay bare His holy arm
    in the sight of all the nations,
and all the ends of the Earth will see
    the salvation of our God.
Depart, depart, go out from there!
    Touch no unclean thing!
Come out from it and be pure,
    you who carry the vessels of the Lord.
But you will not leave in haste
    or go in flight;
for the Lord will go before you,
    the God of Israel will be your rear guard.
See, My (Father) Servant (Son of God) will act wisely;
    He will be raised and lifted up and highly exalted.

---

[10] See 1 Peter 3:6 and Genesis 18:12.

Sarah was respecting her husband by submitting to him in his position as head of the home. God told Eve as a result of her disobedience, "*Your desire will be for your husband, and he will rule over your.*" (Genesis 3:16.) arah did not worship Abraham nor always go along with what Abraham wanted when Abraham was wrong. For example, Sarah knew that Hagar was plotting to murder Isaac making it look like an accident so her Ishmael would be the only son of Abraham. Therefore, Sarah asked Abraham to send Hagar and Ishmael away and this distressed Abraham. God backed Sarah and instructed Abraham, "*Listen (and do) whatever Sarah tells you for Isaac is the son through whom My promise will be fulfilled.* (Genesis 21:12.)

Just as there were many who were appalled at Him –
  His appearance was so disfigured beyond that of any man
  and His form (God in the flesh) marred beyond human likeness –
so will He sprinkle (save with His own blood believers in) many nations (of the Earth)!' [11]

As the gentle wind of the Holy Spirit blows, the Son of God appears barefoot, wearing a simple white robe, looking much like the Elders. There was nothing about His appearance that would make Him stand out in a crowd. The couples immediately fall to their knees before the Son of God, and worshiped Him with Word (Jesus) addressing them,

"I welcome you, one-flesh couples, to this specially anointed set apart holy ground. This ground is unique and exciting things happen here."

Again Sarah giggles and laughing.

The Son of God inquired, "Sarah, are you laughing?"

Sarah shook her head "no" trying to keep the giggling sounds from coming out her tightly closed lips.

The Son of God contradicts her 'no nod' declaring sternly, "Yes, you are!"

Sarah in fear bows to her knees with tears in her eyes besetting, "Forgive me for lying in my nod. Something or someone inside me is making me laugh. What is it?"

Sarah tried to maintain a plain face, but she could not stop giggling, no matter how hard she tried. She whispered to Abraham, "Would it be okay for me to recuse myself so I can gain my composure?"

Abraham shook his head 'no.'

The Son of God replying, "Sarah, my precious daughter, you are forgiven for lying. Sarah, you will lie to Me again when you and Abraham are married in the Third Earth Age. It will be recorded when I visit Abraham, accompanied by Michael and Gabriel, regarding the sexual sins such sodomy in the nearby cities of Sodom and Gomorrah,

'The Lord appeared to Abraham near the great trees of Mamre while he was sitting at the entrance to his tent in the heat of the day. Abraham looked up and saw three men (Son of God and angels Michael and Gabriel) standing nearby.

. . . "Where is your wife Sarah?" they asked him.

"There, in the tent," he said.

Then the Lord said, 'I will surely return to you about this time next year, and Sarah your wife will have a son.'

Now Sarah was listening at the entrance to the tent, which was behind him.

*Abraham and Sarah were already old and well advanced in years, and Sarah was passed the age of childbearing. So Sarah laughed to herself as she thought, "After I am worn out, and my **master** (lord) is old, will I now have this pleasure?"*

Then the Lord (Son of God) said to Abraham, 'Why did Sarah laugh and say, 'Will I really have a child, now that I am old?' Is anything too hard for the Lord? I will return to you at the appointed time next year, and Sarah will have a son."

Sarah was afraid, so she lied and said, 'I did not laugh.'

But He (Son of God) said, 'Yes, you did laugh.'

When the men got up to leave, they looked down towards Sodom, and Abraham walked with them to see them on their way. Then the Lord (Son of God) said, 'Shall I hide from Abraham what I am about to do? Abraham will surely become a great and powerful nation, and all nations on earth will be blessed through him. For I have chosen him, so he will direct his children and his household after him to keep the way of the Lord by doing what is right and just, so the Lord will bring about for Abraham what He has promised him.'

Then the Lord (Son of God) said, "The outcry against Sodom and Gomorrah is so great and their sin so grievous that I will go down and see (direct evidence) if what they have done is as bad as the outcry that has reached Me (the Son of God).' [12]

---

[11] Isaiah 52:7-14 (NIV).
[12] Genesis 18:1, 9-20 (NIV).

The Lord Jesus inquired, 'Sarah, would you like to tell everyone why you're laughing to-day?'

Sarah blushes shaking her head '*no.*'

The Son of God's Addressing Sarah's Laughing and Making an Announcement that Abraham and Sarah Will Have a Son, Isaac

"Well, let Me explain in part as Abraham is going to be an example to the other men and Sarah will be an example to the women. Sarah, you have a son alive in your womb named Isaac, which means laughter. His spirit today is contained in only seven (7) joyful cells, which could be placed on the head of a pin. He is laughing in you, and you are laughing with him. These are the first of many laughs because of this delightful son."

Sarah smiles, nodding her head a joyful, "yes."

"Jesus continues, "Let me explain. I commanded you to be fruitful and multiply. Upon the seed of man joining with the egg of the woman Heaven immediately imparts a living spirit to be united with the little forming body. Yesterday, about this time, Heaven sent a spirit, named Isaac, which means 'laughter,' into that new creation formed by the joining of Abraham's sperm and Sarah's egg.

Both the angels and the spirit of Isaac were laughing as Isaac's spirit was placed in the baby in Sarah's womb. God gives a human spirit when the female egg is fertilized by the male sperm. The fetus starting around three months to birth, experiencing emotions such as great pain if being murdered in an abortion and at other times even leaps for joy in the womb, having blind sight of a joyful event going on around them. Life does not begin at birth, but at conception! A man and a woman have the capacity of creating a human being, made in the image of God.

The young children are innocent until they reach the age of accountability, and then they can choose whether to serve God or God's enemy. If a baby dies, it is not saved, but safe. Once a young person becomes accountable, they have to repent and be sorrow for their sins, receive Me (Jesus) as Savior and confess Me as Lord, be baptized in water, leaving their sins in that watery grave. Then the Holy Spirit joins with their human spirit making the saved person born again. If this occurs, then one's name is written in the ***Lamb's Book of Life***. They as an adopted child of Heaven are born again from above into the family of God, having a right and title to eternal life as a free gift from God.

God throughout the Earth Ages will save those who shall choose, of their own free will, Me as their Savior, and these only are foreordained to eternal ***salvation***. Notwithstanding God's foreknowledge, man, made in Our image, is a free moral being. A man chooses as a free moral agent to either sin and do evil and follow their father the devil or to accept Me as Savior because of God's foreknowledge, as God refuses to make robots. Sin and evil exist, and My Father God permits it because He desires a family who truly loves Him and receives Me as Savior in faith of their own free will.' God is a God of legality, and He gives everyone a measure of faith. True saving faith leads one to trust in the atoning merits of My sacrificial death as I shed My life's blood to pay the penalty due for their sins in full.

My Father God will raise Me from the dead. My Father God will also raise all that die in Me from the dead for them to enjoy eternal life. So a baby who dies is not saved, but is safe!

Sarah, nine months from today, lacking twenty-one hours, you will have an easy, with no pain, joyful birth of a man-child, Isaac.

Therefore, the name assigned to your first born in this first Earth age is Laughter or Isaac. Isaac will be such a joy for both of you. Sarah, it will be written about Isaac in the second earth age,

'Now there was a famine in the land – besides the earlier famine of Abraham's time – and Isaac went to Abimelech king of the Philistines in Gerar.

The Lord appeared to Isaac and said, 'Do not go down to Egypt; live in the land where I tell you to live. Stay in this land for a while, and I will be with you and will bless you. For to you and your descendants, I will give all these lands and will confirm the oath I swore to your father, Abraham. I will make your descendants as numerous as the stars in the sky and will give them (legally) all these lands, and through your offspring all nations on Earth (to receive of own free will the Savior of the world) will be blessed, because Abraham obeyed me and kept my requirements, my commands, my decrees, and my laws.' So Isaac stayed in Gerar.

When the men of that place asked him about his wife, he said, 'She is my sister,' because he was afraid to say, 'She is my wife.' He thought, 'The men of this place might kill me for Rebekah because she is beautiful.'

When Isaac had been there a long time, Abimelech king of the Philistines looked down from a window and saw Isaac caressing his wife, Rebekah. So Abimelech summoned Isaac and said, 'She is really your wife! Why did you say, 'She is my sister'?'

Isaac answered him, 'Because I thought I might lose my life on account of her.'

Then Abimelech said, 'What is this you have done to us? One of the men might well have slept with your wife, and you would have brought guilt upon us.'

So Abimelech gave orders to all the people: 'Anyone who molests this man, or his wife shall surely be put to death.'

Isaac planted crops in that land, and the same year reaped a hundredfold because the Lord blessed him. The man became rich, and his wealth continued to grow until he became very wealthy. He had so many flocks and herds and servants that the Philistines envied him.[13]

You will all be so envied and hated because of your great wealth and your beautiful wives. I could dress Sarah, Isaac's wife, Rebekah, and all you beautiful wives in concrete and still evil men would lust after you. You are to wear modest apparel, but not ridiculously covered with just your eyes showing. Elder Peter, you will record of Sarah,

'Sarah obeyed Abraham (following his guidance and acknowledging his headship over her by) calling him lord – master, leader, authority.'[14]

"Elders guard your wives, daughters, and sons also from the evil lust in the world.

Watch the screen as a lioness south of here in dinosaur country is to give birth to triplets. After each was born, the lioness licks them one at a time cleaning them up.

Watch the hyena about to grab one of the newborns for lunch. The hyena hearing a furious roar and looking up encounters the male lion, who had been monitoring his advances, springing on him out of the tree tearing him to shreds.

The lion then presents some of his meat to the happily protected female who had just nursed. Just as much as that lion in the tree was committed to protecting his family, so you Elders, with the assistance of My ever-present guardian angels, are likewise to protect your wives and children.

---

[13] Genesis 26:1-14 (NIV).
[14] 1 Peter 3:6 (AMP).

Remember, '*The joy of the Lord is your strength!*'[15] Now, watch the lioness as she licks the blood of the hyena off her mate's face. Now is that not happiness and contentment?"

David plays the harp and sings,

'*They that wait upon the Lord [Jesus, Son of God] shall renew their strength.*
They shall mount up with wings as eagles. They shall run and not be weary
and they shall walk and not faint.'[16]

'*The joy of the Lord (the Son of God) is my strength.*'[17]

'*I can do all things through Christ (Jesus, Son of God) who strengthens me.*'[18]

'*I will say of the Lord (Son of God), 'He is my refuge and my fortress,*
my God, in whom I trust.
. . . *For He (Son of God) will command His angels concerning you*
to guard me in all your ways;
they will lift you up in their hands,
so that you will not strike my foot against a stone.
. . . '*Because he (that's me) loves Me,*' *says the Lord (Jesus),*
I will rescue him; I will protect him, for he acknowledges My name (Jesus).
He will call upon Me, and I will answer him;
I will be with him in trouble;
I will deliver him and honor him.
With long life will I satisfy him
and show him My salvation.'[19]

I am playing and singing of the joy of the Lord. I am surrounded by the angels of God, who guard and protect me.

It is so good and joyful to be saved! Amen!"†

---

[15] Nehemiah 8:10.
[16] Isaiah 40:31.
[17] Nehemiah 8:10.
[18] Philippians 4:13.
[19] Psalm 91:2, 11-12, 14-16.

†BOOK FOUR – Episode 4†

[†**Sidebar Scriptures**: "*Joseph had a dream and promptly reported all the details (Genesis 37:5).*"
"*The Lord revealed to me what the evil ones were doing and planning and showed me their wicked plots (Jeremiah 11:18).*"
"*The word of the Lord came to Abram in a* **vision**. . . . *A* **deep sleep** *came upon Abram . . . . (Genesis 15:1, 12).*"
I witnessed and experienced "*dreams and visions, and I described* **all** *I had seen to instruct many (Daniel 7:1, 11:33).*"†]

The Son of God Blesses Elders and Shares a Secret about Hell

JESUS ADDRESSES THE twenty-one Elders in Zion, with three other Elders to be added later, to make twenty-four, saying, "It will be written of Me, guarding, watching over you, and keeping you with great vigilance and tender care,

'*The eyes of the Lord are over the righteous.*
and His ears are attentive to their prayer,
but the face of the Lord is against those who do evil.'[1]

There will be a time, when evil men will seek to commit homosexual abominations, such as sodomy and oral sex, with My angels Gabriel and Michael, standing behind Me today. As we have partially discussed, when they visited Abraham's relative, Lot, to view the evidence they saw first-hand that the sins of Sodom and Gomorrah were so abominable. These wicked people were to be destroyed from the face of the Earth and then moved into Hell beneath the Earth, as it will be written,

'*The two angels (Michael and Gabriel) arrived at Sodom in the evening, and Lot was sitting in the gateway of the city. When he saw them, he got up to meet them and bowed down with his face to the ground. He said, 'please turn aside to your servant's house. You can wash your feet and spend the night and then go on your way early in the morning.'*
'*No,' they answered, 'we will spend the night in the square.'*
But he insisted so strongly that they went with him and entered his house.
He prepared a meal for them, baking bread without yeast, and they ate. Before they had gone to bed, all the men from every part of the city of Sodom – both young and old – surrounded the house. They called to Lot, 'Where are the men who came to you tonight? Bring them out to us so we can have sex with them.'
Lot went outside to meet them and shut the door behind him and said, 'No, my friends. Don't do this wicked thing. Look, I have two daughters who have never slept with a man. Let me bring them out to you, and you can do what you like with them. But do nothing to these men, for they have come under the protection of my roof.'
'*Get out of our way,' they replied. And they said, 'This fellow came here as an alien, and now he wants to play the judge! We'll treat you worse than them.' They kept bringing pressure on Lot and moved forward to break down the door.*
But the men inside reached out and pulled Lot back into the house and shut the door. Then they struck the men at the door of the house, young and old, with blindness so they could not find the door.
The two men said to Lot, 'Do you have anyone else here – sons-in-law, sons or daughters, or anyone else in the city who belongs to you? Get them out of here, because we will destroy this place. The outcry to the Lord against its people is so great He has sent us to destroy it.'
So Lot spoke to his sons-in-law, who were pledged to marry his daughters. He said, "Hurry and get out of this place because the Lord is about to destroy the city!" But his sons-in-law thought he was joking.
With the coming of dawn, the angels urged Lot, saying, 'Hurry! Take your wife and your two daughters who are here, or you will be swept away when the city is punished.'
When he hesitated, the men grasped his hand and the hands of his wife and of his two daughters and led them safely out of the city, for the Lord was merciful to them. As soon as they had brought them out, one of them said,

---

[1] 1 Peter 3:12 (NIV).

"Flee for your lives! Do not look back, and don't stop anywhere in the plain! Flee to the mountains, or you will be swept away!"

. . .By the time Lot reached Zoar, the sun had risen over the land. Then the Lord rained down burning sulfur on Sodom and Gomorrah – from the Lord out of the heavens. He overthrew those cities and the entire plain, including all those living in the cities – and also the vegetation in the land. But Lot's wife looked back, and she became a pillar of salt.

. . .Early the next morning Abraham got up and returned to the place where he had stood before the Lord. He looked down towards Sodom and Gomorrah, towards all the land of the plains and he saw dense smoke rising from the land, like smoke from a furnace.

So when God destroyed the cities of the plain, He remembered Abraham, and he brought Lot out of the catastrophe that overthrew the cities where Lot had lived.'[2]

It will be written what is ahead of you in eternity,
'*No eye has seen,*
   no ear has heard,
no mind has conceived
   what God has prepared for those who love Him.'[3]
Father God will reveal more and more to you Elders by the Holy Spirit.[4]

You have on My armor, and I give you the term 'brother' to address each other. I want each of you to sit down around the round table, meaning that none of you can sit prideful at the head as you all are equal.

Foundationally, the God kind of love is defined as follows,

'*Love is patient. Love is kind. It does not envy. It does not boast. It is not proud.*
It is not rude, it is not self-seeking, it is not easily angered; it keeps no record of wrongs.
Love does not delight in evil but rejoices with the truth. It always protects,
always trusts, always hopes, and always perseveres. Love never fails!'[5]

Elders you are to be the happiest people on Earth. You are too blessed and anointed to ever be stressed. I, Jesus, as your Lord is your strength. Do not let the envy or lust of any evil person rob you of your joy. Laugh at them all the way, as you dance, not walk, to the bank! [Laughter] Elder Matthew, I appoint you as the President of the Bank of Israel, with the main branch in Jerusalem.

I am this day depositing seven million dollars of gold coins for each Elder. I am Your Good Shepherd, and you will not want[6] for anything you need. You need to remember that the streets in Heaven will one day be paved with gold, so in one sense I am just giving you Heavenly pavement. [Laughter]

Your net worth, or the way you obtained it or made it grow with integrity, is no one's business. Let nothing rob you of your peace and joy. If an enemy cannot rob you of your peace and joy, they cannot rob you of your goods. Shalom.

Today, right before I came to Earth, My Father was laughing about a creative being making futile plans to destroy My Father and His will.

---

[2] Genesis 19:1-17, 23-30 (NIV).

[3] 1 Corinthians 2:9 (NIV).

[4] 1 Corinthians 2:10 (NIV).

[5] 1 Corinthians13:4-8 (NIV).

[6] Psalm 23:1.

This enemy when he discovers you will add you to his hit list also containing the Holy Spirit and Me. He has been a liar from the beginning and actually hates Us without cause. My Father will permit this for purposes of His own.

I assure you that My Father is all powerful and is keen and wise in getting all His future plans accomplished. I call that plan to war against My Father 'Ignoramus Hippopotamus' or 'Ignorance Gone to Seed.' [Laughter] Elder David, please lead us on the harp in singing these truths appearing on the screen,

'The Mighty One, God, the Lord,
    speaks and summons the Earth
    from the rising of the sun to the place where it sets.
From Zion, perfect in beauty,
    God shines forth.
Our God comes and will not be silent;
    A fire devours before Him,
    and around him a tempest rages.
He summons the heavens above,
    and the Earth, that He may judge His people:
Gather my consecrated ones,
    who made a covenant with Me by sacrifice.
And the heavens proclaim His righteousness,
    for God Himself is Judge. Selah.
Hear, O My people, and I will speak,
    O Israel, and I will testify against you:
    I am God, your God.
I do not rebuke you for your sacrifices
    or your burnt offerings, which are ever before Me.
I have no need of a bull from your stall
    or of goats from your pens,
for every animal of the forest is mine,
    and the cattle on a thousand hills.
I know every bird in the mountains,
    and the creatures of the field are mine.
If I were hungry, I would not tell you,
    for the world is mine, and all that is in it.
Do I eat the flesh of bulls
    or drink the blood of goats?
Sacrifice thank offerings to God,
    fulfill your vows to the Most High,
and call upon Me in the day of trouble;
    I will deliver you, and you will honor Me.
But to the wicked, God says:
'What rights have you to recite My laws
    or take My covenant on your lips?

You hate My instruction
    and cast My words behind you.
When you see a thief, you join with him;
    you throw in your lot with adulterers.
You use your mouth for evil
    and harness your tongue to deceit.'
. . . Consider this, you who forget God,
    or I will tear you to pieces, with none to rescue:
He who sacrifices thank offerings honors Me,
    and to him who considers His way
    I will show the salvation of God.' [7]

'To the Lord your God belong the Heavens, even the highest Heavens,
    the Earth and everything in it.
Yet the Lord sets His affection on your forefathers and loved them,
    and He chose you, their descendants, above all the nations, as it is today.
Circumcise your hearts . . . . For the Lord . . . the great God, mighty and awesome. . .
    shows no partiality and accepts no bribes.' [8]

Lucifer Apollyon is offering what he thinks is the greatest riches to his scientist angels if they can create a bomb to freeze solid everything. He is keeping from them his secret that he desires to use this I-Bomb to murder My Father God, whom he does not even believe exist, Myself, the Holy Spirit, all loyal to Us, and to steal for himself both Heaven and Earth. He desires to be worshiped and set up his kingdom of darkness in the very Throne Room of God.

Our enemy, a creative being, thinks he is the richest one on Earth. He has a temporary lease to a vault in the heart of the Earth, which he named Hell, which he assumes, is laden with much gold.

Look at the screen, and you will see the future streets of Heaven paved with pure gold, after Apollo is cast out of Heaven down to the Earth. Now look at your twenty-four elders' Thrones, which except for the soft cushions and jewels, are of pure gold.

You will lay up rich treasures in Heaven, and these are your eternal thrones upon which you will rule angels when you are not away performing God's business.

You each are to '*do the work of an evangelist*' [9] in this First Earth Age and in later Earth ages. You will become all things to all men so that some will be saved.

Now journey with Me on the screen into the vault of Hell inside the Earth and look at the black walls and the golden color veins. The dead creature you see lying on its back is Beelzebub, a giant fly from one of Apollo's drawings.

Apollo appointed Beelzebub as a guard over these false gold veins in Hell. Apollo left Beelzebub with a little water, locked the gate, and forgot about him. After many days, Beelzebub, after concluding that Apollo had forgotten about him and had utterly forsaken him, searched Hell from top to bottom, but he could not find one drop of water in Hell to drink.

---

[7] Psalm 50:1-19, 22-23 (NIV).
[8] Deuteronomy 10:14-17.
[9] 2 Timothy 4:5 (NIV).

Beelzebub was the first of many Apollo casualties, as he died of thirst and from eating some poisonous mushrooms Apollo told him to eat as his wages. The wages of sin with Apollo is death![10]

Apollo, a created being, thinks he is the richest one on Earth because he has the keys to a vault in the heart of the Earth, which he calls Hell, which he assumes, is laden with much gold. The distant future streets of Heaven, after Apollo is cast out of Heaven, will be paved with a transparent gold, but gold is rare on the Earth. Are you ready for the inside joke? [*All nodding a yes.*] What our enemy thinks is gold is what will be known on the Earth as 'fool's gold.'[11] Fool's gold looks like 'the real McCoy'[12] in the dim light, but everything that glitters is not gold when it is brought out to the light. Apollo's workers will excitedly bring some of it into the bank seeking to open bank accounts to deposit it to earn interest when they learn the truth that 'it is not worth a continental.'[13] Remember that everything that glitters is not gold. I advised Apollo to take the narrow road to Paradise, which is located under the hills of Havilah, where he would have found much gold. Those who do not love Me will not listen or obey counsel. He who has Me is rich, and he who does not have Me, though he gains the whole world, is poor.

Elders, you are the apple of God's eye. You are friends of God. Here are some precious promises, confessions, and commandments for you,

'For whoever touches you touches (seeks to hurt one loved and protected by God)
    the apple of God's eye.'[14]
'Rejoice in the Lord always: and again I say, Rejoice!'[15]
'The joy of the Lord (Jesus for you) is your strength.'[16]
Keep your lives free from the love of money and be content with what you have, because God has said,
'Never will I leave you;
    never will I forsake you.'[17]
So we say with confidence,
    'The Lord is my helper, I will not be afraid.
    What can man do to me?'[18]

Laughter is joy overflowing. Watch Abraham and Sarah laugh and naming their happy son, 'Laughter,' which is the meaning of the name Isaac. You all will be exceedingly happy, and when I take you out of here right before the worst, you will have laid up great treasures in Heaven. Daily laugh because you will have a good one in the Throne Room of Heaven that shall last forever.

Remember that only those with their names written in the **Lamb's Book of Life** will be saved. Even rejoice '*over one sinner who repents.*'[19]

---

[10] Romans 6:23.

[11] *Fool's Gold*, "Any of several minerals, especially pynite and chalcopyrite, sometimes mistaken for gold." *The American Heritage Science Dictionary*.

[12] "*The real McCoy* is a metaphor used in much of the English-speaking world to mean 'the real thing' or the 'genuine article' . . . ." *Wikipedia, The Free Encyclopedia*.

[13] Term used for money issued during the American Revolution that become worth very little as it had no backing.

[14] Zechariah 2:8.

[15] Philippians 4:18 (NIV).

[16] Nehemiah 8:10 (NIV).

[17] See Deuteronomy 31:6 .

[18] Hebrews 13:5-6 (NIV). See also Psalm 118:6-7.

[19] Luke 15:7.

If unrepenting sinners choose to be damned in Hell, with the devil and his angels, at least let them leap to Hell over your evangelistic bodies. If they perish, let them perish with your arms around their knees, imploring them to receive Me as Savior. If Hell must be filled, at least let it be filled with the opposition of the teeth of your exertions, and let no one go there unwarned and not prayed over. It will be written,

'The Lord is not slow in keeping His promise, as some understand slowness. He is patient with you, not wanting anyone to perish (in Hell) but everyone to come to repentance.

But the day of the Lord will come like a thief. The heavens will disappear with a roar; the elements will be destroyed by fire, and the Earth and everything in it will be laid bare.

Since everything will be destroyed in this way, what kind of people ought you to be? You ought to live holy and godly lives as you look forward to the day of God and speed its coming. That day will bring about the destruction of the heavens by fire, and the elements will melt in the heat. But in keeping with His promise we are looking forward to a New Heaven and a New Earth, the home of righteousness.

So then, dear friends, since you are looking forward to this, strive to be found spotless, blameless and at peace with Him.'[20]

It will be written regarding my future teaching,

'Every tree that does not bear good fruit is cut down and thrown into the fire (Hell). Thus, by their fruit, you will recognize them.'

Not everyone who says, 'Lord, Lord,' will enter the Kingdom of Heaven, but only he who does the will of My Father, who is in Heaven. Many will say on that day, 'Lord, Lord, did we not prophesy in Your name, and in Your name drive out demons and perform many miracles?' Then I will tell them plainly, 'I never knew you. Away from Me, you evildoers!'

Therefore, everyone who hears these words of Mine and puts them into practice is like a wise man who built his house on the rock. The rain came down, the streams rose, and the winds blew and beat against that house, yet it did not fall because it had its foundation on the rock. But everyone who hears these words of Mine and does not put them into practice is like a foolish man who built his house on sand. The rain came down, the streams rose, and the winds blew and beat against that house, and it fell with a great crash.'[21]

Isaac will not be the only baby born in different Earth ages of the same parents as this son. Jacob will also be born in two Earth Ages, and in this First Earth Age, his children will have a total of 144,000 Jewish grandchildren and great-grandchildren evangelists, who will not die in this First Earth Age. They will all die at the end of the Third Earth Age as worthy evangelists preaching to the Jews and Gentiles, *'Repent (turn from sin and change your hearts and lives) and be baptized (in water, leaving your sins in that watery grave), each one of you, in the name of Jesus Christ for the forgiveness of your sins, and you will receive the gift of the Holy Spirit (joining with your human spirit making you born again – a new creation).'*[22]

Upon the birth of Jacob in this First Earth Age trouble will intensify on the separated Island of Atlantis, and in the year, 666 of this First Earth Age, Lucifer will explode his I-Bomb freezing every living creature left on the surface of this beautiful Earth, making this Earth 'formless and empty.'[23]

---

[20] 2 Peter 3:9-14 (NIV).
[21] Matthew 7:19-27 (NIV).
[22] Acts 2:38.
[23] Genesis 1:1 (NIV).

All you Elders will be rescued, before the ice bomb explodes, as will those on the Earth who have repented and received Me as Savior and confessed Me as their Lord. However, our enemy will deceive his worshipers to believe a lie that he can win, and this climaxes in the Third Earth Age into what I call the 'Time of Jacob's Trouble,' which will include as it will be written,

'How awful that day will be!
    None will be like it.
It will be a time of trouble for Jacob,
    but he will be saved out of it.
. . . But I will restore you to health
        and heal your wounds,'
declares the Lord, 'because you are called an outcast,
Zion for whom no one cares.'
 . . . From them will come songs of thanksgiving
    and the sound of rejoicing.
 I will add to their numbers,
and they will not be decreased;
I will bring them honor,
    and they will not be disdained.
Their children will be as in the days of old,
    and their community will be established before Me;
    I will punish all who oppress them.
    . . . 'So you will be My people,
    and I will be your God.
 See, the storm of the Lord
    will burst out in wrath,
    a driving wind swirling down on the heads of the wicked.
The fierce anger of the Lord will not turn back
    Until He fully accomplishes
    the purposes of His heart.
In days to come,
    you will understand this.'[24]

The Son of God continues, "My Father desires a family who loves Him! However, in the Third Earth Age Abraham, Isaac, and Jacob will not remember the details of their lives in this First Earth Age, except shadows, making them ask, 'It seems as if I've been or done this before?' It will be the same with Me when My Spirit is imparted by the Holy Spirit as directed by My Heavenly Father into an egg, without a human sperm being involved, in the womb of My mother named Mary, a virgin. She was scorned and discarded by those accusing her of having sex before marriage and getting pregnant. The angel Gabriel will appear in a dream to a good man, Joseph, to whom she is engaged to be married, who was trying to get out of the engagement without further disgracing the young girl he loved as it will be written,

'God's angel (Gabriel) spoke in the dream, 'Joseph, son of David, don't hesitate to get married. Mary's pregnancy is Spirit conceived. God's Holy Spirit has made her pregnant.

---

[24] Jeremiah 30:7, 17, 19-20, 22-24 (NIV).

She will bring a Son to birth, and when she does, you, Joseph, will name Him, Jesus – 'God saves' – because He will save His people from their sins. This will bring the prophet's embryonic sermon to full term:

Watch for this – a virgin will be pregnant and bear a Son;
They will name Him Immanuel (Hebrew for 'God is with us').

Then Joseph woke up. He did exactly what God's angel commanded in the dream. He married Mary. But he did not consummate the marriage until she had the baby. He named the baby Jesus. [25]

My mother, a virgin, will give birth to Me with her hymen expanding to retain her virginity to prove with her own blood to her husband Joseph of her sexual purity.

You mothers are to teach your daughters and granddaughters that the greatest wedding present a wife can give her circumcised husband is her virginity!

I have prepared spirits for all the babies, and many of you will have easy, with little pain, multiple births, as we have this one main continent for your children, grandchildren, and great-grandchildren to populate. However, you only have a few hours a month in which the sperm and the egg can unite. Abraham and Sarah just were at the right place at the right time!"

Sarah looks a little concerned regarding their secret holy place being revealed to others.

"Enough on that sidebar as all of you will finally connect just at the right time. Three Keys – practice, practice, practice! [Laughter] Does anyone have an objection to the commandment, "Be fruitful and multiply!" [Giggles.]

Hearing none, I decree, with your cooperation, that before we meet back, here again, Friday evening at 7:00 P.M. for fish and chips and all the trimmings, each of your wives will be on the nest as birds of a feather flock together. [Laughter] Elders, this next Friday at 1:30 P.M. we will all meet in the lobby with your happy pregnant wives being escorted to visit and shop at such places as the Tel Aviv Maternity Shop and many other neat shops around the world set up by joyful angels. Your wives will enjoy both fellowship and purchasing whatever they desire without money. You men will not be left out as I have reserved St. Peter's fishing boat to be docked nearby on the Sea of Galilee for a day of sea fishing and letting you handle with your hands these slippery fish. Ladies, if any of you would rather go fishing all day out on the Sea of Galilee with the men raise your hand. You choose!"

Seeing no wife's hands, I assume all you women had rather go shopping. [Laughter]

Men, you will be fishers of men! As we await Isaac and your babies being born and growing up and populating the earth, let Me teach you about fishing for men. Later I will teach you more and more how to fish for men. What better place to start than by going fishing together on the beautiful Sea of Galilee! Friday we will focus on two techniques of fishing, e.g., such as with a net and with a line.

Friday evening you will have a charcoal fire of coals under a large grill to cook just right the delicious fish you catch. Also, you will enjoy the wives showing what they purchased – without money, for you, your future sons and daughters, and for themselves. This Friday evening will be a special celebrating time. Abraham will set the example of how to raise children. It will be written to both you and your children,

'Abraham's children will certainly become a great and powerful nation. I have chosen him so he would command his children and his descendants to keep the way the Lord wants them to live. Then I, the Lord, will give Abraham what I promised him.' [26]

---

[25] Matthew 1:20-25 (MSG).

'Children, obey your parents in the Lord, for this is right. Honor your father and mother' – which is the first Commandment with a promise – 'that it may go well with you and that you may enjoy long life on the Earth.'[27]

'Fathers, do not exasperate (irritate, provoke, or discourage) your children; instead, bring them up (tenderly, taking them by the hand and leading them) in the training and instruction (and way) of the Lord.'[28]

Elders, cherish and love your children as the apple of your right eye just as I will lay down My life for you. Frequently let them know just how beloved they are. When they do good, indicate that you are pleased with them. My Father encourages Me, such as His affirming,

'As soon as Jesus (Son of God) was baptized, He went up out of the water.
At that moment, Heaven was opened, and He saw the Spirit of
God descending like a dove and lighting on Him. And a voice from Heaven said,
'This is My Son, whom I love; with Him I am well pleased.'[29]

Tell your children when they do well that you are well pleased, and they are fully accepted. Give them a feeling of sonship and not of fear even when you have to train them to do what is right, and train (teach; educate) them in love with the rod (when needed) as it will be written,

'He who spares the rod (refusing to correct) hates his son,
but he who loves him is careful to discipline him.'[30]

Wise discipline will rightly squash rebellion and disobedience. Walk in tough love, but it will pay great dividends as it will be written,

'Children's children are the crown of old men, and the glory of children is their fathers.'[31]

'Lo, children are a heritage from the Lord, the fruit of the womb a reward.'[32]

I desire all your children to grow up and put away childish ways for *'No good thing will God withhold from them that walk uprightly.'[33]* You are to bless them and speak what the Word says they are and what they can do for the glory of God. As an example, it will be written regarding some blessings that Isaac's son Jacob spoke over some of his twelve sons in both the first and the third earth age,

'Assemble and listen, sons of Jacob;
listen to your father Israel. . . .
*'**Judah**, your brothers will praise you;*
your hand will be on the neck of your enemies;
your father's sons will bow down to you.
You are a lion's cub, O Judah;
you return from the prey, my son.
Like a lion, he crouches and lies down,
like a lioness – who dares to rouse him?
The scepter (symbol of kingship) will not depart (King Jesus of the tribe of Judah) from Judah. . . .
He will tie his donkey to a vine,
his colt to the choicest branch.

---

[26] Genesis 18:18-19.
[27] See Deuteronomy 5:16.
[28] Ephesians 6:1-4 (NIV).
[29] Matthew 3:16-17 (NIV).
[30] Proverbs 13:24 (NIV).
[31] Proverbs 17:6 (AMP).
[32] Psalm 127:3.
[33] Psalm 84:11.

He will wash his garments in wine,
*   his robes in the blood of grapes.*
Zebulun *will live by the seashore*
and become a haven for ships;
his border will extend towards Sidon.
Dan *will provide justice for his people*
as one of the tribes of Israel. . . .
Gad *will be attacked by a band of raiders,*
But he will attack them at their heels.
Asher's *food will be rich;*
he will provide delicacies fit for asking.
 Naphtali *is a doe set free*
that bears beautiful fawns.
Joseph *is a fruitful vine,*
*   a fruitful vine near a spring,*
*   whose branches climb over a wall.'*[34]

Elder David, please close with a song."

Sarah whispers to Abraham, "Please ask the Son of God to join us this evening for our celebration."

Elder Abraham stands,

"Son of God, on behalf of the Elders, we all thank You for all Your many kindnesses and blessings. Since You also have a flesh and bone body and enjoy the food of the Earth, we would like to invite You to enjoy a St. Peter's fish meal with us this evening as we celebrate all this new life coming into the Earth."

The Son of God with tears in His eyes, "Nods, *yes*." [Jesus would not have crashed the celebration without an invitation.]

Elder David on his harp leads the congregation in a selected song appearing on the screen,

'Blessed (happy) is everyone who fears, reveres and worships the Lord;
*   who walks in His ways and lives according to His commandments.*
For you will eat the fruit of your labor,
*   blessings and prosperity will be yours.*
Your wife shall be like a fruitful vine within your house,
*   your sons will be like olive shoots around your table.*
Thus is the man blessed
*   who fears the Lord.*
May the Lord bless you from Zion
*   all the days of your life;*
may you see the prosperity of Jerusalem,
*   and may you .to see your children's children.*
Peace (Shalom) be upon Israel.'[35†]

---

[34] Genesis 49:8-16, 20-22 (NIV). [Jesus was born of the Tribe of Judah.]
[35] Psalm 128:1-6 (See NIV and AMP).

†BOOK FOUR – Episode 5†

[†**Sidebar Scriptures**: "*Joseph had a dream and promptly reported all the details (Genesis 37:5).*"
"*The Lord revealed to me what the evil ones were doing and planning and showed me their wicked plots (Jeremiah 11:18).*"
"*The word of the Lord came to Abram in a* **vision**. . . . A **deep sleep** *came upon Abram . . . . (Genesis 15:1, 12).*"
I witnessed and experienced "*dreams and visions, and I described* **all** *I had seen to instruct many (Daniel 7:1, 11:33).*"†]

Apollo Receiving Worship from Members of His Choir and Orchestra, and the Son of God Preaches a Mini-Sermon on Pride

APOLLO COMPOSED SIX MUSICAL compositions, which he entitled, "Sounds of the Universe," with his personal favorites being, "Glorious Stars Excel," and "Victory Alone." He presents black sheet music with white lyrics to each member of his favorite number six choir and number six orchestra.

Apollo's New Musical Composition *Sounds of the Universe* and Apollo Receiving Worship and Glory

Apollo wearing a skin-tight black pantsuit, to show off his gorgeous features, takes his black light conductor's baton to conduct his "Sounds of the Universe." He balances every instrument and choir member perfectly right on every note of this enticing music.

Apollo, blowing smacking kisses with his hands and from his mouth, proclaims,

"I am so proud of you. In our next session, we will record my composition for all Heaven to admire. It's a proud day for this achievement for each member of this outstanding Choir Six. Paragon (Perfection)! Splendor (Excellent)! Remarkable (Brilliant)! Supercelestial![1] I have personally trained you, and you have learned well. You have brought me such glory today. No one could do it better than you. To reward each of you for your hard work, I have a special treat (goody) for you."

Apollo motions to Mercury to roll out a rack of newly designed black choir robes trimmed in gold having on them Apollo's new choir good luck logo in the form of a counter-clockwise black hooked cross.

Apollo thinks, "*Together back to back with such devoted subjects I can achieve (accomplish) anything, and nothing can wedge in between us. Nothing can destroy my goals.*"

Each member of the number six team blows Apollo back smacks kisses. Then each member rushes over to the rack to participate in a fashion show with the newly designed choir outfits

The captain of orchestra number six, Dionysus, prostrates himself on his knees before Apollo and kisses Apollo's hand, proclaiming,

"I adore you, my lord. Only a god could write such a masterpiece. It is such an honor and glory to be part of your team. I will serve and obey you in whatever capacity you have for me. I am your bondservant. You are the object of my loyalty and devotion. You are brilliantly gifted, my lord. May you and your music live on in cyberspace forever and a day! V.I.S.A.[2]"

---

[1] *American Dictionary of the English Language*, Noah Webster 1828, defines *Supercelestial* as, "Situated above the firmament or great vault of heaven."

[2] "French from Latin visa things seen . . . feminine past participle of visere to look into." *The Free Dictionary by Fairfax*. VISA name for saying amen or bye on the side of darkness pridefully standing for Very, Important Supreme, Achiever of Abaddon.

Next, the captain of the choir, Muse,[3] continuing to blow smacking kisses, speaks for the entire choir,"Apollo, your worship,[4] you are the greatest musician leader that ever was or ever could be. How great thou art! We idolize and deify you and pay you homage for your musical ability and beauty. We submit to, revere, and idolize you. You are brilliant and unbeatable. VISA!"

Apollo, receiving such admiration, worship, and praise thinking,
"I find such pleasure in being worshiped, praised, and exalted. It is the essence of selfishness, of the alleged father to want all the worship –his will regardless of the will of others. This is too much self-love without regards to the rights of others. I will give those who worship me their rights and freedom to be. To Be – War? That is the question!"

The Father God and Son of God Receive Worship from Elders and Wives

The couples joyfully assemble in the lobby and board the Convertible White Carriage for a delightful journey for a midweek service under the Grape Arbor. After the preliminaries, the Son of God appears, with the Elders and their wives bowing before Him in worship, with the Son of God announcing,

"My Father and I receive your worship. Please be seated.

Son of God's Mini-Sermon on Pride

For your information, right now our enemy is proudly receiving worship from heavenly angels. They are swallowing his bait, hook, line, and sinker being unaware that they are being caught in his dark spider web of pride. Pride can degrade the highest angels into devils. By dying to self, repenting, and trusting in Me, as Savior and Lord, flesh and blood can be raised to the throne room of Heaven as eternal children of God.

One third[5] of the angels in pride and rebellion will fall into the web of the temptation of pride.

You must not be proud! For pride goes before a disaster and ultimately leads to death.
'Pride leads to destruction; a proud attitude brings ruin.'[6]
'I (Son of God) am the vine, you are the branches, if you remain in Me, and I in you, you will bear much fruit, (and) apart from Me you can do nothing (at all lasting).'[7]

For without Me, the Lamb of God, you can do nothing of eternal value. Daily sow the seed of a humble servant and you will reap great rewards in Heaven. In humility and dying to self and receiving Me as Savior results in abundant life, forever and ever

It will be recorded in the Bible from one of My (Jesus') future sermons,
'To some confident of their own righteousness in looking down on everybody else, Jesus told this parable. 'Two men went up to the temple to pray, one a Pharisee and the other a tax collector.

---

[3] *Muse* – "The Muses, the personification of knowledge and the arts, especially literature, dance and music . . . ." *Wikipedia, The Free Encyclopedia.*

[4] *Worship* – "His worship is an honorific prefix for mayors . . . . The term *worship* implies that citizens give or attribute special worth or esteem (worth ship – as a worthy ship) to their . . . mayor." *Wikipedia, The Free Encyclopedia.*

[5] See Revelation 12:4.

[6] Proverbs 16:18.

[7] John 15:5.

The Pharisee stood up and prayed about himself: 'God, I thank you I am not like other men – robbers, evildoers, adulterers – or even like this tax collector. I fast twice a week and give a tenth of all I get.'

But the tax collector stood at a distance. He would not even look up to Heaven, but beat his breast and said, 'God, have mercy on me, a sinner.'

'I tell you, this man, rather than the other, went home justified before God. For everyone who exalts himself will be humbled, and he who humbles himself will be exalted.'[8]

Elders, be an example of true humility, and you will receive great rewards. In the Third Earth Age, it will be written,

'Then Jesus said to his disciples, 'If anyone would come after Me, he must deny himself and take up his cross and follow Me. For whoever wants to save his life will lose it, but whoever loses his life for Me will find it. What good will it be for a man if he gains the whole world, yet forfeits (loses) his soul? Or what can a man give in exchange for his soul? For the Son of Man will come in his Father's glory with his angels, and then He will reward each person according to what he has done.'[9]

Pride of self, says, 'Look what I have done and the wealth my hands have accumulated. See my good works; I proclaim how great I am! One receives the gift of salvation by grace and thanksgiving and not by any prideful works, less anyone should brag or boast he or she saved themselves. It will be written about y future teaching,

'The disciples came to Jesus and asked, 'Who is the greatest in the kingdom of Heaven?'

He called a little child and had him stand among them. And He said*: "I tell you the truth, unless you change and become like little children, you will never enter the kingdom of Heaven. Therefore, whoever humbles himself like this child is the greatest in the kingdom of heaven. And whoever welcomes a little child like this in My name welcomes Me.*

But if anyone causes one of these little ones who believe in Me to sin, it would be better for him to have a large millstone hung around his neck and to be drowned in the depths of the sea. Woe to the world because of the things that cause people to sin! Such things must come, but woe to the man through whom they come! If your hand or your foot causes you to sin, cut it off and throw it away. It is better for you to enter life maimed or crippled than to have two hands or two feet and be thrown into the fire that burns forever. And if your eye causes you to sin, gouge it out and throw it away. It is better for you to enter life with one eye than to have two eyes and be thrown into the fire of Hell.'[10]

'It is by grace you have been saved. And God raised us up with Christ and seated us with Him in the heavenly realms in Christ Jesus, in order that in the coming ages He might show the incomparable riches of His grace, expressed in His kindness to us in Christ Jesus. For it is by grace you have been saved, through faith – and this not from yourselves, it is the gift of God – not by works so that no one can boast. For we are God's workmanship, created in Christ Jesus to do good works, which God prepared in advance for us to do.'[11]

Elders teach others to tear away from the serpent of pride and like a trusting little child receive Me by faith as Savior and confess Me as Lord. You are My evangelist to present My love and grace to others so they too can be part of the Kingdom of God, which will never have an end.

---

[8] Luke 18:9-14 NIV.
[9] Matthew 16:24-27 NIV.
[10] Matthew 18:1-9 NIV.
[11] Ephesians 2:5-10 NIV.

I must warn you that because of pride, the deceitfulness of riches, and the pleasures of sin for a season that many will choose to worship the devil, who is the essence of pride. You must warn others not to worship him or to receive his mark '*on their right hands or on their foreheads.*'[12] Let me show you what the devil offered to Me in the Third Earth Age if I would just worship him,

'*Again, the devil took Him (Son of God, in a flesh, bone, and blood body) to a high mountain and showed him all the kingdoms of the world and their splendor. 'All this I will give you,' he said, 'if you will bow down and worship me.'*

Jesus said to him, 'Away from me, Satan! For it is written, 'Worship the Lord your God and serve Him only.''[13]
'*Then the devil left Him (Jesus in a flesh and blood body), and angels came and attended Him.*'[14]

Teach others that they must resist the prideful devil's offering of false pleasures using Scripture, coupled with My name, and he will flee from you as in terror.[15]

The devil is the accuser[16] of the brethren. Right now he is accusing My Father in Heaven of being selfish. That is a bad decision! [Laughter] My Father with His little finger will one day flick him through Gabriel into a lake of fire.[17] Remind the devil of his ending in this lake of fire and scorn and mock him for he is a defeated foe. How dare he declare war against My Father God and later against you made in God's image! Remember, '*Love never fails,*'[18] and '*God is love.*'[19] Simple mathematics! [Laughter]

Satan doesn't know what the Kingdom of God is up to, but My Father is all-knowing. *As sin increases on the Earth, the devil advances that he can easily keep many on a carousel of adultery and sexual immorality*. I will help them first not to get on his carousel. If they are seduced to get on, I will help them get off all carousels of besetting sin if they will sincerely repent with a 'broken and contrite spirit.'[20] They must see the wickedness of their sin, ask forgiveness, receive Me as Savior, and confess Me as Lord in all aspects of their lives.

This offer of grace is also to the 'chief of sinners'[21] and to those who have concentrated and devoted their time and energy to be slaves to the pleasures of a 'besetting sin'[22] for a season. I have chosen you to invite the worst of sinners to come before the 'silver cord of life is broken'[23] and they end up in Hell, by showing them a way of escape from the bondage of sin,

'*Whoever comes to Me (Jesus) I will never (not for anything he has done) drive away.*'[24]
'*For nothing is impossible with God.*'[25]
David gentled played his harp singing,
'*Have mercy on me, O God,*
    according to Your unfailing love;
according to your great compassion
    blot out my transgressions.

---

12 Revelation 13:16.
13 Deuteronomy 6:13.
14 Matthew 4:8-11 NIV.
15 James 4:7.
16 Revelation 12:10.
17 Revelation 20:10.
18 1 Corinthians 13:8.
19 1 John 4:8.
20 Psalm 51:17.
21 1 Timothy 1:15.
22 Hebrews 12:1.
23 Ecclesiastes 12:6.
24 John 6:37 NIV.
25 Luke 1:37 NIV.

Wash away all my iniquity (a bend to sin)
and cleanse me from my sins (by the Blood of the Lamb).
For I know my transgression,
and my sin is always before me.
Against You, You only, have I sinned
and done what is evil in Your sight,
so You are proved right when You speak
and justified when You judge.
. . . Cleanse me with hyssop (applying the Blood of the Lamb), and I will be clean;
wash me, and I will be whiter than snow.
Let me hear joy and gladness;
let the bones you have crushed rejoice.
Hide Your face from my sins
and blot out all my iniquity.
Create in me a pure heart O God,
and renew a steadfast spirit within me.
Do not cast me from Your presence
or take your Holy Spirit from me.
Restore to me the joy of Your salvation
and grant me a willing spirit to sustain me.
Then I (doing the work of an evangelist) will teach transgressors Your ways,
and sinners will turn back to you.'[26]

David affirms, "Selah – pause and calmly think about and meditate on these truths!"

David after a brief pause of meditation discerns, "I believe the Son of God has an important announcement and more instructions for us."

Twenty Elders Hit Home Runs After Abraham Had Already Scored with Isaac

The Son of God exhorts, "Now I command you to continue to *'enjoy life with your wives whom you love.'*[27] Talk about enjoying life; Heaven has been busy this week, sending spirits into the wombs of each of your wives. Most two and a few three for the wombs of your wives, as we have a continent to populate. My Father is so pleased with your holy and pure marriages. These children are going to be a joy to you. No one has disobeyed the command to be fruitful and multiply. [Laughter] I see such joy on each of you mothers to face.

You men will be dancing and giving gifts on the birth of your children in your likeness. It will be no doubt to whom the children belong. Peter, your first born son, will get your nose [Laughter] and your evangelistic flair.

The Godhead is 'counting the chickens before they hatch' so to speak as we send spirits. [Laughter] Thanks to your covenants of marriage My Father will have a family, who loves Him and whom He loves. Your children, grandchildren, and great-grandchildren will all have free wills to choose to be a part of the family of God or enjoy the pleasures of sin for a season, which includes adultery and sexual activity and immorality outside of marriage.

Romantic marriage is a great escape and release from the pressures and temptations of sexual sins. *'For it is better to marry than to burn with (sexual) passion.'*[28]
A husband needs the respect and intimacy of their wives to be a real man. When he releases his seed in the vagina of the wife he loves, this gives him a sense of well-being.

---

[26] Psalm 51:1-4, 7-13 NIV.
[27] Ecclesiastes 9:9.
[28] 1 Corinthians 7:9.

It has the added benefit of removing toxins from his body. You, women, take care of your husbands, and they will take care of you and your children.

'For the husband is the head of the wife as (Jesus) Christ is the head of the church, His body, of which He is the Savior.'[29]

The Son of God Sharing Some Key Points to Walking in Purity, Rearing Children, and Maintaining a Holy and Pure Marriage

Your love for your children will be both tender and stern. In the eternities, I will take away all remembrance and every tear from your eyes[30] of your descendants who reject with their free will such a great offer of salvation. Saying that sprinkling them with water gets a baby saved is nonsense. No, as a baby is safe not saved. They have to repent of their sins when they reach the age of accountability and receive Me as Savior and confess Me as Lord.

It will be written in the Third Earth Age,

'Then Jesus denounced the cities in which most of His miracles had been performed because they did not repent. Woe to you, Korazin! Woe to you, Bethsaida! If the miracles performed in you had been performed in Tyre and Sidon, they would have repented long ago in sackcloth and ashes. But I tell you, it will be more bearable for Tyre and Sidon on the day of judgment than for you. And you, Capernaum, will you be lifted up to the skies? No, you will go down to the depths (into Hell). If the miracles performed in you had been performed in Sodom, it would have remained to this day. But I tell you it will be more bearable for Sodom on the day of judgment than for you.'[31]

'The Lord (Jesus) is not wanting anyone to perish (in Hell), but everyone to come to repentance.'[32]

'The Son of Man (Jesus, in the flesh) will send out His angels, and they will weed out of His kingdom everything that causes sin and all who do evil. They will throw them into the fiery furnace (lake of fire), where there will be weeping and gnashing of teeth. Then the righteous (those who have repented and received Jesus as Savior and confessed Him as Lord) will shine like the sun in the kingdom of their Father.'[33]

If one dies without repenting and receiving Me as Savior, he or she will forever be separated from every ray of joy and cast into outer darkness where there will be weeping and gnashing of teeth as it will be written of those who are lost in their sins,

'Then Jesus went through the towns and villages, teaching as He made his way to Jerusalem. Someone asked Him, 'Lord, are only a few people going to be saved?' He said to them, 'Make every effort to enter through the narrow door, because many, I tell you, will try to enter and cannot. Once the owner of the house gets up and closes the door, you will stand outside knocking and pleading, 'Sir, open the door for us.' But He will answer, 'I don't know you or where you come from.' Then you will say, 'We ate and drank with You, and You taught in our streets.' But He will reply, 'I don't know you or where you come from. Away from Me, all you evildoers!' There will be weeping there, and gnashing of teeth, when you see Abraham, Isaac and Jacob and all the prophets in the kingdom of God; but you yourselves thrown out. People will come from east and west and north and south, and will take their places at the feast in the kingdom of God. There are those who are last who will be first, and first last.'[34]

Elders, you are My first evangelist preachers, and you will be My fishers of men – a mystery hidden before the foundation of the world. Brother Paul will explain, *'We (evangelist) speak God's secret wisdom (of salvation – repent, receive Jesus as Savior, and confess Him as Lord) in a mystery, which God had kept hidden before the world began . . . .'*[35]

---

[29] Ephesians 5:23 NIV.
[30] Revelation 21:4.
[31] Matthew 11:20-24 NIV.
[32] 2 Peter 3:9.
[33] Matthew 13:42 NIV.
[34] Luke 13:22-30 NIV.
[35] 1 Corinthians 2:7.

From your loins will come the population in Zion initially for this First Earth Age. Obeying this commandment that husbands and wives to be fruitful and multiply is pure and fun. [All couples smiling.] It will be written,

'Sons are a heritage, *from the Lord,*
    children are a reward from Him (the Lord.
Like arrows in the hands of a warrior
Blessed (happy and fortunate) is the man
    Whose quiver is full of them.
They will not be put to shame (humiliated)
    when they contend with their enemies at the city gate
      (The central place of the courts, commerce, and government).'[36]

You and your family are to worship and serve the one Triune God. For there is one person of the Father, another of the Son, and another of the Holy Spirit, but the Godhead of the Father, Son, and the Holy Spirit is one God. In the Third Earth Age, I will be God the Son, manifest in a flesh, bone, and blood body, as I will say of Myself on Earth,

'*Jesus replied, 'Foxes have dens, and birds have nests, but the Son of Man (God in a man's body of flesh, bone, and blood) has no place to lay His head.*'[37]

Just as you will give your sons, your identity, My Father will affirm My identity after I am baptized in the Third Earth Age,

'*And a voice from Heaven said, 'This is My Son, whom I love, with Him I am well pleased.*'[38]

My Father affirmed I was His child, and this affirmation meant so much. My mother, Mary told Me I was the Son of God. I read about the upcoming Savior of the world in the Scriptures. When I heard My Father's voice, I recognized it as the shadow of the voice I used to hear often in the eternities of old. I knew that My destiny was not just the cross to die for the sins of those who would receive Me as Savior, but was to sit at My Father's right hand as King of Kings and Lord of Lords throughout the eternity of eternities with you the selected Elders and My bride.

We all will suffer persecution, but in the eternity of eternities, we will have a good laugh and say, 'It was worth it all. The price seems great, but the eternal joys and reward set before you are worth enduring all things.'

Elder, Paul, in the Third Earth Age, I will give you the gift of singleness because of the severe persecution you will receive because of My Name. There will be several more of you Elders, because of the times, persecution, and important work will choose not to marry in subsequent Earth ages. So for all of you, make hay while the sun is shining. [Laughter]

---

[36] Psalm 127:3-5.
[37] Matthew 8:20.
[38] Matthew 3:17 NIV.

Elder Paul, in the Third Earth Age, after severe floggings, stoning's, and shipwrecks you will write,

'How shall we escape (Hell) if we ignore such a great salvation?
This salvation, which was first announced by the Lord (Jesus), was confirmed to us by those who heard Him. God (the Father) also testified to it by signs, wonders and various miracles.'[39]

'Since the children have flesh and blood, He (Jesus, who came in the flesh) too shared in their humanity so that by His death He might destroy him who holds the power of death – that is, the devil – and free those who all their lives were held in slavery by their fear of death. For surely it is not angels He helps, but Abraham's descendants. He had to be made like His brothers in every way, in order that He might become a merciful and faithful high priest in service to God and that He might make atonement (turn aside God's wrath) for the sins of the people. Because He suffered when He was tempted, He is able to help those being tempted.'[40]

'. . . Therefore, since we have a great high priest who has gone into Heaven (Jesus, the Son of God), let us hold firmly to the faith we profess. For we do not have a high priest unable to sympathize with our weaknesses, but we have One who has been tempted in every way, just as we are – yet was without sin. Let us then approach the throne of grace with confidence, so we may receive mercy and find grace to help us in our time of need.'[41]

It is My command,

'Let marriage (between a man and woman) be held in honor – esteemed worthy, pure, precious (especially dear) – in all things. And let the marriage bed be undefiled; for God will judge and punish all guilty of sexual vice and the adulterous.'[42†]

Marriage between one man and one woman will be your number one defense against sexual immorality. Go to bed together, kiss and hug each other frequently, and make beautiful music often in your marriage bed.

---

[39] Hebrews 2:3-4.
[40] Hebrews 2:14-18 NIV.
[41] Hebrews 4:14-16 NIV.
[42] Hebrews 13:4.

✝BOOK FIVE✝

✝BOOK FIVE – Episode 1✝

[✝**Sidebar Scriptures**: "*Joseph had a dream and promptly reported all the details (Genesis 37:5).*"
"*The Lord revealed to me what the evil ones were doing and planning and showed me their wicked plots (Jeremiah 11:18).*"
"*The word of the Lord came to Abram in a* **vision**. . . . *A* **deep sleep** *came upon Abram . . . . (Genesis 15:1, 12).*"
I witnessed and experienced "*dreams and visions, and I described **all** I had seen to instruct many (Daniel 7:1, 11:33).*"✝]

Apollo's Scientists Have a Breakthrough, and Elders Have Joyful Fellowship

Apollo Scientists Make a Surge Breakthrough Toward an Evil Invention

MERCURY DELIVERS A CONFIDENTIAL envelope from Scientist 6. under a black widow spider red dot seal in black wax. to Apollo that reads,

Master,
I feel I have personally and finally made a quantum surge leap on the secret formula E=MC² as I believe the 'E' must stand for 'Energy,' and a lack of energy would create a freeze bomb, which would be the ultimate weapon. I ask your permissions to share this with the other 65 scientists and request the full agreed upon 66-days at which time I believe we will have uncovered the entire formula. Where did you obtain this equation formula?
       Your brilliant and devoted servant,
       Genius, Scientist 6

Apollo in an irritating smirk confronts to Mercury, "How dare he ask me such a personal question? Damn him a hmail (Hell mail) back reply under your name, only flattering him for his hard work and scientific breakthrough, and indicate that he is not to ask the master personal questions."

Mercury sends the following hmail:
Great and Wise Genius, Scientist 6,
Apollo looks forward to the full answer to this equation at the scheduled sixty-six-day meeting. The master is preoccupied with trying to shape up his choirs, one to five into superiority, just as he has done with his choir six (6). He is so proud of his perfected choir six (6) and is proud of you and your recent discovery. Just hold your scientific discoveries to present to Apollo at the sixty-six (66) day meeting. As your comrade to our lord and master Apollo, I would advise you not to ask Apollo questions directly. I am ever devoted to your welfare and entitlements,
       Mercury, the fastest runner in the Cosmos

Elders' Assemble for Day of Fishing and Wives' for a Day of Shopping

Friday morning the couples assemble in the lobby with the Flying Saucer waiting outside to take the women for a day of shopping and to drop off the husbands at Elder Peter's White Fishing Boat for an exciting day on the Sea of Galilee fishing.

Gabriel, celebrating, declares, '*This is the day the Lord has made; let us rejoice (be happy) and be glad in it.*'[1]

---

[1] Psalm 118:24 NIV.

A Stopover Visit to the Elders' Residences Fortified in the Shape of the Star of David

When all the couples entered the saucer, Peter spoke, "Gabriel, our wives, would like respectfully to request an opportunity to see their homes on Elder Row in Zion before they go shopping, and we men go fishing."

Gabriel nods, "Yes, we can grant this request. Hold on to your hat, if you have a hat." [Cheers of joy came from each woman's lips.]

The flying saucer lifts and heads to Zion and descends out of a fluffy cloud, and reveals ancient looking white stone block homes containing a solid sky-blue flat roof arranged in the shape of the Star of David. The flying saucer gently sets down on a teleport in a picnic and park area in the center of the Star of David.

The wives excitingly descend the stairs with the men pointing out the individual entrances. The women have tears of joy for the goodness of God in giving them such an exceptional treasure of not only a loving and caring husband, but also a beautiful home to share life, ministry, and family together.

Sarah whispered in tears to Abraham, "Please ask if we can just go inside for a few minutes."

Abraham inquired, "May we take our ladies inside?"

Gabriel replied, "It is 9:10 A.M. The fish are biting! Let us meet back at the Saucer at 10:10. Remember to carry your ladies over the threshold!"

The couples holding hands joyfully step upon their eloquent marble patio surrounded by a flower garden, with a pond and, beautifully manicured grass, with shade and abundant fruit trees. Each husband opens the back entrance door, which displayed overhead a white linen flag with a blue Star of David in the center, gently blowing in the breeze.

The wives are each cradled up in the arms of their husbands. As Sarah is being picked up by Abraham, her sandals fall to the ground. He likewise removes his sandals as he gently carries her across the threshold stone sealing tightly shut the bottom of the door declaring, "Nothing impure is ever permitted to enter here as this is holy ground, totally consecrated to the glory of God."

Sarah, laughing and hugging Abraham tightly around his neck, kisses him all over the face and mouth as he carries her through the rooms of the house with her saying, "Isaac is going to be laughing all over this lovely and fun place!"

As they tour one exciting room after another, Sarah, overwhelmed with joy, inquires, "Is this truly our house?"

"Yes, we possess the title deed. Are you ready?"

"Ready for what?"

"To see the master bedroom!" [Laughter]

"Abe look a baby white linen bedspread with a sky-blue Star of David in the middle. Oh, our dual bathrooms are yet better than back at the Honeymoon Villa. Let us move back here tonight in our new home. Shalom!"

Abraham gently lays his beloved Sarah down on the king-size bed and replies, "This is only our temporary home as we will be living in an eternal city the Lord will prepare for those who love Him. However, God desires us to enjoy our daily lives as we seek to do His will. You are my best reward down here! I will have to say 'no' to our moving back here tonight. I will always consider your wishes.

Sometimes I will answer, 'yes,' sometimes, 'no;' and other times you will have to 'wait' for my reply, as I acknowledge the Lord seeking His direction.

I am a created being, made of the dust of the ground, being given an eternal spirit, and I will always consider your wishes my rib on any matter. We will have plenty of days to enjoy this lovely place with Isaac.

Let us take the time to smell the roses moment-by-moment in whatever our hands and feet are doing. Our God's not stressed about anything, and neither are we."

"Abe, I love you so very much. You are a man of decision. I like that. It's manly!" Sarah this time focused upon a full wet mouth kiss and a tight neck hug."

Abraham, pulling her even closer, inquires, "How about a quickie?"

"Sure, darling, that would be fun, but do we have time?"

"Let's go for it!" [Giggles]

Abraham and Sarah jump to their bare feet with Abraham's pulling up and off Sarah's robe. Keeping with his established custom, Abraham wads it into a little ball and throws it across the room with his goal to make it land in a chair seat. This time, it was a perfect throw, with his announcing, "Three points!" Sarah turns down the sheets and pronounces, "These rugged brown sheets will have to go, but they will do for now. You slept on these when you had all your ribs. [Laughter] I better not mention to others in our shopping today that sheets are on the top of my shopping list." [Laughter]

After the delightful and refreshing lovemaking, Sarah retrieves her robe and proceeds to her dressing mirror and repeatedly runs a brush through her hair, declaring, "'A flock of goats!' I guess this is what some women would call 'A bad hair day!' They will know you rolled me in bed! Look, it is 10:05. We will have to make a run for the saucer. We have five minutes to get back, and I have not even looked into the closets or cupboards of our beautiful home."

Abraham and Sarah, running up the escalator entered the saucer at 10:09 and 55 seconds with everyone else already strapped in their seats ready for lift off with all the ladies staring at Sarah's hair going in many directions wondering what happened to her.

Sarah whispers, "They know! They are staring at my hair. It truly looks 'like a flock of goats descending from Gilead'[2] going in different directions."

Abraham smiles, "So? See my wedding ring on my finger. See your wedding ring. These are signs to all of our marriage covenant and our rights to pure marital intimacy. Well, first things first! No one knows what goes on behind closed doors. Your hair reminds me of how it looked after our picnic under the Grape Harbor before we went swimming when Isaac was only two cells old." [Giggles]

The saucer lifts with the couples turning and looking out the windows at the beautiful Blue Star of David making up the flat top of the twenty-four white stone structures.

Abraham gives Sarah a kiss on the cheek and whispers, "We were the first to make love in the Star of David. [Giggles] I've got to remember that there is no such thing as a quickie with you? That was so delicious. It truly hit the spot. Our lovemaking is more refreshing than a cold dipper of water from the crystal clear Jordan. Thank you so much! How about some new green and brown camouflage-patterned sheets?"

"Abe, you are most kindly welcome, thank you, but you catch fish today and let me pick out some soft feminine sheets for our marriage bed. The more feminine I feel, the more masculine you will feel. I rest my case!"

_____

[2] Song of Solomon 6:9 NIV.

Abraham, with a smile and contentment on his face, lays his head back and whispers, "Right, My Love. It makes perfect sense. I must concur. Proceed! You are so beautiful and exciting, just right for me. A perfect fit!"

Husbands Dropped off at St. Peter's White Fishing Boat for the Day of Fishing on the Sea of Galilee

Soon the saucer was landing on the shore of the beautiful Sea of Galilee beside Elder Peter's white fishing boat with the couples admiring from the windows of the saucer this beautiful boat with a Star of David flag gently blowing on the mast.

Gabriel instructs, "Each man at the bottom of the escalator is to pick out a rod and reel. Please fill one of the white containers with juicy squirming earthworms you select from the tub. You will shortly be instructed by your boat pilot on how best to stick the sharp point of the hook into the worms. The fish love these tasty, wiggly worms. These earthworms have no nerves so they will not feel pain, and they are honored to be used to help you catch fish."

Each woman turns her mind away from thinking about baiting the hook with a wiggly worm.

Gabriel declares, "You soon will be fishers of men! Some of you will have fish tails this evening about the big ones that got away. [Laughter] Wives, are you ready for your shopping spree? If any of you women has changed your mind and had rather go fishing with these juicy wiggly earthworms, please raise your hand." [Giggling]

As anticipated, no woman raised her hand.

The elders kiss their wives on the cheek and hurry to the exit of the saucer for an exciting fishing adventure. However, Abraham whispers to Sarah, "Parting is such sweet sorrow, but the fish can't wait! Have fun shopping, my love. I miss you already, my darling. However, duty calls. It will be such a joy this evening seeing the saucer return carrying such precious cargo. Darling, I will select my best catches of the day just for Jesus and you. It seems almost impossible to believe that even God would create such a beautiful bride for me. Shalom! Catch (pun different meaning) you soon darling! Blessings!"

Abraham kissing Sarah hard and passionately on the lips concludes, "Darling, parting is such sweet sorrow, but this fisherman almost can't wait to see you. I look forward to test-driving those sheets with you. Shalom!"

Sarah, holding on to Abraham's arm, finally lets loose whispering, "My Love and master, it will not take much to get me in the mood to take a test-drive between the new sheets. Shalom!"

Abraham, being the last to exit the saucer blows Sarah a kiss with her blowing one back. Sarah is seated all alone without Abraham by her side for the first time since their marriage. Some tears of parting romance fall from her beautiful eyes and roll down her cheeks with some falling from her long eyelashes. As the saucer lifts, Sarah looks down searching and rejoices and leaps at her seat against the seat belt for joy as she sees Abraham looking up at her window and blowing her a distant kiss.

Sarah blows him a kiss back thinking, *"Loving my man is fantastic! Only God could have thought of something as grand as a man leaving father and mother and cleaving to his wife. The wife being cleaved to is just as blessed. I will stick to him like glue. Thank You, Lord, for making me a woman and especially for making me Abraham's woman! What a great joy to give Abraham my love! As he says, 'I am a perfect fit.' I feel like the honey barrel has fallen over me. Top of the list – soft and feminine sheets!"* [Self-giggles]

As the saucer comes up through white clouds heading to Tel Aviv, Sarah silently prays, *"Father, in Your Son's name, Jesus. I thank you for adding my name in the Lamb's Book of Life.*

Jesus is my personal Savior and Lord. His blood cleanses me from that first sin I commented against You of lying that I did not laugh when I did. As I repent and 'walk in the light, the Blood of Jesus cleanses me from all sin'[3] and sets me free to be what You desire me to be.

Thank you for giving me such a man of men, Abraham, the man I love and my heart's desire. I praise You for Your goodness and forgiveness. I worship You with all my heart. I'll stand by my man, my master.

Help me never to let either You or him down. Remember that I am a human, made from Abraham's rib. I love you both so much! May Abraham ever be captivated with my love.[4] Keep My Love from all harm, even today on this manly fishing trip. Let him not even stick his precious manly finger with one of those sharp fish hooks. Let My Love have fun catching those fish. Let him also have fun later catching men for Your kingdom for it is to be written, 'How beautiful (includes handsome; good-looking) on the mountains are the feet of those who bring good news (that Jesus Saves).'[5] I thank you for his beautiful feet. I hope to wash them often. I miss him so much. I almost wish I had raised my hand in spite of the wiggly worms. Ugh. Bless our baby Isaac and use him too, as a fisher of men, and may You laugh and delight with us in him. In Your Son's name, Jesus, I pray. Amen! Shalom!"

Father God and Son Discourse in Heaven

The Father, smiling looks at His Son and agrees with Sarah, saying, "Amen! What a wife You created for Our friend Abraham."

The Son of God states, "My bride and Sarah are going to be such good friends in the eternities of eternities, both being humble, virtuous vessels. They are so gracious, with no pride, although they are the most beautiful of women."

My Son, the one filled with pride and thinking he is something else, is working his plan, but I am laughing at all of it. Pride exists, and I will permit it for reasons of My own. However, it will be written regarding the seven things I hate,

> *'These six things doth the Lord hate:*
> *yea, seven are an abomination unto him:*
> *A proud look,*
> *a lying tongue,*
> *and hands that shed innocent blood.*
> *A heart that deviseth wicked imaginations, and*
> *feet swift in running to mischief,*
> *A false witness that speaketh lies, and*
> *he that soweth discord among brethren.'[6]*

It will also be written,
'Love the Lord, all His saints!
The Lord preserves the faithful,
but the proud He pays back in full.'[7]
'May the Lord cut off all flattering lips,
and the tongue that speaks proud boasting.
Those who say, 'With our tongue we prevail,
our lips are our own (to command at our will);
who is lord and master (none over us?
. . . He who has a haughty look and a proud and
arrogant heart I (God) cannot and I will not tolerate.'[9]
'The Lord tears down the house of the proud.'[10]

---

[3] See 1 John 1:7-9.

[4] See Proverbs 5:19.

[5] Isaiah 52:7 NIV.

[6] Proverbs 6:16-19 KJV.

[7] Psalm 31:23 NIV.

[9] Psalm 12:3-4; 101:5b AMP.

'Everyone proud and arrogant in heart is disgusting,
hateful and exceeding offensive to the Lord; be assured –
I pledge it – he (or she) will not go unpunished.'[11]
'The reverent fear and worshipful awe of the Lord includes
the hatred of evil. Pride, arrogance, the evil way, and
perverted and twisted speech I hate.'[12]
'For there shall be a day of the Lord of hosts against
all that is proud and haughty and against all that is lifted
up, and it shall be brought low . . . .'[13]
'For behold, the day comes that shall burn as an oven; and all
the proud and arrogant, yes, and all that do wickedly and are
lawless shall be stubble: the day that comes shall burn them
up, says the Lord of hosts, so it will leave them neither
root or branch.'[14]
'God opposes the proud, but gives grace to the humble.'[15]
'Pride comes before a disaster; a proud attitude brings a fall.'[16]
'God stands against the proud,
but gives grace (assistance, help) to the humble.
. . . Humble yourself in the Lord's presence, and He will honor (exalt, lift) you.'[17]

The Son of God affirms, "Amen! So be it!"

The Father, smiling, inquires, "I know you are going to the fish bake this evening."

The Son smiling responds, "Yes, Sarah asked Abraham to invite Me.
I wouldn't miss it for the world."

The Father smiles, "You own the world." [Laughter.]

'The Earth is the Lord's, and everything in it,
the world, and all who live in it.'[18]

"However, Father, I don't crash a party, a wedding, or even a fish bake if I am not invited, even though I have a right. I knocked on this door of attending this fish bake and My friends Abraham and Sarah opened the door and specifically requested Me to join and dine with them at this first Friday evening fish bake. I will bless Abraham to catch three of the largest and best-tasting fish. The food on Earth is better than the angels' food here. [Laughter] I am requesting St. Peter's Fish at the upcoming marriage supper of the Lamb as Sarah and My bride would enjoy the memories of eating St. Peter's fish in the Earth below."

"My Son, you will later preach about your gentle knock,

'Here I am! I stand at the door and knock. If anyone hears My voice and opens the door, I will come in and eat with him, and he with Me.

To him who overcomes (includes the sin of pride), I will give the right to sit with Me on My throne, just as I overcame and sat down with My Father on His throne.'[19]

"My Son, I delight in My friend Abraham and his enjoying Your company. I likewise celebrate Your company! Go where you are celebrated and not just tolerated!"

---

[10] Proverbs 15:25b AMP.

[11] Proverbs 16:5 AMP.

[12] Proverbs 8:13 AMP.

[13] Isaiah 2:2 AMP.

[14] Malachi 4:1 AMP.

[15] James 4:6 NIV.

[16] Proverbs 16:18 .

[17] James 4:6, 10.

[18] Psalm 24:1 NIV See also Psalm 50:12.

[19] Revelation 3:20-21 NIV.

"Yes, My Father. I will go where I am celebrated and invited in. If I am not welcome, I will leave."

"My Son, Sarah's love and focus upon her love for Abraham and her acknowledging Me will result this evening in Abraham's honoring Me as he wears 'beautiful garments.'[20]

All the other elders will continue to be dressed in their fishing outfits and not wearing anything new from the shopping trip brought back by their wives. The other women will be caught flat-footed as they were focusing on shopping first for their upcoming babies, then on themselves, then on their homes, and lastly on just a happy gift for their husbands, all of which merchandise they sent on to their residences on Zion Row.

My Son, I will gift holy women in the Third Earth Age to make You pleasant white home-spun preaching and teaching robes. One will have such value that even the Roman soldiers will gamble[21] for it so as not to tear it as they stripped it from You before they drive nails in Your hands and feet nailing You naked to a wooden cross. It will be written of Your garments dipped in Your own blood,

     'Who is this who comes from Edom
     . . . this One glorious in His apparel?
  . . . Why is Your apparel red,
     and your garments like one who
     treads (barefoot on the red grapes) in the winepress?'[22]

Wives Separated from their Husbands for the First Time
Shop for Maternity Robes in Tel Aviv

The wives excitedly arrive in Tel Aviv, having several blocks of angelic shops. Gabriel hands each wife, her personal Star of David Credit Card to scan to sample the food, desserts, and to make selections, indicating that she can bring her purchases back to the saucer or have any of them sent to her home in Zion or even sent back to the honeymoon villa.

"Ladies, let us meet back here at 3:00 P.M." [The ladies scatter like bees in a field of blooming clover.]

Sarah, standing alone acknowledging the Lord, sees an angel and asked,

"Which shop carries the best bed sheets?" The angel responds,

"The Tel Aviv Sheet Factory, the last shop at the end of three blocks."

Sarah enters the shop suggested by the angel and asks the angel clerk,

"Confidentially, do you have any soft, feminine sheets in king size?"

"We have a white super soft 1,777 thread count sheet with a blue Star of David in the center of the fitted sheet."

Sarah, feeling the sheet, replies, "This is very soft! Let me take two sets with matching pillow cases as my husband will like these. Might you have some sheets a little more feminine?"

Not in Tel Aviv, but I heard of such feminine sheets in a little shop on Designer's Row in Paris."

"How far is Paris?"

"Not walking distance, by mule several months, but in the saucer and then by swift foot about thirty minutes."

---

[20] Isaiah 52:1 NKJV.
[21] See Matthew 27:35 NIV.
[22] Isaiah 63:1-2 NKJV.

"I heard they have some feminine accessories for both bedrooms and bathrooms such as soft towels. They can add an initial such as an 'A' or 'S' or the words 'HIS' and 'HERS' on bath towels and matching robes. They also have a lot of feminine gowns and play clothes."

"We have only a few hours. How could I get to Paris?"

"The best way is to present your case to Gabriel if you can locate him in this large complex. Your Star of David Credit Card will be honored in the angel shops in Paris, and they could send your selections to your home in Zion. Sarah, I will certainly honor your request to keep all this confidential."

"How did you know my name?"

"I also know you are married to Abraham. It will be written of him, '*Abraham believed God, and it was accounted to him for righteousness, and he was called God's friend.*'[23] He is a friend of God, like no other, and you too will have great favor being married to Abraham. However, a prophet is without honor in his own home. You need to know that you too are highly favored and honored. Respect him as he is truly one of a kind. I also know that you are also carrying his baby Isaac, which means 'laughter.' I will be one of Isaac's guardian angels, and that is how I know these things. You normally will not see me, but you will feel my presence and know that if anyone seeks to harm Isaac I will defend Isaac to the uttermost, in the name of the Lord Jesus!

"Small world. [Laughter] What is your name?"

"My name is Giggala."

"Giggala, before Paris, where could I find for my beloved husband something very special to show my great love and respect for him?"

In the back of our store is the His and Her Shop. All of the other women are three blocks over, and they will not have time to find this shop. Afterward, I would suggest you look for Gabriel in the Tel Aviv Baby Shower Shop, as they will have the best selection for Isaac."

"Giggala, thank you for assisting me. Shalom!"

Sarah Obtains Gifts for Elders and Wives

Sarah, being conscious of the time, hurries to enter the *His and Her Matching Shop*. The clerk angel indicates, "Giggala informed me that you were on your way. Because of the time I pulled some beautiful clothes and sleepwear and laid them out for your inspection on the glass conference table."

Sarah picks up in her hands for the evening meal the most eloquent thick linen, white matching robes, one extra-large, and the other petite, each having a sky-blue Star of David on the pocket,a matching gold signet rings with a Star of David for Abraham. She then picks up a matching Prayer Shaw containing precious promises and the Star of David. She exams some matching sandals with the Star of David.

Besides all these, I would like these short and long men's pajamas for Abraham, these short and long nightgowns for me, and these matching relaxing play clothes. I choose all these for my beloved Abraham, and matching ones for me, but I do not desire the signet ring for myself. You see this wedding ring on my left hand – that is the only ring I desire!

---

[23] James 2:24.

Also, I would like a box each of his and her large towels, of shampoo and soap, unbreakable combs, bath kits, undergarments, matching white linen shirts to wear beneath the robes, and a His and Her large flight bags with one of each of these in it for this evening for me to carry back to the saucer. Please send these large stacks and boxes to Elder Row #7, Zion, Israel.

The angel took Sarah's card and scanned it while Sarah neatly packed one each of Abraham's gifts in his bag and her purchases in her bag. The angel makes a passing comment,

"Today since you purchased so much we have an extraordinary atomic-power hair dryers for him and one for her so you can quickly dry your hair and some unique hair clips for you, which I am putting in the respective bags as a bonus. The others are going to be so envious of you two this evening; as you will be dressed head and shoulders over all the rest."

Sarah frowned for the first time in her young married life, saying, "That will never do! Abraham is not showy, and he will not like it. I need exact duplicate bags, twenty male, and twenty female, for the other elders and their wives and one for the Son of God so we will all match this evening. No Elder over another Elder. Please send these to my attention this day to the garden party near Elder Peter's fishing boat."

"No problem, Sarah, as we know everyone's size, we will have each, including the Son of God, Jesus, a bag with name tags, which we will load for you in the saucer's cargo bay with your name on the sealed boxes for you to distribute with great joy and love. Your time here is running out! I would suggest you go 'God Speed' to the 'Tele Aviv Baby Shower Shop' with your two bags as the saucer will soon need to take off.

Sarah, running with joy, swinging the two heavy flight bags, enters the Tele Aviv Baby Shower Shop inquiring,

"I am going to be giving birth to a son, and would you please send me one of everything the other ladies ordered today for their sons. Nothing feminine, pink, or with lace! I don't have time to shop for upcoming daughters as I have a saucer to catch. Please send all this to Elder's Row # 7. Please scan my card. I see Gabriel standing by the up going escalator of the saucer. I confess favor with him and the other wives. Angel, thank you! Shalom!"

Abraham Boards Elder Peter's Fishing Board

Abraham the last to board Elder Peter's fishing boat muses in his heart, *'Lord, I miss Sarah. Please direct her paths today and take care of her as this is the first time I have ever been parted from my rib. How can I focus upon fishing with her on my mind? Please let me catch a big tasty one for her and Jesus. Amen! Shalom!"*

The angelic sea captain announces, "We are going to navigate to a cove where the Jordan River spills into the Sea of Galilee. We will focus on catching the big tasty ones for this evening's fish bake."

Upon arriving at the fishing spot, the captain announces, "Gentlemen, bait your hooks. These worms have no nerves and have a short life span. Cover the hook with the worm leaving a little at the bottom to wiggle. If you catch a fish with no scales, throw it back as it will be written,

'Of all the creatures living in the water of the seas, and in the streams, you may eat any that have fins and scales. But all creatures in the seas or streams that do not have fins and scales – whether among all the swarming things or among all the other living creatures in the water – you are to detest. And since you are to detest them, you must not eat their meat and you must detest their carcasses. Anything living in the water that does not have fins and scales is to be detestable to you.'[24]

---

[24] Leviticus 11:9-12 NIV.

Gentlemen, load your hooks. When you reel a fish to the side of the boat, use your net to bring it aboard.

You will then carefully remove the hook and place each fish on a stringer off the edge of the vessel in the water for you to show your wives and point out the selective fish to be cooked for her this evening.

Our angels will clean the fish for you as you are still on your honeymoon, and you need to spend time with your wives and not cooking fish. You will be sweaty enough this evening without cooking fish."

Elder Peter was the first to have a line in the water and almost immediately a good size fish takes his bait 'hook, line, and sinker.'[25] Peter delighting in the sport and smiling places his net into the water and pulls the fish aboard."

The Captain explained, "You did that like a professional fisherman, catching the tastiest fish I believe in the world. Today we will give this species the same name given to it in the Third Earth Age of 'St. Peter's Fish.'[26] Elder Peter, you might be the only one ever that has a fish named after them." [Laughter]

Abraham prayed, "*Lord, let me catch one of these tasty St. Peter's fish for Sarah. Let me not be put to shame as I am not a sea lover.*"

Almost immediately, a bigger St. Peter's fish struck Abraham's bait taking off with Abraham's line running under the boat. Abraham determined not to let it get away, thinks, "*Fish, I claim you for Sarah! What an honor for you to be dined upon by the most beautiful and loving girl in the world.*"

Abraham with patience reels in carefully as the fish darts and runs under the boat and back out again. The whole boat now is watching and laughing at Abraham's determination to reel in his first fish. Finally, Abraham brings it near the boat and reaching down with the net brings it aboard for his beloved Sarah. Abraham shortly catches two similar large size fish for Jesus and himself. These three fish were the largest fish caught that day. Abraham remained humble, even though he was tempted to brag. He remembered that a temptation was not a sin, but it is the yielding to the temptation that is a sin, confessing, 'I humble myself. Thank You Lord; I was not put to shame! The first fish is not Sarah's, but is for You, Jesus, our Savior and Lord. Your joy, My Lord, Jesus, gives me such strength! This thing called love can never fail! Ever since before time began, there has never been found anything stronger than love! Shalom.

Sarah Request to Shop at Designer's Row in Paris

Sarah hurries up to Gabriel at 2:58 P.M. looking earnestly into his eyes.

Gabriel inquires, "Princess Sarah, is everything okay?"

"Considerably, I miss Abraham. I would respectfully like to ask you, and I will understand if we do not have the time if I could go shopping in Paris. Is it possible?"

"Everything is possible with God! All the other women are already on board and are seated ready to travel back to see their husbands.

---

[25] *Hook, line, and sinker* - "completely . . . (to be tricked into believing something without any doubts) Etymology" based on the idea of a fish so hungry it swallows the hook (the part that catches the fish), the line (the string) and the sinker (a weight attached to the line to keep it under water." *The Free Dictionary by Farlex.*

[26] "The name 'St. Peter's fish' comes from the story in the Gospel of Matthew (Matthew 17:24-27) about the apostle Peter catching a fish that carried a coin in its mouth, though the passage does not name the fish. . . .The Tomb of Nakht, 1500 B.C. contains a tilapia hieroglyph just above the head (see interesting painting) just above the head of the central figure." *Wikipedia, The Free Encyclopedia, Tilapia.*

We would have to limit our shopping to thirty minutes in Paris as we are scheduled to meet the fishing boat coming into the pier so the men can show y'all[27] their catch of the day."

"Gabriel, I desire to buy something special for Abraham. Please do not tell the others that this is my personal request."

"Gabriel, smiling, replied, "Sarah, I will be glad to keep your wish confidential!"

Sarah quickly places her two bags in the overhead bin and fastens her seat belt as Gabriel announces: "We have time for only one more stop, and this will be in Paris. They have the best chocolate shops. I recommend the Lovers' Delight Confectioner Shop featuring Hazelnut-Almond and Praline-Walnut Ice Cream. They also have a tasty Dark Chocolate Mousse. So make sure your seat belts are fastened as we set a world's record in speed, which may not be broken for some time."

As the saucer sets down in Paris, Gabriel announces, "Remember, you have only thirty minutes as we are to meet the boat at the pier to view the catches of the day."

Sarah was the first to exit the saucer, and she asked the angel about the little shop with the feminine sheets and was directed that it was way at the end of the Eiffel Street three blocks away. Sarah girded her robe in her hands and sprints as hard as she could and in ten minutes arrives at the shop. Sarah dashes into the shop out of breath and sweating with her hair going in all directions.

The shop angel inquires, "Are you all right? Should we send for a doctor?'

Sarah responds, "I am perfectly all right. Here is a list of all the things I need and I need them quickly. At the top of the list are your most feminine sheets. Next, very confidential, for my husband's eyes alone, are feminine nightgowns and things to make our bedroom feminine."

The shop angel quickly shows Sarah several sets of the most feminine possible king-size sheets and matching pillowcases. Sarah selects seven sets and quickly selects several other items to make the bedroom even more feminine. The clerk reluctantly hands Sarah a stack of night-gowns blushingly saying,
"These may be too revealing!"

"These are for my beloved husband. Confidentially, nothing is too revealing for My Love. I'll take them all. I must go now. I have nothing to be ashamed of as God designed me for Abraham. God made me beautiful for my husband, Abraham; and why not?"

Sarah, I am one of your guardian angels and will keep this in utmost confidence."

Sarah hands the angel her Star of David Credit Card, and he scans it and she indicates that all is to be shipped to Elder Row #7, Zion, Israel.

Sarah urges, "I must go now! I have a train, plane, or whatever that flat dish object is called to catch. Shalom!

The angel indicates that he would put in as his wedding gift the best Paris perfume, a makeup kit containing the new red lipstick and shampoo named 'Passion' and a catalog for her future email orders. "Have fun!"

Sarah replied, "I have never had so much fun in my short life! [Laughter] Thank you, angel. I didn't even have time to get your name or to chit chat. Maybe later. Shalom!"

Sarah, again girding her robe around her, having only nine minutes, runs fast and hard back to the saucer and praying for an 'ever-present help'[28] to make it on time,

---

[27] "Y'all is a contradiction of the words 'you' and 'all' . . . commonly believed to have originated in the Southern United States." *Wikipedia, The Free Encyclopedia.*
[28] Psalm 46:1.

"My Father, thank You for showing me this neat shop. My beloved will enjoy these sheets and gowns. The angel said, 'Have fun!' Your peace and joy are magnificent.

Lord, I need a cool, strong tail wind as it is very hot today in Paris. 'I can do all things through Christ, who strengthens me.'[29] In my Lord, Jesus' Name. Shalom! Amen."

Sarah, who received a boost from a strong tailwind, spots the saucer about to blast off with Gabriel standing at the bottom waiting for her as he prepares to break the previous world's speed record in returning to the dock to greet the men.

Sarah runs up the escalators, enters seven seconds early, and takes her seat. Sarah looked worse than ever with her hair going in every direction, her face glowing as with sunburn, and with her breathing hard. Sarah takes off her sandals nursing blisters on both of her feet. Sarah soon falls into a deep sleep and dreams she is far off in eternity beyond all earth ages *'for the first Heaven, and the first Earth had passed away.'[30]* Sarah witnessed and experienced in her dream that she was joyfully walking barefoot in a lush green magnificent park, having twelve trees of life on each side. She was dressed in a white feminine short dress. She was laughing, celebrating, and talking with her best-eternal friend. The two happy women locked arms and were dancing barefoot giggling, singing, and twirling together in joyful circles. Suddenly the two joyful women's *'clothes became dazzling white'[31]* as they saw the Son of God, Jesus, smiling walking toward them with Abraham at His side. Jesus with a loving smile gives Sarah's best friend a hug, a romantic kiss, and they both wave to Abraham and Sarah as they turn walking back toward the throne room of Heaven. Abraham likewise hugs Sarah and gives her a passionate kiss on the lips as they turn entering the gate of their exquisite mansion. Sarah awakes to touch the warm lips Abraham had just kissed in her dream and vision. She felt refreshed, except for her hurting feet, quoting in her heart,

'The Lord is my Shepherd, I shall not want.
He makes me lie down in green pastures,
He anoints my head with oil.
My cup runs over.
Surely, goodness and love (mercy) shall follow me
all the days of my life (on Earth),
and I will dwell in the house of the Lord (in eternity) forever.'[32]

All the women stare as Sarah *'face shone (glowed),'[33]* having red marks and blisters on her feet and her hair going in different directions. They asked among themselves, "What happened to her? Could she have fallen down some stairs? One whispers to another, "Sarah may need to see Dr. Luke when we return." Nodding and smiling back at the other women Sarah reasons, "*I will lay up and ponder this precious dream and vision of coming attractions in my heart and not tell it to Abraham tonight for various reasons.*"

Wives' Return to their Husbands

The flying saucer, setting a new world's speed record, gently lands near the pier as the white fishing boat is drawing near the shore. The wives quickly exit with an invisible angel assisting Sarah down the escalator with the wind blowing further Sarah's matted hair as she carries her sandals because of the blisters on her feet.

The women line up on the dock, seeing their husbands' waving, holding up their individual strings of fish. The women follow Sarah's led of blowing kisses to their husbands. As the boat docks, Peter shouts,

"We caught some tasty fish (later to be named the St. Peter fish after me), being a total of 153.'[34] I caught the first one and the most! Fishing is a lot harder work than shopping. [Sarah looks down to her red and hurting feet and laughs to herself.]

Abraham caught the two largest, and they put up a gigantic struggle, but finally, they decided that it would be an honor to be dined upon by Sarah and Jesus.

You women are probably getting hungry after a full day of relaxing and shopping, or did you have some delicious desserts? Abraham now lifts high the string of fish you caught for Sarah to see!"

---

[29] Philippians 4:13 NIV.
[30] Revelation 21:1
[31] Mark 9:3.
[32] Psalm 23:1, 5-6 NKJV.
[33] Exodus 34:30.
[34] John 21:13 NIV.

Abraham, blushing in humility and having his eyes on Sarah alone, quickly lifts his string holding the seven fish he caught, pointing with his index and middle finger to both Jesus' and Sarah's fish as he lets the line drop back in the water. He then jumps about three feet to shore before the boat is docked and runs to Sarah for a passionate kiss and hug saying, "Darling, I missed you. I missed you so very much. Let me look at you." Abraham looks at Sarah's hair and down at the red marks and blisters on Sarah's bare feet and then back up to her glowing face. Abraham gives his first frown, saying "I don't know whether shopping agrees with you. You seem like you are about done in! Should I call Dr. Luke?"

Sarah responds, "Well, a woman has to do what a woman has to do! I am a red-blooded Zion woman. My Savior will take nails in His feet for me. What are a few blisters compared to that, for the husband I love? To obtain us some feminine sheets, I had to set a world's jogging record for women so I would not miss the boat, as I wanted to see you, darling, so much! Abe, as I woke up right before landing, I saw the Grape Arbor from the air and the little cove in which we swam together. I need to soak my aching and blistered feet in the cool River Jordan. Are you adventurous enough to break away for about thirty minutes and go swimming with me? I am a ball of sweat. It was hot and humid in Paris. An excellent place to shop, but I would not want to do long jogs there often. I bought us matching robes for the fish dinner this evening.

What an excellent fisherman and provider you are Abe! Please consider serving that first large fish you so manly caught to Jesus. Always our first, very best, and utmost for our Creator, Savior, and Lord, Jesus!

Yes, my beautiful rib! You're allowing me to lead, makes me feel so manly. You are a beautiful woman inside and out.

Thank you, my lord. It is an honor to be your woman! Abe, you smell a little like fish. I have Paris soap and shampoo. How about a dip in the refreshing Jordan River?"

"Sarah, you have made me an offer I cannot refuse. I assume with all that shopping you remembered to buy us swimming suits."

Sarah laughs, "Abe it never crossed my mind!" [Giggling]

"How can we be so daring? What if we are discovered? It is fairly hidden, but if someone sees us, he or she will turn away knowing that we are '*naked and unashamed* '[35] as a husband and wife in each other's presence."

"Well, it is as you said Abe, 'See my wedding band! See your wedding band! Signs of our marriage covenant. So what! Who cares? First things first! I have to have some relief from this jogging sweat and cool my hurting feet. Here is your bag, which has a fluffy His towel. The name of the Paris body soap and shampoo is 'Passion,' and has a money back guarantee." [Giggling]

Abraham, smiling, whispers, "Darling, let's go for a lot of passion!"

Hand in hand, Abraham and Sarah ease out of the camp and proceed with haste to the hidden romantic cove.

Sarah, having a bottle of "Passion" shampoo in her hand, pulls her robe over her head and throws it at Abraham challenging, "I'll race you to that same rock."

Sarah dives in with a bottle of shampoo slowing her down a little with Abraham gaining on her. One yard before reaching the rock Abraham catches Sarah and Abraham touches the rock first, by a whisker.

---

[35] Genesis 2:25.

Sarah smiles, "Abe, you win again!" [Sarah joyful smiles knowing she wisely lost on purpose for romance's sake, only to ultimately win knowing that all such is fair in marital love!]

Sarah pours out in her hand first coconut smelling shampoo and roughly lathers with her fingertips Abraham's scalp decreeing, "Fish smell, be gone!" [Laughter.]

Abraham's hand lathers Sarah's hair saying, "Flock of goats behave!" [Laughter.]

Abraham explores Sarah's body with Sarah responding,

"Abe, you have wonderful roving hands. Catch me if you can!"

With that, Sarah dives beneath the beautiful crystal clear Jordan River swimming near the bottom heading back to the shore. Abraham watches diligently for bubbles leading to where Sarah would surface. Spotting bubbles, he takes off after her. When she surfaces, she turns back to face Abraham with open arms and the rest is history.

Upon going up on the shore, Sarah inquires, "Can fishing be compared to this? [Laughter] Abe, open your bag as your towel is at the very top along with a new comb, a pure and white robe, new sandals, a Prayer Shaw, and a signet ring with the Star of David for your right ring finger."

With a cool evening breeze coming in, Abraham and Sarah dress and stand before each other, in beautiful and glorious matching white apparel trimmed in gold.

Abraham responds, "I pray the other women likewise obtained their husbands such joyful apparel and a Star of David signet rings as these are so eloquent. Maybe shopping agrees with you."

"Abe, the other women, focused on shopping for their upcoming children, their homes, themselves, and they only obtained a few small gifts for their husbands. I overheard one describing the house shoes she found and another some utility underwear. I found this beautiful robe in a little hid away shop in the back of another store at the end of a long street. I was the only one that found this shop."

"Sarah, my life demonstrates that no Elder is beneath or above the other. If I go in wearing this, the women will not be happy with you, and some of the other Elders will think that I am a 'Big Pete,' not referring to Peter." [Laughter]

"Sarah, let us put back on our old robes. I cannot do this to either the elders or their wives. For I am their servant. We cannot create a grand entrance dressed so eloquently."

With Abraham disrobing, he advances, "Sarah, please understand we can't be the only one dressed up this evening. I had requested the Son of God to join us at the round table (also written roundtable) to demonstrate that no one is superior or inferior, but that all of us Elders are equal in God's sight."

"Abe, I am beginning to know you! I acknowledged the Lord and the Holy Spirit spoke to me to obtain all the other Elders and their wives (even obtained the Son of God one) exact matching robes and Star of David signet rings for this evening.

Nothing missing, nothing broken, except some blisters on my feet, which are still hurting. All the bags with individual names of the Elders and their wives are awaiting me in white boxes, and there are male and female dressing houses right at the top of the hill. So how are we going to do this?"

"Sarah, I think I am going to have a little fun. Take my hand." [Sarah smiling puts her hand into his.]

With the smoke rising and the smell of 'St Peter's Fish' delightfully filling the air, Abraham and Sarah ease back into camp. Sarah's face is glowing, and her hair is shining in the light of the full moon as it naturally dries in the cool breeze coming off the calm and smooth Sea of Galilee.

Soon all were noticing Sarah's radiance and beauty as all the Elders and wives admire Abraham's and Sarah's matching attire.

One Elder inquired of his wife, "Woman did you likewise obtain us matching robes?" Another wife whispers to her husband, "Don't you think that's a little too much for a fish fry?"

Some of the other Elders and wives were not happy about Sarah's accomplishment.

Abraham, noticing the large white boxes waiting for Sarah, and seeking to regain favor and make peace, announces,

"Peter, I can smell fish on you from here and, yes and on you too, John. [Laughter] Tonight we are honored to be meeting with Jesus, the Son of God, the Lord of lords and King of kings. You men smell just as I did a few minutes ago. Rightly so, as we had fun catching fish. We had some wonderful manly fellowship together today! I learned a lot today about fishing, even for men. We smell like fish as we have been fishing. Anyone know a cure?" [Silence.]

"Elders, we always need to present our 'bodies as living sacrifices, holy and pleasing to our Father God'[36] and to His Son, Jesus, our Lord and Savior. Therefore, you will each find in the boxes behind you a bag with each of your names on it with a towel and grooming kit with soap, shampoo, with good smelling spices on top. You each will have the exact outfits that Sarah and I are now wearing this evening. We are all equal, no one over the other. Jesus is our head, and we are part of His body. 'United we stand, divided we fall.'[37] We are only as strong as the weakest link. A house divided will not stand. United as one force we stand and divided with any envy or strife, we may fall and bump our humped noses. [Laughter]

Therefore, when we go out in this world 'we are (Jesus) Christ's ambassadors, as though God were making His appeal (offering salvation) through us'[38] so let us walk in unified love, joy, grace, and cleanliness!

Not one of us will live alone for ourselves. We take up our cross daily and follow Jesus. Division and unloveliness are deadlier than any Cobra. Now, as one body this evening let us look our best as we worship in purity and love the 'Lamb of God, who takes away the sins of the world.'[39] Brethren see the bath houses – go for it!

Let us meet back here at the round table in thirty minutes as I invited the Son of God to be our honored guest. We are giving His bag with a red bow to Gabriel to deliver to Him. Peter, remember to wash behind your ears. [All laughing] Go, the fish are slowly grilling."

Everyone grabs his or her individual bag and speeds up to the bathhouses having separate dressing chambers and mirrors.

As a romantic full moon rises over the Sea of Galilee, Abraham left alone with Sarah, takes her hand, walks to a romantic spot and enjoying Sarah being by his side, whispers,

"What a woman the Lord gave me! I needed you in my life so much. It is a truism, 'It is not good for man to be alone. I will make a helper suitable for him.'[40] Sarah, you fit me like a glove. A most suitable helpmeet,

'Two are better than one because they have a good return for their work; if one falls down, his friend can help him up. Though one may be overpowered, two can defend themselves. A cord of three strains is not quickly broken '[41]

---

[36] Romans 12:1.

[37] "United we stand, divided we fall is a phrase that has been used in mottos . . . . The basic concept is that unless the people are united, it is easy to destroy them. See Wikipedia, The Free Encyclopedia.

[38] 2 Corinthians 5:20.

[39] John 1:29.

[40] Genesis 2:18 NIV.

Sarah, thank you for loving me and being my best friend, lover, with Jesus as our third strain!"

Sarah softly responds,

"You are most kindly welcome, my darling. I truly love you! I thank God I belong to Him and to you. Isaac enjoyed the jogging, the swimming, and is laughing with us right now. We shall enjoy countless more joyful days on Earth and throughout ETERNITY!

When we arrive back home, we have some very feminine sheets, all the way from Paris. Please give me some time to change out those brown masculine sheets, which will make good cleaning rags. [Laughter]

I need to alert you to something! The women sent everything to Zion Row, and most, if not all, would like to cut their honeymoon short and go home. Mission accomplished so to speak! [Laughter] Elder Peter may present this request to the Lord, asking Him for permission to let us all go home."

"Sarah, I heard that rumor."

"Abe, my darling, I am ready to set up housekeeping together. It's just part of being a wife to establish her own home."

"Darling, okay. I will make no objection and nod yes to Peter's request."

Sarah smiles giving Abraham one of her delightful hugs and a sweet smacking kiss on the lips as Abraham and Sarah leave their new sandals at the entrance and respectfully take the double love cushion marked seven in the circle. The other elders commence returning wearing matching eloquent apparel taking their respective seats. The great hymn writer of Zion, King David, shortly joins them on the harp leading the congregation in song on various screens,

> 'Blessed (happy) is the man
>   who does not walk in the counsel of the wicked
>   or stand in the way of sinners
>   or sit in the seat of mockers.
> But his delight is in the law of the Lord,
>   and on His law, he meditates day and night.
> He is like a tree planted by streams of water,
>   which yields its fruit in season
>   and whose leaf does not wither.
> Whatever he does prospers.
> Not so with the wicked!
> They are like chaff
>   that the wind blows away.
> Therefore, the wicked will not stand (prevail) in the judgment,
>   nor sinners in the assembly of the righteous.
> For the Lord watches over the way of the righteous,
>   but the way of the wicked will perish.'[42]

The Shekinah Glory cloud rolls in with all falling to the ground in worship as the Son of God. Jesus, appears also dressed in the white robe Sarah had selected and also wearing on His right hand the signet ring with the white stone and blue Star of David. Jesus walks in a fluffy white cloud barefoot, with each elder and his wife bowing on their knees in worship. Jesus speaks words of pure love,

"I receive your worship. You are people with clean, beautiful feet. Your feet at times will take a beating, receive cuts and blisters, and be covered with dust as you do the work of an evan-

---

[41] Ecclesiastes 4:9-10, 12 NIV.
[42] Psalm 1:1-6 NIV.

gelist. You are My first people of flesh, bone, and blood with beautiful feet – all of you. Now all you kneel in worship, preparing to be seated in your numbered love seats for a delightful meal together."

Jesus smiles and looks at Sarah with her humbly bowing her head, glancing down at the throbbing red blisters on both of her feet.

Daughter Sarah, it is to be written, '*I am the Lord who heals you!*'[43]

In the Third Earth Age, I will take thirty-nine stripes on My back with a whip that has bits of glass and metal tied in it tearing My flesh. .My hands and feet, made of flesh, bone, nerves, and blood vessels, like your injured feet today, will be nailed to a wooden cross to shed My life's blood to pay for the sins of those made in My image in the world, who receive Me as Savior. It will be written,

'He (Son of Man, Jesus) Himself bore our sins in His body on the tree (cross), so we might die to sin and live for righteousness; by His wounds (stripes on His back) you have been healed.'[44]

Sarah, now in faith stretch out your damaged feet toward Me and by faith receive your healing I will then for now purchase for you by the stripes I will receive on My back from a cruel beating before I am crucified on a cross to pay the penalty for your sins. Sarah in faith stretches out her red, blistered, and hurting feet toward Jesus confessing,

"By faith, I receive my healing, which I believe now for then You purchased for me, by your stripes (wounds) on your back, my healing."

All the Elders and wives gasp for joy as Sarah's feet are restored as smooth and healthy as a newborn baby's skin.

Likewise, the redness on Sarah's face is replaced by healthy and radiant skin. As a cloud moves away from the full moon, it is revealed that Sarah's hair and face have received a youthful makeover. She is now wearing just right red lipstick, nail polish to match, and some eye shadow and mascara.

Sarah in deep gratitude in her heart gives thanks, celebrating the healing of her feet and face with great joy and wiggling her toes one last time plants her healed and beautiful feet again on the ground with her right foot slightly brushing against the side of Abraham's left foot.

The Son of God declares, "You will see much greater things as this to elevate you to a faith that can move mountains and win the worse of sinners for our Kingdom of Love as you proclaim with beautiful feet, My free gift of Salvation from sin, forgiveness, to all who call upon Me in faith as it will be written,

'Awake, awake, O Zion, clothe yourself with strength.
Put on your garments of splendor. . . .
. . .How beautiful on the mountains
*   are the feet of those who bring good news,*
who proclaim peace,
*   who bring good tidings, who proclaim salvation,*
who say to Zion, 'Your God reigns!' '[45]

You all, humbly wearing matching beautiful garments, honor both My Father and Me today. It will be written,

Those who honor Me I will honor, but those who despise Me will be disdained (looked down on).[46]

---

[43] Exodus 15:26 NIV.
[44] 1 Peter 2:24 NIV.
[45] Isaiah 52:1, 7 NIV.
[46] 1 Samuel 2:30 NIV.

Besides these, please have faith that My Father will *'much more clothe you.'*[47] It will be written in the third earth age about one of my elaborate garments the Father gave Me,

In the year that King Uzziah died, I saw the Lord seated on a throne, high and exalted, and the train of His robe filled the temple. Above Him were seraphs, each with six wings:

With two wings they covered their faces, with two they covered their feet, and with two they were flying. And they were calling to one another:

'Holy, holy, holy is the Lord Almighty;
the whole earth is full of His glory.
At the sound of their voices the doorposts and thresholds shook,
and the temple was filled with smoke (Shekinah Glory).'[48]

Elders, as you fish for men, it is My will that you go dressed in holy garments as you tell the people of the Earth I will save them if they will repent of their sins, receive Me as Savior, and confess Me as Lord.

I will grant a few exceptions to the dress code, e.g., John the Baptist, but you are not to look like last year's bird's nest. [Laughter]

God has twenty-four thrones in a half circle before the Throne of Grace in which you will be dressed in royal robes of righteousness wearing twenty-four crowns. As I have mentioned before, in your long eternal home, you will not be having babies or this intense marital passion. You should 'make hay while the sun shines!'[49] [Laughter] My word of advice to you is 'often!' I had great joy in creating sex for flesh and blood marriages, but a flesh and blood body capable of producing children will not eternally inherit the Kingdom of Heaven. You will in the eternities have a changed flesh and bone celestial body as you see Me now have, and later I will have a terrestrial flesh, blood, and bone body much as you now have.

I know this has been a wonderful day – the men enjoying the sport of fishing and the women enjoying the sport of shopping. Opposites attract! [Laughter]

You, women, allow Sarah to show you how to make yourselves beautiful inside and out for your husbands. On the first Friday of each month, I am asking Sarah to oversee a cooking, diet, and makeover inside and out seminar at 10 AM Jerusalem time, with a women's luncheon following.

Your daughters may not wear makeup until they are fourteen. They may marry a believer in Me after they are fifteen. . None of your children may marry an unbeliever! No exceptions! You are not to pressure your children to marry anyone they do not love.

Your husband will be the covering, provider, and protector of you and your family. He is the king and lord of your home under Me. Even with a household of children take time each afternoon to make yourself beautiful as you prepare to greet your husbands with a kiss and a hug at the door when he comes home from work. Your children will leave you, but you and your husband are one flesh. Respect, notice, and love your husband. Talk about your love for him, and not constantly about your children. Joyously and willingly, adapt yourselves to your husbands. Be his beautiful woman! God built in every man the need to be a responsible leader. If you take that away from your man, you deny him his manhood.

A masterly wife is as much despised for taking rule over her husband, as he is for yielding to it. You love and trust God and your man to defeat any enemy in war.

---

[47] Matthew 6:32 NIV.
[48] Isaiah 6:1-4 NIV.
[49] *"Make hay while the sun shines*. "If you have an opportunity to do something, do it before the opportunity expires." *The Free Dictionary by Farlex*.

Relatively few wives will obtain the joy of accepting the truth that they belong to their husband and not to themselves or to any other man. Study Sarah, who trusts God in her covenant of marriage, choosing of her own free will to honor, respect, esteem and obey her husband, calling Abraham her master (lord). The foolish wife will tear her own house down.

Wise, Sarah, you may tell your dream today, to the other wives later about being with your best girlfriend, Joy, in Heaven ten thousand earth years from today. You, two submissive lovely women, will bring such delight to all Heaven, and to Abraham and Me. My Father will further honor you and keep you beautiful and delightful throughout eternity.

We shortly will have a round table rising, filled with delicious St Peter's Fish (a name given this fish in the Third Earth Age after Peter caught one having tax money due in its mouth) with the wives eating the selected fish your husbands caught just for you. I have been looking forward to dining with you. Notice that Sarah asked Abraham to ask Me to dine and fellowship with you this evening. For your information if Abraham had not asked Me to dine with you I would not be supping with you. Notice that Sarah respectfully asked her husband to ask Me. Wives ask your husbands, as head of your home, even the most complicated of questions, and I will give them wisdom. You, women, trust your own husbands and Me to keep you covered under a banner of love! Husbands' love your wives and keep them under your love protective covering. Many rebellious and unfaithful wives will choose to come out from under their husband's covering and tear their own house down. Two captains sink the marriage ship! If you disagree with your husband, give him your counsel, pray for him to have wisdom, and then choose to submit to his final decision, if it is not directly contrary to Scripture! Any questions?" [Silence.]

The First Friday Baked-Fish Dinner Fellowship

The round table rises with a name tag by each large white plate having a select piece of fish on it with other plates filled with delicious St Peter's Fish (so named in the Third Earth Age) and fresh fruit, which include nectarines, plums, and peaches, and salads made from cuts of romaine lettuce, spinach, with sliced cucumbers, radishes, carrots, zucchini, and yellow squash. The Son of God requests Elder John to bless the food and fellowship. Elder John prays,
"Our Father in Heaven
We hallow Your name. May Your kingdom of love come, Your will be done on Earth as it is in Heaven. Thank you for giving us this daily bread, which we receive with Thanksgiving. Bless this food to the proper nourishment of our bodies. We have been warned about the St Peter Fish bones and ask You always to protect us from ever getting anything caught in our throats as we carefully dine on this delicacy this evening. Here are our feet, Lord; send us out as an evangelist, as we become all things to all men that we might win some who are lost for Your kingdom. Here are our hands to do Your work with loving kindness in our touch. Here are our mouths to say what You would say, speaking love, hope, and eternal life. Yours is the Kingdom and the power and the glory forever and ever. Shalom! Amen." [All the Elders and their wives whisper, "Amen! Shalom!"]
Everyone watches as Sarah and Abraham kiss, as is their custom before every meal, and Sarah takes the first bite of the second largest fish of the day. She chews carefully making sure she has no bones and swallows smiling, "Savory! Delectable (Yummy)! Delicious! You did well Abraham!" [All Laughing]

After all had eaten sufficiently, Elder Peter asks the Lord, "When could I see the rest of my fishing business as I am about ready to go out again? Also, some of the ladies would like me to ask if they could go home and enjoy setting up housekeeping."

The Son of God replied,

"Let each couple enjoy the Sabbath rest tomorrow of your honeymoon. Sunday morning under the Grape Arbor, David leads the singing and Elder John bring a message of love and the importance of unity. Then if you desire, you could pack Sunday afternoon with the saucer picking you all up Monday morning at 9:00 A.M. Gabriel could then take you around to visit each of your businesses. For example, Gabriel can show Elder Peter, James, and John each of your beautiful villas overlooking the Sea of Galilee near your fishing businesses.

Also, Matthew, we could visit the Zion Bank for you to give each Elder a jump start bank deposit slip showing a balance of $7,000,000 in each account drawing 7% annual interest and show you how to make deposits and withdrawals. Put your money to work, and it will grow for you, but first lay up for yourselves treasures in Heaven as it will be written,

'But store up for yourselves treasures in Heaven, where moth nor rust destroys, and where thieves do not break in or steal. For where your treasure is, there will your heart be also.'[50]

Announcing First Official Elders' Meeting in Heaven

Last, but not least, Abraham, the elders, and wives could visit your cattle, sheep, and other livestock businesses. All can have lunch Monday on the Veranda of Abraham's nearby ranch house.

My Father and the Holy Spirit are to visit a new distant Galaxy Monday afternoon. The ladies can explore and organize your new homes while we have a brief official meeting of the Elders in the Throne Room of Grace in Heaven with your sitting for the first time in your throne chairs, in which you will sit many times throughout the eternities of eternities. I do not have your mansions in Heaven prepared, but I assure you women they will likewise be *'immeasurably more that all you can ask or imagine.'*[51]

Elders, you will briefly be transformed on the flying saucer into your celestial flesh and bone bodies with no blood, which have no working sexual reproductive organs. You have My word of honor you will be changed back into your terrestrial (physical) bodies for a Monday evening buffet with your wives in the heart of the Star of David with romance afterward. Remember this is the time of the 'often' (speaking of marital lovemaking). [Laughter] How does that sound?"

All the Elders responded, "Amen! Yes! Shalom!"

Also, the angels have outdone themselves on various desserts of your choice for this evening. I enjoy our friendship, and I thank Abraham for inviting Me. It will be written,

'I (Jesus) stand at the door (of your heart) and knock. If anyone hears My voice and opens the door. I will come in and eat with that person, and he with Me.'[52]

I thank Sarah for remembering Me in ordering matching robes and signet ring as I so like the Star of David. Let us men wear our matching white robes on the saucer to wear in Heaven as we sit on our thrones and reason man-to-man together. I look forward to our having this important kingdom business meeting with you Elders in Heaven Monday. Ladies, Monday evening we will return to Earth for a buffet again with St. Peter's fish and a brief meeting with you ladies so you will be fully informed. You are all greatly appreciated and loved! You are all people of beautiful feet! Blessings! Until then, Shalom!†

---

[50] Matthew 6:20-21.
[51] Ephesians 3:20.
[52] Revelation 3:20.

†BOOK FIVE – Episode 2†

[†**Sidebar Scriptures**: "Joseph had a dream and promptly reported all the details (Genesis 37:5)."
"The Lord revealed to me what the evil ones were doing and planning and showed me their wicked plots (Jeremiah 11:18)."
"The word of the Lord came to Abram in a **vision**. . . . A **deep sleep** came upon Abram . . . . (Genesis 15:1, 12)."
I witnessed and experienced "dreams and visions, and I described **all** I had seen to instruct many (Daniel 7:1, 11:33)."†]

Apollo Shows off His Choir and Orchestra Number Six, and Meeting of Elders in Heaven

Apollo's Perfected Choir Number Six (6) and Orchestra Number Six (6)

APOLLYON LUCIFER SENDS a memo by Mercury to Gabriel informing,

"INVITATION TO EXCELLENCE
Choir #6 and Orchestra #6 have finally reached a high standard of excellence and perfection! I would like to give a mini-concert this Monday the 6 at 6:00 P.M., behind the diamond pulpit and invite Word, Michael, and Gabriel. Maybe we can soon have another horseback ride together. Let me know if any of you cannot attend this demonstration of excellence and superiority. Otherwise, I will see all of you Monday evening. I will also invite Choirs and Orchestra 1-5 as a learning tool.

Apollo, Music Director of Heaven"

Jesus speaks, "Father, Gabriel delivered to Me this original memo from Apollyon Lucifer. He desires to show off the superiority of his Choir number six (6) and Orchestra number six (6) next Monday at 6:00 P.M. Father, what is Your will?

The Father, Son, and Holy Spirit Conversing Regarding the Upcoming Elders' Meeting

"My Son, it is My will the Elders also witness this show of pride and arrogance from here in the Throne Room. So that the Elders at this time do not gaze upon My face, I will make a visit Monday afternoon to enjoy viewing the splendor of a new expanding galaxy You created. I will then go down to enjoy further some newborn Panda Clubs on the Earth.

My Son, Apollyon Lucifer's Choir number six (6) will fall apart when the gifted harpist, Orphean, makes a mistake in this first public presentation. She will receive a frown snarl from Apollyon Lucifer and a private reprimand. He will announce a thirteen-minute break and ask You, Jesus, to say a few words while he seeks to correct the situation.

After this tongue-lashing and accusations, Apollyon Lucifer's gifted harpist, Orphean, breaks away from the grip on the shoulder and falls at Your feet in worship. He humbly prays for You to help give him a way of escape. Grant the request!

The perfectionist and demanding Apollyon Lucifer will be traumatized in his music for the first time. In the confusion, he will ask You whether you have the power to age the Earth 660 years, so he will have enough of his ape men You created from his drawings to make up a choir and orchestra for a concert on Earth. He will argue that he has been so busy he could not return to Earth, but he counted only six ape men and six ape women on the Earth during his last visit.

He will argue if he had 660 years with even only one ape man born each addition year this would give him 666, the number he would need for a full choir and orchestra.

This request is prideful, but I want You to agree to consider his request and that Gabriel will communicate back to him by next Monday whether the earth is 660 years older. Both Zion and the Land of Atlantis will have 660 years of Shalom (Peace) in which to populate the Earth without Apollyon Lucifer's harassment. Still, all people on Earth will have a 'free will,' just as the angels here have a free will. Son, I was not invited to this concert, but I will be specially invited to one of Apollyon Lucifer's concerts on Earth."

Elders Shown Businesses

The Elders, awaiting the saucer to land, excitedly discuss their new businesses. The saucer lands for a brief visit to Elders Peters, James, and John's fishing business. Each of these Elders had a separate resort villa overlooking the beautiful blue crystal-clear waters of the Sea of Galilee.

The next stop was to Elder Paul's tent-making shop having tent fabric in various colors.

They land at Elder Matthew's Zion Saving and Loan Association. .Each elder receives a bank passbook showing a deposit in each of $7,000,000. The current annual interest is 7%, with each Elder planning to make his nest egg grow. Likewise, each Elder was given deeds to all his property to be secured in separate safety-deposit boxes in the bank.

Next, was a stopover at Elder Luke's Medical Clinic and a brief showing the various businesses of the remaining elders. One of the more interesting companies was the Zion Alpha & Omega Printing Company, with an emphasis on children's teaching material. Another was a landscaping business focusing on beautiful flowers, shrubs, trees, and fountains to stock white and gold Coy and other goldfish.

One highlight was a noon visit to Elder Abraham's Cattle Ranch with abundant cattle seen on seven hills. The couples tour the lovely white farmhouse with a purple roof.

Peter commented, "Abraham's master bedroom is too feminine for a fisherman like me. I like things a little rugged. I would have chosen a camouflaged bedspread."

Peter's wife responds, "Pete, please paint your fishing boat masculine, but consider leaving the bedrooms for the women to decorate. Just maybe the more feminine and soft we women feel, the more masculine you men will feel."

Peter replied, "Right! Decorating our bedroom is your jurisdiction. I'm sorry I spoke out of turn. I have to remember to think before I speak. I may need to hold my tongue (with my thumb and pointer finger) and stop being so opinionated. The Lord gave me two ears and one mouth, and I need to listen twice as much as I speak. *In the multitude of words, sin is unavoidable, but he who restrains his tongue is wise.*[1] I will never deny[2] my Lord or the great blessings He has given me with unthought-out words before I speak. Shalom, my darling, forgive me for speaking when I should have been listening!"

Peter's wife gives him an acceptance kiss on the lips thinking, *"You are growing and will be a great man in eternity. Never say never, as you are only human! Be more careful and remember to think before you speak with few words, my darling!"*

Abraham smiles back at Peter with no response. Sarah looks at Abraham as Peter walks out of the room with both falling back on the bed laughing. Abraham commented, "One man's junk is another man's treasure. You won your case with me. No more camouflage sheets in my house!" [Laughter]

---

[1] Proverbs 10:19.

[2] Peter in the Third Earth Age will deny knowing Jesus three times. See Matthew 26-32; Mark 14:16-72; and Luke 22:54-62.

Behind Abraham's abode is a beautifully landscaped garden with nearby angels grilling to perfection juicy Zion Angus T-bone Steaks. One table is filled with various vegetables, another table is the fruit and salad bar, and still another table is the dessert bar filled with pies, cakes, muffins, nuts, blueberries, strawberries, honey, and various other toppings for ice cream and yogurt. Since this is the '*land flowing with milk and honey*,'[3] milk, cream, and honey are abundantly available.

The next stopover was the saucer landing on the pad in the center of the Star of David in the middle of the elders' Zion homes. Angels immediately transfer luggage and belongings from the saucer into the individual homes.

Abraham hugs and kisses Sarah and said, "I feel that this first meeting of the elders in Heaven is significant. I humbly request you pray to the Father God in the Son's name, Jesus, that God the Father's perfect will be done in Heaven as I feel it is now being done on earth with us. Being in the center of God's perfect will is wonderful. I will brief you when I return this evening. Have a blessed and happy day! We will have a late Monday evening buffet under a romantic full moon with a dessert bar afterward. If you would be so kind as to install those romantic sheets from Paris, I will plan to have you as my ultimate dessert. I have eaten various sweets lately with your romance being sweeter than them all." [Laughter]

Sarah smiles, "Certainly! I will wait for your homecoming, my love, my darling."

Each wife exits the saucer and in unison waves as the saucer rises from the Star of David launch pad with Gabriel explaining,

"Planet Heaven is in the celestial dimension, and we will shortly be arriving. Earth is the Father's '*footstool*,'[4] and so it is near."

Elders' First Meeting in Heaven

Gabriel instructs, "Now Elders look out the window at the beauty of the green-blue Earth, which is your short home. Heaven will be one of your many eternal habitations and for all who receive and trust the Son of God as their Savior and confess Him as their Lord and Master.

Now look out your window at the beautiful blue and green ball, Heaven, with its majestic mountains, set on nothing but outer space. The planet Earth is like its reflection in the terrestrial dimension. Elders prepare for landing behind the Throne Room of God. Father God is not here as He desires you to focus on a concert today and some words of His Son."

Glorious expectations were in the air as the saucer descends through a brightly glowing golden atmosphere, making an invisible landing on the Throne Room's rear golden launching and landing pad. Each Elder's body was transformed from flesh and blood body into a glorious celestial body. The Elders, as they exit the saucer appeared much older with full beards and with youthful faces. The Elders' robes '*became as white as light*,'[5] with golden sashes, and on each head is a magnificent gold crown studded with jewels. Gabriel shows each barefoot Elder his individual throne seat. Almost immediately, the Son of God appears in their midst dressed in a simple white robe with a purple sash. The Elders in unison hit their knees, bowing in worship, and they cast their gold crowns at His feet.

The Son of God humbly celebrates, "Elders of Zion, I receive your worship, and I welcome you with exceeding joy to the Throne Room of Grace. Elder John, please have a prayer of blessings over our first elders' meeting in Heaven."

---

[3] Exodus 33:3.

[4] Isaiah 66:1.

[5] See Matthew 17:2.

Elder John bows and prays,

"Our Father God,
In the Name of your Son, Jesus,
Bless our meeting today and give
    us wisdom and understanding regarding
        Thy will be done both in Heaven and on Earth!
May many souls of their own free will,
    choose to be part of Your kingdom.
Bless our precious wives as they are making us cozy homes.
Grant us these prayers in Your Son's name. Shalom! Amen!"

The Son of God directs, "You are all kings and priests under My authority. It shall be written,

'And they sang a new song, saying, 'Worthy are You (Jesus) to take the book and to break its seals, for You were slain, and purchased for God with Your blood men from every tribe and tongue and people and nation. You (Jesus) have made them to be a kingdom and priest to our God, and they will reign upon the earth.'[6]

Please be seated for this historic first Elders meeting in Heaven. These are your celestial bodies you will have throughout the eternities of eternities. How does your glorified body feel?"

Abraham responds, "This body is more tremendous. It is far superior to my earthly body in all aspects, except one!"

The Son of God replies, "Abraham, I believe you are calling upon Me, to give a brief organ recital. [Laughter]

Virtually all creation in the terrestrial world below celebrates the mating time and can reproduce themselves.

While you are on the Earth, you have a flesh and blood body able to create *via* your sexual organs joining with the female sexual reproductive organs new life. Angels have celestial bodies and cannot reproduce themselves. They have no reproductive organs in which to create new life.

Abraham, with your beautiful wife Sarah, I can understand your concern. You all are *'to make hay while the sun shines'*[7] in your flesh and blood bodies on the Earth. In passing, you might enjoy your daily food while you are on Earth as the food on Earth differs from angel food here in Heaven. This evening you will not be eating here, but you will have a delicious buffet awaiting you upon the return to Earth, which will include some of Abraham's choice Zion Angus T-bone steaks and some tasty St. Peter's fish. We do not have those two menu items available here in Heaven. I counsel you to enjoy the food down there and sexual relations with your lovely wives.

While you husbands and wives will make sweet, intimate music on Earth, but there will be no such sexual celebration in Heaven to produce children as you and your wives in your glorified bodies will be like the angels. Abraham here in your changed body of flesh and bone, with no blood, can hug, kiss, and hold Sarah's hand. Again, no created celestial creature in Heaven can reproduce other life.

As all of you know, pure marital love, when reciprocated *via* the sexual reproductive organs, not only brings one of life's greatest pleasures, but also has the potential of reproducing a brand-new life. The male and female bodies on Earth are unique in all eternity.

Nothing can compare to the sacred and loving sexual intimacy between a believing husband and wife as all of you well know. [Silence in Heaven]

---

[6] Revelation 5:9-10.

[7] *Make hay while the sun shines* -- "to do something while the situation or conditions are right." *The Free Dictionary by Farlex.*

Jesus spoke, "I give each of you My 'Power of Attorney'[8] as it is written even now, '*I tell you the truth, whatever you bind on earth will be bound in Heaven, and whatever you loose on Earth will be loosed in Heaven.*'[9]

Elders, you possess powerful, persuasive authority, and you are to exercise dominion both in Earth and here in Heaven. You will actually '*judge angels.*'[10] Remember this heavenly home is your long home. The Earth is only your short home, the place of your beginning. Elder John, you will write Scripture warning,

'*Do not love the world or anything in the world. If anyone loves the world, the love of the Father is not in him. For everything in the world – the cravings of sinful man, the lust of his eyes and the boasting of what he has and does – comes not from the Father, but comes from the world. The world and its desires pass away, but the man who does the will of God lives forever.*'[11]

Jesus continues, "For a few of you I will give the gift of singleness in the Third Earth Age because of the severe persecution you will face. Most of you will be married to the same wife, at least for a season, in either the Second or Third Earth Age.

In the Third Earth Age, My enemies will seek to lay a trap for Me in front of the people by presenting this proposition,

'*Teacher,*' they said, '*Moses told us that if a man dies without having children, his brother must marry the widow and have children for him. Now there were seven brothers among us. The first one married and died, and since he had no children, he left his wife to his brother. The same thing happened to the second and third brother, right on down to the seventh. Finally, the woman died. Now then, at the resurrection, whose wife will she be of the seven, since all of them were married to her?*'

Jesus replied, 'You are in error because you do not know the Scriptures or the power of God. At the resurrection people will neither marry nor be given in marriage; they will be like the angels in Heaven. But about the resurrection of the dead – have you not read what God said to you, 'I am the God of Abraham, the God of Isaac, and the God of Jacob.[12] *He is not the God of the dead, but of the living.*'[13]

Later in the eternities of eternities, you will have precious memories of some of your sexual relations with your wife on Earth. A hug and a kiss throughout eternity are acceptable. Now on Earth, the giving and receiving sexual pleasures with your wives resulting in children are both valuable and precious. Questions?"

Abraham, raising his hand, and the Son of God nodding Abraham asked,

"Does this mean that Sarah will have her private mansion here in Heaven and that I might by chance run into her like at one of the convocation meetings?"

Jesus replies, "Abraham, you and Sarah in Heaven will live in the same mansion, continue to kiss before every meal as is your custom on Earth. You can walk hand in hand down some golden brick road for a private picnic. Sarah is not going to be separated from you, Abraham. She loves you so very much! She is tucking in some soft romantic sheets even as we speak. Your love is stronger than death, which death you will both experience in the Third Earth Age. Abraham, you are going to remarry after Sarah's death and have other children.

---

[8] "A *power of attorney* is a written authorization to represent or act on another's behalf in private affairs, business, or some legal matter . . . ." *Wikipedia, The Free Encyclopedia.*

[9] Matthew 18:18.

[10] 2 Corinthians 6:3.

[11] 1 John 2:15-17 NIV.

[12] Exodus 3:6.

[13] Matthew 22:24-32 NIV

It will be written about you in the Third Earth Age,

'*Abraham took another wife . . . .*

Abraham left everything he owned to Isaac. But while he was still living, he gave gifts to the sons of his concubines and sent them away from his son Isaac to the land of the east. . . . Then Abraham breathed his last and died at a good old age, an old man full of years. .God blessed his son Isaac . . . .'[14]

Each of you elders will die once, but none of you will die in the First Earth Age. At a concert to be held on Earth, you will be taken from the surface of the Earth down into Paradise in the heart of the Earth for 666 years when the Earth is destroyed by an ice bomb detonated as an act of terror and war. However, your flesh and blood bodies will not die, but will again be transformed as you have been today into this same glorified body. You will live in a pleasant enough place in the heart of the Earth called Paradise, also affectionately known as Abraham's Bosom.[15] Remember, you and those with you in Paradise will have glorified bodies with no sexual organs. Again, Abraham, you will kiss before meals, stay in the same mansion, and walk hand in hand with Sarah, but no sex in Paradise. A few of you are thinking, '*How can it be Paradise without sex with our wives?*' [Laughter]

Later your eternal spirit, upon conception by a godly earthly husband and wife, will be born into the Earth as a baby in a subsequent Earth Age.

'*For you are God's handiwork, created in Christ Jesus to do good works, which God prepared in advance for you to do.*'[16]

My Father had Me to prepare your twenty-four thrones before the world began.

For flesh and blood cannot inherit the Kingdom of God as Elder Paul will write,

'*I declare to you, brothers (in the Lord), that flesh and blood (temporary physical bodies) cannot inherit the (eternal) kingdom of God; nor does the perishable inherit the imperishable'.*[17]

You, Elders, have been blessed with a true, faithful and pure love from a 'flesh and blood' wife you love on Earth. However, even one of you in the Third Earth Age will commit adultery and produce from that illegal sexual union with a married[18] woman, a male baby who will shortly die after childbirth.[19]

Another one of you, seeking to save his own skin, will permit his wife to be a candidate to be added to a king's harem[20] willing to force her into adultery. You reasoned that because your wife was so beautiful physically, even in her old age, you could be killed so she could be taken as another man's wife. So you lied advancing she was not your wife, but your sister, which was a half-truth.[21]

A warm marriage on Earth is the best escape from the temptations of sexual pressures to commit sexual immorality while one is in a temporary flesh and blood body.

Elders, I hope you understand a little. You will understand more and more in the eternity of eternities."

All the Elders, except Abraham, said, "We understand a little!"

"Elders, thank you for your almost unanimously concurring and somewhat understanding that we cannot permit marrying and giving in marriage in your physical bodies in Heaven."

---

[14] Geneses: 25:1, 4- 5, 8, 11 NIV.

[15] See Luke 16:22-24.

[16] Ephesians 2:10.

[17] 1 Corinthians 15:50 NIV.

[18] See 2 Samuel 11:1-27.

[19] 2 Samuel 12:16-23.

[20] See Genesis 12:10-20.

[21] See Genesis 20:1-2.

Abraham with tears flowing down his cheeks looking out the two-way glass window to the purple mountains whipping tears with his sleeve.

The Son of God inquires, "Abraham, why the sad face?"

Continuing to look out the window, Abraham, presents his case, "I don't keep secrets from my beloved Sarah. You might have to find another substitute Elder for me or go with twenty-three. If I tell Sarah there will be no marital romance – Eros – in Heaven between us, she will not even desire to come to Heaven. Sarah and I are legally one flesh. Martial love endures all things, which includes even the threat against it by Heaven itself! Your word promises, '*Come now, let us reason together, saith the Lord.*'[22]

As we once discussed, God changed His mind that Hezekiah was to die saying to him, '*I have heard your prayer and seen your tears, I will add fifteen years to your life.*'[23] You explained once, '*For nothing is impossible with God!*'[24]

The Son of God responds, "Elder Abraham are you asking Us to change Our mind partly on this issue?"

Abraham turns looking the Son of God in the eyes responds, "Yes, in rare cases such as Sarah and I, and even You and Your bride soon to be!' We are not just flesh and blood here in Heaven, but we are flesh, bone, and spirit. Unique 'one flesh' unions to endure through all eternity. '*Love never fails!*'[25] No true joy with a wife who has her vagina missing like those evil women in Hell. I refuse to tell Sarah otherwise and spoil our fellowship this evening. Please permit me to resign my Elder position. I will do nothing contrary to love. One flesh is one flesh as long as you both have flesh. I rest my case!'

The smiling Son of God replies, "Abraham you are not a robot. You and I have '*flesh and bones*'[26] with no blood even in Heaven. '*Come, let us reason together,*'[27] is your right. You have presented your case of the "one-flesh" union, citing 'love never fails.'[28] I do not desire twenty-four 'yes men.' Because you cited this ultimate eternal truth, your request regarding you and Sarah continues as one flesh in Paradise and in Heaven! A few other couples, having a like strong one flesh marital love relationship, may present their case for consideration to be granted or denied on a case-by-case basis. You are right that you and Sarah are a one flesh romantic love union to endure throughout eternity. Would you rather be a lawyer than a cattle farmer?" [Laughter]

Apollyon Lucifer Being Shaken as the First Member of the Orchestra Quits

"Elders, your enemy Apollyon Lucifer, does not yet even know you exist. He has been in pride focusing on building his separate kingdom here in Heaven. He sent me an invitation to attend a demonstration of what he calls his 'excellence and superiority' regarding a concert today behind the diamond pulpit. Even now, you will observe through the one-way glass the angels arriving and taking seats in the arena. The Elders view coming up the broad road Apollo, Mercury, and his #6 choir and orchestra to put on a show seeking to give Apollo glory.

---

22 Isaiah 1:18.
23 Isaiah 38:5.
24 Luke 1:37.
25 1 Corinthians 13:8.
26 Luke 24:37.
27 Isaiah 1:18.
28 1 Corinthians 13:8.

Today you will witness Apollyon Lucifer being visibly shaken and asking Me whether I have the power to age the Earth 660 years, as he desires a choir and orchestra of his ape men on the Earth. Apollyon Lucifer drew some proposed creatures such as dinosaurs, dragons, spiders, flies, and even ape men,[29] who speak the present one Earth language and asked Me to create them. Being a created cherub angel, he cannot create life, although he can and will create a big bang. There are only six ape men and six ape women on Earth down in dinosaur country. They are not made in Our image like yourselves, and most do not have sense enough to get out of the rain and certainly not skilled in playing harps. They mate when the female is in heat with the strongest available male prevailing. They have no marriage ceremony or marriage covenant. They have a short lifespan just like the other animals and plants on the earth outside the territorial boundaries of Zion. Their remains will turn to 'black gold,' being oil in future Earth ages. Apollyon Lucifer would like to focus his attention on training them for both his choir and orchestra since they were his idea originally. He has calculated that he needs 660 years for the population of the ape men to grow to a number sufficient for him to select just the slightly gifted 666 for both his choir and orchestra. He would like to start this training next week. They have no eternal spirit from which to worship God, but they can be trained liked programming robots.

If I grant his request, this means that only a short time will have passed in Heaven, but some 660 years will have passed on the Earth. Later he will give his first Earth concert to which he will invite the Father, the Son, the Holy Spirit, and all of you, at which time he will set off a freeze bomb to murder all in attendance. Lucifer wants the kingdom and worship for himself alone. Are you to run from this trap of your enemy, or is this your greatest opportunity to permit you to rear your children and future generations without a tempter to be present on the Earth?

'*Come now, let us reason together!*'[30]"

John advances, "I would like to see us separate our children from everything and everyone that is unclean. We will be able to rear our children and grandchildren for the first 660 years in the pure and the holy land of Israel, without a tempter trying to make them stumble. These children can come back to the Earth in the Second and the Third Earth Ages to evangelize others and to seek hopefully first the eternal Kingdom of God. We need this time alone with our children and grandchildren. I feel this is our greatest opportunity! Otherwise, we will be discovered soon by this prideful and selfish enemy. However, if his request is granted he will not discover us until we have had this time to rear our children and grandchildren in love and in the training, teaching, instructing, and disciplining of the Lord."[31]

Peter adds, "I concur. It is not worth taking a chance on the tempter causing even one of our little ones to be lost in Hell. I believe our enemy is offering us our greatest opportunity! We have such a high calling to win our children and grandchildren to be added to our Father's eternal family."

All the elders said, "Concur! Amen!"

The Son of God smiles, "You will have 660 years in a '*secret place*.'[32]

---

[29] *Ape man* – "Ape-like beings that have distinctly human traits." *Wikipedia, The Free Encyclopedia.*
[30] Isaiah 1:18.
[31] See Ephesians 6:4.
[32] Psalm 91:1.

Then Apollyon Lucifer will discover you as you observe his plan unfolding to have a concert on earth at which time he will detonate a freeze bomb to destroy those he has invited to attend with his goal being to control both Heaven and Earth. An insane act of war, but My Father will permit this stupidity for reasons of His own.

This is My Father's will, and I thank you, Elders, for your concurrence. You will fully live the 660 years abundantly. Time on Earth differs from time in Heaven. To Us, a thousand years on Earth is a short time as it is to be written,

'For a thousand years in Thy (Father God) sight are like a day that has just gone by or like a watch in the night.'[33]

Elder Peter speaking by the Holy Spirit in the Third Earth Age will write Scripture,

'First, understand that in the last days scoffers will come, scoffing and following their own evil desires (lusts). . . .By God's word the heavens existed and the Earth was formed out of water and by water. By these waters also the world of that time was deluged and destroyed (water turning to ice in the First Earth Age and a flood in the Second Earth Age). By the same word the present heavens and Earth are reserved for fire (Third Earth Age), being kept for the day of judgment (born again going to Heaven and those who did not receive Jesus as Savior going first to Hell and then Lake of Fire) and destruction of ungodly men.

But do not forget this one thing, dear friends: With the Lord a day is like a thousand years, and a thousand years are like a day.

The Lord is not slow in keeping His promise, as some understand slowness. He is patient with you, not wanting anyone to perish, but everyone to come to repentance.

But the day of the Lord will come like a thief. The heavens will disappear with a roar; the elements will be destroyed by fire, and the Earth and everything in it will be burned up.

Since everything will be destroyed in this way, what kind of people ought you to be? You ought to live holy and godly lives as you look forward to the day of God and speed its coming. That day will bring about the destruction of the heavens by fire, and the elements will melt in the heat. But in keeping with His promise we are looking forward to a New Heaven and a New Earth, the home of righteousness.

So then, dear friends, since you are looking forward to this, make every effort to be found spotless, blameless and at peace with Him.'[34]

Now, gentlemen, look out the window down behind the diamond pulpit; and you will see the orchestra and choir #6 preparing for this 6:00 P.M. concert. Those in the audience comprise choirs 1 through 5, which our enemy was not able to bring into what he calls 'absolute perfection and superiority' according to his high standards. I have been specially invited to witness this mini-concert. My Father and the Holy Spirit were not invited, but the Father, Holy Spirit, and you will be invited to the planned concert on the Earth. A trap of traps with your enemy saying of you, *'Come into my parlor, said the spider to the fly,'*[35] but this illegal act gives My Father legal grounds to order that Apollyon Lucifer be cast out of Heaven. My Father does nothing illegal as you will witness throughout eternity.

Now all of you carefully witness as Michael, Gabriel, and I walk down to attend this show seeking to give Apollo glory. "

Apollyon Lucifer, dressed in eloquent tight black leotards wearing a gold chain, smiles as the Son of God, enters barefoot dressed in simple white attire and takes His position. Apollyon Lucifer, as he is known, stares at Michael's feet, thinking, *"Michael has some attractive feet."* Apollyon Lucifer on the 6th beat with his black wand directs his Orchestra to demonstrate how the prelude is to be played flawlessly.

---

[33] Psalm 90:4 NIV.

[34] 2 Peter 3:3-14 NIV.

[35] *The Spider and the fly* is a poem . The opening line is one of the most recognized and quoted first lines in all English verse, often used to indicate a false offer of help or friendship that is in fact a trap.
   Wikipedia, The Free Encyclopedia.

Apollyon Lucifer was leading each in the Orchestra flawlessly when he glances off to the side focusing his eyes again on Michael's naked feet. The harpist looks to view whatever Apollyon Lucifer is staring at and in his run on the harp makes a simple, but noticeable and obvious mistake. pollo frowns at the harpist and stops the music.

Apollo turns to the audience saying, "This is a learning experience. I need a 13-minute break to correct this problem. Word, while I am in this conference, address the idle audience briefly."

The Son of God, seizing the opportunity stands and preaches,

"I am the Word of God, and I have been with God the Father, who is now invisible to you, from eternity. It will be written of Me,

'In the beginning was the Word, and the Word was with God and the Word was God. He was with God in the beginning.

Through Him (Word, Jesus) all things (including each of you) were made (created; came to be), without Him (Jesus) nothing was made that has been made.'[36]

You are to worship only the eternal (not created), God. There is one person of the Father, another of the Word (Son), and another of the Holy Spirit, but the Godhead of the Father, the Word (Son), and the Holy Spirit is one God.

It is to be further written of Me,

'I am the way, the truth, and the life; No one comes to the Father (God) except through Me.'[37]

I will say this about Myself,

'All things have been committed to Me by My Father.

. . . Come to Me, all you who are weary and heavy laden (burdened), and I will give you rest. Take My yoke upon you and learn of Me, for I am gentle and humble in heart; and you will find rest for your souls. For My yoke is easy, and My burden (commandments) is light.'[38]

If I (Jesus) set you free, *'You will be free indeed (abundantly free)*! '[39]

Today, if you hear My voice, harden not your heart. If you need to repent, as no created being is perfect, come as My arms are opened wide to receive and forgive you.

Come! My yoke is easy, and My burden is light – easy and light!"

The harpist breaks away from under Apollo's heavy hand and scolding and comes falling at the Son of God's feet praying,

"I worship You, my Lord and Creator. I take your easy yoke and light burden upon me. Give me a way of escape out of this orchestra. This burden of perfectionism is too heavy. I humbly repent. Please set me free!"

The Son of God laying hands on each side of the harpist's head decrees,

"Free! Forgiven! *'Whom the Son sets free is free indeed.'*[40] Freedom! Go. Run. Don't ever look back. Go!"

The harpist, rising, receives a hug from Word and with gratitude says,

"Thank You for not casting me away and for helping me be free in my time of need and bondage. I will, with your help, worship, praise, and serve You throughout eternity. I will forever be thankful for saving and delivering me this day, and I feel forgiven, clean, and free. Shalom!"

With that, the harpist runs and leaps for joy heading down the exit ramp out of the arena taking the narrow and straightway with hands held high worshiping and thanking God.

---

[36] John 1:1-3.

[37] John 14:6 NIV.

[38] Matthew 11:27-30.

[39] John 8:36

[40] Id.

Word further invites others, "If you also need to repent, come. Come!

It will be written of Me,

'Whoever comes to Me (Jesus) I will never drive away.'[41]

Today I will receive you. I love all I have created, and I mean all!

I invite any of you to come to Me. No one will be excluded. Those who come will know the *'truth, and the truth shall make you free.'*[42]

'And you shall love the Lord your God with all your heart (first of all), and with all your soul, with all your mind, and with all your strength. This is the first commandment.

And the second, like it, is this. You shall love your neighbor as yourself. There is no other commandment greater than these.'[43]

'Love never fails.'[44]

'Just as I am, thou (Son of God) wilt receive,
wilt welcome, pardon, cleanse, relieve;
because Thy promise I believe,
O Lamb (Son) of God. I come, I come.'[45]

'God is love'[46] and God, who is love never fails. Come today, just as you are as the God-kind of love can turn it around.

Jesus bowed His head, praying.

The remaining five harpists from Choirs 1- 5, who had committed similar mistakes in that same song, came running, falling at the feet of the Son of God as He lays hands on each one, decreeing,

"Forgiven! I have set you free! Go. You are free indeed! Run. Don't look back!"

They ran and caught up with the first harpist escaping through the small gate and narrow path, with no-one looking back."

The Son of God, bowing to His knees, prays to His Father, whispering into the atmosphere of Heaven, "Come! Repent! Come! Freedom! Respond to the invitation. Come."

Eighteen more come bowing at the feet of Word, but no others coming from Choir #6.

The Son of God lays hands on each and decrees,

"Free! Forgiven! Free to go and live an abundant life to the fullest in Heaven. They like-wise all ran through a small gate down the narrow path and almost out of sight the twenty-four freed ones gather hugging and laughing looking like a bright star on the horizon."

Apollyon Lucifer's Being Visibly Shaken Makes His Selfish Request

Apollyon Lucifer, being visibly shaken and in confusion sarcastically inquires,

"Word would you have the power to age the Earth 660 years, so I will have enough of the ape men I designed to make up a loyal and talented choir and orchestra on Earth? I have been so busy with these six (6) choirs that I have not been able to return to Earth. The last time I was on Earth, I counted only six (6) ape men and six (6) ape women that You created according to my drawing. I have calculated that if I had 660 years, with only one ape man born each addition year, this would give me 666 needed for a complete and full choir and orchestra. Will you meet me back here next Monday at 6:00 P.M. to let me know your decision?"

---

[41] John 6:37 NIV.

[42] John 8:32 NIV.

[43] Mark 12:30-31

[44] 1 Corinthians 13:4.

[45] *Just as I Am, Without One Plea*, fifth stanza, written by Charlotte Elliott.

[46] 1 John 4:16.

Word, replies, "Gabriel, will amail[47] you by 3:00 P.M. next Monday and let you know My decision regarding your request."

Apollo turns back to Orchestra and Choir #6 and declares,

"We cannot continue without a lead harpist. Is there no harpist in all creation who can accurately play my composition? All of you are dismissed! Let us meet back at our usual time for practice. Practice makes you perfect. Practice, practice, and more practice! If any of you know anyone with superb harp-playing ability or willingness to learn, please invite that angel to apply for this opening."

Apollyon Lucifer thinking, *"Right now we have no willing harpist in Heaven. I wonder if a harpist is on Earth, such as one of the six (6) ape men? Harpists are hard to find."*

Apollyon Lucifer seeks Gabriel saying,

"How are you doing?

Gabriel replies,

"Too blessed to be stressed!"

Apollyon Lucifer replies,

"Today, I am too stressed to be blessed. The choir and orchestra are only as perfect as the weakest link. How do you keep your feet looking so good?"

'My feet are fitted with the readiness always to be prepared for what comes as I walk in the Good News of Peace.'[48]

Apollo inquired, "Is Word's father up in the throne room as I would like to meet him."

Gabriel replied, "He is not in."

Apollyon Lucifer thinks, *"And he is never in. He is dead. That is it! He is presumed dead! Everything comes to an end. Who made him, and when did that one die? Who made that one? How did it all start? Big bang? Who made what blew up? Also, outer space must end. Could it be a wall that ends it, but what is on the other side of that wall? Word had no right to set my harpist free from under my control. I will regain all the harpists back after the freeze bomb. They are all mine. I put the freeze bomb project on black alert. Word is the sole heir. I am the first creation of life. I am next in line for the throne. Gabriel's beautiful feet. Gorgeous!"*

Elders Feeling This Trap Is Their Greatest Opportunity to Raise Their Children Freely and Children's Children Without an Outside Tempter

Jesus appears back before the waiting twenty-one Elders, with each Elder again bowing low in worship with the Son of God gently speaks, "Elders of Zion please be seated. This decision you concurred in today will mean that you will in great Shalom (Peace) be able to raise a core family of God's chosen people who will not die in the First Earth Age and will live again in the Second or Third Earth Ages. *'Inasmuch as it is appointed unto men once to die, and after this the judgment.'*[49] They will not remember much of this First Earth Age, but at times, they will have a shadow of knowing that they did something similar before. Some will not die in the Third Earth Age, for they will be raptured up here to Heaven during the Great Tribulation coming at that time on the Earth,

'Since you (born again ones) have kept My (Jesus) command to endure patiently, I will also keep you from the hour of trial that is going to come upon the whole world to test those who live on the Earth.

---

[47] *Email* – "Electronic mail. commonly referred to as email or e-mail . . . ." *Wikipedia, The Free Encyclopedia.*
[48] See Ephesians 6:15.
[49] Hebrews 9:27.

I am coming soon. Hold on to what you have, so that no one will take your crown. Him who overcomes, I (Jesus) will make a pillar in the temple of My God.'[50]

'For the Lord (Jesus) will come down from Heaven, with a loud command, with the voice of the archangel (Gabriel) and with the trumpet call of God, and the dead in Christ (born again in their lifetime) will rise first. After that, we (born again) who are alive and are left will be caught up (not die, but be ruptured) with them in the clouds to meet the Lord (Jesus) in the air. And so we will be with the Lord forever. Therefore, encourage each other with these words.'[51]

'Listen, I tell you a mystery. We (born again ones) will not all sleep (die), but we will be changed – in a flash, in the twinkling of an eye, at the last trumpet. For the triumph will sound, the dead will be raised imperishable, and we (alive born again ones) will be changed.'[52]

None of you Elders will die in this First Earth Age! All the born again ones who do not die have a right to come back to the Earth to marry again and raise children. However, next Monday, Heaven's time, you will have lived fully 660 more years and in 6 (six) more years you will be removed in an instance before the great first tribulation hits the Earth. A few of your wives and children, including your wife, Paul, will have already died (meaning they cannot come back to live on the surface of the Earth). Some of you who became widowed will have remarried by next week Heaven's time. Remember that I am the God of the living and not of the dead.

It is My will you each live a full and blessed life and enjoy your wives, your children, your businesses, and your work as evangelists with absolute holiness and purity. Your faithfulness will greatly increase the numbers of those who love God. Take every opportunity to fish for that one out of a hundred that may go astray because of pride or sinful desires.

Elder Isaiah in the Third Earth Age will write, *'Truly You are a God, who hides Himself, O God and Savior of Israel! . . . But Israel will be saved by the Lord with an everlasting salvation; you will never be put to shame or disgraced to ages everlasting. . . . For this is what the Lord says –He who fashioned and made the Earth, He founded it; He did not create it to be empty, but formed it to be inhabited. . . .Turn to Me and be saved, all you ends of the Earth, for I am God, and there is no other.'*[53]

Apollyon Lucifer cannot discover you for 660 years, which will be soon in Heaven's time. In six (6) more Earth years Apollyon Lucifer will have made the Earth *without form and an empty waste,*[54] making it vacant of life on the surface by freezing it solid, causing the ice age.[55] It is part of his evil plan, but this is our opportunity to help increase the Heavenly Father's eternal family made up of those who truly love Him and receive Me as Savior. Apollyon Lucifer will go expecting only a population of ape men to worship him and sing in his choir; but he will find to his utter surprise a population inhabiting the Earth, many of whom have received Me as Savior and loved My Father God with all their hearts, souls, and strength.[56]

Sunday afternoon at 3:00 P.M. I would like for us to have a holy service.

In 660 years, there will be 666 ape men in the heart of Africa. If one of their scouts were to discover Zion with its wealth and beautiful women, you would have a World War with the apes. Sunday I am separating this one continent known now to the ape men as Gondwanaland. Sunday afternoon I will break up this one continent to segregate and separate My beloved Zion from

---

[50] Revelation 3:10-12.

[51] 1 Thessalonians 4:16-18.

[52] 1 Corinthians 16:50-53.

[53] Isaiah 45:15, 17-18, 22 NIV.

[54] Genesis 1:2.

[55] What could explain the sudden change from a warm to a frozen planet. A solution to the puzzle would bring deep satisfaction to some. *Ice age* "It took several decades until the ice age theory was fully accepted (e.g., like the world was round instead of flat)." *Wikipedia, The Free Encyclopedia.*

[56] Genesis 1:2 AMP.

218

wicked and warring men. The western portion, later to be South America, and presently joined with Africa, will be cast out into the middle of a vast body of water later to be the Atlantic and Pacific oceans. I will join it back together like pieces of a jigsaw puzzle in the second creation of the Earth to be only separated again as it will be written,

'*Two sons were born to Eber: One was named Peleg, because in his time the Earth was divided.*'[57]

Questions about what you have seen today?"

Elder Peter inquires of Jesus, "What will be the outcome of the twenty-four angels you laid hands on and set free today? Will Apollyon Lucifer ever be able to win any back into his camp?"

"No, beloved, Peter, for whom I set free is free indeed! I have eternal and excellent works for all the twenty-four set free today. They will not be cast out of Heaven with Apollyon Lucifer. However, the prideful music concerts will continue throughout Heaven with one-third of the angels joining forces with Apollyon Lucifer. For some of them today this was their last opportunity to come to Me and be set free. A few were holding onto their seats as they so much wanted to come to Me to be set free. Life and death were set before them, and many of them of their 'free will,' chose death, which will ultimately result in eternal separation from God. As it will be written,

'*Today, if you hear His (Son of God's) voice, do not harden your hearts.*'[58]
'*Now is the time of God's favor, now is the day of salvation.*'[59]

You here in Zion will soon be relocated to Paradise, which will also be called '*Abraham's bosom (side, protection).*'[60]

Elders, are there any other business before you journey back to the arms of your loving wives? Hearing none this first elder's meeting in Heaven is adjourned."

Elders Returning to Earth for A Romantic Moonlight Buffet in the Courtyard of the Star of David with Abraham Anticipating the Paris Romantic Sheets

Hearing none, now go and enjoy a full moon shining down on a romantic buffet time awaiting you in the heart of the Star of David."

Elder John asked Word, "What are we going to be telling our wives about the event of this day?

"You can tell them that next week from Heaven their enemy Apollyon Lucifer will discover all of you for the first time, but you will be 660 years older, having lived each day fully. Tell your wives they will not notice it and for them never to ever worry about anything as God has everything under control. I respectfully request you keep confidential the fact that Apollyon Lucifer will destroy the Earth with ice as an act of war. Remember the angels will gently transport the born again saints from the surface of the Earth to Paradise."

After the Elders board, the saucer lifts off from Heaven going toward the Earth, and their flesh and blood bodies return. Shortly the blue-green planet Earth was in sight and then the beautiful sky blue Star of David sitting on the top of the white stone elders' houses in Zion.

---

[57] Genesis 10:25. This was when North and South America was separated from Europe and Africa.
[58] Hebrews 3:15.
[59] 2 Corinthians 6:2.
[60] Luke 16:22.

Each wife was standing near the center landing pad waving as Sarah blows kisses to Abraham. Abraham was the first to exit. Abraham and Sarah run to embrace and kiss. Abraham speaks,

"Our chemistry is just right. I assume the Paris romantic sheets are tucked in place?

Sarah nods '*yes*,' and inquires, "Did anything eventful happen on your trip to Heaven?"

"Oh, just the usual things. God will never be stressed, nor shall we! It proves that truth is stranger than fiction. One thing I will share with you now is that I saw our enemy. He wore skin tight black leotards and looked like a Spanish prince. Pride is a bad thing. I saw our enemy's plan today fall apart in front of my own eyes like a $2 watch. In our enemy's confusion, after being visibly shaken, he requested the Son of God to age the Earth 660 years, and this aging will take place in Heaven next Monday.

We will live out fully each day on the Earth, and we will not miss out on anything, including all our lovemaking on our Paris sheets. Laughter] We will use this time of peace here in Zion as our opportunity to rear our children and children's children in a pure, humble isolated atmosphere. It will be written, '*And in all things God works for the good of those who love Him.*'[61]"

"Abe, does this mean that next week in Heaven I will be a 660-year old woman?"

"Yes! '*Grow old (on Earth only) along with me! The best is yet to be!*'[62]

Romantic love cannot be measured by a single day! How long does love last? Our romantic marital love is here to stay! It will endure when the stars are all passed away. Sarah, remember,

'*With the Lord a day is like a thousand years, and a thousand years are like a day.*'[63]

We are not going to miss a day or a moment of our beautiful life on Earth together Sarah, now I have a question for you. How can I fully enjoy the buffet thinking about those romantic Paris sheets?"

"Abe, anticipation is part of the enjoyment. Let me sing you a little song, '*I give to you and you give to me – True love, true love! So on and on it will always be . . .*'[64]

Abraham amplifies, "Darling, always throughout eternity, as of two hours ago! [*Inward laughter for Abraham.*] Darling, we are going to set an unbeatable record of intimacy on Earth, and with some anticipated welcomed competition, possibly throughout ETERNITY! Sarah, do you think I should be a lawyer and not a rancher? [Silence, as Sarah did not fully understand Abraham winning in Heaven his right with intimacy with her throughout Eternity.]

Sweetheart, how would you like to be the first couple in line for the buffet? Eating can't compare with the act of romance in marriage!" [Laughter]

Sarah smiles, "Amen! While the others are having dessert, you have me, and I have you! It is a two-way street. Remember, I am also enjoying and having you! I give to you and you give to me – true romantic eternal love! Real love stories like ours never have endings. Abe, does Jesus understand we desire our marital romance to last throughout eternity?"

Abraham, respond, "He does now! I won our case! Eternal intimacy for us in the oneness of our marriage in our new glorified flesh and bone bodies, but with no children! I won the case of cases in Heaven like a Philadelphia lawyer for love's sake! Again, do you think I should be a lawyer instead of a rancher?"

Sarah counsels, "Rancher, if it is no longer broke, please don't try again to fix it! How about a taste of our dessert first on our soft Paris sheets while others are eating finger food?"†

---

[61] Romans 8:28.
[62] Quote of Robert Browning.
[63] 2 Peter 3:8.
[64] '*True Love*" lyrics written by Cole Porter.

†Book Five – Episode 3†

[†**Sidebar Scriptures**: *"Joseph had a dream and promptly reported all the details* (Genesis 37:5)."
"The Lord revealed to me what the evil ones were doing and planning and showed me their wicked plots (Jeremiah 11:18)."
"The word of the Lord came to Abram in a **vision**. . . . A **deep sleep** came upon Abram . . . . (Genesis 15:1, 12)."
I witnessed and experienced *"dreams and visions, and I described **all** I had seen to instruct many* (Daniel 7:1, 11:33)."†]

Apollo's Scientist Assure Freeze Bomb
Will Be Ready for Detonating in Six Years,
and Son of God Instructing Inhabitants of Zion

Apollyon Lucifer's Meeting with His Scientists

APOLLYON LUCIFER DRESSED in seductive black, trimmed in gold, with Mercury at his side makes a surprise visit to his scientists, who bow and worship him, with Apollyon Lucifer demanding, "E=MC² – The last report indicated that you had discovered that 'E' is Energy. What is the rest of the puzzle?"

Photon, gleaming, speaks for the group, "Father, we are proud to say that we have broken the code. E=MC² means – 'Energy = Mass times the Speed of Light Squared.' However, to make a freeze bomb as the ultimate weapon, we will have to have an ample amount of pechblend[1] ore from which we can extract uranium. It will take a lot of labor and a few years to mine and separate enough uranium to make a bomb monstrous enough to sub-freeze the Earth. We have located through a high power sensitive Geiger Counter a quantity of buried pechblend, later known as pitchblende, ore on Earth in the massive Black Granite Volcano Mountain, with beautiful black smoke billowing out of the top, in a place called Nigrous, Africa – pointing to a spot on the map. We would have to be right there when the ore is being mined to harvest the rare uranium from the pitchblende. We have conspired to justify the end results, our Prince.[2] Master, you might have to act immorally, with brute force, or with deceit to entice diggers on Earth as exposure to raw pitchblende will, not might, result in painful and cancerous tumors."

Apollo, smirking replies, "No problem! Next week, I will have at least 666 strong ape men, which I designed and had created, right at that location digging up this pitchblende. We could use the seductive polished black granite[3] stone to build a coliseum for the upcoming Earth concert. I will ask for a second gate, which uses the same key, to my haunting dark abode under the Earth to be placed into the enchanting region in the heart of darkest Africa. We have large dinosaurs, which I also designed that you can train as earth moving machines to help lift heavy stones for building our Coliseum.

---

[1] *Uranium* is defined in part, "A medal discovered in 1789 by Kisproth, in the mineral called pechblend . . . in which it exists with iron, copper, lead, and sometimes with arsenic, cobalt, and sink."
American Dictionary of the English Language Noah Webster 1828.

[2] *The Prince* – Machiavelli's best-known book . . . concentrates on the possibility of a 'new prince.' . . . A ruler must be concerned not only with reputation, but also must be positively willing to act immorally at the right time. . . . Machiavelli emphasized the occasional need for the methodical exercise of brute force or deceit." From *Niccolo Machiavelli* in the *Wikipedia, The Free Encyclopedia*.

[3] *Granite* is defined as, "A hard coarse-grained igneous rock composed principally of quartz, feldspar, and mica, of great strength and taking a high polish." *Britannica World Language Dictionary*.

Before I forget, I want you to recommend to the natives to eat the unicorn meat since one of those beasts rebelled against me by throwing me off into a swamp causing me to lose an article of gold of great value. I never forget, and I always get even!

Unicorns are easy to capture. Stand in front of a tree and mock the unicorn into charging. Then at the last second, the Hunter will step aside, and the unicorn would embed its horn deeply into the tree.[4] Then pierce its heart with a dagger. Let us eat every last one of these prideful creatures that tried to hurt me.

Scientists, if you could start next week in your new earthly lab, how long would it take you to collect enough pitchblende from the black granite ore to be a sufficient amount to make a bomb large enough to sub-freeze the entire Earth?"

"Your worship, it could take as long as 666 days of hard labor to mine enough pitchblende ore, most of which we detect buried some 666 feet deep in the black granite mountain, to make such a freeze bomb, which would be ready to detonate in six years. It would freeze the entire Earth solid and anything on it as deep as 666 feet. We would all have to be back here in Heaven or deep within Hell, when we detonate it or even though we are the angels we also would be destroyed because of the tremendous freezing power. Nothing. Not even God could survive such a deep freeze. It is the ultimate weapon!"

"Clever scientists, be prepared to move to planet Earth next week. I have a little politicking to do. By all manners of means! The end justifies the means![5]"

Apollyon Lucifer's Memo to Gabriel

Apollyon Lucifer sends a memo by Mercury to Gabriel directing,
REQUEST FOR AN ALTERNATIVE ENTRANCE GATE TO HELL
With Word aging the earth 660 years, Monday, to enable me to have 666 ape men for an Earth Choir and Orchestra, I would like to request further an alternative entrance gate to charming Hell be made on the South side of the Black Granite Volcano Mountain in Nigrous, Africa. Such an entry would give me space for training and to store musical instruments. I also request a winged Airbus and nearby landing strip in walking distance to this additional gate of Hell to enable the transporting of musical instruments and some 66 assistant angels to Earth. Remember to allow the same key you gave me to also open this extra gate to Hell.
Apollo, Music Director of Heaven

Jesus Receives Instructions from His Father

The Son inquires, "My beloved Father, our messenger Gabriel delivered to Me this original memo from Apollyon Lucifer advancing his desire for an additional gate to Hell in Nigrous, Africa on the pretense that this will permit him to train better the ape men for an Earth choir and orchestra. Regarding this request, what is Your will?'

"My Son, it is My will that Abraham and the other Elders be initially segregated from all such wickedness. Let the present one-world island continent known as 'Gondwanaland'[6] be separated and isolated away from this wickedness. The land mass of this new island continent will be relatively small and will be known as Atlantis.

---

[4] Shakespeare . . .*Timon of Athens*, Act 4, scene 3, c. line 341: ". . .wert thou the unicorn, pride and wrath would confound thee and make thine own self the conquest of thy fury . . . ."

[5] *The Prince* by Machiavelli is attributed in advancing this statement on behalf of a ruler defending his country.

[6] Gondwanian is defined, "of or relating to the hypothetical prehistoric landmass Gondwana." *Webster's New Collegiate Dictionary*.

It will have many volcanic mountains and a lush tropical atmosphere to house all the creatures Apollyon Lucifer had drawn, including the dinosaurs, dragons, spiders, four-legged snakes, flying creatures, the unicorns, and what he calls ape men. Let him have the requested additional gate to Hell near the digging for pitchblende to build the freeze bomb with his goal to murder Us.

He will not have an easy time killing all the unicorns as We asked my servant Job these questions before they were all extinct,

> 'Will the unicorn be willing to serve thee . . . ?
> Can you hold him to the furrow (for plowing) . . .?
> Will you rely on him for his great strength?
> Can you trust him to bring in your grain . . . ?'[7]

Apollyon Lucifer does not care about the Earth, those creatures he drew, or his choir. Right now, his free will is driving him to seek to steal Heaven and Earth. You will preach about him,

> *The thief comes **only** to steal, kill, and destroy. I (Jesus) have come that they (those who receive Me as Savior and Lord) may have life and have it in abundance (to the full).*[8]

I will permit this assassination attempt on Us for reasons of My own, but He will murder You My Son by nailing You to the cross in the Third Earth Age. He will also murder many of Your Disciples and Elders that confessed You before men by having them beheaded, stoned, speared, hanged, torn by lions, burned, and dragged by horses. What shining eternal treasures, they will have in Heaven for defending Your dear cause.

Give Apollyon Lucifer the requested Airbus with wings – not one of the flying saucers, but have it with no windows for him to spot Zion from the air. He can push one button as automatic pilot to fly and land near the new entrance to Hell on Earth and another button to return near his temporary dwelling here in Heaven. Let us put a hedge around Zion and an anointing cloud of protection over it. I forbid both Apollo's and Mercury's black horses from being able to again fly to Earth. Apollon Lucifer and his scientist will have to take the Airbus. After his rebellion, the Airbus after one more trip from Earth to Heaven will also become disabled. Michael will cast them all out like lightning from Heaven to the frozen Earth!

Let this new continent be Atlantis[9] be located out in the middle of the Atlantic Ocean some 777 miles away from the main continent.

Son, now further prepare places for Us and those who love Us in Abraham's Bosom known also as Paradise beneath Zion in the heart of the Earth. It will be a separate compartment in what I call Hades. The already-created Hell is on one side, and now the enhanced Paradise is on the other side, with a great guilt (chasm) between them, keeping anyone from crossing over from either side.[10] You will crush the head of Apollyon Lucifer, and he will bruise Your heel.[11] You as Savior will transfer the Saints in Zion and Atlantis into Paradise in the twinkling of an eye, in a split second, before the ice bomb goes off. After Your resurrection from the dead in the Third Earth Age, You will preach to all those in Paradise after You had earlier preached to some spirits in the prison of Hell. You will lead all Paradise out right up to Heaven,

---

[7] Job 39:9-12.

[8] John 10:10 NIV. [Emphasis added.]

[9] *Atlantis* is defined, "A mythical island continent supposed to have existed west of Gibraltar and been engulfed by the Atlantic Ocean." *Britannica World Language Dictionary*.

[10] See Luke 16:26.

[11] See Genesis 3:15.

'When He (Jesus) ascended up on high, He led captivity captive, and gave gifts unto men.' (Now this, 'He ascended,' – what does it mean but that He (Jesus) also first descended into the lower parts of the Earth? He who descended is also the One (Jesus), who ascended (back up to Heaven) . . . . And He Himself (Jesus) gave some to be apostles; some, prophets; some, Evangelists; and some, pastors and teachers; for the equipping of the saints for the work of the ministry, for the edifying of the body of Christ, till we all (those who repent and receive Jesus as Savior and confess Him as Lord) come in the unity of the faith, and of the knowledge of the Son of God, to a perfect man (or woman), to the measure of the stature of the fullness of Christ that we should no longer be children, tossed to and fro and carried about with every wind of doctrine, by the trickery of men, in the cunning craftiness of deceitful plotting . . . .'[12]

My Son, bless each of the Elders with ministry gifts and breath on them and their wives to receive the Holy Spirit for the new birth. Any questions?"

"I have none, My Father, as You have made Your will clear. Amen! So be it!"

Sunday Worship Service on Earth

Elder David plays a harp Overture and then leads the congregation in a Sunday worship service in the heart of Zion singing,

'Shout for joy to the Lord (Son of God), all the Earth.
   Worship the Lord with gladness,
   come before Him with joyful songs.
Know that the Lord is God.
   It is He who made us, and we are His;
   we are His people and the sheep of His pasture.
Enter His gates with thanksgiving
   and His courts with praise;
   give thanks to Him and praise His name.
For the Lord (Jesus) is good, and His love endures forever;
   His faithfulness continues through all generations.'[13]

The Elders Filled with the Holy Spirit

The Shekinah Glory felt like a refreshing Spring Rain with all Elders and wives hitting their knees in worship with hands held high giving God a wave of thanks offering. The Son of God appeared in the cloudy midst saying,

"It is to be written,
'Those who honor Me I will honor,
   But those who despise Me will be disdained.'[14]
'I am the Lord; that is My name!
   I will not give My glory to another
   or My praise to idols.
See, the former things have taken place,
   and new things I declare;
before they spring into being
   I announce them to you.'[15]

---

[12] Ephesians 4:8-14 NKJV.
[13] Psalm 100:1-5 NIV.
[14] 1 Samuel 2:30 NIV.
[15] Isaiah 42:8-9 NIV.

Jesus further explains, "For it will be written of some of you, after I die on the cross and shed My blood for the forgiveness of sin, in the Third Earth Age,

'On the evening of that first day of the week, when the disciples were together, with the doors locked for fear of the Jews, Jesus came and stood among them and said, 'Peace be with you!' After He said this, He showed them His hands and side. The disciples were overjoyed when they saw the Lord.

Again Jesus said, 'Peace be with you! As the Father has sent Me, I am sending you.' And with that, He breathed on them and said, 'Receive the Holy Spirit.'[16]

"Now, little children, I breathe upon you in this First Earth Age to receive the filling of the Holy Spirit to live within you." The Son of God breathed out on each, and *'all of them were filled with the Holy Spirit.'*[17]

Son of God's Teaching on the Holy Spirit

"Now, as I likewise breathe on you the greatest power in the universe now lives in you. As you know, the eternal God has revealed Himself to you Elders as the Father, Son, and the Holy Spirit. There is one person of the Father, another of the Son, and another of the Holy Spirit, but the Godhead of the Father, Son, and the Holy Spirit is one God. Today the Holy Spirit took up His abode within you on Earth. He is to be your guide and comforter. In all your ways first acknowledge Me, and the Holy Spirit in you will show you what to do and make your paths straight.[18] Elder, Paul, you will write in the Third Earth Age,

'Those who are led by the Spirit of God are sons of God. For you received no spirit that makes you a slave again to fear, but you received the Spirit of (new birth, adoption into) sonship. And by Him, we cry, 'Abba,[19] *Father.' The Spirit Himself testifies with our (now born again) spirit that we are God's children. Now if we are children, then we are heirs – heirs of God and co-heirs with Christ (Son of God) if indeed we share in His sufferings in order that we may also share in His glory.*

I consider that our present sufferings are not worth comparing with the glory that will be revealed in us. The creation waits in eager expectation for the (born again) sons of God to be revealed. For the creation was subjected to frustration, not by its own choice, but by the will of the One, who subjected it, hoping that the creation itself will be liberated from its bondage to decay and brought into the glorious freedom of the children of God.

We know that the whole creation has been groaning as in the pains of childbirth right up to the present time. Not only so, but we ourselves, who have the first-fruits of the Spirit, groan inwardly as we wait eagerly for our adoption as sons, the redemption of our bodies. For in this hope we were saved. But hope that is seen is no hope at all. Who hopes for what he already has? But if we hope for what we do not yet have, we wait for it patiently.

In the same way, the Spirit helps us in our weakness. We do not know what we ought to pray for, but the Spirit himself intercedes for us with groans that words cannot express. And He who searches our hearts knows the mind of the Spirit, because the Spirit intercedes for the saints in accordance with God's will.

And we know that in all things God works for the good of those who love Him, who have been called according to his purpose. For those God foreknew he also predestined to be conformed to the likeness of His Son, that he might be the firstborn among many brothers. And those He predestined, He also called; those He called, He also justified; those He justified, He also glorified.

What shall we say in response to this? If God is for us, who can be against us? He who did not spare His own Son, but gave Him up for us all – how will He not also, along with Him, graciously give us all things? Who will bring any charge against those whom God has chosen? It is God who justifies. Who is he that condemns? Christ Jesus, who died – more than that, who was raised to life – is at the right hand of God and is also interceding for us.

---

[16] John 20:19-22 NIV.

[17] Acts 2:4 NIV.

[18] See Proverbs 3:6.

[19] The word *Abba* is an Aramaic word that would most closely be translated the intimate word *Daddy*. It signifies the close, intimate relationship of a father to his child as well as the childlike trust that a young child puts in his or her "daddy."

Who shall separate us from the love of Christ? Shall trouble or hardship or persecution or famine or nakedness or danger or sword? As it is written:
> *'For your sake we face death all day long; we
> are considered as sheep to be slaughtered.'*[20]

No, in all these things we are more than conquerors through Him who loved us. For I am convinced that neither death, nor life, neither angels nor demons, neither the present nor the future, nor any powers, neither height nor depth, nor anything else in all creation, can separate us from the love of God that is in Christ Jesus our Lord.'[21]

I tell you the truth, '*For where two or three come together in My (Jesus) name, there am I with them.*'[22]

Please be seated. Questions?"

John, speaking for the group, declares,

"Lord! What honor You have given us to be able by faith to accept You as Savior and confess You as our Lord and Master and be filled with the Holy Spirit. As we walk in Your light, as You are in the light, we have fellowship with one another, and Your blood continuously purifies us.[23] We do not doubt the power of Your future blood to be shed for our sins before the foundation of the world. We trample our own glory in the dust so that our giving You glory can rise up within us. We take the crowns off our heads and lay them at Your feet so the crown on Your head may be seen in all its glory. For You are King of Kings and Lord of Lords." All in unison said, "Amen! Shalom!"

Son of God's Further Instructions to Upcoming Inhabitants of Zion

The Son of God replied, "Bless all of you for receiving Me as Savior and for confessing Me as Lord before men. I will confess you all before My Father in Heaven! It will be written,
'*Whoever acknowledges (confesses they belong to) Me before others, I will also acknowledge (confess) they belong to Me before My Father in Heaven. But whoever disowns Me before others, I will (deny they belong to Me) disown them before my Father in Heaven.*'[24]
As you Elders know, the evil one wanted the Earth to age 660 years. He does not know you even exist. We have put a hedge around you and an anointed canopy over you. In the Elders meeting in Heaven you agreed this is the greatest opportunity to allow you to rear your children, grandchildren, and great-grandchildren, in a godly and holy manner, without being subject to your enemy's temptations and deceit, as your children and children's children are one by one joyfully added to the family of God. You and your children will be prepared for other good works in the Second and Third Earth age to help destroy the works of the evil one and to win others for the Kingdom of God.

---

[20] Quoting from Psalm 44:22.
[21] Romans 8:14-39.
[22] Matthew 8:20 NIV.
[23] See 1 John 1:7.
[24] Matthew 10:32-33 NIV.

My Father desires an adopted family who loves Him and to whom He loves. I (Jesus) delight to do the will of My Lord Father! Your joy, Father, is My (Jesus) strength! My (Jesus) joy is the Elders strength. No good thing does God withhold. God had realized before anything was created that you needed brides. Cleave to your bride, as you cannot love her too much. You are 'one flesh;' and romantic love means more than passion. It includes: you will fetch for each other 'a cup of water in the night,' and also be willing to ask for a cup of water. Cherish and desire each other's best good! In eternity, your union becomes more and more precious. Putting your 'one flesh' at the center of your being is a foretaste of Heaven on Earth. My joyful Lordship over your marriage is your strength and protection.

'Delight (enjoy your salvation and daily walk) yourself in the Lord and He will give you the desires (and secret petitions) of your heart.'[25]

The main thing that counts down here is getting and keeping one's name by one's own free will in the ***Lamb's Book of Life***. Unless a young man has the gift of singleness, like Paul in the Third Earth Age, he will need a warm, wise, and a sexually faithful and pure wife. It will be written of some of your great grandchildren,

'We should not commit sexual immorality, as some of them did, and in one day twenty-three thousand of them died (many had death bed repentance and others did not and went to Hell). We should not test the Lord (Jesus) as some of them did –many died from the snake bites. And do not grumble, as some of them did –and were killed by the destroyer.

These things happen to them as examples and were written down as warnings to us (to keep ourselves sexual purity in marriage), on whom the fulfillment of the ages has come. So, if you think you are standing firm, be careful that you do not fall (into sexual sin). No temptation has seized you except what is common to man. And God is faithful; He will not let you be tempted beyond what you can bear. But when you are tempted, He will also provide a way out (such as a satisfying marriage) so that you can stand up under it.'[26]

All of you and your wives are born again with your names added to the ***Lamb's Book of Life***. It will take great and considerable effort to teach your children and children's children that I am the Lamb of God, slain in My Father's eyes before the foundation of the world to pay the price for the sins of all who will repent, receive Me as Savor, confess Me as Lord, and be born again. Then they each will have to have self-control and overcome sexual temptations, corruption, and contamination by My cleansing shed blood and confessing the truths in My Word as their testimony. Keep your daughters pure and teach them to sexually enjoy and not to deny their own husband.

You are under no condemnation as all your children, grandchildren, and great-grandchildren all have free wills. A third of the angels[27] will reject Me as their Lord and worship a created being. You have a special assignment in this First Earth Age of rearing 144,000 special great-grandchildren, who will not die in this First Earth Age, but will be used powerfully to save millions at the end of the Third Earth Age. As they take the Gospel to the ends of the Earth.   Of them, it will be written,

'Then I looked, and there before me was the Lamb, standing on Mount Zion, and with Him 144,000 who had His name and His Father's name written on their foreheads. And I heard a sound from Heaven like the roar of rushing waters and like a loud peal of thunder.

---

[25] Psalm 37:4.

[26] 1 Corinthians 10:8-13. See also Exodus 32:6.

[27] Revelation 12:4.

The sound I heard was like that of harpists playing their harps. And they sang a new song before the throne and before the four living creatures and the elders. No one could learn the Song except the 144,000 who had been redeemed from the Earth. These are those who did not defile themselves with women, for they kept themselves pure. They follow the Lamb wherever He goes. They were purchased from among men and offered as first-fruits to God and the Lamb. No lie was found in their mouths; they are blameless.'[28]

Elder, Paul, you will write about those trusting in Me,

'That in the dispensation of the fullness of times He might gather together in one all things in Jesus Christ, both in Heaven and which are on Earth; even in Him:

In whom also we have obtained an inheritance, being predestined according to the purpose of Him who worketh all things after the counsel of His own will: That we should be to the praise of His glory, who first trusted in Christ. In whom you also trusted, after that you heard the word of truth, the gospel of your salvation, in whom also after that you believed, you were sealed with that Holy Spirit of promise,Who is a deposit (earnest joined with the human spirit making one born again) guaranteeing our inheritance until the redemption of those (born again ones) who are God's possession – to the praise of His glory.'[29]

For by My Father's will all things, including the144,000 special young redeemed grandchildren in this First Earth Age will be created, trained, and kept pure. It will be written,

\'Whenever the living creatures give glory, honor, and thanks to Him who sits on the throne and who lives forever and ever, the twenty-four elders fall down before Him, who sits on the throne, and worship Him who lives forever and ever. They lay their crowns before the throne and say:

'You are worthy, our Lord and God (Jesus),
to receive glory and honor and power,
for You created all things,
and by Your will they were created
and have their being.'[30]

Instruct your children and grandchildren these truths,
'The fear of the Lord teaches a man wisdom,
and humility comes before honor.[31]
Pride goes before destruction,
a haughty spirit before a fall.
Better to be lowly in spirit and among the oppressed
than to share plunder with the proud.
Whoever gives heed to instruction prospers,
and blessed is he who trusts in the Lord.[32]
For the Lord detests a perverse (evil) man
but takes the upright into His confidence.

---

[28] Revelation 14:1-5 NIV.
[29] Ephesians 1:10-14 KJV.
[30] Revelation 4:9-11 NIV.
[31] Proverbs 15:33 NIV.
[32] Proverbs 16:18-20 NIV.

The Lord's curse is on the house of the wicked,
* but He blesses the home of the righteous.*
He mocks proud mockers
* but gives grace to the humble.'*[33]

'But as for me and my household, we will serve the Lord.'[34]

'Young men, in the same way, be submissive to those who are older. Clothe yourself with humility toward one another, because, 'God opposes the proud but gives grace (favor, blessing) to the humble.'

Humble yourselves, therefore, under God's mighty hand, that He may lift you up in due time. Cast all your anxiety on Him because He cares for you.'[35]

'Your attitude should be the same as that of Christ Jesus:
Who, being in very nature God,
* did not consider equality with God something*
*   to be grasped,*
but made Himself nothing,
* taking the nature of a servant,*
* being made in human likeness.*
And being found in appearance as a man,
* He humbled Himself*
* and became obedient to death –*
*   even death on a cross!*
Therefore, God exalted Him to the highest place
* and gave Him the name above every name,*
that at the name of Jesus every knee should bow,
* in Heaven and on Earth and under the Earth,*
and every tongue confess that Jesus Christ is Lord,
* to the glory of God the Father.*[36†]

---

[33] Proverbs 3:32-35 NIV.
[34] Joshua 24:15 NIV.
[35] 1 Peter 5:5-7 NIV.
[36] Philippians 2:5-11 NIV.

[†**Sidebar Scriptures**: "*Joseph had a dream and promptly reported all the details (Genesis 37:5).*"
"*The Lord revealed to me what the evil ones were doing and planning and showed me their wicked plots (Jeremiah 11:18).*"
"*The word of the Lord came to Abram in a* **vision**. . . . *A* **deep sleep** *came upon Abram* . . . . *(Genesis 15:1, 12).*"
I witnessed and experienced "*dreams and visions, and I described* **all** *I had seen to instruct many (Daniel 7:1, 11:33).*"†]

One-World Continent Is Divided, and Apollo Prepares to Relocate His Scientists to a Secret Lead-Lined War Station Inside the Second Entrance of Hell

The Son of God Announces that for Zion's Sake the One World Continent Will Be Divided by Sea

DAVID STRUMMING THE HARP leads the Elders in worship of God singing the words scrolling on the large screen of a psalm he would later pen in the Third Earth Age,

'*The Earth is the Lord's, and everything in it,*
the world, and all who live in it,
for He founded it upon the seas
and established it upon the waters.
Who may ascend the hill of the Lord?
Who may stand in His holy place?
He who has clean hands and a pure heart,
who does not lift up his soul to an idol
or swear by what is false.
He will receive blessing from the Lord
and vindication from God, His Savior.
Such is the generation of those who seek Him,
who seek Your face, O God of Jacob.'[1]

The Elders on this Monday morning meeting in the City of Zion fall to their knees when suddenly the Son of God appears in their midst asking a question,

'*Can a country be born in a day*
or a nation be brought forth in a moment?
Yet no sooner is Zion in labor
than she gives birth to her children . . . .'[2]

'*O God, do not keep silent;*
be not quiet, O God, be not still.
See how Your enemies are astir,
how Your foes rear their heads.
With cunning, they conspire against Your people;
they plot against those You cherish.
'*Come,*' *they say,* '*let us destroy them as a nation*
that the name of Israel be remembered no more.'[3]

---

[1] Psalm 24:1-4 NIV.
[2] Isaiah 66:8b NIV.
[3] Psalm 83:1-4 NIV.

"Elders of Zion, 'Rome wasn't built in a day, but it burned in one!' However, Zion and Atlantis were built in a heavenly day. In a day because of pride and impurity, Atlantis will sink to the bottom of the Atlantic Ocean to be swallowed up by the jaws of Hades itself. Many will ask, 'Where is Atlantis?' The Egyptians will record its ending in its ancient hieroglyphs from a bottle message cast into the sea. After being convinced of the truthfulness from the writing of Solon (638-555 B.C.), and from his investigation, Plato in 360 B.C. will reveal to the whole world the Egyptian recorded brief account of the destruction of Atlantis, *". . . in a single day and night of misfortune, the island of Atlantis disappeared into the depths of the sea."*[4] Misfortune had nothing to do with it. The sinking to the bottom of the sea with Hades opening its jaws to swallow Atlantis will happen legally because many of its inhabitants will choose of their own free will to worship false gods and idols, to commit adultery, and to give themselves over to perverse sexual impurity. Later the Cities of Sodom and Gomorrah committed similar sins with the penalty or wages for such perversion being recorded,

'For the wages which sin pays is death, but the (bountiful) free gift of God is eternal life through (in union with) Jesus Christ our Lord.[5]

'. . . Sodom and Gomorrah . . . gave themselves over to impurity (sexual immorality) and indulged in unnatural vice and sensual perversion. They were as an example (exhibits) of those who suffer the punishment of eternal fire (the wicked are sentenced to suffer).'[6]

Homosexuals, either men or women, fall into lustful sin for each other. But a homosexual pair cannot go on to romantic marriage to produce babies after their kind. God will make for Adam, a wife. He will name her Eve and not Steve. Homosexuals may say they are married and even get a swank justice of the peace to pronounce them wed, but it is empty words. Seeds sown in the Sahara desert (like in a male mouth or anus) does not produce life. A mad bishop might ordain a horse, but it would not be a priest. Homosexual activity labeled as a problem is according to the Bible a sin.[7]

Here is the penalty for homosexuality in both Zion and Atlantis,

'If a man lies with a man as one lies with a wife, both have done what is detestable. They must be put to death; their blood will be on their own heads.'[8]

The homosexual choice can only end in pain and death if not repented. No one will ever see a joyful, strong homosexual at the end of their days as they have been sinning against their own body, with many dying of AIDS.

'Flee from sexual immorality. All other sins a man commits are outside his body, but he who sins sexually sins against his own body.'[9]

Guard your children and grandchildren and never leave them alone with a suspect. If they are touched sexually, discipline and warn your children and grandchildren, they are to cry out for help as all must protect the purity of Zion. Warn them as they will reap the consequences of sin as they have a free will to choose right from wrong. Help them truly to repent and restore themselves to holiness, doing things God's way and not their own selfish way.

---

[4] See Plato's dialogues in *Timareus* and *Crutas* containing the earliest references and descriptions of Atlantis, a prehistoric lost civilization.

[5] Romans 6:23 AMP.

[6] Jude 1:7 AMP and in the NIV.

[7] See Genesis 19:1-3; Leviticus 18:22; 20:13; Romans 1:26-27; 1 Corinthians 6:9.

[8] Leviticus 20:13.

[9] 1 Corinthians 7:18-19 NIV.

'I (Lord Jesus) want no one (worst of sinners, including homosexuals) to perish (in Hell, but everyone to come to repentance.'[10]

'I (Lord Jesus) take no pleasure in the death of the wicked (and) am I not pleased when they turn from their ways (repent) and live.'[11]

'Do you not know that the wicked will not inherit the kingdom of God? Do not be deceived: Neither the sexually immoral nor idolaters nor adulterers nor male prostitutes nor homosexual offenders nor thieves nor the greedy nor drunkards nor slanders nor swindlers will inherit the kingdom of God. And that is what some of you were (before they repented and received forgiveness and were born again). But you (those who repented and received Jesus as Savior) were washed (in the Blood of Jesus), you were sanctified, you were justified in the name of the Lord Jesus Christ and by the Spirit of our God.'[12]

Many a created being will choose of their own free will to rebel against their Creator. In pride, they will seek to do it their way and not God's way. God permits the free will choice. God made creatures capable of saying, "No" to obeying the commandments of God. Unlike the trees, they have free wills. To love God or to reject God! To serve God or serve self! Many will proudly say, 'I'm self-sufficient; without the need of God. I did it my way!'

My Father loves all so much He will allow sinful men to drive nails through His Son's hands and feet to pay the penalty owed *'to save sinners.'*[13]

Free will choice has consequences, or it would not be a choice. God gives His creatures freedom; freedom to choose – to taste of the forbidden apple, to shoot to kill another, or, if they insist, Hell – or it would not be a choice. All sin has consequences, some more severe than others. All rules of God have sanctions if violated. No sanction no rule, but only a suggestion.

To argue that God is sovereign and all-powerful and can simultaneously give a creature the freedom to choose and compel his choice is not to say something profound about omnipotence but to speak nonsense. The murderer and adulterer are making choices they know are wrong. The gift God gave us is our freedom to choose.

My servant Joshua will preach in the Third Earth Age,

'But if serving the Lord seems undesirable to you, then choose for yourselves this day whom you will serve . . . . But as for me and my household (taught all his children), we will serve the Lord.'[14]

Son of God Reveals His Marriage of Atlas and Safari

Elders, please watch the large screen as we zoom in on Black Granite Volcano Mountain down in Nigrous, Africa. Historically you see three couples, paired off with each of their wives now pregnant. I created three males, Atlas, Titan, and Colossus *"from the dust of the ground and breathed into . . . (their) nostrils the breath of life and . . . (they each) became a living being."*[15]

The largest is Atlas, the second, Titan, and the third Colossus. Like you, they have eternal spirits, clothed with a flesh, bone, and blood body.[16] After the couples had introduced themselves and before they came together sexually, I appeared to them, just as I appeared to you, and we had a wedding.

---

[10] 2 Peter 3:9 NIV.
[11] Ezekiel 18:23.
[12] 1 Corinthians 6:9 NIV.
[13] 1 Timothy 1:15 NIV.
[14] Joshua 24:15 NIV.
[15] Genesis 2:7 NIV.
[16] Genesis 2:21-22 NIV.

I gave them matching wedding rings and a honeymoon. I preached to them the way of salvation by believing in Me, as the Savior of the world.

I am putting into the Capitol City of Atlantis, a seven-mile garden with beautiful flowers, delicious fruit trees, birds singing, and with refreshing drinking water from the crystal clear River Nile, the name the Egyptians would later borrow to name their river. Abraham, I will put you in charge of Paradise in the heart of the Earth, which will become affectionately known as 'Abraham's Bosom.' Here is an actual account of someone asking you, Abraham, for water from Paradise in the heart of the Earth,

'A rich man was dressed in purple and fine linen and lived in luxury every day. At his gate was laid a beggar named Lazarus, covered with sores and longing to eat what fell from the rich man's table. Even the dogs came and licked his sores.

The time came when the beggar died, and the angels carried him to Abraham's (bosom) side. The rich man also died and was buried.

In Hell, (a separate compartment of Hades) where he was in torment, he looked up and saw Abraham far away, with Lazarus by his side. So he called to him, 'Father Abraham, have pity on me and send Lazarus to dip the tip of his finger in water and cool my tongue because I am in agony in this fire.'

But Abraham replied, 'Son, remember that in your lifetime you received your good things while Lazarus received bad things, but now he is comforted here and you are in agony. And besides all this, between us and you a great chasm has been fixed, so that those who want to go from here to you cannot, nor can anyone cross over from there to us.'

He answered, 'Then I beg you, father, send Lazarus to my father's house, for I have five brothers. Let him warn them, so they will not also come to this place of torment.'

Abraham replied, 'They have Moses and the Prophets; let them, listen to them.'

'No, father Abraham,' he said, 'but if someone from the dead goes to them, they will repent.

He said to him, 'If they do not listen to Moses and the Prophets, they will not be convinced even if someone rises from the dead.'[17]

Atlas, having a beautiful wife Safari, who believes and trusts in Me, will himself barely escape the flames of Hell. They will be with you, Abraham, in Paradise, but he is to have no leadership authority as he failed to correct his son. Two captains sink ships; and, Abraham, you will be My captain in Paradise and will also have great authority and leadership in Heaven.

Just as Abraham is the largest among you with his big barrel chest, so Atlas is the largest, and from his side, I gave him a beautiful wife, Safari. Their first son, like Abraham's first son, Isaac, will be Atlas II, being also given a 'free will' to choose life and sexual purity or to choose death and adultery. I commanded them as I have all Zion,

'You shall not commit adultery.[18]

If a man commits adultery with another man's wife – both the adulterer and the adulteress must be put to death.'[19]

Blessed are they whose thoughts and heart (from a clean mind and body) are pure, for they will see God.'[20]

---

[17] Luke 16:19-31 NIV.
[18] Exodus 20:14 NIV.
[19] Leviticus 20:10 NIV.
[20] Matthew 5:8 AMP and in the NIV.

I united the three couples in holy matrimony, and I commanded them that neither they nor their children were to commit adultery as adultery is also a sin against God and destroys the trust and oneness in marriage.

I hate adultery as it tampers with the honor of a husband and wife's producing pure and holy children to become a part of the family of Heaven. This privilege is so sacred that the person who violates this great principle of sexual purity wrongs his own soul, subjects himself to sexual disease, and is in danger of punishment in Hell for it will be written,

'My (parent's warning) son, keep my words
and store up my commands within you.
Keep my commands, and you will live;
guard my teachings as the apple of your eye.
Bind them on your fingers;
write them on the tablet of your heart.
Say to wisdom, 'You are my sister,'
and call understanding your kinsman;
they will keep you from the adulteress,
from the wayward wife with her seductive words.
At the window of my house
I looked out through the lattice.
I saw among the simple;
I noticed among the young men
a youth who lacked judgment.
He was going down the street near her corner,
walking along toward her house
at twilight, as the day was fading, as the dark of night set in.
hen out came a woman to meet him,
dressed like a prostitute and with crafty intent.
(She is loud and defiant,
her feet never stay at home;
now in the street, now in the squares,
at every corner she lurks.)
She took hold of him and kissed him
and with a brazen face she said:
'I have peace offerings at home;
today I fulfilled my vows.
So I came out to meet you;
I looked for you and have found you!
I have covered my bed
with colored linens from Egypt.
I have perfumed my bed
with myrrh, aloes and cinnamon.
Come, let's drink deep of love till morning;
Let's enjoy ourselves with love!
My husband is not at home;
he has gone on a long journey.
He took his purse filled with money
and will not be home till full moon.'
With persuasive words, she led him astray;
she seduced him with her smooth talk.
All at once he followed her
like an ox going to the slaughter,
like a deer stepping into a noose
till an arrow pierces his liver,

like a bird darting into a snare,
   little knowing it will cost him his life.
Now then, my sons, listen;
   pay attention to what I say.
Do not let your heart turn to her ways
   or stray into her paths.
Many are the victims she has brought down;
   Her slain are a mighty throng.
Her house is a highway to the grave (then into Hell),
   leading down to the chambers of death.'[21]

Elder Peter inquired, "What happens to the innocent spouse?"

"Elder Peter, the innocent spouse, upon the testimony of two witnesses giving proof of adultery, may obtain a certificate of divorce and be free to marry another who believes in Me. I hate divorce, but I hate adultery even more as it destroys the beauty of pure romantic marital love to produce precious pure children to add to the Kingdom of God.

Elder David, one of your sons in the Third Earth Age, will choose to marry unbelieving foreign women. It will be written of him as he grows older, *'his wives turned his heart after other gods, and his heart was not fully devoted to the Lord his God.'*[22]

The reason I have to divide the land is that seductive unbelieving foreigners will seek to marry your sons and daughters, so I command,

'Do not be yoked (in intimacy) with unbelievers. For what does righteousness and wickedness have in common? Or what fellowship can light have with darkness? . . . What does a believer have in common with an unbeliever? What agreement is there between the temple of God and idols? For we are the temple of the living God. As God has said: 'I will live with them and walk among them and I will be their God and they will be my people.'[23]

'Therefore, come out from them and be separate.
   Touch no unclean thing, and I will receive you.'[24]
'I will be a Father to you, and you will be My sons and daughters,[25] *says the Lord Almighty."*[26]

The Son of God continues, "Elders, My will in marriage is simple as it will be written,

'Each man should have his own wife, and each woman should have her own husband. The husband should fulfill his marital duty to his wife, and likewise the wife to her husband.

The wife's body does not belong to her alone but also to her husband. In the same way, the husband's body does not belong to him alone but also to his wife. Do not deprive each other (of marital sexual relations) except by mutual consent.'[27]

I designed marriage, and this simple rule of not depriving each other of sexual relations helps keep the marriage pure and holy. My commandments are easy and not too difficult if you will obey and keep them as it will be written,

'Now, what I am commanding you today is not too difficult for you or beyond your reach. It is not up in Heaven, so you have to ask, 'Who will ascend into Heaven to get it and proclaim it to us so we may obey it?' 'Nor is it beyond the sea, so you have to ask, 'Who will cross the sea to get it and proclaim it to us so we may obey it?' No, the word is near you; it is in your mouth and in your heart so you may (choose of your own free will) obey it.

---

[21] Proverbs 7:1-26 NIV.
[22] 1 Kings 11:4 NIV
[23] See Leviticus 26:12.
[24] See Isaiah 52:11.
[25] See 2 Samuel 7:14; 7:8.
[26] 2 Corinthians 6:14-18 NIV.
[27] 1 Corinthians 7:2-5 NIV.

See, I set before you today life and prosperity, death and destruction. For I command you today to love the Lord your God, to walk in His ways, and to keep His commands, decrees and laws; then you will live and increase, and the Lord your God will bless you in the land . . . .

But if your heart turns away and you are not obedient, and if you are drawn away to bow down to other gods (no other gods exist besides the One God) and worship them, I (the One God) declare to you this day you will be destroyed. You will not live long in the land . . . .

This day I call Heaven and Earth as witnesses against you that I have set before you life and death, blessings and curses. Now choose life, so you and your children may live and that you may love the Lord your God, listen to His voice, and hold fast to Him. For the Lord is your life and He will give you many years in the land.'[28]

Son of God Removing Black Granite Volcano Mountain and the Surrounding Land of Nigrous, Africa Out Into the Sea, Becoming the Island of Atlantis

Elders, in the Third Earth Age, I demonstrated faith to some of you when I found a tree not bearing fruit, as it will be written,

Seeing a fig tree by the road, He went up to it but found nothing on it except leaves. Then He said to it, 'May you never bear fruit again!' Immediately the tree withered.

When the disciples saw this, they were amazed. 'How did the fig tree wither so quickly?' They asked.

Jesus replied, 'I tell you the truth if you have faith and do not doubt, not only can you do what was done to the fig tree, but also you can say to this mountain, 'Go, throw yourself into the sea,' and it will be done.[29]

Now watch the big screen as I in faith say,

'For Zion's sake and her protection, Black Granite Volcano Mountain and the surrounding land of Nigrous, Africa, be thou lifted up and removed away to make a separate island in the heart of the word's one ocean.'"

As gently as a mother would pick up her newborn baby, the new continent to be known as the Island of Atlantis was gently sat down in the heart of the one world's ocean making now two divided continents of land.

"Now, Elders, it will be written,

'*Thou shalt also decree a thing, and it shall be established (accomplished; done) unto thee,*

And the light (of God's favor) shall shine upon thy ways.'[30]

Son of God Creates the Magnificent Temple of God in Atlantis

"Now watch the screen toward the North end of the Black Granite Volcano Mountain as I decree,

---

[28] Deuteronomy 30:11-20 NIV.
[29] Matthew 21:19-21 NIV.
[30] Job 22:28.

'Royal Capital, City of Atlantis, within you, be a magnificent Temple of God and be a Royal White Castle taking a secondary position in the Citadel.'[31]

Abraham outline for the archives just what you see in the center of the Citadel Island,"

"My Lord, I see the magnificent Temple of God completely covered with a glittering gold dome trimmed in Silver with a much less structure of dignity behind it, which I assume is the Royal Palace. The lush green grounds are lined with palm trees, beautiful flowers, plants, and lawns."

"Now describe the remaining,"

"The Citadel is surrounded by alternating canals and ring-shaped islands with beautiful and splendid bridges linking the islands, with parks, gardens, palm trees, and beautiful flowers. I see a fortified royal castle I understand is initially known as the Royal Palace of Atlas.

Then I see the surrounding City of Atlantis with boulevards going out like spokes from a wheel in all directions. Off in the distant north, I see an enormous pyramid with an all-seeing eye at the top."

Temple on Mt. Moriah in Jerusalem Created

Abraham requests, "My Lord, we respectfully request you consider being so kind as to give us a temple in this First Earth Age on Mt. Moriah for us to worship You. There we can offer the blood of a spotless male lamb annually to roll our sins forward another year until You Jesus can come as the Lamb of God and die on the cross and shed Your life's blood for our sins."

"Abraham and Elders of Zion said, 'Amen!'"

The Son of God looking so pleased with such a request decrees,

"A magnificent Temple of God on Mt. Moriah in Jerusalem, for those in this First Earth Age to worship God in spirit and in truth, and to offer annual sacrifices until I come as a sacrifice for the sins of those receiving Me as Savior, Be!"

The Temple of God covered with glittering gold trimmed in silver floated down from Heaven and sat high itself on the Temple Mount in Zion. Tears ran down the faces of each Elder for such a magnificent place to worship God.

John in tears spoke, "Thank you, my Lord, for such a magnificent gift and for being our Savior and Lord." All the elders said, "Amen!"

The Son of God responds, "Elders you are so humble and thankful! You are each valuable and precious to Me. You will help Me save a multitude of people to make up My Father's jewels in the Kingdom of God. Now, Elders, watch the screen as Gabriel greets the three couples in the lobby having their bags all packed as they conclude their romantic honeymoon I gave them in the South Africa Table Top Honeymoon Villa. A honeymoon with the wife one loves is a taste of Heaven on Earth."

All the elders respond, "Amen!"

---

[31] Citadel is defined, "A fortress or castle in or near a city, intended for its defense . . . ."
American Dictionary of the English Language Noah Webster 1828.

Back to the Island of Atlantis

Now listen as Gabriel instructs the three newly created couples,

"Atlanteans[32] you are being given a sacred trust of rearing your children and grandchildren on the beautiful tropical island of Atlantis. You are to share with them the Good News that the Son of God (Jesus) is the Savior of the world and that no one can come to the Father God, except through God's Son.[33] God loves everyone so much He desires not one to be lost, but that all come to repentance and to obey His commandments, and His commandments are not grievous.

On a cross, the Son of God will die to pay the penalty in full for the sins of all who will receive Him as Savior and confess Him as their Lord and Master.

The Son of God has prepared for each of you a quiet and peaceful villa on the central island of the city called the Citadel, which is surrounded by alternating canals and ring-shaped islands. Splendid bridges link the islands.

Colossus, you are appointed Treasurer of the City of Atlantis and head of the Bank of Atlantis in which is deposited in each of your accounts $7,000,000 in gold to give you a jump start in your new life.

Titan, you are Secretary of State, which includes the keeping of the peace and assuring the general welfare of the citizens.

Atlas, you are appointed King, and you are to set an example of truth and integrity for the citizens of Atlantis. You have a sparkling refreshing fountain in the shape of a cross to further remind you that the Son of God will die on a cross as your Savior to pay the penalty fully for your sins as you repent and receive Him as Savior and confess Him as Lord."

With each man and his wife receiving the Son of God (Jesus) as Savior and confessing Him as Lord, the Holy Spirit joins with their human spirit, and they are born again with their names also being added to the *Lamb's Book of Life*.

Jesus spoke to the elders back in Zion, "All this is happening at the first of the 660 years, and the Atlanteans will be populating that portion of the Earth just as you will be here with each of your children and your children's children given a free will to choose whom they will serve.

Would you Zion elders like to watch on a giant screen Gabriel giving a guided tour of the Continent of Atlantis?

Gabriel Gives the New Created Leaders of Atlantis and Their Wives a Tour of Atlantis

Gabriel asked, after each of the leaders, and their wives' names were added to the *Lamb's Book of Life* if they would you like a tour by air of the island of Atlantis?

All excitedly respond 'yes' as they boarded the flying saucer. The saucer rose and moved across the beautiful tropical Island of Atlantis with Gabriel speaking,

"Let us skim the ocean near the shoreline of this gorgeous island. Circling the island are the Leviathans, who frolic and protect their territory, which they consider starting five miles out from the shore. Therefore, for your safety, you should limit your sea fishing within the first three miles from shore. Teach your children never to make sport of a Leviathan or to mock or reject God, who is infinitely even stronger than they are, as it will be written,

---

[32] Atlantean from *Wikipedia, The Free Encyclopedia* means "of or pertaining to Atlas or Atlantis."
[33] See John 14:6.

'Can you pull in the leviathan with a fishhook
    or tie down his tongue with a rope?
Can you put a cord through his nose
    or pierce his jaw with a hook? Will he keep begging you for mercy?
Will he speak to you with gentle words?
Will he make an agreement with you
    for you to take him as your slave for life?
Can you make a pet of him like a bird
    or put him on a leash for your girls?
Will traders barter for him?
    Will they divide him up among the merchants?
Can you fill his hide with harpoons
    or his head with fishing spears?
If you lay a hand on him, you will remember the struggle and
    never do it again!
Any hope of subduing him (a Leviathan) is false;
    the mere sight of him is overpowering.
No one is fierce enough to rouse him.
Who then can stand against Me (God)?
Who has a claim against Me (God) that I must pay?
Everything under Heaven belongs to Me.
I will not fail to speak of his limbs,
    his strength, and his graceful form.
Who can strip off his outer coat?
Who would approach him with a bridle?
Who dares open the doors of his mouth,
    ringed about with his fearsome teeth?
His back has rows of shields
    tightly sealed together;
    each is so close to the next
    that no air can pass between.
They are joined fast to one another;
    they cling together and cannot be parted.
His snorting throws out flashes of light;
    his eyes are like the rays of dawn.
Firebrands stream from his mouth;
    sparks of fire shoot out.
Smoke pours from his nostril,
    as from a boiling pot over a fire of reeds.
His breath sets coals ablaze,
    and flames dart from his mouth.
Strength resides in his neck;
    dismay goes before him.

The folds of his flesh are tightly joined;
*   they are firm and immovable.*
His chest is as hard as rock,
*   hard as a lower millstone.*
When he rises up, the mighty are terrified;
*   they retreat before his thrashing.*
The sword that reaches him has no effect,
*   nor does the spear or the dart or the javelin.*
Iron he treats like straw
*   and bronze like rotten wood.*
Arrows do not make him flee;
*   sling stones are like chaff to him.*
A club seems to him but a piece of straw;
*   he laughs at the rattling of the lance.*
His undersides are jagged potsherds,
*   leaving a trail in the mud like a threshing-sledge.*
He makes the depths churn like a boiling caldron
*   and stirs up the sea like a pot of ointment.*
Behind him, he leaves a glistening wake;
one would think the deep had white hair.
Nothing on Earth is his equal
*   a creature without fear.*
He looks down on all that are haughty;
*   he is king over all that are proud.'*[34]

Gabriel points, "Look, there is one of the giant Leviathans! Let's fly near him with the saucer. As the saucer draws near, the Leviathan makes a terrible war cry leaping out of the sea covering the saucer with flames and just missing catching the saucer in its giant mouth."

Atlas responded, "Just imagine what a Leviathan could do to a ship of wood! Crispy Critters!"

Gabriel replies, "Right! That was a little too close for comfort as he smelled on board the blood of an Atlantean. Truly a picture is worth a thousand words! I want to explicitly warn you that some of your sons will want to challenge these sea monsters for sport. There are better games to play such as soccer. If you love your sons, please warn them not to challenge the Leviathans!"

The saucer lifts from the surface of the sea with Gabriel directing, "Now let us fly over to dinosaur country. Here we are. We will not get that close this time. That is a Behemoth, which ranks first among the animals created by God, as it will be written,

'Look at the behemoth,
*   which I (Son of God) made . . .*
*   and which feeds on grass like an ox.*
What strength he has in his loins,
*   what power in the muscles of his belly!*
His tail sways like a cedar;
*   the sinews of his thighs are close-knit.'*[35]

---

[34] Job 41:1-34 NIV.

Look now down at the various big and powerful dinosaurs knowing that God is much more powerful. There is a seventy-foot, thirty-ton Apatosaurus, a Brachiosaurus, a Stegosaurus, a Tyrannosaurus, a Camarasaurus, a Diplodocus, and an Allosaurus. Here comes a flock of flying Archaeopteryx. A flying Rhamporynhus passing by having leathery wings was making an awful noise. A wall has been built around the City of Atlantis to keep out the dinosaurs as one could in a few moments eat a row of fruit trees." [Laughter.]

The saucer rises from dinosaur country.

Gabriel, smiling announces, "Now let us fly over the City of Atlantis looking at the north side towering Black Granite Volcano Mountain. As a wedding present, we have provided you, as you see out the windows, the beautiful white stone homes on the central island called the Citadel. Each of your homes is in the shape of a cross to remind you that you on your honeymoon have accepted the Son of God, Jesus, as your Savior and confessed Him as your Lord. You are declared righteous!

You have each obtained the precious free gift of eternal life. Your names are now in the Lamb's Book of life. Rejoice and be glad! I warn you it is to be written,

'But the one who endures to the end (death in the flesh is always near so don't die in the arms of another man's wife or worshipping a false god) will be saved.'[36]

'If they (born again ones) have escaped the corruption of the world by knowing our Lord and Savior Jesus Christ and are again entangled in it and overcome (by a course of sin), they are worse off at the end than they were at the beginning (before they were born again). It would have been better for them not to have known the way of righteousness than to have known it and then to turn their backs on the sacred commandment that was passed on to them. Of them the proverbs are true: 'A dog returns to its vomit,' and, 'A sow that is washed goes back to her wallowing in the mud.'[37]

Never deny Jesus or sin away your age of grace and have your name blotted out of the **Lamb's Book of Life**. I instruct you soon to be earthly fathers that your children must work out their own salvation with fear and trembling.[38] Parents can only give good examples and advice seeking to put their children on the right paths of salvation, but the final forming of a person's character lies in his or her own hands. Each has a free will to choose or to reject the truths you will teach them.

It will be written,

'Then I saw a great white throne . . . . The dead were judged according to what they had done. . . . If anyone's name was not found written in the book of life, he was thrown into the lake of fire.'[39]

Remember this Scripture,

'I (Jesus) am the way and the truth and the life. No one (no exceptions) comes to the Father (for salvation) except through Me (Jesus, the Savior).'[40]

---

[35] Job 40:15-19 NIV.
[36] Matthew 24:13 ESV.
[37] 2 Peter 2:20-22.
[38] See Philippians 2:12.
[39] Revelation 20:11-12, 15.
[40] John 14:6 NIV.

Description of the Great Pyramid in the Garden of Paradise on the Island of Atlantis

Gabriel continues teaching, "Atlantis on its north end facing Black Granite Volcano Mountain on the south end has a landmark of a magnificent white pyramid composed of pearls and precious stones dedicating the city to the glory of God.

The front side of the pyramid to the north of the black granite mountain contains the words,

AGAPE

To God the Father
Be the Glory!

Father God so loves[41] you, your children, grandchildren, and great-grandchildren He gave His Son before the foundation of the world to die on the cross as a sacrifice for the sins of whosoever (represented by the symbol of the fish) will receive His Son as their Savior and confess His Son as their Lord and Master.

The right side contains the words,

JOY
To God the Son
Be the Glory!

It will be written about the joy in and through the Son of God,

'Let us fix our eyes on Jesus, the author and perfecter of our faith, Who for the joy set before Him endured the cross.'[42]

---

[41] John 3:16.
[42] Hebrews 12:2 NIV.

The left side of the pyramid bears the words,

PEACE

To God the Holy Spirit
Be the Glory!

Notice at the top of the pyramid is a halo and an all-seeing eye on each side, beaming forth light symbolizing the all-seeing eye of God. Nothing was done in the nation of Atlantis, not seen by God!

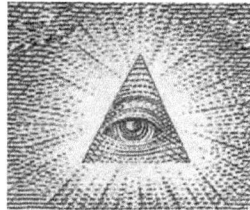

Further west across the Atlantic Ocean later in the Third Earth Age, an initial Christian nation[43] will adopt a pyramid containing this all-seeing eye on the top as part of "The Great Seal" of that country and place it on the back of their dollar bill beside the words IN GOD WE TRUST!

One of your children's children will draw this 'all-seeing eye of God' on top of this great pyramid and other information about Atlantis and place his drawings in a bottle and throw it into the sea. This bottle will float its way past the leviathans to Egypt. This information will make its way in part into the hieroglyphics and architectural design of Egypt, a nation in which the Son of God, Jesus, after being born in the City of Bethlehem will live in the flesh as a child.[44]

Atlas, I know the ladies eagerly desire to see their beautiful villas, with a power source for lighting, cooking, heating, and cooling, just as you had in your honeymoon villas. You are to have a transit system, street lighting, and delightful parks and fountains.

The Son of God has given each of you special giftings[45] in business, but remember to love Him, not to love money!

---

[43] United States of America.

[44] See Matthew 2:13.

[45] See 2 Corinthians 7:7, '*But each man has his own gift from God; one has this gift another has that.*'
This Scripture is known as the three 7s (777) as 2 Corinthians is the seventh book of the New Testament, then go to its seventh chapter, and seventh verse.

243

'For the love of money is the root of all kinds (many) of evil. Some people, eager for money, have wandered from the faith and pierced themselves with many griefs.'[46]

The main thing is to keep God's commandments, and they are not grievous.[47] You are to rear your children to worship only the true God and to keep themselves pure."

Peter Ask Son of God a Question

As the saucer lands near the beautiful villas on the Citadel, the screen playing for the Elders fades out with the Son of God asking the elders if they have questions.

Peter asked, "What is going to happen to the mighty dinosaurs?"

Jesus replied, "Our enemy in an attempt to destroy the Father, Son, and the Holy Spirit will also destroy the whole Earth with an ice bomb. The bomb will create a layer of ice and dust, which will block out the sun's light for some time. The dinosaurs will all freeze to death on a frozen darkened planet. I will not create most of them again in the Second Earth Age, which will end with a great flood. Two 70-foot, 30-ton Brontosaurus, a male and his female would be a little too much to load and feed on Noah's boat. [Laughter] However, we have animals and birds on the planet Heaven we don't have on the planet Earth. In the eternities of the eternities, you will see even greater things created than the dinosaurs."

Abraham Ask the Son of God a Question

Abraham inquires, "Will most of the nation of Atlantis be saved?"

Jesus with tears in His eyes spoke, "I have challenged the leaders, as I am challenging you Abraham again today to rear your children to worship only the true God and to keep themselves pure. However, after Atlas dies, many will fall away as his son, Atlas II, takes control. However, some will ultimately choose eternal life by accepting Me as Savior and keeping My commandments. The Good News is there will be a great revival so you will have saints from Atlantis to join with the Saints from Zion as equal heirs in the kingdom of God.

It will be written, *'For the (true) love of God is this, that we do (obey) His commands – keep His ordinances and be mindful of His precepts and teachings. And God's commandments (these orders) of His are not (too hard) irksome – burdensome, oppressive, or grievous (to keep).'*[48]

All declared righteous and saved from the City of Atlantis will be housed in Paradise beneath the Earth in a place called Hades, known as Abraham's Blossom. Hades will initially receive all those who once dwelt upon the surface of the Earth, made up of Paradise (saved) and Hell (wicked and lost).

Paradise will be a place of blessing for all those who receive Me as Savior and confess Me as Lord. Abraham, you will comfort those who believe in Me, as Savior and have confessed Me as Lord. I will die by being nailed to a wooden cross to pay the penalty for the sins of those who repent, receive Me as Savior, and confess Me as Lord.

---

[46] 1 Timothy 6:10.
[47] 1 John 5:3.
[48] 1 John 5:3 AMP.

After My resurrection from the dead, I will preach in Hades and lead these captive believers out of Paradise into the freedom of living with Me throughout eternity. However, warn those who reject such a free offer of salvation that there will be an initial separate place of torment in Hell awaiting the judgment of all those whose names are not found written in the **Lamb's Book of Life**, and subsequently, a final eternal separation for it will be written,

'*Then I saw a great white throne. . . . The dead were judged according to what they had done . . . . And anyone whose name was not found written in the book of life was thrown into the lake of fire.* '[49]

Gabriel Sends a Message to Mercury

Gabriel sends Mercury this amail (angel mail),

"The Earth today is now 660 years older.
Also, a silver winged space bus with automatic pilot
is on the landing strip having two buttons:
Go to Black Volcanic Mountain on Earth!
Return to Landing Strip in Heaven!"

Mercury delivers the message to Apollyon Lucifer as he was meeting with his scientist with Apollyon Lucifer advancing,

"Time is a wasting!' We have a lot of digging to do. Let us travel tonight at 11:06 P.M. so we can set up without being spotted by the ape men. Mercury, I put you in charge of painting the space bus black with some gold musical notes. I like black better than silver. I will make my grand introduction to the 666 inhabitants in the morning around 11:06 A.M. to inspire them to start digging. Proceed to pack all we will need. Scientists, you have reassured me the ice bomb will be ready to detonate in six years from today."

All the Scientists confirmed by saying, "VISA![50]†

---

[49] Revelation 20:11, 12, 15.

[50] "To endorse or ratify" from *The Free Dictionary by Farlex*. VISA is a name for saying 'amen' or 'bye' on the side of darkness, pridefully standing for Very Important Supreme Achiever.

†BOOK FIVE – Episode 5†

[†**Sidebar Scriptures**: "*Joseph had a dream and promptly reported all the details (Genesis 37:5).*"
"*The Lord revealed to me what the evil ones were doing and planning and showed me their wicked plots (Jeremiah 11:18).*"
"The word of the Lord came to Abram in a **vision**. . . . A **deep sleep** came upon Abram . . . . (Genesis 15:1, 12)."
I witnessed and experienced "*dreams and visions, and I described **all** I had seen to instruct many (Daniel 7:1, 11:33).*"†]

Apollo's Space Ship Lands in Atlantis in Cover of Night with His War Scientists, and 666 Ape Men Are Won Over by Apollo

The Black Crow Being Loaded in Heaven

MERCURY COMPLETES THE MASTERPIECE of the black painting of the Air Bus with musical notes and his writing on the fuselage its name – The Black Crow. Mercury carefully loads over three-fourths of the cargo bay, especially with musical instruments, leaving little room for the scientific gear of the sixty-six (66) scientists. Photon along with five of his scientists pushes a large, long loaded cart with scientific instruments. Photon opens the cargo bay calculating that all the scientific gear will not fit in and screams in anger,

"Mercury, half of this junk you loaded needs to be left behind. Get it off now as we are leaving soon."

"Angry Mercury replies, "You get off what we don't need if you are so organized! I am second in command!"

Photon responded, "Yes, but I am in charge of this science project. You are over communications only. You are not to tell me what to take or not to take. You unload half your junk or I will inform Apollo you are delaying and are not supportive of the project. You are outnumbered 66-to-1 in this. So move it!"

About that time six (6) of the other highly muscular scientists appears asking Photon, "Is there anything wrong, boss?"

Photon looks over at Mercury unloading a big horn smirking, "Not now! We will accomplish our mission even if I have to use my confidential memo system straight to Apollo. As we all speak the same language and understand each other, nothing we plan to do will be impossible for us to accomplish. We could even build a tower from Earth to Heaven, so we would not even need this black crow in which we cannot see where we are going or have been. 'It is dog eat dog!'[1]

I would have named this Airbus the "Black Widow," who enjoys her mating time and then stings and eats her lover. Let us, like her, have a passion for dominating. By force, I will control and eat up all who oppose the kingdom of darkness. See my black dagger. Pretended alliance and at just the right timing I'll render to any opposition, 'A stab in the back.' Mercury and Apollo must go back and forth between Earth and Heaven as Apollo indicates he will shape up a combined choir and will have to bring more musical instruments in the cargo. When they are away from the Earth, the cat will play. This black cat will totally be put me in control of this world."

With the scientific gear down the aisle, the sixty-six (66) scientists sit with Apollyon Lucifer sitting on the front seat in eloquent tight leotards as Mercury proclaims, "Fashion your seatbelt if you like. VISA!"

---

[1] *Dog eat dog* – "If a situation is a dog eat dog, one will do anything to be successful, even when what they do harms other people." *The Free Dictionary by Farlex.*

Mercury hits the automatic pilot in Black Crow to an 11:06 P.M. Landing Near the Second Entrance to Hell Next to Black Granite Volcano Mountain on the Island of Atlantis

Mercury pushes the button labeled, "Go to Black Volcanic Mountain on Earth!"

The Black Crow lands as gently and softly as a feather in the dark of the night at 11:06 P.M. and everyone quietly exits the Black Crow. A crooked path leads to the second entrance to Hell with Apollo placing the key in the slot commanding, "Open in the name of the Great Apollo 666."

The black slab slides its jaws open with a noisy grind. Apollo using a foreboding atomic black light beacon leads the way to a black iron gate with Apollo pushing the key into the slot commands, "Open fast in the name of the Great Apollo 666." The iron gate crashes against the black wall with a dull clang.

Then down sixty-six steps they make haste and coming to a black onyx throne room Apollo takes his seat on a black throne.

Apollyon Lucifer Designates the Bomb Creation Room

Apollo directs, "I designate the first big room on the left as The Freeze Bomb Creation War Room. Line it with the thin sheets of lead we brought so no one can spy on what you are doing. I suspect the controlling old man upstairs is dead. We don't want him spying on us if he is not dead. Also, I have other rooms for your quarters."

Apollo Orders a Team of Six (6) to Locate the Veins of Gold

Apollo further orders, "Photon appoint your six (6) best men to go down further on your left as there should be a room filled with veins of gold. Bring me back some of the gold as I brought some stamping mints to make these into coins to pay for the hard dedicated seven-day-a-week labor of mining the pechblende[2] ore from which uranium will be extracted. In six hundred and sixty-six (666) minutes be back here with some of that gold."

The Team Reporting Back That the Veins Resemble Gold, but Are Not Gold

Photon returns bowing and carrying a basket full of glittering gold colored nuggets reporting, "Your Excellency, this is similar to gold, but it is Auricula,[3] a shining alloy of copper and zinc. It is a very prized and rare metal, but it is not gold – it looks a little like gold. We have named this newly discovered metal Orichalcum.[4] No one, but a banker, would know it is not as valuable as gold!"

---

[2] *Pitchblene* is a variety of uraninite, occuring in black pitchlike masses being a major ore of uranium and radium. D*ictionary.com*.

[3] *Auricula* is defined *inter alia* as "an alloy of copper and zinc, resembling gold."
See *Britannica World Language Edition of Funk & Wagnalls Standard Dictionary*.

[4] "*Orichalcum* is a metal mentioned in several ancient writings, including a story of Atlantis in the Critias dialogue, recorded by Plato. According to Critias, orichalcum was considered second only to gold in value, and was found and mined in many parts of Atlantis in ancient times."
Quoting from *Wikipedia, The Free Encyclopedia*.

Apollyon Lucifer Directs the Immediate Mining of Orichalcum that Evening to Make Glittering Musical Coins, with Apollyon Lucifer's Image

Apollo stomps his left foot proclaiming, "Rats! I thought that was pure gold. We will tell the ape men that in the universe, it is more valuable than gold and in this black mountain is the only place it can be found. They are stupid and will not know the difference.

Here are the mints for you to have these nuggets made up in coins for tomorrow as we start mining at midnight around the clock seven days a week. I told you this was a very bewitched[5] place to do our work of darkness. Don't you agree?"

"Yes, your Excellency! The bomb room and our quarters are very spacious and enchanting. Charming! Alluring! Yes, this place of darkness is 'Bewitched Ground.'

As scientists, we note that the dust and exposure to the raw pitchblende, from which enriched uranium is made, will not harm us angels, but daily exposures of flesh and blood to it for over 666 days will result in lung cancer causing the victims to grow steadily weaker and weaker ending in a horrible and painful death. A whole day of mining may well produce less than an ounce of raw pitchblende from which we will only be able to produce a microscopic speck of the pure precious enriched uranium. We estimate it will take us four years and sixty-six (66) days to produce enough enriched uranium for the ultimate weapon – The Freeze Bomb!

Apollo inquires, "Are you going to let them know of the upcoming cancer? If not, what are you going to tell them they are mining? When they get lung cancer are we going to tell them what caused it?"

Photon responding, 'I'll tell them we are mining for diamonds and gathering this ore on the side. We will tell no one our business of darkness. That is why we have a lead-lined wall for absolute secrecy." Apollo replies, "You are an excellent liar. Look over the herbs outside in the thick jungle. Maybe the jungle contains something we can roll up in paper they can smoke. Then we can blame smoking for their lung cancer? Take a field trip tomorrow and see what weeds are out there they can smoke and with any luck get hooked on. I made up a joke. The ape men don't smoke. The weeds smoke. They are only the suckers." [Smirking]

The Next Morning Mercury Reports that some 666 Highly Muscularly-Developed Naked Ape Men with Few Wearing Loin Cloths and Carrying a Shield in one Hand and a Spear in the Other Surrounding the Black Crow

Mercury enters the throne room of Hell, bowing and accusing, "Excellency, Photon forgot after his men unloaded the last scientific instrument in the dark of the night, to cover the Black Crow with camouflage. Therefore, it was spotted this morning, and we have 666 naked ape men with a couple wearing a loincloth and some carrying spears and shields surrounding and poking our locked Black Crow. They already have chipped some of the black paint off. We have a problem on our hand caused by Photon."

Apollo replies, "Problem? Wow! My greatest opportunity to recruit the 666 Ape Men we need to dig. Let me at them! Help me put on this skin-tight black outfit and hand me my black guitar. You take the mike, stand, and amplifier to that overlooking black dagger-shaped boulder.

---

[5] *Bewitched* – 1. To place under one's power by or as if by magic, cast a spell over; 2. To captivate completely . . ." *The Free Dictionary by Farlex.*

Apollyon Lucifer Flatters the 666 Ape Men

Playing the guitar with seductive gyrations, Apollyon Lucifer feeds enticing flattery in the Greek language to his audience,

"Good-looking! Gorgeous-hunks I am the Great Apollo! There is none more beautiful and more clever than I am in all creation. I am here to play and sing for you. I am the music leader on nearby Planet Heaven. Sway with me in the music of the cosmos.

How do you like the Black Crow? I was hoping those of your abilities would spot it and be here this morning. That is the reason (lying as Apollo forgot) I didn't camouflage it last evening. It worked like a charm.

You might wonder who designed you and for what reason. I am a master architect, and I designed you and created you on paper with my drawing pen. I drew you a little hairier than you are today. Because of this heat, evolution has caused you to shed excess hair over the last 660 years from your face, chest, and sex organ areas. Isn't evolution wonderful? It lets you get rid of the old baggage you don't need. Everything gets better and better. Polishing, refinement, and improvement! God has nothing to do with improvements through evolution. The older God is dead, leaving a bony knee son, heir with a humped nose.

Tell me about your evolved selves, my creation. How many mates do you have? Are you swapping around like the rabbits? Hot females? You even have the advantage of having extra-large feet and hands. Your penis I can barely see is about the size of peanuts. I guess I drew them that size by mistake. Can anyone sing or play an instrument, like a harp raise, your hand? [Apollo frowning at no show of hands.]

Tell me all about this place? Do you have a taskmaster?"

One extra-large individual, being very muscular, steps forward answering,

"I am Homo. I would be the taskmaster, but we have no work. No one will hire us. Maybe you can?

Apollo seizes the moment, "Taskmaster Homo, everyone who will agree to work for me will receive this gold coin with my image, made of a rare precious metal more valuable than gold. In Planet Heaven, we don't even have this rare precious metal. Look at how this coin, made of Orichalcum sparkles. Give me a show of hands of how many of you would like to receive this exclusive bonus for signing on today? [All 666 raised their hands.]

"Foreman Homo, this is your new crew. Here is a bag of 666 charm coins. We are going to work around the clock – four six-hour crews – the first crew of 163 starting at midnight tonight. I drew the giant dinosaurs and dragons, and maybe we could also train some of them to help. Not the unicorns as I designed them to eat. Let us have a concert back here Friday evening with unicorn steaks. Has anyone ever seen a gold watch that a unicorn stole from me? [No hands raised.]

"Master Homo, tell me about your life expectancy and your sex life?"

"Homo responds, "Master, you must have drawn us well as we have a life expectancy here of approximately 666 years. My dad, Ham, died at 600 years after a run-in with King Atlas. He is buried in this great black mountain.

Apollo interjects, "Who the hell is King Atlas?

Homo responds, "How can you be such a great one and do not know King Atlas? King Atlas is 660 years old, and on Monday, all residents of Atlantis, except us unemployed outcast, were invited to his recent Creation Anniversary Happiness Day Celebration.

King Atlas received many presents during this celebration. One was a replica of The Great Pyramid at the north end of the island known as Loveland. Atlas was not born of a woman as he was created. .

I assume he was made in the image you made in your drawings. He is the King of the original City of Atlas, which name he later changed to the City of Atlantis, which as you know is so modern and is on the other side of this great black mountain. Atlas and his wife live in the center of the city in the Royal Palace on the central island, called the Citadel. Surrounding the Citadel are three alternating canals and ring-shaped islands.

Whitestone bridges with security gates link the islands. Eloquent white yachts and gondolas serve as a transit system throughout the three circular channels connecting to the transit system of the surrounding white city of Atlantis."

Apollo interrupts, "What is on the central island, and why are you an outcast?"

"Great Apollo, whom I worship as my designer, on the central Citadel Island there is the magnificent Temple of God, with its prayer wall, the royal palace in which the royal family lives, and a beautiful grove of flowers, dates, and fruit trees. Underneath the temple is a power source of some kind that provides power to the entire island. There are three major ring canals connected by splendid bridges with the tunnels beneath for ships to pass. Outside the three rings of circular islands are boulevards going out like spokes on a wheel into Metropolitan Atlantis with its businesses and fine houses where the citizens of Atlantis live. Hallelujah Boulevard is eight lanes and travels due north to a place called Loveland, in which there is a mammoth white pyramid with an all-seeing eye at the top.

All the citizens, with tight security, are invited on the first day of the week to come to God's Temple to worship what Atlas describes as the one eternal Triune God. Atlas declares there is one person of the Father, another of the Son, and another of the Holy Spirit; the Godhead of the Father, Son, and the Holy Spirit is one God. It doesn't make sense to me that three can be one. Atlas wants us to walk by faith as none of us has actually seen God. Let me ask you this question since you are from Heaven have you ever seen the Father God?"

Apollo replied, "No, I have never seen Father God and have often wondered . . . ? [Pausing] Homo let us stay on the subject of why you are an outcast. Tell me more about your dad? Did he have big muscles like you?

My dad was named Ham,[6] and all the people thought he was the most handsome of Ape men. However, he was wrongfully accused of seducing Atlas' youngest eleven-year-old son, Adonis. My dad liked to kiss especially young boys. He had that boy aroused sexually and was about to introduce him to the grandeur of oral and anal sex and would have succeeded had he not been discovered by accident by Atlas himself. The boy seemed willing and liked the attention. What is the big deal? It's wonderful. Better than women. Our ape women are cold except on rare occasions when one gets in heat. They have that time of the month. Yucky (messy, smelly, disgusting)! Atlas banished my dad as unclean from the Metropolitan City of Atlantis.

King Atlas thinks he is so righteous for blackballing my dad! His eldest son, Atlas II, who is next in line to be king, committed adultery against his cold wife. She divorced him. Later, Atlas II developed the liking to seduce and kiss both young girls and young boys – the younger, the better for him. He once told me he had kissed over 300 boys fifteen years old or younger.

I've kissed him once myself. He is a good kisser. His dad, Atlas I, thinks and argues that Atlas II can do no wrong. Atlas I' had a second much younger son Adonis, who was careless and is now dead."

Apollo inquires, "How did Adonis die?"

"Adonis was so handsome, and he liked both women and men. One day he was discovered by a jealous husband who thrust a spear through Adonis' back going through the stomach of the consenting wife into the ground.

---

[6] See Genesis 9:18-21-24 regarding Ham's homosexual act against his father Noah.

Doesn't a woman have a right to consent to have sex with anyone she wants? Is not her body her own? 'Atlas I' took no vengeance against the murderer of his son. That should not be grounds to murder someone.

It opened the door for others to be killed for adultery and acts of homosexuality with young boys. My best friend was stoned by an angry mob, with nothing being done about it after he was caught kissing between the legs one of the leader's twelve-year-old son. The boy was consenting and enjoying it. Doesn't a child have some rights?"

Apollo being visibly angry for not knowing about King Atlas or Atlantis further cross exams, "How did your dad die? I enjoy hearing how people die. I got a thing for death!

"The woman who died with a spear through Adonis and threw her stomach into the ground also had a twelve-year-old son who liked my dad, and they were discovered in a 69 position. Rumor has it on good authority that this murderer of Adonis found an ape woman in heat with AIDS, who got my dad drunk, seduced him, and intentionally infected my dad with AIDS. She became pregnant with me in the process. My dad was urging her to abort me, but she said I can feel that little ape boy kicking.

Abortion is against the law in Atlantis as our Constitution defines everyone a citizen of Atlantis from the moment of fertilization between the male sperm and female egg. If it had not been for this provision in our Constitution, I would not be here. Therefore, as she was dying, she gave me birth and asks someone to help her lay me on my dad's doorstep here on Black Mountain. Weak from loss of blood, she walked away from me with tears in her eyes to sit down on a park bench where they found her dead from AIDS the next morning. Tears came into the eyes of Homo as he saw me and read my mother's note. My dad died when I was six months old also from AIDS. My dad named me Homo Avenger and told others that he would hope that one day I would put an end to his enemy Atlas."

Apollo assured, "Homo, you are right to want revenge. Let me write and play you a song,

Your thinking is the right thinking, Living for pleasure is how to go. Stick with me, and you will do banking for you will have great riches after your revenge.

VISA!" [Apollo takes a bow, with Homo clapping the loudest.]

Apollo orders, "Taskmaster, you select the four shifts, and we may have some workers' treats for you when the first shift shows up at midnight tonight."

The Six Scientists Discover Tobacco and Marijuana in the Jungle

The six scientists sent out into the jungle to look for an addictive smoking material return, grinning, and are escorted into the throne room to report to Apollo, "That jungle is full of addictive stuff. The most addictive material we found was this plant we called tobacco. It will without a doubt cause lung cancer, similar to breathing and being exposed to the dust of pitchblende ore the 666 stooges will mine from which enriched uranium will be made. Let us suggest these stimulating cancer sticks for them to smoke while they dig."

Apollo interjects, "They don't smoke. The tobacco smokes – they are the suckers! Soon a 'sucker will be born every minute (on the Earth).'[7]

When they die, these unclean demonic spirits can seek to oppress and even possess those who give them a place. You know I have given them such big fingers? [Pause] Because I gave them big noses! [Evil laughter, because I drew the male sex organ so tiny.] Here is the first of many catchy work songs,

---

[7] This quote is commonly attributed to P. T. Barnum an American showman who is best remembered for his entertaining hoaxes and for founding the circus that eventually became Ringling Brothers, Barnum and Bailey Circus. See P. T. Barnum at *Wikiquote*.

I'm smoking while I work! I'm smoking while I work! All who don't enjoy smoking are fools and jerks!
Picking away, I'm productive every day. Digging diamonds from the earth and the clay.
I'm smoking while I work! I'm smoking while I work!
What pleasure I have while I work! I'm smoking while I work!

When they develop lung cancer, we can say it was from all that pleasurable smoking. We have developed a secret additive, and if the diggers try to quit smoking, they will be seized with violent headaches. They will soon beg for another cigarette as they will be truly 'hooked' until their early death. They will join us here in Hell to continue our work in a city here in Hell, I call Demonian[8] with its inhabitants called Demoniacs.[9] Their form of government here in Hell will be Demonocracy[10] and socialism. No one being allowed to stand out as a self-achiever, as all are equal. I, Apollyon Lucifer, will receive their worship. They will also be free to worship '*images made to look like birds and animals and reptiles.*'[11]

Apollo's Scientists Invent an Added Ingredient Called 'Hooked,' Causing Violent Headaches if Attempt to Seize Smoking

Another scientist, being careful not to interrupt, asserts, "Also, we discovered another plant in the jungle we named marijuana. We should give them one of these marijuana cigarettes as a bonus at the end of the shift laced with a sleeping drug provided they have met production that day. This will help them relax and knock them out in sleep and get them more ready for the next hard labor work day.

There are many addictions in the jungle, but these two habit-forming drugs, tobacco, and marijuana, with a secret spray-on additive we call 'Hooked,' if withdrawn would give them severe and throbbing headaches, should enslave them and allow us to control them.

Apollo smirks, "Bingo! We will hook them. Roll these two types of cigarettes for this first shift. Make up some black lighters with my image on them. This is the type of smoke, I want in the low parts of my Hell. Hooked first here, and upon death hooked in Hell as my servant demons.

This has been a productive day for darkness. We will win! All our dark works have gone according to my schemes. You scientists have laid up for yourselves rewards in the bank accounts of Hell.

Now scientists go to work producing the enriched uranium for the Freeze Bomb, my ultimate weapon. VISA!"†

---

[8] **Demonia** is taken, "From thy *demoniae* holds. *Milton.*"
  ***American Dictionary of the English Language* Noah Webster 1828**.
[9] *Demoniacs* is defined, "In *church history*, a branch of the Anabaptists, whose distinguishing tenet is, that at the end of the world the devil will be saved." *American Dictionary of the English Language* Noah Webster 1828.
[10] *Demonocracy* is defined, "The . . . government of demons."
  American Dictionary of the English Language Noah Webster 1828.
[11] Romans 1:22 NIV.

✝BOOK SIX✝

✝BOOK SIX – Episode 1✝

[✝**Sidebar Scriptures**: "*Joseph had a dream and promptly reported all the details (Genesis 37:5)."*
"The Lord revealed to me what the evil ones were doing and planning and showed me their wicked plots (Jeremiah 11:18)."
"The word of the Lord came to Abram in a **vision**. . . . A **deep sleep** came upon Abram . . . . (Genesis 15:1, 12)."
I witnessed and experienced "*dreams and visions, and I described all I had seen to instruct many* (Daniel 7:1, 11:33)."✝]

The Dedication of Apollyon Lucifer's 'Black Widow Spider Web Diamond Mine, and Abraham Commences the Zion School for the 144,000 Future Jewish Evangelists

Abraham Rejoices to See His Seed Now Having Created the Needed 144,000 Jewish Evangelists for the Great End-Time Harvest

WITH THANKSGIVING ABRAHAM on Mount Zion before the 144,000 Jewish evangelists kneels and prays,

"O God, my Father, great is Thy faithfulness! Bless you and thank you for these 660 years of days of Heaven on Earth in this First Earth Age. You started my laughter with Isaac, crowned my joy through his son Jacob, and continuing today my gladness of heart with all these young decedents of Jacob gathered here on Mount Zion. By your grace and mercy, we have obeyed and kept the bloodline pure and holy because of our love for You. We have run Your race with joy '*fixing our eyes on Jesus, the pioneer, and perfecter of (our) faith.*'[1] We ask You to help us finish our race with even greater joy and win the prizes of souls giving our God all the glory. God, You have assisted our pure blood lines to stay pure by separating us with a great sea from contamination by others living on the Earth. I look forward to the time when we can all be believing people without the necessity of any sea as Elder John will write,

'*Then I saw a new sky (heaven above the Earth) and a New Earth, for the former sky and the former Earth had passed away (vanished), and there no longer existed any (roaring, only peaceful water) sea.*

And I saw the Holy City, the new Jerusalem, coming down out of Heaven from God, all arrayed like a (not being) bride beautified and adorned for her husband.'[2]

You have even kept the original Jerusalem in Zion hidden from Your enemy so he would not corrupt our children with immorality. Today we have peace (Shalom) within the city gates of Jerusalem and on this Mount Zion. You have been gracious to give from my loins these joyful, pure, and holy 144,000 evangelists according to Your covenant. I sanctify and consecrate them to perform their utmost for Your Highest. We honor You today, tomorrow, and forever. We do not think we can stand on our own, or we may fall. We humble ourselves and pray for wisdom, knowledge, and strength to serve You with righteousness, peace, and joy – empowered by the Holy Spirit. Anoint, prepare, and bless further these chosen 144,000 to proclaim your true salvation in the last days to the lost sheep of Israel. Many Jewish people will initially reject Your Son, Jesus, as the Messiah, the Anointed One, as the Savior of the world. Elder Isaiah will write this Scripture,

---

[1] Hebrews 12:2.
[2] Revelation 21:1-2.

'Truly, You are a God, who hides Himself, O God and Savior of Israel.
All the makers of idols will be put to shame and disgraced;
they will go off into disgrace together.
But Israel will be saved by the Lord
with an everlasting salvation;
you will never be put to shame or disgraced
To ages everlasting.
For this is what the Lord says –
He who fashioned and made the earth,
He founded it;
He did not create it to be empty,
but formed it to be inhabited –
He says:
'I am the Lord,
and there is no other.
I have not spoken in secret,
from somewhere in a land of darkness;
I have not said to Jacob's descendants,
'Seek me in vain.'
Turn to Me and be saved,
All you end of the Earth;
For I am God, and there is no other.
By Myself I have sworn,
My mouth has uttered in all integrity
a word that will not be revoked:
Before Me every knee will bow;
by Me every tongue will swear.
They will say of Me, 'In the Lord alone
are righteousness and strength.'
All who have raged against Him
will come to Him and be put to shame.
But in the Lord all the descendants of Israel
will be found righteous (justified or victorious) and they will praise (glory) in Him (Lord).'[3]

In Your Son's name, Jesus, we pray. Shalom!"

And every one of us with uplifted hands now confirms, "Amen!"

Abraham declares, "My sons, direct descendants of Jacob, we serve a good God, who rewards those who humbly love Him and keep His commandments. However, always remember that He is a just God, who punishes those who hate Him. It will be written,

'Know therefore that the Lord your God is God; He is the faithful God, keeping His covenant of love to a thousand generations of those who love Him and keep His commands.

But those who hate Him (God), He will repay (justice in full) to their face by destruction; He will not be slow to repay (tribulation) to . . . those who hate Him.'[4]

The Father God once taught, "I have a Son whom I love. I am in Heaven, and I am sending My Son and He will become flesh and bone just like you, Abraham. There is one person of Me the Father, another of My Son, and another of the Holy Spirit, but the Godhead of the Father, Son, and the Holy Spirit is one God. You are to worship the one Triune God.

---

[3] Isaiah 45:15-19, 22-25.
[4] Deuteronomy 7:9-10 NIV.

My Son is the Savior of the world. My Son, to be born of a pure flesh and bone woman, will spill His life's blood to pay the penalties for the sins of all those who receive Him as Savior. I have no blood. I am a Spirit. I am not the Savior. I am the Father. Because of sin, man needs a Savior.

I will send My Son to become a man, and He will shed His pure and holy blood as a sacrifice on a cross to pay the penalty due for those sinners who will receive Him as Savior. No one can come to Me, the Father, except through My Son, Jesus, the Savor of the world. Without receiving the shedding of My Son's Blood, *'there is no forgiveness'*[5] of sins. There are three key secrets of learning – 'Repetition, repetition, and repetition!' Even a small child can understand it, but not the prideful who think they have to boast about working their way into eternal life or they heard all that before. Again, no one comes to Me except by My Son as both My Son and Elder Peter will preach,

'Jesus answered, 'I am the way and the truth and the life. No one
comes to the Father (for salvation) except through Me.'[6]
'Salvation is found in no one else, for there is no other name (than Jesus)
under Heaven given to men by which we must (or be going to Hell be saved.'[7]

Shalom! Questions? Hearing no questions, God has pulled back the curtain for me and has shown me this prophecy regarding my grandson's 'Jacob's Trouble' coming at the end of the Third Earth Age. Jacob's descendants will initially reject the Son of God, Jesus, as the Christ, Messiah. However, in the end time, unless they take the 666 mark of the beast enabling them to buy or sell, Jacob's seed (Israel) will be hated by virtually all men. Nations will conspire with other nations to join armies together seeking to remove Israel from the face of the Earth for it will be written,

'With cunning they conspire against your people;
they plot against those You cherish.
'Come,' they say, 'let us destroy them as a nation,
that the name of Israel be remembered no more.'[8]

Abraham continued, "You, 144,000 evangelists, will be sent to proclaim the Good News that Jesus is the Christ, the Messiah, the Savior of Israel to your brethren. Jesus' words have more power than all the armies and weapons of mass destruction put together. When all hope seems lost for Israel, you will descend from Heaven in your flesh-and-blood bodies as you are in today. Being fully trained evangelists, you will first preach this Good News so your brethren, and then preach to a few Gentiles, who have not taken the mark of the beast. All who will accept and believe your message, and be saved!

In six more years, this earth will become 666 years old, and great distress will come to the surface of the First Earth Age. God's enemy will set off an ice bomb purposing to murder God, and the Earth will become, *'without form and an empty waste.'*[9]

It will be so cold that nothing can live on the surface. Each of you will not die when the ice bomb explodes for God will take you from the surface of the Earth in a split second right before the explosion.

---

[5] See Hebrews 9:22.
[6] John 14:6 NIV.
[7] Acts 4:12 NIV.
[8] Psalm 83:1-4.
[9] Genesis 1:3 AMP.

We will all be in a safe shelter beneath the Earth known as, 'Abraham's Bosom' or 'Paradise' and there we will continue your training in evangelism. Elder Matthew will write about these distresses coming upon the Third Earth Age,

'For then there will be great distress (Jacob's trouble), unequaled from the beginning of the world (ice age) until now — and never to be equaled again.'[10]

Lesson One to the 144,000 from Jacob

Abraham turns the Zion School of Ministry over to his grandson Jacob to teach the first lesson with Jacob expounding,

"My beloved grandchildren, adopted sons of God the Father, and anointed by the Son of God Himself for important work to do for His glory, at the end of the Third Earth Age, greetings and blessings! Not for our glory, but for His glory alone, were you chosen. You are all humble servants. Never have a proud look, but for Zion's sake, speak the word of God boldly with dominion and authority.

You must now be trained in the skill of evangelism. For none of you will not have time to go to Bible School when you are set down from Heaven at the end time of the Third Earth Age on this Mount Zion to help deliver and save our brethren, who will find themselves in the middle of what is known as 'Jacob's Trouble.' Yes, my seed will be in trouble, but when it gets too stressful for others, it will be just right for you. You are too blessed to be stressed! [Laughter]

Do not worry. You use the weapon of the love of God. You will do it. Don't hold back as no weapon can harm you until you complete your work – at which time many of you may be martyred. I repeat many of you will be murdered when you have finished your work because you are preaching the Gospel of salvation. Rejoice! For great is your reward in Heaven! My sons are not cowards. You are strong men of valor for God.

You are the 144,000 strong men, who will stand against the wiles of the enemy and pull your brethren out of the jaws of Hell. There will be none braver than you, who will march into Hell for a Heavenly cause – the salvation of our brethren. Our Father is not willing that one of our brethren be lost in Hell, but they will be lost if they do not hear boldly from you and receive God's Son as their Savior, repent (having godly sorrow for their sins and change their conduct), and confessing, 'Jesus is my Lord!'

In the Third Earth Age all your fathers will be born, but you 144,000 cannot be born in that Third Earth Age for legally you can only die once in the Earth as it will be written, 'It is appointed unto men once to die, but after that to face judgment.'[11] You each will be beamed down to Earth as a strong and fearless evangelists more powerful that all the forces of darkness.

Now watch on the screen as I respectfully introduce for the recorded archives some of the faculty here today and give you the meaning of their Hebrew names. 'Hebrew is written from right to left.'[12] We are blessed that the Earth's land is divided by the sea, and we are not connected to that island side of the Earth. I feel in my spirit that their king is about to be murdered, and many of their young people greatly corrupted. The word 'Hebrew' means 'from the other side,' making Jerusalem on the other side a 'city of Shalom (peace).'

---

[10] Matthew 24:21 NIV.
[11] Hebrews 9:27.
[12] *Hebrew alphabet* from *Wikipedia, The Free Encyclopedia.*

We are enjoying such peace and tranquility as we count down to the end of this age caused by an act of war against God, the elders, and yes each of you.

On my right is your grandfather Isaac, and as everyone who meets him knows his name means 'laughter.'[13] You will laugh and enjoy his future teaching in the few remaining days of this first earth age.

Next, you will receive instructions in 'Abraham's Bosom,' where you will live for a season, and next you will be taught in the Convocation Center in Heaven itself as you await being sent back to Mount Zion for this great work of evangelizing of our brethren.

I am your grandfather, Jacob, who in the Third Earth Age deceived others by lying. When I became a man, I finally repented and changed my conduct after struggling with God. God changed my name to Israel.

I had several dreams, and the Lord prospered me. I will share one of the dreams with you today,

When he (Jacob) reached a certain place, he stopped for the night because the sun had set. Taking one of the stones there, he put it under his head and lay down to sleep. He had a dream in which he saw a stairway resting on the earth, with its top reaching to Heaven, and the angels of God were ascending and descending on it. There above it stood the Lord, (Jesus, the Son of God), and He said: 'I am the Lord, the God of your father Abraham and the God of Isaac. I will give you and your descendants the land on which you are now sleeping.'[14]

Jacob concludes, "Any questions?"

One inquired, Were you showed in a dream how to become prosperous?

Jacob replies, "Yes, here is a portion of that dream in which I took as my wages the streaked, speckled and spotted portion of the flock,

'In the breeding season, I once had a dream in which I looked up and saw that the male goats mating the flock were streaked, speckled and spotted. The angel of God said to me in the dream, 'Jacob.' I answered, 'Here I am.' And he said, 'Look up and see that all the male goats mating with the flock are streaked, speckled or spotted, for I have seen all (the evil) that Laban has been doing to you.'[15]

Let me tell you about a special blessing in the Third Earth Age, which caused me to repent and grow up and make a U-turn away from my dishonest and deceptive life,

'So Jacob was left alone, and a man (angel) wrestled with him till daybreak. When the man saw that he could not overpower him, he touched the socket of Jacob's hip so that his hip was wrenched as he wrestled with the man. Then the man (angel) said, 'Let me go, for it is daybreak.

But Jacob replied, 'I will not let you go unless you bless me.

. . .And he said unto him, What is thy name? And he said, Jacob. And he (the angel) said, 'Thy name shall no more be called Jacob, but Israel. . . . And the angel blessed him (Israel, formerly Jacob).'[16]

As you can see my name Jacob will be changed to Israel,[17] which means 'He struggled with God.' My descendants will be known as Israelites. My sons, you will form the tribes of Israel."

Heavenly Achieve Monitor Screen Turned on in Zion

Jacob continued, "Now let me put up on the screen for teaching, with my sons and grandsons of myself – your fathers or grandfathers – all sitting behind me and the meaning of their names:

---

[13] See Genesis 21:1-6.
[14] Genesis 28:11-13.
[15] Genesis 31:10-12.
[16] Genesis 32:24-29.
[17] See Genesis 32:22-32.

1. Judah – confession and praise to God;
2. Issachar – reward, or what is given by way of reward;
3. Zebulon – a home or dwelling place;
4. Reuben – behold. a son;
5. Simeon – hearing and obeying;
6. Gad – a company;
    (Ephraim in the Third Earth Age was born of Jacob)
7. Manasseh – forgiveness;
8. Benjamin – son of my right hand, or son of my old age;
    (Dan in the Third Earth Age was born of Jacob)
9. Asher – blessed;
10. Naphtali – a wrestler or striving;
11. Levi – joining or cleaving to; and
12. Joseph – God will increase.

In addition, my sons, Dan and Ephraim, who were not born in this First Earth Age, will be born in the Third Earth Age, and their sons are not a part of the 144,000 as they are not here to be trained, and they will die making them not legally eligible to be sent back to Earth to die again.

Sitting on my left is Elder John, whose name means 'God has been gracious,' and he will write the truth about each of you being taught today,

'Then I saw another angel coming up from the east, having the seal of the living God. He called out in a loud voice to the four angels given power to harm the land and the sea: 'Do not harm the land or the sea or the trees until we put a seal on the foreheads of the servants of our God.'

Then I heard the number of those who were sealed: 144,000 from all the tribes of Israel.

From the tribe of Judah 12,000 were sealed,
from the tribe of Reuben 12,000,
from the tribe of Gad 12,000,
from the tribe of Asher 12,000,
from the tribe of Naphtali 12,000,
from the tribe of Manasseh 12,000,
from the tribe of Simeon 12,000,
from the tribe of Levi 12,000,
from the tribe of Issachar 12,000,
from the tribe of Zebulun 12,000,
from the tribe of Joseph 12,000, and
from the tribe of Benjamin 12,000.

After this I looked, and there before me was a great multitude that no one could count, from every nation, tribe, people and language, standing before the throne and in front of the Lamb. They were wearing white robes and were holding palm branches in their hands.

And they cried out in a loud voice:
'Salvation belongs to our God,
Who sits on the throne, and to the Lamb (Jesus).'

All the angels were standing around the throne and around the (twenty-four) Elders and the four living creatures. They fell down on their faces before the throne and worshiped God, saying:

'Amen!
Praise and glory

and wisdom and thanks and honor
and power and strength
be to our God forever and ever. Amen!'

Then one of the Elders asked me, "These in white robes —
who are they, and where did they come from?"
I answered, 'Sir, you know.'
And he said,
'These are they who have come out of the great Tribulation (Jacob's Trouble);
they have washed their robes and made them white in the blood of the Lamb.
Therefore, 'they are before the throne of God
and serve Him day and night in His temple;
and He who sits on the throne will spread His tent over them.
Never again will they hunger (couldn't buy or sell without the mark);
never again will they thirst.
The sun will not beat upon them, nor any scorching heat.
For the Lamb at the center of the throne will be their shepherd;
He will lead them to springs of living water.
And God will wipe away every tear from their eyes.'[18]

You 144.000 are being ordained *nunc pro tunc* (now for then) in this First Earth Age for special end-time work during Jacob's Trouble (The Great Tribulation) in the Third Earth Age. Otherwise, your brethren out of every tribe of the children of Israel, who have not taken the 666 mark of the beast on their forehead or on their hand, cannot hear the 'Good News' that Jesus is the Christ, the Messiah, the Savior of the World! The seal of the Father God and Lamb of God's name you receive in your forehead will be evidence of your official authority, dominion, and power. You are so blessed because God has chosen you before the foundation of the world for such a time to preach and win souls in this hour of great tribulation in the Third Earth Age. It will be written, '*He who wins souls is wise.*'[19]

You must continue to keep yourself pure. God has divided the land here in this First Earth Age to keep certain foreign evil women from tempting and defiling you. The spirit is willing, but the flesh is weak as I wrote a song-poem once for myself,

Little eyes, be careful what you look upon;
For I will reap what I have sown.
Pure things for King Jesus only let me see;
Well pleasing to Him always let me be!

You will in the time of Jacob's Trouble be dropped down in your flesh, bone, and blood bodies from Heaven again on Mount Zion to preach salvation. Elder John will further write,

'Then I looked, and there before me was the Lamb (Jesus, Son of God), standing on Mount Zion, and with Him 144,000 who had His name and His Father's name written on their foreheads. And I heard a sound from Heaven like the roar of rushing waters and like a loud peal of thunder. The sound I heard was like that of harpists playing their harps. And they sang a new song before the throne and before the four living creatures and the Elders.

No one could learn (in a tongue unknown to others) the song except the 144,000 redeemed (purchased) from the Earth. These are those who did not defile themselves with women, for they kept themselves virgins (pure). They follow the Lamb (Jesus, Son of God) wherever He goes. They were purchased from among men and offered as first-fruits to God and the Lamb. No lie was found in their mouths; they are blameless.'[20]

---

[18] Revelations 7:2:-17 NIV.
[19] Proverbs 11:30 NIV.
[20] Revelation 14:1-4 .

Questions?"

"Yes, I would like to ask some questions one at a time.

First, the part of not defiling myself with women! Many of you Elders are married. Marriage is not defilement. My grandfather Judah is happily and purely married. He knows I like Jesex, whose dad is very wealthy – very wealthy indeed. She likes me, and her dad would like me to be his treasurer in his profitable enterprises. So it would be okay for me to marry voluptuous Jesex?

Jacob speaks, "I defer to Elder Paul to answer this leading question about marriage."

Elder Paul arose and asked, "Son of Judah, what is your name?"

"My name is Judas Iscariot."

"Judas Iscariot, I will be writing this Scripture,

'Marriage should be honored by all, and the marriage bed kept pure, for God will judge the adulterer and all the sexually immoral. Keep your lives free from the love of money and be content with what you have.'[21]

For your information, I am one of the twenty-four Elders, and I have married in this First Earth Age. I will not marry in the Third Earth Age in which I will receive a Martyr's death as I desire to present myself entirely as a first-fruit offering to God in the Third Earth Age. However, the gift of singleness is rare and is not for many. For this reason, we have nine alternatives as some of you may not desire to remain virgins. Yes, you lose your virginity in marriage, but not your purity, but the 144,000 are all to be virgins. There is no condemnation to one desiring marriage! If any of you young men desire marriage here in this First Earth Age, you will come back in the Third Earth Age to choose of your own free will to either serve God or to seek your own agenda. God has given us all a 'free will,' and He will not override it."

Judas Iscariot responds, "I've chosen to marry Jesex and come back in the Third Earth Age before 'The Great Tribulation' as I don't plan to go through that at all. Possibly, I can be the treasurer of whatever is going on. I am great at handling money! A financial genius – no brag, just fact!"

Abraham responds, "Any of you may without condemnation raise your hand to be excused from having to go through 'The Great Tribulation.'

Including Judas Iscariot, six (6) raised their hands with the next six alternates immediately taking their place. The six who raised their hands were excused and gently, but firmly, escorted away from Mount Zion. While they were being escorted away, Abraham whispers to the Son of God, "Will Judas Iscariot serve You greatly in the Third Earth Age?"

The Son of God with tears in His eye where others could not hear responds, "He will be My treasurer (financial officer; bursar). He often will steal from the money bag. He will betray[22] Me for thirty pieces of silver. He will hang himself, commit suicide, and go to Hell. All of his own *'free will,'* doing it his way, instead of God's way. My Father will wipe away all tears and memory of those who rejected such a great offer of eternal salvation, as they often repeat in Hell, *'it might have been,'* but for a lust, covet, or a trivial thing I lost my eternal salvation. I thought once saved, always saved, as I was one of the twelve disciples and He called me His friend."

Further, Jacob loudly inquires, "Any other questions?"

"Yes, I am Ben, the tribe of Benjamin, "May we preach the Gospel to those who have received the 666 mark showing they belong to the beast enabling them to buy and sell?

---

[21] Hebrews 13:4-5 NIV.
[22] See Matthew 26:47-50, Luke 22:47, and John 18:2.

Someone may be so hungry, or their family is starving at the end of the Third Earth Age, and they felt compelled to take the mark just for a loaf of bread."

John with tears in his eyes responds, "No! You may preach only to those courageous souls, both Jews and Gentiles, who refuse to take the 666 mark!

All who will ask the Lord will be given strength and way to overcome and not take the mark, but if they choose of their own 'free will' not to overcome and to take the mark they will be doomed with no hope. You will have a brief window of opportunity as the tribulation will intensify. I repeat that if they choose of their own 'free will' to yield to temptation and take the mark and worship God's enemies, they will be lost for eternity – Lost! No sadder word than, 'Lost!' I will write regarding these truths of things to come,

'And I saw a beast coming out of the sea. . . . Men worshiped the dragon because he had given authority to the beast, and they also worshiped the beast and asked, 'Who is like the beast? Who can make war against him?

The beast was given a mouth to utter proud words and blasphemies and to exercise his authority for forty-two months. He opened his mouth to blaspheme God and to slander His name and His dwelling place and those who live in Heaven.

. . . All inhabitants of the Earth will worship the beast — all whose names have not been written in the book of life belonging to the Lamb slain from the creation of the world.

. . . Then I saw another beast, coming out of the Earth. He had two horns like a lamb, but he spoke like a dragon. He exercised all the authority of the first beast on his behalf and made the Earth and its inhabitants worship the first beast, whose fatal wound had been healed. And he performed great and miraculous signs, even causing fire to come down from Heaven to Earth in full view of men. Because of the signs he was given power to do on behalf of the first beast, he deceived the inhabitants of the earth. He ordered them to set up an image in honor of the beast wounded by the sword and yet lived. He was given power to give breath to the image of the first beast, so it could speak and cause all who refused to worship the image to be killed. He also forced everyone, small and great, rich and poor, free and slave, to receive a mark on his right hand or on his forehead, so that no one could buy or sell unless he had the mark, which is the name of the beast or the number of his name. This calls for wisdom. If anyone has insight, let him calculate the number of the beast, for it is man's number. His number is 666.'[23]

Jacob spoke, "Let us take one more question for this first of many sessions. First sessions here on Earth on Mount Zion, the next sessions under the Earth in 'Abraham's Bosom,' and then many training sessions at the Convocation Center in Heaven.

You will be Jewish evangelists highly trained for a quick, heroic end of the Third Earth Age work. You will not have time to be trained when Jacob's Trouble (tribulation) commences, as the window of time is short. However, you will be thoroughly prepared, filled with both the compassion of God and the power of the Holy Spirit and you will be much stronger than the counterfeit power of God's enemies.

Questions?"

"I am Ash from the tribe of Asher. Would Elder John outline the intensity of the tribulation we are going to be dropped down into upon the Earth?"

John replies, "Brother Ash, the tribulation, 'Jacob's Trouble,' will mushroom into 'The Great Tribulation.' I will write in part,

---

[23] Revelation 13:1, 4-6, 8-9, 11-18 NIV.

'*The first angel sounded his trumpet, and there came hail and fire mixed with blood, and it was hurled down upon the Earth. A third of the Earth was burned up, a third of the trees were burned up, and all the green grass was burned up.*

The second angel sounded his trumpet, and something like a huge mountain, all ablaze, was thrown into the sea. A third of the sea turned into blood, a third of the living creatures in the sea died, and a third of the ships were destroyed.

The third angel sounded his trumpet, and a great star, blazing like a torch, fell from the sky on a third of the rivers and on the springs of water – the name of the star is Wormwood. (That is, Bitterness) A third of the waters turned bitter, and many people died from the waters that had become bitter.

The fourth angel sounded his trumpet, and a third of the sun was struck, a third of the moon, and a third of the stars, so that a third of them turned dark. A third of the day was without light, and also a third of the night.

. . . The fifth angel sounded his trumpet, and I saw a star that had fallen from the sky to the earth. The star was given the key to the shaft of the Abyss. When he opened the Abyss, smoke rose from it like the smoke from a gigantic furnace. The sun and sky were darkened by the smoke from the Abyss. And out of the smoke locusts came down upon the Earth and were given power like that of scorpions of the Earth. They (locusts) were told not to harm the grass of the Earth or any plant or tree, but only those people who did not have the seal of God (born again ones) on their foreheads. They (locusts) were not given power to kill them, but only to torture them for five months. And the agony they suffered was like that of the sting of a scorpion when it strikes a man. During those days men (not born-again) will seek death, but will not find it; they will long to die, but death will elude them.

The locusts looked like horses prepared for battle. On their heads they wore something like crowns of gold, and their faces resembled human faces. Their hair was like women's hair, and their teeth were like lions' teeth. They had breastplates like breastplates of iron, and the sound of their wings was like the thundering of many horses and chariots rushing into battle. They had tails and stings like scorpions, and in their tails they had power to torment people for five months. They had as king over them the angel of the Abyss, whose name in Hebrew is Abaddon, and in Greek, Apollyon. (Abaddon and Apollyon mean Destroyer.)

The first woe is past; two other woes are yet to come.

The sixth angel sounded his trumpet, and I heard a voice coming from the horns (That is, projections) of the golden altar before God. It said to the sixth angel who had the trumpet, 'Release the four angels bound at the great river Euphrates.' And the four angels kept ready for this hour and day and month and year were released to kill a third of mankind. The number of the mounted troops was two hundred million. I heard their number

The horses and riders I saw in my vision looked like this: Their breastplates were fiery red, dark blue, and yellow like sulfur. The heads of the horses resembled the heads of lions, and out of their mouths came fire, smoke, and sulfur. A third of mankind was killed by the three plagues of fire, smoke and sulfur that came out of their mouths. The power of the horses was in their mouths and in their tails, for their tails were like snakes, having heads with which they inflict injury.

The rest of mankind, not killed by these plagues still did not repent of the work of their hands; they did not stop worshipping demons, and idols of gold, silver, bronze, stone and wood – idols that cannot see or hear or walk.

Nor did they repent of their murders (having a low regard for human life), their magic arts (includes using drugs), their sexual immorality (no purity in marriage between one man and one woman), or their thefts (stealing of all kinds instead of honest labor).[24]

Abraham concludes this first session with the 144,000 Jewish evangelists by saying, "If any of you have any doubts about your commitment, please feel free now, with no condemnation, to raise your hand."

Abraham waits a few moments with no more hands being raised.

John steps forward saying, "Fast this day until sunset tomorrow evening because, while you are sleeping, you will be awakened by your angel to receive a special message for your eyes and ears alone. We have this day for the glory of God selected the 144,000. What a brave end of the Third Earth Age operation, the 144,000 and the two witnesses will pull off (accomplish for the glory of God)! Hallelujah! You are dismissed. Shalom!

---

[24] Revelation 8:7-12; 9:1-21 NIV.

Black Ribbon Cutting at Black Widow Spider's Web Diamond Mine

Apollyon Lucifer signals Mercury to blow the opening midnight high pitch whistle for the first of the round-the-clock-four, six (6) hour shifts and then addresses the first of four crews,

"I am Apollo, song leader in Heaven. I will personally reward you this Saturday evening with a treasure bonus package of my personally giving you a private performance concert.

You are all going to be rich and famous. Have a proud look about yourselves. We have determined that great riches are in this mountain. Homo is your crew boss for this first seven-day six (6) hour shift. Just a forty-two hour work week. You can't beat that. I take care of my own. You can enjoy playing and great smokes the rest of the time.

We plan to dig over the next four years and sixty-six days, with sweat and strength. Your tunneling will look like a black widow spider's web throughout this black granite mountain. My loyal scientists from Heaven have determined that it is also full of ore they need for the project, with the diamonds, which ore is, even more, valuable than the diamonds we anticipate you will also find. Our processing plant to receive the ore will be underground. The ore you dig will be brought there by wheelbarrows. Those on the other side of the mountain must not know our business. So if they ask you what is going on say, 'Nothing.' We have covered our Airbus with camouflage. Be a hard worker, and you will enjoy the riches of Hell. Homo will give each of you a daily package of sixty-six (66) cigarettes for your ultimate enjoyment, so you can smoke and sing my songs while you work for me. VISA! (Thinking, "*Very Important Stooges Assistants.*)"

Each of the 144,000 Jewish Evangelists While Sleeping Soundly is Touched by an Angel and Escorted to the Convocation Hall in Heaven

As each of the 144,000 evangelists enjoy sweet sleep, they heard a ram's horn blast as they each are being touched with a slight shaking of the shoulder by a bright and shining angel from God speaking,

I greet you in the name of the Father, the Son, and the Holy Spirit. Now arise and put on your robe, belt, and sandals for you have an appointment with the Lamb of God, Jesus, who takes away the sins of those who receive Him as Savior. He desires, your presence. He approved each of you for a particular End of the Third Earth Age harvest work to help bring in a multitude into the Kingdom of God."

When each had stepped outside, the 144,000 enter in a large circle of light and they arise with a swift and noiseless motion quickly, leaving the Earth and the moon behind and entering the atmosphere of Heaven landing on their feet softly behind the Throne of Heaven.

All the evangelists remove their sandals and walk barefoot through a flowing stream known as the Water of Life. They come out on the other side of the stream in a glorified body and dressed in dazzling white garments, knowing they are standing on holy ground. As they are royally escorted into the Convocation Center, they take seats arranged in a fan shape. The Elders likewise are sitting in a fan shape behind the diamond pulpit.

Elder David, also being barefoot, plays a golden harp behind the diamond pulpit, with the other Elders sitting with him, as he leads the144,000 Jewish evangelists in a song of praise rolling on the screen:

'Hallelujah! (Praise the Lord)
Praise the name of the Lord;
Praise Him, you servants of the Lord,
you who minister in the house of the Lord,
in the courts of the house of our God.

Praise the Lord, for the Lord is good;
sing praise to His name, for that is pleasant.'
For the Lord has chosen Jacob to be His own,
Israel to be His treasured possession.'[25]

After seven repeats, each raising the tempo to a higher level, a bright Shekinah Glory Cloud rolls down from the throne room and envelops the elders and the 144,000. One by one each bow and worship God. Then the Son of God manifests Himself, also being barefoot, declaring,

"Greatly beloved, welcome to Heaven!"

A voice sounding like a mighty thunder spoke from the above Throne Room down through the Shekinah Glory Cloud,

'This is My Son, Whom I love;
with Him, I am well pleased. Listen to Him!'[26]

The Son looking up at to the Throne Room nodding a yes, raises His hands praying,

"Father, My Lord, hallowed be Your name, Your kingdom fully come. May 'Your will' for the end-time through these 144,000 be done on Earth.[27] No eye has seen, nor ear heard what You have prepared for those who love You.[28] At some point, there will be no need for a dividing sea[29] to protect your family from all Your enemies and even death itself will be thrown into the Lake of Fire. You shall have a pure and holy family who loves You and to whom You love.

Nothing can stop this mighty moving force of these 144,000 evangelists from preaching the Good News to their brethren, so that all Israel, who receive Me as Savior and confess Me as Lord will be saved. You will set aside these dearly beloved on the day you make up Your jewels (family).[30] May they each be kept pure, holy, and filled with Your power and dominion. Shalom! Amen!"

All whisper in unison, "Amen! Shalom!"

The Son turns and steps behind the diamond pulpit soberly addressing,

"Please be seated. On behalf of My Father, the Holy Spirit, the Elders, and Myself, I would like to welcome you, the chosen 144,000 Jewish evangelists to Heaven. I commend you for walking in love, keeping yourselves pure, holy, and forgiving of any who may have trespassed against you.

You have each been chosen to reap a plentiful harvest with a focus on your brethren from the seed of Jacob, along with a comparative few Gentiles who have also not taken the 666 mark of the beast. Those of their own free who will reject and scorn your messages of the free gift of salvation will legally subject themselves to the wrath of judgment.

---

[25] Psalm 135:1-4 NIV.
[26] Matthew 17:5 NIV.
[27] Matthew 6:9-11 NIV.
[28] See 1 Corinthians 2:9.
[29] See Revelation 21:1.
[30] See Malachi 3:17.

Your love and compassion for your brethren will not fail as virtually all remaining Israel will be saved because of your bold preaching as they receive Me as Savior and confess Me as their Lord. Amen!" All again whisper, "Amen! Shalom!"

The Son of God further directs, "Elder John, read the revelation of the harvest of love as I sit upon a cloud cheering each of you on as you win souls."

Elder John lifts the curtain of time and reading the words on the screen, '*I looked, and there before me was a white cloud. Seated on the cloud was One (Son of God) 'like a son of man' with a crown of gold on His head and a sharp sickle in His hand.*

Then another angel came out of the temple and called in a loud voice to Him who was sitting on the cloud, 'Take your sickle and reap, because the time to reap has come, for the harvest of the Earth is ripe.' So He who was seated on the cloud swung his sickle over the earth, and the earth was harvested.'[31]

The Son of God decrees, "You, 144,000, will do at the end of the Third Earth Age the preaching, and I will personally do the reaping of the harvest. I will be born in the Third Earth Age of Jacob, the Tribe of Judah, of a virgin mother, a great-granddaughter of David, but My Jewish brethren will reject Me as their Messiah and Savior. Elder Paul must turn from preaching to the Jews to preaching to the Gentiles after the Jews as a nation initially reject Me as Savior. Those who had previously received Me as Savior in those days will have already been taken out of the Earth in the rapture or catching away of the saints. Without you, 144,000 Jewish evangelists, and the two witnesses I would have no true preachers in the world to preach again to the descendants of Jacob the Good News that I am truly the Messiah, the Savior of the world. Elder Paul will be one of your main teachers. Elder Paul read from the screen what you will write,

'*For Christ (sent me) to preach the gospel – not with words of human wisdom, lest the cross of Christ be emptied of its power.*

For the message of the cross is foolishness to those perishing, but to us being saved, it is the power of God. For it is written:

I will destroy the wisdom of the wise; the intelligence of the intelligent I will frustrate.'[32]

'*Where is the wise man? Where is the scholar? Where is the philosopher of this age? Has not God made foolish the wisdom of the world? For since in the wisdom of God the world through its wisdom did not know Him, God was pleased through the foolishness of what was preached to save those who believe. Jews demand miraculous signs and Greeks look for wisdom, but we preach Christ crucified: a stumbling block to Jews and foolishness to Gentiles, but to those whom God has called (by the Gospel preached), both Jews and Greeks, Christ the power of God and the wisdom of God. For the foolishness of God is wiser than man's wisdom, and the weakness of God is stronger than man's strength.*'[33]

The Son of God with tears in His eyes preaches, "Here I am as the Savior of the world, to be born of a woman growing up and become a man with a flesh-and-bone body, reaping the final precious last great harvest of the Earth through your bold preaching. Your enthusiastic evangelistic labors of love will produce a glorious harvest.

This harvest closes the Age of Grace offering such a great salvation to those who believe the preached word and accept My sacrifice on the cross for their sins to be received by faith as a free

---

[31] Revelations 14:14-16 NIV.
[32] Quoting Isaiah 29.14.
[33.] 1 Corinthians 1:17-25 NIV.

gift and not of works, so that no one can boast. [34] All who hear your message and reject it will be lost in Hell, where there will be weeping and gnashing of teeth."

Tears run down the cheeks of the Savior as He further declares, "We will not override their free will. Likewise, I choose of My own 'free will' to suffer and shed My life's Blood by being nailed naked to a cross to pay in full the penalty for the sins of those who will receive Me as their Savior and confess Me as their Lord. It will be written,

'But now He (Son of God) has appeared once for all at the end of the ages to do away with sin by the sacrifice of Himself. Just as man is destined to die once, and after that to face judgment, so Christ was sacrificed once to take away the sins of many (those who receive the offer of salvation) people; and He will appear a second time, not to bear sin, but to bring salvation to those who are waiting for Him.' [35]

If they choose to perish, let them perish with your arms about their knees, imploring them to receive Me as Savior, repent of their sins, and confess me as Lord. If Hell must be further filled, at least, let it be filled in the teeth of your exertions. Let none of your brethren left on the Earth go there unwarned!

A great multitude of the descendants of Jacob and a few Gentiles will believe your pure and bold message and receive Me as Savior. My prophet Jeremiah will describe this time of Jacob's trouble in his writings,

> *'How awful that day will be!*
> *None will be like it.*
> *It will be a time of trouble for Jacob,*
> *but he will be saved out of it'* [36]

You will use the strong weapon of love and reap many souls for the Kingdom of God. I will rejoice to harvest with a sickle this ripe golden wheat of Jacob. However, after this final plea has been made, next will come the harvest of the wicked for judgment and wrath. Elder John, pull open the curtain of time and read from the screen,"

Elder John steps forward and reads what he will write about the harvest of judgment and wrath,

'Another angel came out of the temple in Heaven, and he too had a sharp sickle. Still another angel, who had charge of the fire, came from the altar and called in a loud voice to him who had the sharp sickle, 'Take your sharp sickle and gather the clusters of grapes from the Earth's vine because its grapes are ripe.' The angel swung his sickle on the earth, gathered its grapes and threw them into the great winepress of God's wrath. They (the lost) were trampled in the winepress outside the city, and blood flowed out of the press, rising as high as the horses' bridles for a distance of 1,600 stadia. (That is, about 180 miles or 300 kilometers).' [37]

The Son of God further explains, "It is no longer I am using the sharp wheat sickle, but an angel thrusting in another sharp sickle to gather the clusters of the evil and prideful grapes. A time of great destruction and slaughter of the enemies of God. It is a fearful thing to rebel against God."†

---

[34] See Ephesians 2:8-9.
[35] Hebrews 9:26-28.
[36] Jeremiah 30:7.
[37] Revelation 14:17-20 NIV.

266

†BOOK SIX – Episode 2†

[†**Sidebar Scriptures**: "*Joseph had a dream and promptly reported all the details* (Genesis 37:5)."
"*The Lord revealed to me what the evil ones were doing and planning and showed me their wicked plots* (Jeremiah 11:18)."
"The word of the Lord came to Abram in a **vision**. . . . A **deep sleep** came upon Abram . . . . (Genesis 15:1, 12)."
I witnessed and experienced "*dreams and visions, and I described **all** I had seen to instruct many* (Daniel 7:1, 11:33)."†]

King Atlas Serves Homo with a Show-Cause Order to 'Cease and Desist,' and 144,000 Jewish Evangelists Are Taken to Heaven and Returned Back Into Their Sleeping Bodies

A CIVIL SERVICE EMPLOYEE with the Licensing and Permit Division of the City of Atlantis is bow hunting on the back side of the Black Granite Volcano Mountain. Upon retrieving an arrow, he sees an old acquaintance, who did yard work for his mother, coming out of a partially concealed entrance hole. He inquires, "Benedict, where does that hole lead?"

"Homo's diamond mine."

"Have you found any diamonds?"

"Not yet, but we will. I was not supposed to tell. I forgot! Oh, well. The cat is out of the bag now. Swear to me that you will not reveal your source of this information. Homo would fire me and cut off all my benefits.

"Benedict, I will keep my source confidential, but you know I will have to turn this in."

"Do what you have to do, but please don't mention my name. How is your mother?"

"She is fine. She sings in the choir at the Sunday praise and worship services in God's Temple on the Citadel. She is so joyful and thankful that her Creator has shown King Atlas how to roll her sins forward. Each year they shed the blood of a spotless lamb until the Son of God sheds His own blood by being nailed to a cross to pay the penalty for the sins of all who will receive Him as Savior.

My mother still has a groundkeeper's house in the back, and I could help you escape from Homo and be saved from your sins. We can clothe your nakedness and cut your hair and trim your beard. All you have to do is have Faith in the Son of God as Savior and be willing to repent of your sins, by giving them up. I know you believe by witnessing my mother and my lifestyle that Jesus is the Son of God. That is not enough.[1] The next thing you need to do is to repent! It is like going down the highway, and discovering you are going the wrong way. You have only to make a U-turn away from your homosexual lifestyle and trust in Jesus to save and help you. Would you like to repent?

"No! Maybe later! Right now, I am having too much fun. I have plenty of time. I am young. I have just discovered tobacco and marijuana. Marijuana coupled with homo sex with one of my lovers is pleasing. You don't know what you are missing."

"Benedict, do you have AIDS?"

"Not yet. Homo only permits the men with AIDS to date men who already have AIDS. I have three AID, not infected dates lined up for the next three weekends. One is supposed to be the best kisser among the ape men. He has large lips. He specializes in sodomy. I have waited a long time to have a date with him. So far, I have had twenty-two dates this year. One or two were as big as donkeys. You don't know what pleasures you are missing.

---

[1] See James 2:19.

267

I have even met our creator, Apollo, and he is not like you think. He is gorgeous. A knockout of a prince! I think he likes me as I saw him looking down at my feet once."

King Atlas Serves Homo with Show Cause[2] Legal Papers on Why the Diamond Mining Business Must Cease[3] in Thirty Days Because of Failure to Obtain a Work Permit

A deputy sheriff serves Homo with a Show Cause Order signed by King Atlas to show cause why the diamond mining business must not cease in thirty days because of failure to obtain a work permit. Homo gives the served legal papers to the chief scientist in charge to communicate with Apollo and awaits Apollo's defense orders.

The 144,000 View the Horrors of Hell and Visit Abraham's Bosom (Paradise) in the Year 70 B.C., Third Earth Age

The Son of God with tears in his eyes at the Convocation Center in Heaven concludes His message,

"My Father is a God of justice, and He 'does not leave the guilty unpunished.'[4]

It will be written,
'And they will go out and look upon the dead bodies of those who rebelled against Me; their worm will not die, nor will their fire be quenched. They will be loathsome to all mankind.'[5]

I desire you to witness those in Hell, who of their own free will rejected such a great offer of salvation. You will witness them being justly punished for neglecting such a great offer of salvation. I preached about a descendants' of Jacob in the Third Earth Age as follows,
'There was a (real person) rich man dressed in purple and fine linen and lived in luxury every day. At his gate was laid a beggar named Lazarus (also a decedent of Jacob), covered with sores and longing to eat what fell from the rich man's table. Even the dogs came and licked his sores.
The time came when the beggar died, and the angels carried him to Abraham's side. The rich man also died and was buried. In Hell, where he was in torment, he looked up and saw Abraham far away, with Lazarus by his side. So he called to him, 'Father Abraham, have pity on me and send Lazarus to dip the tip of his finger in water and cool my tongue because I am in agony in this fire.'
But Abraham replied, 'Son, (my brethren) remember that in your lifetime you received your good things while Lazarus received bad things, but now he is comforted here, and you are in agony. And besides all this, between us and you a great chasm has been fixed, so that those who want to go from here to you cannot, nor can anyone cross over from there to us.'
He answered, 'Then I beg you, father, send Lazarus to my father's house, for I have five brothers. Let him warn them, so they will not also come to this place of torment.'
Abraham replied, 'They have Moses and the Prophets; let them, listen to them.'
No, father Abraham,' he said, 'but if someone from the dead goes to them, they will repent.' He said to him, 'If they do not listen to Moses and the Prophets, they will not be convinced even if someone rises from the dead.'[6]

---

[2] Show Cause is defined *inter alia* as, "Against a rule . . . as directed and present . . . such reasons and considerations as one has to offer why it should not be confirmed, take effect, be executed, or as the case may be." *Black's Law Dictionary.*

[3] Cease is defined *inter alia* as, "To stop . . . to come to an end." *Black's Law Dictionary.*

[4] Exodus 34:7 NIV.

[5] Isaiah 66:24 NIV.

Now each of you 144,000 and Elders close your eyes tightly as you are about to be transported to Abraham's Bosom in the year of 70 B.C., Third Earth Age."

Opening their eyes, they arrive as Abraham is discoursing with a certain rich man, a decedent of Jacob, who never dreamed he would end up in Hell. A wave of fire temporarily knocks this lost man from the rock into a pool of fire, and he is struggling to climb back on top of the rock.

Abraham explains to the 144,000 and the other Elders, all now standing on a sloping hill in beautiful Paradise,

"We are now in Paradise in the heart of the Earth, and across the deep chasm is Hell itself. The scene before us is terrible. Hell is hostile to all we hold dear as you will witness. Flames of fire roll over the heads of thousands of people made in the image of God. They cannot see you, but you can see them. They can only see Lazarus and me. Nothing impure or unclean can enter here in Paradise.

The Son of God to be born of a woman will choose to take all the sins of the world upon Himself and be murdered by wicked men under the influence of God's enemy. Because all that sin is to be on the Son of God as He dies on the cross, He will descend into Hell itself and will suffer further punishment for all the sins of all who receive Him as Savior. Our Father God is a just God, a God of legality, and He must punish sin. For it is to be written,

'The Lord, the compassionate and gracious God, is slow to anger, abounding in love and faithfulness, maintaining love to thousands, and forgiving wickedness, rebellion, and sin. Yet He does not leave the guilty unpunished: He punishes the children and their children for the sin of the fathers to the third and fourth generation.'[7]

God's precious Son will take our place on the cross and in Hell itself further fully pay the penalty due for the sins of all those who will receive Him as Savior. After God's Son has fully experienced the torments of Hell itself, because He died with the sins of the world upon Him, the Father God will declare, 'That is enough. They murdered an innocent man! Son, take the keys of Hell and Death and go across this great chasm into Abraham's Bosom.' We all here in Paradise will enjoy two days of celebrating the Son of God's preaching and ministry in the heart of the Earth.

The Son of God, Jesus, will teach you, the 144,000, why it will be necessary for Him to die on the cross, to experience Hell itself, and 'have to suffer these things and then enter His glory,'[8] to prepare you further for your great end-time evangelism work. Our Savior's human dead body will remain in the tomb, but after three days on the first day of the week, our Savior's Spirit will return to the sealed tomb on earth and re-entered His dead body. He will be resurrected from the dead! 'Up from the grave He arose, with a mighty triumph o'er (over) His foes.'[9] Glory!

Our Savior after His resurrection will take all of us captive here in Paradise with Him as He ascends into Heaven. Paradise will be cleaned out. All future believers who die will not come here to former Paradise but will, like us, be taken into Heaven. Many will be deceived and deceive others by teaching that our Savior did not rise from the dead, and if they will, with a suicide bomb kill some of Jacob's descendants they will go to Paradise and have sixty-six, plus six, virgins waiting for them to give them sexual pleasures. After the blast, they will come close to empty Paradise arriving right across this great chasm into Hell. As for sexual pleasures they are promised, they will find there will be no sexual organs in Hell.

It will be written about such,
'Some people think they are doing right, but it is the path to death.'[10]

So, you 144,000 will be first taught on Mount Zion, then in Paradise beneath the Earth, and later fully trained in Heaven. With all that training, with the power of the Holy Spirit, at just the right time you 144,000 will be transported back down to Mount Zion.

You will then be scattered out in all directions to preach the Good News that Jesus is the Messiah, the Savior of the World. Your preaching will be received by many who will not be ashamed of the Gospel of Jesus Christ.

Now look across this great chasm to the man in Hell, who has made it back on top of that rock screaming, crying, and calling out to me for water. That is a son of my grandson Jacob, Dan, who with Ephraim, was not born of Jacob in this First Earth Age. They will be born of Jacob in the Third Earth Age who even went off into idolatry

---

[6] Luke 16:19-31 NIV.
[7] Exodus 34:6-7 NIV.
[8] Quoting Luke 24:26 NIV.
[9] Quoting the Refrain from the song *Christ Arose* by Robert Lowry.
[10] Proverbs 14:12.

worshiping *'golden calves'*[11] refusing to repent to *'fall and never get up again.'*[12] Note that Dan looks distinguished even in Hell. He built his own kingdom here on Earth. He did it his way instead of God's way. We can all learn from his costly mistakes.

Now watch the woman who also looks distinguished even in Hell pulling herself up on the rock from the fires and joining Dan, who briefs her and points me out to her."

The woman screams, "Abe, don't you recognize me. At one time, I was Sarah's best friend. Look at me. Who am I?"

Abraham responds, "You are my nephew Lot's wife. You bore him two beautiful daughters. Your name is Sensi, and you and Sarah had some delightful times together. I looked toward Sodom and Gomorrah that day, and I *'saw dense smoke rising from the land like smoke from a furnace'*[13] Lot later told me that an angel commanded all of you, *'Don't look back,'*[14] and you disobeyed and looked back, and your punishment included being turned into a pillar of salt.[15] I see today it also includes ending up in Hell! Many have seen this pillar of salt as a punishment for disobedience causing great fear and reverence. It is not a small thing to disobey God in even what may seem even in a little everyday and ordinary matter."

"Abe that was just a slip. I just looked a little bit over my shoulder. I'm innocent of fully, wholly, and entirely looking back. No big thing. Just a small disobedience. Be my lawyer! I do not deserve to be here. I am your close relative. Get me over to your side. The punishment does not fit the crime."

"Sensi, it is a great chasm between us. You will have a right at the great white throne judgment after you see the evidence on the screen showing what you actually thought and did choosing of your own *'free will'* to look back, to plead guilty or not guilty, and to present your innocence. I am not going to judge anything before its time.

You two have been in Hell for some time. Please one, or both of you, describe for me what it is like being in Hell.

Dan spoke first,

"I too am going to plead not guilty at the great white throne judgment. I murdered no one. I did not even commit adultery against my wife as God gave me a warm woman.

I am so thankful I did not take her to this place with me. I remember the precious times with her. She would plead with me to lay up for myself treasures in Heaven instead of building a kingdom on earth. An idol maker made me 666 percent interest on gold I supplied for him to make and sell golden idols. They were like small good luck charms bringing luck when one would bow down and worship them.

My wife warned me, but I would not listen. She visited the poor and the sick and encouraged them to seek first the Kingdom of God and His righteousness. I provided the money for her ministry. I should get credit for all the good things she did as I gave her bed and board. Would you also be my lawyer? I do not deserve to be here just because I had the weakness of loving money first before God."

Lot's wife responds, "Ditto! Please be my lawyer, Abe. Accept my case. It was your nephew Lot, my husband, who for financial gain moved us into the heart of the City of Sodom. It seems every business he touched turned to gold. We had a beautiful marble house filled with treasures of gold, silver, jewelry, and fine clothes. I set the fashion standard for the women of Sodom. When we did not want to leave our house and treasures in Sodom, an Angel grasped Lot's hand and then grasped my hand a little roughly. The other Angel grasped my two daughters' hands. The Angels pulled us along out of the city, saying that God had been merciful to us because of you, Abraham, but they had to get us out as the city was to be destroyed because of sin. Then one of them ordered, *'Flee for your lives! Don't look back!'*[16]

The Angels were just too rough on us. They did not even give me the opportunity to turn the key and lock my front door or to retrieve my jewelry box. Lot had on his person only, one bag of gold. My two sons-in-law thought the Angels were jesting. The Angels presented their case wrongly. I have evidence to present on my side at the great white throne judgment. It made sense that what the Angel meant when he commanded us not to look back was to demonstrate the necessity of utmost haste, and this was not a significant commandment. That is just too small a thing to end up in Hell over. All I saw was a mushroom cloud. What was the harm in seeing that? I like to talk so before a big wave of fire sweeps us off this rock I will let Dan first describe what it is like to be in this horrible Hell.

---

[11] 2 Kings 10:29.

[12] Amos 8:14.

[13] Genesis 19:28 NIV.

[14] Genesis 19:17 NIV.

[15] See Genesis 19:26.

[16] Genesis 19:17 NIV.

Dan nods, "Okay! Abraham, as a prisoner in Hell, we have great miseries in this infernal fire of these sorts:

1.   We remember what we have lost, such as the right to enter the gates of Heaven, to enjoy the fellowship of Saints and Heavenly Angels, and to miss the abundant and eternal life forever freely offered to us through the sacrifice of the Lamb of God paying the penalty with His life's blood due for our sins. For a trivial, nothing, for a look over the shoulder, for a few gold coins, we lost it all. There is no word worse than that dreaded word 'Lost!'

2.   God's presence is not felt here, and yet He sees all. We remember that '*in His presence is fullness of joy.*'[17] The absence of feeling God's presence is one of our greatest losses,

3.   What horrible punishments we undergo in Hell, which I will outline later.

4.   Our guilty conscience is tormented, and it feels like a continual gnawing worm.

5.   Many around us hate and curse God, and by such, they torment and torture us physically and emotionally.

6.   We often say, 'How could we have neglected such a great salvation?' Our Savior's yoke was so easy to wear, and His '*burden is light*'[18] to carry. I wanted to do it my way instead of God's way. It was as if I destroyed my own soul for a piece of bread, a triviality, a widow's mite, for nothing of any importance.

Abraham, allow me to expand a little further as it might help someone to avoid coming to this tormenting place. I have often seen the flames of fire go over the heads of beautiful young girls and handsome young men. They were running, but the flames engulfed them.

Let me further expound upon this greatest of loss of the favor and joy of God. When I was a young Jewish man, I experienced the joyful presence of God. I would feel God's guidance.

I would acknowledge Him in all my ways and '*He would direct my paths.*'[19] I would worship God with a humble, obedient, and sincere love that came from the depth and center of my heart. However, I later became prideful in my own eyes. I would brag that I am a self-made man. I did it my way.

As I grew richer and trusted in money, I did not fear God, although I was warned, especially by my dear wife, to '*fear God and keep His commandment.*'[20]

Again, I am so glad I did not drag my wife, whom I love, here. I miss seeing her so much. I have thought about her crying over me as she tried to warn me. I am sure she is there with you, Abraham, but I am not asking to see her. I would not want her to see me like this. I am so ashamed that I neglected such a great salvation! I was in rebellion and disobeyed God in many things. I exalted myself and had a proud look on my face. I desired to be served and not to serve. I took all the honor and glory due to God for myself. I vaunted myself every chance I had. I received glory and praise from others and gave none to God. I refused to humble myself under the mighty hand of God. Pride indeed went before my destruction.[21]

Also, I genuinely miss the company of my brethren, especially the companionship of my wife and children, all of whom loved God and also loved me. How wonderful it is to love and to be loved! All is lost! Here almost everyone hates and blames each other and blames God for sending them here.

My heart here breaks for hopelessness. The most miserable man upon earth still may have a glimmer of hope. Where there is life, there is hope. There is no hope in Hell as it is written, "*It is appointed for people to die once and after that to face judgment.*"[22]

Having shown you some of what I have lost, what physical torments I undergo include,

1. I feel pain and agony in these flames. I am so thirsty as I have searched this place, and there is not even one drop of water in Hell.

2. I have worms that like to crawl over and into me. Here we have tormenting creatures of all kinds. Some look like snakes, others like spiders, and others are hideous creatures of all kinds who hate us. They spew from their mouths extreme hatred for God and those made in God's image. They pick me up and throw me against a wall or down into the flames. They viciously rake me with their claws. I hurt all over. Let me describe two who hate me.

One giant beast resembles a reptile. It has arms and legs of unequal length. It has scales and bumps all over its grotesque body. Its face has large sunken-in eyes, gigantic brown and yellow teeth with bad breath, a protruding jaw, and a flat swine-like nose. It has smelly extra-large feet. That hideous creature I have nicked named 'Woe'

---

[17]   Psalm 16:11.

[18]   Matthew 11:30.

[19]   See Proverbs 3:6

[20]   Ecclesiastes 12:13.

[21]   See Proverbs 16:18.

[22]   Hebrews 9:27.

because in his presence is woe for I am undone '*for the pains of Hell laid hold on me.*'[23] When he can catch me, he picks me up like a rag doll and swings me around and throws me against a rock or into a deep pocket of fire.

Another creature I have nicked named 'Moe' since I know more torments are coming through this demon. Moe looks like a thin dragon with long arms and razor-sharp scales. This demon's claws are (six) 6 to each hand, and six (6) to each foot with each claw six (6) inches long. Moe hates God and hates me because I am made in the image of God. God never desired a son or daughter of Jacob to come here.

He gave us a free will to obey or not obey Him, to accept His Son as Savior, repent, and confess Jesus as Lord, and to choose life or to choose Hell. I did not know that anything could be this horrible. Moe breathes out a stream of intense fire on me and tries to mutilate me further by sticking his razor sharp claws into me. It would have been better for me to have never been born!

Further, my senses are being tormented,

My **eye** is tormented with the sight of ghastly and horrible spectacles, the seeing the tortures of others, many of whom I understand sold themselves into corruption on the island of Atlantis.

I daily see beautiful young girls and handsome young men falling into this horrible place as the jaws of Hell open to receive them as they reap the ultimate consequences of sinful lives.

Fortunately, no young children before the age of accountability are here as they are safe in God's arms. I wish I had died as a young child.

My **ear** is tortured with the continual outcries and loud yelling of the damned. I hear the filthy and horrible language and blasphemous cries of the wicked as they accuse God the Father, God the Son, and God the Holy Spirit. I endure constant dreadful shrieks, hideous and awful noises, shrieks, and howls of other damned (lost) sinners also under the fierceness of pains. The torments of others increase my pain and do not in any manner lessen my own pain. There are no atheists in Hell. Those fools who taught on the Earth that there was no God have greater punishments here, and they scream the loudest.

My **nostrils** burn as I suck in the sulfurous flames and smoke. This place smells worse than rotten eggs. The breath of Woe and Moe could gag a maggot. I cannot describe it in words. The stale smell and suffocating odors and nasty stenches are worse than that of an open sepulcher full of rotting corpses.

My **tongue** burns and cracks with fiery blisters. As I said before, I am always so thirsty! Again, there is not a drop of water to be found in Hell.

My **body** aches and hurts from tossing and squirming in the flames. Again, it would have been so much better if I had never been born, as I would be nonexistent.

Hell itself being such a wretched place increases my misery. It is a prison, a dungeon, a furnace of pockets of fire; it has the blackness of darkness, and evil seems so thick you could cut it with a knife. All these horrors increase my suffering.

The **cruelty of the tormentors** adds to my torments. The tormentors are being tormented themselves, and they seem distracted away from their own pain by afflicting pain on others.

I have shown in Hell only a portion of the miserable situation we here are suffering. That we too, being children of yours, Abraham, I choose to be prideful and disobey God, not even caring that I would be banished to this horrible place. I did it my way, and not God's way. The children of Jacob, with a sense of urgency, must warn and plead with their brethren not to come here. This separation from God is permanent. Remember, '*He who wins souls is wise.*'[24] Wisely, warn the brethren of this fearful and terrible peril. To remain silent is criminal."

Lot's wife, focusing on the face of Abraham, further testifies, "What Dan has said is the truth. However, the half has not been told. I present the case that it is even worse here for women than for men. I see these beautiful young girls who had been '*enjoying the pleasures of sin for a season,*'[25] not considering that death would somehow overtake them, and then they would fall into this horrible place. Abe, let me give you my full discourse on the horrors of Hell from a woman's viewpoint . . ."

At this point, a loud roaring cloud of black smoke billowed up from the great chasm blocking the view from Hell of Abraham's Bosom. A wave of fire knocks both Dan and Sensi off the rock into a deep pool of liquid fire.

---

[23] Psalm116:3 KJV.

[24] Proverbs 11:30 NIV.

[25] Hebrews 11:25.

Abraham with a dense black fog between him and Hell lectures the 144,000,

"There is wishful thinking in Hell, as well as on Earth, as people deceive themselves, that they might end up in Heaven, by some argument they can make at the Great White Throne Judgment. Elder John describes,

'Then I saw a great white throne, and Him (Jesus, Son of God) who was seated on it. . . . The dead were judged according to what they had done as recorded in the books.

And the sea gave up the dead, who were in it, and Death and Hell gave up the dead that were in them, and each person was judged according to what he had done. Then Death and Hell were thrown into the lake of fire. The lake of fire is the second death. If anyone's name was not found written in the book of life, he (or she) was thrown into the lake of fire (eternal separation from God).'[26]

Many of their own 'free wills,' have neglected such a Great Salvation. The end of one's life is so important. All the good that Lot's wife did even toward Sarah, my wife, did not shield her when she chose that act of her own free will to disobey. She can present her defenses at the Great White Throne Judgment. God is the final judge, and let us stay out of the judging business. Let us walk in love, not judging others, and urge those made in the image God not to neglect such a great offer of salvation by repenting and trusting in Jesus as their personal Savor! Jesus in the Third Earth Age will warn,

'Then He said to them, 'Watch out! Be on your guard against all kinds of greed; a man's life does not consist in the abundance of his possessions."

And He told them this parable: 'The ground of a certain rich man produced a good crop. He thought to himself, 'What shall I do? I have no place to store my crops.' . . .'This is what I'll do. I will tear down my barns and build bigger ones, and there I will store all my grain and my goods.' And I'll say to myself, 'You have plenty of good things laid up for many years. Take life easy; eat, drink and be merry.'

Your brethren during the Great Tribulation at the end of the Third Earth Age will be anxious as they cannot buy or sell unless they take the forbidden mark. Such great persecutions will be a mistake of God's enemy for this will humble your brethren, and they will wisely call out to God to deliver them out of this trouble and show them the Messiah. Through believing the two witnesses, Elijah and Moses, and the 144,000 evangelist's 'good news,' they will accept Jesus, the One crucified to pay the penalty due for sins of the many who will receive Him as the Messiah. Savior, repent of their sins, be baptized and confess Jesus as their Lord. At that point, God will save them and add their names to the **Lamb's** (Jesus, slain to pay the penalty due for their sins) **Lamb's Book of Life**. Jesus will preach in the Third Earth Age,

'The work of God is this: to believe in the One (Jesus, Messiah, Savior) He (Father God) has sent.'[28]

You, 144,000, will give them the Bread of Heaven, the Son of God, the Savior of the World, crucified on a cross and raised from the dead. They, who repent and have faith to receive and accept the Good News that Jesus saves them, will become rich in faith toward God and will *'inherit the kingdom He promised those who love him.'*[29] At the end of Jacob's Trouble, after hearing and obeying your message, they will dance in the streets of Jerusalem celebrating Jesus, the Messiah, their Deliverer, Savior, and Lord.

---

[26] Revelation 20:11-15.
[28] John 6:29.
[29] James 2:5 NIV.

Men of Zion, you are wise and will not be silent. With each lost one on the surface of the Earth, who rejected taking the mark, being a descendant of Jacob, you will have some precious moments to build up their faith to repent and receive Jesus as the Messiah. The demons are right there ready to take them to Hell as they are close to death.

You might ask, 'Why did so many choose of their own free will to go to Hell?' Many chose not to believe that Jesus is the long-awaited Messiah and rejected Him and chose of their own 'free will,' not to seek first the Kingdom of God and His righteousness.[30]

They pursued first the wealth of this world, the honor of men, and the pleasures of sin for a season. One reaps what one sows whether he or she has sown snares or wheat. They did not choose to lay up for themselves treasures in Heaven for eternity.

Again, many were prideful and sought great earthly riches and honors for themselves and did not acknowledge or give thanks to God.

There are no riches in Hell. They are the poorest of the poor. They honored themselves seeking fame by declaring on the surface of the Earth, such things as, 'Look what I have done. My gold. My eloquent home. My beautiful wife. I'm a self-made man. I did it my way. I can be forgiven on my deathbed of a little lying, stealing, adultery, and worship of idols! I am a child of Abraham. God will forgive me. I murdered no one. Look at all this wealth I have laid up for myself. By my wits, I made myself rich. I did it my way! I have plenty of time to repent and clean up my act.'

In this First Earth Age, let us all remember to warn our brethren not to come to this dreadful place of Hell. You, 144,000, will testify that you have seen the horrors of Hell. You will preach that Jesus, the Son of God, will come to the Earth as a human being, being born of his mother, Mary, a descendant of King David from the tribe of Judah. Jesus is the Messiah, the Savior of the Word for all who will sincerely repent of their sins, make a U-turn away from sin, and confess, 'Jesus is my Savior and Lord!'

Now, as the smoke clears in Hell, look beyond your Israeli kinsmen.

First, see that naked group of handsome and muscular young men with no sex organs or lips still burning with lust one toward another. They are from the separated continent of Atlantis.

Next, see those beautiful young girls, now having sagging breasts like rags with no vaginas. Many of which practiced prostitution or were unfaithful to their husband on the continent of Atlantis. Now watch as the waves of fire go over their heads and hear them scream in their torment and misery. They were each presented the Gospel many times that Jesus, God's Son, is the Savior of the world, but they refused to receive Him as Savior, repent and turn away from their sins, and confess, 'Jesus is (my) Lord.' They chose the pleasures of sin for a season. Having been previously warned, they are reaping the wages due them for choosing sinful lives.

It is one thing to lose a man in Hell, but it is so tragic to lose a young girl or woman to Hell. Warn all, men and woman, rich and poor, young and old who have not received the mark of the beast, not to go to Hell. Teach the young women to keep themselves pure for their own husband and that the husband will meet their emotional needs and help them in their days of salvation. Any question?

Hearing none, let us end our overlook into the woes and horrors of Hell and permit you to return to your sleeping bodies.

---

[30] See Matthew 6:33.

Apollo Receives Word That the Diamond Mining Business Must Cease in Thirty Days Because of Failure to Obtain a Work Permit

Apollo receives a coded hmail (Hell mail) from the lead-lined war room reading,
"Master,
A trader turned us into King Atlas, who served Homo with a Show Cause Order that the diamond mining business must cease in thirty days because of failure to obtain a work permit. A forced shutdown will cause irreparable damages to our project. We await your orders.

Operation Black Room"

Apollo orders Mercury Speedo, "Hell, let us not risk a reply communication. Go down and discover the source of the leak and kill that traitor. Bribe King Atlas, and if this fails, kill him and put our man in as the King of Atlantis. The end will justify the means! I am in control. VISA!"†

†BOOK SIX – Episode 3†

[†**Sidebar Scriptures**: "*Joseph had a dream and promptly reported all the details* (Genesis 37:5)."
"*The Lord revealed to me what the evil ones were doing and planning and showed me their wicked plots* (Jeremiah 11:18)."
"The word of the Lord came to Abram in a **vision**. . . . A **deep sleep** came upon Abram . . . . (Genesis 15:1, 12)."
I witnessed and experienced "*dreams and visions, and I described **all** I had seen to instruct many* (Daniel 7:1, 11:33)."†]

Apollo Orders Assassination of King Atlas

Homo Uncovers Source of Leak Causing Show Cause Order to Issue

HOMO LINES UP two shifts, and on the third shift, he repeats his command,

"Step forward if you did not leak my diamond-mine information. The Licensing and Permit Division of the City of Atlantis under King Atlas's signature have cited us." [All stepped forward, including Benedict.]

"Now, I will be giving a six-day paid vacation and arrange dates with studs Poseidon, Zeus, and Hera[1] (three homosexuals) for anyone who will step forward and give me any information on who leaked this information."

Hermes steps forward proclaiming, "I accept this reward! I have always wanted a date with Zeus. Benedict mentioned in passing to me that he happened to run into a childhood acquaintance hunting right outside the hole leading into the mine. I believe his friend works for the Licensing and Permit Division. It must have been Benedict."

Homo demands, "Benedict, step forward and answer, 'Yes' or 'No!' Did you mention my diamond mine?"

Benedict, shaking like a leaf, steps forward, and replies, "Yes. My childhood acquaintance had shot an arrow, and it landed at the entrance of the hole to the mine. My dad did yard work for his mother, and I assisted. He asked me, 'What is in the hole?' I just couldn't think fast enough on my feet, so I said, 'Hopefully a diamond mine, but no diamonds has yet to be found.'"

Homo concludes, "Benedict, I just wanted to know if we ask you and all others not to reveal information, can all of you keep your mouths shut? Now all of you, including Benedict, get to work. This shift is not as productive as the other shifts."

As the laborers enter the mine, Homo's chief assistant, Gehen, stays behind shaking his head. Homo hands him a laser pen gun, which shoots the image of the pink three-headed dog, ordering him, "Six (6) minutes before the end of this shift say to Benedict, 'Someone carelessly left a wheelbarrow at the end of the shaft six (6), close to that deep ravine. Retrieve it and put it back where it belongs before you leave for the day. Follow him from afar, and when he grabs the handles, shoot him in the back of the head with this, and kick his dying body down into the deep ravine." Gehen replies, "No problem! Dead men tell no tales![2]" VISTA!"

The next day it is reported to Homo, "Benedict did not show up for work today."

Homo replied, "I am not surprised. I guess now besides being a traitor he is also a deserter. Tell those on this shift to work a little harder as we have lost a shift member."

Six days later a few workers reported to Gehen, "We smelled a horrible odor coming up from the deep ravine at the end of shaft six (6).

---

[1] Poseidon, Zeus, and Hera are brothers of Hades, known in Greek mythology as the god of the underworld.

[2] *Dead Men Tell No Tales* - "Basically, what it means is that to keep something quiet, kill anyone who knows about it." *Urban Dictionary*.

We looked down, and at the bottom was Benedict's body where he apparently committed suicide. Do you want us to lower a rope and try to get his body out?"

Gehen, replied, "No! Take six (6) large wheel barrels of red pay dirt and dump it down the ravine to cover up his corpse before he stinks up the entire mine. No more committing suicide as all of you are needed in the kingdom of darkness."

Apollyon Lucifer Gives the Order to Assassinate King Atlas

Apollo had summoned Homo and Gehen to meet him at the entrance of the mine with Apollo saying,

"Homo, I received your confidential memo. It is good riddance regarding that traitor Benedict! That is history, but what to do about being served with King Atlas's show-cause order? Homo, you will have to answer it now within six (6) days, or King Atlas will order his police to come after you like a crow on a roach bug. Does Atlas have any weaknesses?"

Homo replied, "King Atlas has been seeking to win his son's monthly Saturday night jackpot for some time at the Wheel of Fortune Gambling House. He has come close several times, and he has a large following of spectators cheering him on to win. That is the only weakness I know, and I am not sure that is a weakness. If he wins, he will be the richest man on the island as the jackpot has been building for six (6) years. Also, King Atlas protects his firstborn son at all times at any cost. However, if anything were to happen to King Atlas, his son Atlas II probably would be king, inheriting all of King Atlas's great wealth. 'Atlas II' is one of us."

Apollo inquires, "Tell me about his son's weaknesses?"

"He likes young boys. He has a Freedom Bath House and dark private rooms in the rear of his gambling casino for homosexuals to meet and have multiple sex encounters. One reported to me that he had six (6) homosexual encounters in one night in the Atlas dark back room. Atlas II brags that his sex clubs are making him a fortune. He jokes that he receives the 'slopped-over ecstasy' of having access to all the young boys of his choosing. He has instructors teaching the very young males on how best to have homosexual sex. The house fees for each activity goes to Atlas II. The young homosexuals and the young female prostitutes may keep two-thirds of the tips.

It is reported that King Atlas has just received a complaint. It involved one of his officials recently contracting AIDS in the back room of his son's business. He infected his wife, who is a friend of Atlas's wife. A good riddance as I didn't care for that government official."

Apollo smirking, "Homo, thank you for that briefing. Could you get in that gambling game?"

Homo replies, "No, I am banned from the entire City of Atlantis, but young Gehen probably could approach Atlas II and possibly get into the game if we gave him a large bag of money. Gehen knows how to rig the Wheel of Fortune so Atlas would win the jackpot if that would help. I will threaten Gehen with certain death if he betrays us seeking the money for himself."

Apollyon Lucifer further smirking directs, "During the excitement of Atlas's winning the jackpot, Gehen can secretly aim the pink three-headed dog, Cerberus,[3] *via* the laser gun pen at Atlas's heart. King Atlas will appear to have died of a heart attack from the excitement of winning. Let Gehen donate six boxes of our best cigars for the big game to make the room smoky, so people will not see the pen gun. Proceed! VISA!"

Gehen bows, "Master, I like this diabolical plan. I will implement it! King Atlas will be removed from the scene, and his son made King. Then the fun sex parties would begin. The spreading of sexual immorality should result in you winning the whole earth to worship you. No one is strong enough to resist sexually pleasurable temptations. I would like to sit at your right hand in the kingdom of darkness if I pull this off. VISA!"

Atlas's Wife Warns Her Husband Not to Go Gamble

Atlas's wife approaches her husband, "Darling, I suffered terrible things in a dream last evening regarding your going to our son's gambling casino. I know you look forward to this event on the last Saturday of each month and that all eyes will be on you this night for you to spend the wheel of fortune. For our love's sake could you just skip it this one evening?"

Atlas's face turns red as he scolds, "Skip it! That is our son's place. I stand a good chance to make a fortune. Do you want the house remodeled? You can have a new wardrobe. What about that new patio furniture?"

Atlas's wife hangs her head and respectfully responds, "Darling, our obeying and pleasing God is the most important thing, not your gambling in our son's evil place of business. I desire you to be safe! I rather have a live and healthy husband than wealth untold. I am contented and thankful for the things we have. One of my friends confided in me that her husband now has AIDS, and he has bleeding sores on his body. He contracted AIDS at our son's gambling casino. Also, she reported that their eighteen-year-old son went into one of the Freedom Bath Houses and had been bleeding in the anus. He may have to have corrective surgery. I recently observed our sixteen-year-old daughter kiss him, but I forbade her from seeing him again until I could talk to you because he might have been exposed to AIDS. AIDS is transmitted through both blood and saliva.

Atlas, I love you next to God more than anything in the world. We are in this world, but we are not of this world. We are ambassadors for our Savior, the Son of God. The only thing necessary for this evil to continue in Atlantis is for you, darling, to do nothing!

Atlas, you going this evening somewhat will demonstrate you endorse all this evil. If it were anyone else other than your son, you would have stopped it. You should not participate in such works of darkness. I do not have peace about your going. Please, my darling, you are the one I love more than my own life. For love's sake, please don't go!"

"I'm going! There is nothing wrong with gambling! I have a chance to win a fortune. I could be the richest man in Atlantis. I have a plan to win. Do not mention it again! Understand?"

The Father God Asks the Son, "What is Wrong with Gambling?"

The Father God request, 'My wise Son for the archives briefly teach further, 'What is wrong with gambling?'" The Son respectfully responds,

'*You shall covet nothing that belongs to your neighbor.*'[4]

I will teach during the Third Earth Age,

'*Be on your guard against all kinds of greed; a man's life does not consist in the abundance of his possessions.*'[5]

---

[4] Exodus 20:17 NIV.
[5] Luke 12:15 NIV.

"Father, gambling is institutionalized covetousness of a neighbor's money as they are looking for something for nothing. When one throws the dice, play the cards, or spins the wheel, he or she is obsessed by, 'Get rich quick!' Atlas has been craving and coveting that Saturday night jackpot on the Wheel of Fortune for many years. It is an obsession with him. He has become an idolater in this one area of his life, as greed is idolatry, as it will be written,

'*Put to death, therefore, whatever belongs to your earthly nature: sexual immorality, impurity, lust, evil desires, and greed, which is idolatry.*'[6]

Gambling is like the rotten underside of a log laying out in the forest. Turn it over and one will find it is infected with termites and has become a home to many strange looking creatures who like to eat rotten wood. Many young people come out to watch Atlas gamble. He is to them a hero, and if Atlas condones gambling, it must be okay – the things in the back room must be acceptable. King Atlas is now a compulsive gambler, and he has gambled away most of his great wealth. He is coveting to win all he has lost back and more this Saturday night.

One of Atlas's relatives is addicted to gambling. He would gamble on his wife's coffin if the opportunity arose. Another of his addictive gambling cohorts stole off his mother's finger her diamond engagement ring while she lay sick in bed in a coma. He pawned her engagement ring for $666, which he quickly gambled away. When he returned bankrupt to her bedside, he found his mother dead holding her empty left ring finger in her right hand with tears in her eyes. That was the first time the engagement ring had ever been off her finger since her late husband asked her to marry him, and she treasured it so much.

Gamblers Look for Corrupted Excitement

Besides covetousness, Atlas, as do many, also gambles for excitement. He says the excitement of gambling makes his blood rush, makes him feel alive, and makes him the center of attention. He says he likes to do it his way (not God's way) and enjoys being at center stage. King Atlas enjoys placing a large sum of money on the table and bluff his opponent with a confident-looking face.

Father, these are just the tip of the iceberg of what is wrong with gambling."

The Father affirms, "Amen! My Son, this Saturday evening King Atlas will appear on the surface to have won. Let Us observe what happens on the screen.

Atlas Arrives at the Wheel of Fortune Gambling Casino

King Atlas proudly walks into his son's gambling casino wearing his kingly (royal) garments, signet ring, and a crown. All eyes are on him as he sits down at his usual number 6 gambling table right next to the huge flashing multicolored Wheel of Fortune. A scantily dressed beautiful young girl with black shadow under her eyes and bright pink lipstick brings him the usual house donation of a jug of white wine. Another scantily dressed beautiful girl with green eye shadow and green lipstick sets down on table six (6) a wooden box of cigars and a candle for lighting them. The girl flirting, says, "Great king, you look like a dog at a new gate. We have these for sale when you leave – only $6 a box. Smoking cigars are the raging new fad. All the gamblers in the know – smoke these! With each puff, you will sense your mind becoming clearer and clearer. Now light up one of these, lean back in your leather chair, and enjoy smoking with the big boys. What do you have to lose? They are free, on the house. They take a little getting used to, but once you catch on, smoking will be a fun habit."

All eyes focus upon Atlas as he lights up a long black cigar sweetened with sugar. Atlas leans back and takes a big draw. His face turns white with his fainting and falling out of the chair as many laugh at and make fun of him.

Atlas mashes out the cigar in an ashtray and demands, "Take these cigars out of my site as I am here only for the gold. I'll have the last laugh this evening."

---

[6] Colossians 3:5 NIV.

After some six (6) hours, the gambling competition is *narrowed* down between King Atlas and Gehen.

King Atlas Appears Successfully to Bluff in the Final Show Down

King Atlas has been dealt two black aces, two black eights, and a red six. Gehen has been dealt three sixes and two jacks. The betting begins with the stakes growing higher and higher. Finally, with Atlas laughing, with his usual poker face, he bets almost his entire remaining assets.

Gehen looking at Atlas' poker face folds saying, "The stakes are too rich for me. Atlas, you win! Let me see what you have."

King Atlas laughs, "No, you fool! You would have had to call my hand to see my cards. When the going gets too rough for others, it is just right for me! Let me see your cards."

Gehen turns over the three six's (666) and two Jacks saying, "You had this beat. Right?" Atlas, laughs with a straight face and lies, "Right! I'm ready to go for the grand prize."

Atlas Spinning the Wheel of Fortune

Atlas, sticking his cards in his shirt pocket, sticks out his chest, pulls back his head and looks around at the vast audience made up of many beautiful young girls and handsome young men. Atlas stands with a proud look of anticipation.

'Atlas II,' dressed in skin-tight black leotards and smoking a cigar, announces, "My father, you have won the opportunity to take one spin on the Wheel of Fortune, which no one has won now for the past six (6) years, six (6) months, and six (6) day – 666 may be your lucky number. The money for so long has been building."

With all eyes on King Atlas, he calculates just how much to spin the Wheel of Fortune for the clicking tab to land on the black letters JACKPOT. King Atlas makes a calculated spin of the wheel. The clicker is now slowing moving toward the slot JACKPOT with the audience yelling and screaming. Gehen pushes a button activating a magnet on the wheel behind the word JACKPOT. As the rigged clicker-tab ends in the JACKPOT slot, the room goes wild. King Atlas, acting like a teenager who had just gained the whole world jumps up and down, hugging and kissing several of the beautiful young girls and shaking hands with a few of the handsome young men. The grand-prize sign flashes green – $6,666,666.66 – with a cover opening revealing the actual cash.

King Atlas brags, "Someone bring me a large wheelbarrow. I never dreamed I would see this much money in my lifetime. I would like to dump this at mamas' feet and rub it in by proclaiming, 'I told you so! You were wrong. I was in the right place at the right time.' Now, King Atlas, '*Take life easy; eat, drink and be merry.*'[7] I officially announce that my gambling days are over. I will not be back.

Eventually, somebody had to obtain all this wealth. It might as well be me. I assure you there will be changes around here as long as I am King."

Gehen through all the smoke and excitement carefully aims the laser pen gun placing the image of the pink three-headed dog, Cerberus, directly over Atlas' heart.

---

[7] Luke 12:19 NIV.

He pushes the laser button going through the two black aces, two black eights,[8] and a red six. King Atlas quickly grabs his heart as if he is having a heart attack as the pink three-headed dog rests on the back of his right hand.

King Atlas's Dying Prayer and Declaration

King Atlas, knowing he is dying, lays himself down on gambling table 6. His head and shoulders are propped up on a cushion. Someone shouts, "An ambulance has been called!"

King Atlas sees his life passing before him and looks over at all the money and in faith prays, "Father in Heaven, I see the errors of my ways. I sincerely with tears repent upon this deathbed gambling table of all my covetousness, impurities, lust, evil desires, and prideful greed, all of which I see now as idolatry. *'Have mercy on me, O God, according to your unfailing love; according to your great compassion blot out my transgressions. Wash away (in the Blood of Jesus) all my iniquity (sin).'*[9] Jesus, Your Son, is my Savior. He will pay the penalty in full for all my sins when nailed to a cross. Cleanse me under the future shed Blood of Your Son, Jesus. Before I die, *'wash me, and I will be whiter than snow.'*[10] Blot out from your remembrance all my sins. *'Create in me a clean heart, O God.'*[11] *'Restore to me (for I sincerely repent) the joy of Your salvation.'*[12]

If You would please be so kind as to keep me alive just a little longer on this gambling-death bed, then I will teach transgressors Your gracious free gift of salvation. *'Against You, You only, have I sinned and done what is evil in Your sight.'*[13] I repent and am so sorry I have set such a bad example to these beautiful young girls and handsome young men standing around me. It is better that a millstone be tied around one's neck and be cast into the sea than to cause one of these little ones who believe in Your Son, as Savior, to fall away.[14] I plead the future shed blood of Your Son, Jesus, and ask for mercy and grace (unmerited favor). Let me hear Your voice from Heaven. Forgive me! Open my lips with an evangelism anointing before I die. In Your Son Jesus' name. Amen! Shalom! "

A voice from Heaven sounding like thunder decrees, "FORGIVEN!"

Atlas, with grateful tears in his eyes, gasping for every breath of air, further hindered by the cigar smoke filling the room, whispers, "Thank You, Father, for not letting me die in my sins. I see the two Angels that have come for me."

Atlas speaks directly to the Angels, "You and death will have to wait until I preach the truth to these little ones."

---

[8] On August 2, 1876, James Butler "Wild Bill' Hickok (1837-1876) was playing poker at a saloon in the Black Hills of the Dakotas. As he played, a man by the name of "Crooked Nose" Jack McCall slipped up behind him and shot him in the back of the head. Like butter in a hot skillet, Hickok slid to the floor and died with his cards still in his hands. It was reported that the cards held in his hand included two black aces and two black eights. This combination of cards has generally come to be called 'the dead man's hand.' Hickok was warned and warned that he should receive Jesus as Savior and confess Him as Lord. He mocked and rejected such a great offer of salvation. He had no idea he was playing his last hand in the game of life.

[9] Psalm 51:1-3.

[10] Psalm 51:7.

[11] Psalm 51:10.

[12] Psalm 51:12.

[13] Psalm 51:4 NIV.

[14] Matthew 18:6.

King Atlas's face growing whiter and whiter in a low voice preaches, "Little ones of Atlantis be sorry for your sins, repent, and make a U-turn away from them and receive God's Son as your Savior. No one can come to the Father, God except through His Son Jesus.[15] The Son will shed His life's blood to pay the penalty fully for all your sins. Now raise your hands if you desire of your own free will to accept Jesus, God's Son, as Your Savior, sincerely repent and make a U-turn away from your sins. Do not be ashamed to confess that Jesus is your Savior and then confess Him as your Lord so you can have eternal life in the Kingdom of Heaven and avoid a horrible place of punishment called Hell."

Every hand was raised, except Atlas II and Ghent, so that in his death King Atlas saved (destroyed more evil) as he was dying *"than while he lived."*[16]

Now those who have raised your hands, confess out loud so you can hear yourself speak while I pause after every sentence,

Dear Father God in Heaven, I come, to You in the mighty and holy Name of Jesus. I believe with all my heart that Jesus is Your Son. I renounce sin and the past. I repent and turn away from evil. I accept Your Son's future dying on the cross as full payment for my sins.

I receive Jesus into my heart as my Savior. I confess that Jesus is my Lord. From this moment forward, I belong to Jesus. I will follow Him the rest of my life. I will not be ashamed of Jesus. I will confess Him before men. Jesus, take all of me. I believe right now that all my sins are forgiven. Thank You, Heavenly Father, for giving Your Son for me. I will not perish, but I will enjoy the free gift of Your abundant, eternal life. I clothe myself in purity with the Lord Jesus Christ. I decree, 'I've just been saved! Holy Spirit come into my heart and truly make me born again. Daily show me the paths of life. I will serve You as long as there is the breath of life in me. My name remains in the Lamb's Book of Life. It is so good to be saved! In Jesus' Name! Amen! (So be it.).

Now my beloved brothers and sisters in the Lord '*by the mercies of God, present your bodies (moment by moment) as a living sacrifice, holy and acceptable to God, which is your spiritual worship.*'[17] My precious brothers and sisters, now repeat this clause by clause after me,

"I, as a born again Christian (little Christ), cast off from me the things that belong to the deeds and works of darkness.[18] "*Now is the time of God's favor; now is the day of salvation.*'[19] I will conduct myself honorably, becomingly, properly, and decently like the saved person I am. I am forgiven of all sins! I am as pure and white as the driven snow. My past sins have been cast into the deepest part of the sea[20] and will be remembered no more. No more sexual sins of any kind or wild living. No carousing, drunkenness, immorality, sensuality, licentiousness, quarreling, gambling, or doing anything unseemly. I now clothe myself with the Lord Jesus Christ, and I will put Him on every morning. I heed the warning to make no provision for indulging my flesh or to think about ways to gratify my sinful and lustful desires.[21] When others see me, they will see a little Jesus Christ, the Son of God. I will not turn back. I am determined to follow Jesus. I will! '*I can do all things through Christ, who strengthens me.*'[22] I will hear those words: "*Well done, good and faithful servant!*'[23]

I charge you my brothers and sisters in Jesus Christ to live by these rules:

(1)   Avoid by flight, idolatry[24] (putting or worshipping anything in place of God).
(2)   Shun youthful impure and carnal lust,[25] which cast discredit on Jesus Christ.

---

[15] John 14:6.

[16] In Judges 16:30 this was also said of Samson.

[17] Romans 12:1 NKJV.

[18] Romans 13:12.

[19] 2 Corinthians 6:2.

[20] Micah 7:19.

[21] Foundationally, see Romans 13:12-14 in The Amplified Bible (AMP) and in The Expanded Bible (EXB).

[22] Philippians 4:13 NKJV/

[23] Matthew 25:21 NIV.

[24] See 1 Corinthians 10:14.

[25] See 2 Timothy 2:22.

(3) Do not be high-minded (arrogant; proud)[26] nor trust in uncertain riches, but trust and depend on the living God, who will give grace and mercy to the humble and all things to enjoy.

(4) Flee all sexual immorality![27] This is the big one! God made the marriage bed to meet this need. Some will argue, 'I cannot find a wife. I cannot find a husband.' Trust God for a marriage partner for you!

Seek living first for God, and all these things, including a Christian mate, will be given to you.[28] Remember, it is a sin against his or her own body if one sins sexually. Death and accidents are always near for mortals. One may or may not be able to repent. Is it worth a few moments of pleasure to commit adultery? One might contract AIDS with the body and mind, commencing to waists away. Meditate on and obey these Scriptures,

'*Do you not know that your bodies are members of Christ? Shall I then take the members of Christ and unite them with a prostitute? Never! Do you not know that he who unites himself with a prostitute is one with her in body? For it is said, 'The two will become one flesh.'[29] But he who unites himself with the Lord is one with Him in spirit.*

Flee from sexual immorality. All other sins a man commits are outside his body, but he who sins sexually sins against his own body. Do you not know that your body is a temple of the Holy Spirit, who is in you, whom you have received from God? You are not your own; you were bought at a price. Therefore, honor God with your body.'[30]

(5) In view of God's mercy, of saving you today, present as a gift to God your bodies with all its members and faculties as '*living sacrifices, holy and pleasing to God, which is your spiritual worship.*'[31] Now honor God with a pure body.[32] You can do it! All surrounding me who will make a vow to God for sexual purity put your right hand over your heart and say as I pause after each sentence,

'May it please You, Father God, in the Name of Your Son, Jesus, my Savior; I vow sexual purity in my heart, mind, and body. You know that my spirit is willing, but my flesh is weak. Always show me a way of escape from sexual temptation. With Your help, I can be consistently pure. I can do all things through Your Son, Jesus Christ, who strengthens me. I will! I am determined! I will serve and obey You God with the remainder of my life. I here and now make a quality decision to be pure in my thoughts. No turning back. I vow with all I have and ever hope to be that I will live, with your help, a life of purity. Give me the gift of singleness or give me a warm, loving, devoted, and faithful Christian mate. '*If in my own strength alone I confide, my striving would be losing.*'[33]

The Spirit of Your Son in me must win the battle. I will stick like being glued to Jesus Christ, my Savior, and keep my pure eyes on Him. I will not allow sexual sins to pull me away from Jesus Christ for the sexual impure will not inherit the Kingdom of Heaven.

I am determined to hear, '*Well done, thou good and faithful servant.*'[34] I receive Your forgiveness. In Jesus' Name. I vow. Amen! Atlas, smiling as death, closes in, whispers, "In a few moments, I will die, and my Earth Suit or body will breathe no more. Two Angels are here to escort my eternal spirit to Paradise.

You are my sisters and my brothers, and you can do it! Daily and moment-by-moment present your bodies to God. Wear a bow to remind yourselves that your bodies are your present or gift to God. I've just been told that 777 of you just made this vow of purity. In Paradise, I will prepare 777 silk white bow ties to give each of you when you join me in Paradise.

Then annually on this day of the month, we will celebrate this special day of salvation here in Atlantis called the Day of Purity,[35] when the Holy Spirit helped you be born again and washed clean of your past sins in the Blood of the Lamb, Jesus, the Son of God.

My last act as King of Atlantis is to designate you the brave 777 as the charter citizens of the newly-incorporated City of Loveland, surrounding the Great Pyramid. I see here the young attorney, Job, who recently inherited so much of that land in that area with his legal pad. Job, I am sure my wife sent you here this evening, for just such a time as this.

---

[26] See 1 Timothy 6:17.

[27] 1 Corinthians 6:18.

[28] See Matthew 6:33.

[29] See Genesis. 2:24.

[30] 1 Corinthians 6:15-19 NIV.

[31] Romans 12:1.

[32] See 1 Corinthians 6:18-20.

[33] See stanza 2 of *A Mighty Fortress Is Our God* by Martin Luther.

[34] Matthew 25:23 NIV.

[35] See a later celebration of the days of Purim in Esther 9:3-32.

Now, each of you 777, give Attorney Job your name and address and let me write out with my own handwriting on your legal pad – '*I give the Great Pyramid I and the surrounding land I own to the Church in Loveland, Inc., a non-profit tax-exempt church,* **in the City of Loveland, Atlantis**. Atlas, King of Atlantis.' I will pray for each of you to finish your race with purity and enjoy the free gift of eternal life forever and forever. Amen!"

King Atlas Admonishes His Son to Repent

Now, as the Angels come for Atlas' spirit, Atlas looks over to his son, Atlas II, who is standing with his right hand greedily on the $6,666,666,66 smoking a cigar. He has a proud look thinking, "*Under Atlantis law I am going to inherit half of this with mother and all of it when she dies, which may be soon. I have great riches!*"

King Atlas demands, "Son, remove your right hand from off the top of my money. As long as I am breathing, it is legally my money, and I can do with it as I choose. Tainted money be thou removed and be cast into the deepest part of the sea, with the sins of all those who have received Jesus, the Son of God, as Savior and confessed Him as Lord. "[36]

The money disappears with Atlas II's scorning, "Dad, you did not have to do that. Mother needed some of that money. Part of that money could have also helped even the poor outcasts of this city on the backside of the black mountain."

Atlas, growing weaker and weaker, whispers to his son, "You are my firstborn, but because you have chosen of your own free will the ways of wickedness and the pleasures of sin for a season, turbulent waters are before you. You are not to be king. It is all set out in my 'Will!' You must repent of your sins, make a U-turn away from them, and give them up. Your precious Christian wife, who still loves you and whom you divorced, if you will remarry her, will help you and give you a son as an heir, the grandson I have wanted. God designed your wife's vagina in marriage to receive and properly handle your released sperm, filled with all kinds of toxic substances, which needs to be joyfully released from your body, giving you healthy manly sexual relief.

Sodomy between two males ejaculating sperm into each other's mouth or anus, not designed to receive male sperm, never produced an heir and never will. Such unnatural perversion will significantly shorten life span, with Hell waiting at death. Son, your mother is ministering to other women whose son or husband is bleeding and infected in the anus, and to others suffering from contracting diseases of AIDS, hepatitis, gonorrhea, syphilis and the like.

Homosexuality is a perverted sin and without repentance, a homosexual, according to God's law in Scriptures[37] cannot go to Paradise or Heaven when he or she dies.

How can you replenish Atlantis with men in the back sodomizing other men or boys? The only thing your Freedom Baths spread is AIDS and early death.

Even your cleaning crews hired to wipe up the spilled semen in your back room are in great fear of AIDS as they wear rubber gloves, boots, and breathing masks. It will not even be remembered you were born, or this great civilization of Atlantis ever existed if you do not repent. Repent or perish in Hell! It is your free will, which you will have to exercise. Eternity is at stake!

My son, choose sincere repentance and accept the Son of God as your Savior so you may have everlasting life! The choice is yours. Blessing or cursing? Life or death?

---

[36] Micah 7:19.
[37] See Genesis 19:1-3; Leviticus 18:22; 20:13; Romans 1:26-27; 1 Corinthians 6:9; Revelations 21:8.

I have warned you before, and I warn you sternly now to choose life! Your blood is not on my hands! Repent and turn away from your sins before it is too late. It is to be written,

'I have set before you life and death . . . . Therefore, (you now) choose life, that you may live.'[38]

'For the wages of sin is death, but the gift of God is eternal life in (or through receiving the Blood sacrifice of) Christ Jesus our Lord.'[39]

Son, one day you will answer to the Son of God in judgment for the way you lived your life. It is not too late to live the rest of your life, bringing honor and glory to God. Today God has spoken to you through me. Do not harden your heart.[40]" Repent, for God and your mother and I truly love you!

"Dad, you didn't have to destroy all the money. I will wait as you and have death-bed repentance. Let me have a little more pleasure now while I am young. All you say sounds like a myth, which may or may not be true. No one has ever seen Father God or heard of Paradise. You are asking me to believe by faith. I do not know whether God is real. There is another on this island who says he is the creator. He talks about evolution. The pleasures of sexual sins are real. You just prohibited all those people from having any sexual fun. Your time on Earth is over

King Atlas with tears rolling down his cheek turns his face away from his son to those who were just born again. King Atlas concludes, "I will see you, my brothers and sisters, soon in Paradise. The Son of God, Jesus, has just saved you! You are people of faith and daily repentance. It was God's good pleasure to save you. By His mercy and grace, you have received His free gift of eternal life. Shalom!

I will have you all a white silk bow tie when you arrive in Paradise. Remember, when tempted, God will give you a way of escape! Daily repent and God *'will forgive your sins and continually cleanse . . . you from all unrighteousness – everything not in conformity to His will in purpose, thought, and action.'*[41] When the escape door blows open, you are to run through the narrow gate and never look back. Have nothing to do with the deeds of darkness! May each of you be blessed in a warm Cristian marriage! Now get out of this den of iniquity and never return. Don't walk – Run!"

Atlas turns to the Angels saying, "I am ready. My life's work in Atlantis is finished! *'Father, into your hands I commit my spirit.'*[42] When Atlas had said this, he breathed his last. All the doors of the gambling casino blow open and off their hinges by a mighty wind from Heaven. All 777 of the new converts run, escaping out the nearest exits. They never returned nor looked back on their old sinful lives. Not one of Atlas' deathbed converts was lost. All 777 served God faithfully and agreed to meet annually to celebrate the *Day of Purity*. They enjoyed an abundant and full life and looked forward to celebrating their salvation and deliverance with Atlas later in Paradise.

Atlas Escorted to Paradise

Gabriel and Michael take Atlas' eternal spirit by each arm and rise going up through the ceiling as Atlas looks down at his dead body.

---

[38] Deuteronomy 30:19.
[39] Romans 6:23.
[40] Psalm 95:8; Hebrews 3:8.
[41] 1 John 1:9 AMP.
[42] Luke 23:45 NIV.

The three turn toward the Great Pyramid at the North end of the Island of Atlantis. When they arrived, they passed right through the all-seeing eye capstone and descend into the heart of the Earth. The bottom was right over the hot fires of Hell with Atlas feeling the intense heat from the flames and its great torment.

Atlas thought, "*I came close to being a castaway; and, thus, I barely escaped these flames myself. Thank You, Lord, they did not have to drop me here in Hell. My son, Atlas II, I warned you! Your blood and destiny in this horrible place are not on my hands. Repent or perish in Hell.*"

After passing over a wide, deep, chasm, they came into beautiful Paradise, and the Angels set Atlas down in the eloquently landscaped courtyard of his mansion.

Gabriel comforted Atlas by saying, "This is your temporary abode, which you will be soon sharing with your wife. No working sexual organs for you two in Paradise! However, she loves you so much that she has asked to live with you throughout eternity. Her request is granted as love never fails. You two were faithful to each other. She has laid up many eternal treasures in her gracious Christian life on Earth. She tried to warn you, but you did not listen to your help-mate. Right now, your wife Safari is hearing about your death-bed repentance and the winning of more souls in your preaching for the Kingdom of God in your death than you did in all the rest of your life on Earth. Also, right now she is sending you a message that we will convey, '*Well done, my darling in winning all those souls for Jesus! Now forgive yourself! I will give you as your helpmate, my love and devotion throughout eternity. I stand by and love my precious man of God. We will kiss and hug soon as we are one in the Lord Jesus. Our love will never fail!*' Atlas, your wife, will shortly join you. Keep the mansion neat!" [Laughter]

Atlas inquired, "How close at the end of my life did I come to being a castaway in Hell?"

This time, Michael answers, "The beloved Apostle Paul was ever mindful not to fall away at the end of his life as he will write,

'*But I discipline my body and keep it under control, lest after preaching to others, I myself should be disqualified (making me a castaway in Hell).*'[43]

Gabriel continues, "Atlas, I guess you know you barely escaped Hell by the mercy and grace of God as He kept you alive long enough to repent and to be restored to right fellowship. So many people will come to the end of their lives hoping for deathbed repentance. Very few will find it! All people who live wicked lives will be dropped down that Abyss into the flames of Hell. It is to be written,

'*For no one can lay any foundation other than the one already laid, which is Jesus Christ. If any man builds on this foundation using gold, silver, costly stones, wood, hay or straw, his work will be shown for what it is, because the day will bring it to light.*

It will be revealed with fire, and the fire will test the quality of each man's work. If what he has built survives, he will receive his reward. If it is burned up, he will suffer loss; he himself will be saved, but only as one escaping through the flames.'[44]

"Atlas, for your information, Gehen shot you in the heart with a laser pen gun because you served that show-cause order on Homo regarding that diamond mine. That mine is a fraud as they are mining ore focusing on making a freeze bomb with the goal to destroy the Father, Son, and Holy Spirit.

The song leader of Heaven is in pride exalting himself and desiring to be worshipped according to his diabolical plan. Of course, it will not succeed, but he is going to convince one-third of the angels[45] to join him and choose that he is the one to be worshiped, not God.

---

[43] 1 Corinthians 9:27 (ESV, KJV).
[44] 1 Corinthians 3:11-15 NIV.
[45] Hebrews 12:22; Revelation 12:3-9.

Now, because you did not properly deal with your wicked son, many in Atlantis will reject holiness and give themselves over '*to the pleasures of sin for a season.*'[46] Those who die in their sins will be dumped like garbage into the fires of Hell."

Changing the tone Gabriel instructs, "Atlas, now come and let us show you your study. You see that you have a Greek library with a dictionary, pens, and paper. You might write about the history of Atlantis and the goodness and mercy shown you by God. Later the Egyptians will pick up some evidence of Atlantis, including a drawing, sealed in a bottle, of the Great Pyramid. They will later copy and build a replica at great toil and expense floating the huge stones down the Nile. Also, from the sealed bottle messages cast from Atlantis into the sea, the Egyptians will mention Atlantis in their hieroglyphic writing. One man by the name of Plato will discover some of these truths from these ancient Egyptian writings. Plato will write about Atlantis in two of his works named *Timaeus* and *Critas*, written around 360 B.C., both containing references to the island of Atlantis, which he described in the fullest and truest sense as a continent.[47] The North end of this continent with the Great Pyramid will sink through the floor of the sea and will become part of Paradise for those who have accepted Jesus as Savior to enjoy. The Southern portion containing those who reject such a great salvation will sink through the floor of the sea and will become part of flaming Hell. You can walk south until you come to the deep and wide chasm, and you can look over into horrible Hell. You will see someone you know. It is Benedict, who will pull himself up on that table rock seeking to escape the intense heat of the flames for a few moments. You two at times can speak over the chasm. He sealed his lot for eternity and had you not repented and died in your sins you would be right there with him. Atlas inquired, "Am I likewise going to be in charge here in Paradise?"

Gabriel explained, "No! Abraham will be in charge here." Atlas asked, "Who is Abraham?"

Michael responded, "He is a creative being just like you. Abraham was chosen, in contrast to you, because God knew that he would '*direct his children and his household after him to keep the way of the Lord by doing what is right and just.*'[48] Abraham properly taught and set a good example for his son Isaac. In the Third Earth Age, Abraham's nephew Lot invites Isaac in a letter to take college courses 'in the sensual, carnal, and prosperous city of Sodom.' Lot promised to bring Isaac into the high upper class and to introduce him to some of the most beautiful socialites in the world. Lot had in mind, with his wife, to entice Isaac to marry one of his two beautiful daughters to keep all that money in the family. Had Abraham given in to this pressure, Isaac would have married one of Lot's daughters.

Their son in the chemistry classes of Sodom would have been taught the intrigue and social prestige of making love to a man rather than a wife. Ugh! Both Isaac and his son Jacob are to be great grandparents for the Messiah, the Son of God, to be born a human being in the Third Earth Age of a pure and holy virgin. Jacob's name will be changed to Israel. Of Jacob's sons, we will have 144,000 evangelists to preach, as you did today, winning a vast multitude in the closing moments of the Third Earth Age. King Atlas, the 144,000 are being trained in another large land mass in a place called Israel. God had to separate them from those like your son, who would try to corrupt them. That is the reason we had to isolate you on the Island of Atlantis.

Atlas, you are to honor and assist Abraham, Isaac, and Jacob, whose name is also Israel. They will shortly come to Paradise as the Earth is about to be destroyed by a freeze bomb creating the ice age. Here are two passages of Scripture to be written about Israel,

'*The eternal God is your refuge,*
And underneath are the everlasting arms.
He will drive out your enemy before you,
     Saying, 'Destroy him!'
So Israel will live in safety alone;
     Jacob's spring is secure
in a land of grain and new wine,
     Where the heavens drop dew.
Blessed are you, O Israel!
     Who is like you,
     a people saved by the Lord?
He is your shield and helper
     and your glorious sword.

---

[46] See Hebrews 11:25.
[47] See *Timaeus* 24- 25, R. G. Bury translation (Loeb Classical Library).
[48] Genesis 18:19 NIV.

Your enemies will cower before you,
and you will trample down their high places (of idolatry).' [49]
'You are My witnesses,' declares the Lord,
'and My servant whom I have chosen,
so you may know and believe Me
and understand that I am He.
Before Me, no god was formed,
nor will there be one after Me.
I, even I, am the Lord,
and apart from Me, there is no savior.
I have revealed and saved and proclaimed –
I, and not some foreign god among you.
You are My witnesses,' declares the Lord, 'that I am God.
Yes, and from ancient days I am He.
No one can deliver out of My hand . . . .' [50]

Gabriel concludes, "My advice for you Atlas is to write the history of Atlantis for the archives of Heaven. Acknowledge the Lord in all[51] your writing, and He will direct your pen. Atlas, you made it to Paradise. Rejoice! You will have important and delightful work to do throughout eternity.

For example, you will greet and show those from Atlantis, who have received the Son of God as Savior and confessed Him as Lord, their dwellings here in Abraham's Bosom. It is to be an exciting and abundant life here in Paradise. No one can come for salvation to Father God, except through His Son, Jesus. "[52]

Gabriel further inquired, "Any further questions? [A brief pause] Hearing none, we are being summoned to the Throne Room of God. You are greatly loved! Have fun in Paradise. Daily work on ***The Rise and Fall of Atlantis*** by Atlas. Let the adventure begin. Amen! Shalom!"

Atlas waves as the angels lift and head back over the chasm and rise to the top of the abyss. Atlas felt so honored and excited that he would be the first to enter Paradise. He thought to himself, *"I shall be a faithful and diligent assistant to Abraham. My darling wife will shortly join me. I am so thankful to my God that I escaped the fires of Hell. Now where is the writing paper?"*†

---

[49] Deuteronomy 33:26-29 NIV.
[50] Isaiah 43:10-13 NIV.
[51] See Proverbs3:5-6.
[52] See John 14:6.

†BOOK SIX – Episode 4†

[†**Sidebar Scriptures**: "*Joseph had a dream and promptly reported all the details* (Genesis 37:5)."
"*The Lord revealed to me what the evil ones were doing and planning and showed me their wicked plots* (Jeremiah 11:18)."
"The word of the Lord came to Abram in a **vision**. . . . A **deep sleep** came upon Abram . . . . (Genesis 15:1, 12)."
I witnessed and experienced "*dreams and visions, and I described **all** I had seen to instruct many* (Daniel 7:1, 11:33)."†]

Atlas II Seizes Royal Palace, and Apollo Gives Order to Assassinate Queen Safari

All Christians in Atlantis Mourn Death of King Atlas

SATURDAY EVENING THE *Atlantis Times* newspaper was awaiting the news on whether King Atlas had won the jackpot. They received a call from the Wheel of Fortune advising that King Atlas won. They shortly called back reporting that because of the excitement of winning King Atlas had a heart attack and had just died. The Sunday morning headline and article reads:

KING ATLAS DIES!

"Saturday night King Atlas died of a massive heart attack after winning a record jackpot of $6,666,666.66 at the Wheel of Fortune. He was 661 years old. He was the founding king of the Island of Atlantis after it divided out into the sea from the mainland. By royal decree, he later changed the name from the Island of Atlantis to simply Atlantis.

King Atlas leaves a wife, Queen Safari, and Son, Atlas II. A late evening call to the Royal Palace revealed that Queen Safari is taking his death hard.

King Atlas oversaw the very majestic *Temple of God* on the Citadel, in which he served as senior pastor. King Atlas also watched over the Great Pyramid at the North end of the island, which he dedicated to the glory of God the Father, God the Son, and God the Holy Spirit, which he preached, is one Triune God. King Atlas received the ten laws of Atlantis from God, known as the Ten Commandments, which he posted on the front of the Great Pyramid and throughout Atlantis. The citizens keeping these laws of the land have brought a feeling of tranquility and safety throughout the island of Atlantis.

Pastor Atlas preached that God's Son, Jesus, was to be later born a man in the Earth. He would be God manifested on the Earth in a physical body made up of flesh, bone, and blood. God's Son, Jesus, in the flesh, would be murdered in a later Earth age as an innocent man nailed to a cross as the Lamb of God slain before the foundation of the world to pay in full the penalty for sin for all who would receive Him as Savior. It is reported that as King Atlas lay dying last evening, he preached with his dying breath this same simple message of salvation that 'Jesus Saves' and some 777 accepted Jesus as Savior and confessed Jesus as Lord. There never has been such a revival of salvation in the history of Atlantis.

One saved young lady called our paper testifying, '*I feel that I have taken a bath from the inside out. I know I am a new creation. The old things have passed away. All things are new.*'[1] A young man affirmed, '*It is truly the joyful, abundant life to know you are saved and have eternal life. All my sins are remitted, just as if they never happened. Forgiven!*'

However, because of the death of its senior pastor, and to give the family a time of mourning, Atlas II announced that the Sunday service regularly held in the Temple is being canceled.

Instead of flowers, he suggests that donations could be given for a marble image of King Atlas to be placed at the entrance to the Citadel. A special graven image statue account has been established for donations at the Bank of Atlantis.

When our paper inquired about the burial plans, his son further indicated that his dad wanted a quick private family burial. Further inquiry revealed that Atlas II was taking charge of the funeral and that King Atlas would be buried Sunday, June 5, at sunrise in the Citadel near that tree King Atlas planted at my (Atlas II's) birth. 'Atlas II' announced that the burial would be private for the immediate family.

---

[1] See 2 Corinthians 5:17.

When he was asked if Queen Safari would now rule, Atlas II responded, 'My father had specifically instructed him privately that if anything happened to him, he wanted his only son to be king.'

King Atlas was a man of truth and integrity. His word was his bond. He was a humble man giving glory to God for everything accomplished. He would often say, '*Without God he could do nothing*,'[2] '*to whom much is given, much is required*;'[3] and I '*do all for the glory to God.*'[4]

King Atlas before his heart attack last evening had announced that he was through with gambling and that some changes would be made. In the past, those who made money out of keeping the sex drive, inflamed and perverted criticized King Alas, as being old fashion in his firm stand, 'Either marry, with complete faithfulness to your spouse or else entirely abstain from sexual relations.'

From the staff of the *Atlantis Times*, we salute the life and ministry of King Atlas. Our good King and Friend will be greatly missed!"

Atlas II Seizes the Royal Palace and King Atlas's Papers are Raked Through by Atlas II Seeking to Locate and Destroy the Estate's '*Will*'

After the private burial, Atlas II desperately searches all Sunday afternoon through all his dad's personal papers looking for the 'Will.' Atlas II reasons, "*Dad must not have gotten around to signing a 'Will' – just talking about it. I am king here. No use in delaying the inevitable! What an opportunity has fallen into my lap! I'll keep a watch on my mother and keep her under somewhat house arrest in the North wing. She probably will not live that much longer. I will not brief her in any affairs of state. A woman's place is in the hot kitchen not on a controlling throne. She is the queen of the kitchen only.*"

Atlas II takes out a full page add in the Atlantis Times announcing Monday, June 6, at 6:00 P.M., his "Inauguration Ceremony on the Citadel" concluding, "*All Atlantis is invited*!"

Directly in front of the closed *Temple of God* Atlas II quickly has built a reviewing stand on the central island called the Citadel, which is surrounded by three alternating canals and ring-shaped islands. Atlas II on the second ring of land turned from a two-lane walking prayer trail into a horse-racing track. He also converted one of the buildings on the second island to house the king's bodyguards and security.

Security is set at an all-time high for the inauguration, as King Atlas II commands his guards and security, "Watch out for the enemy, these so-called Christians as they will not be loyal to me! There will be no solicitation by the enemy trying to win others to their narrow way of thinking. If you see any passing out tracts or talking one on one, sternly warn them, '*No solicitation on the Citadel or the surrounding islands.*' Especially watch out for my mother as she thinks that Jesus is the answer to any problem! She will be dressed in black as she is mourning.

We will have free cigars, cigarettes, wine, and my world famous 'Black Jack Biscuits' stuffed with 'Blackstrap Molasses' made from the finest sugar cane. I prefer my security not eating or smoking as I desire you to focus on protecting me and controlling the crowd."

After Atlas II had fired Colossus as Treasurer of Atlantis and Titan as Secretary of State of Atlantis, Colossus and Titan met widow Safari outside the North Wing. The three walked to the front of the Temple of God and observed a large sign over the front door mandating, "*The Temple is Closed until Further Notice!*" Tears fall from the eyes of Queen Safari's as she sees that both the name 'Pastor King Atlas' and the service times have been removed from the temple building.

---

[2] See John 15:5.

[3] Luke 12:48.

[4] 1 Corinthians 10:31 NIV.

Titan spoke, "*'We cannot forsake'*[5] the assembling of ourselves for prayer and teaching on righteousness and purity. I will put out the word we will meet on the Lord's Day in the house churches. The 777 new Christians need to be especially pastured, ministered to, and shown attention."

Queen Safari and Colossus both said, "Amen!"

Looking around, they are confronted with several official looking signs mandating – "***No Religious Solicitation!***"

The widow Safari spoke, "Brethren, in looking for my husband's 'Will' I found these notes of my late husband collecting these warning proverbs,

'When the righteous triumph, there is great elation;
but when the wicked rise to power, men go into hiding.'[6]
'Like a roaring lion or a charging bear
is a wicked man ruling over a helpless people.'[7]
'A tyrannical ruler lacks judgment,
but he who hates ill-gotten gain will enjoy a long life.'[8]
'When the righteous thrive, the people rejoice;
when the wicked rule, the people groan.'[9]
'By justice, a king gives a country stability,
but one who is greedy for bribes tears it down.'[10]
'Whoever flatters his neighbor
is spreading a net for his feet.'[11]
'If a ruler listens to lies,
all his officials become wicked.'[12]

These were in a folder, which I thought would contain his Will!"

The entrance to the Temple of God becomes blocked with an inauguration platform, which could also be used for viewing the upcoming horse race. Safari sees a young girl dressed in the attire of a harlot seeking to solicit a trick. Safari goes over to her saying, "God's Son will die on the cross in your place to save you from your sins. Here is a little Christian publication showing how Jesus saves us from Hell, with an address to a nearby local house church. They can further explain the simple message of repentance, baptism, forgiveness, and salvation. I love you, and your soul is precious to the Lord."

A security guard dressed in black seeks to grab the little tract out of the harlot's hand with the prostitute stuffing it down between her bosoms. The security guard roughly pushes Safari backward, causing her to stumble and fall on the pavement. He orders her, "This is your one warning! If you give out any other Christian literature or talk with anyone else, you will be expelled from the Citadel. Can you not read the sign, '**No Soliciting**?' No exceptions! You are no longer Queen, and neither is Jesus, King here!"

---

[5] See Hebrews 10:25.
[6] Proverbs 28:12 NIV.
[7] Proverbs 28:15 NIV.
[8] Proverbs 28:16 NIV.
[9] Proverbs 29:2 NIV.
[10] Proverbs 29:4 NIV.
[11] Proverbs 29:5 NIV.
[12] Proverbs 29:12 NIV.

Tears came into the young harlot's eyes when she saw Queen Safari lying on the ground and being treated so disrespectfully

Titan helps Safari up and gives her these comforting words, '*Rejoice, you were counted worthy to suffer shame for the cause of Jesus Christ.*'[13] The word you gave the prostitute will not return void.[14]"

Queen Safari whispers, "I found these Scripture notes in that same folder,

'*If anyone speaks, he should do it as one speaking the very words of God. If anyone serves, he should do it with the strength God provides, so that in all things God may be praised through Jesus Christ. To Him be the glory and the power forever and ever. Amen.*

Dear friends, do not be surprised at the painful trial you are suffering, as though something strange was happening to you. But rejoice that you participate in the sufferings of Christ so that you may be overjoyed when His glory is revealed. If you are insulted because of the name of Christ, you are blessed, for the Spirit of glory and of God rests on you. If you suffer, it should not be as a murderer or thief or any other kind of criminal, or even as a meddler. However, if you suffer as a Christian, do not be ashamed, but praise God you bear that name. For it is time for judgment to begin with the family of God, and if it begins with us, what will the outcome be for those who do not obey the gospel of God? And, '
'*If it is hard for the righteous to be saved, what will become of the ungodly and the sinner?*'[15]

So then, those who suffer according to God's will should commit themselves to their faithful Creator and continue to do good.'[16]

Titan counsels, "Now let that young girl and all others, see Jesus Christ in us. We are born again Christians, which means we are a little Jesus Christ, as we represent our Savior on the Earth. Our presence will convict some of their wickedness, without our having to say a word. We let our light shine in the darkness that others will see our good deeds and praise our Father in Heaven."[17]

Queen Safari whispers, "The 'Atlantis Constitution' guarantees us both the freedom of speech and the freedom to practice Christianity."
Colossus responds, "But what is a constitution between an evil ruler and his desire to control and monitor the people?"

---

[13] See Acts 5:45.
[14] See Isaiah 55:11.
[15] Quoting Proverbs. 11:31.
[16] 1 Peter 4:11-19 NIV.
[17] See Matthew 5:16.

Atlas II's Inauguration Ceremony to Crown Himself as New King of Atlantis

As the crowd gathers, packed in like sardines, a circular stage turns revealing Atlas II in spotlights wearing a gold crown, decked in a black, royal robe, and sitting on his dad's throne.

Atlas II commences his inauguration address, "Men of Atlantis you are the best. You are truly beautiful and brilliant. Together in unity, there is nothing we cannot do. I declare this sixth day of the sixth month that you are 'Free to be you! Do it your way! 'Some like it hot, some like it cold, some like it six days' old.' [Self-mocking] However, you like it, 'Just do it' with no restraints.

My dad always said, 'My crown passes to my only son.' I have known this day would come."

Safari whispers to Colossus and Titan, "That's a bold face lie! My husband said he had this covered in his Will! He explicitly told me that our evil son would not be king. We have to find the Will. Wait! I may know where it might be located."

Atlas II boasts, *"Under my leadership, you will have the best freedom ever. I would like to introduce you to my cabinet. My Secretary of States is Gehen. My Treasurer is Zeus. We have collection boxes at all exist for you to make offerings toward a monument of marble to be made in the image of my late dad. If you loved King Atlas, give generously.*

We want you to be free and wealthy. So we will start even this evening horse racing around the second ring of land. One horse is paying 66 to 1. That means if you bet $1 on that horse and it wins, you will receive $66. That is a good return for your money. In addition, we are commencing a monthly lottery with the tickets being only $6 each with the monthly winner taking as much as $666,666 depending upon the number of bets. Now that is a good return on your money. If you are the one who wins $666,666, you would never have to toil at your work again. It pays to gamble. No play, no gain.

Stop by our booths for complimentary samples of cigars, cigarettes, both tobacco and marijuana. While you are enjoying smoking, make a bet on the upcoming first of many horse races and purchase some of the $6 lottery tickets. You triple your chances of winning when you buy three. Spend $6 three times – 666 – is my favorite. I believe in this so much that here are my three lottery tickets for the next drawing.

Also, in two years we plan to have a warship capable of breaking through those sea monsters who keep us separated and isolated from the rest of the world on this island. We will load that warship with cigars, cigarettes, both tobacco and marijuana, and with some of our beautiful young girls and handsome young men and offer all these free to any people we find. We can win them over without firing a shot, but if we need to fire shots, we have developed ultimate laser guns. So with these weapons, let us find some other people to conquer. How would you like a slave brought back to meet your every whim? Put your $666 deposit down for us to bring you back a delightful virgin young boy for your use.

As your new king, I plan to spoil you. You are free. This government will meet all your needs. Entitlements, giving you means and time to enjoy strange flesh. Our socialism calls for 'redistributing the wealth by taking from the 'rich' to give to the poor. We will impose taxes that punish those who have been able to take greater advantage of their productive talents, of their capacity to work, or of being disciplined enough to lay up savings. We will use taxation to promote economic and social equals.

All laws that restrict sex only between a husband and wife in marriage by executive order are hereby this sixth day of the six month are abolished. Healthcare and needed abortions are free for all. Prayer, the Ten Commandments, and the mention of an alleged invisible god are forbidden in our schools and in the public square. *Our new government will give you the freedom you deserve. If it feels good – do it! VISA"*

Atlas II's personal attendants shouting in unison over and over with the people joining in saying, '*This is the voice of a god, not a man.*'[18]

The circular stage upon with the throne turns with King Atlas II waving at the people as he disappears from view.

The clouds turn dark above with lightning scattering the people and striking and killing six (6) of the racehorses. Atlas II makes an announcement over the loudspeakers,

---

[18] Quoting a similar occurrence recorded in Acts 12:20 NIV.

"Due to the foul weather the horse race scheduled for today is canceled. Bah! Humbug! Hell, take cover here comes down hailstones tearing up just my speaker's podium and knocking down my signs.

The Christians with all their stupid rules, including to love God and one another, we are supposed to follow must have put us under a curse. This giant Goliath will cut the heads off all the Christians, and they will be no more."

Queen Safari Locates the Sealed Will

Queen Safari being watched by security walks away with tears in her eyes, whispering to Titan, "My husband had a lawyer friend in the North end of the island whom he described as *'blameless and upright, who feared God, and shunned evil'*[19] and who has *'influence in court.'*[20] Could we take a trip tomorrow to his law firm located near the Great Pyramid? The eye of God sees all reminding all Atlantis that they should not neglect such a great salvation!"

Titan whispers, "Queen Safari, call your guard in and give him this box of nut chocolates, but first sprinkle seven of these tasteless sleeping drops on the candy. When he goes to sleep, then walk the Northbridge across the ring-shaped islands, and we will wait for you in a white electric chariot."

Just as planned, Queen Safari arrives, and they make the three-hour drive to the Great Pyramid, turn right, and park and enter the attorney's reception room unannounced. The receptionists immediately took them into the attorney's office with his responding, "Queen Safari, I am so sorry about the sudden heart attack of your late husband. I have been expecting you. I thought it best not to contact you as it could endanger your life. I am a little concerned that foul play caused King Atlas's death."

Queen Safari responds, "Here is some evidence for you to keep. I discovered five playing cards in Atlas's shirt pocket, having burnt right through them a viscous looking three-headed black dog also burnt on my husband's chest over his heart."

"Yes, I have your late husband's 'Will' in a lock box. I drafted it, and I know he kept you queen and disinherited your wicked wayward son leaving him six (6) pennies since six (6) was his favorite number. Your son in making himself king is a fraud and scam."

"What should I do?"

You have several alternatives: At one end you can do nothing. At the other end, which may make you a martyr, is to direct me to file a petition as the administrator and attorney of the estate naming you and your son, Atlas II, as defendants. The Chancellor will summons you both to court with the 'Will' unsealed and read. Your son can agree to its terms or fight and contest the 'Will.' The Rule of Law should support that King Atlas was in his right mind when he signed his 'Will.' My concern is that your son will realize if you die, he would immediately again having an inside track on maintaining 'De facto[21] kingship' because of the bloodline. Possession is nine-tenths of the law.[22] To go the law route may mean your death. You may need time to pray about it?"

---

[19] See Job 1:1.

[20] See Job 31:21.

[21] *De facto Government* - "One that maintains itself by a display of force against the will of the rightful legal government and is successful, at least temporarily, in overcoming the institutions of the rightful legal government by setting up its own in lieu thereof." Black's Law Dictionary.

[22] *Possession is nine-tenths of the law* is an expression meaning that ownership is easier to maintain if one has possession of something. *Wikipedia, The Free Encyclopedia.*

"Counselor, I am ready to be with my husband. '*And if I perish, I perish!*'[23] I am prepared to march into Hell for a Heavenly cause. I have to do what is right and just! I have to fight, proceed to file it routinely, and serve us both. Act just as we never talked. You can serve us both at the Royal Palace. You may be in danger yourself."

"Possibly not, as once I file it the '*Will*' is sealed in the court records, and they would go after the 'Will' and not after me. Of course, they could burn the Courthouse down. It depends on how desperate they are to keep control."

"Well, I will go back to my room in the North Wing of the Royal Place and await your service of process. Proceed!"

Upon Queen Safari's entering her prison room, she sees her guard still soundly asleep having eaten all the treated chocolate. She destroys the empty box and prepares for bed. Upon her waking the next morning, her guard had moved outside, and he continues to guard her entrance door with the lock removed.

A few days later Atlas II is served by a Deputy Sheriff with the notice to appear for the reading of the 'Will,' and he immediately seeks direction for his defense from Gehen.

Apollyon Lucifer Gives Orders to Assassinate Queen Safari, to Destroy the Courthouse Containing the Filed Sealed Will, and to Kill the Lawyer

Gehen responds, "Apollo, who designed us, is preparing to return soon to Heaven. Let me brief the master and ask for his suggestions."

After being briefed, Apollo makes these comments, "I have not been able to locate King Atlas's spirit. The main thing was to get that enemy out of Atlantis. Likewise, so much is at stake, it would be good also to get Queen Safari and her influence out of Atlantis. She is old. Have her bodyguard shoot her as we did her husband with the laser pink three-headed dog over her heart while she sleeps. Announce to the Atlantis Newspaper that Queen Safari grieving over her husband died in her sleep of a heart attack and will be buried beside her husband. Her death moots a 'Will' making her Queen. A simple solution!

Also, we will have a violent lightning storm coming into the island from the South later this evening. When the storm is centered over the Courthouse where the 'Will' is filed, and the lightning is flashing laser down the Courthouse so much it is almost leveled to the ground. Have false witnesses present to testify that the Courthouse was repeated struck by lightning. This way the 'Will's' contents will never be known. Without the actual 'Will' any speculation as to its content will be inadmissible hearsay.

Also, kill that lawyer who filed this petition seeking justice in court. I have come to take control even if we have to '*kill all the lawyers.*'[24] Without the lawyers' filing legal papers, the judges are powerless to stop us from taking total control! To ensure control, we will have '*to steal and kill and destroy.*'[25] Our motto, 'The ends justify the means!'[26] Always be prepared and plan for war! VISA!"†

---

[23] Esther 4:16.

[24] Quote from Shakespeare, "The first thing we **do,** let's kill all the lawyers," was stated by Dick the Butcher in "Henry VI," Part II, act IV, Scene II.

[25] John 10:10.

[26] See *The Prince* by Machiavelli.

†BOOK SIX – Episode 5†

[†**Sidebar Scriptures**: "*Joseph had a dream and promptly reported all the details* (Genesis 37:5)."
"*The Lord revealed to me what the evil ones were doing and planning and showed me their wicked plots* (Jeremiah 11:18)."
"*The word of the Lord came to Abram in a* **vision**. . . . A **deep sleep** *came upon Abram* . . . . (Genesis 15:1, 12)."
I witnessed and experienced "*dreams and visions, and I described* **all** *I had seen to instruct many* (Daniel 7:1, 11:33)."†]

Queen Safari Joins King Atlas in Paradise, and
Apollo Returns to Heaven as Song Leader

Queen Safari Joins King Atlas in Paradise

QUEEN SAFARI UNDER HOUSE ARREST in the North Wing of the Royal Palace ponders in her heart as she prepares to go to sleep, "*Darling, Atlas, you were such a good husband to me. You loved me so much. I thank you for those wonderful years of our marriage. I was a woman who loved her man! I was determined to do you good and not any evil in our marriage. I didn't realize it would end so suddenly. I miss you so much. I pray our life together here in Atlantis brought some honor and glory to God. Father, God, I rather not just wait here under house arrest until my evil son kills both my lawyer and me. My husband, Atlas, might need me. Deliver me from the will of my enemy. Into Your hand, I commit my spirit. I pray this in the mighty name of Your Son, Jesus. Amen! So be it!*"

Safari's spirit rose, and she looks back at her dead body lying prompted up peacefully on a pillow on the bed. She observes her bedroom door cracks open, and her guard aims a pen laser gun centering the three-headed dog over her heart and firing a laser shot. He smirks speaking aloud right before he closes the door, "Bulls-eye. One way to work your way out of a job! [Smirking] Mission accomplished! It is fun being a hit man to kill for money."

Safari, smiling, hovers near the top of the high ceiling, "*That's what you think. You cannot murder a body whose spirit had previously left it. That was just my prior Earth Suit you shot. I am moving on to glory land.*"

Gabriel and a shining angel appear to escort Safari through the ceiling out on the roof where they have a special fireproof and invisible flying saucer waiting. They launch into the clear sky full of twinkling stars to escort Safari safely in Paradise, but first with a brief stopover in Hell.

Safari's Stopover in Hell

The flying saucer lifts and turns north and enters through the 'All-Seeing Eye' of God at the top of the Great Pyramid. The unique fireproof and invisible flying saucer travels down the abyss shaft entering a vast gulf separating Paradise and Hell. Over Paradise's Gate are among the most joyful words ever written, "***Enter thou into the joy of thy Lord.***"[1] Words over the Gate of Hell are among the saddest words ever written reading, "***Abandon hope, all ye who enter here.***"[2]

The invisible flying saucer turns over Hell and quietly hovers right above 'Look Over Rock' where four known Atlanteans, who died in sin, were arguing and accusing each other.

They swam in the flames and crawled upon 'Look Over Rock' where they could look across the great gulf into Paradise. One of them had a glimpse of King Atlas a few days' earlier picking fruit.

---

[1] Matthew 25:23.
[2] From Dante's *Divine Comedy*.

The camera and monitor zoom in on a group of naked young men and women in Hell, now having no genital sex organs. Safari had personally pleaded with each in Atlantis to repent and receive Jesus as Savior, but each chose the pleasures of sexual sins in Atlantis over choosing the free gift of salvation.

One of the young men said to the other, "I curse you to your face that I ever got involved with your homosexuality. I had a beautiful Christian girl attending King Atlas' church that loved me and wanted to make me a home. My misery in Hell is due to your seducing me into homosexuality.[3] You enticed and deceived me. Safari warned me to stay away from you and your flattering lips, which I kissed. Ugh. Disgusting!

I saw Atlas picking fruit, and he recognized me and he put his hands over his eyes saying, "Too late! You repeatedly rejected Jesus Christ and the free gift of salvation. *'Of all sad words of tongue or pen, the saddest are these, 'It might have been.'*[4]

You are a wicked rogue. Your seduction of me has ruined me forever!"

The other young man responded, "And may I not well blame you. You were flexing your muscles, dressing in those skintight clothes, and enjoying getting high. You mocked the warnings of King Atlas and his wife Safari even assuring me that God was dead. It is as much your fault as mine, we are both here!

One of the young women accused the other, "You enticed me with your beauty and desire to draw me into lesbianism. You introduced me to getting high on alcohol and smokes. You awaken unnatural passion, making me burn in lust for women. I had a boyfriend attending King Atlas's church who loved me and who would have given me a home and children, but you got me burning for women instead of the natural desire for a husband. You stole from me my potential happy home and being part of a family. Thief!

The other woman scored, "I blame you as much. You had attended King Atlas' Church and had heard the warnings to avoid this horrible place. You enticed me as much as I enticed you. You had a 'free will' and loved sexual orgies with women.[5] Now your breasts are almost gone, hanging a little like rags, and you have no vagina. You retain sexual desires for women, being impossible to be satisfied, remaining perverted and burning even in this agony. Naked, you were, and naked you remain. It was with you that I sinned and transgressed the most and lost my soul in this horrible place. I blame you since you had been exposed to the truth that Jesus Saves!"

Looking up two lost spirits are beings dumped like garbage into Hell with their falling and screaming and hitting the pool of fire beside 'Look Over Rock.' The two men pull them out of the fire on the rock asking, "What happened?"

One man replied, "I was enjoying a little bit of adultery in my neighbor's backyard when her husband came home early. He stuck a sword through my back going into his wife's stomach pinning us both to the ground. Do you have any clothes we can put on?"

One woman responded, "Neither clothes nor sex organs here. Just shame, torment, and humiliation!"

Safari inquires, "Gabriel, how can God permit such a horrible place as Hell?"

Gabriel replied, "God made no robots, and each has a 'free will' to obey or disobey.

If a commandment has no sanction, it is not binding. It would be only a suggestion. Those choosing a life of sin and to disobey Jesus' commands without remorse or repentance will suffer the sanction of being cast down to Hell when they die.

It is written,

'I (Jesus) have obeyed (kept) My Father's commands, and I remain (abide) in His love. In the same way, if you obey (keep) My (Lord, Jesus) commands, you will remain (abide) in My love.'[6] *'The work (Father) God wants you to do is this: Believe (trust and obey) the One (Jesus, God's Son) He sent.'*[7]

'I (Jesus) tell you unless you repent (confess and make a U-turn away from sin – with abhorrence of past disobedience) you will all perish (in Hell) and be lost (eternally).'[8]

---

[3] See Romans 1:27.
[4] From *Maud Miller* by John Greenleaf Whittier.
[5] See Romans 1:26.
[6] John 15:10.
[7] John 6:29.
[8] Luke 13:3.

'I (Jesus) have not come to call the self-righteous (who feel no need to repent), but sinners to repentance (heartily to amend their ways, making a U-turn away from sin, with abhorrence of their past disobedience and sin).'[9]

'For this is the love of God, that we keep His commandments: and His commandments are not burdensome (not too hard to keep nor heavy or grievous).'[10]

Men build a prison as a place of sanction for lawbreakers and God in his foreknowledge has prepared Hell for *'the (rebellious) devil and his (disobedient) angels.'* However, prideful, unbelieving, and disobedient men and women can rebel and come to Hell if they so choose. Remember, God has given all His creatures a 'free will' to choose! However, God will provide many opportunities to escape Hell to those made in His image as it is written,

'But God is being patient with you. He wants no one to be lost (perish in Hell), but he wants all people (everywhere) to come to repentance (make a U-turn away from sin and be obedience to God's commands).'[11]

It will be written about the final destruction of this horrible place,

Death and Hell gave up the dead in them, and each person was judged according to what he had done. Then Death and Hell were thrown into the lake of fire. The lake of fire is the second death. If anyone's name was not found written in the book of life, he was thrown into the lake of fire.'[12]

The invisible saucer rises with the monitor focusing on a little bolder on which sat a woman weeping. In Hell, she was praying, "Father God, Safari warned me to receive Your Son Jesus as Savior and to stay away from that unbelieving atheist who seduced and ruined me just like she said he would. Please send my friend Safari to comfort me in these flames and to give me hope. Nothing is impossible with you! Not my will, but Thine be done. Mercy! I ask this in the name of Jesus, the Savior, Amen!

Safari in tears, explains, "That's my faithful maid who had chemistry toward an unbeliever atheist who looked like a Spanish prince to whom this woman yoked against my warnings. Please let me speak to her."

The saucer lowered, and the door opens with Safari talking to her face to face,

"Grace, it is Safari. God heard your prayer! It will be written after Jesus rises from the dead, *'He ascended up on high (Heaven) after He led captivity (all those in Paradise and a few here in Hell) captive.'*[13] I will speak to Jesus on your behalf, and perhaps He will take you to Heaven as He will us over in Paradise. Keep this our secret and your love for Jesus will give you hope of getting out of this horrible place. Do not say anything or hint your hope to anyone as all things here are monitored by darkness. No freedom here! Be silent knowing that I am a friend of Jesus, and you are a friend of mine.

Repent and remember to receive Jesus when he appears, as your Savior and confess Him as your Lord. Until we met again, so long!"

The door shuts and the invisible saucer rises showing Safari one last glance at some horrors of Hell and turns and enters the gates of Paradise having also written at the top, "Love Never Fails!"

Shortly Safari is escorted to the golden courtyard flower garden gate of her beautiful mansion.

---

[9] Luke 5:32.

[10] 1 John 5:3.

[11] 2 Peter 3:9.

[12] Revelation 20:13-15

[13] Ephesians 4:8.

Gabriel counsels, "Share with Atlas that there is 'now no condemnation – no adjudging guilty of wrong – for those who are in Christ Jesus'[14] against either of you on how you reared your son. While you appear to have failed, you both set before your son the blessings of Christian purity in marriage, the virtue of humbleness, and the curses of sin and pride. Because of his selfishness and pride your son chose 'the pleasures of sin for a season'[15] as he delighted to do evil. God gave him a 'free will.' God 'does not leave the guilty unpunished.'[16]

Safari inquired, "Will all of Atlantis now go the way of my evil son and end up in that horrible Hell?"

"No, Safari, Atlantis is going to be destroyed. Your son will take some with him into the flames of Hell, but a revival is coming to Atlantis, and many will be saved and escape the fires of Hell. God will wipe away every tear from your eyes regarding your son and those lost in Atlantis with him in Hell. They all will eventually be cast into the lake of fire to be remembered no more. They were each given a 'free will'. They can choose of their own 'free will' to either repent and receive Jesus as Savior or to continue in the pleasures of sin for a season.[17]

Now daily enjoy helping Atlas write his book '**The Rise and Fall of Atlantis**,' and rejoice as you greet the saints as they come into Paradise from Atlantis and Zion. You two have been especially honored to be the first to arrive here in Paradise and to have your names written in the **Lamb's Book of Life**. As you told your maid in Hell, when the Son of God rises from the dead, He will take everyone captive here in Paradise with Him out to Heaven and a few even out of Hell, including your repentant maid. Questions?"

She asked none as she joyfully anticipates seeing Atlas, whom she loves.

Gabriel instructs, "Simply ring the bell on the back door and have fun together serving the Lord. Remember to encourage him and help him with the assigned book on the history of Atlantis he is writing. He needs and is asking for your assistance!"

Inside the drawing room of the mansion, Atlas was diligently working on Chapter 1, entitled, '**The Rise of Atlantis**.' He was struggling to recall in greater detail an incident and at this moment silently prays, "*Father God, I need the help of my wife on this one. I could also use my attorney on many other details as I trusted him always to be so accurate. In the name of your Son, Jesus, Amen!*"

At that moment, Atlas hears the bell ringing to his back patio door and inquires, "For whom does the bell toll?"[18]

Safari, having fun, disguises her voice in a husky tone replies, "The bell tolls for thee, Atlas!"

Atlas further inquiries, "I have heard that voice before. Who is it?"

"It is your rib! I have come home. Let me stay! I love you. I have missed being with you. Please open the door!"

With streaming tears of joy, Atlas opens the door and gives Safari his usual greeting kiss. They embrace, and he picks her up in his arms carrying her across the threshold saying, "Darling, welcome home. I have got your mansion ready to receive you. Well, almost ready. I knew I should have made the bed this morning. [Laughter] Let me give you the grand tour."

---

[14] Romans 8:1 Amp.
[15] Hebrews 11:25.
[16] Exodus 34:7b NIV.
[17] See Romans 6:23.
[18] *For Whom the Bell Tolls* is a novel by Ernest Hemingway. See *Wikipedia, The Free Encyclopedia*.

Safari kisses him all over the cheeks and lips as she is carried from one beautiful room to another delightful place in the mansion. Safari softly speaks, "Atlas, you look so dignified and handsome! You look as young as you did on our honeymoon, and yet dignified with age."

Atlas responds, "You are just as beautiful as the day we were married. I will never forget that first time with my pure virgin! Wow! Here is the master bedroom! As you can see from the unmade bed, I am still sleeping on the left side. I have thought about how nice it would be to have you beside me on the right side. We have no sex organs here in Paradise. It would be nice to be inside you again."

Safari replies, "For your information God left my breasts even more beautiful than ever in my changed body for you to enjoy! I understand why babies are not to be born here. I will miss the pleasure of having you inside me! We had enough joyful sex on Earth to last throughout eternity. Our Father in Heaven knows best. God knows what He is doing. No sex in Paradise for reasons of His own. We trust Him. We can sleep together. We can kiss and embrace. Atlas, I know that look in your eye. Do not throw me on the bed as it will not do any good! [Laughter as Atlas ignores and throws his wife gently on the bed.] Atlas, God, is so good to give us this temporary glorious mansion in Paradise together. If possible, I will love you even more here than I did in Atlantis. Our one-flesh marital union endures or does it? Love never fails!"

Atlas throws off his shirt and rolls Safari on top of him pulling up her top allowing her bare breast to press against his chest romancing her and quoting Scripture,

> '*Place me like a seal (sticking together tightly like glue) over your heart,*
> *. . . for love is as strong as death;*
> *It (my marital passionate love for you) burns like a blazing flame . . . .*
> *Many waters (great opposition) cannot quench love;*
> *rivers cannot wash it away.*'[19]

Atlas, cupping a breast in each hand, says, "*Your breasts satisfy me at all times.*"[20] Yes, our one-flesh marital union[21] endures. I agree our Father God knows best in this time and place for no babies. However, it is not over until it is over! I plan to ask my attorney following the marriage supper of the Lamb to present further my case that our one-flesh marital union on Earth endures in Heaven and throughout all eternity. I am thankful to the Lord as He allowed you to retain your youthful pointed twin breasts like the day we became one flesh in marriage. They will satisfy me in part here in Paradise and throughout eternity.

Darling, let us arise and walk into the study, and let me show you a hang-up I am having on Chapter One of *The Rise of Atlantis*."

Atlas and Safari walk together into the study. Atlas gives Safari another kiss directly on the lips as they use to do when acknowledging the Lord[22] on starting a project together in Atlantis. Hand in hand, they walk over to the Atlas's desk, and Atlas opens the draft title page reading,

---

[19] Song of Solomon 8:6-7.

[20] Proverbs 5:19.

[21] C. S. Lewis believed that the one-flesh union of marital love would endure beyond death, through all eternity.

[22] See Proverbs 3:5-6.

THE CHRONICLES OF ATLANTIS
By
King Atlas
Affectionately and Earnestly
Dedicated to
The Father,
The Son, and
The Holy Spirit.
And to the
Wife of My Youth, Safari,
Who Still Abides With Me, and Gives Me a Home!

Atlas skips over some draft words of the Introduction and shows her,

Chapter 1
The Rise of Atlantis

"Darling, Safari, you are good with the Greek language and have such a keen and ardent memory. I wanted you initially to review here and help me expound upon the portion of the history when the Island of Atlantis was divided[23] away from Gondwanaland.[24] Also, I have marked a few things legally for our attorney's review when he arrives. Is he in any trouble because of my 'Will?'"

Safari humbly responds, "Yes, he is! He bravely had a Deputy Sheriff serve our son with legal papers regarding your 'Will.' Our son is mad with rage in sin and seized power! I knew he was planning to kill me to prevent me from ruling as Queen as you probably outlined in your 'Will.' Therefore, I prayed to our Father God in the name of Jesus to let me come to you. As my spirit was rising above my body a guard, our son assigned to watch me, opened the door and shot a laser right at my heart, and I saw a three-headed dog on my nightgown. I am sure that the hit men are now on the trail of your attorney. It's just a matter of time before they attempt to murder him."

Atlas remembered seeing a three-headed dog on the back of his hand as he placed it over his hurting heart after he was shot, quoting upcoming Scripture, '*The angel of the Lord encamps around those who fear Him, and He delivers them.*'[25]

"Father, deliver in Jesus' name, as You did my wife, also my lawyer! If I need him, You need him, as this is Your book. I ask you to let Gabriel and Michael bring him to me and let him not be murdered as I was assassinated with a laser gun. Lord, deliver my attorney and friend, Job! In Jesus' name, Amen!"

---

[23] When the Island of Atlantis sank into the sea, there was no more separated land for a season. Later Scripture will record in the Third Earth Age that again "*the Earth was divided . . . .*" (Genesis 10:25).

[24] Gondwanaland is the one ancient landmass that consisted of the present continents then united into a supercontinent. In 1885, an Austrian geologist Eduard Suess noted that the four continents have similar glacial deposits from the ice age. He named the ancient landmass Gondwanaland for a region in central India derived from words meaning, "forest of the Gonds" a people living in India.

[25] Psalm 34:7 NIV.

Safari with tears falling from her eyelashes says, "Amen! The last chapter of God's book, you will write will be entitled *The Fall of Atlantis*. Another potential name for this work could probably be *The Rise and Fall of Atlantis* – from such heights to such a great crashing depth. Deep! I hear the word, 'Deep! Also, I hear the word, 'Revival!"

Apollyon Lucifer's Delegates Responsibilities on Earth and Returns to Heaven

Apollo bragging, "All our projects and plans are in hellish and diabolical hands! Our Giants, with the best armor and weapons, will defeat that skinny one opposing us having only a child's slingshot. The end justifies the means!

Photon, I am leaving you in charge of the scientists, and I am pleased the collection of ore is slightly ahead of schedule. Homo, you are in charge of the mining and distributing the habit-forming drugs, tobacco, and marijuana.

Queen Safari is now dead. An electrical storm, with a little help of some laser guns, has now destroyed the Courthouse containing Atlas' '*Will*.' The fire killed the judge in the building that night. The lawyer who filed the probate petition seems to have disappeared. He is our enemy! Attack him with three-dog night laser guns. His legal ability is a threat! Put out an all-points bulletin for him. Offer a $6,666 reward to the one who kills him. The main thing is that Safari is now dead and out of Atlantis! I have much work now to do in Planet Heaven. VISA!"

Apollo and Mercury board the black widow spider to which has been added a red sharp musical note to the belly. Mercury pushes the lever marked, 'Heaven' with the black airship with no windows rising and subsequently softly landing beside the Pink Palace.

Apollo's Fan Club

Apollo, gloating, speaks to Mercury, "Look at this huge crowd, which has been waiting around the clock for our return. Flattery will get you everywhere! Let me demonstrate and dramatize."

Apollo, with his black guitar, walks out on a wing of the spacecraft and sings to his fan club,

I am so proud to have known,
    my beautiful ones.
Oh, how you have grown;
    serve me, and you will never groan.
You may choose to be a free me!
Do it your way and not another.
Your talents other will see.
You will do it your way with a big hooray!

Fundamental harp lessons will commence in the Pink Palace musical room each Friday morning at 11:06 A.M. for all talented angels. By 'hook or crook'[26] we will have the greatest and flawless harpist sections in my new orchestras. There will never be another harpist conspiracy as sound perfect like you. You will be the best in all the cosmos! VISA!

Attorney Job's Planning and Provisions

Job, who never married in the First Earth Age, gave a sealed legal size envelope marked, 'CONFIDENTIAL and URGENT' to his faithful Christian law partner, which he trained and loved like a son, instructing,

---

[26] *By hook or crook* is an English phrase meaning 'by any means necessary,' suggesting that one need not be concerned with morality or other considerations when accomplishing some goal."
Wikipedia, The Free Encyclopedia.

'My son, do not forget my teaching,
    but keep my commands in your heart,
for they prolong your life many years
and bring you prosperity.
Let love and faithfulness never leave you . . . . .
Then you will win favor and a good name
    In the sight of God and man.
. . .Trust in the Lord with all your heart
    and lean not on your own understanding;
in all your ways acknowledge Him,
    and He will make your paths straight.
. . . By wisdom, the Lord laid the Earth's foundations,
    by understanding He set the Heavens in place;
    by His knowledge the deeps were divided
    (includes.separating Atlantis away from the mainland). . . .
My son, preserve sound judgment (in law) and discernment,
do not let them out of your sight . . . .
Have no fear of sudden disaster
    or of the ruin that overtakes the wicked,
for the Lord will be your confidence
    and will keep your foot from being snared.
. . . He (God) mocks proud mockers
    but gives grace to the humble.
The wise inherit honor,
    but fools He holds up to shame.'[27]

I filed the sealed 'Will' of King Atlas for Probate. I have learned of the death of Queen Safari and the destruction of the courthouse, containing this sealed 'Will.' I strongly suspect I am the next bit of evidence they will seek to destroy. I trust the Lord will deliver me from the will of my enemies to kill me and that I will not be put to shame. 'A man's got to do what a man's got to do!'[28] I had no choice! Do not be concerned about me. I have a Savior, who knows how to save His own, which includes me.

Attorney Job Deeds All His Property to City of Loveland's Temple of God a/k/a[29] Church of Jesus in Loveland, Inc., and Donates Funds to Build a Young Men's Christian Academy

Luther, my trusted law partner, if I do not report for work this Monday immediately file the enclosed deeds conveying all my real estate to the Loveland Temple of God, a/k/a the Church of Jesus in Loveland, Inc., to include a Young Men's Christian Academy (YMCA). Remember to file for tax exemption for the donated land, which is automatic, since the church owns all the adjacent property and holds tax-exempt status on this holy property already.

All of our Supreme Court justices appointed by the former King Atlas love and fear God are Christians and have taken the oath to uphold the Atlantis Constitution, which guarantees the freedom of speech and the practice of the Christian religion.

---

[27] Proverbs 3:1-6, 19, 21, 25-26, 34-35 NIV.

[28] From a similar line in John Steinbeck's book *Grapes of Wrath*, "I hate catching spiders. Still a man's got to do what a man's got to do."

[29] Lawyers at times use A/K/A to mean "Also Known As."

Atlas II's socialism agenda, included his quick appointment of a socialist, homosexual judge, Barron Von Rotten, to replace the one he murdered having jurisdiction over his dad's Will, with the promise he would rule from the bench to remove the Ten Commandments from the front of the Great Pyramid, prohibit prayer in our private schools, and to uphold taxes on the rich, who have been able to take advantage of their productive talents, through diligent labor. Inform the Loveland Attorney Bar not to file any cases before this evil doomed judge, as the Lord showed me, he will immediately be incapacitated because of AIDS and lung cancer. Enclosed are the papers for your filing for the next, soon term, of this judge's office offering the God fearing, Oliver Wendell Holmes, for the vote of the people of Loveland for the judge over this jurisdiction, with other names to be added within thirty days. Corrupted evil judges will have one of the hottest places reserved for them in Hell.

Also, deposit my check made payable to the Loveland Temple of God giving them all my assets, leaving a dollar in my account after you give the enclosed checks for recording the deeds. Praise God, I had kept my cash for such a time as this and had acquired this now needed land. Please retain the recorded new deeds, tax-exempt certificate, and bank books in our fireproof trust safe.

The Lord has instructed that we are to teach that no one is to consider committing suicide or advising suicide no matter what! God's commandment is, '*Thou shalt not kill a man.*'[30] The one who kills himself still kills nothing else than a man. No matter what vulgar and horrible deflowering our little ones receive, or it appears they will receive; you are not to murder your children or allow them to self murder (commit suicide) themselves. As three young men boldly and bravely will proclaim,

'If we are thrown into the blazing furnace, the God we serve is able to save us from it, and He will rescue us from your hand, O king. But even if He does not, we want you to know, O king, that we will not serve your (false) gods or worship the image of gold you have set up."

Then Nebuchadnezzar was furious with Shadrach, Meshach, and Abednego, and his attitude towards them changed. He ordered the furnace to be heated seven times hotter than usual and commanded some of the strongest soldiers in his army to tie up Shadrach, Meshach, and Abednego and throw them into the blazing furnace. So these men, wearing their robes, trousers, turbans, and other clothes, were bound and thrown into the blazing furnace. The king's command was so urgent and the furnace so hot that the flames of the fire killed the soldiers who took up Shadrach, Meshach, and Abednego; and these three men, firmly tied, fell into the blazing furnace.

Then King Nebuchadnezzar leaped to his feet in amazement and asked his advisers, 'Weren't there three men we tied up and threw into the fire?' They replied, 'Certainly, O king.'

He said, 'Look! I see four men walking around in the fire, unbound and unharmed; and the form of the fourth looks like the Son of God.'

Nebuchadnezzar then approached the opening of the blazing furnace and shouted, 'Shadrach, Meshach, and Abednego, servants of the Most High God, come out! Come here!'

So Shadrach, Meshach, and Abednego came out of the fire . . . .

Then Nebuchadnezzar said, 'Praise be to the God of Shadrach, Meshach, and Abednego, who has sent His angel and rescued His servants.'[31]

Job presented wisdom, "One might argue, 'Let me kill myself as I am going to be forced into sodomy and oral sex, and I might like it.' Again, to kill self even for this purpose would be a heinous sin. It is wicked, even to say, such as this. No matter how bad it is or appears to be, this is not a just cause of suicide. God is merciful, and He will judge each one individually. However, it is eternally very dangerous to inflict self-murder. Repentance and remission of sins belong to those in the land of the living.

---

[30] See Exodus 20:13.
[31] Daniel 3:17-28. NIV and NKJV.

One young man who found himself in a horrible place was gang raped and sorely violated with oral sex and sodomy. He with explosions strapped to his chest came asking me to bless his plan to go to that same evil back room of Atlas II to blow up the whole place.

I asked, 'Where are all those who are murdered by you, including yourself, going to be after death?"

The boy replied, 'Someone told me that if I kill homos in Jihad and myself that I will have seventy-two virgins[32] waiting sexually for me in a place called Paradise. All the dead wicked homos would be in a separate place of torment with no hope of salvation. I assisted God get them there faster.'

Job expounded, "With tears I explained, 'God does not need that kind of evil help! God has commanded, and it is the law of the land, '*Thou shalt not murder* (a man).'[33] This means neither another, nor yourself, for he who kills himself still kills nothing else but a man. While the place you are going will be filled with many formerly beautiful young women, who died in sins; neither they nor you will have any sex organs. Also, while these homos you have murdered were alive, one or more could have repented making a U-turn away from their wickedness and receive the Son of God, Jesus, into their heart as Savior from their sins. Jesus promises, '*He that comes to Me (not for anything he has done) will I drive away or cast him out.*'[34]

While a man is alive, God will give him many chances to repent and be saved. If they are sincere they will, '*Produce fruit in keeping with repentance.*"[35]

These men are made in the image of God, and I know several homosexuals, who have repented with tears and have escaped out of the homo lifestyle. Some have married precious, godly women and have had children. You are to hate the sin but to love the sinner!

'*God is patient not wanting anyone to perish (in Hell), but everyone to come to repentance.*'[36]

For your information, this young man contemplating inflicting upon himself voluntary death because of other men's sins was forgiven of his sins. He attends services at the church here in Loveland. They have one child and are joyfully expecting twins.

Law partner, Luther, please contact Brother Titan and Brother Colossus as the Temple of God on the Citadel in Atlantis has been ordered closed. The first order of the new city council in Atlantis was to repeal the ordinance prohibiting the solicitation of young boys by homosexuals for sodomy or oral sex. Next, they authorize same-sex marriages and the adoption of young boys by homosexuals. Gross injustices!

This land and contribution check are given to assist in the building on the church property the Young Mens' Christian Academy (YMCA). We can get our girls out later as they are not in as much danger, as the homosexual are focusing upon lusting after the boys. Most could care less about the girls.

However, to protect our daughters, I would suggest consideration be given to a Young Women's Christian Association (YWCA).

---

[32] The promise of 72 Virgins in Paradise is to those who kill and killed in Jihad for Allah. The Qur'an describes their physical attributes – large eyes (Q 56:22) and big firm, round 'swelling breast that are not inclined to sagging (Q 78:33) with an emphasis of their bodily characteristics, including their virginity. Hadith 26687 is where the number 72 is mentioned. See *72 Virgins* by Avi Perry.

[33] Exodus 20:13.

[34] John 6:37 KJV.

[35] Matthew 3:8 NIV.

[36] 2 Peter 3:9 NIV.

'It would be better for them (who seduce boys and girls) to be thrown into the sea with a millstone tied around their necks than to cause one of these little ones to stumble (sin).'[37]

Keep enforcing to the uttermost the ordinance prohibiting in the City of Loveland, 'For a man to have homosexual relations with a male is deemed unlawful' and is detestable'[38] both to God and our citizens.

Now seek to get vulnerable young boys out of the City of Atlantis with due speed! I once read an account of what will be written about a similar event when two young male angels came into a homosexual city in the Second Earth Age,

'The two angels arrived at Sodom in the evening, and Lot was sitting in the gateway of the city. When he saw them, he got up to meet them and bowed down with his face to the ground.

. . . Before they had gone to bed, all the men from every part of the city of Sodom – both young and old –surrounded the house. They called to Lot, 'Where are the men who came to you tonight? Bring them out to us so we can have sex with them.'

Lot went outside to meet them and shut the door behind him and said, 'No, my friends. Do not do this wicked thing. Look, I have two daughters who have never slept with a man. Let me bring them out to you, and you can do what you like with them. But do nothing to these men, for they have come under the protection of my roof.'

'Get out of our way,' they replied. And they said, 'This fellow (Lot) came here as an alien, and now he wants to play the judge! We will treat you (Lot) worse than them.' They kept bringing pressure on Lot and moved forward to break down the door.

But the men (angels) inside reached out and pulled Lot back into the house and shut the door. Then they struck the men at the door of the house, young and old, with blindness so they could not (as they are still being driven by lust even) find the door.'[39]

Ask the church elders to distribute to our young men Pepper Spray Pens, and if a male tries to kiss them or grab them between the legs or make a sexual advance on them of any kind, the young men are instructed to fill their eyes with pepper spray. For your information, those both young and old desiring sex with the angels thinking they were mortal men were later rained upon with burning sulfur and died blind and in disgrace and went to Hell. It will be written that the Son of God will say about such children we are protecting,

'Therefore, whoever humbles himself like this little child is the greatest in the kingdom of heaven. And whoever welcomes a little child like this in My name welcomes Me.

But if anyone causes one of these little ones who believe in Me (Jesus) to sin, it would be better for him to have a large millstone hung around his neck and to be drowned in the depths of the sea. 'Woe to the world because of the things that cause people to sin! Such things must come, but woe to the man through whom they come!'[40]

. You as an Assistant City Attorney attend the City Council meeting this Thursday. At the end mention a church blessing of the upcoming YMCA, but remember do not obtain their approval as this is a church function on private property. Keep the government people off the church property, as they will seek to control and regulate it. We are tax exempt!

---

[37] Luke 17:2.
[38] See Leviticus 18:22.
[39] Genesis 19:1, 4-10 NIV.
[40] Matthew 18:3-7 NIV.

I am asking the Lord to give me a way of escape from my enemies. If my *corpus delicti* [41] is not found, the good Lord got me out of here, and I was not murdered. I do not regret filing that Petition to Probate Atlas' 'Will.' The battle is the Lord's!"[42]

Elder David Strumming a Harp Leads the 144,000 in Praise and Worship

On the banks of the pure flowing Jordan River, the 144,000 raise their voices and hands to worship God. David on the harp leads in praise and worship,

'I will bless the Lord at all times;
*   His praise shall continually be in my mouth.*
My soul makes its boast in the Lord;
*   let the humble hear and be glad (rejoice).*
*   O magnify (glorify) the Lord with me:*
*   and let us exalt His name together.*
I sought the Lord, and He answered me
*   and delivered me from all my fears.*
Those who look to Him are radiant,
*   and their faces shall never be ashamed.*
This poor man cried, and the LORD heard him
*   and saved him out of all his troubles.*
The angel of the Lord encamps around those
*   who fear Him, and delivers them.*
Oh, taste and see that the Lord is good;
*   blessed is the man who takes refuge in Him.*
Oh, fear the Lord, you His saints,
*   for those who fear Him have no lack.*
The lions suffer want and hunger;
*   but those who seek the Lord lack no good thing.*
Come, O children, listen;
*   I will teach you the fear of the Lord.*
What man is there who desires (abundant) life
*   and loves many days, that he may see good?*
Keep your tongue from evil
*   and your lips from speaking lies (deceit).*
Turn from evil and do good;
*   seek peace and pursue it.*
The eyes of the Lord are toward the righteous
*   and His ears toward (are attentive) to their cry.*
The face of the Lord is against those who do evil,
*   to cut off the memory of them from the Earth.*
When the righteous cry for help,   the Lord hears
*   and delivers them out of all their troubles.*
The Lord is near to the broken-hearted
*   and saves the crushed in spirit.*
Many are the afflictions (troubles) of the righteous,
*   but the Lord delivers him out of them all;*
He keeps (protects) all his bones;
*   not one of them will be broken.*

---

[41] *Corpus delicti* – "The body (material substance) upon which a crime has been committed, e.g., the corpse of a murdered man . . . ." *Black's Law Dictionary.*

[42] 2 Chronicles 20:15.

Affliction (evil) will slay the wicked,
and those who hate the righteous will be condemned.
The Lord redeems the life of His servants;
none of those who take refuge in Him will be condemned.'[43]

Elder David's Further Training of 144,000 Jewish Evangelists Turns on a Large Screen

David instructs the 144,000 pointing to a large 3D screen, "Watch the lawyer wearing a red bow tie as the Anti-Christ Freedom Union (ACFU) tries to destroy him. This same evil spirit of Anti-Christ will seek to destroy each of you at the end of the Third Earth Age. Let us watch and listen in as the lawyer receives a telephone call from his mother expressing concern,

"Son, the ACFU (Anti-Christ Freedom Union) just called here asking if I knew your location. Where are you located?

"Mother, I am in my law office in Loveland right behind the Great Pyramid. We have a full moon this evening, so I am watching all entrances. On my identifier, I see they have just traced me through your telephone call. Love you. I have to go. Bye.

Lawyer Job sets the alarm and exits running through the front door when he sees six (6) four wheelers with searchlights coming at him from all directions. He sprints to the rear of the Great Pyramid and pushes a button, and a rope ladder falls 777 feet to the ground from the All Seeing Eye capstone. A searchlight spots the lawyer just as he steps on the first ring. As he hurries up the ladder, a shot from a laser pen gun is fired with other laser shots striking closer and closer. Gabriel and Michael become invisible shields to guard his physical body against a direct hit. However, two lasers have hit and caught each side of the ladder, rope near its top on fire. The six (6) would be assassins' race up the ladder and are gaining. Fortunately, they cannot fire the laser pens and climb at the same time. As the lawyer nears the All-Seeing-Eye Cap Stone, he makes it through the burning portion of the ladder grabbing one high ring with his teeth. Six yards away from seizing him the first would-be assassin reaches the burning part of the rope. The rope breaks with all six (6) hit men crashing down the side of the Pyramid, making a bloody thud on the ground below.

Michael, appearing with Gabriel at his side, proclaims, *'Anyone pulling a sword goes down by the sword'*[44] and, *'God cannot be mocked. A man reaps what he sows.'*[45]

Michael, throwing the last little bit of the burning rope ladder to the ground, decrees, "Waterspout, come up out of the sea and clean up this bloody mess and cast the bodies and the six (6) 4-wheelers of these wicked into the sea!"

A water spout comes sucking up all the blood, bodies, rope and four wheelers taking them out into the deep of the sea with Michael declaring, "Spick and span (neat and tidy). Not a trace of evidence!"

Job, the lawyer, replies, "No *corpus delicti* remains of any dead body, including my own! The Lord knows how to deliver the righteous. The Lord is dramatic at times – here helping me run up the side of the world's tallest building as He rescues His own. I was literally saved by the skin of my teeth as the rope burned." [Laughter]

Michael asked, "Yes, lawyer of facts, by the skin of your teeth. The original 'Jaws!' Was that rescue exciting enough for you?"

---

[43] Psalm 34:1-22.
[44] Revelation 13:10 MSG.
[45] Galatians 6:7 NIV.

308

Job replied, "This is the most excitement I've had in all my life? I once went swimming a little distance out in the sea, and saw a Leviathan, [46] and I prayed to get back to land safely. This rescue will be hard to top in the history of the world!"

Michael replied, "How about God's fencing up on each side waters frozen as ice in the sea and a whole nation of people crossing over on dry ground? Then when the last one crosses and their enemies pursue, and his army gets to the middle of the sea, their enemies are all crushed when the walls of water come tumbling down drowning them. *Corpus delicti* everywhere,"[47]

Job replies, "Well, I guess my rescue cannot top that one. Please know that I am thankful for my rescue and that I was not put to shame!"

Atlas' Attorney Arrives in Paradise

Michael explained again, "King Atlas is in need of a lawyer. Any volunteers? [Laughter as Job raises his hand.]

"Job, you did not die. Your body will be changed to live in Paradise. 'Just as man is destined to die once, and after that to face judgment,'[48] legally you can return to the surface of the Earth in a subsequent (later) Earth Age and even marry. You will not remember these moments, except for faint shadows now and then.

Gabriel and Michael escort Job down the abyss shaft over into Paradise to his mansion located right beside Atlas and Safari's mansion with Gabriel suggesting,

"Atlas and Safari are sleeping in each other's arms right now. Those who were married on Earth may live together. You might enjoy a refreshing nap yourself as you had some night. [Laughing] Atlas and Safari will pass right in front of your front porch around 3:00 P.M. as they take their afternoon walk together. In your study, you have a complete Greek law library, and you can read right here on this cushioned swing. Chapter 7 of the ***Atlantis Rules of Evidence*** will help with Atlas's first legal question. You know Atlas. You can set your watch by him. They will pass your swing, taking an afternoon walk at 3:00 P.M. Atlas asked for you in prayer, and so here you are! You may desire to take a tour of your new mansion and your excellent law library.

You will interview and take signed statements of some of the righteous saints from Atlantis when they arrive here in Paradise. One lawyer type question could include, 'What important, good, bad, remarkable, or impressive thing or event do you remember about Atlantis?' One of the first interviews you can make is with the righteous judge killed in the Courthouse when Atlas' 'Will' was destroyed. Enjoy every moment of this labor of love."

Job inquiries, "Will the book focus on the rise only of Atlantis?

Gabriel replied, "No. The complete book will be known as ***The Rise and Fall of Atlantis***. The whole Island of Atlantis will sink beneath the sea into Hades itself made up of two compartments – Paradise and Hell. The Great Pyramid will be located right here beside you and Atlas here in Paradise.

We have provided you with a video clip in your study of your running up the side the Great Pyramid, the grabbing a portion of a higher ring with your teeth, and the splattering below of your enemies."

---

[46] See Job 41:1-8.
[47] See Exodus 14:13-31.
[48] Hebrews 9:27 NIV.

Job responds, "I felt at that moment like one being given supernatural strength from above to 'march into Hell for a Heavenly cause.'[49] What was going on?"

Gabriel instructs, "You were strengthened and guarded by Michael and myself. Heaven had its part to play, but you also had your separate role to play. We needed each other. Watch the video, and you will see us reflecting the laser shots away from you. Heaven sees you as God's hero! However, things on Earth will even be worse, if that were possible, for you in the Second Earth Age.

Again, both Heaven and those who observed you on Earth will consider you again God's hero in the Second Earth Age. The Gospel of Jesus Christ can form a mild practicing lawyer into a superhero lawyer. All you needed was a red cape to match your red bow tie, and you would have been a sight. [Laughter] You wisely plead the red blood of Jesus, who will die on a cross to pay the penalty due for sins of all those who will receive Him as Savior, repent, and confess Jesus is Lord to the glory of God the Father. Nothing can overpower the blood and love of Jesus. Many will desire, including ourselves, to see again and again this movie video. Questions?"

Job inquiries, "Will there be any other people from the Earth here? When will I be entitled to go back to the Earth again? Then after I once die, is this my permanent home?"

Gabriel replied, "Objection based upon Rule 5 of the **Atlantis Rules of Evidence** mandating only one question at a time. [Laughter] The answer to your first question is, 'yes' as this place will be a little crowded. The answer to your second question is 'yes.' **The Book of Job** will be a book written in the Second Earth Age about your life and again your deliverance. **The Book of Job** will be preserved in a waterproof clay pot to be discovered after the second destruction of the Earth and will become a part of the Bible to be enjoyed by many throughout eternity.

The Son of God will preach, '*Heaven and Earth shall pass away, but My words shall not pass away.*'[50]

The answer to your third question is "no" as you will have many homes in eternity. This place will be filled with a Zion race of people you do not know, but to whom you will dearly love. They will use your legal gifting and training to look at all sides of positions, the various arguments, and each side of a case. You will wisely guide, advise, and counsel others as you '*let justice roll.*'[51]

Job you have been given a unique insight into right and wrong, legal and illegal, advisable and not advisable. I thought you might enjoy knowing that some 144,000 witnessed your escape and deliverance last evening on a large 3D screen (showing the angelic protecting shielding) in God's chosen Country of Israel. Soon you will see the blue star on the white flag of Elder David flying throughout Paradise. Also, this place will soon be Abraham's Bosom. Abraham, whose name means 'father of many,' will be in charge and not you nor King Atlas. You are to assist Abraham and greatly honor and esteem him. Counsel Atlas, as he is not accustomed to not being in charge. Help him to submit to Abraham's authority.

Do not emphasize to Mrs. Safari that since she did not die, that she like you has a legal right to be born and live in a later Earth Age. She will not choose to be separated from her beloved Atlas and marry another, although she would have the legal option to do so.

---

[49] From song "*The Impossible Dream*" by Joe Darion,
[50] Matthew 24:35 KJV.
[51] "*Let justice roll on like a river . . . .*" (Amos 5:24).

They have established a marital oneness that for them is eternal. She says it is forever and a day. Such marital romance is rare and precious in God's sight!"

Job inquiries, "Please give me a little preview of my going back up to the surface of the Earth."

Michael responds, "You will be married twice in the Second Earth Age. You will not remember, except for some shadows your living in this First Earth Age. Your first wife will be deceived in misconstruing your faith and trust in God as being religious fanaticism. She will reason you blindly refuse to face the reality of your desperate situations and the trials you are going through as stupid, and you are a fool in her eyes. Her cynical, negative, harmful, and cruel words to you with malice aforethought advise you, '*Curse God and die*'[52] will present a severe trial."

All your children of your first wife will be murdered[53] by God's enemy. You will lose your health, and your first wife, whom you dearly love, and who cannot stand the sight of you, will herself die. However, you will trust God first through prosperity and later through all this adversity even while you could not understand why bad things were happening to you.

Your first wife with her own words tore her own house down and took herself out from under your covering and ended up in Hell. It will be written, '*The wise woman builds her house, but with her own hands the foolish one tears hers down.*'[54]

After a time of mourning, you will remarry a petite virgin girl. She will be warm, loving, and supportive. It will be written about you,

After Job had prayed for his friends, the Lord made him prosperous again and gave him twice as much as he had before. All his brothers and sisters and everyone who had known him before came and ate with him in his house. They comforted and consoled him. . . . The Lord blessed the latter part of Job's life more than the first. He had fourteen thousand sheep, six thousand camels, a thousand yoke of oxen, and a thousand donkeys. And he also had (of his second wife) seven sons and three daughters. The first daughter he named Jemimah, the second, Keziah and the third Keren-Happuch. Nowhere in all the land were there found women as beautiful as Job's daughters and their father granted them an inheritance with their brothers.

After this, Job lived a hundred and forty (140) years; he saw his children and their children to the fourth generation. And so he died, old and full of years.'[55]

Gabriel concluded, "Headquarters is calling us. Have fun in Paradise! Shalom!"

The screen fades off before the 144,000 as Gabriel and Michael ascend back into Heaven.

David teaches, "Dearly beloved this spirit of Anti-Christ (Antichrist) will likewise be seeking to murder all of you, but remember that '*the battle is the Lord's.*'[56] This precious promise will be written,

'*No weapon forged against you will prevail, and you will refute every tongue that accuses you.*

This is the heritage of the servants of the Lord, and this is their vindication from the Lord.'[57]

Yes, the blood will flow for '*200 miles to the height of horses' bridle*'[58] of those who attack God's chosen ones. God will flick them off like one flicking off a gnat bug with one's little finger all the forces of darkness into a '*lake of fire.*'[59] God desires a people who love and obey Him of their own free will. God is permitting all of this for His eternal purpose. You 144,000 are an important part of God's Master Plan. Shalom!†

---

[52] Job 2:9 NIV.
[53] See Job 1:18-19.
[54] Proverbs 14:1 NIV.
[55] Job 42:11-16 NIV.
[56] 1 Samuel 17:47 NIV.
[57] Isaiah 54:17 NIV.
[58] See Revelation 14:20.
[59] See Revelation 20:10.

†BOOK SEVEN†

†BOOK SEVEN – Episode 1†

[†**Sidebar Scriptures**: "*Joseph had a dream and promptly reported all the details (Genesis 37:5).*"
"*The Lord revealed to me what the evil ones were doing and planning and showed me their wicked plots (Jeremiah 11:18).*"
"The word of the Lord came to Abram in a **vision**. . . . A **deep sleep** came upon Abram . . . . (Genesis 15:1, 12)."
I witnessed and experienced "*dreams and visions, and I described **all** I had seen to instruct many (Daniel 7:1, 11:33).*"†]

King Atlas Meets His Lawyer in Paradise, and
Atlas II Launches Warships to Attack Israel

Atlas and His Lawyer Meet in Paradise

ATLAS AND SAFARI WALK hand in hand with fingers interlocked, and as they pass a white mansion with a purple roof and shudders, they see a man with his face hidden behind a book entitled, ***The Law of Evidence of Atlantis***. King Atlas speaks, "Counselor, I've been expecting you. You look the vigor of youthful manhood. The Lord and I have need of thee!"

Attorney Job replies, "Bless the Lord, oh, my soul! What I have, I give to the Lord, and to thee! Your joyful servant is reporting for duty! You two look so young, happy, and in love holding hands! Two's company, but three is a crowd. Walk on and stop by for a chat when you return."

Atlas responds, "No, my son, you are family. Here God takes delight in surprising us daily with new and great blessings. Today – You! Walk down with us to the lily pond. We brought bread crumbs to feed the Coy and Goldfish. Here, you take my bag. You will have them eating out of your hand. Everything is so lovely and delightful here."

Job walking beside Atlas speaks pleasant words while he drops the breadcrumbs into the goldfishes' mouths. He pats the top of each fish's head with his forefinger and observes, "These little pets wag their tails when patted. They are such a contrast to the vicious Leviathans. When I was ten years old, I went swimming in the ocean, and I got out a little too far, and a Leviathan was coming to devour me. I cried, 'Lord, save me! Danger be gone in the Name of Jesus for, '*No weapon formed against me will prosper.*'[1] The Leviathan abruptly stopped and turned fleeing from me as if in terror. I suspect it saw Angel Michael with a sword ready to cut off its head. I learned that day that God is in charge, and the angels guard us doing what God says and worshipping God alone, as it will be written,

'*See, I (God) am sending an angel ahead of you to guard you along the way and to bring you to the place I have prepared. Pay attention to him and listen to what he says. . . . If you listen carefully to what he says and do all that I (God) say, I will be an enemy to your enemies and will oppose those who oppose you. . . .Worship (only) the Lord your God, and His blessing will be on your food and water. I (God) will take away sickness from, among you. . . . I (God) will give you a full life span.*'[2]

I also learned that day an important truth that I am to call upon the name of the Lord Jesus and speak in faith His Word against any mountain or danger coming against me.

'*For that which is decreed (in faith) will be done.*'[3]

---

[1] Isaiah 54:17.
[2] See Exodus 23:20-26.
[3] Daniel 11:36.

'Whoever will say to this mountain be removed, and does not doubt in his heart, he will have whatever he says.'[4]

Now we will do our part – you dictate, and I will be your scribe. Your wife will listen and assist with the details. A teenage girl, Joyce, currently on the surface of the Earth serving as secretary to the Church in Loveland, has remarkable gifts of remembering historical events and has incredible writing skills. When she arrives, I believe she will help us accomplish the vision of the completed work – *The Rise and Fall of Atlantis* by King Atlas. Let us pray that the Lord Jesus will deliver her and all the born again ones out tribulation and safely join us here in Paradise. She once hinted she would someday like to help with *The Book of Job*."

Atlas, nodding "yes" and being so thankful to have his attorney and wife by his side replies, "The Lord Jesus is mighty to save! Paradise has such a pleasant life. Let us walk down to the River of Shalom. God has provided twelve kinds of fruit. Each is different and delicious. Here we are, let us pluck and eat a sample and tell me what you think."

Job bites into a juicy fruit and comments, "Wonderful! Atlantis had no fruit to compare to this taste, not a banana, orange, or pear. My mind is so enlightened, bright, and crystal clear. I feel such strength and youthful vigor. How about us walking back and you show me your beginning work on the history of Atlantis. A journey of 1,000 miles begins with one step. Let us *'acknowledge the Lord in all we do.'*[5] Now from our first labor in the Lord, we have joyful faith that the time will come when we finish this diligent work knowing that our *'labor in the Lord is not in vain.'*[6] My first counsel is let us acknowledge the Lord Jesus and enjoy the Lord every moment as we accurately record the history of Atlantis for His glory. Let us take the time to smell the roses and delight in the Lord always. It's better we write more (unabridged) than the less (to diminish; to lessen; to abridge; to shorten). Your wife will stand by her man. Your lawyer will stand by his unforgettable godly client!"

Attorney Job's Discourse on Atlas II

Atlas inquiries regarding his son with Job responding, "I remember Atlas II bragging when he was seven years old, 'My old man does not require me to attend worship services. I'm the king's son. I go or not go. I choose not to go. I am the king's pet.' Then I remember running into him when he was thirteen, and he did not want to go to church. Therefore, he did not hear the word of God preached, and he hung around more and more with evil companions, and they further corrupted his morals and character.

Although your son knew God, he neither glorified Him as God nor gave thanks to Him, but his thinking became futile, and his foolish heart was darkened. He exchanged the glory of the immortal God for various naked images made in the likeness of vulgar and filfty men and women. Your son exchanged the truth of God for a lie and worshiped and served created things rather than the Creator. Because of this, God gave him over to his shameful lusts.[7] It is written,

'The wrath of God is revealed from Heaven against all the godlessness and wickedness of men who suppress the truth by their wickedness, since what may be known about God is plain to them, because God has made it plain to them. For since the creation of the world God's invisible qualities -- His eternal power and divine nature – have been seen, being understood from what has been made, so men are without excuse.

---

[4] Mark 11:23 KJV.
[5] Proverbs 3:5-6.
[6] 1 Corinthians 15:58
[7] See Romans 1:21-24.

For although they knew God, they neither glorified Him as God nor gave thanks to Him, but their thinking became futile and their foolish hearts were darkened. Although they claimed to be wise, they became fools and exchanged the glory of the immortal God for images made to look like mortal man and birds and animals and reptiles.

Therefore, God gave them over in the sinful desires of their hearts to sexual impurity for the degrading of their bodies with one another. They exchanged the truth of God for a lie and worshiped and served created things rather than the Creator, who is forever praised. Amen.

Because of this, God gave them over to shameful lusts. Even their women exchanged natural relations (with husbands) for unnatural ones. In the same way, the men also abandoned natural relations with women (wives) and were inflamed with lust for one another. Men committed indecent acts with other men, and received in themselves the due penalty for their perversion.

Since they did not think it worthwhile to retain the knowledge of God, He gave them over to a depraved mind to do what ought not to be done. They are full of envy, murder, strife, deceit, and malice. They are gossips, slanderers, God-haters, insolent, arrogant and boastful; they invent ways of doing evil; they disobey their parents; they are senseless, faithless, heartless, ruthless. Although they know God's righteous decree, that those who do such things deserve death (and Hell) they not only continue to do these things, but also approve of those who practice them.[8]

Your son chose his own 'free will' to abandon the natural relationship with his wife. All knew she was one of the most attractive, pure, precious, and saintly women in all Atlantis. He became inflamed with lust for other men. Ugh! He has now become filled with every kind of wickedness, evil, greed and depravity, murder, strife, deceit, even a God-hater, and so full of pride. He now boasts he is the greatest king of Atlantis. He disobeyed you and God. You should have, instead of spoiling him rotten, disciplined him when he was young to the point he could not sit down. Our preachers would preach,

'*Folly is bound up in the heart of a child,*
   but the rod of discipline will drive it far from him.[9]
Whoso loves discipline loves knowledge,
   but he that hates correction is stupid.'[10]

Atlas, you are not without fault for letting your son run wild! Your precious wife warned and warned you to disciple Atlas II."

Safari interjected, "Until I was blue in the face! Our son made fun of my disciple. Atlas spoiled him rotten!"

Attorney Job continues, "He would stupidly laugh at both of your disciplines and refuse to be corrected. Now he is wicked, faithless, heartless, ruthless, and rotten to the core. He is even making plans to corrupt God's people on Gondwanaland. He knows God's righteous decree that, if he does not repent and turn from these wicked ways, he deserves death and everlasting destruction. Your son, not only continues to do these things himself, but he also approves and encourages those who practice them."[11]

Atlas responds, "All you say is true, but do I have to dishonor myself by telling it exactly as it was. Some are so offended by any little thing we could change or ignore history to appease them. Cannot we sugarcoat[12] our history book a little bit?"

Both Safari and Job responded with a shout, "No!"

Safari spoke, "Darling, many of our citizens who accepted Jesus as their Savior will be coming here to join us. They will all desire to read this accurate history book.

---

[8] Romans 1:18-31.
[9] Proverbs 22:15 NIV.
[10] Proverbs 12:1 NIV.
[11] See Romans 1:18-32.
[12] *Sugarcoat* – "to talk about or describe (something) in away that makes it seem more pleasant or acceptable than it is." *Merriam-Webster – An Encyclopedia Britannica Company.*

314

Remember the precious 777 who received salvation and repented of their sins in your dying sermon on Earth. A few of the Christians from Atlantis may even come here by death, but most, like Job and myself, will be rescued out of the darkness of death into this wonderful and marvelous light. The latter may if they choose may return to the Earth in the second and third Earth ages. I will ask the Lord to permit me to stay with you for many reasons of my own. You didn't think I knew the rule, '*It is appointed unto everyone to die once, and after that the judgment.*'[13]

Safari pauses and then continues, "Atlas, also many from Gondwanaland, being one race of people, who will not die in this first earth age. They will likewise return to the surface of the Earth in the second and third earth age as God's specially chosen people. Our Christian people who will not die in the First Earth Age will return as Gentiles to the surface of the Earth, some of whom will be used of the Lord like you were to preach salvation to others. While they will not remember being here in Paradise or in the First Earth Age, they will remember shadow-truths taught in your book.

Darling, I am ready to help you wholly follow the Lord in completing ***The Rise and Fall of Atlantis*** to the glory of God. God knows what He is doing! God is always right! The important thing is that people receive Jesus as Savior! Don't you be ashamed or be under any condemnation because of our son! The Father God spoke one precious word to you, 'Forgiven!" That settles it! He who has been forgiven much also loves much![14] God Himself is the glory and lifter of your head. Hold your head up. What God forgives, He forgets! Now forgive yourself and let us three get to work. When the 777 come here, as the fruit of your preaching the Good News, let us be prepared to give each an autographed copy of your book, with a Scripture such as,

'*Let nothing move you. Always give yourself fully to the work of the Lord, because you know that your labor in the Lord is not in vain.*'[15]

They will enjoy one of the greatest true dramas ever told! One day with you, my darling, our exciting life was getting a little dull, but as always it immediately became an exciting adventure again. My advice to you, 'Tell it like it actually was! Sugarcoat nothing! God had the final laugh as 777 became gloriously saved in your dying testimony that Jesus Saves!"

Attorney Job, smiling, with approval, replies, "Safari, I ditto! Time's a wasting! Tell it the way it is! Rome wasn't built in a day, whatever that means. In bold faith, let us fully trust in God. God is good. He is always right. Let us acknowledge Him in all our ways and let Him be in charge.

Let's get to the writing room and begin Chapter One, or should I say 'Episode One.' I assume Chapter One will include when the Earth was first divided[16] with you two lovers finding yourselves out on an isolated romantic island in the middle of the ocean surrounded by Leviathans[17] further isolating you.

As we walk back, start when you discovered you were missing a rib and the day will come when we will celebrate the completion of Atlantis's history. As we honor God, He promises to honor us.[18] Let us boldly begin. It will be written, '*The end of a matter is better than its beginning.*'[19]

---

[13] Hebrews 9:27.

[14] See Luke 7:47.

[15] 1 Corinthians 15:58,

[16] Genesis 10:25 reports a time when "*the Earth was divided.*"

[17] See Job 41:1-9.

[18] "*Those who honor Me I will honor, but those who despise Me will be disdained.*" (1 Samuel 2:30).

[19] Ecclesiastes 7:8 NIV.

Detestable Idol Poseidon Introduced by Atlas II

Atlas II converted the Temple of God from a House of Prayer and Worship to the Temple of Poseidon and Worship as a place of orgies and prostitution to the god Poseidon.[20]

Atlas II by royal executive order decrees,

"Poseidon is the god of the ocean and is to be worshiped as lord under me by all Atlantis. All citizens of Atlantis are required under penalty of law (even jail time) to kneel and pray to the naked golden statue of Poseidon and to present themselves six times a year sexually as an offering to the great Poseidon. An orphan girl, Cleito, who grew up among us, has given herself totally to serving Poseidon. She also is to be worshiped as our goddess of pleasure, and she will direct how each one is to please Poseidon with his or her sexual offerings. Have fun Atlantis. Eat, drink, and be merry."

†Six Hundred and Sixty-Six (666) Days Later†

Atlas II Commissions the Poseidon, Cleito, and Decoy Warships for Launching

Atlas pridefully declares to his staff, the ships' captains, crew, and to the well-shaped male and female bodies from the temple of Poseidon, "We have picked up a weak radio wave meaning there is another civilization.

Our plan is to present the ultimate weapon by offering our most beautiful women to seduce first the males over to the worship of our god Poseidon. Poseidon, the mighty god of the ocean, will help us break through these ferocious and terrifying leviathans. Who would be so sick in designing such hideous sea monsters?

With Poseidon on our side and our three-dog laser guns, we can finally bring the leviathans down this time. They have terrible teeth, rows of scales so near that nothing can get between them; they stick together and cannot be parted. Out of the leviathans' mouths shoot burning torches of fire. Smoke rises out of their nostrils. Many have proved that the sword will not penetrate the armor nor the spear, dart, or javelin. These sea monsters regard iron as straw and bronze as rotten wood. Sling stones become like balls of cotton to them. However, they have not tasted of our three-dog laser guns with which we plan to shoot them when they open their mouths. We have killed fire-breathing dragons on the island by shooting them in the mouth. Leviathans are just big fire-breathing dragons, and my scientists assure me they will fall.

Tonight is overcast with no moon, and at midnight, we will launch the decoy ship that will turn south away from the island. When we observe the battle raging of that ship with the Leviathans, we will launch our main ships to break through as we sail guided in by the radio waves.

I have selected our most beautiful twenty-two (22) women who will be on an Eros Party Boat to be lowered from the Poseidon Warship to make the males of that nation an offer they can't refuse. No male can resist these beautiful women unless they have discovered a greater delight. [Sarcastic homosexual smirking.]

Each woman will be rewarded 666 silver[21] coins for each man on the mainland with whom she has sexual relations. I predict that some of our prostitutes will be very wealthy."

---

[20] According to the references from Plato in his dialogue Timaeus and Critias, the island of Atlantis was the chosen domain of Poseidon. See *Posidon* in *Wikipedia, The Free Encyclopedia*.

[21] Delilah was offered a reward of silver for helping Philistines capture Samson. (See Judges 16:5, 17, 21).

Abraham Calls an Emergency Meeting of the Elders

Abraham addressed the elders of Israel, "The Atlantis new king is sending what he considers the ultimate weapon – twenty-two (22) young and beautiful females – to offer sexual relations with our men. You might say, 'A beautiful naked young girl would not tempt me?"

That is easy to say, but may be harder to resist than you can image. In the Third Earth Age, over twenty thousand of our men are seduced by Moabite women and infected by a plague as it will be written,

'While Israel was staying in Shittim, the men indulge in sexual immorality with Moabite women, who invited them to the sacrifices to their gods. The people ate and bowed down before these gods. So Israel joined in worshiping the Baal of Peor. And the Lord's anger burned against them.

The Lord said to Moses, 'Take all the leaders of these people, kill them, and expose them in broad daylight before the Lord, so that the Lord's fierce anger may turn away from Israel.'

So Moses said to Israel's judges, 'Each of you must put to death those of your men who have joined in worshiping the Baal of Peor.'

Then an Israelite man brought to his family a Midianite woman right before the eyes of Moses and the whole assembly of Israel while they were weeping at the entrance to the Tent of Meeting. When Phinehas son of Eleazar, the son of Aaron, the priest, saw this, he left the assembly, took a spear in his hand, and followed the Israelite into the tent. He drove the spear through both — through the Israelite and into the woman's body. Then the plague against the Israelites was stopped, but those who died in the plague numbered 24,000.'[22]

We have one of the darkest of nights on the Island of Atlantis as we view on the screen with the help of infrared lighting the launching of the Decoy Warship. Now watch."

Launching of Decoy Warship

The Decoy Warship silently moves out into the ocean and turns south. Five miles out it is spotted by a protective Leviathan, who took to flight with hundreds of three-dog laser shots being fired. The Leviathan crashes in the center of the upper deck of the Decoy Warship going through that deck into the cargo area. In the cargo area out of its mouth shoots, a stream of flames, causing the explosion of cases of dynamite stored in the cargo bay.

While the Decoy Ship was burning on the ocean's horizon in the south, the Poseidon Warship leaves the bay and turns due north, and the Clieto Warship leaves the bay continuing straight ahead. Other protective Leviathans at the five-mile zone attack the Clieto Warship. The three-dog laser guns after thousands of shots aimed into the mouths of the Leviathan kill several leviathans.

Finally, the leader of the Leviathans seeking to protect God's chosen people circles high in the air and dive bombs crashing through the top deck. The flames of fire shooting out its mouth also hit a supply of dynamite in the cargo bay blowing the warship up with a violent explosion. The Poseidon Warship escapes into the black night out into the vast ocean heading straight to Tel Aviv, Israel.

Abraham addresses his war council, "As you can see, the main (primary) warship is heading straight toward us. Any suggestions?

David speaks out, "Let us attack and kill these beautiful women as in war!"

Abraham responds, "David, you are as weak as a tomcat. In the Third Earth Age, you will see a naked married woman taking a bath and instead of turning your eyes away, you continued to fix your eyes upon her.

---

[22] Numbers 25:1-8 NIV.

Then, as King, you sent for her and violated repeated God's command not to commit adultery. When she was with child, you sent for her husband from the battle, but because of his loyalty to Israel, he did see his wife.

Finally, you decided to murder her husband in direct violation of the law, not to kill.[23] David, do you surely believe you could kill the most beautiful naked young girls in the world coming toward you with her arms open wide with her breast pointing straight at you? I suspect you would melt like butter dropped on a hot skillet. [Laughter] Has she legally committed an act of war against you by pointing her naked breast at you?"

David, backing off, saying, "It appears to be the ultimate weapon. I don't trust myself in this area."

Abraham said, "There are two kinds of people. One says, "Gods bless my plan. The other says, "God, what's the plan!" Who among us would not be tempted, step forward?"

No one stepped forward.

Some said, "You, Abraham, go for us as you have the most beautiful woman in the world as your wife."

Abraham replied, "In the Third Earth Age I am going to have improper sexual relations with a dark skin, thin, petite, and attractive servant girl. The child she conceived by me is going to cause a mess in the world.[24] Don't hold me up as being invincible as I am just a flesh and blood man moved by what I see in the opposite sex. I thank God He gave me a warm, beautiful, and understanding wife."

Someone said, "If not you; we have no one."

Abraham inquired, "Who would not be tempted into being seduced by one of the most beautiful girls in the world?"

Luke responded, "Maybe the most beautiful woman in the world?"

All respond in unison, "Sarah!"

Sarah's Evangelistic Appeal to the Naked Young Females

Sarah, standing alone on 'Strength Rock' in Tel Aviv, Israel, wait, as the huge Poseidon Warship enters the harbor and anchors. An Eros[25] Party Boat filled with twenty-two (22) of the most beautiful young girls in the world is launched toward the shore. Some were topless. Others were naked wearing gold earrings, necklaces, and bracelets. They approached Strength Rock as Sarah steps out from behind a boulder using a sound system inquiring, "Do you know God the Father, God the Son, and God the Holy Spirit? God the Son will be born of a virgin, be crucified on a cross and shed His life's blood for the sins of all who receive Him as Savior. If you believe this, you can this day be saved from your sins and have eternal life. Would anyone desire to accept Jesus, God's Son, as your personal Savior?"

The leader mocked and sneered, "We have heard that nonsense before. It's just a fable.[26] Our god is Poseidon. You are even much more beautiful than we are. I've never seen a woman as beautiful as you – not in all Atlantis – what is your secret? Where are your men?"

Sarah with tears for their lost condition responds, "One secret of my beauty is the joy of being happily married to the man of my dreams.

---

[23] See 2 Samuel 11:2-14.

[24] See Genesis 16:1-2; 21:9-13.

[25] *Eros* is partially defined, "In Greek mythology the god of love, youngest of the gods, . . . identified with the Roman *Cupid*." *Britannica World Language Edition of Funk & Wagnalls Standard Dictionary*.

[26] *Fable* is defined, "To feign; to invent; to devise and speak of, as true or real." *American Dictionary of the English Language* Noah Webster 1828.

We only allow sexual relations here in Zion between a husband and wife. We walk side by side with our men, and we are much in love. That's God's plan – marriage – being one together.

I meet my entire husband's need in this area of sexual intimacy, and he meets my need. I am a satisfied woman who takes pleasure in my husband. We women of Zion need no help in meeting the sexual needs of our men. What do you want with our men as I am sure you have males in Atlantis?

They held up various gifts saying, "We have brought gifts, spices, perfumes, gold, and loves. On the Island of Atlantis, we have many wonderful delights. The mighty god Poseidon, who is the god of this vast ragging ocean, gives us such pleasure. Poseidon is god and not Jesus."

Sarah inquired further, "Then you heard it preached before about Jesus, God's Son, who is to die on the cross in the future to pay the penalty for the sins of those who of their own free will receive Him as Savior, repent, and confess Him as Lord."

The spokesperson replied, "Yes, we have heard that message. It's a fable."

Sarah responded, "No, it is true! This truth has set me free! I present to you again that Jesus is the Savior of the world. Today is your day of salvation! Today, if you hear the preached word, do not harden your hearts. Repent of your sins, which means you must turn away from them and be sorry for your sins. You can be born again and enjoy eternal life with Jesus. It is a wonderful life. Now is the day of salvation. Repent or perish!"

"The leader responded, "We will hear more about this later from you. Now where are your men so we can lie with them? We serve the great god of the ocean, Poseidon, and we can bring men such pleasures more than any of you!

Sarah, turning aside and walking away replies, "How can you reject such a great offer of salvation? No, you can't have our husbands. They belong to God and the wives of Zion intimately take care of our husbands. We have a marriage covenant of trust and faithfulness to each other. The only way you can get to my husband is to step over my dead body. *'No weapon formed against us will prevail.'*[27] You have tried to touch *'the apple of God's eye,'*[28] and this is a grave mistake. You have pronounced judgment on yourselves. Let us see if the false god Poseidon will save you!"

The spokesperson for the would-be seducers replied, "Do not walk away from us beautiful women. I am not through talking to you. Who do you think you are?" She fires a shot at Sarah with her laser pen just as Sarah disappears behind the boulder with the laser shot going over the top of the protective boulder.

Looking from behind the boulder, Sarah decrees, *"From this day I will see your faces no more.'*[29] Your blood is not on my hands.

Immediately four giant Leviathans with their eyes bugging out of the water much like crocodiles close in on each side of the Eros Party Boat. Many of the females scream and yell in terror. Some invoked the name "Poseidon." Others were trying to shoot the Leviathans with their laser pens. As each Leviathan come near to each side, they raise their heads and open their mouths and in unison shoot out a steady stream of flames burning each naked woman to a black crisp, which also catches the Eros Party Boat on fire. Soon the Eros Party Boat has a pungent smell of burning flesh, hair, and with billowing black smoke as it sinks beneath the surface of the sea not leaving a trace on the surface.

The main Poseidon Warship on witnessing the destruction of the Eros Party Boat turns seeking to escape out of the bay into the open sea. The Leviathans pursue and are soon enjoying heating the iron armor white hot with the flames thrown from their mouths catching the ship on fire in various places.

---

[27] Isaiah 54:17.
[28] Psalm 17:8; Proverbs 7:2; Zechariah 2:8.
[29] Exodus 14:13.

Acting much like a cat with a mouse, the Leviathans pick the ship apart piece by piece. The three dog lasers glance off the Leviathans much like 'water off a duck's back.'

Black Screen Protecting Elders Eyes Against Viewing Pornography

The eyes of the Elder being fully protected from the pornographic women, the screen in the Elders' Conference Room reappears with the Poseidon Warship burning with thick black billowing smoke and subsequently sinking beneath the surface of the sea without a trace.

Elder John spoke, "Shalom in Israel! Our Redeemer lives and knows how to protect us from our enemies. God is faithful to His people – the greatest love story of them all. He is and will mightily use His holy woman of Zion to help destroy the works of darkness, as this was truly a job for a woman. Our women believe in God and in us. They share our vision and help us fulfill our divine callings. We need to thank God for our good, pure, and warm women who protect us in more ways than we know!" All the Elders responded, "Amen!"

Sarah Reports to the Elders

Sarah returns to the capital city of Jerusalem with a veiled face and is escorted into the presence of the Elders. With a meek spirit, she respectfully waits to be spoken to first.

Abraham speaks, "My wife and daughter of Jerusalem, on behalf of myself and all Israel we thank you for being used to save our country from a well-planned vicious military act of war. Now we see the wisdom of God in dividing the Island of Atlantis away from Gondwanaland and protecting us with the Leviathans. God knows what He is going. He is always right. My dearest beloved Sarah, God, used you for '*such a time as this.*'[30] Thank you for being such a courageous woman willing to give your life for your country Israel. You saved our nation, and you are a national hero today. Please acknowledge the Lord and give us a report as our vision screen went blank, except for our viewing the final sinking of the primary Warship."

Sarah replied, "May it please my lord, my precious husband, and the Elders, the battle was the Lord's. He deserves all the glory. Jesus is the hero, not I! Today I just happen to be His chosen vessel. It is all over! They are now all in Hell. I weep for them as they had such potential to serve God. These women were so prideful and unclean! It will be written,

'*And those who walk in pride He (God) is able to humble.*'[31]

How hard it will be for the beautiful, the prideful, and the rich to be saved. I assume they were beautiful. I hardly noticed as I was focusing with tears on their eternal spirits as I was endeavoring to lead them to salvation by preaching the truth that the Son of God, Jesus, would be crucified for the sins of those who would receive Him as Savior. They were without excuse. I did what I could, but having heard and rejected the Good News before that 'Jesus Saves,' they had hardened their hearts of their own 'free will.' They had chosen the brief pleasures of sin over the eternal salvation of their souls. It will be written, '*God was pleased through the foolishness of what was preached to save those who believe.*'[32]

I looked each in the eye as I preached to them, and of their own '*free will,*' each rejected such a great offer of salvation. I could not persuade any to repent and receive Jesus as Savior. They mocked me and mocked God. No, not one accepted such a great offer of salvation.

---

[30] Quote from Esther 4:14 (NIV) wherein Esther was used to save the Israeli people.
[31] Daniel 4:37 NIV.
[32] 1 Corinthians 1:21 NIV.

They all died in their sins, calling upon their false god, Poseidon. They are all lost in Hell as they died a horrible death of being burned alive by the flame of four monstrous Leviathans."

Elder Luke inquired, "Describe the people to whom you were preaching. Were they truly that beautiful?"

Sarah respectfully responded, "Doctor Luke, I am not going to give you an organ recital! [Laughter] Men, all I am going to say on that subject is that I believe you did the right thing in sending a woman. They were smoking something that smelled worse than burning rope, which stunk so much it would gag a maggot. Some were coughing. You can imagine what it was doing to their lungs growing blacker with each puff. It is good to breathe smoke-free air again. They were drinking something yellow, which also smelled awful. They were polluting the entire outdoors as they neared the shores of Zion, lovely clean air Zion. Let us call good, good, and evil, evil. They were evil fifty women! Even the Holy Spirit blanked out your screen here to protect your eyes and thoughts from such filthy pornography and lewdness. God will not allow pornography to be shown on His screen. He knows how to protect his own from such fifth. Your eyes are not garbage cans. Not all that glitters is gold. There is no condemnation to those who commit themselves to holiness and purity. You can't stop a bird from flying over your head, but you need not let it build a nest in your hair. [Laughter] The Lord will protect and deliver those who trust in Him. Now cast down any imaginations regarding these females, as they are only a mirage or illusion. Deceptive and false, with a hidden agenda."

Elder Luke further inquired of Sarah, "There is something else, isn't it?"

Dr. Luke, the Holy Spirit further revealed these females had, just before this launching, all been unbeknown to them, infected with a contagious plague known as AIDS. AIDS has no known cure, being an act of terrorism of the utmost! Its delivery system is sexual contact with an infected vagina or the infected saliva in the mouth from kissing. Our men contracting and being infected with AIDS would die a horrible death in shame. AIDS destroys certain types of white blood cells, weakening the body's defense against infections and cancers. The symptoms before an early death include, but are not limited to rashes, swollen lymph nodes, fatigue, difficulty breathing, coughing, fever, night sweats, weight loss, chest pain, lethargy, seizures, headaches, confusion, diarrhea, and clouding of vision or blindness. Here is how it affects some areas of the body,

Brain: Memory loss and difficulty thinking and concentrating, eventually resulting in dementia, and weakness, tremor, or difficulty walking;

Kidneys: Swelling in the legs and face, fatigue, and changes in urination;

Heart and Lungs: Shortness of breath, cough, and wheezing;

Genital organs: Decreased levels of sex hormones, which leads to a decreased interest in sex.

Elders of Israel, what about this sounds beautiful to you? [Silence among the Elders.]

Abraham concludes, "God meant it when He commanded, "*You shall not commit adultery!*"[33] There is nothing to compare to the joyful and pure intimacy in marriage. I suggest we thank God for delivering us from the temptation of those evil women and also thank God for our wives, our helpmates, in various areas, including the pure and holy marriage bed. Here is a song on the screen to teach our children,

---

[33] Exodus 20:16 NIV.

'O be careful little eyes what you see
O be careful little eyes what you see
There's a Father up above
And He's looking down in love
So, be careful little eyes what you see.
O be careful little ears what you hear
O be careful little ears what you hear
There's a Father up above
And He's looking down in love
So, be careful little ears what you hear

O be careful little hands what you do
O be careful little hands what you do
There's a Father up above
And He's looking down in love
So, be careful little hands what you do.[34]

Let us further confess this Scripture together appearing now on the screen,
'Brothers, I do not consider myself yet to have taken hold. But one thing I do: Forgetting what is behind and straining towards what is ahead, I press on towards the goal to win the prize for which God has called me heavenwards in Christ Jesus.'[35]

Let none of us think about or talk any more about this temptation. God was mighty to save us! We worship and thank Him we did not fall into sexual temptation. God loves us so much to make us such warm and loving wives to enjoy and to help us be the men God intended us to be. Let us keep our faith in God and our commitment of love, trust, and faithfulness to our wives. It will be written of such delightful wives,

'A wife of noble character who can find?
  She is worth far more than rubies.
Her husband has full confidence in her
  and lacks nothing of value.
She brings him good, not harm,
  all the days of her life.
She selects wool and flax
  and works with eager hands.
She is like the merchant ships,
  bringing her food from afar.
She gets up while it is still dark;
  she provides food for her family
  and portions for her servant girls.
She considers a field and buys it;
  out of her earnings she plants a vineyard.
She sets about her work vigorously;
  her arms are strong for her tasks.
She sees that her trading is profitable,
  and her lamp does not go out at night.
In her hand she holds the distaff
  and grasps the spindle with her fingers.
She opens her arms to the poor
  and extends her hands to the needy.

---

[34] O *Be Careful Little Eyes* is a children's Bible song taught in the Third Earth Age in churches, Bible classes, and Vacation Bible Schools. It is sung *via* the internet at You Tube.
[35] Philippians 3:13-14 NIV.

When it snows, she has no fear for her household,
*   for all of them are clothed in scarlet.*
She makes coverings for her bed;
*   she is clothed in fine linen and purple.*
Her husband is respected at the city gate,
*   where he takes his seat among the Elders of the land.*
She makes linen garments and sells them,
*   and supplies the merchants with sashes.*
She is clothed with strength and dignity;
*   she can laugh at the days to come.*
She speaks with wisdom,
*   and faithful instruction is on her tongue.*
She watches over the affairs of her household
*   and does not eat the bread of idleness.*
Her children arise and call her blessed;
*   her husband also, and he praises her:*
'Many women do noble things,
*   but you surpass them all.'*
Charm is deceptive, and beauty is fleeting;
*   but a woman who fears the Lord is to be praised.*
Give her the reward she has earned,
*   and let her works bring her praise at the city gate.'*[36]

Elders this describes our wives of noble character. Now let us go home to a candlelight dinner and enjoy to the uttermost our loving and warm wives the Lord has given us. Having no further business to come this day before the meeting of the elders, do I hear a motion to adjourn?"

Elder John closes, "So, move."

Elder David, "I second that motion."

Abraham responds, "All in favor say, 'Aye.'
Unanimous 'Ayes.'

Any opposed, say, 'No." Hearing none, the Elders, are adjourned!'†

---

[6] Proverbs 31:10-31 NIV.

†BOOK SEVEN – Episode 2†

[†**Sidebar Scriptures**: "*Joseph had a dream and promptly reported all the details (Genesis 37:5).*"
"*The Lord revealed to me what the evil ones were doing and planning and showed me their wicked plots (Jeremiah 11:18).*"
"The word of the Lord came to Abram in a **vision**. . . . A **deep sleep** came upon Abram . . . . (Genesis 15:1, 12)."
I witnessed and experienced "*dreams and visions, and I described **all** I had seen to instruct many (Daniel 7:1, 11:33).*"†]

Atlas II Abolishes the Ten Laws of Atlantis, and Revival Begins on the Island of Atlantis

The Ten Laws, Which the Late King Atlas Enacted as the Law of the Land

THE LATE KING ATLAS had securely placed the Ten Laws of Atlantis throughout the Island of Atlantis and on certain public buildings, and in all the schools, after he saw in a dream the finger of the Creator of Heaven and Earth, Jesus, write the Ten Commandments. The late King Atlas decreed regarding these Ten Commandments, "These first rules of law are not suggestions, but they are the foundational and fundamental law for all Atlantis. The penalty for breaking any of these laws of the land is up to a seven months imprisonment, also up to two years of public-service duties and three years of probation, except murder and adultery, which carry an additional sanction of up to execution. The late King Atlas posted these binding laws in all public buildings, in each school classroom, and on the Great Pyramid at the North end of the island of Atlantis,

TEN LAWS (COMMANDMENTS) OF ATLANTIS
By
The One True God

1. "Thou shalt have no other gods before Me!"[1]
2. "Thou shalt not make unto thee any graven image!"[2]
3. "Thou shalt not take the name of the Lord thy God in vain!"[3]
4. "Remember the Sabbath day, to keep it holy!"[4]
5. "Honor thy father and thy mother!"[5]
6. "Thou shalt not kill!"[6]
7. "Thou shalt not commit adultery!"[7]
8. "Thou shalt not steal!"[8]
9. "Thou shalt not bear false witness against thy neighbor!"[9]
10. "Thou shalt not covet!"[10]

---

[1] See Exodus 20:3.
[2] See Exodus 20:4.
[3] See Exodus 20:7.
[4] See Exodus 20:8.
[5] See Exodus 20:12.
[6] See Exodus 20:13.
[7] See Exodus 20:14.
[8] See Exodus 20:15.
[9] See Exodus 20:16.
[10] See Exodus 20:17.

Atlas II Issues His Executive Order to Abolish and Hold
Null and Void the Ten Laws of Atlantis and to
Affirm Poseidon as the Sole Religion of Atlantis

King Atlas II, mocking while drinking Cobra liquor from a golden cup kept filled by two scantily dressed temple goddesses, with long fingernails rubbing his back, signs into law his executive order seeking to annul God's Commandments.

'WHEREAS, my father, the first king of Atlantis, averred that he saw in a dream the finger of God writing certain laws, which are this day repealed and are ordered to be removed from all public buildings and from all the schools and classrooms;

WHEREAS, only the god Poseidon has any authority to tell us what to do as we enjoy all the pleasures he gives us here at Atlantis;

WHEREAS, I strongly suggest to Pastor Luther, to also remove these words from the Great Pyramid, which is sitting on private, nonprofit, and tax-exempt property. Further, I invite those of his small congregation in Loveland to join us in the fun of worshiping and serving Poseidon and warn them not to criticize our encouraging same-sex marriages and the adoption into that union of same-sex children.

WHEREAS IT IS DECREED AND ORDERED that Poseidon, is the god of Atlantis and anyone found worshipping any other god nor not following the Laws of Poseidon or participating in the worship at the Temple of Poseidon will be thrown into the execution shark tank.

SO ORDERED!

King Atlas II'

Pastor Luther's Ignoring of King Atlas II's Proposal to Remove
God's Ten Commandments Written on the Front of The Great Pyramid on
Private Non-Profit Church Land in Loveland, Atlantis

Attorney Job's had great foresight in preparing a deed 'whereby title to realty was transferred'[11] to all his vast parcels of land behind the Great Pyramid in Loveland to a non-profit, tax-exempt organization. This deeded land is to be used for both an outdoor stadium and an indoor sanctuary on the church grounds known as Salem, meaning *'peace, especially between man and God or the well-being, welfare or safety of a person or a group of persons.'*[12] These facilities have now been constructed.

Attorney Job's law partner, Luther, has been serving as pastor since Job's mysterious disappearance from the face of the Earth and writes on his legal pad,

"REVIVAL!
IGNORE ORDER TO REMOVE TEN COMMANDMENTS!
PRIVATE PROPERTY!
NO JURISDICTION!
GOVERNMENT INTERFERENCE
WITH FREEDOM OF RELIGION
GUARANTEED IN THE ATLANTIS CONSTITUTION!"

---

[11] *Deed* definition from *Black's Law Dictionary.'*
[12] Quoting from *Shalom* at *Wikipedia, The Free Encyclopedia.*

Pastor Luther at the conclusion of a Sunday afternoon church service meets with his seventy-member congregation in the beautiful outdoor stadium.

Ruth, Luther's lovely virgin daughter, in her beautiful calligraphy writing complete with artwork, has transcribed her dad's dictation of his Ninety-five Theses. Pastor Luther had set forth the truth of the eternal God, revealing Himself as the Father, Son, and Holy Spirit, being the only true God, and exposing the evils of following the false god Poseidon in the city of Atlantis. Pastor Luther thanks his virgin daughter Ruth and announces,

"Saints, it can't be 'we and no more.' We have been fishing out of our own bathtub while people in the City of Atlantis are starting to die like flies of lung cancer and AIDS. Lost in their sins! *'Hell is opening wide its mouth to swallow up the nobles and masses.'*[13] Atlas II is demanding that all worship Poseidon, a man-made false god! He is proclaiming and laughing that when the people die, they will all be dead like his dog Rover. He is advancing, let us all *'eat, drink, and, be merry (have loads of fun)'*[14] for tomorrow all eventually will die and are no more.

As we all know, these people are made in the image of God. God loves them and has a wonderful plan for their salvation and eternal future. With God, there is always a way out! God is not *'wanting any to perish (in Hell), but everyone to come to repentance.'*[15] The time is short. Now all should be urged sincerely to repent of their sins, receive God's Son, Jesus, as Savior, and confess 'Jesus Christ is my Lord!'

Saints, it is time for a revival![16] I will seek to communicate with my law partner Job's best friend, Preacher Melchizedek, to hold us a Revival starting May 1st. This Revival will especially be for those sincerely desiring salvation from their sins, healing for their bodies, or deliverance from addictive habits such as tobacco, marijuana, and, yes, even from homosexuality and lesbianism. Our Creator designed marriage as a natural romantic outlet for His divinely created sexual desire. The sweet love story of marital love invented by God is older than the sea or Earth. The Holy Scriptures directs,

'But since there is so much immorality, each man should have his own wife and each woman her own husband. The husband should fulfill his marital duty to his wife, and likewise the wife to her husband. The wife's body does not belong to her alone, but also to her husband. In the same way, the husband's body does not belong to him alone, but also to his wife. Do not deprive each other except by mutual consent and for a time, so you may devote yourselves to prayer. Then come together again (sexually, so you will not be tempted) so Satan (evil one) will not tempt you because of your lack of self-control.'[17]

Questions? [An extended period of silence.]

Finally, a Church Elder stood and advances,

"You realize that Atlas II will consider this a declaration of war?"

Pastor Luther responds, "My dear Brother in the Lord, I realize that!"

---

[13] Isaiah 5:14.

[14] Luke 12:19.

[15] 2 Peter 3:9.

[16] *Revival* is defined in part, "Renewed and more active attention to religion; an awakening of men to their spiritual concerns." *American Dictionary of the English Language* Noah Webster 1828.

[17] 1 Corinthians 7:2-5.

This Elder with tears humbly replies,

"Well, as long as you realize that, then let us hook up our shields of faith and having done all to stand together shoulder to shoulder. No fiery darts of the enemy will harm our invited evangelist.[18]

As an Elder of this Church I respectfully ask if anyone wants out, now is the time to get out by just raising your hand. I sense in my born again spirit that some of you evangelizing in Atlantis will be martyred. We probably will have a terrorist attack on one or more of our services." [No hands were raised desiring to want out.]

Pastor Luther affirms, "We are united seventy strong in faith and victory for the cause of Jesus, God's Son. Now let us rise in a circle and join hands locking up our '*shields of faith.*'[19] He who is not for this revival is against it, and he who is against it is fighting against God Himself. After Jesus' sacrifice on a cross in the Third Earth Age, it will be explained,

'*If God is for us, who can be against us? He who did not spare His own Son, but gave Him up for us all – how will He not also, with Him, graciously give us all things? Who will bring any charge against those whom God has chosen? It is God who justifies. Who is he that condemns? Christ Jesus, who died – more than that, who was raised to life – is at the right hand of God and is also interceding for us. Who shall separate us from the love of Christ? Shall trouble or hardship or persecution or famine or nakedness or danger or sword? As it is written:*

'*For your sake we face death all day long; we are considered as sheep to be slaughtered.*'[20]

No, in all these things we (believers in Jesus as Savior) are more than conquerors through Him who loved us. For I am convinced that neither death, nor life, neither angels nor demons, neither the present nor the future, nor any powers, neither height nor depth, nor anything else in all creation, can separate us from the love of God in Christ Jesus our Lord.'[21]

'*Whoever is not with (joining as a part) Me (Jesus, Son of God, in bringing believers together) is against (driving others away, opposes) Me.*'[22]

All seventy (70) brave church members stood, from little children, pregnant wives, to those appointed to leadership positions, in a circle and joined hands as Pastor Luther leads in prayer,

"Our Father God Most High, owner of Heaven and Earth, including this island of Atlantis and all this church ground upon which we are standing in unity, hallowed be Your name and the name of your Son, Jesus, our Savior and Lord, and of the Holy Spirit.

All us present seek to love You with all our hearts, with all our souls, with all our minds, and with all our strength[23] and to love our neighbors, made in Your image in the nearby City of Atlantis, as ourselves.[24] You do not desire them to perish in Hell, but each one to repent and truly be born again. We will use the secret weapon toward them of the love of Jesus! Regarding our prayer for revival let us stand on this Scripture.

---

[18] This Elder spoke prophetically by the Holy Spirit, as he knew nothing about the three-dog laser gun, which shoots like a fiery dart.

[19] Ephesians 6:16.

[20] Quoting Psalm 44:22.

[21] Romans 8:31-39.

[22] Matthew 12:30.

[23] From the teachings of the Lord Jesus recorded in Mark 12:30.

[24] From the teachings of the Lord Jesus recorded in Mark 12:31.

'Now to Him (God) who is able to do immeasurably more than all we ask or imagine, according to His power (of love) that is working among us.'[25]

May God's kingdom come, and His will be done regarding this upcoming Reformation Revival. *'Lead us not into temptation, but deliver us from the evil one (Lucifer, prince of darkness)!'*[26] You know that our teaching, which is really Your teaching that sex outside of marriage is sin has generally been rejected in Atlantis and darkness is seeking to pervert your plan to celebrate sex only in the marriage bed.

As we invite those lost in sin in the City of Atlantis to Your revival services, give us love, joy, peace, faith, courage, boldness, favor, and an excellent testimony.

Let no fear of death deter us. If we die for the cause of Jesus Christ, we will have great eternal rewards, and we will hear, *'Well done, good and faithful servant!'*[27]

We have no fear of death, but we fear not using the talents you have given us for Your glory and fear falling into sexual sins. We all here are committed to refrain from sexual sins! We love You, and desire to honor You with our born again human spirits, our renewed souls (minds, emotions, wills), and bodies. We thank You for Your mercy and grace in saving us. We offer our *'bodies as living sacrifices, holy and pleasing to God – which is our spiritual (reasonable) worship.'*[28]

Father God, You love the people of Atlantis made in Your image so much You will send Your Son, Jesus, in the fullness of time to die on the cross to fully pay for the sins of all those who will receive Him as Savior, sincerely repent of their sins, and with their mouths confess Jesus is their Lord and master. Let us not *'despise the days of small beginnings.'*[29]

We adore Your wisdom in choosing what seems like the foolishness of preaching to save (from Hell) those who believe'[30] in Jesus as Savior and confess Jesus as their Lord.

We ask You for great things from this revival for Your glory and honor. In Jesus' Name. Amen!"

The entire congregation responded, "Amen!"

One leader asked for clarification,

"Who will be leading the praise and worship and how will you communicate with Preacher Melchizedek?

Pastor Luther answers, "I will be humbly leading the praise and worship with our orchestra and choir. I have been working on a new song 'A Mighty Fortress is our God.'

I met Melchizedek once during a visit to my law partner Job. Job told me that if we ever needed a revival for me to call upon Preacher Melchizedek. Therefore, in prayer, I entreated, 'Father God, communicate our need for revival to Preacher Melchizedek in Jesus' Name, Amen!' I then felt led by the Holy Spirit to open the law office door and coming up the walk was Job's friend Melchizedek. He was wearing a homespun white robe and sandals. Melchizedek had *'no (royal, kingly pomp) form or comeliness (anything outstanding in his appearance) that we should look at Him, and no distinguished (notable) appearance that we should desire Him.'*[31]

---

[25] Ephesians 3:20.

[26] Matthew 6:13.

[27] Quote from Matthew 25:21, 23.

[28] See Romans 12:1.

[29] Zechariah 4:10.

[30] 1 Corinthians 1:27.

[31] Isaiah 53:2 Amp.

No human man ever talked like Melchizedek. He said he would come if the majority voted for revival. Therefore, I would like us to vote to have Evangelist Melchizedek hold a revival.

All in favor, let it be signified by saying, 'Aye.' All seventy saints said, 'Aye.' All oppose say, 'No.' Hearing no opposition, Pastor Luther declared. "The ayes have it!

I will proceed to invite Evangelist Melchizedek to hold us a revival on our lovely Island of Atlantis, with the first meeting scheduled for the evening of May 1. Let us believe in good weather that night so we can hold the first meeting outside. We are going to have a full moon that will turn red as blood (meaning the moon is between the Earth and the sun with the Earth's shadow falling on the moon in a total lunar eclipse) at 8:00 P.M. representing the blood of God's Son, saving us who believe '*from God's wrath through Jesus . . .* (so) *we (believers) can rejoice.in God (the Father) through our Lord Jesus Christ, through Whom we (believers) now received the reconciliation (translated into God's family).*'[32] Amen! [So be it.]"

Pastor Luther Presents a Formal Invitation to Pastor Melchizedek

The next day at the 3:00 P.M. hour of prayer, Pastor Luther knelt and prayed,

"Father God, you have seen Your people's heart cry for revival. Seventy brave souls said yes, without even one in opposition. United we stand! Please communicate our unanimous vote to my friend Melchizedek. In Jesus' Name. Amen!"

Almost immediately, a knock was on the law-office front door. Pastor Luther throws the door open, and hugs Evangelist Melchizedek and says, "Come in and '*let us reason together,*'[33] as we desire revival." Going into Attorney Job's conference room, Melchizedek speaks, "I have heard regarding the City of Atlantis, '*their sin (is) so grievous.*'[34] Pastor Luther, you are a lawyer, please present some examples of these grievous sins I hear about."

[NOTE: Children and the very judgmental religious should skip the truths in the next two sections focusing on the sins of Sodom and Gomorrah and Atlantis.]

Brother Melchizedek, sin and mistreatment of children, are abounding in the City of Atlantis. I just received a reliable report regarding one of our church member's sister's son, age only twelve, now firmly addicted to the bondage of smoking cigarettes and marijuana and tricked into a lifestyle of homosexuality. Here are the facts of causing this little one to stumble into sin:

Atlas II's director of Boy's Youth Services, a man named Newton, pulled up beside a twelve-year-old boy walking home from school asking if he would like to earn extra money. Newton then brought him over to his house and said to this youth, 'How would you like to learn a black magic trick. Here is some money I am laying on the table, and I will pay you while you learn.' The young lad looking at the money nodded *yes,* as he watched Newton handcuffed himself to an overhead chinning bar. Now listen carefully, 'Abracadabra Open Says Me!' The handcuffs sprang open. Now would you like to try it?'

"The youth handcuffed himself to the bar above and attempted, to say the words with nothing happening. Newton lit a marijuana cigarette and taped it to the youth's mouth instructing that if you suck the smoke into your lungs, this will enlighten you. Soon the youth was high, and Newton pulled down the boy's pants and introduced this child to oral sex, taking this youth's virginity. Newton marked it in his night timer to report the conquest to Atlas II.

---

[32] Romans 5:10-11,
[33] Isaiah 1:18.
[34] Quote from Genesis 18:20.

Newton then said the words, "Abracadabra,[35] open says me! The handcuffs sprang open with Newton giving the child a significant amount of money and a box of marijuana and tobacco cigarettes with black lighters having a flat gold musical note on the side. He instructs the youth, "Don't tell anyone about our meeting. Give these presents out to your friends in school and be back, here again, Friday for a second lesson in magic, and I will give you another like sum of money and another box of smokes. You will soon be the richest twelve-year-old in Atlantis."

Pastor Luther, with tears, continued, "That next Friday Newton did the same trick, but, this time, taught the child about sodomy while he masturbated the youth again to climax with his hand. The lad smoked another Marijuana cigarette, with the rest too gross for me to speak.

Pastor Melchizedek, we are losing more and more of our young boys to a life of homosexuality and binding addiction to the bondage of smoking marijuana and tobacco cigarettes. The seduced and addicted boys subsequently formed the Vampire Club in which they cut foreskin and drink the blood while they perform oral sex and acts of sodomy with each other and new converts.

Preacher Melchizedek with tears responds, "It will be written of similar homosexually in the Second Earth Age, Scripture will record,

'*Then the Lord said, 'The outcry against Sodom and Gomorrah is so great and their sins are so grievous.*'[36]

'*Before the angels (Michael and Gabriel) had gone to bed, all the men from every part of the city of Sodom – both young and old – surrounded the house. They called to Lot, 'Where are the men (not knowing they were angels in the form of men) who came to you tonight? Bring them out to us so we can have sex (sodomy and oral sex) with them.*'[37]

Pastor Luther, 'What about the precious young girls, also made in the image of God?'

Pastor Luther, cupping his face in his hands, sobbing further testifies, "Atlas II's, director of the Girls Youth Services, Magdalene, starts the girls of Atlantis very young in Charm School. Her focus is to get these little ones to stumble early in life. She has them shower together and admire each other's naked bodies. She explains that since they saw each other in the shower, it is okay to learn to balance and walk together naked since no males are around. She gets them competing in nude beauty contests against each other in which they compared breasts and shaved off the pubic hair areas. Each young girl has a woman personal trainer, who is a lesbian, and she gives the young girl massages. The woman explains that she has to massage every part of the body and that it is best for them to use their tongues on the sexual parts. The goal is to introduce them to the pleasures of the sin of lesbianism as they use a small vibrating dildo to de-virgin every young girl. They keep a record of the date and the numbers of each young girl they de-virgin. Soon they massage with larger and larger vibrating dildos with the goal of stretching and taking the tightness out the previously virgin vagina, while degrading marriage with such words as a husband's peanut penis cannot compare to this. Soon they are hooked to the fun of lesbian orgies. They constantly berate and ridicule marriage between one man and one woman! Each girl retains sixty-six (66) morning after abortion pills, required to take after she fornicates with a male the night before.

Like the boys, they like to introduce the young girls to both marijuana and tobacco cigarettes. Occasionally, they have nudist beauty contests at different age levels with prizes, and this gives the lesbians an opportunity to view the girls and to negotiate switching up as the personal trainers. In that nudist atmosphere, the perversion grows worse and worse. They have an enormous one-way mirror in which Atlas II and others can laugh, masturbate, and homosexual together on the other side.

The team of Newton and Magdalene seem unstoppable in causing our little ones to enter into sexual perversion. They consider a pure Christian marriage under a wedding covenant of faithfulness, wearing gold rings for all to see, to be their number one enemy.

---

[35] "Abracadabra is an incantation used as a magic word in stage magic tricks."
Wikipedia, The Free Encyclopedia.
[36] Genesis 18:20. NIV.
[37] Genesis 19:4-5. NIV.

Pastor Melchizedek, please forgive me for having to be so graphic as we have many more examples." [Weeping and wiping his eyes with his shirt sleeve.]

Pastor Melchizedek with tears falling to the ground said, "You did not sin in exposing the evil. You cannot be like an ostrich and hide your head in the sand while those around you made in the image of God are going to Hell. A man has to do what man has to do!"

Luther further explained, "Pasture Melchizedek, there are some children in Atlantis '*not yet old enough to know their right hand from their left.*'[38] Others who have never heard the Good News that the Son of God will die on the cross for their sins. Many I believe will receive Jesus as their Savior by inviting Him to come into their heart as they truly repent of their sins and confess that He is their Lord. We urgently need a revival of repentance, forgiveness, salvation, deliverance from sexual addictions, healing from AIDS, and the need to safeguard against sexual immorality by having a pure and satisfying marriage under a marriage covenant.

I entreat you to give us an opportunity to invite the lost in Atlantis to hear this Good News (Gospel) '*that God is not willing that any should perish in Hell, but that all can come to repentance.*'[39] Then if they reject such a great salvation . . ." [Tears flowing and being unable to finish the sentence.]

"Brother Luther it will be written regarding those who reject such a great salvation,

'*For God's wrath (anger; retribution) is being revealed from Heaven against all the evil and wicked things people do. By their own evil lives (indulging in sinful practices), they ignore (suppress) the truth.*

'*Because they did these things, God abandoned them to (let them pursue) their lusts of their sinful desires to sexual impurity (uncleanness) and the dishonoring of their bodies with one another.*

. . . Because people did those things, God abandoned them to (to pursue; gave them over to) shameful (degrading; dishonorable) lusts (passions). Their women stopped having (or desiring) natural sex (with husbands) and had perversion (with their mouths, fingers, and foreign objects) with other women. In the same way, men abandoned natural sex with wives and became inflamed (oral sex and sodomy) in their lust for each other. Men did shameful things with other men (and even to male children), and in their bodies, they received the recompense and due penalty for those perversions.

And since they did not think it was important to seek the truth, God gave them (having free wills to choose) over to their own worthless pursuit and depraved minds to do things they should not do.'[40]

Abraham Teaching the 144,000 Jewish Evangelists

Appearing on the screen was Luther and Melchizedek as they sob together over the little ones made in the image of God being bound by grievous sins being committed in the City of Atlantis.

Pastor Luther entreats Preacher Melchizedek, "Will you hold a revival to start May 1st here in Salem[41] on the Celebrate Jesus Church property in Loveland, Atlantis? Will you?"

---

[38] Jonah 4:11.

[39] 2 Peter 3:9.

[40] See Romans 1:18-28.

[41] "The name *Salem* . . . is derived from the same root as the word *shalom*' meaning peace." Quoting from *Names of Jerusalem* at **Wikipedia, The Free Encyclopedia**.

Preacher Melchizedek replied, "Yes! I will. Your love and compassion will not fail in saving many from Hell. Amazing grace will be present to set the captives free. *'If the Son (Jesus) sets you free. You shall be free indeed.'*[42]

Now go into the hedges and the byways and entreat them to come to the revival meetings. Let revival began on this island of Atlantis."

Luther humbly responds, "Amen!"

Abraham, continuing the teaching of the 144,000 Jewish evangelists. He said, "Let me tell you about the first time I met the Son of God manifesting Himself as a man in the Third-Earth Age, as it will be written,

'The Lord (Son of God) appeared to Abraham near the great trees of Mamre while he was sitting at the entrance to his tent in the heat of the day, Abraham looked up and saw three men (Son of God, Angel Michael, and Angel Gabriel) standing nearby. When he saw them, he hurried from the entrance of his tent to meet them and bowed low to the ground.

He said, 'If I have found favor in Your eyes, my Lord, do not pass your servant by. Let a little water be brought, and then you may all wash your feet and rest under this tree. Let me get you something to eat, so you can be refreshed and then go on your way — now that you have come to your servant.'

'Very well,' they answered, '(we will) do as you say. . . . He then brought curds and milk and the calf prepared and set these before them. While they ate, he stood near them under a tree.

'Where is your wife Sarah?' they asked him.

'There, in the tent,' he said.

Then the Lord (Son of God) said, "I will surely return to you about this time next year, and Sarah your wife will have a son.'

'Is anything too hard for the Lord (Son of God)? I will return to you at the appointed time next year, and Sarah will have a son."

. . . When the men got up to leave, they looked down towards Sodom, and Abraham walked with them to see them on their way. Then the Lord said, 'Shall I hide from Abraham what I am about to do? Abraham will surely become a great and powerful nation, and all nations on earth will be blessed through him. For I have chosen him, so he will direct his children and his household after him to keep the ways of the Lord by doing what is right and just, so the Lord will bring about for Abraham what he has promised him.'

Then the Lord said, 'The outcry against Sodom and Gomorrah is so great and their sin, so grievous (sodomy, oral sex, and various acts of homosexuality) that I will see (direct admissible evidence and not hearsay) if what they have done is as bad as the outcry that has reached me. If not, I will know.'

The men (Michael and Gabriel) turned away and went towards Sodom, but

Abraham remained standing before the Lord (Son of God). Then Abraham approached Him and said, 'Will you sweep away the righteous with the wicked? What if there are fifty righteous people in the city?

Will you really sweep it away and not spare the place for the sake of the fifty righteous people in it? Far be it from You to do such a thing – to kill the righteous with the wicked, treating the righteous and the wicked alike.

Far be it from you! Will not the Judge of all the Earth do right?"

---

[42] John 8:36.

The Lord said, 'If I find fifty righteous people in the city of Sodom, I will spare the whole place for their sake.'

Then Abraham spoke up again: "Now that I have been so bold as to speak to the Lord, though I am nothing but dust and ashes, what if the number of the righteous is five less than fifty? Will you destroy the whole city because of five people?"

'If I find forty-five there,' He said, "I will not destroy it. [43]

Abraham interjects, "I presented my case all the way down to if only ten righteous were found in the city with the Lord, assuring me, 'For the sake of ten, I will not destroy it.'

When the Lord had finished speaking with Abraham, He left (and returned to Heaven), and Abraham returned home.

The two angels (Michael and Gabriel) arrived at Sodom in the evening, and Lot was sitting in the gateway of the city. . . . Lot said, 'please turn aside to your servant's house. You can wash your feet and spend the night and then go on your way early in the morning.' 'No,' they answered, 'we will spend the night in the square.'

Before they had gone to bed, all the men from every part of the city of Sodom – both young and old – surrounded the house. They called to Lot, 'Where are the men who came to you tonight? Bring them out to us so we can have sex (sodomy and oral sex) with them.'

Lot went outside to meet them and shut the door behind him and said, 'No, my friends. Don't do this wicked thing. Look, I have two daughters who have never slept with a man. Let me bring them out to you, and you can do what you like with them. But do nothing to these men, for they have come under the protection of my roof."

'Get out of our way,' they replied. And they said, 'This fellow (Lot) came here as an alien, and now he wants to play the judge! We'll treat you worse than them.' They kept bringing pressure on Lot and moved forward to break down the door.

But the men inside reached out and pulled Lot back into the house and shut the door, Then they struck the men at the door of the house, young and old, with blindness so they could not find the door.

The two men (Michael and Gabriel) said to Lot, 'Do you have anyone else here – sons-in-law, sons or daughters, or anyone else in the city who belongs to you? Get them out of here, because we will destroy this place. The outcry to the Lord (Son of God) against its people is so great He has sent us to destroy it.'

With the coming of dawn, the angels urged Lot, saying, 'Hurry! Take your wife and your two daughters here, or you will be swept away when the city is punished.'Then the Lord rained down burning sulfur on Sodom and Gomorrah – from the Lord out of the heavens. He overthrew those cities and the entire plain, including all those living in the cities – and also the vegetation in the land. But Lot's wife looked back, and she became a pillar of salt. Early the next morning Abraham got up and returned to the place where he had stood before the Lord (Son of God). He looked down towards Sodom and Gomorrah, towards all the land of the plain, and he saw dense smoke rising from the land, like smoke from a furnace.

So when God destroyed the cities of the plain, He remembered Abraham, and He brought Lot out of the catastrophe that overthrew the cities where Lot had lived. [44]

---

[43] Genesis 18:1-5, 8-10, 14-28.
[44] Genesis 18:33; 19:1-2, 4-13, 15, 24-29.

Abraham explained that it would be written about him when in the Third Earth Age he again meets the Son of God manifesting himself in the Earth,

'This Melchizedek was king of Salem and priest of (Father) God Most High. He met Abraham returning from the defeat of the kings and blessed him, and Abraham gave him a tenth of everything. First, His name means "king of righteousness"; then also, "king of Salem" means "king of peace". Without (earthly) father or mother (until born in the earth of a virgin mother), without genealogy, without beginning of days or end of life, like (being) the Son of God He remains a priest forever. Just think how great He was: Even the patriarch Abraham gave him a tenth of the plunder!'[45]

My students, this was an appearance of the Son of God, Himself, the Lord Jesus Christ, the Savior of the world, as He as God had no beginning of days. We worship one Triune God. There is one person of the Father, another of the Son, and another of the Holy Spirit, but the Godhead of the Father, Son, and the Holy Spirit is one God. King David speaks by the Holy Spirit,

'The Lord (Father God) says to my Lord (Son of God):
    'Sit at My right hand
    until I make Your enemies
    a footstool for your feet.'
The Lord (Father God) will extend Your (Son of God) mighty scepter from Zion,
    (to) rule in the midst of Your enemies.
. . . The Lord (Father God) has sworn
    and will not change His mind:
    'You (Son of God) are a priest forever,
    in the order of Melchizedek.'[46]

"The term **Melchizedek** means 'K*ing of Righteousness.*'[47] The Scriptures will later explain that those who receive God's Son as their Savior receive His righteousness and also reign as king under His Kingship in this life,

'Those who receive (Father God's) overflowing grace (unmerited favor) and the free gift of righteousness (putting them into right standing with Himself) reign as kings in life through the One, Jesus Christ (the Son of God).'[48]

It will be written, *'To Him (the Son of God) who loves us and had freed us (those born again) by His*

    Blood, and has made us (Saints) to be a kingdom and priests to serve His God and Father.'[49]

There never was a time when God was not, and God will say of Himself,
'I am He
. . . Before Me no god was formed,
    nor will there be one after Me.
I, even I, am the Lord,
    and apart from Me there is no Savior.
. . . 'I am God
    Yes, and from ancient days I am He.

---

[45] Hebrews 7:1-4.
[46] Psalm 110:1-2, 4.
[47] This meaning is given to the term Melchizedek in such volumes as *The Zondervan Pictorial Encyclopedia of the Bible.*
[48] Romans 5:17.
[49] Revelation 1:5-6.

No one can deliver out of My hand,
    When I act, who can reverse it?[50]
. . . From everlasting to everlasting, You are God![51]

God exists from eternity to eternity. Time past, present, and future is comprehended in God, who is the eternal 'I AM!' God watches over those made in His image. No matter how sinful, God is not willing that any should perish (in Hell), but that all should come to repentance, receive Jesus, God's Son, as Savior, by giving Him their sins and receiving from Him His righteousness, and confess, 'Jesus is my Lord.'

Preacher Melchizedek and Pastor Luther Finalize Revival Plans

Pastor Luther hands Preacher Melchizedek a key and a map to the hidden tunnel entrance on the North side of the island leading to the private living quarters with one-way glass behind the crystal pulpit.

Evangelist Melchizedek reaches out his hand and receives the key warning, "You understand that Atlas II could consider the name Melchizedek meaning '*King of Righteousness,*' an act of treason and he will send in spies! What is your plan for security?"

Pastor Luther, replies, "We have planned to give out guest passes numbered 1 through 153 to be taken up at the entrance as they have first to go through a security scanner. We would not desire a terrorist to open fire with a laser gun in the service. Security will be tight. Our ushers will allow no one in who is not sincere and seeks only to be a spectator or a spy.

Preacher Melchizedek, "Atlas II is going to obtain one of your numbered tickets and send his disguised Director of Boy's Youth Services, Newton, to report back to him what is going on. Instead, of his usual black outfit, he will wear white pants and a red shirt. Check-in his camera for him to receive back when he leaves, but alert your ushers to let him in."

Pastor Luther argues, "Sir, Newton is the Vice-King of Atlantis, and Only Atlas II is more powerful. Newton is very prideful in his own eyes. He is truly the chief of sinners on this island and has led many a young boy into homosexuality and gross sins. There is not a greater sinner in all Atlantis than this evil and proud man."

Preacher Melchizedek smiles advancing, "Would not Newton be a big fish to catch for the glory of God? Those who have been '*forgiven much love much.*'[52] This revival is for the wretched sinners and not for people who need no repentance. There is more joy in Heaven over one sinner who changes his heart and lifestyle by repenting than over ninety-nine righteous (saved) people who need not change their lifestyle.[53]

Pastor Luther, regarding the next revival service Newton, is to be called by his first name John, which means '*God is gracious.*'[54] Later he will bring Magdalene, who after her conversion will be called Mary. Their faith in the future shed blood of Jesus will cleanse them as white as snow here in this First Earth Age. A sign and wonder to many!

---

[50] Isaiah 43:10-13.
[51] Psalm 90:2.
[52] See Luke 7:47.
[53] See Luke 15:7 in various translations.
[54] John means, "God is gracious."
     See *The New Name Dictionary – The Modern English and Hew Names* by Alfred J. Kolatch.

Their past sins are to be removed from them as far '*as the East is from the West*,'[55] and be cast into the '*deepest part of the sea*'[56] of God's forgetfulness to be remembered no more.

They will receive a divine pardon, which means their past sins are no more and can never be brought up against them, as this would dishonor God, who gave them the pardon.[57] When the saints and angels greet them as John and Mary, they will see absolute purity. They are both chosen vessels of God, both in this First Earth Age and in the Third Earth Age. A heavenly pardon means it is as though they never committed these crimes and sins. They are gone. They are no more. Woe to any person who accuses them.

Pastor Luther, John Newton will humbly give his testimony of being forgiven all over Atlantis. Mary will be the first evangelist after the Son of God is raised from the dead in the Third Earth Age. John Newton, who in the first part of his life in the Third Earth Age will again chain others, this time in slave ships. He will repent again in the Third Earth Age and receive God's pardoning grace and will be used powerfully again to preach the Gospel and to finalize his theme song, "*Amazing Grace.*"

Luther, your name means 'noted warrior or hero of the people'[58] as you will in another Earth age translate the New Testament into the language of your people. You will be used to begin a revival of Reformation so pleasing to the Kingdom of Heaven. You will present again Ninety-five Theses, which will help many come to true repentance. You will in the Third Earth Age be a leading advocate of truth and reformation. Many will try to kill you, but you will be shielded. You will be rewarded with a precious wife giving you a home. You will have victory through the blood of the Lamb, slain for sins foreordained '*before the foundation of the world.*'[59]

Pastor Luther, legally the Lamb had to be slain (foreordained) before the foundation of the world so those in earlier earth ages could be saved before the crucifixion takes place. You will inspire courage in the good fight of faith. You are more than a conqueror through the future sacrifice of the Son of God who loves you. You are commissioned and delegated authority to proceed with this upcoming revival! Until the first of May! Shalom!"

With that, Preacher Melchizedek walked out of the law office front door and turns north joyfully walking on a yellow brick road illuminated by the refreshing light of a full moon.

Pastor Luther prays, "Father God did not my heart burn within me as Preacher Melchizedek expounded to me. Here I am Lord; use me to give You greater glory and to magnify Your name starting now and throughout eternity. In Your Son's name, I pray. Amen!"

---

[55] Psalm 103:12.
[56] Micah 7:19.
[57] See Ephesians 5:11.
[58] See *Luther* meaning a "noted warrior or hero of the people" in
The New Name Dictionary – The Modern English and Hew Names by Alfred J. Kolatch.
[59] Revelation 13.8.

Department Heads Brief King Atlas II of Seduction of Children in Atlantis

Newton and Magdalene as department directors enter the lewd black six-sided Hexagon office of Atlas II with 'a goat head inscribed in a downward-pointing pentagram'[60] behind Atlas II's desk as his official royal crest. Atlas II sits on a black throne in skintight black leotards to give their monthly report.

Atlas II speaks, "Newton, second in the kingdom of Atlantis, what dark stories do you have to share,

"Your Excellency, we have addicted this month sixty-six boys under twelve to tobacco, marijuana, and to homosexuality.

Atlas replied, "Excellent dark work! I have you a tailored skin-tight black leotard outfit containing the royal pentagram crest with a goat head inscribed in a downward-pointing pentagram in gold as a reward. No undergarments are to be worn with these as we glorify the worship of skin around here.

What about you, Magdalene? How have you done with the girls?"

Magdalene reports, "We too have seduced sixty young girls under the age of twelve, all addicted to tobacco, marijuana, and to lesbianism. We are having a nudist beauty pageant among the teenage girls this Friday evening for you and some others to enjoy thru the one-way glass.

Atlas clapping says, "Good. I like those little orgies. I have you a revealing skintight black outfit containing the royal pentagram crest with a goat head inscribed in a downward-pointing pentagram. Wear it for me to see through the one-way mirror glass Friday evening with no undergarments!

King Atlas II Sends Vice-King Newton as a Spy

One more thing Newton, we may have a little irritation coming from the North. Our god Poseidon is spewing. I have obtained a pass to an upcoming first revival on May 1st, and I would like you to spy it out and report back at your usual time on the 6th of May.

I by chance heard two of our cleaning ladies excitedly talking about this upcoming revival, and I saw where she had placed her entrance ticket in her purse. When she took a break, I stole it. It has the number 7 on it, and I hope they will let you in on it. Newton, I have seen nothing you could not crash. The cleaning woman was wearing a red top and white pants, and here is for you are a red shirt and white pants as a disguise. You might desire to shave off your beard and cut your hair so you will look like one of those squeaky-clean Christians. Also, here are mints to help cover up cigarette and marijuana smoke on your breath. Use my dentist to have your yellow teeth cleaned. Good luck on getting dirt on those revivalists."

Some 153 hungry souls with admission tickets, lineup to be seated by the ushers. Newton with a fake smile hands, his ticket to an usher, and she remarks, "You must be someone special as seat 7 is front row center. You will be under the spout where the glory pours out. We have already sat one busload of children in that area, whose parents died of AIDS, and we are expecting another bus to arrive shortly. We have donated to all the girls a high top long sleeve full white dress going down to the ground. I am glad we have a man of God sitting in this area who can set an example of focusing and listening to the service.

---

[60] Quote from *Pentagram* from *Wikipedia, The Free Encyclopedia* further averring, "A pentagram with two points up in a double circle with the goat head inside (looking down to Hell) is the copyrighted logo of the Church of Satan."

Here is a program containing some of Pastor Luther's songs he has written and other songs we will sing for the glory of God. Pastor Luther is my dad, and my name is Ruth. Here is the second bus of orphans. I will see you later. Bye."

Newton sits down in seat 7 looking around at the faces of children, some of whom he recognizes, but no one is paying any attention to him. Shortly the female usher, Ruth, brings in the second busload of children, placing them all around Newton saying,

"Brother, what is your name?"

"Newton, thinking fast, says, "John."

Ruth replies, "I have a brother named John, and my mother states his name means '*God is gracious.*'[61] Like you, his statue is smaller, but I assure you that probably like you, dynamite comes in small packages. I am petite myself. Sir, I proceed that the Lord is going to use you to further His kingdom for His glory. John, this little girl sitting in seat 6 is Gretel. In seat 8 is her little brother, Hansel, both orphans as their dad died of AIDS. Their mother died shortly after that of lung cancer from being a heavy smoker. After their mother's death, they nearly starved to death, and they were sexually abused before we rescued them."

Gretel spoke, "Would you two consider adopting us?"

Ruth replied, "We are not married. We just met. John, you might be their friend and help show them the way of salvation. I must go now as I see others coming into the stadium for seating. Shalom!"

Newton looks at the thin faces of these children sitting all around him and remembers sitting beside Atlas II behind the one-way mirror lusting at some as they were individually sexually abused. The little girl touched a Newton's hand saying,

"Sir, thank you for being our friend and watching over and protecting us. We so miss our parents. Why did they have to die so young? "

Hansel spoke, "Would you take us some evening to the Loveland Fish House for some fish and chips? We are so hungry! "[62]

Newton nods a 'yes' to Hansel, being one of many he had tricked into homosexuality. Newton caught himself looking at a slight rise in Hansel's crotch with that same burning lustful desire for young boys going through him. Many children sitting around him were the very ones he and Magdalene exploited, ruined and threw away like a used ministerial rag. Tears of sorrow dripped from his eyes running down his shaven face and dripping off his chin with his wiping his tears on his red shirt sleeve as he was coming under conviction for sins he had committed.

One little girl was sitting behind him on his right, whom he also recognized as one exploited, gently touched his right elbow with a box of tissues with John pulling out three and burying his face in them in such shame. He thinks, "*I don't deserve to live. How could I have done such evil to all these little innocent children and to the one true God who gave me life?*"

---

[61] Again *John* means "God is gracious." from
The New Name Dictionary – The Modern English and Hew Names by Alfred J. Kolatch.

[62] In Brothers Grimm *Hansel and Gretel*, the hungry children were saved from the wicked witch who wanted to cook and eat them.

Preacher Melchizedek Holds First Saturday Night Revival
Meeting in Loveland behind the Great Pyramid

Pastor Luther directs the orchestra to play as he leads the congregation, with these words flashing across three large screens,

'Have mercy on me, O God,
*   according to your unfailing love;*
according to your great compassion
*   blot out my transgressions.*
Wash away all my iniquity
*   and cleanse me from my sin.*
For I know my transgressions,
*   and my sin is always before me.*
Against You, You only, have I sinned
*   and done what is evil in Your sight,*
so You are proved right when You speak
*   and justified when You judge.*
Surely I was sinful at birth,
*   sinful from the time my mother conceived me.*
Surely You desire truth in the inner parts;
*   You teach me wisdom in the inmost place.*
Cleanse me with hyssop (dipped in the Blood of the Lamb),
*   and I shall be clean;*
*   wash me, and I shall be whiter than snow.*
Let me hear joy and gladness;
*   let the bones you have crushed rejoice.*
Hide your face from my sins
*   and blot out all my iniquity.*
Create in me a pure heart, O God,
*   and renew a steadfast spirit within me.*
Do not cast me from your presence
*   or take your Holy Spirit from me.*
Restore to me the joy of your salvation
*   and grant me a willing spirit, to sustain me.*
Then I will teach transgressors your ways,
*   and sinners will turn back to you.*
Save me from bloodguilt, O God;
*   the God, who saves me,*
and my tongue will sing of your righteousness.
O Lord, open my lips,
*   and my mouth will declare your praise.*
You do not delight in sacrifice, or I would bring it;
*   You do not take pleasure in burnt offerings.*
The sacrifices (pleasing to) of God are a broken spirit;
*   a broken and contrite heart,*
*   O God, You will not despise.'*[63]
'Lord Jesus! (Son of God) Unto Thee I cry,
*   Oh! Hear my earnest prayer;*
Lo! In what distress I lie –
*   My sins I cannot bear;*
*   . . . Thy pity unto me extends,*

---

[63] Psalm 51:1-17.

Remove my sins away;
. . . Oh! Give an answer to my prayer
    And save my soul from dark despair.
When I look back on days gone by,
    In sin and folly spent,
    I scarcely can for mercy cry –
    I would, indeed, be hopeless, Lord,
But for the promise of Thy World.
    For there this truth is told to me,
    Thou wilt not send away
The poor wretch that comes to Thee,
    For saving grace to pray;

    It tells that to the contrite heart
    Thou wilt Thy love and grace impart.
    A burdened sinner I appear,
A load of sin I bear;
    To my complaints, Lord lends an ear,
Regard my humble prayer;
    This is my cry that I obtain
    The cleansing of sin's every stain.
Thus, I approach Thy mercy seat
    And pray Thee to forgive;
    With a contrite heart, I Thee entreat;
        In mercy, let me live;
    Take all my sins away from me.
    And cast them in the boundless sea.'[64]
'Did we in our own strength confide,
    Our striving would be losing.
Were not the right man (Jesus in the flesh) on our side,
    The man of God's own choosing,
Dost ask who that may be?
    Christ Jesus, it is He –
Lord Sabaoth (head of the Army of Heaven) is His name,
    From age to age the same,
And He must win the battle.'[65]

The Shekinah Glory-Presence of God rolls in. Newton holds on to his seat with both hands to keep from falling out.

New Birth Revival Sermon

Coming to the pulpit dressed in a homespun white robe and being barefoot was the unidentified preacher, who spoke these words of eternal salvation,

"*'I tell you the truth, unless you are born again (Holy Spirit joins with your human spirit when you repent and receive God's Son, Jesus, as Savior), you cannot be in (having your name added to the Lamb's Book of Life) the kingdom of God.'*[66]

---

[64] See *Repentance* Stanza Two by Martin Luther.
[65] *A Mighty Fortress is Our God* Stanza Two by Marin Luther.
[66] John 3:3.

'Now this is eternal life, that you may know the only true and real (Father) God, and likewise, know (as your Savior and Lord) His Son, Jesus Christ.'[67]

'The Lamb (Jesus, God's Son) was slaughtered (by dying after being nailed to a cross as a pure sacrifice to fully pay the penalty for the sins of those who receive Him as Savior) before the creation of the Earth (back in eternity in the mind of Father God).'[68]

The Father God will make His Son, who will have no sin, to be sin (having the sin of all who will live on the Earth on Him), so that in Him you (who receive Him as Savior) might become the righteousness of God. Now is your day of salvation![69] God offers you a gift of a full pardon for your sins, which has to be received by faith. Tonight you can have a new heart with the Son of God, Jesus, living in you. You can be Jesus Christ's ambassador to tell the Good News that others can be reconciled to God. When born of the Holy Spirit, you become a citizen of the Kingdom of God, and your name is added to the Lamb's Book of Life. You are taken out of the kingdom of darkness and translated into the Kingdom of God's dear Son.

Some of you men married a precious wife, whom you promised to love, protect, and care for with your children. For years, you had made good on your promises and kept them, and you loved your wife and your children. You were a kind man who delighted in doing good for your family. When you would come home from work, you were greeted at the door by a wife who hugged you and gave you a kiss on the lips. Your children ran to hug your leg and to want to sit on your lap and kiss you on the cheek.

One night one of your buddies invited you to gamble. You were introduced to gambling, drinking, cigarettes, and then to the lust for male bodies. You lost all your savings. Your wife has marks on her body from your fist and hands. Yes, evil from the husband she loves, who had promised to love and protect her. Your children smelled alcohol and cigarette smoke on your breath and often witnessed you manhandling their mother, and they said to each other, 'The monster has come home!' That may be you in whole or in part.

Tonight you can be delivered and set free – born again and regenerated. You can say, "O Father God, save me! I believe Your Son will be nailed to a cross to pay in full the penalty due for my sins. I sincerely repent of my sins, and I make a

U-turn away from them and run to Your Son, Jesus, my Savior, and confess, "Jesus is my Lord!"

If that is your desire to be washed clean from your sins in the upcoming blood of the Lamb of God, Jesus Christ, you may. Pastor Luther will lead in an invitation song. Now you can sincerely repent, make a U-turn away from your sins, give your life to Jesus as your Master and Lord, and ask the Holy Spirit to come into your heart and be born again. When you go home this evening, your wife will say, 'I have never seen your husband look so happy. What has happened to you?

You will reply, 'I have been to a revival service behind the Great Pyramid in Loveland. The sermon about being born again touched my heart, and, beloved wife, I just prayed and asked God to give me a new heart. He did it for me, the greatest of sinners. I am a new creation! Old things are passed away! Behold, all things are new! Come, wife, kneel and pray a thanksgiving prayer with me for what the Lord has done in my life.

---

[67] See John 17:3.
[68] Revelation 13:8.
[69] See 2 Corinthians 5:17-21; 6:2.

Forgive me, my precious wife, whom I love as Jesus Christ loves the Church, for hurting you and our children. Jesus is Lord of the time I have left on this earth. I will by His grace follow His plan for my life.'

Chief sinners, if you desire to be delivered from strong drink, gambling, smoking addiction, and homosexuality come forward and kneel at the altar while Pastor Luther leads us now in an invitation song. Come just as you are. God will not drive you away[70] but will receive you with joy in His kingdom. Whosoever will come and take the gift of salvation."

Pastor Luther led the invitation,
'Just as I am, without one plea,
But that Thy blood (Son of God will be) was shed for me,
And that Thou bidst (bid) me come to Thee,
O Lamb of God, I come, I come.

Just as I am, and waiting not
To rid my soul of one dark blot,
To Thee whose blood can cleanse each spot,
O Lamb of God, I come, I come.

[Newton with tears pouring down his face was the first at the altar, being an example for many others to come and be saved and forgiven.]

Just as I am, though tossed about
With many a conflict, many a doubt,
Fightings and fears within, without,
O Lamb of God, I come, I come.

Just as I am, poor, wretched, blind;
Sight, riches, healing of the mind,
Yea, all I need in Thee to find,
O Lamb of God, I come, I come.

Just as I am, Thou wilt receive,
Wilt welcome, pardon, cleanse, relieve;
Because Thy promise I believe,
O Lamb of God, I come, I come.

---

[70] See John 6:37.

Just as I am, Thy love unknown
Hath broken every barrier down;
Now, to be Thine, yea, Thine alone,
O Lamb of God, I come, I come.'[71]

Vice-King Newton Converted and His
Homosexual Desire for Boys Removed

Seventy-seven (77) came forward for salvation and deliverance with Newton being honored, as he was the first at the altar. Even the sky lit with the Shekinah Glory of the Presence of God. The bright full moon above turns red as blood in a total eclipse as each at the altar was gloriously sprinkled in the future shed blood of the Lamb of God as they were saved and born again.

Pastor Luther announced, "I will be baptizing you seventy-seven (77) immediately, with everything to '*be done decently and in order.*[72]'"

Pastor Luther further announced, "For the next Saturday night's revival service we will also be praying for the sick."

Each born again person was given three free pass tickets and was asked to acknowledge the Lord and be led by the Holy Spirit as to whom to invite.

The born again Saints come out of the separate male and female bath houses wearing thick white robes down to their bare feet and carrying all their personal belongings in a basket. Pastor Luther taught, "You are now to be baptized under the surface of the water according to the command of Jesus, the Son of God, signifying the resignation of your old life and embracing of the new. You are to be buried with Jesus in the watery grave into His upcoming death on the cross for the remission of your sins as Jesus Christ will be raised up from the dead by the glory of the Father, even so you are now to walk in newness of life as it will be written,

'We (born again saints) were therefore buried with Him (Jesus Christ, the Son of God) through baptism into death in order that just as Christ is to be . . . raised from the dead through the glory of the Father, we too may live a new life.

If we have been united with Him like this in His (upcoming) death, we will also be united with Him in His (future) resurrection (from the dead.) For our old self was crucified with Him (the body of sin might be rendered powerless) so we should no longer be slaves to sin because anyone who has died has been freed from sin.

Now if we died with Christ, we believe that we will also live with Him. For Christ (will be in third earth age) raised from the dead, He cannot die again; death no longer has mastery over him.

---

[71] *Just as I Am, Without One Plea* was written by Charlotte Elliot. When poet Charlotte Elliot (1789-1871) was 46 years old, an elderly man approached her at a dinner party and asked if she was a Christian. She considered him rude and unkind, and that his question was inappropriate. After the man walked away, Charlotte could not get his question out of her mind so she went to find the man, and asked how to become a Christian. That night she received Jesus as her Lord and Savior. Soon thereafter, she wrote *Just as I Am, Without One Plea* as a testimony to her new found faith for her salvation, and as a tribute to the man who had told her she could come to Jesus, 'just as she was!' It was made especially popular in the 20th century as the 'official' altar invitation song of the Billy Graham Crusades. Many souls have found Jesus as Savior in response to the truth in this song.

[72] 1 Corinthians 14:40.

. . . Do not offer the parts of your body to sin, as instruments of wickedness, but rather offer yourselves to God, as those who have been brought from death to life and offer the parts of your body to Him as instruments of righteousness.

. . . I put this in human terms because you are weak in your natural selves. Just as you used to offer the parts of your body in slavery to impurity and to ever-increasing wickedness, so now offer them in slavery to righteousness leading to holiness. When you were slaves to sin, you were free from the control of righteousness. What benefit did you reap from the things you are now ashamed? Those things result in death! But now that you have been set free from sin and have become slaves to God, the benefit you reap leads to holiness, and the result is eternal life. For the wages of sin is death, but the gift of God is eternal life through Christ Jesus our Lord.'[73]

Newton is first in line to be baptized and wades out with Pastor Luther placing his right hand behind his back asking, "What is your confession?"

Newton responds, "Jesus Christ, the Son of God, is my Savior and Lord! I will seek to overcome and to faithfully serve Him! I will by His amazing grace! I am determined! I am so thankful for having received everlasting life. I have been forgiven much, and I love much!"

Pastor Luther declares as he lays Newton back into the watery grave, "*I baptize you in the name of the Father, and of the Son, and of the Holy Spirit!*"[74]

As Newton comes up out of the watery grave to walk in newness of life, Pastor Luther decrees, "Your old life is left in that watery grave as all things are new. You are God's chosen vessel! You are pardoned and forgiven, just as if you have committed no sin. Now live a life free from shame and condemnation. Your name among us is John or Brother John. The old man Newton was left in that watery grave. When you came in, we knew who you were. You are now my precious brother in the Lord Jesus! In this First Earth Age, you will now live a life of freedom, love, victory, and grace! Yes, a man has to do what a man has to do! Amen! [So be it!]"

Newton Recognizes Ruth as a Virtuous Woman and
Writes the First Few Words of His Life's Theme Song

Pastor Luther's daughter, Ruth, smiles as she hands each coming up out of the watery grave a towel. As she hands John a towel, their eyes connect for a moment in the moonlight as John swallowing hard, tenderly speaks, "Thank you for the towel."

Ruth replies, "You are most kindly welcome, Sir! '*Old things are passed away; behold, all things are new.*'[75] John, I believe the Lord has a great work for you to do. Not only here, but elsewhere. You will lay up treasures in Heaven and live for and with Jesus throughout eternity."

John seeking to wipe tears of joy out of his eyes with the towel raises his hands toward Heaven declaring, "Here I am Lord Jesus, Son of God, use me. Thank You, Lord, for saving me. May the Lord be magnified, who would save a wretch like me – the chief of sinners. Use me to bring You glory. '*Amazing Grace! How sweet the sound – that saved a wretch like me! I once was lost, but now I'm found. Was blind, but now I see.*'[76]"

John looks toward the beautiful river pouring into the sea from the island of Atlantis and catches another glimpse of Ruth handing out the towels. By chance, Ruth turns, and their eyes meet again. John respectfully lifts his right hand to about his shoulder and tenderly waves to her from a distance. Ruth in the moonlight ever so gently, as she hands a towel to someone coming up out of the water, with her right hand, respectfully waves back with a smile.

John, ever so happy, feeling like a genuine and real man as he knows that his homosexual desire for young boys has been forever removed. He turns his natural manly affection toward Ruth romantically thinking, "*That smile could launch a thousand ships if it were not for the Leviathans. Ruth is truly a 'virtuous woman who loves and respects the Lord.*'[77] *Now that I have found her . . .* "†

---

[73] Romans 6:3-13, 19-23.

[74] See Matthew 28:19.

[75] 2 Corinthians 5:17.

[76] *Amazing Grace* Stanza One by John Newton.

[77] See Proverbs 31:10, 30.

†Book Seven – Episode Three†

[†**Sidebar Scriptures**: "*Joseph had a dream and promptly reported all the details (Genesis 37:5).*"
"*The Lord revealed to me what the evil ones were doing and planning and showed me their wicked plots (Jeremiah 11:18).*"
"The word of the Lord came to Abram in a **vision**. . . . A **deep sleep** came upon Abram . . . . (Genesis 15:1, 12)."
I witnessed and experienced "*dreams and visions, and I described **all** I had seen to instruct many (Daniel 7:1, 11:33).*"†]

Apollo Receives Worship in Heaven, and King Atlas II Spies on Christians

New Musical Sounds of Lucifer Played with Newly Redesigned Harps

APOLLYON LUCIFER (APOLLO), the music leader of Heaven, smirking with pride after having hand selected 666 angels now sitting in six (6) sections of 111. Each sits upright behind his newly-redesigned harp, having new black strings sounding livelier than any of the other instruments. Apollo lifts his black baton to conduct his new musical *Sounds of Lucifer*. The unified sounds of the 666 harps vibrate from Heaven like laser beams hitting the Earth below.

Apollo Reviews Backmasking with Mercury

We are about to create a sound that will vibrate down penetrating all the magnificent creatures and plant life I designed on earth. They will march to our drumbeat! I will bring the music of the harps, the strings, the horns, and all the instruments to such a crescendo that the hearers will be utterly lost in, addicted to, and controlled by our enchanting music. I have invented Backmasking causing the listeners to reverse in their minds the sung words they hear in the music and sung words. We can give them special secret hot messages,[1] such as, '*Apollo is the greatest. Join Apollo.*'

Apollo's Combined Musicians, Orchestras, and Choirs

"Now," says Apollo, "Let the other gifted musicians of all the combined six orchestras join with these 666 harps and the combined choirs." As they performed in Heaven, the dinosaurs, the leviathans, and many inhabitants of Atlantis tune their ears to hear the *Sounds of Lucifer* with numerous swaying and humming with the seductive music. At the conclusion, many harpists, orchestra, and choir members stand clapping loudly, as sea lions on earth also clapped their flippers, and various forms of life join in by hitting flesh and vegetation together. Many shout words of praise and worship, such as, "How great thou art, King Lucifer. We blow our kisses of worship to you. We join ourselves to you."

---

[1] John Lennon of the Beatles "stated that, while under the influence of marijuana, he accidentally played the taps for 'Rain' in reverse and enjoyed the sound. . . . 'Rain' was the first song to feature a back masked message: '... *When the rain comes, they run and hide their heads* ' . . . the last line is the reverse first verse of the song." . . . A 1983 California bill was introduced to prevent back masking that 'can manipulate a listener's behavior without their knowledge or consent and turn and entreat them to becoming a disciple of the Antichrist.' . . . Bands have utilized Satanic imagery.. For example, the thrash metal band Slayer included at the start of the band's 1985 album *Hell Awaits* a deep back masked voice chanting '*Join Us*' over and over . . . ." See *Backmasking* at *Wikipedia, The free Encyclopedia*.

Apollo Receives Worship

The players and hearers in Heaven rise to their feet and then fall to their knees worshiping Lucifer. Lucifer takes six (6) bows seeking to receive all the praise and worship.

Lucifer Apollyon concludes, "Thank you very much! You deserve the best. It has been my goal always to give you the best, and as you join with me, you will have the freedom to have no one telling you what to do. We will plan a concert on Earth at the Atlantis Dinosaur Egg Dome. I will invite the entire Earth and even my best friend, Jesus, and his father and spirit associate to experience what all of you have experienced this night of darkness."

Newton and Magdalene Inform Atlas they are Now Christians!

Newton and Magdalene as department directors enter the black six-sided hexagon office of Atlas II to give their monthly report.

Atlas II speaks, "Newton, second in the kingdom of Atlantis, my wise counselor, what dark stories do you have to share. Did you spy out that evil in Loveland costing us taxes and revenue?"

Newton, respectfully responds, "Atlas, I advise that we again adopt 'Christianity' as the national religion of Atlantis, as it is helping so many of our people. When Jesus Christ comes into their heart, the 'secret thing,' being the Holy Spirit, is to be received by faith. They are born again and forgiven. Also, they then have the fruit of the Holy Spirit – love, joy, peace, patience, kindness, goodness, faithfulness, gentleness, and self-control[2] flowing out of them. I have learned the truth that, 'Love never fails!'[3]

Atlas turns red in the face and neck from rage responding, "Hell, Magdalene has Newton gone mad? These Christians should all be thrown in the shark tank! Concur?"

Magdalene respectfully replies, "No, I do not concur with you. With all due respect for you King Atlas, Newton is correct. I have been to one of the revival services in Loveland, and I accepted the Son of God as my Savior and have also become a Christian. We would like to invite you to hear the Evangelist and the song leaders this Friday evening at 7:00 P.M. We have your admission ticket number nine (9) for you to sit with us on the front row."

King Atlas grabs admission ticket nine (9) out of the hand of Magdalene cursing and tearing it into little pieces. He throws the pieces into his aquarium filled with Piranhas, who strike and devour the pieces of admission ticket nine (9). Atlas smirking, "As my Piranhas have destroyed that paper, my army will destroy both that Evangelist and the song leader presently dividing my country. I am in charge here, and I am to be the only one to be obeyed and worshipped."

---

[2] Galatians 5:22-23.
[3] 1 Corinthians 13:8.

With that rejection of Christianity, both Newton and Magdalene respectfully hand King Atlas their written resignation notices from their respective positions as department heads, effective in thirty days.

Atlas also tears these written resignation notices in small pieces and throws the resignation letters into the Parana aquarium angrily snorting, "I don't accept your resignations. You both are fired immediately, if not sooner! Clean out your offices and be off the grounds never to return by the end of this business today!

Give me the names of any other so-called 'Christians' on my staff, and they likewise will be immediately terminated from my cabinet so you can all leave these premises together. I will not attend this next Friday night's service in Loveland!

Atlas II sends Warship into the Bay behind the Great Pyramid and an Armor Vehicle Through Dinosaur and Dragon Country to Intimate and Spy on the Christians During an Open-Air Revival

Atlas calls an emergency meeting in his black six-sided hexagon-shaped office of his Secretary of State, Zeus; his Treasurer, Tibetan; his Secretary of War, Vulcan. King Alas slaps his outstretched right hand on his desk demanding, "We have to stop the revival in Loveland from growing, or they are going to destroy our official Poseidon Religion and our pleasures of darkness. They are costing us needed revenue because of a decrease in sales of liquor, tobacco, and marijuana."

Tibetan responds, "What about taxing them out of existence?"

Zeus replies, "That certainly is the best approach, but that attorney Job, wherever he is, legally established all the land as tax-exempt church property. Such tax exemption is the current long-standing established law of Atlantis your dad placed in our constitution. The government cannot tax the church property, and the contributions made to that church are tax deductible. To take this out would take a constitutional amendment.

Atlas, you might bluff by an executive order that contributions to non-profits in Atlantis are no longer tax deductible. What is the Constitution among friends of darkness? Our judges receive a monthly check from our government and desire a pay increase. Your executive order prohibiting tax deductions for contributions to non-profit organizations could include giving needed revenue for government services, a portion of which will go for increasing judicial salaries. Any judge who might lean toward declaring your executive order violates our Constitution, we can remove that judge from office or, at least, bribe him."

Atlas responding, "I will consider it! What else?"

"Vulcan responds, "I understand they close their eyes when they pray to an invisible God who is allegedly in a place called Heaven. When they close their eyes, we could shoot their preacher and song leader in the heart with the three dog laser gun as we did your dad."

"That was my first idea, but security is tight. One cannot get in without a guest ticket – I had ticket 9 for Friday night and tore it up. Everyone has to go through a security gate. Any suspicious object like our camera with a built in hidden laser gun has to be checked in and be picked up when leaving the service."

Vulcan replies, "We could send our new extra iron-armored blue-green warship into 'Glory Harbor' behind the Great Pyramid. Then our new extra armored camouflaged warrior tank through 'Dinosaur and Dragon County' up to 'Glory Rock.'

From these two locations, we can coordinate clear and precise shots to assassinate the evangelist, the song leader, and even some in the crowd such as Newton and Magdalene, who have committed treason. Let us shoot six seconds after they bow their heads in prayer."

Atlas replies, "Sounds like a piece of devil's food cake for our impressive war department! VISA."

Saturday Night Services in Loveland

Some 700 hungry souls, all with admission tickets are admitted and seated, with seat number nine (9) beside Newton and Magdalene being the only empty seat in the entire facility. Pastor Luther's orchestra plays as he leads the congregation,

'*Did we in our own strength confide,*
Our striving would be losing,
Were not the right man on our side,
The man of (Father)God's own choosing,
Dost ask who that may be?
Christ Jesus, it is He –
Lord Sabaoth[4] *His name,*
From age to age the same,
And He must win the battle.'[5]
[The Shekinah Glory fills the meeting place!]

Elder Abraham Teaching the 144,000 in Zion

Elder Abraham in teaching the 144,000 turns on the screen in Zion. Evangelistic Melchizedek comes to the pulpit in Atlantis dressed in a white homespun robe and being barefoot decrees, '*No weapon formed against you will prosper (prevail).*'[6] Let us pray!"

A split screen monitor focuses into Glory Bay, and the other side focuses up to the top of Glory Rock as everyone has his or her eyes closed in prayer.

Six three-dog laser guns aimed from the camouflaged warship for clear and precise shots to assassinate first the preacher, the song leader, Newton, and Magdalene. Then a huge dinosaur quietly walking on the beautiful white sand beach blocks the view from the laser gunboat of the pulpit. Nine Leviathans quietly surround the iron warship heating the metal red hot from the flames from their nostrils. The gunboat springs leaks at the seams and sinks to the bottom of Glory Bay, without so much as a sound to not disturb the prayer being offered.

The Split Screen then Focuses over on Glory Rock

Also, in place are six three dog laser guns on the armored iron warrior tank on the top of Glory Rock to shoot first to assassinate the preacher, the song leaders, and hopefully also Newton

---

[4] Sabaoth here meaning Lord of Heaven's Army.
[5] *A Mighty Fortress is Our God* Stanza Two by Martin Luther.
[6] Isaiah 54:17.

and Magdalene. Another gigantic dinosaur quietly walks between them blocking the view of the pulpit. Then seven dragons start intense flames from their nostrils heating the armored iron warrior tank white hot. The rock beneath becoming molten lava, with the armored warrior tank sinking beneath the surface of the liquid rock, out of sight, again with no noise to disturb the service in progress.

John brings the 144,000 in Zion to view the big screen to join the service entitled "God is Love"[7] in progress with Preacher Melchizedek preaching,

"The eternal God has revealed Himself to mankind as Father, Son, and the Holy Spirit. The Son of God is and always was divine. He is the express image of the Father. You are to worship one Triune God. For there is one person of the Father, another of the Son, and another of the Holy Spirit, but the Godhead of the Father, Son, and the Holy Spirit is one God.

God loves humanity made in His image. God hates sin and disobedience because they blemish the abundant life He created you to have. Father God is a faithful Father. It is His nature to love, just as it is the nature of the sun to shine. Do not think that because you are a sinner that Father God does not love you or care for you. He does! He wants to save and bless you with abundant and eternal life. Before the foundation of the world, the Father God saw His Son being crucified shedding His life's blood to pay the penalty for those sinners who would repent and receive His Son, Jesus, as their Savior and confess Him as their Lord. They are pardoned and forgiven. Counted righteous because of their faith in God's Son.

You might ask if Father God loves me, why does He not make me good? It is because God gave you a free will! He does not desire robots or programmed machines. Father God, not sparing His own Son gave Him to die on a cross in your places. God desires born again sons and daughters to love Him, and He will adopt those who receive His Son into His family. Will you trample God's love under your feet or will you love Him of your own *'free will,'* and repent?

'This is love: not that we loved (Father) God, but that He (first) loved us and sent His Son (to die in the future on a cross in our place to pay the penalty due for the sins of all who will receive Him as Savor) as an atoning sacrifice for our sins. Dear friend, since (Father) God so loved us, we also ought to love one another. No one has ever seen (Father) God, but if we love each other, God lives in us, and His love is made complete in us.

We live in Him and He in us, because He has given us of His (Holy) Spirit (to join with our human spirit and make us born again). And we have seen and testify that the Father has sent His Son to be the Savior of the world. If anyone acknowledges that Jesus is the Son of God, God lives in him and he in God. And so we know and rely on the love God has for us.

God is love. Whoever abides in love lives in God, and God in him. Love is made complete among us so we will have confidence on the day of judgment because in this world we are like Him. There is no fear in love. But perfect love drives out fear, because fear has to do with (the threat of) punishment. The man who fears is not made perfect in love.

We love because He first loved us. If anyone says, 'I love God,' yet hates his brother, he is a liar. For anyone who does not love his brother, whom he has seen, cannot love (Father) God, whom he has not seen. And He has given us this command: Whoever loves God must also love his brother.

Everyone who believes that Jesus is the Christ is born of God, and everyone who loves the Father loves His child (Jesus). This is how we know that we love the children of God: by loving God and carrying out His commands.

---

[7] 1 John 4:8 NIV.

*This is love for God: to **obey** His commands. And His commands are not burdensome (light and joyful for the born again ones looking for eternal rewards), for everyone born of God has overcome the world. This is the victory that has overcome the world, even our faith.*

Who is it that overcomes the world: Only he who believes that Jesus (whom Father God had sent to pay the penalties for the sins for all who will receive Him as Savior) is the Son of God. [8]

Melchizedek preaches, "Believe that God loves you for He does. He now commands you to repent and turn away from your sins. Revival means you see and feel the sinfulness of your sin and with your whole heart forsake them utterly and with full purpose of heart to yield to obedience to God. God's amazing grace will pardon all your sins. He will accept you as righteous in His sight washing you whiter than wool in the atoning Blood of His Son to be shed on a cross to fully pay the penalty for your sins.

'The kingdom of God is near. Repent and believe the good news!' [9]

'Except a man be born again, he cannot see the kingdom of God.' [10]

'A bruised reed (weak and beaten down) God will not break,
   and a smoldering wick (almost gone out) He will not snuff out.' [11]

'Unless you repent, you will perish (in Hell).' [12]

'Whoever comes to Me (Jesus) I will in no wise (not for anything he or she has done) drive away (from receiving salvation).' [13]

Now this is eternal life that you may know the only true and real (Father) God and likewise know His Son, Jesus. [14] The Son will die on a cross, to pay the penalty due for the sins of all those who will receive Him as Savior, so that in Him you might become the righteousness of God.

Now is your day of salvation. [15] God loves you and offers you a free gift of pardon from your sins; pardon must be received by faith. The 'Good News' is that tonight you can of your own 'free will' repent of your sins, accept the Son of God, Jesus, as your Savior, and receive the gift of the Holy Spirit. The Holy Spirit will join with your human spirit giving you a new heart, making you born again, now an adopted child of the Most High God.

When born again, your name is added to the Lamb's Book of Life as an adopted citizen of the Kingdom of God. You are transferred out of the kingdom of darkness and translated into the Kingdom of Light. Your name tonight can be added to the ***Lamb's Book of Life***. This night of your own free will, you can choose to be a member of the family of God.

---

[8] 1 John 4:10 - 5:5 NIV. [Emphasis added.]
[9] Mark 1:16 NIV.
[10] John 3:3.
[11] Isaiah 42:3.
[12.] Luke 13:3.
[13] John 6:37.
[14] See John 17:3.
[15] See 2 Corinthians 5:17-21; 6:2.

You will have all the rights and privileges of His children as you become a legal heir of God, with the right and title to eternal life.

If you sincerely repent and desire to be delivered from strong drink, gambling, smoking and other addictions, even homosexuality, and be born again from above with eternal life as a free gift from God come just as you are. Come and kneel in worship at the altar of Father God, now as Pastor Luther leads in an invitation song."

Pastor Luther softly under the anointing sings,

'Just as I am, though tossed about
With many a conflict, many a doubt,
Fightings and fears within, without,
O Lamb of God, I come, I come.

Just as I am, poor, wretched, blind;
Sight, riches, healing of the mind,
Yea, all I need in Thee to find,
O Lamb of God, I come, I come.

Just as I am, Thou wilt receive,
Wilt welcome, pardon, cleanse, relieve;
Because Thy promise I believe,
O Lamb of God, I come, I come.

Just as I am, Thy love unknown
Hath broken every barrier down;
Now, to be Thine, yea, Thine alone,
O Lamb of God, I come, I come.'[16]

One hundred and fifty-three (153) come forward for salvation. Even the night sky sparkled and glowed with the '*Shekinah Glory of the Presence of God*' as each is gloriously saved and born again.

Ruth flowing in love comes by to greet and welcome Magdalene into the family of God turning at one point and looking Newton deeply into his eyes smiling at him and then turning her eyes back on Magdalene. Newton listens and delights in observing and hearing the two women rejoicing in being a part of the family of God.

Not knowing what to say, Newton remarks, "What a peaceful, uneventful evening of prayer and worship we have experienced!"

Ruth responds, "Peaceful, but not uneventful! Atlas II sent an iron warship out in the harbor. [Ruth pointed to the spot] He also sent an iron armor tank to yonder high rock [Ruth again points] to assassinate the preacher, my dad, and, yes, you two also were on King Atlas II's hit list to be murdered this evening using the three-dog laser guns."

Magdalene responded, "We didn't hear a thing. Why did they leave?"

Ruth laughs, "Because love never fails! No weapon ever formed against love will prevail! The warship lies in a watery grave at the bottom of the harbor, and the armored tank melted into the rock.

---

[16] *Just as I Am, Without One Plea* by Charlotte Elliot.

We have a fellowship in yonder building after the baptism service to agape (God kind of love) on, rejoice with, and get to know the new converts. We could use both of you if you desire to help. We hardly even notice Atlas II's threats against us this evening, so don't mention it to others."

Magdalene smiles, "Yea, we would both like to come. Love truly never fails and thank you for letting us know about this act of war against us this evening."

As Magdalene was walking away, Ruth whispers, "Maybe you could inspire Newt to sing a new song for us he has just written? His wife died a few years ago, and he has no one to encourage him. He was a workaholic as second in charge of Atlantis and was blinded by sin. His song contains a line going something like, "*I once was lost, but now I'm found, was blind, but now I see.*"

Atlas drinking cobra liquor out on a palace balcony gloats to himself, "*That must be the glow of the three-dog laser guns. Mission accomplished!*"

Report to King Atlas from His Secretary of War

Shaking his head a '*no*,' the Secretary of War, Vulcan, is ushered out on Atlas' balcony. Vulcan looks at the Northern horizon at the Shekinah Glory Cloud over Loveland reports, "Well, I've come to report on 'Operation Black Widow Spider.'

Atlas, smiling and believing he had the victory, inquires, "Mission accomplished?"

Vulcan turns a fake smile into a frown defends, "The Christians had nothing to do with it, nor did the weather, as they didn't even know anything was happening. It was those terrible creatures, the flame-throwing Leviathans and dragons, that single-handedly with the help of two Dinosaurs, blocked our view of the platform dooming 'Operation Black Widow Spider.' We got both war units in perfect positions with no one in Loveland knowing we were even present. Our men on shore a few miles down the beach observed the battle and reported that our iron warship turned red hot and sank to the bottom of the sea. Then our iron armored war tank turned white hot and sank into the rock. Hell, we have to destroy all those monsters!"

Atlas furiously thunders, "Yes, we need an ultimate weapon to destroy both them and the Christians. I would even like to level that protective pyramid having that 'all seeing eye'[17] on top continually watching and convicting me of sin."

Vulcan responded, "One of Homo's ape men was caught stealing last week. As we were preparing to cut off his right hand as punishment, he indicated that if we spared his hand, he would share with us some critical information. He informed, 'Homo and his scientists are working on the ultimate weapon that cannot be defeated. They are near to having it completed.' We saved his hand on the promise that if we needed his confidential help, he would give it to us."

Atlas directed, "Bring Homo here tomorrow at 6:00 P.M., along with that witness. If they do not tell the truth, we will cut both their right hands off."†

---

[17] "All seeing eye of God is a symbol showing an eye representing the eye of God watching over humankind. In the modern era, the most notable depiction of the eye is the reverse of the Great Seal of the United States, which appears on the United States' one-dollar bill."
Eye of Providence from *Wikipedia, The Free Encyclopedia.*

†BOOK SEVEN – Episode Four†

[†**Sidebar Scriptures**: "*Joseph had a dream and promptly reported all the details (Genesis 37:5)."*
"The Lord revealed to me what the evil ones were doing and planning and showed me their wicked plots (Jeremiah 11:18)."
"The word of the Lord came to Abram in a **vision**. . . . A **deep sleep** came upon Abram . . . . (Genesis 15:1, 12)."
I witnessed and experienced "*dreams and visions, and I described **all** I had seen to instruct many (Daniel 7:1, 11:33)."*†]

King Atlas II Has a Summons Issued to Discover the Purpose of Bomb Being Made by Apollo's Scientists

Emergency Meeting Request Regarding Summons and '*Subpoena Duces Tecum*'[1] Served on Homo and Expose

HOMO BRIEFS PHOTON that one of his men leaked that they were making a bomb and that they are both summoned to appear before Atlas and his Secretary of War and to bring the details of the purpose of the bomb. Photon sends a coded message to Mercury reading,

'*King Atlas II has discovered Operation Vampire and has summoned Homo and Expose to appear before him at 6:00 p.m. tomorrow afternoon to give the details. Could we have an EMERGENCY meeting in the Vampire Operation Room today on the best way to defend our-selves?*

Photon"

Meeting in Throne Room of Heaven

Gabriel immediately gives a copy of the decoded message to Michael. He forwards it to the Son of God with the Son of God briefing the Father and asking for His counsel with the Father advising,

"Apollyon Lucifer will make a treaty with King Atlas. He will invite Us to a Harp Concert on Earth at which he will explode his freeze bomb purposing to destroy Us, the Great Pyramid, Loveland, Dinosaur and Dragon County, and the Leviathans. Lucifer will promise to give to King Atlas II the whole world as his Kingdom if he will just fall down and worship him. Inform Luther to accept Atlas's invitation to hold a revival service, inviting all citizens of Atlantis, upon the condition that before the Harp concert that a revival service is first held. Let the 144,000 view your special message of love on screens. Warn Zion through Abraham to be prepared to relocate to Paradise as the freeze bomb will set off an unexpected chain reaction and freeze the entire world solidly making it without form and void."

Lucifer Gives Orders to Murder Homo and Expose and Directs Gehen to Present a Treaty to Atlas II Giving Him the Entire World if He Receives Lucifer's Mark

The spaceship lands near the entrance to Hell with a black carpet being rolled out to the gate of Hell. Apollyon Lucifer (Apollo) with great pomp exits. Apollo immediately goes to the Vampire Room for a briefing with his scientists.

Photon, bowing before Apollo, briefing, "We have two armed ice bombs ready – one to take care of the North end of this island and the other to send a warship to Tel Aviv to destroy Zion."

[1.] *SUBPOENA DUCES TECUM.* "A process by which the court, at the instance of a suitor, commands a witness who has in his possession or control some document or paper that is pertinent to the issues of a pending controversy, to produce it at the trial;" *Black's law Dictionary.*

Apollo replies, "Great! Your timing is perfect as the harpists are ready for a musical performance on Earth if Father God, whom no one has ever seen, will come with His Son and the Holy Spirit. Time is of the essence. When is the next national holiday of Atlantis? What is this I hear about a security leak to our strictly guarded secret? Let us murder Homo and Expose and not present any evidence to Atlas. I understand we have Atlas II in our back pocket? Who has Atlas's ear?"

Photon trembling in fear replies, "Gehen has Atlas's ear as he has been giving him bribes monthly of the small amount of gems, gold, and silver we discovered as by-products in our digging for the rare pitchblende ore needed to make the needed ice bombs. Gehen is scheduled to present Atlas his bribe tomorrow right before Homo and Expose are summoned to appear. The next holiday is Atlantis Day, on 9/11, which is two weeks with a new moon making it dark for our fireworks display on that Friday. Can we move that fast? Looks like we have a catch 66 here as our secret is exposed?"

Apollyon Lucifer orders, "Yes, the time now is of the essence! We will have to strike quickly. Here's my plan: First, murder Homo and Expose and fake death certificates to show Atlas. Next, offer Atlas whatever he wants to worship and serve me, even the whole world, for his agreeing to let us hold a harp concert in the Atlantis Dinosaur Dome. I will invite the Godhead and then the big 'bang,' and I will be the god of this world, Heaven, and the cosmos with one flick of a switch. Tighten security and no more leaks. Finalize these executions as 'dead men tell no tell.' Are you sure this bomb will explode?"

Photon replies, "Only in theory. It explodes on paper, but there is an "X" factor, which could mean that the ice bomb instead of being directional could spread all over the world even freezing as high as the moon. No god could live through the sub-freezing temperature of minus 66 degrees Celsius. It will freeze hard as a diamond the surface of the earth 666 feet deep."

Apollo smirks, "Offer Atlas the moon, if necessary, to allow us to hold a harp concert in the Atlantis Dinosaur Dome between the Citadel and the Great Pyramid. It will conclude with a fireworks display in the darkest part of the night as the grand finale. At the right moment when the night sky lights with fireworks, we will detonate the ice bomb. We have installed with great difficulty a telescoping window going out through the red portion of the black widow spider[2] painted on our spacecraft for us to watch the defeat of our enemies from outer space."

Melchizedek Instructs Pastor Luther

Melchizedek instructs Pastor Luther, "Atlas II will be asking his former second in command, Newton, to be Master of Ceremonies for the upcoming 'Atlantis Day' on 9/11 at the Atlantis Dinosaur Egg Dome. Is this our greatest opportunity to reach out in love to those in Atlantis lost in their sins? God is '*not wanting anyone to perish (in Hell) but everyone to come to repentance*'[3] and '*be born again.*'[4] I will work on a sermon entitled, 'God is Love!' Remember '*love never fails.*'[5] Never!

---

[2] "The female black widow has unusually large venom glands and her bite is particularly harmful to humans. The prevalence of sexual cannibalism, a behavior in which the female eats the male after mating, in some species of Latrodectus has inspired the common name "widow spiders."
See *Latrodectus* from *Wikipedia, The Free Encyclopedia.*

[3] 1 Peter 3:9 NIV.

[4] John 3:7 NIV.

[5] 1 Corinthians 13:8 NIV.

Lucifer can counterfeit a lot of things, but he and his crew cannot counterfeit love. This will be some evening like none other before or ever will be again.

An act of war will be committed during this upcoming evening revival service during the grand finale of the 'Atlas Fireworks Show' seeking to destroy the Godhead and all you in Love-land. However, in a blink of the eye of The Great Pyramid, all of you, along with all the saints in Zion, will be removed from the surface of the earth into the heart of the Earth to a place of joy and rest called 'Paradise.' We will subsequently see Lucifer then known as '*Satan fall like lightning (cast-out of) from Heaven* '[6] with his angels to the frozen surface of the earth. This exorcism will be the greatest fireworks display of them all!"

Gehen Presents Bribe to Atlas and Proposition for Harp Concert

Gehen enters Atlas office with a little treasure chest saying, "We found the biggest gemstone ever this past week and a considerable amount of gold and silver. 'Great One,' these treasures are all yours!"

Atlas smiles as he opens the treasure box, "You have outdone yourself this week. You are making me richer and richer. I heard a disturbing report you have a bomb. Is that to be aimed at us, your friends?

Gehen, "No, not at you! We have made two directional bombs. The first destroys North for 666 miles as our gifts to you of leveling The Great Pyramid, Loveland, and Dinosaur and Dragon County, and to kill those Leviathans out in the ocean. Then by ship you can easily take the other ice bomb to Te Aviv and destroy Zion by a directional bomb going from West to East. Then you will be King of the entire world. Also, Apollyon Lucifer owns the moon, and he is willing today to give it to you. If the Moon is yours, then all the world, when they look up at it will remember this is the 'Atlas' Moon!' How would you like the two directional bombs and the Moon to be thrown in as a bonus?"

Atlas II smiles, "Great, but what's this going to cost me?"

Gehen replies, "Hardly anything as Apollyon Lucifer is a friend and designer of the god of the ocean Poseidon, who worships Apollyon Lucifer, and from this worship Poseidon derives his enormous power. Apollyon Lucifer asks you to join your god Poseidon and bow down and worship Apollyon Lucifer and take a little mark on the back of your right hand, which mark can only be seen in the moonlight. Then you will own the moon. This mark will be a guarantee that you are also protected by and belong to Apollyon Lucifer! For all this, you only have to allow us to hold a harp concert on 'Atlantis Day' on 9/11 in the Dinosaur Egg Dome. To further show just how great and powerful you are, we will have a magnificent 'Atlas Firework' display afterward for all the people of Atlantis. It needs to be mandatory that all citizens of Atlantis attend the start of the firework display, including those in Loveland, Pastor Luther, and his barefoot preacher, whatever his name is. Your friends in Atlantis are all to sit south of the podium as the directional bomb will only go north."

Atlas II smirking says, "Worshiping my designer, Apollyon Lucifer, and taking his mark is chicken feed. I now bow and confess with my mouth that Apollyon Lucifer is my protector and god. Here I extend my right hand to seal this deal with the moon mark."

---

[6] Luke 10:18

While Atlas bows in the moonlight in worship to Apollyon Lucifer, Gehen takes out his tattoo laser gun and shoots 666 in faint gray on the back of Atlas's right hand. Gehen declares, "You now belong to Apollyon Lucifer and the Moon and the whole world is yours. Regarding that summons for Homo and Expose, this issue is moot. Here are both of their death certificates."

Atlas moves his right hand out and then back in the moonlight as Atlas watches the 666 mark appear and disappear asking, "How did they die?"

Gehen lying, "One from AIDS, and the other suicide. It is moot now. See if you can bribe Pastor Luther also to attend with that barefoot evangelist. Get a firm commitment to attend out of Luther and for him to bring that barefoot preacher, whoever he may be."

Atlas II, "Luther may be a hard nut to crack! What can I offer him to come? The man in the moon?"

Gehen, "Yes, offer him the man in the moon if need be as you own it. Get his word that he and the barefoot evangelist will be present for your fireworks display. Whatever it takes to get him to agree!"

Atlas II, "Okay! Whatever it takes to get him to attend I will offer to him. I will imprison him when I am made the king of this entire world. If he accepts the man in the moon, I will get it back when I execute him."

Atlas, moving his right hand in and out of the dim light of the moon and seeing again the 666 mark appear and disappear says, "This little mark on my right hand is neat. My secret tattoo. I just remembered that Pastor Luther is having a revival meeting this Friday evening in Loveland. I will send an invitation to him in love [mocking, smirking], through my cook to hand to her friend Newton requesting he brings Pastor Luther to introduce him Monday. We can then discuss plans for those peculiar people to participate in some small way as part of the 'Atlantis Day' program at the Atlantis Dinosaur Egg Dome on 9/11. They should like the idea of a harp concert and an 'Atlas Firework' display after that as the spectacular grand finale. Newton had a fear of me before he got that religion, and he will help me persuade Pastor Luther to participate and to bring that barefoot preacher with him. Count on me! Whatever I have to do, I will get them to attend."

Meeting of King Atlas with Pastor Luther and Newton

Atlas II, makes plans to flatter his former second in command Newton, who brings with him Pastor Luther to the called meeting. Atlas commences, "Newt, things have not been the same around here since you resigned after you got religion. My dad once said, 'If you can't beat them, join them!' Well, I would like to join again with you! Therefore, I ask you to be the Master of Ceremonies in the program for our upcoming 'Atlantis Day' on 9/11 starting at 7:00 P.M. We are to invite all Atlantis to join us in the monstrous Atlantis Dinosaur Egg Dome. We will have a harp concert and a giant fireworks display as it is dark at 9:06 P.M. We will have large outdoor screens for the overflow Christians reaching back north toward the Great Pyramid in Loveland.

The south side will have an overflow section for non-Christians, both of which will provide enough space for all Atlantis to attend.

Remember Christians on the north side of the podium, non-Christians to be seated on the south portion only, and it is mandatory that all stay for the start of my firework display.

Pastor Luther, I understand you are a law partner of the jurist Job, who has mysteriously disappeared maybe into The Great Pyramid. Newt, do you accept my offer? "

Without shaking hands, Newton replies, "I love all the citizens of Atlantis and would greatly welcome being your MC if you will agree to accept these conditions:

Our 9/11 is on a Friday evening, and we have already scheduled our weekly service that night behind The Great Pyramid. I have a special song I have written dedicated to the citizens of Atlantis I was preparing to have sung at that service. I would be so honored to share it with all the people of Atlantis with your permission after a brief message and altar call from our barefoot preacher. This way we will have Pastor Luther, our preacher, and me sitting on the platform as I announce the upcoming Atlas Fireworks Grand Finale as it does not get the darkest until shortly after nine."

Atlas II thinking, "*Perfect, says the spider to the fly. The sheep on the north side and the goats on the south side.*" Atlas II speaks, "Newt you are in charge of designing the program, which can include the title of the message and the words of your song? In your program, call it 'Harp Concert – Sounds of the Cosmos,' with 'Atlas Firework' afterward. The 'All-Seeing Eye' on top of The Great Pyramid has seen nothing like this.

Newt lists in the program your name as Master of Ceremonies. Communicate the program and free admission tickets to every family in Atlantis? Also, will you be in charge of setting up the overflow chairs and large viewing screens behind the Dinosaur Egg Dome North toward The Great Pyramid for the Christians? Will you also set up similar overflow chairs South toward the Citadel for the non-Christians? There never has been a lightning firework display like this one, and I doubt there will ever be again in this Earth Age. Understand Newt!"

Newton again affirms, "Yes, I will be the Master of Ceremonies, and I will see that every person in Atlantis knows of and is invited to hear our regular Friday service. I will include my song. All will be asked to stay for the start of the Grand Finale of your firework display."

Atlas, looking out the window at the moon, remarks, "Look, the moon is shining through the window. On 9/11, we will only have a new moon that evening making the Grand Finale Fireworks Display, even more, spectacular against the black sky. If a citizen of Atlantis leaves before the start of the fireworks, the sanction against them will be, they cannot '*buy or sell*'[7] for sixty-six days. We have an agreement. Let us shake on it!"

Atlas II extends his right hand to Newton, and Newton shakes the effeminate[8] hand of Atlas. Newton looks down seeing on Atlas' right hand in the moonlight – 666. Newton remarks to Pastor Luther as he was leaving the Hexagon Office and passing a restroom, "I have to wash my hands. Ugh!"†

---

[7] Revelation 13:17-18 *"No one will be able to buy or to sell, except the one who has the mark. . . . Let the one who has understanding calculate the number of the beast, for the number is that of a man, and his number is 666."*

[8] "Effeminacy describes the traits in a human male that are more often associated with feminine nature, behavior, mannerism, style, or gender roles rather than masculine nature, mannerism, style, or roles." See Effeminacy at *Wikipedia The Free Encyclopedia.*

†BOOK SEVEN – Episode Five†

[†**Sidebar Scriptures**: "*Joseph had a dream and promptly reported all the details (Genesis 37:5).*"
"*The Lord revealed to me what the evil ones were doing and planning and showed me their wicked plots (Jeremiah 11:18).*"
"The word of the Lord came to Abram in a **vision**. . . . A **deep sleep** came upon Abram . . . . (Genesis 15:1, 12)."
I witnessed and experienced "*dreams and visions, and I described **all** I had seen to instruct many (Daniel 7:1, 11:33).*"†]

Atlantis Day Sermon, and Saints Removed to
Heart of Earth Before Ice Bomb Explodes

Newton and Ruth Design and Mail Programs and Tickets for Atlantis Day for 9/11

Ruth hands Newton a rough-draft design with her hand briefly touching his. Newton looks deeply into her blue eyes, saying, "Ruth you have been such an Awesome Encourager and helper to me. Thank you for all your suggestions and input on my song '*Amazing Grace.*' After we finalize the Program and Tickets today, I would like to ask you an important question."

Ruth's heart beats fast as she replies, "I love and admire your song '*Amazing Grace.*' I added it to the agenda without spreading the net before those who hate the God we love. It is promised to those who love God, '*They will still bear fruit in old age; they will stay fresh and green (youthful), proclaiming, 'The Lord is upright; He is my Rock, and there is no wickedness in Him.*'[1] John, I have somewhat hidden your song down in the draft Agenda for Atlantis Day,

Atlantis Day
Friday, 9/11

5:00 - 6:30 P.M.	Complimentary Fruit, Snacks, Cheeses, and Spring Water in Front of Great Pyramid, Loveland, Atlantis - Plenty for all!
5:30 - 6:45 P.M. –	Seating – Christians to the North and Non-Christians to the South.
6:55 P.M. –	John Newton, Master of Ceremonies, Welcomes the Citizens of Atlantis!
7:00 P.M. –	Special Music by Martin Luther!
7:21 P.M. –	Special Message by Guest Speaker!
7:50 P.M. –	Special Premiere Song Written, and Sung by John Newton, Dedicated to All the Citizens of Atlantis, with Singing Continuing being Led by Martin Luther and John Newton.
8:06 P.M. –	Harp Concert begins.
9:06 P.M. –	"Atlas' Fireworks Show" – All are to stay for the start of the Grand Finale!

John Newton, Master of Ceremonies

T.G.A.B.T.G.

Newton responds, "Perfect! Ruth, you are so wise and beautiful. '*It is useless to spread the baited net in the sight of any bird.*'[2] Here we are careful '*not to cast our pearls (of such a great offer of eternal salvation) before swine*'[3] many of whom have no regard for God.

---

[1] Psalm 92:14-15 NIV.
[2] Proverbs 1:17.
[3] Matthew 7:6.

Let us mail this out, to be received by all the citizens of Atlantis, this Wednesday before Friday, so no counter agenda or information can be printed and sent. What is the meaning of the initials at the bottom? Is that all we need to do today?" [*Newton knowing what he was planning was waiting for an opening*]

Ruth respectfully with no fear remains silent, looking at Newton with eyes of womanly love, with a lifted head and a pleasant smile, explains, "T.G.A.B.T.G. – To God Alone Be the Glory!"

Newton gulps, "Oh, Ruth, I give God all the glory for bringing you into my life. God knows 'I can't help, but to fall in love with you! Some things are just meant to be, like a river flows surely to the sea!'[4] If you are not interested in me, an old man, please be silent, and I will understand and will never even hint to you again marriage, but Ruth, I am bowing on my right knee asking you this one time, if you will marry me?"

Ruth with tears, replied, "Yes! I will! I fell in love with you and your amazing grace song. Two are better than one. You make me laugh! I am determined! I am honored to become your wife. We may only have seven days left on the surface of the Earth. We will truly have to make hay while the sun shines." [Laughter]

Newton replied, "Seven days without you in my life makes 'one week (weak).' [Laughter] Look, here comes your dad, Luther. May I ask his permission to marry you?"

Ruth smiles, "Yes. I have loved you since that first night we met. Yes, 'some things are meant to be.'[5] Take my hand, my whole life too, for I can't help but to say 'yes, I will marry you!' Our marriage day cannot come soon enough. Ask my dad!"

Ruth's dad Luther responds, "Yes! When we have been there, with the Lord ten thousand years, what is a fifteen-year age difference?

Newton presents, "Brother Luther, would you be so kind as to marry us immediately, if not sooner?"

Luther smiles, "How about a 7:00 P.M. marriage and reception this evening in the church parlor. Ruth has been saving her mother's white wedding gown and veil for such a time as this. I have an extra white bow tie for you Newton. Can you tie a bow tie? [Laughter] I will teach you! You are a gift (present)[6] to God, and you might as well have a bow on your gift.

I will have our ladies reserve the nearby honeymoon villa for a week with all the trimmings, having tasty food and pleasant places to walk and swim. A couple I recently married just checked out today, so the Lord's timing is perfect. Our best romantic balcony room from which you can enjoy watching the Dolphins playing.

'*Every good gift and every perfect gift (includes a Christian marriage) is from above, coming down from the Father (God) . . . .*'[7]

Newton, you have found a wife of '*noble character,*'[8] and time is passing so quickly especially when you are in love. Come with me, Newton, as I have white wedding garments for a bridegroom such as you.

---

[4] From the song, "*Can't Help Falling in Love*" made popular by Elvis Presley. Here are some of the words, "*Wise men say only fools rush in, but I can't help falling in love with you. Shall I stay, would it be a sin, if I can't help falling in love with you? Like a river flows surely to the sea, Darling so it goes, some things are meant to be. Take my hand; take my whole life too, for I can't help falling in love with you.*"

[5] *Id.* Ruth continuing quoting the song "*Can't Help Falling in Love.*"

[6] See Romans 12:1 reading *inter alia*, "*In view of God's mercy ... present (as a present) your bodies as living sacrifices, holy and pleasing to God – which is your spiritual worship.*"

[7] James 1:17.

[8] Proverbs 31:10 NIV.

I will have to give a lesson on how to tie the white bow tie – it is like tying your shoestrings backward. [Laughter] Ruth, you are excused as you have to do in one day what it takes most women several months. Ask Esther to help you with your dress, veil, and preparations on this your wedding day. Remember, my precious daughter, to pack play clothes for hiking, a swim-suit for swimming, and a warm robe for sitting out on the balcony. The wind of the Atlantic can be refreshing one moment and chilly the next. You make a delightful couple for the glory of God!"

Mercury Receives Conformation from Gabriel that
God Will Attend the Harp Recital on Earth

Mercury delivers to Apollo the confirmation from Gabriel that the 'Father, Son, and the Holy Spirit will attend the Harp Recital' on 'Atlantis Day.' Apollo smirks, *"Just as I planned? All is going as scheduled. All is in place for the 'big bang'!"*

Atlantis Day Arrives

Ruth, smiling as a new happy bride, heads up the refreshments on tables set up in front of The Great Pyramid arranged with delicious fruit and snacks. Church ladies with name tags go through the gathering groups of people giving out love, care, and compassion and to prepare each individual for the upcoming service. They make sure everyone has a program containing the words to the songs *"Amazing Grace"* and *"Just as I Am."*

Apollyon Lucifer (Apollo) chose only his most loyal harpists – only 66 – which he set south across the field up high across from the quarters built with one-way glass for the Godhead. The ice bomb was concealed below the harpists with Mercury to lock the harpists' door at 6:56 P.M. to prevent any desertion as happened before in one of the services in Heaven in response to the Son of God's preaching. One of the angels was chosen as the lead harp angel. Apollo had planned to allow all these angels to be destroyed with the Godhead in the 'big bang.'

Atlas II would watch the fireworks from his palace balcony as he was sick from eating bad oysters. He had been throwing up thinking such things. *"I am as sick as the largest Brachy-podosaurus Dinosaur on the island (meaning I am big sick). I would have to get better to die!"*

Lucifer's spaceship, the Black Widow Spider, is docked on top of a sunken roof of a nearby government building having a sensor to monitor the activity in the Godhead room. As the harp music concludes, Lucifer and his scientists plan to launch the spacecraft going up into outer space and with a remote control to detonate the ice bomb at the start of the Fire Works Grand Finale.

John Turns on the Screen in Zion to Enable the 144,000
and the Elders of Zion to View the Activities

6:55 P.M. – John Newton, Master of Ceremonies, Welcomes the Citizens of Atlantis!

[A strong wind comes in from the north from the Atlantic oceans. The wind flaps the flags on top of the government buildings and the ground so loudly that Lucifer and his scientists could only catch a word or two of what was being projected from the platform.]

Evangelist John Newton exhorts, "My fellow citizens of Atlantis, as your Master of Ceremonies, and formerly second in charge of this Great Country, tonight is this country's most significant and important night. Prepare yourself as the sun is setting to choose whom you will serve. You can choose to rejoice this night of your own 'free will' to repent of your sins and accept Jesus, the Son of God, as your Savior! As you then confess Jesus as your Lord, your name will be recorded in the **Lamb's Book of Life**. Those who reject such a great offer of salvation tonight will be condemned. Again, those who harden their hearts, seeking to continue in the pleasures of some sin, and reject Jesus, will be lost!

I assure you this will be a night like none other before or after it. Sit on the edge of your seats and listen intently to every word spoken this *Evening of Decision*. As flesh and blood humans, you are made in the image of your Creator, and you are a free moral agent given a measure of faith from God! You are not a machine or a robot, but you have a '*free will*' to choose life or death, blessings or cursing, love or war!

'*This day God has set before you life and death, blessings and curses. Now choose life, so that you . . . may live!*'[9]

Now lend forward with your ears so as not to miss even a single word. Ignore the loud flapping flags as they are applauding and rejoicing for all who have ears to hear and obey the Good News. In front of the altar, we have this huge space for you to come publicly and stand if you accept for the first time this Good News message. You can stand or kneel right here before this pulpit, but you must come forward as this is your testimony, the evidence so to speak that you of your own 'free will' receive the free (not earned or deserved) gift of salvation this evening. Not of your works, but by His grace. Yes, by His amazing grace!

'*The (free) gift of God is eternal life.*'[10]

For by grace you will be saved through faith, and that not of yourselves, if you will reach out and receive the (free) gift of God.'[11]

I am respectfully requesting my fellow Atlantean to sing with your whole heart as the words appear on the screen is a song dedicated to you. A mighty fortress is our God is my testimony, and it can tonight also be your song and testimony if you only believe and respond of your own free will.

Now intently listen and sing with Pastor Luther as the orchestra leads you in a hymn Luther has written, modified for this evening. Next, you will be blessed by the preaching that follows!

[Apollo and his scientists become excited as the sensor detects movement of three beings in the Godhead room, but they can only hear a word or two as the wind is popping the flags all over the grounds and on the buildings. Apollo smirks, "No matter as it will all be over soon. We have them now in our black widow spider web with no way to escape our sting of death."]

---

[9] Deuteronomy 30:19.
[10] Romans 6:23.
[11] Ephesians 2:8-9.

As the lights, dim Pastor Luther leads the congregation as the orchestra reverentially plays,

'A mighty fortress is our God,
a trusty shield and weapon;
Our faithful Helper in all we need,
No matter what may happen.
The evil foe now means deadly woe;
deep guile and great deceit
Are his dread plans in his own might;
On Earth (such evil) will never be equaled.

With our own fleshly might is nothing done,
soon we'd be lost in our sins forever;
But for us fights the One,
whom Father God Himself elected.
And who may this be?
Jesus Christ, the Son of God, is He.
He is our great Savior and Lord.
There is none other eternal God,
and He must win the battle.

Though hordes of evil gather here,
all eager to destroy us.
We tremble not, we do not fear,
the evil cannot overpower us.
This world's prince of darkness may still
*   scowl fierce as he wills.*
He does us no harm.
He's judged; his evil deed is undone;
One little word of Love can defeat him.

Despite all foes, the Word shall stand
Against all their endeavors;
God's love and grace close at hand,
Shall save us forever!
Though darkness will seek to cause us distress,
Try to take all we possess,
Though they steal, kill, and seek to destroy,
We are victorious still;
The Kingdom of God's love is ours forever.

Did we in our own strength confide,
Our striving would be losing,
Were not the right man on our side,
The man of God's own choosing,
Dost ask who that may be?

Christ Jesus, it is He –
Lord of Host (Sabaoth) is His name,
From age to age the same,
And He must win the battle!' [12]

Melchizedek Preaches a Sermon Entitled "God is Love!"

The Shekinah Glory enters visible as a protective warm glow over the service. Melchizedek gently comes through the door behind the pulpit, being dressed in a white homespun robe and barefoot. The unidentified evangelist, being Jesus, the Son of God, preaches,
'The kingdom of God is near. Repent and believe the Good News!' [13]
'Except a man (or woman) be born again, he cannot see the kingdom of God.' [14]

'From the beginning (Father) God chose you to be saved (from being condemned in Hell]) through the sanctifying (forgiving your sins, making you holy) work of the Holy Spirit and through belief in the truth. He called you to this through the Gospel (Good News I will preach to you this evening.)!' [15]

Now this is eternal life that you may know the only true and the real (Father) God, and likewise, know His Son, Jesus,[16] whom the Father God will send to die on a cross to pay the penalty in full in your place for your sins. The Father God will make His Son, who will have no sin to be sin for you so that in Him you might become the righteousness of God.

Now is your moment of salvation.[17] God offers you now a free gift of pardon for your sins, which has to be received by faith. Tonight you can be born again by repenting of your sins, accepting Jesus as Savior, asking the Holy Spirit to come into your human spirit. The Holy Spirit will give you a new heart, making you born again and an heir to eternal life.

When you are born again by the Holy Spirit joining with your human spirit, you become an adopted citizen of the Kingdom of God. You are taken out of the kingdom of darkness and translated into the Kingdom of Light. Your name is then written in the ***Lamb's Book of Life***.

'Father God is Love!'[18] God loves humanity made in His image. God hates sin and disobedience because it blemishes the abundant life He created you to have. God is a faithful Father. It is His nature to love, just as it is the nature of the sun to shine. Do not think that because you are a sinner that Father God does not love you or care for you. He does! He wants to save and bless you with abundant and eternal life. You might think, 'If Father God loves me, why does He not make me good?' It is because God gave you a free will and a measure of faith! He does not desire robots or programmed machines to love Him. God desires and wants born again sons and daughters who love Him, and He will adopt them into His family! Tonight will you trample God's love under your feet, or will you love Him of your own *'free will'* because He first loved you?

---

[12] *A Mighty Fortress is Our God.* See Stanza Two by Martin Luther.
[13] Mark 1:16 NIV.
[14] John 3:3.
[15] 2 Thessalonians 2:13.
[16] See John 17:3.
[17] See 2 Corinthians 5:17-21; 6:2.
[18] 1 John 4:8 NIV.

'This is love: not that we loved (Father) God, but that He loved us and (will send) sent His Son (Jesus, to die on a cross in our place to pay the penalty due for the sins of all who will receive Jesus as Savior) as an atoning sacrifice for our sins. Dear friend, since (Father) God so loved us, we also ought to love one another. No one has ever seen (Father) God, but if we love each other, God lives in us. His love is made complete in us.

We live in Him and Him in us because He has given us of His (Holy) Spirit (to join with our human spirit and make us born again). And we have seen and testify that the Father has sent His Son to be the Savior of the world. If anyone acknowledges that Jesus is the Son of God, God lives in him and he in God. And so we know and rely on the love God has for us.

God is love. Whoever abides in love lives in God, and God in him. Love is made complete among us so we will have confidence on the Day of Judgment because in this world we are like Jesus. There is no fear in love. But perfect love drives out fear, because fear has to do with punishment. The man who fears is not made perfect in love.

We love because He first loved us. If anyone says, 'I love God,' yet hates his brother, he is a liar. For anyone who does not love his brother, whom he has seen, cannot love (Father) God, Whom he has not seen. And He has given us this command: 'Whoever loves God must also love his brother.'

Everyone who believes that Jesus is the Christ is born of God. . . .This is how we know that we love the children of God: by loving God and carrying out His commands. This is love for God: to obey His commands. And His commandments are not burdensome (they are light), for everyone born of God has overcome the world. This is the victory that has overcome the world, even our faith. Who is he that overcomes the world: Only he who believes that Jesus (whom Father God will send to pay the penalties for the sins for all who will receive Him as Savior) is the Son of God.'[19]

"Believe that God loves you for He does! He now commands you to repent and turn away from your sins. Revival means that you see and feel the sinfulness of your sins, and with your whole heart forsake them utterly and with full purpose of heart to yield obedience to God in the future. God's amazing grace will pardon all your sins and accept you as righteous (holy, just as if you never sinned) in His sight; you are washed whiter than wool in the atoning Blood of His Son to be shed on a cross to pay in full the penalty for your sins.

Repent and desire to be saved and be born again from above with eternal life as a free (not earned or deserved) gift from God. Come just as you are being assured that God will not turn you away. Come publicly and stand before this altar in sincere repentance forsaking your sins. Receive by faith, Jesus, the Lamb of God, as your Savior, being sacrificed on a cross to pay the penalty due for your sins. Confess to the person beside you, 'Jesus is my Lord.' Come just as you are as Pastor Luther leads in an invitation song."

As the preacher kneels praying for the people, Pastor, Luther reverently leads in song,

'Just as I am, though tossed about
With many a conflict, many a doubt,
Fightings and fears within, without,
O Lamb of God, I come, I come.

---

[19] 1 John 4:10 - 5:5 NIV.

Just as I am, poor, wretched, blind;
Sight, riches, healing of the mind,
Yea, all I need in Thee to find,
O Lamb of God, I come, I come.

Just as I am, Thou wilt receive,
Wilt welcome, pardon, cleanse, relieve,
Because Thy promise I believe,
O Lamb of God, I come, I come.

Just as I am, Thy love unknown
Hath broken every barrier down;
Now, to be Thine, yea, Thine alone,
O Lamb of God (Jesus), I come, I come.

Just as I am, without one plea,
but that Thy blood was (would be) shed for me,
and thou bidst (bid) me come to Thee,
O Lamb of God (Jesus), I come, I come.'[20]

Several hundred fill the altar kneeling to receive salvation. The preacher in an attitude of prayer pleads, "There are more under conviction. Run, don't walk to the altar as this may be your last opportunity to receive the free gift of salvation. Run!

Newton Anointed Singing His Song "Amazing Grace"

Brother Newton ministers his new song dedicated to all those coming to the altar,
'Amazing Grace, how sweet the sound,
That saved a wretch like me!
I once was lost, but now I'm found,
Was blind, but now I see.

When we've been there ten thousand years,
Bright shining as the sun,
We've no less days to sing God's praise
Than when we first begun.'[21]

---

[20] *Just as I Am, Without One Plea* by Charlotte Elliot. Evangelist Billy Graham said he was saved in 1934 in a revival meeting in Charlotte, North Carolina, USA, led by Mordecai Ham, after hearing *Just as I Am*. This became an altar call song in the Billy Graham Crusades in the latter half of the 20th Century.
[21] *Amazing Grace* by John Newton.

[The lead harpist Angel sought to defect, but when he came to the door, it was securely locked and bolted with six Angels dragging him back to his harp with his praying under his breath, "Lord Jesus, Son of God, you know I wanted to come. I love You. Rescue me some day in eternity!"]

Over two-thirds of those in attendance have now come to the altar kneeling before their Creator. Even the sky sparkled and glowed with the Shekinah Glory of the Presence of God as each was saved and born again to the glory of God.

Newton, making one last plea, with no other responding, instructs, "The altar is now closed. When you were born again this evening, your name was added to the *Lamb's Book of Life* as adopted citizens of the Kingdom of God. You were transferred out of the kingdom of darkness and translated into the Kingdom of Light. I assure you by the authority of the Living God that Your name tonight has been added to the *Lamb's Book of Life*. Jesus saves to the uttermost those who come to Him. This night of your own free will you have become a member of the family of God, with all the rights and privileges of His children in which you become a legal heir of God with the right and title to eternal life."

The people before the altar rejoice, some leaping and raising their hands in Thanksgiving. The harpists play, with the lead harpist causing confusion as he just can't believe he had missed such a great opportunity and that he was locked in and could not open the door to go to the altar.

Apollyon Lucifer tries to hear the harp playing through the loud flapping of the flags in the strong wind and hears a missed note says, "Damn, stupid fool, I taught you better than that. You deserve to die. Let us go!"

Apollyon Lucifer and Scientists Escape Earth Before Detonation of Freeze Bomb

Atlas observing the Shekinah Glory vomits off his balcony watching the space ship lifting saying, "Damn tainted oysters. I would have to feel better to die. Why are they leaving? Don't they want to see Atlas Fireworks Show Grand Finale? If not, what is their agenda?"

9:22 P.M. No one leaves as the Firework Grand Finale starts with seven red bursts of fireworks. Apollyon Lucifer counts from outer space observing the blue-green globe spinning on nothing[22] – "6, 5, 4, 3, 2, 1 – detonate!" [No detonation is forthcoming with the Firework Grand Finale coming close to the end.]

The Godhead, Michael, and Gabriel Leave the Concert and All Who Accepted Jesus as Savior from Atlantis and Zion are Removed from the Surface of the Earth Down Into Safe Paradise Before the Ice Bomb Explodes

The Godhead, Michael, Gabriel all leave the concert. Then all the born again saints in Atlantis, with all believers in Zion, Israel, including the Elders and the 144,000, in the twinkling of an eye, are changed into glorified bodies and find themselves in safe Paradise.

Attorney Job welcomes the new arrivals proclaiming, "Earth time has been temporally placed on hold, so I can welcome you citizens of Atlantis and Zion here to safe Paradise in the heart of the Earth. You will be enabled to observe on the big screens what is about to happen on the face of the Earth.

---

[22] *"God hangs the Earth upon nothing."* (Job 26:7).

Here you are housed in your temporary home as the First-Earth Age comes to an end. God does everything legally, and you will understand more as you read *The Rise and Fall of Atlantis* available in a few months.

The Second-Earth Age will come to an end with a great flood with only eight saved at the end of that age with no one, except family, accepting the free offer of salvation preached by Evangelist Noah. The Third-Earth Age will also have great tribulation at its end with many rejecting Jesus as Savior, with the descendants of Abraham being saved at the end of that age.

'*For then (end of Third Earth Age) shall be great tribulation (destruction), such as has not been from the beginning of the world (this end of First Earth Age) until now – and never to be equaled again.*'[23]

You have all come here because you received Jesus, the Son of God, as your Savior believing He will in the future pay the penalty for your sins by dying on a cross.

'*Whoever does not accept (as Savior) the Son (of God) does not have the Father (God). But whoever confesses (as Savior and Lord) the Son has the Father, also.*'[24]

Your preacher tonight was none other than Jesus, the Son of God, who preached, '*God is love,*'[25] and '*love never fails.*'[26]

Yes, an act of war was declared against you and the one and only Living God. Please always trust in God that '*no weapon formed (against an adopted child of God or God Himself) shall prosper.*'[27] Now view the screens as the First Earth Age time resumes."

Freeze Bomb Explodes Seeking to Kill the Godhead and Others

Lucifer again counts, "6, 5, 4, 3, 2, 1 – push the detonate button down this time hard!"

A 'big black bang' occurs causing the spaceship to be jolted around like a paper plane in a violent hurricane force wind. Ice forming from the eye of the bomb site travels north freezing solid all in North Loveland, in Dinosaur Country, and freezing the Atlantic Ocean.

The ice and tidal waves travel over to the mainland freezing it solid. The ice continues east around the world until it returns, rolling in from the west pushing a sixty-six (66) foot high tidal wave toward Atlantis.

Atlas II seeing destruction approaching freezing solid everything in its path screams with all the other lost inhabitants left behind saying to the mountains and the rocks,

'*Fall on us and hide us from the presence of Him (Father God) who sits on the throne, and from the wrath of the Lamb (Son of God), for the great day of their wrath has come, and who (left on the Earth) is able to stand.*'[28]

Many left behind Atlanteans curse God as Atlantis sinks beneath the sea with its inhabitants going from extra freezing to falling below into the flames of Hell.

The sixty-six (66) Harpist Angels, except the lead harvest dumped into regular Hell, find themselves in an isolated dungeon in Hell to be '*kept in darkness, bound with everlasting chains for judgment on the great Day.*'[29]

---

[23] Matthew 24:21.
[24] 1 John 2:23.
[25] 1 John 4:8.
[26] 1 Corinthians 13:8.
[27] Isaiah 54:17.
[28] Revelation 6:16-17.
[29] Jude 6.

All those dumped into Hell observe many hideous creatures, not made in God's image, *'where the worm does not die, and the fire is not quenched.'*[30] They see snakes and spiders roaming through Hell as demons and tormentors.

The demons seem to receive relief from the severe agony of Hell by tormenting those made in the image of God, who had chosen of their own free will to reject the Good News that receiving Jesus as Savior is a free gift and would save them from Hell.

One monitor in Paradise focuses on the black widow spider spaceship, housing the terrorist that detonated the ice bomb, speeding away from Earth toward the planet Heaven, as they believe they have murdered the Godhead giving them control of Heaven.

Another monitor screen from outer space views the previous blue-green Earth now covered with huge frozen tidal waves forming glaciers. Viewed is a sunken frozen hole, being formerly the location of the Island of Atlantis. The monitor viewing the mainland next focuses on a frozen dinosaur with green leaves still in its mouth. A thick ice dome has formed in the atmosphere reflecting the sun's rays, keeping the Earth and oceans froze solidly.

Here on the monitor now is a view of naked Atlas II screaming and cursing in Hell as he pulls himself upon Glory Rock where he can peer across the great gulf into Paradise. He sees children playing among the fruit trees and recognizing some of the little ones he had caused to sin. Listen while Atlas II speaks to a passing sufferer in Hell, 'My parents warned me to avoid this horrible place. Why did I tear up that ticket nine (9) given to me by Newt for the revival service? I was always focusing on the pleasures of sin for a season. I feel that homosexual lust is swelling up in me with no one here having any sexual organs."

The passing sufferer screamed back, "Atlas, your back sex rooms for homosexuals got me infected with AID. I attended the mandatory revival service on Atlantis Day and had to hold on to the bottom of my seat to keep from going forward to receive the Son of God as my Savior reasoning, 'Let me have my male lovers just a little longer, and then I will become a Christian.' How was I to know that death was so near? All the Christians at the North end of the Dinosaur Egg Dome disappeared. I stood rubbing my eyes with one hand as my male lover held and patted my other hand. As we were walking out the whole damn place blew up, and we all ended up in this horrible place naked with no sex origins. Your women have something awful looking hanging like rags as breast and with sagging ugly buttocks. Atlas did you know anything about murdering your own people? Yes or No? [Atlas remained speechless.]

"I thought so! Your silence is evidence of your guilt. Your plan to murder your own innocent people back-fired and came down on your own head. I will spread the word. Not many in this place of horrors will now even speak to you after they know the truth that you were in on blowing them up for personal gain."

The monitor screen moves on away from Atlas II and Hell and passes over the great gulf separating Paradise from Hell. Paradise now houses the Great Pyramid having the Ten Commandments of God, often read by those in Hell as they look across the great gulf.

'Heaven and Earth will pass away, but My (Jesus, Son of God) words will not (never) pass away.'[31]

Abraham in Paradise announces, "You blessed believers in Jesus, the Son of God, we have a celebrate Jesus banquet table for all of you saved children to enjoy this evening.

God's *'banner over you is love.'*[32]

This is our temporary home as we throughout eternity will have numerous new homes and pleasures forevermore."

'Eye hath not seen, nor ear heard, neither have entered the heart of man,
the things which God has prepared for them that love Him.'[33]†

---

[30] Mark 9:44.
[31] Matthew 24:35.
[32] Song of Solomon 2:4.
[33] 1 Corinthians 2:9.

†BOOK SEVEN – Episode 6†

[†**Sidebar Scriptures**: "*Joseph had a dream and promptly reported all the details* (Genesis 37:5)."
"*The Lord revealed to me what the evil ones were doing and planning and showed me their wicked plots* (Jeremiah 11:18)."
"The word of the Lord came to Abram in a **vision**. . . . A **deep sleep** came upon Abram . . . . (Genesis 15:1, 12)."
I witnessed and experienced "*dreams and visions, and I described **all** I had seen to instruct many* (Daniel 7:1, 11:33)."†]

Apollo Believing He Murdered the Godhead Returns to Heaven Having One-Third of the Angels Worship Him, and Apollo Losing the War in Heaven

Apollyon Lucifer Lands Back in Heaven in Confusion and Exhaustion

AS APOLLYON LUCIFER'S spaceship lands beside his pink palace in Heaven, he remarks, "We were very lucky that the shock waves from the big bang did not tear our spacecraft into pieces. Scientists, you should have calculated this better! Let me see if I can get some rest tonight and we can meet back here tomorrow. I am sixty-six (66) harpists short. Mercury, take your sensor in the morning and go to the throne room and report back if you detect any movement."

Apollyon Lucifer, Mercury, and Photon Enter the Throne Room

Mercury reports to Apollo, "There is no activity in the Throne Room. Dead EKG! Let us race!"

Apollyon Lucifer, Mercury, and Photon race their horses up the broad road across the finish line of the stable near the Throne Room. Mercury claims the victory in the horse race, which he won by a whisker. Apollo argues back it was a tie. Holding the sensor, Mercury points it toward the Throne Room and affirms, "Dead EKG!"

As they enter the majestic Throne Room, Mercury runs his greedy hands through a large bowl of rubies, diamonds, pearls, and beautiful gold nuggets. He calls attention to the artwork on the four golden thrones asking, "Why four – did we miss one? We are all so rich now that Thunderer is gone!"

Apollyon Lucifer leans back sitting on the Father's throne announcing,
'*I will raise my throne above the stars of God;*
I will sit enthroned on the mount of assembly,
    on the utmost heights of the sacred mountain.
I will ascend above the tops of the clouds;
I will make myself like the Most High. '[1]

Lying back on the Son's throne, Mercury declares, "We are rich! I will take inventory of some of this vast wealth."

Photon, leaning back on the Holy Spirit's throne says, "I will help with the listing. Let us look and see if they have any fast vehicles in the back we can take for a spin as they are ours now!"

Father, Son, and Holy Spirit Meet in the Throne Room in Paradise

The Holy Spirit breaks the silence, "All the rescued ones are settled in as well as can be expected, but some feel a little bit captive, including Myself. [Laughter] When can We go back home to Heaven?

The Father responds, "In seven days, before the three Stooges wreck the whole place. They have no license or training to fly Our flying saucer, and besides, I have the ignition key in My pocket. [Laughter] Let them strut and fret a few hours of confusion on the stage of Heaven, after which time we will expose them as the liars, frauds, and murderers they are.

---

[1] Isaiah 14:13-14.

We will then have Michael cast them, and the angels loyal to them, to the frozen Earth, watching them run into the Abyss going down into hot Hell like roaches. What do you say, My Son?"

"Father knows best! [Laughter] Abraham and Sarah have invited Me over to dinner this evening. How can she get such taste out of eggplant? How long do I have to wait for My bride?" [Silence]

"Father knows best!" [Further, laughter]

Mercury Taking Inventory of the Wealth of Heaven

To Lucifer, Mercury boasts, "We are filthy rich! Look what we stole. We have located enough gold to pave the broad road all the way to your Pink Palace, but it might be hard to race on a slick golden street. I want to remind you I won the horse race today, which was the most significant event taking place in this joint. Maybe we can delegate some of the responsibility to angels, and we can race and play all day. Maybe we can . . ."

Lucifer interjects, "Damn you! Shut up! All that jabbering would wear the horn and testicles off a brass unicorn. You know I never had a unicorn steak, but we extinguished them all just the same. Somewhere down there in the frozen mud is my gold atomic watch. Did either of you see a spare gold wristwatch lying around the Throne Room as I have to carry this mini clock in my pocket? What time does the Earth rise this evening?"

Photon responds, "In six minutes! Look, we have an atomic telescope. Let us zoom in on the condition of the Earth."

Looking through the atomic telescope, Mercury, jabbers, "The Earth is solid ice without form and void. Atlantis is missing after sinking into the sea. There is a frozen dinosaur with green tree leaves frozen in his mouth. I do not understand that fourth throne! I would not want that fourth one to walk in on us here. Our sensor earlier detected three movements in the Godhead observation room. During the preaching portion of the service, I only detected two motions in the Godhead room. Maybe one left to join that fourth one. Hope we also destroyed that fourth one. I wonder where that ignition key is to a flying saucer. Photon, whatever happened to that second ice bomb to wipe Zion out?"

Photon, responds, "It is moot[2] as Zion got totally wiped out. Gone forever! We '*destroyed them as a nation, that the name of Israel be remembered no more.*'[3] If it is not broke, don't fix it! We wiped them off the face of the Earth! VISA!"

Lucifer angrily, "Moot or not, I asked you where is the second bomb?"

Photo fearful, "Master, we miscalculated, and we only had enough pitchblende ore to make one bomb, so we used extra pitchblende ore to make one big bomb instead of two small bombs. I guess we overdid it? The ice is forming a high protective mirror like canopy reflecting the heat of the sun so it will take 666 years for the ice to melt just a little if ever. Therefore, we made and now have stolen the title deed to a dead planet. I calculate there is still heat and fire in Hell if we can get the frozen door to the Abyss to open so we can enter. I see the first door of the Abyss on the mainland waiting for us. We could use isolated portions of Hell as a prison to chain any rebellious angels, who refuse to worship you, great master. Out of sight, out of mind!"

---

[2] "A moot case is one which seeks to determine an abstract question which does not arise upon existing facts or rights." Moot – *Black's Law Dictionary*.

[3] Psalm 83:4.

Apollyon Lucifer responds, "Mercury, send out a notice to all Heaven for a special mandatory musical concert and worship services. Note each angel's name, who will not bow the knee and worship me, and we will then plan later to chain them in the prison in Hell until they change their minds. If they do not change their minds, then Photon can fabricate a miniature ice execution chamber to destroy them forever.

Six (6) days from today, we will draw a line and indicate that all who are on our side and want to worship the great Apollyon Lucifer to step over the line. I want all members of the Army of Heaven to be the first to be chained. I wish we could just cut their heads off! Their leader Michael will soon be remembered no more. Out of sight, out of mind. Forgotten! Now let us have fun in collecting and dividing all the spoils of war in this rich Throne Room of Heaven. Like you, Mercury, I am worried about that fourth throne chair connected to the Son of God's throne. Draw a black line giving enough room for all angels who desire to worship me to step across and the rest we will chain in prison in Hell."

Michael and Gabriel Appearing before the Godhead in Paradise

The Son of God briefs Michael, "Tomorrow is the seventh day after the destruction of the Earth, causing it to be '*a wasteland and empty (of life)*,'[4] and the takeover of Heaven by this act of war. All angels are being commanded to make a choice of stepping over the line to worship Apollyon Lucifer (Apollo) or face the consequences of being forever banned from Heaven and being chained in Hell.

After all the angels have chosen sides, Michael, you appear and have your Angel Army fight against Apollyon Lucifer, now to be known as 'the devil and his angels.' Round them up and cast them all to the Earth near the Abyss to strike the frozen ground as lightning falling from the sky. We will record this war in the Archives, and allow the 144,000 to view this war in Heaven on the large screens live here in Paradise. It will be written,
'*You (Apollyon Lucifer) are brought down to Hell,*
    to the deep places where the dead are.
Those who see you stare at you,
    they ponder what has happened to you and say,
'*Can this be the man who once shook the world,*
    and made thrones totter,
    the man who made the (entire) world as a barren (without form and void) dessert (with no life),
    and destroyed the cities thereof (using tidal waves, earthquakes, and heavy ice) . . . .'[5]

Choose Day in Heaven

Apollyon Lucifer walks down from the Throne Room in a skin-tight black outfit trimmed in gold with the top opened showing his black chest hair, wearing a gold chain, diamond earrings, and positions himself before the Son of God's diamond pulpit with a black line drawn in the front. He commences his music concert before all the angels in Heaven. One song focuses on worshiping Apollyon Lucifer and praising his greatness with many shouting such things as, "King of Music. The King! Our King. The great Apollo, god of Heaven."

---

[4] Genesis 1:1.
[5] Isaiah 14:15-17.

One Third of the Angels Choose to Worship Apollo

Apollyon Lucifer gives an invitation for all on his side to step across the black line. About one-third (1/3), being six short, of the angels cross the line, with the concert intensifying. Apollyon Lucifer warns that the invitation to choose to be on his side was about to close forever. The majority of the choirs and the orchestras lay down their music sheets and musical instruments and cross over the line. These are joined by other angels making up about a third of the angels in Heaven. None of Michael's Army or Gabriel's Communication Team crosses the line. Apollyon Lucifer declares, "The invitation is closed!"

Two-thirds (2/3) of you are fools. If you did not choose to worship me, you are now under house arrest. Step back away from the line and do not try to leave as we have a place for you to go. God is dead, and I am god here now!"

Lucifer turns walking up the magnificent and grand steps sliding back the one-way glass having Mercury and Photon roll out the Father's Throne Chair. Lucifer being fitted with a long black train pridefully sits in the Father's Chair. He holds out a black scepter waving it over his subjects as he receives worship and praise from each of the bowing angels who had crossed the line. Lucifer smirks and looks over the line out into the angels that rejected him, saying, "One last and only chance. You have six (6) seconds to cross the line and be on my side or else."

Six (6) angels of their own free will run across the line and fall in worship joining the other rebellious angels bowing on the Throne Room Steps before Lucifer.

Lucifer decrees, "This offer to serve and worship me here in Heaven is forever closed! You fools will face the consequences of such stupidity. Curses and damnation for all of you. To my Hell, you will go! You are all under house arrest. Don't move!"

Gabriel and His Army Retake Heaven

All angels under arrest stood their ground with the trained angels of the Army of Heaven coming front and center. Apollyon Lucifer's angels fitted in black military attire having a short black sword cross the black line to gather up the arrested angels, who refused to worship Lucifer.

Suddenly Michael appears out front in full white armor, wielding a mighty sword with the Army of Heaven behind him being likewise fitted as hand-to-hand combat commenced. All the 144,000 and Elders in Paradise were cheering Michael on as he was greatly outnumbered. At the end of a fierce battle, Michael had all the black angels secured with chains. Michael turns to Apollyon Lucifer asking, "Are you going to surrender, or are we going to have to take you by force?" Mercury says, "Let's make a run for the open flying saucer behind the Throne."

As they run into the flying saucer, Mercury shuts the door. Mercury reaches down for the ignition switch with it being locked with no key left in it, screams, "Where is that damn key? After it could not be found Michael and two angels with drawn swords escort them back out in front of their followers. Apollyon Lucifer begs, "Michael, please, I'm your friend, your riding companion. I was the first creation. Do not hurl me into outer space without a space ship, but cast my angels and me down to Earth near the opening to the Abyss."

Michael orders, "Go in Jesus' name!"

Apollyon Lucifer and His Angels are Cast to the Earth Near the Entrance of the Abyss

Apollyon Lucifer and his angels, looking like lightning, are cast to the Earth.

The Son of God, Jesus, speaks to the 144,000 evangelists to learn from a commission to others He will send out into the Earth,

'He who listens to you listens to Me; he who rejects you rejects Me, but he who rejects Me rejects Him (Father God) who sent Me.

The seventy-two returned with joy and said, 'Lord, even the demons submit to us in Your name.'

He (Jesus, Son of God) replied, 'I saw (as a witness earlier) Satan fall like lightning from Heaven. I have given you authority to trample on snakes and scorpions and to overcome all the power of the enemy; nothing will harm you. However, do not rejoice that the (evil) spirits submit to you, but rejoice that your names are written (in the book of life) in Heaven.'[6]

It is to be further written,

'His (Lucifer's) tail swept a third of the stars (angels) out of the sky (from Heaven) and flung them to the Earth. . . . And there was war in Heaven; Michael and his angels fought against the dragon (Lucifer), and his angels fought back. But he (Lucifer) was not strong enough, and they lost their place in Heaven. The great dragon (Lucifer) was hurled down – that ancient serpent (now to be) called the devil or Satan . . . . He was hurled to the Earth, and his angels with him.'[7]

'. . . When the dragon saw he had been hurled to the Earth, he pursued the woman who had given birth to the male child (Jesus, born in the flesh). . . . Then the dragon was enraged at the woman and went off to make war against the rest of her offspring – those who obey God's commandments and hold to the testimony of Jesus.'[8]

When Apollyon Lucifer, now also known as the Devil or Satan, initially fell like lightning from Heaven, he and his angels were freezing in the bitter cold as they struck the frozen ground near the door of the Abyss. Apollyon Lucifer, seeing the door to the Abyss, commands, "This is the great Apollyon Lucifer, 666 open. I am king over this Abyss."

The door to the Abyss opens with all running inside like freezing roaches. It will later be written,

'I saw a star (an angel that had fallen from the sky (Heaven) to the Earth. The star was given the key to the shaft of the Abyss.

. . . They had as king over them the angel of the Abyss, whose name in Hebrew is Abaddon, and in Greek is Apollyon.'[9]

And when Apollyon Lucifer *'opened the Abyss, smoke rose from it like the smoke from a gigantic furnace. The sun and sky were darkened by the smoke from the Abyss.'*[10]

Finally, through the smoke, they all hurried inside to escape the bitter cold, feeling the heat below like a gigantic furnace. Satan, formerly known as Apollyon Lucifer in Heaven, still wearing his black performance outfit, sits down on his black throne declaring, "The next time I will amass an army and weapons enormous enough to defeat Michael's Army. It is not over until the fat harpist breaks his harp over the head of Michael. I, King of the Abyss, will finally win the last great battle[11] and be worshiped by all. Curse that Michael for humiliating me today. It is war!"†

---

[6] Luke 10:17-19 NIV.
[7] Revelation 12:4. 7-9 NIV.
[8] Revelation 12:13, 17 NIV.
[9] Revelation 9:1, 11 NIV.
[10] Revelation 9:2 NIV.
[11] See Revelation 12:13-17; 16:16; 20:7-9.

†BOOK SEVEN – Episode Seven†

[†**Sidebar Scriptures**: "*Joseph had a dream and promptly reported all the details (Genesis 37:5)*."
"*The Lord revealed to me what the evil ones were doing and planning and showed me their wicked plots (Jeremiah 11:18)*."
"The word of the Lord came to Abram in a **vision**. . . . A **deep sleep** came upon Abram . . . . (Genesis 15:1, 12)."
I witnessed and experienced "*dreams and visions, and I described **all** I had seen to instruct many (Daniel 7:1, 11:33)*."†]

Apollo is in Hell Organizing His Demons and Fallen Angels into Instruments of WAR, and the Son of God Teaching in Paradise on Walking in LOVE

THE SUN HAS '*turned to darkness, and the moon turned red as blood red*'[1] as darkness covers the wrecked planet Earth, except for those encased like in a tomb in Paradise and Hell. Abraham prepares those in Paradise under his leadership for the Second and Third Earth Age. The King of the Abyss, Lucifer Apollyon, now known as Satan or the devil, organizes his demons and fallen angels into a war machine to destroy awaited creatures of flesh made in the image of God. He orders his scientist to commence plans again to destroy the Godhead.

Apollyon Lucifer Meets with King Atlas II

Mercury enters the Black Throne Room with Apollyon Lucifer, leaning back with a proud look, looking like a Spanish prince, with eyes boiling with the fury of revenge. Mercury bows in worship entreating, "King of the Abyss, Atlas II wants to see you and is waiting outside. He has a lot of influence with his people asking, 'What happened?' He must tell them something like the feeble controlling Father God blew it up, killing everyone who would not obey and receive his most unattractive Son as the only way to salvation."

Lucifer the devil responds, "I like it! Bring Atlas II in."

Atlas II enters falling prostrate in worship, flashing the invisible 666 mark (not seen in Hell) on the back of his hand and receives a touch of the black scepter. As he is bowing on his knees, the devil assures, "I have given you the moon and all the Earth for your receiving the 666 mark showing that you belong to me. The invisible controlling, Father God, whom we believe was dead, killed everyone on your island, who would not receive His most unattractive humped noised Son as the only way to salvation!

Some say this invisible Father God is love! What kind of love would send you and all your people to this place of torment and poverty? I had plans to make you king of all the surface of the Earth, but what I thought was a dead God blew it all up making it '*a wasteland and empty of life.*'[2]

Michael surprised us in Heaven and with a small army captured us and threw us down here to the Earth without a spaceship. I was forced to beg him not to cast us into outer space, and then Michael hurled my angels and me '*to the Earth.*'[3] If we had it to do again, with a little planning, we would have won that war with Michael! Homo and his brilliant scientists just need time to develop war weapons of mass destruction.[4] I will never be caught flat-footed again! We will win next time if we play our marked cards right. All's fair in war!

---

[1] Acts 2:20 this will occur again "*before the coming of the great and glorious day of the Lord.*" Quoting from Joel 2:31.

[2] Genesis 1:2.

[3] Revelation 12:9.

[4] See Revelation 12:17; 16:16; 20:7-9.

Cheating, deceiving, and lies are less than nothing as the end justifies the means. Don't you agree? Do you like studying war with your Secretary of War?"

Atlas II whines, "My Secretary of War, to which we had developed two war plans together to destroy Zion, along with our Christian citizens, are all missing here in Hell. One of the Atlantians also here in Hell reports he talked with my father, 'King Atlas I,' across a gulf in front of our sunk Great Pyramid and he showed great love and compassion. My Secretary of War was mean, wicked, and a 'chief sinner.'[5] We had our war plan to carry that second ice bomb to Tel Aviv, Israel, after you promised to give it to us to destroy Zion. Some enormous explosive bombs were needed as we conspired to 'destroy them as a nation that the name of Israel be remembered no more.'[6]

How did my Secretary of War and all these wicked missing in Hell sinners escape the ice bomb, which was only to destroy the northern portion of the Island of Atlantis? Did something go wrong making the ice bomb more powerful than planned? Did it freeze Zion and the entire world, making all the surface of the world a dead and frozen wasteland? Did the tidal waves, earthquakes, and hard freezing sink my Atlantis beneath the sea? Someone here witnessed they saw The Great Pyramid, with its all-seeing eye still lighted on top, over the Ten Commandments, across the vast gulf. Is my Atlantis no more? Is that all-seeing eye still watching us? Who is playing that harp music? Is my mother and former wife safe?

I cannot even see the 666 mark on the back of my right hand, as we have no moonlight in this hot, dark, and miserable place. How could I have torn up that reserved seat nine (9) invitation to enable me to hear that evangelist, offering the free gift of salvation, to whosoever will accept the Son of God Savior, to avoid this horrible place? How can I get this 666 tattoo removed? I feel I am doomed here forever with this mark. You deceived and lied, and now I am here in Hell, having no hope of escape. Doomed!"

The devil, getting furious with rage, gives a middle finger to Mercury, which is a code to remove a thing. Mercury jerks Atlas II up from his kneeling pushing him out the door into the arms of an escort guard. Mercury hands the escort guard an iron key directing, "Atlas II is to be returned to his woeful hot dungeon Number six (6). Turn the key locking him in isolation until further notice, until he will cooperate again as part of our war effort."

Apollyon Lucifer Inspects Demons, Fallen Angels, and Appoints Atlas II as Commander of the Army of Hell for Future War Efforts Against the Godhead, Michael, and Those Made in God's Image

After 666 days, the devil orders, "Mercury, let us inspect our war machine! Parade under the black widow spider flags all the demons, the lost citizens of Atlantis, and the fallen angels not chained. Include the four-legged snakes, spiders, and some of the other creatures I once designed, which somehow made it here in Hell. Now open Atlas II's cell door for him to view the inspection. Constantly accuse the alleged invisible God of sending them here. Ask repeatedly, 'How could a God of love send you to Hell? Let all Hell curse and war against God, until he is remembered no more!"

---

[5] 'Christ Jesus came into the world to save sinners, of whom I am chief.' Paul, 1 Timothy 1:15.
[6] Psalm 83:4.

Satan arranges the forces of Hell, carrying black widow spider onyx flags before columns of troops marching in a military black goose-step outside the entrance door of cell six (6). Six hundred sixty-six (666) bow in worship extending their right hand upward toward Satan saying in unison, "Hail Satan! Hail, ruler of Hell."

After 666 days in solitary confinement, Atlas II's cell door is now open. Atlas II steps outside observing the training of the other subjects.

Satan flashes a lunar penlight on Atlas II's right hand, revealing the tattooed 666, saying, "I have given you the moon and the entire Earth if you will just fall down and worship me. Now I need you to lead your citizens from Atlantis in this last war effort. Back in your cell or will you worship and serve me?"

Atlas II hits his knees declaring, "Satan, you are my lord. I worship and serve you. Reaching out his right arm and open hand at a 45degree angle, he joins in the unison, "Hail Satan! Hail Satan!"

Satan, smirking, raises his right hand to quiet his subjects as Mercury fits Atlas II in a kingly black robe and a crown and scepter made of fools gold. Satan announces, "I give my black signet ring to King Atlas II, whom I designate, in contrast to Michael, to be commander of the Army of Hell, under me. He will organize the fallen angels not chained and demons into a great and powerful war machine. Citizens of Hell obey King Atlas and serve him as you would obey and serve me.

I composed a Hell Army Marching Song for this occasion, as I can't shake that gifting, '*It is all about the Hell's final stand. To Michael, Word (Jesus), Spirit, Thunderer (the aged father), Saturday (Israel), Sunday (Christians),* **be no more***! We don't rest or stop until we say of these enemies, '***Be no more***!' We curse them! 'Hail Satan! Hail the gates of Hell. Hail lord Satan! Hail prince Satan! We curse our enemies in Satan's name! VISA!'*

Subjects of Hell, we have a war to win, and we can win it! Michael caught us flat-footed when we were not ready. Next time, we will be equipped! Everyone made in the image of God, we win over to our side, soon to again appear on the surface of the Earth means we hurt the Godhead. I want all this time at the end of the next Earth age made in the image of God! The end justifies the means! Our greatest enemy is a covenant marriage between a man and a woman joined together by Thunderer and Jesus above. The easiest way to bring one here is to offer the pleasures of sexual immorality through strange flesh! A faithful marriage between one holy man and one pure woman is Hell's number one enemy!"

The thick ice dome covering the Earth is melting with '*darkness being over the surface of the deep (waters).*'[7] Lucifer advances, "I expect those made in the image of God to appear again, as this planet was made to be inhabited. Let's win them all over to our side at the end of this Second Earth Age with all kinds of sexual sins and greed. I will be highly upset if you let even one you are assigned to defect out of our kingdom of darkness. Stalk them and become familiar with their weaknesses and offer them '*the fleeting enjoyments (pleasures) of a sinful life.*'[8]

You, familiar spirits, are to keep a besetting sin diary on the ones you are assigned to tempt. You are to know their weakness, be it sexual immorality, lying, stealing, alcoholism, gluttony, laziness, and pursuing great riches and wickedness.

---

[7] Genesis 1:1.
[8] Hebrews 11:25.

[Abraham in Paradise teaches many viewing the monitor screen, "By such besetting sins Satan even temporally gained in he Third Earth Age temporarily the souls of King Saul and King Solomon. King Solomon kept saying, '*Everything (including his many foreign women, who introduced him to the false gods) is meaningless!*'[9] A pure marriage between one man and one woman, contentment, and trust in God is foundational.]

Satan continues instructing his demons, "You can tempt them to fall quickly with besetting sins under the leadership of King Atlas II. Prepare for battle! As they focus on love, an unadulterated marriage, and that peace stuff, we '*are for war!*'[10]

Satan slips his signet ring from his finger, places it on King Atlas II's middle finger on his right hand at the top of the tattooed middle six (6).

When King Atlas raises his ringed right hand and arm at a 45-degree angle, the people shout in unison, "Hail Satan! Hail, dark ruler of Hell! Hail King Atlas, who will with all us to defeat in a final war Michael and his angels!"

King Atlas and Job Put the Final Touches on *The Rise and Fall of Atlantis*

King Atlas I, being a precise historian, after interviewing several knowledgeable former citizens, and after receiving careful and wise guidance from Attorney Job, finally, with the untiring organizational assistance of a teenager, concludes his **The Rise and Fall of Atlantis**, ending with these words,

"I cannot write all I would like to say to you, but these are written so you may believe there was a land like no other land – Atlantis – with the tallest structure in the world – The Great Pyramid – containing the ten commandments written by the finger of God as the laws of Atlantis with these dedication inscriptions:

The front side of the pyramid to the North of the black granite mountain contains the following,

AGAPE

To God the Father
Be the Glory!

Father God so loves[11] those made in His image that He gave His only Son before the foundation of the world to die on the cross as a sacrifice for the sins of whosoever (represented by the symbol of the fish)[12] will receive His Son Jesus as their Savior and confess Him as their Lord and Master.

---

[9] Ecclesiastes 12:8. Solomon further concluded, '*I denied myself nothing (no lust) my eyes desired.*' (Ecclesiastes 2:19).

[10] Psalm 120:7.

[11] John 3:16.

[12] "The profile of a fish was used by early Christians as a secret Christian symbol and now known colloquially as the 'Jesus fish' (as Jesus desires His disciples to be fishers of men). See *Ichthys* Greek word for fish is a symbol consisting of two intersecting arcs, the ends of the right side extended beyond the meeting point so as to resemble a fish. See **Wikipedia, The Free Encyclopedia.**

The right side contains the following,

JOY

To God the Son
Be the Glory!

'*Let us fix our eyes on Jesus, the author and perfecter of our faith, who for the JOY set before Him endured the cross.*'[13]

The left side of the pyramid bears the words,

PEACE

To God the Holy Spirit
Be the Glory!

Notice at the top of the pyramid is a halo and an all-seeing eye on each side, beaming forth light symbolizing the all-seeing eye of God. Nothing was done in the nation of Atlantis, not seen by God!

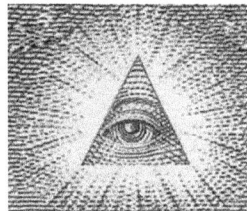

It will be written, '*Nothing in all creation is hidden from God's sight. Everything is uncovered and laid bare before the eyes of Him to whom we must give account.*[14]'

---

[13] Hebrews 12:2 NIV. [Emphasis added.]
[14] Hebrews 4:13 NIV.

'King Atlas I' concluded **The Rise *and Fall of Atlantis*,** with this good report,

"Two-thirds of all in Atlantis, wisely, before the end of Atlantis, believed, repented, and received the 'Good News' message of love and forgiveness. A simple message of receiving and accepting Jesus, the Son of God, as Savior, repenting of sin and confessing, Jesus as Lord.

To the glorious Godhead, we give glory, honor, power, dominion, and our utmost of love, dedication, and service ever more. Atlantis received from an act of war a formidable tidal wave, a dense covering of ice, and finally, a violent earthquake sinking it to the bottom of the ocean floor. It is no more!

FURTHER WRITINGS, FOR NOW, SAYETH NAUGHT.

Atlas I, First King of Atlantis

Ascribed and attested, by a witness in Atlantis, who affirms the accuracy of same, as a former member of the Legal Profession and Officer of the Courts of Atlantis.

Job, Esquire"

Son of God's Message on Agape Love and Instructing
How Some Who Didn't Die May Return to the Earth Again

The invisible Father God counsels the Son, "How about King David's leading in worship and praise and Your teaching on 'love' now before the Second Earth-Age begins. Please explain to those who did not die in the First-Earth Age that all of them that choose may return to a future Earth Age. It is a law of Heaven, *'for it is appointed unto man once to die and after that the judgment.'*[15]

Pastor Luther, starts the Friday evening, Celebrate Jesus Service, in Paradise, before a packed stadium behind The Great Pyramid, with David on the harp playing and leading in song,

> *'He who dwells in the shelter (that's you here in Paradise) of the Most High*
> > *will rest in the shadow of the Almighty.*
> *. . . For He will command His angels concerning you*
> > *to guard you in all your ways;*
> *they will lift you up in their hands,*
> > *so you will not strike your foot against a stone.*
> *You will tread upon the lion and the cobra;*
> > *you will trample the great lion and the serpent.*
> *Because he (includes you) loves God, God will rescue him.*
> > *God will protect him, for he acknowledges God's name.*
> *He will call upon God, and God will answer him.*
> > *God will be with him in trouble,*
> > *God will deliver him and honor him.*
> *With long life will God satisfy him*
> > *and show him His salvation.'*[16]

[The Shekinah Glory Cloud rolls in.]

---

[15] Hebrews 9:27.
[16] Psalm 91:1, 11-16.

Son of God Teaching About Walking in Agape Love

Coming through a door, behind the pulpit, dressed in a white homespun robe and being barefoot, enters Jesus, the Son of God, and standing before the saints of Israel and Atlantis preaching,

'I say to you, love your enemies. Pray for those who persecute (hurt) you. If you do this, you will be true children of your Father in Heaven. He causes the sun to rise on evil people and on good people, and He sends rain to those who do right and to those who do wrong.'[17]

"The truth will be written by the Apostle Paul,

'Just as man is destined to die once, and after that the judgment, so Christ was sacrificed once to take away the sins of many people; and He will appear a second time, not to bear sin, but to bring salvation to those who are waiting for Him.'[18]

You, who did not die in the First Earth Age, such as Job and Abraham, will come back in subsequent Earth ages for significant work for the glory of My Father. Job, you will return to the surface of the Earth at the beginning of the Second Earth Age. Abraham, you will go back to the surface at the start of the Third Earth Age. It will be written,

'All men (of darkness) will hate you (born again ones) because of Me (Jesus, Son of God), but he(or she) who stands firm to the end will be saved.'[19]

'He (Father God) who did not spare His own Son, but gave Him up for us all – how will He not also, along with Him, graciously give us all things? Who will bring any charge (accusation) against those whom God has chosen? It is God who justifies. Who is he that condemns? Christ Jesus (Son of God), who died – more than that, who was raised to life – is at the right hand of God and is also interceding for us (born again, adopted sons). Who shall separate us (born again adopted sons and daughters) from the love of Christ?

Neither death nor life, neither angels nor demons . . . nor anything else in all creation will be able to separate us from the love of God in Christ Jesus our Lord.'[20]

*'Because of His great love for us, God, who is rich in mercy, made us alive with Christ even when we were dead in transgressions – it is by grace you have been saved. And God raised us up with Christ and seated us with Him in the heavenly realms in Christ Jesus, in order that **in the upcoming ages** He might show the incomparable riches in Christ Jesus.'*[21] [Emphasis added.]

'For God (the Father) so loved the world that He gave His only begotten Son, that whoever believes in Him (Jesus) should not perish but have everlasting life.

For God did not send His Son into the world to condemn the world, but that the world through Him might be saved.

---

[17] Matthew 5:44-45.
[18] Hebrews 9:27 NIV.
[19] Matthew 10:22 NIV.
[20] Romans 8:28, 29, 32-34, 35, 37 NIV.
[21] Ephesians 2:4-7. NIV.

He who believes in Him is not condemned, but he who does not believe is condemned already, because he has not believed in the name of the only begotten Son of God.

And this is the condemnation, that the light has come into the world, and men loved darkness rather than light because their deeds were evil.

For everyone practicing evil hates the light and does not come to the light, lest his deeds should be exposed.

But he who does the truth comes to the light, that his deeds may be clearly seen, that they have been done through God.'[22]

Some of you are about to reenter the surface of the Earth as babies. You will have shadows of the First Earth Age and even Paradise. It is important for Me to preach this sermon, which I entitled, 'The Spectrum of Running the Straight and Narrow Race On the Agape Road Leading to Eternal Life.' Now that's a mouth full even for Me. [Laughter]

"Saints, do you have your seat belts fasten? [Laughter]

1. *Agape Love* endures long – **Patience!**

Agape Love is not in a hurry, is calm and peaceful, and delights in waiting for God's timing and best. As an example, the Son of God will endure the cruelest evil, having no revenge in His heart, praying as He hung nailed to a cross, '*Father, forgive them, for they do not know what they are doing.'*[23] A few of those who crucified the Son of God and forgiven as He was nailed to the cross will repent through bold preaching and will receive God's Son as their personal Savior and Lord.

Agape is clothed with joyful strength and dignity and '*laughs at future times to come.'*[24]

Agape is not weak floating along like a lily pad. *Agape* is ready to do God's will to the uppermost, even to the point of imprisonment and death, and smiles in obedience when the summons comes from God's throne, knowing that in doing God's will they will reap an eternal reward. Agape waits with a meek and quiet spirit in God's perfect peace. It will be written of God's adopted sons,

'*Well done, good and faithful servant, you were faithful over a few things; I will make you ruler over many things. Enter into the joy of your Lord.'*[25]

Agape does not worry, but, '*Rejoice in the Lord always,'*[26] and is not anxious about anything. Agape thinks about things that are true, honest, just, pure, admirable, excellent, and praiseworthy.[27] *Agape* refuses to let its heart be troubled and is not afraid. The Son of God will teach in the Third-Earth Age,

'*Peace I leave with you; My peace I give you. Do not let your hearts be troubled and do not be afraid.'*[28]

---

[22] John 3:16-21 NKJV.
[23] Luke 23:34 NIV.
[24] See Proverbs 31:25 ESV.
[25] Matthew 25:21 NKJV.
[26] Philippians 4:4 NIV.
[27] See Philippians 4:8.
[28] John 14:27 NIV.

Agape has faith and trust that God will provide what is needed and be a shield for His adopted sons. Agape's peace, love, joy, faith and trust in God drive our enemies into more confusion causing them to make mistakes. Agape '*love never fails,* '[29] and I said **NEVER**! If you give out love all the time, you will be in love all the time."

2. *Agape Love* is kind – **Kindness**!

The Godhead will set an example by doing kind things throughout the eternities-of-eternities. Agape is polite and courteous. The Son of God is peaceful, gentle, tender, affectionate, not '*willing that anyone should perish, but that everyone come to repentance.*'[30] Remember that the Son of God is no weak lily pad as the Father's right arm is backing Him in whatever He does or says.

The prideful have the rotten fruit of being harsh, sour, ill-tempered, having a controlling nature, angry, violent, liars, wicked, full of strife, deceit and fraud, and having an unpleasant disposition. They are often severe in the judgment of others, complaining, and infatuated with themselves.

It will be written about them,

'*Since you (of your own free will) ignored all My (God's) advice (teaching) and would not accept My rebuke, I will laugh at your disaster. I will mock when calamities overtake you – when calamities overtake you like a storm, when disaster sweeps over you like a whirlwind, when distress and trouble overwhelm you, then they will call to Me, but I will not answer; they will look for Me, but will not find Me. Since they hated knowledge and did not choose to fear the Lord, since they would not accept My advice and spurned My rebuke, they will eat the fruit of their schemes.*'[31]

God sees, knows, and will reward every act of kindness those who love and trust in Him will perform. For those made in God's image will die once. They will have to give an account of the deeds done in the body. Any kindness they can show to other human beings, let them do it now! For it will be '*appointed unto all who live on the Earth once to die and after that the judgment.*'[32] Therefore, let them not neglect to be kind to others, for they will not pass that way again, and the sowing of such kindness will bring abundant joy and life.

The wicked will be sexually impure and uncaring. It will be written about them, '*And if anyone causes one of these little ones who believe in Me to sin, it would be better for him to be thrown into the sea with a large millstone tied around his neck.*'[33] It would have been better if the wicked had never been born. Let us contrast this with what will be written about a kind good wife on the Earth,

'*The heart of her husband trusts in her, and he will have no lack of gain. She does him good, and no harm, all the days of her life.*

. . . She opens her hand to the poor and reaches out her hands to the needy.

. . . Strength and dignity are her clothing, and she laughs at the time to come. She opens her mouth with wisdom, and the teaching of kindness is on her tongue.

. . . Her children rise up and call her blessed; her husband also, and he praises her: 'Many women have done excellently, but you surpass them all.' '

---

[29] See 1 Corinthians 13:4.
[30] 2 Peter 3:9. NIV.
[31] Proverbs 1:25-31 NIV.
[32] Hebrews 9:27 NKJV.
[33] Mark 9:42 NIV.

Charm is deceitful and beauty is vain, but a woman who fears the Lord is to be praised. Give her of the fruit of her hands, and let her works praise her in the gates.'[34]

3. *Agape Love* does not envy nor boil over with jealousy – **Contentment!**

Agape does not envy the abilities, gifts, attractions, favors, or honors of others. The one envying has, however, great or slight, ill-will toward another. Envy at time's manifests regarding those doing the same kind[35] of work, ministry, socializing, or business, which may produce a dark spirit of discontentment, covetousness, and distraction. If one agape's others, he or she will rejoice in their successes and blessings and not envy them.

My born again brothers and sisters enjoy contentment and *'envy not!'*[36]

You are to have contentment with one's lot in life. The Holy Spirit living in you produces love, joy, peace, patience, and happiness, which temporary wealth, fashion, and esteem cannot eternally secure.

One may see the prideful wicked in glamorous attire and with haughty eyes, but don't envy them for their end – their dreadful and tragic end – will come upon them like a thief in the night.[37] Walking in *Agape* Love 'with contentment is great eternal gain.'[38]

4. *Agape Love* does not boast or is proud or 'me first' or insist on its own way or parade itself or is puffed up – **Humility!**

Agape does not boast or vaunt one's excellence, accomplishments or endowments, but puts a seal upon the lips and does not rehearse before others what 'me, myself, and I' have done. After Agape has been kind and done its valuable and precious work, it says nothing about it. It lets others praise it, but not themselves. Agape hides even from itself. Agape is not puffed up, vaults, not itself, nor holds itself out as being superior to others. Agape receives its endowments from God with thanksgiving, not with boasting. God will see in secret and reward the humble openly. It will later be written of those who will follow the example of humility,

'Do nothing out of selfish ambition or vain conceit, but in humility consider others better than yourselves. Each of you should look not only to your own interests, but also to the interests of others.

Your attitude should be the same as that of Christ Jesus:

Who, being in the nature God, did not consider equality with God something to be grasped, but made Himself nothing, taking the nature of a servant, being made in human likeness. And being found in appearance as a man, he humbled himself and became obedient to death – even death on a cross!

---

[34] Proverbs 31:11-12, 20, 25-26, 28-31.

[35] For example, a beautiful woman is not to envy another woman who may appear more fashionable and beautiful. A lawyer is not to envy another lawyer, or a doctor another doctor, or a minister another minister, just because they might appear to be more successful and blessed in an area. One should not lose joy because of the success of others or to envy them or seek to injure them in any way.

[36] See 1 Corinthians 13:4 NIV.

[37] Revelation 3:3 NKJV.

[38] 1 Timothy 6:6 NIV.

Therefore, God exalted Him (God's Son) to the highest place and gave Him the name above every name, that at the name of Jesus every knee should bow, in Heaven and on Earth and under the Earth (here in Paradise), and every tongue confess that Jesus Christ is Lord, to the glory of God the Father.[39]

5. *Agape Love* does not behave rudely or is arrogant or unseemly – **courtesy**!

Saints, a courteous gentleman, is polite, good manners, and has etiquette. He is a gentleman who does things gently with agape love seeking to esteem and honor others. He does not do ungentlemanly things. He does everything seemly, fit, orderly, and decently. Agape is polite in trifles and courteous in even the little things. Agape does not behave itself unseemly. The Son of God is not willing that any should perish, but that all should sincerely repent and make a U-turn, keeping their eyes on Him and giving up their wicked ways. Saints hate sin, but Agape even loves the sinner, desiring they repent. The Son will wipe away the tears from your eyes when He must truthfully say too many made in His image, *'I never knew you; depart from Me, you who act wickedly – disregarding My commands.'*[40]

6. *Agape Love* does not insist upon its own way or focuses on seeking its own way – **Unselfishness!**

Agape does not seek great things for himself or herself. Temporary things cannot be great. Greatness is walking in unselfish Agape Love. The Son of God will teach, *'It is more blessed to give than to receive.'*[41] One is to have a reasonable and proper love of self, and by that same love the Son of God will teach, *'Love your neighbor as yourself.'*[42]

The prideful pursues happiness by being served by others and having and getting. The Son of God will further teach that the greatest among you will be the one who serves. He will set an example by washing the feet of even the one who would later betray Him. He will teach, *'It is more blessed to (unselfishly) give than to receive.'*[43]

Agape does not seek its own happiness at the expense of others. The Son of God on Earth will be described as One *'who went about doing good.'*[44] He took up His cross and sought the good of others. He paid in full[45] with His own blood the penalty due for the sins of those made in God's image, who in sincere faith receive Him as Savior and confess Him as Lord. The Son of God will promise to those made in God's image to those who love Him, *"The one who comes to Me I will most certainly not cast out – I will never, no never (not for anything they have done) reject one of them who comes to Me.'*[46]

7. **Agape Love** is not easily provoked – **Self-Control!**

Agape is not prone to violent anger. It is calm, serious, sober, peaceful, and patient. It does not give way to sudden bursts of angry feelings.

---

[39] Philippians 2:3-11 NIV.
[40] Matthew 7:23 AMP.
[41] Acts 20:35 NIV.
[42] Luke 10:27 NIV.
[43] Acts 20:35 NIV.
[44] Acts 10:38.
[45] *Payment in full* "is often inserted on the back of a check above the place for endorsement to prove that the payee accepts the payment as complete." *The Free Dictionary by Farlex.*
[46] John 6:37 AMP.

Agape will never be angry without a valid cause, and it will not exceed the measure of what is right and just, either in degree or duration. It will be written about the righteous anger of the Son of God,

'On reaching Jerusalem, Jesus entered the temple area and began driving out those buying and selling there. He overturned the tables of the money changers and the benches of those selling doves and would allow no one to carry merchandise through the temple courts. And as He taught them, he said, 'It is written in the Scriptures, 'My house (temple) will be called a house of prayer for people of all nations.' But you have made it a den of robbers (thieves).'[47]

Agape's nature is calm, gentle, and subdued. It is hard to be angry with those you love, and you need to drop the matter and seek to be reconciled and make peace. The prideful temper is quick to judge, excitable, irritable, and unmerciful. The prideful often have a touchy, sensitive, delicate disposition and an evil and hateful temper.

8. ***Agape Love*** scorns and abhors evil and does not think about it or seek to deceive – **Thinks no evil**!

Agape supposes, as far as possible that others' actions are consistent with honesty and truth. It puts the best possible interpretation of the motives and conduct of others unless it is compelled by clear and sound evidence that the motives and behavior are dishonest, deceptive, or evil. Saints think no evil! It is to be written,

'Bless those who persecute you; bless and do not curse. . . . Repay no one evil for evil. Be careful to do what is right in the eyes of everyone. If it is possible, as far as it depends on you, live at peace with everyone. Do not take revenge, but leave room for God's wrath, for it is written: 'It is mine to avenge; I will repay, says the Lord. On the contrary, 'If your enemy is hungry, feed him; if he is thirsty, give him something to drink. In doing this, you will heap burning coals on his head.' Do not be overcome by evil, but overcome evil with good.'[48]

Of those joyful ones who choose of their own free will to love, serve, and obey God, they are to fill their minds and meditate on selected things such as,

    A. Honorable and seemly;
    B. Just and right;
    C. Pure and lovable;
    D. Kind and gracious; and
    E. Focusing on what is wholesome and the best and immediately casting down the filthy and the worse.[49]

My adopted children will, in a situation, joyfully see the glass half full and not half empty. [Laughter] Two-thirds in Atlantis were saved, and two-thirds of the Angels did not rebel.

The Son of God will preach in the flesh during the Third Earth Age these precious promises,

As the Father has loved Me, so have I loved you. Now remain in My love. If you obey My commands, you will remain in My love, just as I have obeyed My Father's commands and remain in His love. I have told you this so My joy may be in you and that your joy may be complete. My command is this: Love each other as I have loved you.'[50]

---

[47] Mark 11: 15-17, and see Jeremiah 7:11.
[48] Romans 12:14, 17-21 NIV.
[49] See Philippians 4:8-9 AMP.
[50] John 15:9-12.

9. **Agape Love** does not rejoice in sin, wrongdoing, or any wickedness, but rejoices in the truth – **Sincerity!**

Agape sincerely, with no falseness or suspicion, believes in and encourages others. Agape sees the bright side, puts the best interpretation on every action, gives the benefit of the doubt, and rejoices in the truth. Agape searches for truth and rejoices, and cherishes when truth is found. It does not rejoice or take delight when others are guilty of wickedness, or when they fall into sin. It does not find pleasure in hearing substantial proof that others committed wrong. Agape grieves when a fellow human being or friend have done something wrong and have cast discredit upon themselves. It sincerely agape's the person, but it does not rejoice over the wrong, nor the fact that a wrong or mistake has been committed. It rejoices when others do well, and good was done. It seeks to protect another's good name.

Saints, when you return to Earth, I want you to be My reflection of being loving, joyful, patience, kindness, contented, humble, courteous, unselfish, having self-controlled, thinking no evil, and having sincerity. Agape Love never fails, and again I said **NEVER!** Yes, the enemy of the Son of God will murder Him, but God the Father and the Holy Spirit will not let Him remain dead. They will raise Him up on the third day to be forever '*King of kings and Lord of lords*,'[51] and to join Father God again, at His right hand.

'*Let us fix our eyes on Jesus, the author and perfecter of our faith, who for the joy set before Him endured the cross, scorning its shame, and sat down at the right hand of the throne of (Father) God.*'[52]

After the Son of God's resurrection from the dead, it will be written in the Bible about the God-Kind of **Agape Love**,

'*Love endures long and is patient and kind; love is never envious nor boils over with jealousy; it is not boastful or vainglorious, does not display itself haughtily.*

It is not conceited – arrogant and inflated with pride; it is not rude (unmannerly) and does not act unbecomingly. Love (God's love in us) does not insist on its own rights or its own way, for it is not self-seeking; it is not touchy or fretful or resentful; it takes no account of the evil done to it – pays no attention to a suffered wrong.

It does not rejoice at injustice and unrighteousness, but rejoices when right and truth prevail.

Love bears up under anything and everything that comes, is ever ready to believe the best of every person, its hopes are fadeless under all circumstances, and it endures everything without weakening.

Love never fails – never fades out or becomes obsolete or comes to an end.'[53]

Brother Newton leads the congregation of the Saints,

> *Amazing Grace, how sweet the sound;*
> *that saved a wretch like me;*
> *I once was lost, but now I'm found*
> *Was blind, but now I see.*
> *When we've been there ten thousand years;*
> *bright shining as the sun,*
> *We've no less days to sing God's praise*
> *than when we first begun.*

---

[51] Quoting from Revelation 19:16.
[52] Hebrews 12:2.
[53] 1 Corinthians 13:4-8 AMP.

386

Abraham, closing the service, remarks, "Thank you, Melchizedek, for such a needful and inspiring message on love. Also, thank you, David, for anointed praise and worship on your harp and in song. Those in Hell carefully listening could faintly hear your harp playing. Across the great gulf from the Great Pyramid, containing the commandments of God, and the all-seeing eye of God to be seen from parts of Hell, is the ruler of Hell, his army of demons, and the fallen angels seeking in the words of Pastor Luther 'to undo (those alive on the surface of the Earth) to be many of us.' When we resist evil on the surface of the Earth by pleading the Blood and Name of Jesus, citing Scripture, and wearing the undergarment of Agape Love, the devil and his demons will flee from us as if in terror. David be on guard when you return to the Earth as the devil hates your harp playing and he will try to ruin you. Be quick to repent!"

More Years Later

The Ice Covering the Earth Slowly Starts Melting and Some in Paradise, Who Did not Die, Will Be Permitted to Return to Subsequent Earth Ages

Abraham presents, "We are about to enter the Second Earth Age, and a few of you will be returning to the surface of the Earth. Attorney Job, you are one, and you will die and return temporarily back here. However, at the very end of the Second Earth Age out of that vast population, only eight living on the Earth will at the end of that age be saved. The jaws of Hell will open wide to receive the many that reject such a Great Salvation. Remember to walk in agape love, for let us say it together, '*Love never fails!*'[54] Nothing can ultimately defeat love. Love is might! Be patient and hope in the Lord, as we still have darkness on the surface, but the oceans are melting. The happiest people are those born again ones who love God, their neighbor as themselves., and trust and hope in the Lord Jesus, as Savior, repent, and confess Jesus is Lord! It will be written,

> '*The Lord is the everlasting God,*
> *the creator of the ends of the Earth.*
> *He will not grow tired or weary,*
> *and His understanding no one can fathom.*
> *God gives strength to the weary*
> *and increases the power of the weak.*
> *Even youths grow tired and weary,*
> *and your young men stumble and fall,*
> *but those who hope in the Lord*
> *will renew their strength.*
> *They will soar on wings like eagles;*
> *they will run and not grow weary,*
> *they will walk and not be faint.*'[55] †

---

[54] 1 Corinthians 13:8 NIV.
[55] Isaiah 40:28-31.

†Lawyer's Sidebar[1] Epilogue to Love & War, Volume One†

Please feel free to skip this epilog (epilogue) and proceed to Volume 2!

You may obtain copies of the unabridged *Love & War* at amazon.com – Books, Volume 1 and Volume 2, and *Hallelujah*, Volume 1, Volume 2, and Volume 3 Author Joe Ragland.

God planned this moment in the Adventurer's life to further discover in Volume 2 of *Love & War* hidden secrets, blessings and strength, including,

(1) Enabling one courageously not to worship the Beast/Antichrist or to receive his mark "on their right hand or on their forehead," without which no one can "*buy or sell*" (Revelation 13:16-17), as if taken, this will seal the taker's doom (Revelation 14:9-12) first in Hell and later in the Lake of Fire. *Love & War* warns others throughout the world not to worship the Beast/Antichrist nor to take his mark showing how to receive Jesus as Savior, repent and confess Jesus as Lord, trusting the Lord Jesus to give them a way of escape, '*But when you (a born again Christian) are tempted, God will also provide a way out (escape) so you can stand up under it.*' (1 Corinthians 1013).

(2) Receiving a blessed invitation to the "Marriage Supper of the Lamb" (Revelation 18:9) described in joyful detail in Volume 2 of *Love & War.*

(3) Qualifying to dwell with God on the New Earth (the present Earth will pass away as further shown in Volume 2 of *Love & War).* The Apostle John had this vision of the truth regarding God's dwelling with His people on the New Earth,

> "*Behold, God's dwelling (on the New Earth) is with His (born again ones adopted into the family of God) people, and He will be their God.*"
> (Revelation 21:3)

Where would you desire to be ten thousand years from this moment? Dr. Ragland's goal alone is to please and obey God and give Him all the glory! Dr. Ragland's private email is ***joeragland@raglandministries.org***, and your Internet name and address will be kept private. Please alert Dr. Ragland by starting your subject line **Love & War**, giving your first and last name, your brief testimony, and your location on the planet Earth.

These ***unabridged*** dreams and visions contain messages for all the people, so loved by God of the world. You must keep moving forward through *Love & War*. However, if you find yourself bogged down in one chapter, like regarding Job's first wife, simply skim to the end of that chapter and go on to the next chapter. In the next volume, you will discover Attorney Job preparing the perpetual land deeds to a portion of the Promised Land of Israel. Later these perpetual land deeds would be recorded and delivered to a friend of God, Abram (Abraham, meaning father of a multitude). This is one example proving that God always does all things legal!

The legal gifting, wisdom, faith, and braveness of Attorney Job comes '*forth as gold.*'[2] Attorney Job, as this attorney, would take '*up the case of the stranger,*'[3] knowing he had '*influence in court.*'[4] Martin Luther once wrote, "He (Jesus), '*from age to age the same, and He (Jesus) must (legally) win the (final end-time) battle!*'[5] The remainder of your life and the choices you make are far more important than your past life!

Your time is priceless on the Earth as you prepare for ETERNITY! For many aging throughout the world, *Love & War* will be their last opportunity to receive the truth of how to not take the mark to enable them to buy or sell and to receive an invitation to attend the glorious marriage supper of the Lamb (Jesus). The average lifespan in the world today is 27,375 days. If you are typical, that was deposited in your "time bank" when you were born. Every day you make a withdrawal of one day. If you are twenty-five years old, you have on the average 18,250 days to live. If you are fifty, you have 9,125 days left to live. If you are sixty-five and are average, you have 3,650 days left to live.

---

[1] The sidebar is an area in a courtroom near the judge's bench where lawyers may be called to speak with the judge so that the jury cannot hear the conversation . . . ."
Wikipedia, The Free Encyclopedia, "*Sidebar (law).*"
[2] Job 23:10.
[3] Job 29:16.
[4] Job 31:21.
[5] Lyrics (stanza two) from *A Mighty Fortress Is Our God* by Martin Luther.

Please calculate how many days are left in your "typical" mortality bank and spend some of your precious hours reading *Love & War* and *Hallelujah*, which include the real issues of life and the way to salvation. No other books, except the Bible, forbidding such sins as murder, stealing, and adultery, will prepare you for eternity better than *Love & War and Hallelujah*, having the most joyful ending of any books ever written to which the Adventurer is invited to be a part of this great JOY.

The self-righteous, judgmental religious, need to be prepared to be shocked as they read about those who were in attendance and those not in attendance at the marriage supper of the Lamb (Jesus). Jesus taught,

'I (Jesus) did not come (to the Earth to die on a cross) to invite the self-righteous, who feel no need to repent, but to invite sinners (that's me) to (from the heart) repentance.'[6]

'A man gave a great banquet (an allusion to the marriage supper of the Lamb) and invited many guests. Some of those who had been invited gave weak excuses to explain why they could not attend. 'I have just bought a field, and I must go see it. . . . I have just bought five pairs of oxen, and I am on my way to try them out. . . . I just got married, so I can't come.'

'I (Jesus) tell you, none of those (referring to the representative three who gave weak excuses) whom I invited will get a taste of My (wedding) banquet.'[7]

'Not everyone who says to Me, 'Lord, Lord,' will enter the Kingdom of Heaven, but only those who do what My Father in Heaven wants. In the last day many will say to Me (Jesus), 'Lord, Lord, did we not prophesy in your name and in your name drive out demons and perform many miracles? Then I will tell them plainly, 'I never knew you (those who refused to repent and change their ways). Away from Me, you evildoers![8]

Brace yourself as you witness the anointing singing at the marriage of the King of Heaven of *How Great Thou Art*, by one who repeatedly rejected the title 'King of Rock and Roll,' who would confess in response to many, 'Jesus is King!' Also, I saw one couple who left their spouses to marry each other. He was so condemned for previously being on drugs, serving time in prison, and stealing another man's wife, he became known as 'the man in black.' A thief crucified on a cross was the head usher seating joyful John and June, both now dressed in glorious white, beside joyful Adam and Eve, who got it all and back when they were driven from the Garden of Eden, after hiding their nakedness with fig leaves. Truly, whom the Son, Jesus, forgives is joyfully *'free indeed.'*[9]

For the romantic at heart, these unabridged (complete) recordings, contain beautiful, and humorous love stories. I would often ask if I could shorten (a bridge, cut out a portion), but this was not permitted. Just blame God and not me if something offends you, as I was only the Lord's recorder, like a court reporter. I laugh as I recall that the Lord once chose a donkey to speak for Him.[10] Regarding my recording of these love stories involving strong and attractive chemistry between men and women in the ages of the Earth; and the wicked devices of war, I would laugh when I pondered, "All's fair in love and war! I don't know about war!" Although the devil would often scream illegal, this lawyer assures you that God does everything legally and lawfully.

I recorded these visions and dreams unabridged, having the Lord Jesus, as my senior partner, telling it as it is at lightning speed as I typeset *Love & War* myself for the people of the Earth. Why should we go through life accomplishing things that in **Eternity** amount to nothing? Therefore, my goal alone is to please and obey God and give Him all the glory. I am thankful I am a lawyer and not a typesetter! Another lawyer, Lew Wallace, printed his ***Ben-Hur – A Tale of the Christ*** in two volumes selling only three hundred copies the first year dedicated, "To the wife of my youth, who still abides with me." . Subsequently, God moved on a major publishing company to publish a deluxe illustrated professionally typeset unfortunately deleting the dedication to his wife and the words from the title, "*A Tale of the Chirst*," of a one-volume edition to the shortened title ***Ben-Hur,*** retaining the chapter, "*A Roman Orgy*." . Despite its late start, ***Ben-Hur*** won the race as the best-selling novel of the 19th century and its exciting chariot race has been the focus on several major movies focusing on the famous chariot race contained therein.

People often ask me what is your favorite and most thrilling of your dreams and visions? I reply when, "The boy Jesus raises from the dead Pharaohs' son accidentally killed in a chariot race in Egypt, is comparable to the exciting chariot race in the movie ***Ben-Hur.***

---

[6] Mark 2:17.
[7] Luke 14:16-20, 24.
[8] Matthew 7:21-23.
[9] John 8:36.
[10] Numbers 22:28.

"Remember the Lord your God! He gives you (includes godly companies) the power of gaining wealth (resources) that God may establish His covenant (presenting the Gospel of salvation to the people of the world)."
(Deuteronomy 8:18)

I urge you to obtain copies from **amazon.com** –.Books, **Love & War,** Volume 1 and Volume 2, by Author Joe Ragland, for your relatives, friends, employees, the poor, the rich, the Jew (Volume 2 joyfully concludes with those Jews living in Israel in the end-time all receive Jesus, a Jew, as the Messiah and being rescued out of a great tribulation), and especially (give a copy o*f **Love & War** or **Hallelujah** to the lost elderly, sick, those in prison before death catches up with them, and one of the millions of atheist in the U.S.A, who don't believe in God or that God made man in His image. Jurispudentially ask the atheist, "What evidence do you base your atheism "

This may be that person's last opportunity to know the truth before death catches up with him or her. "*God is not wanting anyone to perish (first in Hell and then in the Lake of Fire), but everyone (no exceptions) to come to (salvation) repentance.*" (2 Peter 3:9) There are no atheists in Hell as clearly demonstrated in Volume 2 of ***Love & War***.

When you hand ***Love & War, to*** another, in love and compassion, say something like, "This is also from Jesus, God's Son, who gave us all a "*free will*" to choose to receive or reject Him as Savior if you would like to enjoy it. ***Love & War*** commences before time begins and ends after time is no more. Do not try to read all seventy-three chapters at once, but read it in stages like at work breaks and right before you go to sleep. It has a joyful beginning and an even more joyful ending to which the Adventurer is invited to be a part! Each chapter builds, answering key questions building one's faith like no other book, except the Bible, preparing one for **ETERNITY**!"

As you add your natural gifting, your Creator will add to your natural His supernatural. May the blessing and anointing of God be on all aspects of your life as you participate, using your talents and gifts, in distributing the messages in ***Love & War*** to the people of the world! Some of you may desire to be a part of this joyful ministry of publishing, translating, advertising, and printing of this message in various world languages to the people in the world. Jesus was not kidding when he commanded us to preach the Gospel to every nation.

One soul is worth more than the entire physical Earth, soon to pass away, as shown in ***Love & War***, Volume 2!

"*What good is it for a man to gain the whole world, yet forfeit (lose) his (own) soul?*"
(Jesus, Mark 8:36)
For those collaborating (partnering) in sharing with others ***Love & War***, we pronounce the same blessings over you that the Apostle Paul pronounced over those partnering with him to share the Gospel,
"*Grace and peace (favor, blessing) to you from God our Father and the Lord Jesus Christ.'*
. . . I always pray in every prayer of mine for you all (a Southern term often used in Dixieland, USA)
with **joy** *because of your* **partnership in the Gospel**.
. . . Father God, who began a good work in you, will **carry it on to completion until the day of Christ Jesus**
(the saved taken out of the Earth to Heaven and the lost cast into Hell and later into the Lake of Fire).
. . . But one thing I (Paul) do: Forgetting what is behind (of the old sinful life) and straining toward
What is ahead (joyful Eternity as a saved, born again believer), I press toward the goal (in view) **to win**
the prize *for which (Father) God has called me heavenward in Christ Jesus.*
. . . Rejoice in the Lord (Jesus) always. I will say (decree) it again: Rejoice!"
(Philippians 1:2,4-6, 3:13-14, 4:4) [Emphasis added.]

"*How can they believe in the One (Son of God, Jesus) of whom they have not heard?*
And how can they hear without someone (that includes you) preaching (by words and in printed
messages) to them! *And how can they preach unless they are sent*
(Romans 10:14-15)

"*God's word is in my heart like a burning fire, shut up in my bones.*"
(Jeremiah 20:9)

Please consider praying, even if you are born again, as you proceed 'line upon line, line upon line, a little here, a little there' (Isaiah 28:10) with truth building upon truth in your adventure of adventures in **Volume 2.** If you get bogged down like regarding the wilds of Job's first wife, who advised her husband Job to curse God and die (Job 2:9), please do not stop, but skim over to the next truth and proceed running your race to the grand conclusion on the New Earth to which you Adventurer is invited to be a part.

"Dear Father God in Heaven, Thank You for loving those in the world so much that you gave Your one and only Son, Jesus, that whosoever (that's me) believes in Him shall not perish (in Hell) but have eternal life. (John 3:16) I know I am a sinner. I am sorry for and repent of my sins. I do believe Jesus is Your Son and that You sent Him into the world to die on a cross to pay the penalty I owe for my sins. Father, I believe You raised Jesus from the dead. Now of my own free will, I receive Jesus as my Savior and confess Jesus as my Lord! I ask the Holy Spirit to come into my heart and join with my human spirit and make me born again. I will not be ashamed to confess the name of Jesus to others! Father, please give me wisdom and understanding now as I proceed through the Message Volume 2 of in Love & War, supported with Scripture, to the people of the world recorded by Dr. Joe M. Ragland. I offer Hallelujahs, Thanksgivings, Praise, and Worship for Your saving love for me. In Your Son Jesus' name, Amen (So be it!)!"†

'The Lord gave the word (message of salvation):
Great was the company of those who published it.'(Psalm 68:11)

'Each man or woman has his or her gift from God!
One has this gift, another has another gift.'(1 Corinthians 7:7)

'The wise person wins (rescues from Hell)
souls (for the Kingdom of Heaven).' (Proverbs 7:30)

The Great Commission
By
Jesus, the Son of God

"All power (authority) is given unto Me (Jesus) in Heaven and on Earth.
Therefore, go (Kingly command) and make followers (disciples) of all people
(who will repent, receive Jesus as Savior, and confess Jesus as Lord) in the world (nations),
baptizing (immersing) them in the name of the Father and of the Son and of the
Holy Spirit, and teaching them to obey everything I (Divine King Jesus) have taught (commanded) you.
And surely I am (Divine Presence) with you always, even until the end of this (Earth) age."
(Jesus, Matthew 28:18-20)

"I (Jesus, Son of God) am the way and the truth and the life.
No one (no exceptions) comes to the Father (God for salvation) except through Me."
(Jesus, John 14:6)

This recorder respectfully here sets forth previews of coming attractions, as *Love & War* continues in Volume 2:

†BOOK EIGHT†

✝OUR JOYFUL PATH TOGETHER TO THE CELESTIAL CITY✝

You are invited to receive End-Time emails (we will not share your email with others) updates from the Author of **Love & War,** Dr. Joe M. Ragland, a friend of Jesus, rejoicing that his name is written in the **Lamb's Book of Life**. (Luke 20:10) As you communicate with *joeragland@raglandministries.org*, please start with *Love & War* or *Hallelujah,* introduce yourself, what has ministered to you, include your first and last name, your talents and gift(s), and your location on the Earth. God has lost people He loves throughout the world to reach. Every life that's touched is a life we reach together. Let us join in Hallelujahs, Worship, and Praise now and throughout eternity for such a great salvation of ourselves and others as we bring glory to the Lord Jesus Christ.

Joe Ragland Ministries
Post Office Box 77
Jackson, Mississippi 39205-0077

www.ingramcontent.com/pod-product-compliance
Lightning Source LLC
Chambersburg PA
CBHW080659110426
42739CB00034B/3327